Xcode 6
Start to Finish

Developer's Library Series

Visit **developers-library.com** for a complete list of available products

---

T he **Developer's Library Series** from Addison-Wesley provides practicing programmers with unique, high-quality references and tutorials on the latest programming languages and technologies they use in their daily work. All books in the Developer's Library are written by expert technology practitioners who are exceptionally skilled at organizing and presenting information in a way that's useful for other programmers.

Developer's Library books cover a wide range of topics, from open-source programming languages and databases, Linux programming, Microsoft, and Java, to Web development, social networking platforms, Mac/iPhone programming, and Android programming.

Xcode 6
Start to Finish

iOS and OS X Development

Fritz Anderson

✦✦Addison-Wesley

New York • Boston • Indianapolis • San Francisco
Toronto • Montreal • London • Munich • Paris • Madrid
Capetown • Sydney • Tokyo • Singapore • Mexico City

Many of the designations used by manufacturers and sellers to distinguish their products are claimed as trademarks. Where those designations appear in this book, and the publisher was aware of a trademark claim, the designations have been printed with initial capital letters or in all capitals.

Xcode is a trademark of Apple, Inc., registered in the U.S. and other countries.

The author and publisher have taken care in the preparation of this book, but make no expressed or implied warranty of any kind and assume no responsibility for errors or omissions. No liability is assumed for incidental or consequential damages in connection with or arising out of the use of the information or programs contained herein.

For information about buying this title in bulk quantities, or for special sales opportunities (which may include electronic versions; custom cover designs; and content particular to your business, training goals, marketing focus, or branding interests), please contact our corporate sales department at corpsales@pearsoned.com or (800) 382-3419.

For government sales inquiries, please contact governmentsales@pearsoned.com.

For questions about sales outside the United States, please contact international@pearsoned.com.

Visit us on the Web: informit.com/aw

Library of Congress Cataloging-in-Publication Data
Anderson, Fritz.
    Xcode 6 start to finish : iOS and OS X development / Fritz Anderson.
        pages   cm
    Includes index.
    ISBN 978-0-13-405277-9 (pbk. : alk. paper)
    1. Mac OS. 2. iOS (Electronic resource) 3. Macintosh (Computer)—Programming. 4. iPhone (Smartphone)—Programming. 5. Application software—Development. I. Title.
    QA76.774.M33A534 2015
    005.4'46—dc23
                                                            2015004190

ISBN-13: 978-0-13-405277-9
ISBN-10: 0-13-405277-3

Text printed in the United States on recycled paper at Edwards Brothers Malloy in Ann Arbor, Michigan.
First printing, June 2015

Editor-in-Chief
Mark L. Taub

Senior Acquisitions Editor
Trina MacDonald

Senior Development Editor
Chris Zahn

Managing Editor
John Fuller

Full-Service Production Manager
Julie B. Nahil

Copy Editor
Stephanie Geels

Indexer
Ted Laux

Proofreader
Kathleen Allain

Technical Reviewers
Duncan Champney
Chuck Ross
Dan Wood

Editorial Assistant
Olivia Basegio

Cover Designer
Chuti Prasertsith

Compositor
Lori Hughes

❖

For the Honorable Betty Shelton Cole,
a tough old broad

❖

Contents at a Glance

Contents

Acknowledgments

Only part of the effort that went into putting *Xcode 6 Start to Finish* into your hands was spent at a text editor. I am indebted to those without whom this book could not have been made. Many of them appear in the formal production credits; they deserve better-than-formal thanks.

Trina MacDonald went through enormous pains to turn a new edition around quickly in the face of the many changes in Xcode. This was not a sure thing; she made sure it happened. Thank you.

Lori Hughes stepped in with skill and good humor to give us a head start in getting the manuscript ready to go on a tight schedule. Julie Nahil, the production manager, stepped in early to make this possible, in addition to her job-title work of turning the manuscript I submitted into the book I'd hoped for.

Olivia Basegio made sure the contracts, correspondence, (and advance payments!) all got through. She guided the reviewers through their work while the book was still in unassembled pieces on the ground.

The reviewers, Chris Zahn, Gene Backlin, and Josh Day, saved me much embarrassment, and made this a much better work than it started. Errors remain. Some are intentional, some not; they are all my own.

Stephanie Geels, the copy editor, made the prosecution of typos, grammar, and which instance of a particular word gets which typeface, more fun than you'd think. In fact, fun.

A full-time day job is not an author's best friend (except for the part about paying the rent). Alan Takaoka, my boss in the Web Services department of IT Services, The University of Chicago, got me three- and four-day weekends while I wrote. I promised to keep all my meetings and deadlines while I worked on the book, but somehow none of them fell on a Monday or Friday. Cornelia Bailey, who manages most of my projects, kept rescheduling them.

Bess and Kate bore more than daughters should of my doubts and frustrations, and were simply confident that I would do fine—which was all they needed to do.

About the Author

Fritz Anderson has been writing software, books, and articles for Apple platforms since 1984. This is his fifth book.

He has worked for research and development firms, consulting practices, and freelance. He was admitted to the Indiana bar, but thought better of it. He is now a senior iOS developer for the Web Services department at The University of Chicago. He has two daughters.

Introduction

Welcome to *Xcode 6 Start to Finish*! This book will show you how to use Apple's integrated development environment to make great products with the least effort.

Xcode 6 is the descendant of a family of development tools dating back more than 20 years to NeXT's ProjectBuilder. It started as a text editor, a user-interface designer, and a front end for Unix development tools. It has become a sophisticated system for building applications and system software, with a multitude of features that leverage a comprehensive indexing system and subtle incremental parser to help you assemble the right code for your project, and get it right the first time.

That much power can be intimidating. My aim in *Xcode 6 Start to Finish* is to demystify Xcode, giving you a gradual tour through examples that show you how it is used day to day. Don't let the gentle approach fool you: This book will lead you through the full, best-practices workflow of development with Xcode 6. There are no "advanced topics" here—I'll show you version control and unit testing in their proper places in the development process.

How This Book Is Organized

First, a word on my overall plan. This is a book about developer tools. If it teaches you something about how to use the Cocoa frameworks, or something about programming, that's fine, but that's incidental to showing you the Xcode workflow. There are many excellent books and other resources for learning the frameworks; you'll find many of them listed in Appendix B, "Resources."

Every tour needs a pathway, and every lesson needs a story. The first three parts of this book demonstrate Xcode through three applications—a command-line tool, an iOS app, and an OS X application—that calculate and display some statistics in American football. None of the apps are very useful; the graphical apps run almost entirely on sample data. But they demand enough of the development tools to give you a solid insight into how to use them.

Xcode supports some technologies, like Core Data and OS X bindings, that are *not* for beginners. *Xcode 6 Start to Finish* dives straight into those techniques, ignoring conceptually simpler approaches, so I can demonstrate how Xcode works. Other "advanced" techniques, like unit testing and version control, appear at the points where best practices require them. This will be the workflow as Xcode supports it.

I'm using applications for iOS and OS X as examples, but read both Parts II and III, even if you're only interested in one platform. The applications are only *stories*; the techniques apply to both platforms.

First Steps

In Part I, I'll take you from installing Xcode and running your first project through basic debugging skills. You'll work through a small command-line application. The application may be simple, but you'll learn foundational skills you'll need before adding the complexity of graphical apps.

- **Chapter 1, Getting Xcode**—Some things to consider before you download Xcode 6; two ways to download and install it.
- **Chapter 2, Kicking the Tires**—Your first look at Xcode, setting up a trivial project and running it.
- **Chapter 3, Simple Workflow and Passive Debugging**—Write, build, and run a simple application, and respond to a crash.
- **Chapter 4, Active Debugging**—Take charge of debugging by setting breakpoints and tracing through the program. I'll show you how to organize your workspace.
- **Chapter 5, Compilation**—A pause to describe the process of building an application.
- **Chapter 6, Adding a Library Target**—Add a library target to a project, and learn how to build a product from multiple targets.
- **Chapter 7, Version Control**—Why source control is important, and how to take advantage of Xcode's built-in support for versioning through Git and Subversion.

The Life Cycle of an iOS Application

Part II tells the story of a small iPhone app, and how to use Apple's developer tools to build it. It introduces you to the graphical editor for user interfaces, and shows how to profile an app to optimize its speed and memory burden.

- **Chapter 8, Starting an iOS Application**—You'll start by creating an iOS project, and learn the Model-View-Controller design at the core of Cocoa on iOS and OS X alike.
- **Chapter 9, An iOS Application: Model**—Design a Core Data schema and supplement it with your own code.
- **Chapter 10, An iOS Application: Controller**—Create a controller to link your model to the on-screen views. On the way, I'll tell you about refactoring, and Xcode's continual error-checking.
- **Chapter 11, Building a New View**—Design the user-interface views for your app with the integrated Interface Builder, and take advantage of source-code completion.

- **Chapter 12, Auto Layout in a New View**—In Xcode 6, Auto Layout is more about getting things done than fighting the tools. Learn how to make Cocoa layout do what you want.

- **Chapter 13, Adding Table Cells**—While adding an in-screen component to your app, you'll debug memory management, and control how Xcode builds, runs, and tests your apps through the Scheme editor.

- **Chapter 14, Adding an Editor**—Add an editor view, and get deep into Storyboard.

- **Chapter 15, Unit Testing**—Unit testing speeds development and makes your apps more reliable. I'll show you how Xcode supports it as a first-class part of the development process.

- **Chapter 16, Measurement and Analysis**—Use Instruments to track down performance and memory bugs.

- **Chapter 17, An iOS Extension**—Create a system-wide extension and a shared library to bring your app's value beyond its own screen.

- **Chapter 18, Provisioning**—Behind the scenes, the process of getting Apple's permission to put apps on devices is complicated and temperamental. I'll show you how Xcode saves you from most of the pain, and give you a few tips on how to get out if it backs you into a corner.

Xcode for Mac OS X

Part III shifts focus to OS X development. Some concepts are more important to OS X than iOS, but you'll be learning techniques you can use regardless of your platform.

- **Chapter 19, Starting an OS X Application**—Carrying iOS components over to OS X; what the responder chain is, and how Interface Builder makes it easy to take advantage of it.

- **Chapter 20, Bindings: Wiring an OS X Application**—As you build a popover window, you'll use OS X bindings to simplify the link between your data and the screen. You'll also encounter autosizing, a legacy technique for laying out view hierarchies.

- **Chapter 21, Localization**—How you can translate your Mac and iOS apps into other languages.

- **Chapter 22, Bundles and Packages**—You'll master the fundamental structure of most Mac and iOS products, and how both platforms use the Info.plist file to fit apps into the operating system.

- **Chapter 23, Property Lists**—Learn the basic JSON-like file type for storing data in both OS X and iOS.

Xcode Tasks

By this point in the book, you'll have a foundation for digging into the details of the Xcode toolset. Part IV moves on to topics that deserve a more concentrated treatment than Parts II and III.

- **Chapter 24, Documentation in Xcode**—How Xcode gives you both immediate help on API, and browsable details on the concepts of Cocoa development. Find out how you can add your own documentation to the system.
- **Chapter 25, The Xcode Build System**—I'll show you the fundamental rules and tools behind how Xcode goes from source files to executable products.
- **Chapter 26, Instruments**—Using Apple's timeline profiler, you can go beyond basic performance and memory diagnostics to a comprehensive look at how your program uses its resources.
- **Chapter 27, Debugging**—How to use breakpoint actions and conditions to eliminate in-code diagnostics. You'll also find a tutorial on the `lldb` debugger command set, for even closer control over your code.
- **Chapter 28, Snippets**—A roundup of tips, traps, and features to help you get the most from the developer tools.

Appendixes

The appendixes in Part V contain references to help you master the build system, and find help and support.

- **Appendix A, Some Build Variables**—The most important configuration and environment variables from Xcode's build system.
- **Appendix B, Resources**—A compendium of books, tools, and Internet resources to support your development efforts.

About Versions

This book was finished in the fall of 2014. *Xcode 6 Start to Finish* is written to early versions of 10.10, iOS 8.2, and Xcode 6.2.

About the Code

Xcode 6 Start to Finish has many examples of executable code—it's about a system for creating code and running it. My goal is to teach *workflow.* What the code itself does is practically incidental. In particular, be aware: **Much of the code in this book will not run as initially presented.** *Xcode 6 Start to Finish* is about the development process, most of which (it seems) entails prosecuting and fixing bugs. You can't learn the workflow unless you learn how to respond to bugs.

So I'll be giving you buggy code. You may find it painful to read, and if you try to run it, it will be painful to run. Trust me: It's for a reason.

Also, sample code for this book is available at `informit.com/title/9780134052779` (register your book to gain access to the code). You'll find archives of the projects in this book as they stand at the end of each chapter. With very few exceptions—I'll make them very clear—if you want the project as it stands at the *start* of a chapter, you should use the archive for the *end* of the previous chapter.

The chapter archives do not include version-control metadata. If you are following along with the examples, and using Git (or Subversion) for your work, copy the changes into your own working directory. If you replace your directory with a sample directory, you'll lose your version history.

Conventions

This book observes a number of typographic and verbal conventions.

- Human-interface elements, such as menu items and button labels, are shown **like this**.
- File names and programming constructs are shown `like this`. This will sometimes get tricky as when I refer to the product of the "Hello World" *project* (plain text, because it's just a noun) as the *file* `Hello World`.
- Text that you type in will be shown `like this`.
- When I introduce a new term, I'll call it out *like this*.

I'll have you do some command-line work in the Terminal. Some of the content will be wider than this page, so I'll follow the convention of breaking input lines with backslashes (\) at the ends. I'll break long output lines simply by splitting them, and indenting the continuations. When that output includes long file paths, I'll replace components with ellipses (. . .), leaving the significant parts.

For its first 20 years, the Macintosh had a one-button mouse. (Don't laugh—most purchasers didn't know what a mouse *was*; try pushing the wrong button on an old Mac mouse.) Now it has four ways to effect an alternate mouse click: You can use the right button on an actual mouse (or the corner of the mouse where the right button would be); you can hold down the Control key and make an ordinary click; you can hold down two fingers while clicking on a multi-touch trackpad (increasingly common even on desktop Macs); or you can tap at a designated corner of a multi-touch trackpad. And there are more variations available through System Preferences. Unless the distinction really matters, I'm simply going to call it a "right-click" and let you sort it out for yourself.

Part I

First Steps

## 1

Getting Xcode

If you want to use Xcode, you must install it. Developer tools were bundled into OS X in the early days, but now you must download it, drag the Xcode application into your /Applications folder, and start it up.

Before You Begin

Before you do anything, be sure you can use Xcode 6. There are two considerations.

Developing for Earlier Operating Systems

When Apple brings out a new version of Xcode, it includes software development kits (SDKs) for the latest version of iOS (8) and the versions of OS X that it can run on (Mavericks 10.9 and Yosemite 10.10). In theory, that isn't much of a constraint: You can still target earlier OSes; the SDK does the right thing to adapt itself to the earlier versions.

However, there are some APIs that don't make the cut. (An earlier, incompatible version of libcrypto was dropped in OS X 10.6 after warnings more than a year in advance.) The same with PowerPC development: If you need to do that, get a Mac that can run 10.6 and use Xcode 3.2.6. I'll explain how use the xcode-select tool to switch your system between versions of Xcode in the "Command-Line Tools" section of Chapter 25, "The Xcode Build System."

> **Note**
>
> People have asked whether they can pluck SDKs from earlier Xcode installations and drop them into Xcode 6. Ultimately it doesn't work: The older SDKs rely on compilers and runtime libraries that are not available in Xcode 6, and Xcode 6 assumes that its SDKs are built to support the tools it does have. To quote an Apple Developer Tools engineer, "Xcode receives zero testing in these unsupported configurations."

Requirements

Apple is cagey about what the operating requirements are for Xcode, and that's understandable, because it depends on your usage and preferences.

- Xcode 6 runs on OS X Mavericks (10.9) and Yosemite (10.10).
- The download will be about 2 GB.
- How much disk space the installed Xcode takes up depends on what documentation sets and supplementary tools you download. A fresh installation is about 6.5 GB; 9 GB is not uncommon with options.
- Xcode 6 can be *run* in 2 GB of memory, but don't expect to do much more than look at it. For the examples in this book, 4 GB should be enough, but for medium-sized projects, my rule of thumb is that you'll need about 3 GB, plus another 750 MB for each processor core in your machine. Get more RAM if you can; I don't know anybody who has reached the point of diminishing returns.
- Xcode is a 64-bit Intel application. The minima for this book are 64-bit, dual-core, and 1.2 GHz. More is better.
- Bigger—particularly, wider—displays are better. I'm writing on a MacBook Air with 1,440 points' horizontal resolution. With the display-management techniques I'll show you, it's comfortable most of the time. And with my 15" Retina MacBook Pro set to show the maximum content, I have no complaints.

The bottom-of-the-line Mac mini on sale as I write this ($599 in the U.S., plus display, keyboard, and mouse) is fine for the purposes of *Xcode 6 Start to Finish*, as are most Macs sold since 2010.

> **Note**
>
> *Xcode 6 Start to Finish* was written using Xcode up through version 6.2 on a Mac running OS X 10.10 Yosemite, with allowances for Swift 1.2. If you're using Mavericks, be aware that the appearance of the windows won't match what you see in the illustrations, and some exercises—Mac storyboards in particular—will not be possible without Yosemite.

Installing Xcode

For most purposes, obtaining Xcode 6 is very easy: Find it in the Mac App Store (MAS), enter your Apple ID and password, and download it. It's free. See "Downloading Xcode," later in this chapter, for another option, and why you might need it.

Once the download is complete, Xcode will be in your /Applications folder.

> **Note**
>
> Want to see everything you got? Right-click the Xcode icon in /Applications, and select **Show Package Contents**. You'll see the directories and files behind the pseudo-file representing Xcode. Poke around all you like, but don't make any changes.

There's no step three. There are no installation options—there's no installer. In earlier versions, developer tools were put in a /Developer directory at the root of the boot volume (or the one you selected in the installer). No more: All the tools you need for basic iOS and Mac development are contained in Xcode itself.

Most of the documentation *isn't* installed. Xcode will download it the first time you run it. It's not practical to bundle it into the Xcode download: It runs hundreds of megabytes, it changes more frequently than the developer tools, and you may not want it all. The **Downloads** panel of the Preferences window controls the downloads.

One advantage of MAS distribution is that once the App Store application knows it has installed Xcode, it can alert you to updates. When you accept an update, the App Store sends only the components that changed, greatly reducing the download time. Downloads smaller than 100 MB are not unknown.

Command-Line Tools

As installed, Mavericks and Yosemite contain executable files in /usr/bin that have the names of common development tools—make, gcc, clang, and so on. Open-source projects that must be built before being installed expect to find those tools in that directory. But they aren't the actual programs that go by those names. They are trampolines; when you run them, they hand off to the real programs elsewhere in the system:

- To the tools embedded in the Xcode application package, if Xcode is present.
- To the tools in /Library/Developer, if present. This is where the contents of the optional command-line tools package go.
- If none can be found, the trampoline program will offer to download and install the command-line tools package. You can also do this by executing sudo xcode-select --install.

In any case, the executable files in /usr/bin will always be trampolines.

So if you're running Xcode 6, you don't need a separate package of developer tools. The system will act as though they were there already—and your Xcode and command-line builds will use the same tools, which should make most developers a lot less nervous.

If you don't want Xcode 6, don't install it. Run one of the tools, or go to http://developer.apple.com/downloads and grab an installer; be sure to get the version that goes with your version of OS X.

Removing Xcode

Your life has changed. The honeymoon is over. You've had your look, and you're done. You've decided to edit a theatrical feature and you need the space. You're giving your Mac to your daughter in art school. For whatever reason, you're done with Xcode. How do you get rid of it?

In the early days of Xcode, this involved uninstall scripts and directory deletions. Now, you just drag the Xcode application into the Trash, and you're done. Almost.

The reason uninstallation was so complicated in earlier Xcodes was that you had to get rid of the tools, libraries, headers, and frameworks that Xcode would infiltrate throughout the system. The scripts ran down the inventory and rooted out each item.

But remember what I said earlier about the command-line tools: The tools and other files are all inside Xcode. Everything else out in the system is a trampoline to those files. Throw away Xcode, and you'll have gotten rid of what previously had been infiltrations...

...unless you installed the stand-alone Command Line Developer Tools package. You can find those in `/Library/Developer/` along with some large documentation libraries. Delete that directory. Do the same with `~/Library/Developer/`.

Apple Developer Programs

Anyone can pick up Xcode 6 for free and start developing OS X and iOS software. If your interest is in distributing Mac software on your own, your preparation is done: Build your apps, put them on the Net, and God bless you.

However, if you want to distribute your work on the Mac or iOS App Store; assure users with Gatekeeper that your Mac apps are safe; or even test your iOS app on a device, you have to go further. You'll need to pay for a membership in the Mac or iOS Developer Program. (If you need to, you can join both.)

Apple's policies and methods for joining developer programs are subject to change, so the best I can do for you is to give an overview. Start by browsing to `http://developer.apple.com/`. Prominently featured will be links to join the iOS and Mac developer programs. The programs will give you:

- Access to prerelease software, including operating systems and developer tools.
- Access to the parts of the developer forums (`http://devforums.apple.com/`) that cover nondisclosed topics.
- Two incidents with Developer Technical Support (DTS), Apple engineers who can advise you on development strategies and help you with troubleshooting. This is the only official, guaranteed way to get help from Apple. If you have the time, by all means go to a developer forum or mailing list first (you'll find lots of leads in Appendix B, "Resources"), but if that fails, DTS is the best choice.
- The right to submit your applications for sale in the Mac or iOS App Store.
- In the case of iOS, the right to load your app into a device for debugging purposes (see Chapter 18, "Provisioning," for details).
- In the case of OS X, a Developer ID certificate that enables users who use Gatekeeper to install your app.

Make your choice (whichever you choose, you'll be offered both programs), and you will be taken to a page with an **Enroll Now** button, citing the cost of a year's membership ($99 in the United States as I write this).

The next step is to establish your status as a "registered Apple developer." Registered developers have few privileges beyond having a persistent record with Apple that can be used to sign up for developer programs. (There are a limited number of resources to which your assent to terms and conditions entitles you, such as access to the released-product sections of the developer forums.) If you're already registered, say so, and skip to the signup process. If you're not, present your Apple ID (such as you might be using with iTunes) or get one, fill out marketing and demographic questionnaires, and assent to the terms and conditions of Apple programs. They'll send you an email you can use to verify your contact information.

Once that's done, you're given your choice of programs. Select all you are interested in and can afford; the iOS and Mac programs incur separate charges, and there's no discount. There's also a free Safari program, which allows you to develop and sign extensions for the desktop Safari web browser.

Next you'll have program-specific licenses to agree to. When that's done, you're a member.

Downloading Xcode

The App Store download is convenient, but it's not for everybody. New versions of Xcode—even point releases—may drop features on which you may have relied. Xcode supports keeping more than one copy of the application on your computer, but the App Store *doesn't*. When you accept an update from the App Store, it seeks out older versions, wherever they may be, and deletes them. You'll have to take control of the process yourself.

> **Note**
>
> See Chapter 25, "The Xcode Build System," for the `xcode-select` and `xcrun` command-line tools that support using multiple versions of Xcode.

If you're a developer program member (even a member of the free program), you have access to `http://developer.apple.com/downloads`. Use the checkboxes to narrow the listing to developer tools. You will find every Xcode toolset going back to 1.0 (a 584-MB CD image for OS X 10.3). The currently released version of Xcode will be near the top. Download it.

If you want a version that Apple has not put out as a public beta, you'll have to go to either the iOS or OS X developer center, log in with your paid developer-program credentials, select the prerelease section, and receive a Mac App Store redemption code. This will get you the first prerelease version of Xcode, which the Mac App Store application will update.

You'll end up with a compressed disk-image (`.dmg`) file. Double-click it to reveal the Xcode application. Drag it into `/Applications`, or wherever you like. If you want to preserve an earlier version, rename that copy first.

Updates carry two penalties compared to the MAS method: You'll have to keep track of their availability yourself, and you'll have to download the whole toolset again. No incremental updates for you.

> **Warning**
>
> Apple's official position is that Xcode 6 is the only version it will support on Yosemite. Historically, Apple has been very conservative with the word "support" as it applies to

> previous versions of developer tools on newer operating systems. My interpretation is that Developer Tools has enough on its hands building a major version of Xcode without exhaustively testing and revising the version they were making obsolete. Maybe it works, maybe it doesn't, but Apple isn't going to stand behind it.

Additional Downloads

Download files for early versions of Xcode topped out at 3 GB. The Xcode 4.3 image was just over half that size, 1.8 GB.

One way Apple keeps download sizes down is to provide only stubs for OS X and iOS documentation. The first time you run Xcode, it triggers a download of the full documentation sets. This annoys people who want 100 percent functionality after installing Xcode aboard airplanes, but there's really no alternative: Not everybody needs every documentation set. Further, Apple updates its documentation much more often than it updates Xcode, so even if the download included full documentation, you'd have to pull in the current docs anyway.

Another trick for reducing download size is to recognize that not everybody needs every development tool. Apple has broken seven toolsets out into downloadable archives. Not only does this keep these files out of the main download, it allows Apple to free them from the release cycle of Xcode itself.

Here are the available packages as I write this:

- Accessibility—Tools for auditing and testing accessibility support of your Mac applications.
- Audio—Applications for examining Core Audio units, plus headers and sample code.
- Auxiliary—Help Indexer (create Mac application help books), Repeat After Me (refine your text-to-speech translations), and tools for creating new dictionaries for the Mac Dictionary application.
- Command-line tools—Commands you can use from the Terminal application for classic-style development; this is how you'd get the tools without needing Xcode even to install them.
- Dashcode—Apple's visual editor for HTML5/CSS/JavaScript to be used as OS X Dashboard widgets, and for iOS-like web applications.
- Hardware IO—Probes for USB and Bluetooth, as well as the Network Link Conditioner, which allows you to degrade network performance and reliability to simulate mobile connectivity in the iOS Simulator.
- Graphics—OpenGL development tools, and the Quartz Composer builder for chains of image and video filters.

If you want one of the supplemental toolsets, open Xcode and select **Xcode → Open Developer Tool → More Developer Tools. . . .** Your default browser will be directed to the developer downloads site, with the search string set to **for Xcode -**, which will show you what's available.

When you find what you need, click the disclosure triangle to show a description of the package and a link to download it. You'll be asked to read and accept the general license for Apple's developer tools. Agree, and the download will start.

What you'll get is a `.dmg` disk image containing applications and installers. Drag the apps into `/Applications`, or wherever else you find convenient—they will not appear under the **Xcode** menu.

In addition to the specialized toolsets, there are other components like device-debugging software and simulators for back versions of iOS. Use the Preferences window, **Downloads** panel, **Components** section to download and install them if you need them.

Summary

Apple has tried to strike a balance between making Xcode easily available to everybody, and providing choices about what and how much to install. The free installation from the Mac App Store will get you everything you need to get started with iOS and OS X development. If your needs are more specialized—if you need older versions, or customized toolsets—the developer downloads site has it all.

2

Kicking the Tires

Now you have Xcode. It's time to start it up and see what it looks like.

Starting Xcode

You'll find Xcode in the /Applications directory, just like any application. You'll be using it constantly, so you'll want to keep it in the Dock at the bottom of your main screen. Drag Xcode to the Dock—take care to drop it *between* icons, and not *on* one.

Now click the Xcode icon. It bounces to show Xcode is being launched. It will bounce for a very, very long time. And then it will stop bouncing, and nothing will happen.

The first time any OS X application is launched, the system examines the application bundle to verify that it matches its cryptographic signature. A typical application has as many as 2,000 files to check, imposing a delay that is noticeable if you pay attention.

Xcode 6 has some 188,000 files. OS X must validate all of them. This takes minutes. Apple now displays progress bars for lengthy verifications, which at least assures you that something is happening. Eventually, Xcode is ready for business.

The first time you run any of Apple's developer tools—even through the command line—you'll be asked to read and accept a license agreement for the tools and SDKs. It's no different from any other click-through license process.

Next, Xcode will ask you for permission to install the "additional components" it needs. Permit it, and present an administrator's credentials. Those components overlap the iTunes frameworks, so you may be asked to close iTunes.

Once the progress window clears, you are greeted with the "Welcome to Xcode" window (see Figure 2.1).

If this is the first time you've ever run Xcode, the table on the right will be empty ("No Recent Projects"); as you accumulate projects, the table will contain references to them, so you have a quick way to get back to your work. When you accumulate projects in this list, you'll be able to select one, but Xcode doesn't reveal any way to open it. The trick is to double-click the item, or press the Return key.

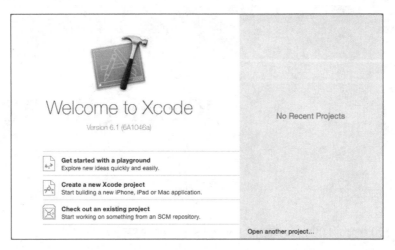

Figure 2.1   When you launch Xcode, it displays a "Welcome" window with options for creating a new project, reopening a recent one, or fetching a project from a source-control repository.

You have four other options:

- **Get started with a playground**. A *playground* is a file that accepts code in the Swift programming language, and interprets it interactively—it's not just a type-and-print console. A playground displays all the results of your code in real time: The results of your code appear instantly, and any changes you make will be reflected in the whole file.

- **Create a new Xcode project**. This is obvious enough; it's how you'd start work on a new product. You're about to do this, but hold off for the moment. You could also select **File →New →Project. . .** (⇧⌘N).

- **Check out an existing project**. Xcode recognizes that source control management is essential to even the most trivial of projects. Your development effort might start not with your own work, but with collaborative work pulled in from a source repository. Use this link to get started.

- **Open another project. . .** (at the bottom of the "recents" list). This will get you the standard get-file dialog so you can select any Xcode project file you want. You can do the same thing with the **File →Open. . .** (⌘O) command.

If you need to get back to the Welcome window, select **Window →Welcome to Xcode** (⇧⌘1). If you're tired of seeing this window, uncheck **Show this window when Xcode launches**. (The checkbox appears only when your mouse pointer is over the window.)

> **Note**
>
> "Show this window when Xcode launches" is not quite accurate. If you had a project open when you last quit Xcode, it will reopen when you start it up again, and the Welcome window won't appear.

Hello World

Just to get oriented, I'm going to start with the simplest imaginable example project—so simple, you won't have to do much coding at all.

A New Project

Click the **Create a new Xcode project** link. Xcode opens an empty Workspace window, and drops the New Project assistant sheet in front of it (see Figure 2.2). Select **OS X → Application** from the list at left, and then the **Command Line Tool** template from the icons that appear at right. Click **Next**.

The next panel (Figure 2.3) asks for the name of the project and the kind of command-line tool you want.

1. Type **Hello World** in the **Product Name** field. This will be used as the name of the project and its principal product.
2. Xcode should have filled in the **Organization Name** for you, from your "me" card in Contacts. If you listed a company for yourself, that's what will be in the field; otherwise, it's your personal name. Xcode will use this as the name of the copyright holder for all new files.
3. Virtually all executable objects in the OS X and iOS world have reverse-DNS-style identifiers that are used to uniquely identify them. The **Organization Identifier** is the leading portion of those reverse-DNS names, to be used by every product of this project. For this example, I used com.wt9t.
4. By default, Xcode infers the unique **Bundle Identifier** from the organization identifier and the name of the product. You'll see later how to change this if you have to.

Figure 2.2   The New Project assistant leads you through the creation of an Xcode project. First, you specify the kind of product you want to produce.

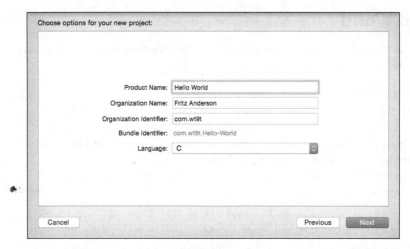

Figure 2.3   The **Options** panel of the New Project assistant lets you identify the product and what support it needs from system libraries.

5. The **Language** popup prompts Xcode on how to fill in the system libraries the tool will use. This is just a plain old C program, with no need for C++ or Apple-specific support, so choose **C**.

Click **Next**; a put-file sheet appears, so you can select a directory to put the project into. For this example, select your Desktop. One more thing—*uncheck* the box labeled **Create Git repository on. . . .** Source control (Chapter 7, "Version Control") is a Good Thing, but let's not deal with it in this trivial example. Click **Create**.

If you look on your Desktop, you'll find that Xcode has created a folder named `Hello World`. The project name you specified is used in several places.

- It's the name of the project *directory* that contains your project files.
- It's the name of the project *document* (`Hello World.xcodeproj`) itself.
- It's the name of the *product*—in this case a command-line tool named `Hello World`.
- It's the name of the *target* that builds the product. I'll get into the concept of a target later; for now, think of it as the set of files that go into a product, and a specification of how it is built.
- It's the name of the *target's* directory inside the *project's* directory.

When you've made your choices, Xcode unmasks the workspace for the Hello World project (Figure 2.4). Don't look at it too closely just yet. Xcode starts you off with a view of the settings that control how `Hello World` is to be built. This is useful information, but for now, it's just details.

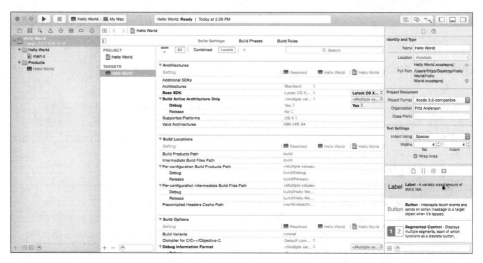

Figure 2.4   Once set up, the Hello World project window fills in with a list of source files and a
display of the options that control how the application will be built.

More interesting is the program code itself. The left column of the window is called
the *Navigator area*. Find `main.c` in the list, and click it (see Figure 2.5). The Editor area,
which fills most of the window, now displays the contents of `main.c`. This is the code for
the canonical simplest-possible program, known as "Hello, World."

The Navigator area displays many different things in the course of development—it's
not just a file listing. It can display analyses, searches, and build logs. Which list you see
often depends on what Xcode wants to show you; you can make the choice yourself by
clicking the tiny icons in the bar at the top of the Navigator area. Hovering the mouse
pointer over them will show you the names of the various views.

As this book goes on, you'll meet all of them. For now, you care only about the
"Project" navigator, the file list Xcode starts you out with. Feel free to click the other

Figure 2.5   Clicking the name of an editable file in the Project navigator displays its contents in
the Editor area.

icons, but to keep up with this example, be sure to return to the Project navigator, as shown in Figure 2.5.

Quieting Xcode Down

But first.

Xcode is a toolset that contains everything its creators could think of to provide a powerful, helpful environment for writing iOS and OS X applications. Often, you barely need to begin a task, and Xcode will offer to finish it for you. It will usually be right. I use these features all the time. I recommend them.

You're going to turn them all off.

Automatic completions and indentations and code decorations and code fixes are great, once you know what's going on, but an automaton that snatches your work out of your hands, however helpfully, is straight out of *The Sorcerer's Apprentice*. Better to start with what *you* want to do; once you're confident of what that is, then you have the discretion and control to direct Xcode as it helps you.

So you're going to damp Xcode down a bit. You'll do all of this in Xcode's Preferences window, which you can summon with **Xcode →Preferences...** (⌘ **comma**). The Preferences window is divided into panels, which you select with the icons at the top of the window.

To start, make sure the **General** panel is visible. Under **Issues**, uncheck **Show live issues**.

Next, select the **Text Editing** panel, which has two tabs. Select the **Editing** tab, and uncheck **Show: Code folding ribbon**, and all the options under **Code completion:**.

In the **Indentation** tab, turn off **Line wrapping: Wrap lines to editor width** and the **Syntax-aware indenting** section.

Now Xcode will mostly stay out of your way as you explore.

Building and Running

The program in `main.c` would run as is, but we have to trick Xcode into keeping its output on the screen long enough to see it. Add a few lines after the `printf` call so it looks like this:

```c
int main(int argc, const char * argv[])
{
    // insert code here...
    printf("Hello, World!\n");

    /*******************************************
     *  Pause, so the console doesn't disappear
     *******************************************/
    char    dummy[128];
    fgets(dummy, sizeof(dummy), stdin);
```

```
        return 0;
}
```

Now we can run it. Select **Product → Run** (⌘R).

A heads-up window ("bezel") appears almost instantly, to tell you "Build Succeeded." (If Xcode is in the background, a notification banner will appear saying the build succeeded, and identifying the project and product involved.)

So. What happened?

Hello World is a console application; it just writes out some text without putting up any windows. Xcode captures the console of the apps it runs in the Debug area, which popped into view when you ran the program (Figure 2.6). The Debug area includes a console view on the right. It says Hello, World! (Figure 2.7).

Click in the console to make it ready for text input, and press the Return key. Hello World exits, and the Debug area closes.

Note

If the Debug area didn't hide itself as soon as an application terminated, we wouldn't have had to add that fgets() call. That's easy to change; see the "Behaviors" section of Chapter 4, "Active Debugging."

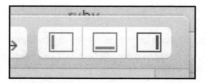

Figure 2.6   The **View** selector in the toolbar shows and hides the Navigator, Debug, and Utility areas (left to right) of the project window. Clicking a button so it is highlighted exposes the corresponding area. Here, the Navigator and Debug areas are selected.

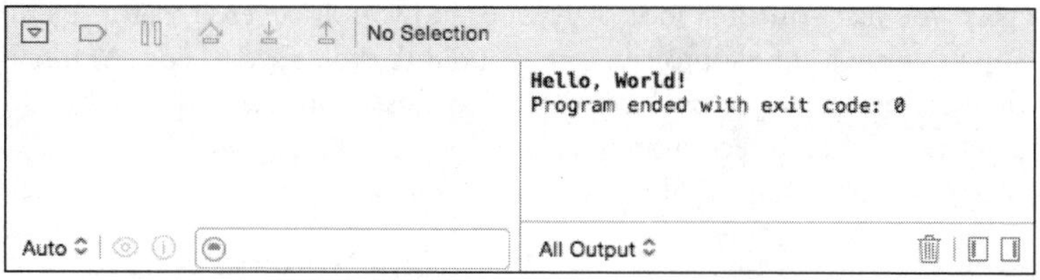

```
 ▽  ▷  ‖   △  ⤓  ⤒  │ No Selection
                              Hello, World!
                              Program ended with exit code: 0



 Auto ↕ │ ◉ ⓘ  ⦿          All Output ↕          🗑 │ ▯ ▯
```

Figure 2.7   Opening the Debug area after running Hello World shows the eponymous output.

The Real Thing

What Xcode just produced for you is a real, executable application, not a simulation. To prove it, open the Terminal application (you'll find it at `/Applications/Utilities/Terminal`, and you'd be well advised to add Terminal to your Dock). In Xcode, find the `Hello World` product in the Project navigator by clicking the disclosure triangle next to the Products folder icon. Drag the `Hello World` icon into the Terminal window, switch to Terminal, and press the Return key. (The path to a file deep in a directory for build products is remarkably long, but Terminal takes care of the necessary escaping.) "Hello, World!" appears.

If you want access to the executable file itself, select it in the Project navigator, then **File → Show in Finder**—also available in the contextual menu you get by right-clicking the `Hello World` icon. A window will open in the Finder showing you the file.

You're done! You can close the Workspace window (**File → Close Project**, ⌥⌘W) or quit Xcode entirely (**Xcode → Quit Xcode**, ⌘Q).

Getting Rid of It

There is nothing magical about an Xcode project. It's just a directory on your hard drive. If you don't want it any more, close the project, select its enclosing folder in the Finder, and drag it to the Trash. It's gone. It won't even show up in the Recents list in the Welcome to Xcode window, or in the **File → Open Recent** menu.

That's it.

Okay, yes, the build products of the project will still stick around in a warren of directories inside `~/Library/Developer/Xcode/DerivedData`. They aren't many or large in this case, but there's a principle involved.

If you want them gone, the best way is to close the project window, open the Organizer window (**Window → Organizer**), select the **Projects** panel, select the "Hello World" project, press Delete, and confirm the deletion in the ensuing alert sheet. All trace of the build products is gone.

Summary

In this chapter, you had your first look at Xcode, and you discovered that it doesn't bite. You saw how to create a simple project, one you didn't even have to edit. You saw what happens when you run a project in Xcode, how to close a project and quit Xcode, and at last how to get rid of the project entirely.

Next, we'll start doing some real work.

3

Simple Workflow and Passive Debugging

This chapter begins your use of Xcode in earnest. Here's where I introduce the problem that is the basis for all of the example code in this book.

The problem is the calculation of *passer ratings*. In American/Canadian football, quarterbacks advance the ball by throwing (passing) it to other players. The ball may be caught (received, a good thing) by someone on the quarterback's own team, in which case the ball is advanced (yardage, more is better), possibly to beyond the goal line (a touchdown, the object of the game); or it may be caught by a member of the opposing team (intercepted, a very bad thing).

But those are four numbers, and everybody wants a figure-of-merit, a single scale that says (accurately or not) who is the better passer. The National Football League and the Canadian Football League have a formula for passer ratings, yielding a scale running from 0 to (oddly) 158.3. A quarterback who rates 100 has had a pretty good day.

Creating the Project

As in Chapter 2, "Kicking the Tires," you'll start with a command-line project. Start Xcode and click **Create a new Xcode project**, or select **File → New → Project. . .** (⇧ ⌘ N). In the New Project assistant sheet, select an OS X Command Line Tool, and name the tool **passer-rating**; for **Language**, once again choose **C**.

Another difference: When you are shown the get-file sheet to select the location for the new project, check the box labeled **Create Git repository on**, and select **My Mac**. Git is a *version-control system*, an essential part of modern development. You'll learn all about it in Chapter 7, "Version Control," but now is the time to start.

> **Note**
> Are you ever going to change anything in a project? Get it under version control. Seriously. Your work will be safer, and you'll do it faster.

Again, you'll be shown target settings, which you can ignore for now. Instead, mouse over to the Project navigator at the left side of the Workspace window, and select `main.c`.

Delete everything in the `main()` function but its outer braces, and replace the body of the function so the file reads thus (keep the comments at the top of the file):

```c
#include <stdio.h>
#include "rating.h"      //  Yet to create; initially an error

int main(int argc, const char * argv[])
{
    int         nArgs;
    do {
        int         comps, atts, yards, TDs;
        printf("comps, atts, yards, TDs: ");
        nArgs = scanf("%d %d %d %d %d",
                      &comps, &atts, &yards, &TDs);
        if (nArgs == 5) {
            float  rating = passer_rating(comps, atts, yards, TDs);
            printf("Rating = %.1f\n", rating);
        }
    } while (nArgs == 5);

    return 0;
}
```

You'll notice that as you type closing parentheses, brackets, and braces, the corresponding opening character is briefly highlighted in yellow.

The rating calculation itself is simple. Put it into a file of its own: Select **File → New → File...** (⌘ N). You'll be presented with the New File assistant sheet; see Figure 3.1. Navigate the source list on the left, and the icon array on the right thus: OS X → Source → C File.

Click **Next**, and use the save-file sheet that appears to name the file **rating** (Xcode will append .c automatically).

The save-file sheet has two custom controls. The **Group** popup lets you place the new file in the Project navigator (the source list at the left of the project window). Roughly, groups are simply ways to organize the Project inspector list; they have no influence on how the new file will be placed on-disk. Make sure the passer-rating group is selected.

Second is **Targets**, a table that for now has only one row, **passer-rating**. A target is a group of files and settings that combine to build a product. A file that isn't part of a target isn't used to build anything. Make sure that **passer-rating** is checked.

> **Note**
>
> It's easy to get the target assignment wrong. Xcode 6 sets the same targets for new files as the ones for the last files that were added. If you forget to set the proper targets, you won't know about it until your app fails to build or mysteriously crashes because a needed resource wasn't included.

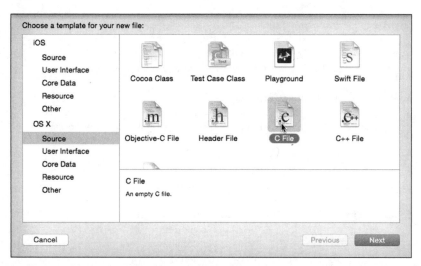

Figure 3.1   The New File assistant sheet offers many templates you can use to start a new file. Select the category from the source list on the left, and pick the template from the array of icons on the right.

Here's what goes into `rating.c`:

```c
#include "rating.h"

static
double pinPassingComponent(double component)
{
    if (component < 0.0)
        return 0.0;
    else if (component > 2.375)
        return 2.375;
    else
        return component;
}

float
passer_rating(int comps, int atts, int yds, int tds, int ints)
{
    //  See http://en.wikipedia.org/wiki/Quarterback_Rating


    double      completionComponent =
                    (((double) comps / atts) * 100.0 - 30.0) / 20.0;
    completionComponent = pinPassingComponent(completionComponent);
```

```
double      yardageComponent =
                 (((double) yds / atts) - 0.3) / 4.0;
                 //  intentional bug
yardageComponent = pinPassingComponent(yardageComponent);

double      touchdownComponent =
                 20.0 * (double) tds / atts;
touchdownComponent = pinPassingComponent(touchdownComponent);

double      pickComponent =
                 2.375 - (25.0 * (double) ints / atts);
pickComponent = pinPassingComponent(pickComponent);

double retval =   100.0 * (completionComponent +
                          yardageComponent +
                          touchdownComponent +
                          pickComponent) / 6.0;
return retval;
}
```

Note

You see a few bugs in this code. Well done. Throughout this book, I'm going to give you some buggy code to illustrate debugging techniques. Just play along, okay?

By now, you've missed a couple of braces, and you are tired of tabbing to get the extra level of indenting. Xcode can do this for you—it's among the features I had you turn off in the last chapter.

Open the Preferences window (**Xcode → Preferences**, ⌘ **comma**) and select the **Text Editing** panel. In the **Editing** tab, check **Code completion: Automatically insert closing "}"**. In the **Indentation** tab, check **Syntax-aware indenting: Automatically indent based on syntax**.

Now type an open brace in your code, at the end of a line. So what, it's a brace. Now press Return. Xcode adds two lines: Your cursor is now at the next line, indented one level, and a matching closing brace appears on the line after that.

Finally, you've noticed that both main.c and rating.c refer to a rating.h, which notifies main() of the existence of the passer_rating function. Press ⌘ N again, and choose Header File from the source files. Name it **rating**, and put this into it:

```
#ifndef passer_rating_rating_h
#define passer_rating_rating_h

float passer_rating(int comps, int atts, int yds,
                    int tds, int ints);
#endif
```

> **Note**
>
> Place header files wherever you like among the project groups, but don't add them to any targets. There are exceptions; if you need to do it, you'll know. Chapter 6, "Adding a Library Target," has more.

Click **Create**.

Building

That's enough to start. Let's try to run it. It's easy: Click the **Run** button at the left end of the toolbar, or select **Product** → **Run** (⌘ R). It doesn't matter if you haven't saved your work; by default Xcode saves everything before it attempts a build. Xcode chugs away at your code for a bit... and stops.

- A heads-up placard flashes, saying "Build Failed."
- The Navigator area switches to the Issue navigator, which shows two items under `main.c`. (If the Issue navigator doesn't appear, click the fourth tab at the top of the Navigator area.) One is tagged with a yellow triangle (a warning), and the other with a red octagon (an error). These include descriptions of the errors (Figure 3.2, top).
- When you click one of the items, the editor highlights two lines in `main.c`. The line that triggered the warning is tagged in yellow, with a banner describing the warning; the error line is in red, with a banner of its own (Figure 3.2, bottom).

It seems the only place where I remembered about interceptions was the format string of the `scanf` call. The compiler was smart enough to match the number of format specifiers to the number of arguments of the `scanf` and complain. Similarly, I left off the last parameter to `passer_rating`, which is an outright error.

> **Note**
>
> For a compiler, an *error* is a flaw in your source that makes it impossible to translate your code into executable form. The presence of even one error prevents Xcode from producing a program. A *warning* indicates something in your source that *can* be translated but will probably result in a bug or a crash when you run it. Experienced developers do not tolerate warnings; there is even a compiler option to make a build fail upon a warning just as though it were an error. Don't ever ignore a warning.

> **Note**
>
> Need a reminder of what `passer_rating` does with its parameters? Try this: While `main` is visible in the Editor area, hold down the Command key and point the mouse at the symbol `passer_rating`. You'll see it turns blue and acquires an underline, as if it were a link on a standard web page. Click it: The editor jumps to the declaration of `passer_rating`. You can jump back by clicking the back-arrow button in the upper-left corner of the editor; by pressing ^ ⌘ ←; or by swiping right across the editor area with two fingers, if you've enabled the gesture in System Preferences. (Option-clicking the name

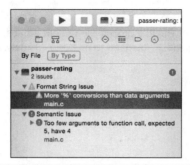

Figure 3.2   (top) When Xcode detects build errors, it opens the Issue navigator to display them. (bottom) Clicking an issue focuses the editor on the file and line at which the issue was detected.

gets you a popover that tells you `passer_rating` was declared in `rating.h`. More on this in Chapter 24, "Documentation in Xcode.")

You can dash off a fix very quickly:

```
do {
    int        comps, atts, yards, TDs, INTs;
    printf("comps, atts, yards, TDs, INTs: ");
    nArgs = scanf("%d %d %d %d %d",
                  &comps, &atts, &yards, &TDs, INTs);
    if (nArgs == 5) {
        float   rating = passer_rating(comps, atts, yards,
                                       TDs, INTs);
        printf("Rating = %.1f\n", rating);
    }
} while (nArgs == 5);
```

To be conservative (I don't want Xcode to run the program if a warning remains), **Product →Build** (⌘B) will compile and link `passer-rating` without running it. You needn't have worried: It compiles without error, displaying a "Build Succeeded" placard.

Note

The Issues navigator will show a warning or two. Let's play dumb and carry on.

Running

Now you have something runnable. Run it (**Run** button, first in the toolbar; or ⌘**R**).

There is a transformation: The Debug area appears at the bottom of the window; and the **View** control in the toolbar highlights its middle button to match the appearance of the Debug area (Figure 3.3).

The right half of the Debug area is a console that you'll be using to communicate with the `passer-rating` tool. If all has gone well, it should be showing something like this:

comps, atts, yards, TDs, INTs:

...which is just what the `printf()` was supposed to do. `passer-rating` is waiting for input, so click in the console pane and type:

10 20 85 1 0 <return>

Something went wrong. `passer-rating` crashed. `lldb`, the debugging engine, takes control, and the debugging displays fill up.

- In the Navigator area, the Debug navigator appears, showing the status of the program when it crashed. The upper part of the navigator contains performance bar charts that will be useful when you get to more complex projects. Ignore them for the moment.

  What's left is a *stack trace*, showing the chain of function calls that led to the crash. The top line, labeled 0, is the name of the function, `_svfscanf_l`, where the crash occurred; if you click it, you can see the assembly code (the source isn't available) focused on the very instruction that went wrong. The next line is `scanf`, which you recognize as the function you called from `main`, the function on the next line.

  Xcode identifies `main` as your work by flagging it with a blue head-and-shoulders icon. Click that line to see what your code was doing when the crash occurred.

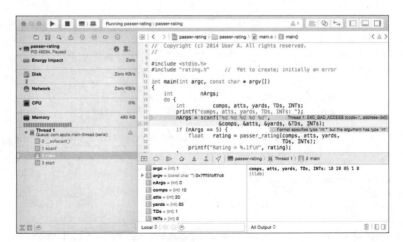

Figure 3.3   Running an app in Xcode opens the Debug area (at the bottom of the project window).

- In the Debug area at the bottom of the window, the left-hand pane fills with the names of variables and their values. You see, for instance, "**atts** = (int) 20," which is just what you entered. Chapter 4, "Active Debugging," discusses this more.

- The Editor area has the most interesting change: A green flag at the left margin and a green banner at the right of the call to `scanf`. The banner says, "Thread 1: EXC_BAD_ACCESS (code=1, address=0x0)." The message may be truncated; you can see the full text in a tooltip that appears if you hover the mouse cursor over the banner.

Note

Xcode has a lot of these banners; often they are the only way it will convey important messages. You will probably set your editor fonts to the smallest you can comfortably read so you can see more of your work at once. The banners are one line high, and their margins take up some space, so the text in them may be *smaller* than you can comfortably read. The only solution is to select larger fonts for everyday use; see the **Fonts & Colors** panel of the Preferences window.

Simple Debugging

EXC_BAD_ACCESS entails the use of a bad pointer, perhaps one pointing into memory that isn't legal for you to read or write to. (The 64-bit virtual-memory management on OS X and modern iOS is set so any address that might be derived from a 32-bit integer is illegal, making it harder to cross `ints` and pointers.) Reexamine the line in `main` that crashed the application and allow a scale to fall from your eyes:

```
nArgs = scanf("%d %d %d %d %d",
              &comps, &atts, &yards, &TDs, INTs);
```

`scanf` collects values through pointers to the variables that will hold them. This call does that for all values except `INTs`, which is passed by value, not by reference. One of the warnings I had you ignore said exactly that: "Format specifies type '(int *)' but the argument has type 'int'." Simply inserting an &

```
nArgs = scanf("%d %d %d %d %d",
              &comps, &atts, &yards, &TDs, &INTs);
```

should cure the problem. Sure enough, running `passer-rating` again shows the crasher is gone:

```
comps, atts, yards, TDs, INTs: 10 20 85 1 0
Rating = 89.4
comps, atts, yards, TDs, INTs: <^D>
```

With the **^D** keystroke, the input stream to `passer-rating` ends, the program exits, and the Debug area closes.

You ordinarily wouldn't want to run or debug a program under Xcode if another is running. Instead, you'd like the incumbent app to clear out. There are four ways to do this.

- Simply let the app exit on its own, as you did when you used **^D** to stop `passer-rating`, or would by selecting the **Quit** command in an OS X application. But this doesn't work for iOS apps, which in principle never quit. You'll have to use one of the other techniques.
- Click the **Stop** button in the toolbar.
- Select **Product → Stop** (⌘ **period**).
- Tell Xcode to run an application, the same or a different one, and click **Stop** in the alert sheet that appears. See Figure 3.4.

That alert sheet also offers an **Add** button, which will run and debug the new process without quitting the old one. Xcode will start a new execution context: You can switch between them using the jump bar at the top of the Debug area, and the **Stop** button in the toolbar becomes a menu you can use to select which instance to stop.

> **Note**
>
> Don't check the **Do not show this message again** box. There will come a time when you want to continue the execution of a program you are debugging, and rather than clicking the tiny button the debugger provides, you'll go for the large, friendly **Run** button in the toolbar. That time comes to me frequently. The add-or-stop sheet is the only thing standing between you and the ruin of your debugging session.

For the moment, you're done: The `scanf` call will return fewer than five inputs if the standard input stream ends. You end it as you would in a terminal shell, by pressing **^D**.

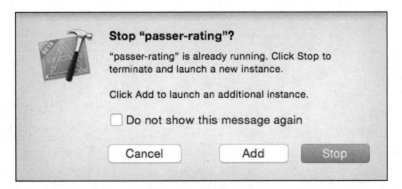

Figure 3.4   When you tell Xcode to run an application while it already has an application running, it displays a sheet asking what you want to do with the existing app. Normally, you'd click **Stop**, but there is also the option to **Add** the new instance to run concurrently with the old one.

> **Note**
>
> **M** and **A** badges are accumulating in the Project navigator. These have to do with version control. Nothing is wrong. Patience! I'll get to it in Chapter 7, "Version Control."

Summary

This chapter stepped you up to writing and running a program of your own. It introduced the first level of debugging: what to do when your program crashes. It turns out that Xcode offers good facilities to help you analyze a crash without you having to do much. You accepted Xcode's guidance, quickly traced the problem, and verified that your fix worked.

But we're not done with `passer-rating`. There are still bugs in it, and this time you'll have to hunt for them.

## 4

Active Debugging

In passer-rating, you have a program that runs without crashing. This is an achievement, but a small one. Let's explore it a little more and see if we can't turn it into a program that works. This entails a small test, and maybe some probing of the inner workings.

A Simple Test Case

Run passer-rating again. Give it the old data set if you like, for a short, mediocre game; but also try a rating for a quarterback who didn't play at all:

```
comps, atts, yards, TDs, INTs: 10 20 85 1 0
Rating = 89.4
comps, atts, yards, TDs, INTs: 0 0 0 0 0
Rating = nan
comps, atts, yards, TDs, INTs:
```

H'm. Not what you expected. It doesn't crash, but it's wrong. A performance in which a passer never passed should be rated zero. passer-rating gave a rating of "nan," which is a code for "not a number." That indicates a logical error in how the math was done.

Now is the time to use the Xcode debugger to examine what is actually happening in passer-rating. Don't stop passer-rating—the debugger lets you instrument your application without changing it.

Going Active

In your previous encounter with the debugger, it took control over passer-rating when a fatal error occurred. This time, you want the debugger to take control at a time of your choosing. By setting a *breakpoint* at a particular line in passer-rating, you tell the debugger to halt execution of the application at that line, so that the contents of variables can be examined and execution resumed under your control.

Setting a Breakpoint

The easiest way to set a breakpoint is to click in the broad gutter area at the left margin of the source code in one of Xcode's editors. Select **rating.c** in the Project navigator to bring that file into the editor. Scroll to the first line of the `passer_rating` function and click in the gutter next to the line that initializes `completionComponent` (see Figure 4.1, top). On the screen, a dark-blue arrowhead appears in the gutter to show that a breakpoint is set there. You can remove the breakpoint by dragging the arrowhead to the side, out of the gutter; you can move the breakpoint by dragging it up or down the gutter.

You can also set a breakpoint at whatever line the editor's insertion point or selection is on by selecting **Debug → Breakpoints → Add Breakpoint at Current Line** (⌘ \\).

> **Note**
>
> If you're keyboard oriented, you can select among the navigators by pressing ⌘ *n*, where *n* is the number of a tab in the Navigator area. Of course, you'll still need the mouse to use the navigator.

There are three ways to avoid a breakpoint. The first is simply to drag it out of the gutter, but if you'll want to restore it, you won't have a marker for the line you were interested in. If you just want to turn off a breakpoint, click on the dark-blue arrow; it will turn pale, and the debugger will ignore it (see Figure 4.1, bottom).

Finally, there is a button in the Debug area's control bar (use the middle segment of the **View** selector at the right end of the toolbar to expose the Debug area) shaped like a breakpoint flag. It's a toggle: When it's blue, the debugger will honor all active breakpoints. When it's gray, the debugger will ignore all breakpoints. Even if the master breakpoint control is off, the debugger will take control if the program crashes.

> **Note**
>
> The Breakpoint navigator (the seventh tab in the Navigator area) lists all of the breakpoints in your project. You can disable or delete breakpoints, or navigate to the corresponding code.

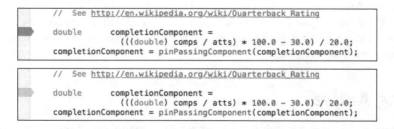

Figure 4.1   (top) Clicking in the gutter at the left edge of the editor sets a breakpoint at that line of code. When the application reaches that line, execution will pause, and the debugger will display the state of the program. (bottom) Clicking an active breakpoint will preserve its place in your code, but the debugger will ignore it. The breakpoint arrow dims to show it is inactive.

You don't have to stop and relaunch a program to start debugging it actively: Setting a breakpoint doesn't change your code, and it doesn't change the executable that was compiled from it. Now that the breakpoint is set, return to the debugger console, where passer-rating still awaits your input, and enter those five zeroes again.

Xcode hits the breakpoint, and responds much as it did for that EXC_BAD_ACCESS error: The Debug navigator shows a stack trace from main to passer_rating, the variables pane in the left half of the Debug area displays the variables in their current state, and a green banner appears in the editor with the label "Thread 1: breakpoint 1.1." At the left margin, just outside the gutter, is a green arrowhead; as you go along, the arrowhead marks the line currently being executed.

> **Note**
>
> The Debug area consists of two panes: variables on the left, and console on the right. A control to show either or both is at the bottom-right corner of the Debug area.

The Variables Pane

Turn your attention to the variables pane. There will be five lines flagged with a purple **A** to designate function arguments and one flagged with a blue-green **L** for the local variable completionComponent. The arguments are all shown as "(int) 0," as you'd expect from the numbers you supplied. The local variable, completionComponent, is also a zero, but typed double.

But wait a minute, there's more than one local variable. Where are the rest? The debugger tries to narrow the list of variables to the ones that are interesting at the moment. yardageComponent is uninteresting because it hasn't been set yet. You don't need to see the garbage value. If you do want to see everything, use the popup menu at the bottom left of the variables pane and select **Local variables** (Figure 4.2, top).

Expose all of the local variables so we can set the values to something that will make it easier to see when they change: Click the line for each one and press Return (double-clicking works as well). Type -1 and press Return again (Figure 4.2, bottom).

> **Note**
>
> There's another way to examine the values of variables as they are displayed in the editor view. Hover your mouse pointer over a reference to the variable, and Xcode will show a popover view containing at least the value, and in the case of complex types like structs and objects, some accounting of the contents. In the case of graphical values, the QuickLook (eye) button will even show you the graphic. It's very powerful and will probably be your first resort as you debug. I'm using the variables pane because it shows all variables continuously and allows you to change them.

Stepping Through

You're ready to watch passer-rating execute. Just above the variables pane is a bar containing a series of controls (Figure 4.3). All controls have menu equivalents, most of them in the **Debug** menu.

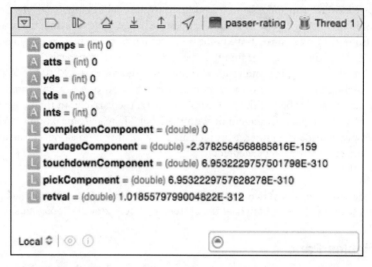

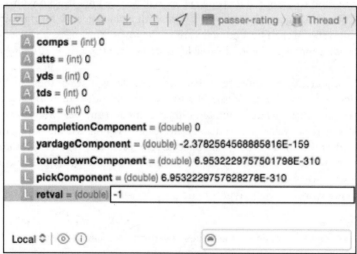

Figure 4.2   (top) When you set the scoping popup at the bottom left of the variables pane to **Local,** you can see all of the arguments and local variables in the current function. (bottom) Double-clicking the value portion of a variable's line allows you to change values on the fly.

Figure 4.3   The bar at the top of the Debug area provides controls for advancing the execution of the program and navigating through its state.

1. The **Hide/Show Debug Area (⇧ ⌘ Y)** button reduces the Debug area to just the debugging bar, and expands it again.
2. The **Activate/Deactivate Breakpoints (⌘ Y)** button enables or disables all of the breakpoints in your project.
3. **Continue (⌃ ⌘ Y)** lets the program run until it hits another breakpoint or crashes.
4. **Step Over (F6)** executes the current line and stops at the next one.
5. **Step Into (F7)** proceeds with execution until it enters the next function called on this line; you'll resume control on the first line of that function.
6. **Step Out (F8)** proceeds with execution until it leaves the current function; you'll resume control in the caller.
7. **Simulate Location** sets the location your app will see when it uses Core Location. This is a popup menu with a selection of common locations throughout the world. You can specify a location of your own by providing a JSON GPX file describing it.
8. A jump bar traces the state of the program from the process to the thread to the current location in the stack trace. Each step allows you to examine a different process, thread, or level in the call stack, and each step presents a submenu so that you can set all three levels with one mouse gesture.

> **Note**
>
> Your Mac may be set up so that the F-keys are overridden by hardware-control functions like volume and screen brightness or intercepted at the system level for other functions. Review the settings in the **Keyboard** tab of the **Keyboard** panel in System Preferences if you want to clear these keys for Xcode's use. Holding down the **fn** key switches the function keys between the two uses.

You're interested in seeing what `passer_rating` does, line by line. Click the **Step Over** button (the arrow looping over an underscore). The green arrowhead jumps to the next line, and something changes in the variables pane: `completionComponent`'s value changes to `NaN`. So now you know: The result is poisoned from the first calculation. Even if the other values are good, a `NaN` in any part of a calculation makes the result a `NaN`, too.

The next line calls `pinPassingComponent`; does that cure the error? Click **Step In** (the arrow pointing down into an underscore). The arrowhead jumps up the page to the first line of `pinPassingComponent`. Step through. You'll find that as `component` fails each of the tests in the `if` statements (`NaN` doesn't compare to anything), the arrow follows execution, jumping over the lines that don't get executed. Stepping through the final `return` jumps execution to the exit point of the function, and then to the next line of the caller.

Fixing the Problem

The problem in `passer-rating` was obvious: I never accounted for the possibility of zero attempts. Time to get back to `rating.c` and make the fix.

Behaviors

But if you've been following along, you'll find some annoyances:

- When `passer-rating` finishes, the Debug area goes away, and you can't inspect its output. You'll have to go to the toolbar and expose it again. A slight pain, but still a pain.

  It was worse in the case of `Hello World`, because without the `fgets()` call, the program would have exited so quickly the debugger console would have closed before you could see it had opened.

- If `passer-rating` were slightly different, and didn't display a prompt before `scanf()` accepted input, you'd never see the debugger at all. The debugger bar would appear at the bottom of the window, but the program would apparently hang until you expanded the debugger and typed something in. Xcode displays the debugger only when the program prints something.

- Xcode does open the debugger in response to output, but the Debug *navigator* doesn't show, unless it had been showing before.

- *But*, stopping for a breakpoint *does* switch to the Debug navigator.

Opinions may differ on these points, and maybe there's a majority for each separately. But it's unlikely that most users will be satisfied with the combination.

Xcode provides a solution. What I've just described is the default, but you can replace the default. Xcode lets you set *behaviors* to control what it does when certain events occur.

> **Note**
>
> If this is not the first time you've used Xcode, it's likely you've touched the default behaviors already, and you aren't seeing what I am. The points are still the same.

Examine the **Behaviors** panel of the Preferences window (Figure 4.4). You'll see the available events listed on the left, divided into building, testing, running, graphical analysis, searching, integration builds, and file unlocking. You're interested in the **Running** → **Starts** event—what happens when your application runs under the debugger.

What you'd like is for the Debug area to appear whenever you run your application for debugging. By default, Xcode does nothing special when you trigger a run: However your project window is configured is how it will stay, and you won't get any sort of notification.

If, instead, Xcode presented the full debugging interface without waiting for break points or output, you'd get your full application status from the start. Here's how you do this.

1. Check the box next to the **Show/Hide navigator** item.
2. Be sure the first popup menu says **Show**.
3. Select **Debug Navigator** in the second popup.
4. Check the box next to the **Show/Hide...debugger** item.
5. Select **Show** from the first popup, and **Current Views** from the second. You can also force the debugger to show either or both of the variables and console panes.

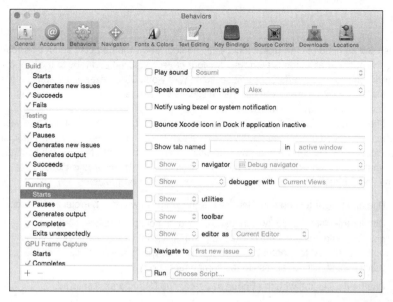

Figure 4.4   The Behaviors panel of Xcode's Preferences window lets you determine what Xcode will do in response to certain events.

The **Starts** row in the behaviors table now has a check next to it. Its actions now match the ones for the **Pauses** and **Generates output** actions, but there's no harm in it, and if you change your mind about **Starts**, you won't have to do anything to get back to where you were.

At the end of the run, I'd like to hide the Debug area and resume the use of the Project navigator *unless* the app wrote something out; I'd be interested in seeing that. Leave the **Completes** behavior as it is by default: **Show** navigator **Project Navigator**, and **If no output, hide** debugger.

> **Note**
>
> There's another way to refer to the debugger output of a program. The last tab of the Navigator area, labeled with a speech balloon, opens the Report navigator. It contains the results of every major operation you've performed recently, including debug sessions. If there are more than one, you can examine and compare each of them.

Try it: Run `passer-rating` one more time, enter some data, get a result, then press **^D** to terminate it. The Debug area and Debug navigator appear when the run starts; when it ends, the Project navigator reappears, but the Debug area remains because `passer-rating` wrote into the console. Success.

Tabs

You also see an option in the **Behaviors** panel labeled "Show tab named," and it's tempting. True to the notion that Xcode is a browser for your project, you can add tabs to the window, each of which provides a different perspective on your work. Other text-editing applications can put separate files in each tab, but that misconceives Xcode's model. The feature is much more powerful but, in a way, also fragile.

Select **File** → **New** → **Tab** (⌘ T) to switch to a new tab. It starts with the same content you had when you issued the command. Try selecting a different file in the Project navigator, and use the toolbar's **View** control to expose the Utility area (on the right). Now switch back to the original tab: Not only does it show the original file, but the Utility area is closed.

Imagine another use. You might have tabs for three different purposes:

- One for straight text-editing: Nothing but the Editor view and the Project navigator.

- One for Interface Builder, which takes up a lot of horizontal space: Navigator hidden (you'd use the jump bar to navigate); Assistant view (the middle "tuxedo" button of the **Editor** control) to show the code for the view's controller; and the Utility area shown for access to the component library.

- One for debugging, with the Debug navigator and Debug area displayed.

You can name tabs: Double-click on the tab's label (by default it shows the name of the file being displayed). It becomes editable, so you can name the tabs "Edit," "Interface Builder," and "Debugger," respectively.

With *that*, you can open the **Behaviors** panel to set the **Completes** action to **Show tab named**, with the name of your "Edit" tab. Just remember to uncheck the **Show navigator** and **Debug Navigator** actions; the tab is already set up for that. The effect is that you can set changes in the window's appearance and function that are much more complex than the simpler options in the **Behaviors** panel.

This is great, as far as it goes, but it's unstable. The same freedom that lets you set each tab as you like doesn't prevent your changing that tab, losing the effort you put into arranging it and focusing it on the right type of file. If you have any behaviors lingering (such as exposing build issues or showing the Debug area), a simple build-and-go could ruin your carefully constructed Interface Builder tab, unless your system of tabs and behaviors changes to a separate context at every event.

The Fix

At last, we get around to repairing `passer_rating`. After all this business with behaviors and tabs, the fix is an anticlimax. Just add this to the start of `passer_rating`:

```
if (atts == 0)
    return 0.0;
```

⌘ **R** runs `passer-rating` one more time. Enter 0 0 0 0 0 at the prompt, and sure enough, you are rewarded with **Rating = 0.0**. Press ^**D**; the Debug area goes away, and the Navigator area returns to the Project navigator. Just what you wanted.

Summary

In this chapter, you used Xcode's debugger to take charge of `passer-rating` to track down a bug. You set a breakpoint, stepped through, into, and out of functions, examining and changing variables as you went.

You also picked up a couple of skills—setting behaviors and tabs—that make it easier to get control of Xcode's habit of changing its windows on its own initiative. On the way, you came to a crucial insight: Xcode isn't meant to be just a source editor; it is a browser on the whole flow of your development effort.

Now I'm going to take a break from that flow to have our first, focused view on what the Xcode tools are doing.

## 5

Compilation

Before continuing, let's review how computer programs get made. If you're coming to Xcode from long experience with GNU Make or another development environment, this discussion will be very familiar to you. Bear with me: I'm going back to basics so every reader will be on a par for what they know about the build process.

Programmers use *source code* to specify what a program does; source code files contain a notation that, although technical and sometimes cryptic, is recognizably the product of a human, intended in part for humans to read. Even the most precise human communication leaves to allusion and implication things that a computer has to have spelled out. If a passer-rating tool were to refer to the local variable `yardageComp`, for example, you'd care only that the name `yardageComp` should consistently refer to the result of a particular calculation; the central processor of a computer running an application, however, cares about the amount of memory allocated to `yardageComp`, the format by which it is interpreted, how memory is reserved for the use of `yardageComp` and later released, that the memory should be aligned on the proper address boundary, that no conflicting use be made of that memory, and, finally, how the address of `yardageComp` is to be determined when data is to be stored or retrieved there. The same issues have to be resolved for each and every named thing in a program.

Compiling

Fortunately, you have a computer to keep track of such things. A *compiler* is a program that takes source files and generates the corresponding streams of machine-level instructions. Consider this function, which calculates two averages and sends them back to the caller through a results `struct`:

```
void calculate_stats(Results * results)
{
    int     n = 0, nScanned = 0;
    double  sum_X, sum_Y;
    sum_X = sum_Y = 0.0;
```

```
    do {
        double      x, y;
        nScanned = scanf("%lg %lg", &x, &y);
        if (nScanned == 2) {
            n++;
            sum_X += x;
            sum_Y += y;
        }
    } while (nScanned == 2);
    Results     lclResults = { .avg_X = sum_X/n
#if CALCULATE_AVG_Y
        , .avg_Y = sum_Y/n
#endif
    };
    *results = lclResults;
}
```

CALCULATE_AVG_Y is defined as 1 or 0, depending on whether the function is to calculate the average of the y values it reads. With average-y included, these 22 lines translate into 54 lines of assembly code (the human-readable equivalent of the bytes the processor would execute):

```
_calculate_stats_100000e40:
    push        rbp
    mov         rbp, rsp
    push        r15
    push        r14
    push        r13
    push        r12
    push        rbx
    sub         rsp, 0x28
    mov         r14, rdi
    lea         rdi, qword [ds:0x100000f82]  ; "%lg %lg"
    lea         rsi, qword [ss:rbp-0x50+var_32]
    lea         rdx, qword [ss:rbp-0x50+var_24]
    xor         al, al
    call        imp___stubs__scanf
    xorps       xmm1, xmm1
    cmp         eax, 0x2
    jne         0x100000ecb
    xor         ebx, ebx
    lea         r15, qword [ds:0x100000f82]  ; "%lg %lg"
    lea         r12, qword [ss:rbp-0x50+var_32]
    lea         r13, qword [ss:rbp-0x50+var_24]
```

```
xorps       xmm2, xmm2
nop         word [cs:rax+rax+0x0]
addsd       xmm1, qword [ss:rbp-0x50+var_24]
```

. . .

Note

For the record, this code was produced by the Xcode 5 version of the `clang` compiler with optimization set to -O3.

I've cut this off at the first 25 lines; you see the kind of output involved. It's not very instructive unless you live with assembly every day. Fortunately, I have the useful Hopper Disassembler, which can reconstruct a C-like function from the byte stream:

```
function _calculate_stats_100000e40 {
    r14 = rdi;
    rax = scanf("%lg %lg");
    xmm1 = 0x0;
    if (rax == 0x2) {
        rbx = 0x0;
        r12 = &var_32;
        r13 = &var_24;
        xmm2 = 0x0;
        do {
            xmm1 = xmm1 + var_24;
            var_16 = xmm1;
            xmm2 = xmm2 + var_32;
            var_8 = xmm2;
            rax = scanf("%lg %lg");
            xmm2 = var_8;
            xmm1 = var_16;
            rbx = rbx + 0x1;
        } while (rax == 0x2);
    }
    else {
        xmm2 = 0x0;
    }
    asm{ divsd    xmm1, xmm0 };
    asm{ divsd    xmm2, xmm0 };
    *r14 = xmm2;
    *(r14 + 0x8) = xmm1;
    return rax;
}
```

You lose the variable names, but you can see the outline. Even at this level, you notice a difference between the machine code and the source: The compiled function calls scanf() *twice*. The read-and-calculate loop in the original function is controlled by whether scanf(), in the loop, returned two values. That determination is made at the bottom of the loop, but that's *after* the input is added to the sums, so the original code guards the calculations in the middle of the loop by testing whether there are two inputs. The compiler simplified the loop by making an extra call to scanf() before the loop starts, eliminating the need for the big if block in the middle.

By now you've seen an important point: Your source is *your* expression of what your code does, but if you let it, the compiler will substantially rearrange (*optimize*) it to meet some criterion—usually speed, but sometimes size or memory pressure. Its only obligation is to ensure that the emitted code has the same effect. But in the line-by-line details, if you were to step through optimized code, the program counter would jump apparently randomly around the lines of your code.

There's more. Let's set the CALCULATE_AVG_Y macro to 0, which does nothing more than remove the final use of sum_Y. The inner loop (while scanf() returns 2) becomes:

```
do {
    var_16 = xmm1;
    var_8 = var_32;
    rax = scanf("%lg %lg");
    xmm1 = var_16;
    xmm1 = xmm1 + var_8;
    rbx = rbx + 0x1;
} while (rax == 0x2);
```

If you puzzle this out, you'll see that sum_Y *isn't there at all*. The compiler saw that, even though the variable was used to accumulate a sum, nothing else used it. There's no point in doing the sum, so it removed sum_Y completely. If you were to trace through this function in the debugger, you wouldn't be able to see the value of sum_Y, because there is no value to see.

Fortunately, you can turn optimization off completely, and the reconstructed loop would look almost identical to what you wrote, including the summing of the sum_Y value that will never be used:

```
function _calculate_stats_100000e70 {
    xmm0 = 0x0;
    var_56 = rdi;
    var_52 = 0x0;
    var_48 = 0x0;
    var_32 = xmm0;
    var_40 = xmm0;
    do {
        rax = scanf("%lg %lg");
        var_48 = rax;
        if (var_48 == 0x2) {
            var_52 = var_52 + 0x1;
            var_40 = var_40 + var_24;
            var_32 = var_32 + var_16;
        }
```

```
    } while (var_48 == 0x2);
    asm{ divsd        xmm1, xmm2 };
    var_0 = var_40;
    var_8 = 0x0;
    rax = var_56;
    *rax = var_0;
    *(rax + 0x8) = var_8;
    return rax;
}
```

This setting (-O0) is what Xcode uses for debugging builds.

When imagining the tasks a compiler must perform in producing executable machine instructions from human-readable source, the first thing that comes to mind is the choice of machine instructions: the translation of floating-point add operations into addsd instructions or expressing the do/while loop in terms of cmpl, je, and jmp. Even this simple example shows that this isn't the whole story.

Another important task is the management of *symbols*. Each C function and every variable has to be expressed in machine code in terms of regions of memory, with addresses and extents. A compiler has to keep strict account of every symbol, assigning an address—or at least a way of getting an address—for it and making sure that no two symbols get overlapping sections of memory. Here's how the assembly for the unoptimized version begins:

```
    push        rbp
    mov         rbp, rsp
    sub         rsp, 0x40
    xorps       xmm0, xmm0
    mov         qword [ss:rbp-0x40+var_56], rdi
    mov         dword [ss:rbp-0x40+var_52], 0x0
    mov         dword [ss:rbp-0x40+var_48], 0x0
    movsd       qword [ss:rbp-0x40+var_32], xmm0
    movsd       qword [ss:rbp-0x40+var_40], xmm0
```

In its analysis of calculate_stats, the compiler budgeted a certain amount of memory in RAM for local variables and assigned general-purpose register rbp to keep track of the end of that block. The 8-byte floating-point number x (var_40) was assigned to the memory beginning 40 bytes into that block; y was assigned to the eight bytes before that. The compiler made sure not to use that memory for any other purpose.

In the optimized version, the sums don't even get stored in memory but are held in the processor's floating-point registers and used from there. Register xmm1, for instance, holds the value of the sum_x variable. Once again, the compiler makes sure that each datum has something to hold it, and that no two claims on storage collide.

In an Xcode project, files that are to be compiled are found in the Target editor: Open the Navigator area on the left side of the window and select the first tab to display the

Project navigator. The item at the top represents the project and all its targets. Select your product's name from the TARGETS list.

The files to be compiled in the build of the target are listed in the "Compile Sources" build phase under the **Build Phases** tab. See Figure 5.1.

```
call        imp___stubs__scanf
```

This line is the translation of the call to the `scanf()` function. What sort of symbol is `imp__stubs_scanf`? Examining a full disassembly of an application using `scanf()` won't tell you much: It traces to a location named `imp__la_symbol_ptr__scanf`, which is initialized with a 64-bit number. The compiled application does not contain any code, or any memory allocated, for `scanf()`.

And a good thing, too, as `scanf()` is a component of the standard C library. You don't want to define it yourself: You want to use the code that comes in the library. But the compiler, which works with only one `.c` or `.m` file at a time, doesn't have any way of referring directly to the starting address of `scanf()`. The compiler has to leave that address as a blank to be filled in later; therefore, in building a program, there has to be an additional step for filling in such blanks.

The product of the compiler, an *object file*, contains the machine code generated from a source file, along with directories detailing what symbols are defined in that file and what symbols still need definitions filled in. Objective-C source files have the suffix `.m`; object files have the same name, with the `.m` removed and `.o` (for object) substituted. Libraries are single files that collect object files supplying useful definitions for commonly used symbols. In the simplest case, a library has a name beginning with `lib` and suffixed with `.a`.

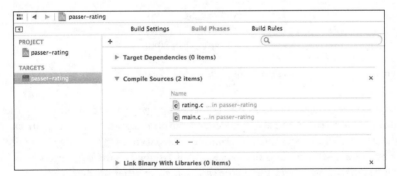

Figure 5.1   Selecting the project icon in the Project navigator displays an editor for the project and its targets. The **Build Phases** tab of the Target editor is a table showing the steps in building the target. Click the disclosure triangle in a phase's header to display the files that go into that phase. Even a simple build has a "Compile Sources" phase (upper) containing every file to be transformed into object files; and a "Link Binary With Libraries" phase (lower) to designate precompiled system and private code to bind into a finished product.

The process of back-filling unresolved addresses in compiled code is called *linkage editing*, or simply *linking*. You present the linker with a set of object files and libraries, and, you hope, the linker finds among them a definition for every unresolved symbol your application uses. Every address that had been left blank for later will then be filled in. The result is an executable file containing all of the code that gets used in the application. See Figure 5.2.

This process corresponds to the "Link Binary With Libraries" build phase in the application's target listing. This phase lists all of the libraries and frameworks against which the application is to be linked.

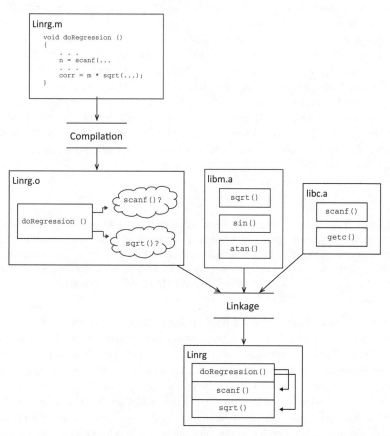

Figure 5.2   The process of turning source code into an executable binary, ruthlessly simplified. You provide source code in `Linrg.m` (top left); compiling it produces an object file, `Linrg.o`, that contains your translated code, plus unresolved references to functions `calculate.c` doesn't define. Other libraries (the notional `libm.a` and `libc.a`) contain machine code for those functions. It's the job of the linker to merge your code and the other functions you requested into a complete executable program (bottom).

> **Note**
>
> Sharp-eyed readers will have seen that the linkage phase shown in Figure 5.1 contains no
> libraries at all. There are two reasons: First, most C compilers will link programs against
> the standard C library without being told to. Second, `clang` implements the *modules*
> extension to C-family languages, which can add libraries to the linkage task whenever one
> of their headers is used. See the "Precompilation" section later in this chapter for details.

Dynamic Loading

Actually, it's one step more complicated than that. Standard routines, such as `scanf()`,
will be used simultaneously by many—possibly hundreds—of processes on a system.
Copying the machine code that implements `scanf()` into each application is a pointless
waste of disk space. The solution is *dynamic loading*: The application leaves the addresses of
common library functions unresolved even in the final executable file, providing the partial
executable code along with a dictionary of symbols to be resolved and the system libraries
to find them in. The operating system then fetches the missing code from a library that is
shared system-wide, and links it into the executable when the application runs.

Dynamic loading saves not only disk space, but RAM and execution time. When a
dynamic library—a collection of object files set up for dynamic linking and having the
prefix `lib` and the suffix `.dylib`—is loaded into physical memory, the same copy is made
visible to every application that needs it. The second and subsequent users of a dynamic
library won't incur memory or load-time costs.

> **Note**
>
> The iOS operating system relies on dynamic libraries for shared services just as any
> modern operating system does. iOS 8 brings dynamic libraries to apps, as well, in the form
> of frameworks (see Chapter 17, "An iOS Extension"). A framework is useful because it
> integrates the code and resources for a library into a discrete bundle that a developer can
> link into his applications. Application extensions, which allow iOS apps to provide services
> to other apps, are delivered as frameworks.

If dynamic libraries don't get linked with the application's executable code until run
time, why do they figure in the linkage phase of the build process at all? There are two
reasons. First, the linker can verify that all of the unresolved symbols in your application
are defined somewhere and it can issue an error message if you specified a misspelled or
absent function. Second, the linker-built tables in the dynamically linked code specify not
only the symbols that need resolving but also what libraries the needed definitions are to
be found in. With files specified, the dynamic loader does not have to search all of the
system's libraries for each symbol, and the application can specify private dynamic libraries
that would not be in any general search path.

Xcode and Clang

A traditional compiler sticks to what I've just described: It's a command-line tool that
starts, reads your source code, writes some object code, and then stops. That's what `gcc`,

the Free Software Foundation's widely used compiler, which Xcode provided or simulated through Xcode 4, does.

However, gcc had become hard to live with. gcc is. . .mature. Apple needed new features in C and Objective-C to make Cocoa programs more reliable and easier to write. It had been extending gcc for years, and publishing its contributions, but making significant changes to a code base with many stakeholders and dependencies is very slow business, and some of Apple's needs were practically inexpressible in the gcc code base.

Also, gcc is published under the GNU General Public License, which requires all code linked with GPL code to be open source as well. There's nothing wrong with this, but Apple's goals were different: It hoped to integrate its compiler technology into much of its own software, for which it does not want to publish the source.

Apple's solution was a new open-source compiler engine in the form of a linkable library, llvm, first introduced in Xcode 3.2. llvm's first major product was the C-language-family compiler clang, but there was much more in store.

- The Xcode text editor links to llvm to get continuous information on the state of your code from the same parser that will translate it into your product. Open the Preferences window (**Xcode** →**Preferences. . . ⌘ comma**) and set **Issues: Show live issues** to display warnings and errors as you enter your code.

- The llvm library is linked into lldb, the debugging engine under the Xcode debugger. lldb lets you enter source-code statements on its command line; it will compile them—compatibly with the code being debugged, because it's the same compiler—and inject them into the process you're debugging.

- OpenCL, the OS X facility that harnesses graphics-chip computing power for massively parallel computation, relies on storing C-like source code in the client program. It has to; GPUs are all different. The OS uses llvm to convert the source text into the binary for the system's GPU.

- Vendors providing bridges between Cocoa and "managed" or interpreted languages link the llvm library to their own compilers to translate relatively slow interpreted code to CPU-native code.

Adopting llvm allowed Apple to make tremendous leaps in its development systems. Before, the Objective-C language changed very little over the course of decades—a fine language, but new uses and new insights into code translation were making it less and less efficient and safe than it could have been. In the years since, llvm has allowed clang to develop deep insights into the developer's code, with all that implies for the quality of diagnostics and generated code.

Local Analysis

The insight the previous generation of compilers have into source code is confined to a certain scope, no finer than a single line, no broader than a fairly large function. They can tell you what line an error occurred on; clang can specify the *token*. They can tell you that a symbol you used isn't known; you can ask them to flag certain coding practices for you to double-check. clang can offer to correct the spelling, and recode expressions that it *knows* are problematic in the context, which can be very broad.

clang can be made to know about conventions and other constraints on your code. A common idiom in Cocoa programming is for a method to accept a pointer to the pointer for an NSError object. If an error occurs, the method can fill the reference with an error object, thus passing it back to the caller. However, such methods always offer to accept a NULL pointer, in case the caller wants to ignore the error detail.

Consider this Foundation command-line program, which implements a simple class with three methods:

```
#import <Foundation/Foundation.h>

static NSString * const MyErrDomain = @"MyErrDomain";

@interface MyClass : NSObject
- (void) doSomething;
- (BOOL) methodWithErrorRef: (NSError **) error;
@property(nonatomic, assign) BOOL   somethingWrong;
@end

@implementation MyClass

- (instancetype) init
{
    self = [super init];
    if (self) {
        _somethingWrong = NO;
    }
    return self;
}

- (void) doSomething { self.somethingWrong = YES; }

- (BOOL) methodWithErrorRef: (NSError **) error
{
    NSError *   justInCase =
            [NSError errorWithDomain: MyErrDomain
                                code: -1 userInfo: nil];
    *error = justInCase;            //  Line 29

    [self doSomething];
    if (self.somethingWrong)
        return NO;
    else
        return YES;
}
```

```
@end

int main(int argc, const char * argv[])
{
    @autoreleasepool {
        MyClass *       object = [[MyClass alloc] init];
        NSError *       error;
        if ([object methodWithErrorRef: &error]) {
            NSLog(@"Method on %@ succeeded", object);
        }
        else {
            NSLog(@"Method on %@ failed", object);
        }
    }
    return 0;
}
```

> **Note**
>
> Notice that `methodWithErrorRef:` fills the `error` output with a catchall error object before it knows whether an error occurred. Methods that accept `NSError*` references are allowed to do that. Callers *must not* try to determine whether something went wrong by examining the returned `NSError`. It may be present, but not valid. Only the method's return value can tell you whether it failed.

`MyClass` is about as simple as it can be, just enough to have a method that appears to do something, and accepts a pointer to an `NSError*` pointer. Make `clang` take a really close look at it: Select **Product → Analyze** (⇧⌘B). Soon the Issues navigator appears with one blue-flagged entry, which in the log appears as:

```
main.m:29:9: warning: Potential null dereference.
    According to coding standards in 'Creating and
    Returning NSError Objects' the parameter may be null
        *error = justInCase;
        ~~~~~~~~~~~~~~~~~~~~
```

So that's a nice feature—Apple taught `clang` about one of its coding standards, and `clang` alerts you when you violate one. It will even identify the character position (the = assignment operator) where the error occurred. (The editor will show a red caret at that position.)

Cross-Function Analysis

It goes beyond nice. In `main()`'s call to `methodWithErrorRef:`, replace `&error` with `NULL`. Repeat the analysis.

The coding-convention error flag is joined by a "logic error." Click the disclosure triangle in the Issues navigator, and step through the details it contains:

1. In `main()`, "Passing null pointer value via 1st parameter 'error'"
2. "Calling 'methodWithErrorRef:'"
3. In `methodWithErrorRef:`, "Entered call from 'main'"
4. "Dereference of null pointer (loaded from variable 'error')"

The original flag was for an in-place violation of a coding convention. This is a warning of an *actual* programming error arising from an *actual* execution path that `clang` traced across two methods. See Figure 5.3.

> **Note**
>
> Between the banners and the Issues navigator, it can be hard to see the full text of error, warning, and analysis messages. The banners often run out of room, even with the tiny font they use, and the Issues items show only the first few words of the messages. You can do better: Open the **General** panel of the Preferences window, and set **Issue Navigator Detail:** to **Up to Ten Lines**. That should be plenty of room.

Indexing

Project indexing was a marquee feature of Xcode 1, and remains at its core. In the background, Xcode examines your code base, and all of the system files you use, to collect the type and place-of-definition of every symbol. That information is used so:

- The editor can give a unique color to each construct on the screen.
- You can jump directly to the declaration of a symbol by command-clicking on it. The gesture works on the semantic unit—command-clicking the first part of

```
int main(int argc, const char * argv[])
{
    @autoreleasepool {
        MyClass *object = [[MyClass alloc] init];
        if ([object methodWithErrorRef: NULL]) {       1. Passing null pointer value via 1st parameter 'error'
            NSLog(@"Method on %@ succeeded", object);   2. Calling 'methodWithErrorRef:'
        }
        else {
            NSLog(@"Method on %@ failed", object);
        }
    }
    return 0;
}
```

```
- (BOOL) methodWithErrorRef: (NSError **) error      3. Entered call from 'main'
{
    NSError *justInCase =
    [NSError errorWithDomain: MyErrDomain
                        code: -1 userInfo: nil];
    *error = justInCase;        4. Dereference of null pointer (loaded from variable 'error')
                                Dereference of null pointer (loaded from variable 'error')
    [self doSomething];
    if ([self somethingWentWrong])
        return NO;
    else
        return YES;
}
```

Figure 5.3   Even early on, `clang` could warn of programming errors that arise from program flows as they actually occur, even between functions. Expanding a logic error message will show arrows demonstrating exactly the path that will lead to the error.

`fileExistsAtPath:isDirectory:` will pick up the whole method name and won't bounce you to `fileExistsAtPath:`.

- You can click in a symbol, and then on the indicator that appears next to it, to command **Edit All in Scope**; editing the one symbol will change all other instances, but only those that refer to the same object.

- The Symbol navigator (second tab in the Navigator area) can show you a directory of the symbols defined in your project, jumping you to the definition of each. This works even for `@property` directives: They normally create hidden methods to set and examine the property. The Symbol navigator shows the implicit methods.

- The new facility for changing documentation comments into live help text can choose which documentation among identically spelled methods it should show.

- The refactoring feature can operate on all instances of a complex symbol (like a multipart method name), and only those, without the limitations of a search for text or patterns.

- The Assistant editor can be set to display all callers or callees of the method selected in the main editor. This makes possible the trick of moving callers of an obsolete method over to a new one by simply stepping through the callers and converting them until the caller list is empty.

Before the transition to `llvm`, Xcode had to fall back on its own parser, which could be made to match the behavior of the `gcc` compiler only with difficulty. With a slower indexing parser (and, yes, slower computers), it was common to have re-indexing interrupt your workflow. Creating an index for a large project still takes time (though you can continue work while it happens), but after that, you won't notice it. `llvm` guarantees that the indexer and `clang` work from the same sophisticated code model.

Swift

All very nice for Objective-C and other C-family languages. But that was not all.

`clang` had made coding for Apple platforms about as efficient and reliable as possible—if you can tolerate some drawbacks:

- Objective-C is C. Any legal standard C program is a legal Objective-C program. (This is not true between C and C++.) C was intended to be a convenient, portable way to write assembly code for minicomputer operating systems. Assembly code owns the machine it runs on—if the developer wants to declare a ten-byte array and traverse all of memory from it, forward and back, the developer knows best. That's not just an invitation to disaster for application programmers, it's an all-comers street fair. But a language that restrains it is not C.

- A tool for coding the bare minimum of an operating system can't assume, or prefer, any one method of managing system resources; in particular, C does not, and cannot, care about dynamic memory management. The standard C library provides routines like `malloc()` and `free()` for claiming blocks of memory, but they're just functions; the language itself doesn't know that they do anything special. A language that enforces memory-management practices is not C.

- In Objective-C, method dispatch—choosing the proper code to execute a message to an object—is *always* done on the assumption that any method might have an independent implementation, whether from subclass overrides or independent classes' parallel adoption of a method. This degree of flexibility, called *duck-typing*, is powerful, but in practice it's rarely needed. A smart compiler might convert lone-implementer methods into direct-address functions, but a C-family compiler rarely knows enough about the whole program to do it. Java and C++ let (or force) the programmer to provide that information, but a language that does that is not C.

- Code generation and programming techniques have advanced since the late 1970s. We know more, and we have the computing power to make them practical: Generic functions and data types; compilers that are free to choose among radically different implementations and resource strategies for the same code; passing executable code across functions—as parameters *or* function returns—as freely as any other data; control structures (such as `switch`es) that can test for more than whether two byte patterns are identical. And more. There have been decades of progress since the fundamentals of C++ and Objective-C were set.

  Especially with `llvm` at its disposal, Apple has managed to wedge some of these ideas into a language that remains compatible with C: Cross-function code analysis (in certain circumstances); blocks; properties and Automatic Reference Counting. But the language still has to be C, with its limitations on analysis, safety, and expression.

The obvious solution is to create a language that is transparent, safe, and expressive—but can express the old Objective-C data structures and design patterns. Not an easy task. At WWDC 2014, Apple announced its solution: the Swift programming language.

I can't get deep into describing Swift; previous editions of this book avoided discussion of languages and techniques beyond their influence on the Xcode workflow. But Swift is "strange" enough that I want to give you a taste of what Swift can do that is at least difficult to express in Objective-C.

- Generic functions, which express pure algorithms without having to specify in advance what data types they handle.

- Type inference, by which Swift can enforce rigid data typing without requiring explicit type declarations in many cases.

- Closures, raw blocks of executable code that can be passed around, called, or even created, while a program runs. (Functions are just a special case of closures.)

- Currying, a technique for specializing a function by creating a new one that fixes some of its parameters. The resulting function accepts the other parameters (classically only one) and returns the result of the original function.

You noticed in Chapter 3, "Simple Workflow and Passive Debugging," that the
components of a passer rating are pinned to an interval no less than 0.0 and no greater
than 2.375. This was done by adding a function `pinPassingComponent()` to enforce
exactly that interval. This is how the same thing might be done in Swift:

```
/******************** Generic pinner: *******************/

/* Given a value, make it no less than a lower bound, nor more
   than an upper. The three values need only be of the same type,
   and that type must conform to the Comparable protocol.

   Comparable promises a type responds to the < operator, plus
   the == operator from Equatable; the other relations follow
   from those.
*/
func pinComparables<T:Comparable> (value: T, lower: T, upper: T)
                              -> T
{
    if value < lower { return lower }
    else if value > upper { return upper }
    else { return value }
}

pinComparables(-8.0, 0.0, 2.375)    // => 0
pinComparables(1.5, 0.0, 2.375)     // => 1.5
pinComparables(7.0, 0.0, 2.375)     // => 2.375

/******************** Pinner factory *******************/

/* Given a lower and upper bound, return a closure
   that takes a single argument of the same type, and
   returns the pinned value.
*/
func limitPinner<T: Comparable> (lower: T, upper: T)
                            -> (T -> T)
{ return { value in pinComparables(value, lower, upper) } }

/* The new function has the bounds baked-in; the only
   variable is the value to be pinned to those bounds.
*/

/*************** Floating-point pinner: ****************/

let pinPassingComponent = limitPinner(0.0, 2.375)
// => a new function, (Double -> Double)
```

```
println("below: \(pinPassingComponent(-3.3)), " +
        "above: \(pinPassingComponent(3.3)), " +
        "within: \(pinPassingComponent(1.7))")
)
// => below: 0.0, above: 2.375, within: 1.7
```

That's a lot of trouble just to confine a Double to an interval, though that didn't stop me from including it in Utilities.swift in the sample code for the chapters to come. But it doesn't stop there. String is also Comparable:

```
/******************* String pinner: ********************/

let stringPinner = limitPinner("Cornelia", "Josh")
// => (String -> String)

for name in ["Alan", "Fritz", "Oren"] {
    println(name + ": " + stringPinner(name))
}
// Alan: Cornelia
// Fritz: Fritz
// Oren: Josh

/* All that was necessary was to pass the limits to limitPinner().
   Swift inferred the type for limitPinner(), and therefore
   pinComparables(), yielding a (String -> String) function
   specialized for that range.
*/
```

Fine, if strange, but what about dates? In Swift, you represent them by the Foundation (Objective-C) class NSDate, but NSDate is not Comparable; if you applied pinComparables() to dates, the Swift compiler would reject it.

But you can *make* it Comparable:

```
/************ Define < and == for NSDate: **************/
/* Swift lets you define operators, even your own, like "<*>". */
public
func == (one: NSDate, another: NSDate) -> Bool
{ return one.compare(another) == .OrderedSame }

public
func < (one: NSDate, another: NSDate) -> Bool
{  return one.compare(another) == .OrderedAscending  }

/************* Now NSDate is Comparable: **************/
extension NSDate: Comparable, Equatable {}
```

```
/***************** Define some dates: ******************/
// Easy way to convert String to NSDate (en_US locale):
let shortFormatter = NSDateFormatter()
shortFormatter.dateStyle = .ShortStyle

/*****************  A macabre date span: ****************/
let fBirth = shortFormatter.dateFromString("12/3/1955")
let fDeath = shortFormatter.dateFromString("7/15/2017")

/***** Create a pinning function for the life span: *****/
let inFritzsLifetime = pinnerFunction(fBirth!, fDeath!)

/******************** Some other dates: ****************/
let pearlHarbor        = shortFormatter.dateFromString("12/7/1941")
let cBirthday          = shortFormatter.dateFromString("12/23/1973")
let probeReachesNeptune = shortFormatter.dateFromString("8/9/2025")

inFritzsLifetime(pearlHarbor!)          // => NSDate of 12/3/1955
inFritzsLifetime(cBirthday!)            // => NSDate of 12/23/1973
inFritzsLifetime(probeReachesNeptune!)  // => NSDate of 7/15/2017
```

> **Note**
>
> If you study Apple's documentation of the Swift language, you can find every technique I used here, but not everything you will, sooner or later, need to know about the Swift standard library. In Appendix B, "Resources," I'll point you to sites where you can browse the full library, but there is a shortcut: Add `import Swift` to any playground, hold the Command key down, and click `Swift`. Xcode will present a complete listing of classes, structs, and protocols, with comments to document most of them. Module `Darwin` for the UNIX layer works, too, but isn't as informative.

The first release of the Swift compiler is . . . a first release. Apple Developer Tools is nowhere close to the ideal implementation. However, some things can be inferred from the logical structure of the language and what it means for its potential:

Swift gives the compiler enough discretion that it can generalize or specialize code as needed. For instance, the same function might be dynamically dispatched, provisioned as a fixed-address routine, or copied into the caller inline, depending on how it is used in the whole program, not on the developer's guess. That is only one example of many. The logical structure of the Swift language makes it possible to generate code that runs *faster* than C++, until now the gold standard for speed in an object-oriented language. That's in principle; it isn't there yet.

Using Swift, and Why

Part I of this book sticks to C to simplify the concepts. Once we get into development for iOS and OS X, we'll be working exclusively in Swift.

There is a reason: Apple has gone through this sort of transition before, through four processor architectures (at least six, if you count iOS), two byte sexes, two application frameworks, three desktop operating environments, and even a flirtation with Java. The old ways are supported, even generously, even for years. But in time, the old way falls off. Objective-C is not going away soon; probably not for years. But Apple has made clear that Swift will make your apps, and therefore its products, more stable, secure, and responsive than Objective-C can.

Cocoa itself, Foundation especially, isn't going anywhere: `NSDate` and its family, for example, give Swift a core library other new languages take years to mature into. If you seek the missing features in the Swift standard library, look around you: They're in Cocoa.

But: Over time, Apple will be making advances in its hardware and API; it will set priorities on how to make them easier for developers to support; it will choose how to allocate its OS and tools efforts. It's pretty clear that while Objective-C is dominant today, sooner or later Swift will come first.

For new development, use Swift unless compelled not to. That includes products already built in Objective-C: Apple has made the bridge between the two languages as gentle as it can be.

Of course, I've had nearly 40 years to say this sort of thing about dozens of Apple technologies that have long since sunk from memory.

Compiler Products

Object files are the principal products of the compilation process: You're most often interested only in building something you can run and test. But sometimes, the compiler will identify issues or produce results that, with all diligence, you can't make sense of. In such cases, it's useful to see what the compiler did on the way to translating your code.

Also, the build process will produce files that encapsulate repetitive tasks, like compiling common header files. These, too, are compiler products.

Intermediate Products

When you are tracing bugs—or are just curious—you may need to see what the compiler has done in the steps between your source and the executable product. Xcode provides a way to do this.

C-family compilers were originally run in three stages, each feeding the next. Modern compilers merge the steps to gain a better understanding of how to generate the best code, but notionally the steps are still there, and you can get the products of each:

1. The *preprocessor* takes your code and outputs the "real" source after making simple string substitutions. When it finds `#include` and `#import` directives, it inserts the contents of the included files into the output stream. Macros from `#define` directives are expanded and substituted into the stream. Conditional directives admit or block sections of code in the input file.

You can see the results of the preprocessor by clicking on the **Related Items** menu (at the left end of the jump bar above the editor) and selecting **Preprocess**. The editor shows the full interpreted stream of the current source file. This can be long, but you can track down bugs by making sure that the code you thought you were compiling, and the symbols you thought you were using, are really there. Choosing **Preprocess** from the root item in the jump bar of the Assistant editor will display a preprocessed version alongside the file you are editing. Also, you can issue **Product → Perform Action → Preprocess**.

2. The parser/generator takes the "simplified," preprocessed code, reduces it to logical constructs (parsing), and produces the assembly source for a machine-language program that does what the original source directs (code generation).

There are three ways to call for an assembly listing.

- Selecting **Assembly** from the **Related Items** menu, which drops down from the small array-of-rectangles button at the left end of the jump bar (Figure 5.4), replaces the editor's contents with the translated code.

- The **Product → Perform Action → Assemble** command does the same thing.

- Selecting **Assembly** from the Assistant editor's jump bar will show the assembly for whatever file is in the Standard editor.

> **Note**
>
> This is not a disassembly like the one I began this chapter with. It is not derived from the final executable stream of the completed product. It is a representation of the compiler's understanding of your code, and features annotations that relate back to `clang`'s knowledge of your source.

> **Note**
>
> Unfortunately, as of Xcode 6.3, neither the Assistant editor nor the Related Items menu will produce assembly or disassembly listings for Swift code. Full support for Swift is a work in progress; code refactoring is another example. You can expect these features to come back as time goes on.

3. An assembler reads the assembly source and reduces it to executable bytes in an object file, with references to be filled in by the linker. The `otool` command-line tool has a plethora of options for examining object files and libraries, with dis-assemblies and file layouts, and limited options for editing. The nm tool is useful for examining the symbol tables in a library. See man `otool` and man nm for details.

> **Note**
>
> The three-step translation process has no meaning in Swift: There is no preprocessor, and the compiler can't determine exactly what code to generate until it has analyzed the whole program.

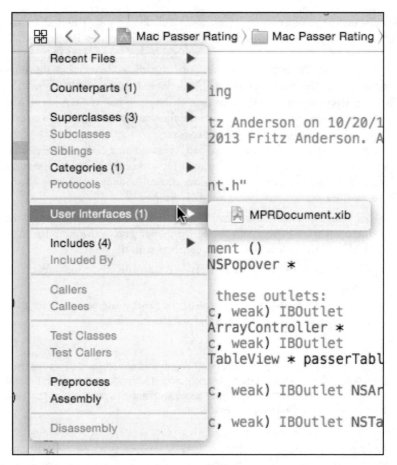

Figure 5.4   The small item at the left end of the jump bar above any editor view is the anchor for the **Related Items** menu, offering many alternative views of the file displayed in the editor.

Precompilation

Mac and iOS applications draw on *frameworks*, packages of dynamic libraries, headers, and resources that define and link to the operating systems, human interface services, and other services. Frameworks entail huge numbers of large header files. In early days, it made sense for programmers to speed up builds by carefully choosing the system headers they included, but the Cocoa frameworks are so interdependent that that isn't possible. (In fact, Apple emphatically warns against trying to pull pieces out of frameworks.)

Prefix Headers

Framework headers are usually the first things a C-family implementation file imports, either directly or through headers of its own. You can set a *prefix file* to be injected into the source stream of all your files; in fact, when you instantiate an iOS or OS X project, Xcode generates a `.pch` file and sets up the build settings to inject it. A typical prefix file looks like this:

```
#ifdef __OBJC__
    #import <Cocoa/Cocoa.h>
#endif
```

That's convenient, but doesn't solve the problem of speed if the prefix is to be read and converted every time you compile a file. The `.pch` extension gives a clue to the solution: The file's intended purpose is as source for a *precompiled header*; if you opt for precompilation, `clang` will read the `.pch` and save its parsing state. All subsequent uses of the prefix header will reload that saved state, saving you the time that repeating the compilation would have taken. There is another build setting for precompilation, and by default, it is on.

> **Note**
>
> Again, this is C-family; Swift depends on modules and API it pulls in automatically from other source files.

Modules

The `clang` supplied with Xcode 5 added *modules* to the C-family languages. The designers saw a problem: Notionally, the `#include` and `#import` directives that have been a part of C since its inception are nothing more than commands for pouring the uninterpreted text of one file into another. The included file defines symbols and macros that the compiler applies in the order it sees them. If you reorder the includes in your source files, the reordering of the definitions could change their meanings. Further, because you could insert defines among your includes, there is no way to be sure you can share precompiled inclusions among implementation files; even the same sequence of includes could yield completely different code.

The `llvm` engineers' response is a system of modules, to be added to the C-family programming languages. Unlike header files brought in by the preprocessor, each module is a discrete unit and can come into the compilation state as completely parsed units. Swift is designed exclusively for modules, which are usable unchanged for Swift and Objective-C alike.

There is a price: For the full benefit, you can't modify the effects of included headers by interleaving your own macro definitions. (It forces the compiler to generate a unique module file for just that case.) If you ever found it a good idea to do that, it's because bad design in the headers forced you. If you deliberately exploited order dependencies among your header files, you were insane, and should have stopped.

For a concrete instance, the C standard libraries might be encapsulated into an umbrella module called `std`, and you could request only the parts you want by asking for sub-modules like `std.io` or `std.strings`. You can invoke the module feature directly by replacing your framework includes and imports with the `@import` Objective-C directory, so

```
#import <Foundation/Foundation.h>
```

becomes

```
@import Foundation;
```

Command-clicking the module name will take you to the framework's umbrella header.

Unfortunately, none of the living authors of the many billions of C/C++/Objective-C source files are going to amend them to replace preprocessor directives with `@import` directives. For legacy code, when `clang` sees an `#include` or `#import`, it tries to build a module on the fly and use the module from then on.

Apple has modularized the system libraries, so the worst of the `#include`-and-recompile cycle has already been eliminated. If you examine the preprocessed version of your source, you'll find that the contents of the system headers have been replaced with "implicit imports." If you want to pre-build modules of your own, you can describe the structure by providing a `module.map` file.

The `module.map` file does something else: It associates libraries with each module. If you `#include`/`#import` a header from a modularized framework, you don't have to add the framework to the "Link Binary With Libraries" build phase.

Swift adds another level: Objective-C code is subject to namespace collisions when objects from different libraries unwittingly adopt the same names. If you're lucky, the linker will detect the duplicate definitions and refuse to emit an executable file. If not—as may be the case with the dynamic symbols used throughout Objective-C—you won't know until your app makes very strange errors in very strange places.

For this reason, Swift code uses modules to confine symbols to the modules that define them (even the public ones). Your own application is a module, with a name based on the app name: The ASCII alphanumerics go through unchanged, and everything else is replaced by an underscore.

If you use a symbol from another module in a way that might give rise to a conflict, Swift will require you to prefix the symbol with the name of the defining module: If you have a class named `Parser`, and you use a library `XMLParser` that provides its own class `Parser`, you can safely refer to the library class as `XMLParser.Parser`.

Xcode 6's new-project and -target templates for Objective-C are set to use modules by default. If you want the automatic linking feature as well, set "Link Frameworks Automatically" to **Yes**—that's the default, as well.

I've left many of your questions unanswered; visit `http://clang.llvm.org/docs/Modules.html` to learn more.

Summary

This chapter was a short but essential review of what happens when you compile and link a program. You saw how compilation not only translates your code into machine-executable code, but also transforms it. The biggest task in building an executable is not translation, but the bookkeeping involved in allocating space to data and code and how it culminates in the linkage phase. Linkage can be done all at once, as in a static linker, but iOS and OS X rely heavily on dynamic linkage, where much of the heavy work is done as the program starts running.

6

Adding a Library Target

The passer_rating function is a tremendous achievement—and hard-won. It plainly has applications beyond that simple command-line tool, so let's encapsulate its services for use in other programs.

All right, no, it isn't, but doing so will introduce some important skills. So, you can create a static library (an archive of reusable code) for passer_rating, moving its code from the passer-rating tool into the new library, and linking it back into the tool.

Adding a Target

You don't need to start a new project to create a library—it's better if you don't. Open the passer-rating project in Xcode and click the top entry, representing the project, in the Project navigator. This brings up the Project/Target editor.

Like all editors, it has a jump bar at the top. The next bar contains the tabs that organize the target's settings. At the very left end is a button with a triangle on it. This opens the master list of the objects the Project/Target editor can work on. If you don't see the master list on the left side of the editor, click this button to disclose it. The list contains listings for the project itself, and for the sole target, passer-rating (Figure 6.1).

At the bottom of the master list is a **+** button. Click it.

This produces a New Target assistant sheet, which organizes the available templates in the way you've already seen for projects and files.

1. In the column on the left, select **OS X → Framework & Library**.
2. You're given a choice of linkable targets. Pick **Library** (passer_rating doesn't involve anything more than standard C, and doesn't need the dynamic linkage provided by a framework), and click **Next**.
3. Name the product. You may be aware that Unix static libraries have names of the form lib*name*.a. Don't worry about that; just provide the base name **passer**, and the build system will take care of naming the file.
4. Select **None (Plain C/C++ Library)** from the **Framework** popup.
5. Select **Type: Static**, and accept **Project: passer-rating**.
6. Click **Finish**.

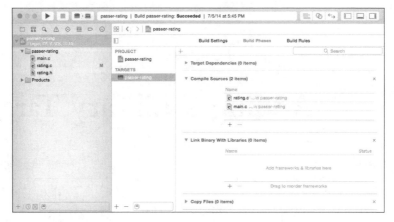

Figure 6.1   Click the button on the left end of the Project/Target editor's tab bar to disclose the master list of objects the editor can work on.

The Editor area is filled with a Target editor for the new "passer" target. For simple targets like C libraries and tools, the editor has three tabs:

- **Build Settings** lets you set all the options that control how the target is to be built. Even for so simple a library, there are quite a few of these. You can cut down by selecting the **Basic** and **Combined** filters. There is at least one all-caps setting that Xcode calls "User-Defined." These refer to clang. Xcode treats them this way because the passer library doesn't contain any source files yet, and Xcode doesn't know about clang until something in the build process uses it.

- **Build Phases** is something you saw before, in Chapter 5, "Compilation." It describes the components of the target and how they will be converted for use in building it. This is the first thing Xcode will show you when you create a target.

- **Build Rules** allow you to change the tools the Xcode build system uses to process files into the target. You can define rules of your own so you can add custom files and processes, but most developers never bother with it. You can learn more in Chapter 25, "The Xcode Build System."

Select the **Build Phases** tab.

Targets

What have you done? What is a target? Let's step back from the details of the Target editor.

A *target* describes a single build process in Xcode: It has a specific product, a specific set of files that go into the product, and a specific set of parameters for the build process.

Targets are organized into *build phases*. A build phase accepts files that are members of its target and processes them in a particular way. Source files (.c, .m, .swift, and .cpp files, most commonly, but other files for other compilers, as well) go into a "Compile Sources" phase; libraries, into a "Link Binary With Libraries" phase; and so on.

> **Note**
>
> Chapter 25, "The Xcode Build System," covers build phases and their role in the Xcode build system in detail.

You can change the files and settings as much as you like, but the type of the product, which determines what build process will be used, can't change. If you've started a static library, for instance, and then decide you need a dynamic library instead, you're out of luck. You have to create a new target for a dynamic library and add the source files again.

Target Membership

Targets consist of a product (which you specified), build settings (which you've accepted), and member files, of which the passer target has none. You'll have to add something—specifically `rating.c`.

Adding Files to a Target

There are three ways to do this.

- Click the project item in the Project navigator, and select the library target, passer, from the Targets list. Select the **Build Phases** tab. Find `rating.c` in the Project navigator, and drag it into the "Compile Sources" phase. The label will show that there is one item in the phase, and the phase will open to show `rating.c` in the list (Figure 6.2).

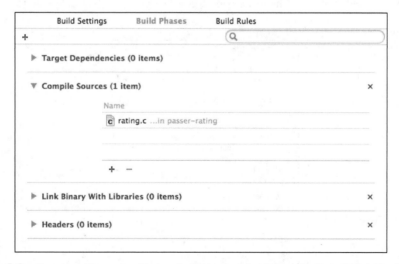

Figure 6.2   You can add a source file to a target by dragging it from the Project navigator into the "Compile Sources" phase. This gives you the most control of the role the file will play in the build process.

- Undo that by selecting `rating.c` in the Compile Sources table, and clicking the – button at the bottom of the table (or pressing the Delete key), so you can try another way.

> **Note**
>
> Removing a file from a build phase, even all build phases, won't delete the file or remove it from your project.

  Now click the **+** button at the bottom of the Compile Sources table. A sheet containing the project outline drops down. Click `rating.c`, and then the **Add** button. If you click **Add Other. . .** , you can select files on-disk and add them to the build phase and the project in one step.

- The third way is to come at it file-to-target: Click `rating.c` in the Project navigator. Then expose the Utility area by clicking the right-hand segment of the **View** control at the right end of the toolbar. Make sure the first tab, the File inspector, is selected. The File inspector lets you control the way Xcode treats the selected file (or files; if you select more than one in the Project navigator, the settings will affect all of them). One of the sections is **Target Membership**, listing all the targets in the project. For `rating.c`, click the checkbox for the passer target (Figure 6.3).

The advantage to working from the build-phase end is that you have control over which phase a file goes into. Yes, `.c` files should almost always be compiled, but suppose you were creating a programmer's editor for OS X that has file templates embedded in it. Your `TemplateFile.c` file *looks* like C source—it is—but you want it bundled as a text file, not compiled as source. The phase you want is "Copy Files" (available only for

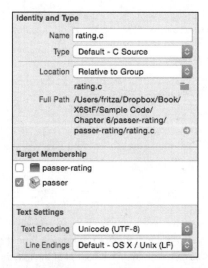

Figure 6.3   A table in the File inspector lets you select which targets a file is to contribute to.

application and bundle targets), not "Compile Sources." If you start from the build phase, there's no ambiguity.

Working from the file's end of the chain has an advantage of its own: If your project has many targets, the checkboxes allow you to set all memberships at once, without having to visit the Target editors and hunt for the files. Xcode will guess which build phases they should go into, but its guesses are usually correct.

When you create a new file, using **File → New → File. . .** (⌘ N), you get a shortcut to assigning targets from the file end: The save-file dialog for the new file includes a picker for the targets to which you want to add it. Similarly, when you add files, **File → Add Files to. . .** (⌥ ⌘ A), you're given a target picker. Again, Xcode will guess at the build phases (Figure 6.4).

> **Warning**
> The target picker may not be set for the targets you expect. This is easy to miss, and the resulting errors will puzzle you.

However you added `rating.c` to the `passer` library, remember to *remove* it from the passer-rating target. The whole point of having a library is that clients don't have to include the source for the services it provides.

Figure 6.4   The save-file sheet for creating a new file includes a table for selecting the targets the file is to contribute to. The table is always set to the last-selected set of targets.

Headers in Targets

What about `rating.h`? You can't add it to an application target from the file end: Headers themselves aren't compiled—they merely contribute to implementation files. If you want them inside an application bundle for some reason, you can drag them into the "Copy Bundle Resources" phase.

`rating.h` *can* be added to a *library* target. You can choose the role the header plays in your product:

- **Project**, if it's to be visible only inside your project, as an element in a build.
- **Public**, if it's to be installed somewhere like `/usr/local/include`, or the `Headers` directory of a framework.
- **Private**, if it's to be installed in the `PrivateHeaders` directory of a framework.

One of the phases the **Build Phases** tab of the target editor is "Headers." This phase is available only for library and framework targets. Expanding it reveals sections for the **Public**, **Private**, and **Project** categories. The process is the same as for adding files to the other build phases: Drag the header from the Project navigator into the proper role; or click the **+** button to choose a header from a browser. The latter method will put the selected header into the project category, but you can drag it to the one you want.

A Dependent Target

Next to the **Run** and **Stop** buttons in the toolbar is the **Scheme** control, which sets the target and CPU architecture to be used for actions like running a product. Select **passer – My Mac**, then select **Product** → **Build** (⌘ B). Xcode builds the library, and reports success.

Now switch the scheme popup to **passer-rating – My Mac**. Click **Run**. The build fails. Let's see why. Select the Report navigator (last tab at the top of the Navigator area). The navigator lists all the events in the recent history of the project; the top item should be the build you just attempted. Select it; you'll see a summary of the build, including an item carrying a red **!** icon.

That item says the problem occurred at the "Link" step. Click the stack-of-lines button at the right end of the item to reveal the transcript for that part of the build. The last part is the linker's complaint:

```
Undefined symbols for architecture x86_64:
  "_passer_rating", referenced from:
      _main in main.o
ld: symbol(s) not found for architecture x86_64
clang: error: linker command failed with exit code 1 (use -v to see
               invocation)
```

In other words, `main()` uses `passer_rating`, but the linker couldn't find that function. See Figure 6.5.

Figure 6.5   The Report navigator lists all of the problems that arose in your build. Clicking on an issue displays the location of the problem. In this case, the error came at the link phase, so the editor displays the link command and the error messages it printed.

This makes sense: You removed `rating.c`, and therefore `passer_rating`, from the passer-rating target, and you haven't told that target where to find it. Yes, the file and the library product are still in the project, but it's the passer-rating target, not the project, that determines what files go into the `passer-rating` tool.

> **Note**
>
> Chapter 25, "The Xcode Build System," shows in-depth how to interpret build transcripts.

Adding a Library

So you need to correct the passer-rating, which means going to the Target editor. You know the drill: In the Project navigator, select the passer-rating project at the top of the list. In the targets list, select passer-rating, and then the **Build Phases** tab.

You want to link `libpasser.a`, the product of the passer target, into `passer-rating`. It's straightforward: Open the "Link Binary With Libraries" build phase, and click the **+** button. A sheet appears with a two-section list. The first section, titled "passer-rating Project," lists the libraries the project produces—in this case, only `libpasser.a`. Select it and click **Add**.

> **Note**
>
> A popup containing **Required** and **Optional** appears next to the name of `libpasser.a`. Always use **Required** until you have enough experience to know why you wouldn't.

> **Note**
>
> If you're building a Cocoa (iOS or OS X) application, you can also add libraries in the Linked Frameworks and Libraries section of the **General** tab in the Target editor.

Now click **Run**. The build succeeds, passer-rating runs, and when you enter some test data, it works. Everything is great.

Implicit Dependencies

In a more traditional build system, your work would not be finished. Suppose you added a printf() call to rating.c. The change in the file would cascade to a rebuild of libpasser.a.

And there the changes would stop. Such build systems have to be told when a product (such as passer-rating) must be updated in response to a change in a constituent library. Changing rating.c would not get the updated library linked into passer-rating, and when you run it, there would be no call to printf().

Xcode is subtler than that. When it sees the product of a library target used in another target, it knows to bring the library up-to-date, so the target that uses it gets the latest version. This is almost always what you want.

If it's not what you want (usually because you have to keep compatibility with an old project), use the Scheme editor. Open it by selecting **Product → Scheme → Edit Scheme...** (⌘ <). (On U.S. keyboards, this amounts to ⇧ ⌘ **period**.) The Scheme editor controls the environment in which targets are built and run.

Make sure passer-rating is selected in the popup at the top of the editor sheet that slides down, and select **Build** from the master list. Uncheck **Find Implicit Dependencies**. Click **OK** when you're finished.

Now you can choose which targets (dependencies) will be rebuilt when the consumer target is rebuilt. In this example, click the top item in the Project navigator to open the Target editor for the passer-rating target, and disclose the "Target Dependencies" phase. Click the **+** button to select the passer target, and **Add** it to the dependency list.

Then remove it, go back to the Scheme editor, and enable implicit dependencies again. There's no point in making yourself crazy.

Debugging a Dependent Target

One more thing. Suppose you develop a new interest in libpasser.a and want to debug it as it is called by the command-line tool. The tool and the function are produced by different targets; does that matter?

See for yourself: Set a breakpoint at the assignment to completionComponent. Run passer-rating.

Sure enough, the debugger stops the application at the breakpoint. Xcode will consolidate the debugging information across the targets that go into the current executable.

Summary

You've divided the `passer-rating` application into a main executable and a static library. It hardly deserves it, but it's just an example.

On the way, you created a target to assemble and build the files needed for the new library, and distributed files between the library and the main program. You added the `libpasser.a` library product to the main passer-rating target.

You saw that Xcode does right by you in two important ways: Adding the library to the application target not only linked the library into the application, it ensured that the library is always brought up-to-date when the application is built. And, it incorporated the debugging information from the library so you can examine the working of the library while the application is running.

Next, a chapter about hygiene.

7

Version Control

There isn't much to the passer-rating project—less than a hundred lines of source, plus the contents of the project file—but you have already invested time and trouble in it. So far, you've only created three files, but soon you will be moving on from *creation* to *change*. If you're like most programmers, you are conservative of the code you've written. An old function may no longer be required, but it may still embody an insight into the underlying problem.

One solution might be simply to keep all of the obsolete code in your active source files, possibly commented out or guarded by `#if 0` blocks, but this bloats the file and obscures code that actually *does* something. Once the revisions get more than one layer deep, it can be difficult to track which blocked-out stretch of code goes with which.

A *source-control* (or *version-control*) system is a database that keeps track of all of the files in a project and allows you to register changes to those files as you go. Version control frees you to make extensive changes secure in the knowledge that all of the previous versions of each file are still available if you need to roll back your changes.

You may have heard of version control and concluded that it's only for large projects with many developers. It is true that it makes it much easier to manage large code bases and to coordinate the efforts of large teams. But even if you work alone:

- You will still make extensive changes to your source.

- You will still need to refer to previous versions.

- You will still need to revert to previous versions to dig yourself out of the holes you dug with those extensive changes.

- You will find it easier if you can make changes cleanly, rather than trying to make sure you caught all the obsolete code in comments and `#if 0` blocks.

- You will likely need to work on more than one computer, each of which will contribute different changes to your code base.

As I said in Chapter 3, "Simple Workflow and Passive Debugging," if you are going to change your code, *ever*—if you save a file more than once—you ought to put it under version control. Xcode 6 makes it easy.

> **Note**
>
> Xcode 6 supports two version-control systems: Subversion and Git. Subversion is in wide use, but it has been overtaken by distributed systems like Git. Most open-source projects are now shared through public services like GitHub, or private repositories on the Net. Xcode's workflow has centered on Git since Xcode 4. I regret it, but for simplicity's sake, I'm only covering Git.

Taking Control

So I've convinced you. You want to get your project under source control. How do you start?

If you took my advice in Chapter 3, you've started already. When you place a new project on disk, Xcode offers a checkbox, **Create Git repository on**, followed by a pop-up menu that defaults to **My Mac** (Figure 7.1). You checked it. The passer-rating/ directory contains a hidden .git/ directory that indexes the project, and Xcode tracks the files you add and edit.

If you used the Welcome window (**Window → Welcome to Xcode**, ⇧⌘1), you may have chosen **Check out an existing project**, which would have led you through the process of cloning a remote repository into your local storage. The cloning process creates a .git directory, and the copy is under the control of the local repository.

There is a third option. If you've registered an Xcode server in the **Accounts** tab of the Preferences window, the **Create Git repository on** popup will include the name of that server. If you select it, Xcode will still create a .git directory for a local repository in your project directory, but it will also negotiate with your server to set up a remote repository on that machine. Other developers (or your other computers) will then be able to coordinate their work with a central copy of the project.

> **Note**
>
> Xcode Server is a feature of Yosemite Server. The server-management application includes a configuration panel for Xcode, just as it does for mail and the web. Yosemite Server is a simple add-on (early versions of OS X Server were pricey replacements for the retail OS) costing about $50 in the Mac App Store. As a paid member of the Mac Developer Program, you can download the current version for free.

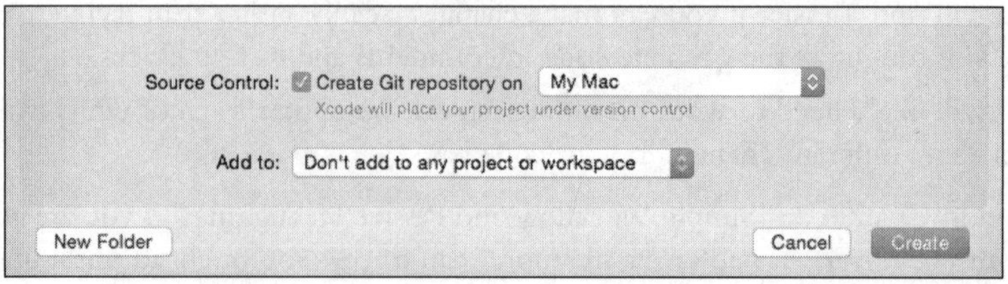

Figure 7.1   When you create a project, Xcode offers to create a local Git repository to control it.

Creating a Git Repository by Hand

Most of the time, you'll use the automated methods for creating or retrieving a local repository, and you don't have to think about it. Still, you must know how to bring an existing project under control if Git had never touched it.

There's one optional step I recommend: Create a `.gitignore` file to tell Git that certain files and directories are off limits. They won't be included in mass additions to the repository, and they won't be listed in status messages as unmanaged. It's simple. Open the Terminal application (`/Applications/Utilities/Terminal`) and get busy:

```
$ # Focus on the project's directory:
$ cd /path/to/my/project
$
$ # Enter the contents of the file, closing with control-D
$ cat > .gitignore xcuserdata/ .DS_Store ^D
$ # Want to add other files?
$ # Include them in that last command,
$ # or append them to the existing .gitignore
$ # with "cat >> .gitignore" (two carets).
$
```

> **Note**
>
> Apple's distribution of Git already knows to ignore some files and directories.

> **Note**
>
> Xcode 6 and Yosemite do a bit of legerdemain with command-line developer tools like `git`. See "Command-Line Tools" in Chapter 1, "Getting Xcode."

```
$ # Add a Git repository to this directory:
$ git init
Initialized empty Git repository in
   /Users/xcodeuser/Desktop/MyProject/.git/
$
$ # Tell Git you want to control everything in "." (this
$ # directory tree), except for what's in .gitignore:
$ git add .
$
$ # Tell Git to record the files you added,
$ # logging it as "Initial commit"
$ git commit -m 'Initial commit'
[master (root-commit) f0d59bf] Initial commit
9 files changed, 819 insertions(+)
create mode 100644 .gitignore  ...
```

This is all you need do so far as Git is concerned, but if the project was open while you did it, Xcode won't notice. You'll have to quit and restart Xcode before the **Source**

Control menu recognizes your project, and source-control status flags appear in the Project navigator.

Part of the metadata Git attaches to the files it tracks is the name and email address of the person who made each change, line by line. The first time you try to commit to a Git repository, if you have not configured your name and address, Git will balk and demand that you make the settings. It will give you examples of the commands you will have to issue.

If your first-ever repository was created by Xcode, this presents a problem. The first thing Xcode does with a new project is to commit almost all the files it instantiates from the project template. That commit will fail if you haven't set your Git identity. Xcode will display Git's message in an alert sheet, and the commit will not have gone through. You'll have to fix it in Terminal:

```
$ # Focus on the project directory (use your own path)
$ cd /path/to/my/project
$
$ # Set your metadata (your own address and name)
$ git config --global user.email "xcodeuser@example.com"
$ git config --global user.name "Xcode User"
$
$ # Do the commit Xcode couldn't
$ git commit -m 'Initial commit'
```

> **Note**
>
> Once the local repository is in place, you can also make up for the lack of a link to a remote repository. See the "Working with Remote Repositories" section later in this chapter.

The State of Your Files

Xcode presents a model of source control that is close to that of the version-control system you chose. Subversion and Git are different; I'll show you how Git sees files, and how Xcode reflects that view.

In Git's world, a file can be in one of six states.

- **Ignored**—The file's name matches a pattern in the `.gitignore` file. Git will never attempt to manage it, unless you explicitly add it to the repository.

- **Untracked**—Git sees the file, but it's neither in the repository nor staged for adding to the repository. There is no history of its previous contents. The `git add` command *stages* it for entry into the repository.

- **Modified**—In a way, a modified file isn't much different from an untracked one: Its contents won't go into the repository until it is staged. However, its previous contents *are* in the repository and can be compared against the current version, or restored. It, too, can be readied to commit its contents with the `git add` command.

- **Staged**—The file has been designated (with `git add`) for inclusion in the next commit. Why doesn't the `add` command simply put the modified/new contents into the repository? Because you usually make logical changes to your project in more than one file—a method in an `.m` file, its declaration in a header, and its use in other `.m` files—and it doesn't make sense to register or roll back changes that are only partway made. When you stage a file, you're assembling it into a conceptual group that will arrive in the repository all at once.

- **Unmerged**—You changed the file and attempted to pull in changes from another repository, and the two sets of changes couldn't be reconciled. Git marks the file to highlight the conflicts, and warns you if you attempt a commit without resolving the conflict. When you modify and restage the file, Git takes it that the conflicts are resolved and stops complaining.

- **Unmodified**—The file's current state, as registered with `git commit`, is what's in the repository. So far as Git is concerned, there's nothing more to be done with it unless you want to inspect or restore an earlier state. When you edit and save the file, it becomes "modified," and the `add`/`commit` cycle begins again.

If you delete a file, that counts as a modification. `git rm` will stage the deletion for the repository. If you move or rename a file, that's equivalent to a `git rm` of the file at its old location or name, and `git add` at the new one. `git mv` will do it all in one step. However you do it, Git will notice that the "old" and "new" files are identical, and the file's track in the history will be unbroken.

How Xcode Works with Git

Xcode's view of a Git repository is slightly different, because its demands as an IDE require another layer of abstraction. As Xcode presents them, files have six states.

- **Unmodified**, with no badge on the file's entry in the Project navigator. The file's history is in the repository, and you haven't saved any changes.

- **Modified**, with an **M** badge. The file is in a repository, but you've changed your working copy since it was last committed. Git will see these files as "modified," but not "staged." Xcode's version-control model has no "staged" status. When you commit a revision, Xcode lets you choose which files to include in the commit, and stages and commits them at the same time.

- **Added**, with an **A** badge. You've created a new file in the project (**File → New → File...**, ⌘N), or added an existing one and copied it to the project directory (**File → Add Files to...**, ⌥⌘A). Xcode *will* stage added files, but will still let you withhold them from a commit.

- **Renamed**, with an **A+** badge. You've moved or renamed a file in the project. Xcode stages such files, but will still let you withhold them from a commit.

- **Conflicted**, with a red **C** added to any other status indicator. When you merge changes from another repository into your own, it may not be possible to determine which lines from which files are to survive the merge—more on this soon. Xcode flags these with a **C** and will refuse further commits until you use **Source Control →Mark Selected Files as Resolved** to clear the conflicted state. Git's approach is slightly different: It tracks conflicted files, but clears the conflicts when you edit and stage them.

See "Merges and Conflicts," in this chapter, for how you can resolve conflicts in a file.

- **Unknown**, marked **?**. The file is in the project directory, but not in the repository. This is equivalent to Git's "untracked" state.

Your First Commit

If you created a Git repository along with your project, Xcode has already done your first commit—all of the source files, and all of the configurations that aren't one-user-only are already in the repo.

But what about the first commit *you* do? Set up an experiment:

1. If you didn't have Xcode create a repository for the passer-rating project, use the techniques I just showed you to add one.
2. Open the passer-rating project.
3. If you just now created the local repository (and possibly restarted Xcode), the Project navigator will be full of files marked **M**. Otherwise, make a change to one of the files and save it; the file will pick up the **M** badge in a few seconds.
4. Select **Source Control →Commit. . .** (⌥⌘C). A sheet will appear (Figure 7.2) showing your changes and offering a text-editing area for your notes on what you changed.

> **Note**
>
> The Commit editor, which shows the changes you're committing in a file, is a real editor. You can make last-moment changes, and those will be a part of the file as it is committed.

Working with Remote Repositories

Git is a *distributed* source-control system. To simplify, every developer has a repository containing the whole history of the project. The repositories are peers; in principle, none of them are authoritative. The concept that Subversion has of a single repository feeding the truth to clients in the form of snapshot copies of the project has no *inherent* expression in Git.

However, it's common to have such a central repository for a project, one on a machine that is continuously available, is backed up, and has a stable hostname and IP address. That way, multiple developers, or a single developer with more than one computer, can keep each other current.

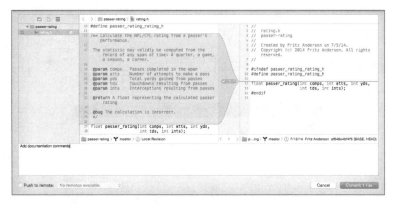

Figure 7.2   The Commit editor sheet contains a variant on the Comparison editor. It highlights the changes made in each file. The source list on the left side of the window allows you to withhold files by unchecking them. The file to be committed can still be edited. The area at the bottom receives your message describing the new revision. Xcode will not permit you to complete the commit without a message.

Usually these are "bare" repositories, `cloned` or `inited` with the `--bare` option so they do not include the literal set of controlled files that developers would have in their working copies.

Note

A local working copy may be associated with more than one remote repository, but let's keep it simple.

Xcode has three ways to deal with remote repositories.

- **Cloning an Existing Repository:** The remote is known to exist. You can clone it by selecting **Check out an existing project** from the Welcome window (⇧ ⌘ 1). The **Source Control → Check Out. . .** command has the same effect. Obviously, the remote repository was there; you wouldn't have a clone otherwise.

- **Creating a Repository with Xcode Server:** The remote does not exist, but Xcode can make it exist. If you have an Xcode server registered in the **Accounts** tab of the Preferences window, you can ask the server to create a bare repo for you. If your project has a local repository in its working copy, you can select the working copy in the **Source Control** menu, and then **Configure. . . .** The Configure Repository sheet will drop down; select the middle tab, **Remotes**. Click the **+** button at lower left and select **Create New Remote. . . .** You'll be asked to identify the Xcode server from a list of the ones you registered in the **Accounts** preferences and to give it a name for local reference. (The name has to be usable by the Git tools; Xcode will reject names that don't fit the need.) See Figure 7.3, top right.

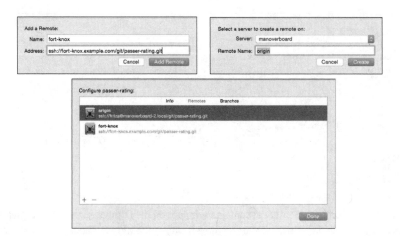

Figure 7.3   Using the Configure Repository sheet (bottom) available for a project in the **Source Control** menu, you can add an existing repository as a remote (top left), or negotiate a completely new repository with an Xcode server (top right).

Xcode logs into Xcode Server and negotiates the creation of the repo, and the server does the rest. Push your working copy onto the remote (**Source Control** →**Push. . .**, and select the remote and branch). You're done. On the server, the Server control application's **Xcode** panel shows the new repository (Figure 7.4).

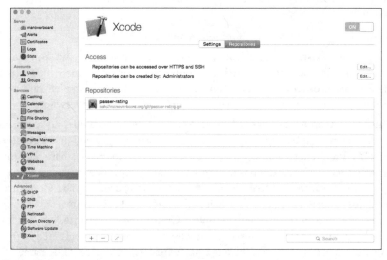

Figure 7.4   Adding a repository to an Xcode server from Xcode adds the new repo to the list in the control application on the server.

- **Adding a Reference to a Repository:** Selecting **Add Remote...** from the **+** button in the Configure Repository editor shows a simple dialog sheet that asks you for a local name and a URL for a repository (Figure 7.3, top right). Xcode updates your working copy's configuration with the pointer to the remote. Xcode will show the remote and its branches whenever you push or pull files with it.

  Add Remote... has exactly the same effect as the most common variant of `git remote add` on the command line. That includes the fact that this is only a local, named *reference* to a remote repository. Creating the reference in Xcode does not ensure that the repo exists or is reachable.

Setting Up a "Remote"—Locally

You don't need a fancy purpose-made server to work with a remote repository. You don't even need another machine. You can do everything I'm going to show you in this chapter using a "remote" that's nothing more than a local file directory.

You're going to create a "bare" (no working files) repository in `/Users/Shared/`, marked as "shared," where all users can get at it. Open the Terminal, and do this:

```
$ # Work on the "Shared" user
$ cd /Users/Shared
$
$ # Create a directory for Git repositories...
$ mkdir git
$
$ # ... and work on that
$ cd git
$
$ # Create a shareable, bare repository named passer-rating.git
$ git init --bare --share=all passer-rating.git
Initialized empty Git repository in /Users/Shared/git/passer-rating.git/
$
$ # The directory contains just the repository infrastructure
$ ls -1 passer-rating.git/
total 24
-rw-rw-r--    1 fritza  staff    23 Jul  7 15:56 HEAD
drwxrwsr-x    2 fritza  staff    68 Jul  7 15:56 branches
-rw-rw-r--    1 fritza  staff   171 Jul  7 15:56 config
-rw-rw-r--    1 fritza  staff    73 Jul  7 15:56 description
drwxrwsr-x   11 fritza  staff   374 Jul  7 15:56 hooks
drwxrwsr-x    3 fritza  staff   102 Jul  7 15:56 info
drwxrwsr-x    4 fritza  staff   136 Jul  7 15:56 objects
drwxrwsr-x    4 fritza  staff   136 Jul  7 15:56 refs
$
```

With this, `/Users/Shared/git/` includes a repository named `passer-rating.git`. It's a "bare" repository because there is no working directory containing files you can edit and check in, and there never will be. Its sole purpose is to hold work from other clients.

The --shared flag tells Git that whenever it makes changes to the repository, they should be given filesystem permissions that preserve other users' access to the repo.

> **Note**
>
> Readers have felt cheated that this "remote" repository isn't on a different machine, but that's not what the term means in Git. A remote repository is one that isn't your local repo. It doesn't matter where it is—it could even be another subdirectory of your home account. Simply add an item to the Repositories list in the **Accounts** panel of the Preferences window, and enter a URL—file, ssh, http, whatever—giving the host and path for the repo, and your credentials to access it. Once the link is established, Git hides the details of where the remote actually is. As I write this book, I'm using a repo on an Xcode server because it fits my workflow and I want to demonstrate some other features, but you can follow along with a file remote and see no difference.

> **Note**
>
> What, by the way, is a Git server? Git transactions can take place over HTTP or HTTPS, but the most common setup for small teams is a Unix box running an ssh server, on which the stock Git package has been installed. That's it. There is no software package that is a "Git server." And not every remote repository is a server, anyway—all repos are peers, and it's perfectly legitimate to push and pull revisions with another developer's local repository. There are far too many variants to cover in this book; I'll recommend complete guides later in this chapter and in Appendix B, "Resources."

Return to your passer-rating project in Xcode, and from the **Source Control** menu, select your local repository and branch, and then **Configure passer-rating...** (or whatever your local is named). The Configure Remote editor appears as I showed earlier in this chapter. In the **Remotes** tab, select **Add Remote...** from the **+** popup menu. Name the remote **origin** (the expected name for the primary remote) and enter the URL `file:///Users/Shared/git/passer-rating.git`.

You're now ready to use the origin repository using exactly the same techniques no matter where it's located.

Pushing to the Remote

New bare repositories have absolutely no content, and if you try to clone (retrieve a new copy) from one, you'll get an error message from Git. You have to push your files into the remote, thus filling its database with your files and the history they accumulated back to the creation of your local repo.

If you got here by adding a regular remote repo by hand, you weren't sure the remote existed or was reachable—that's not how Git works, it's just a convenience name for a URL. When the push dialog appears, Xcode pauses briefly before filling the remote/branch popup. In that period, Xcode *does* verify that the remote exists and accepts connections; if it doesn't, Xcode won't add it to the popup. See Figure 7.5.

Click **Push**. The dialog will show an activity spinner as the push is negotiated with the remote and your changes are transferred. When it's done, a green checkmark badge appears briefly, and the sheet retracts.

Figure 7.5   Selecting **Source Control** → **Push. . .** drops a concise dialog with which you can designate what remote, and branch within the remote, you want to push to. If you have a local branch that the remote does not, the popup menu will include the option of creating the branch on the remote.

Merges and Conflicts

All your work so far has been done under one user account on your Mac; call that "User A." Let's imagine that User A is working with User B. For the sake of example, User B will be played by a second account on the same Mac. In practice, your collaborators will be other people—or you—using different computers.

User B doesn't have a copy of the passer-rating project, but we've already seen how easy it is for her to get one. She can

- Open the Welcome to Xcode window (⇧ ⌘ 1), and select **Check out an existing project**; or
- Select **Source Control** → **Check Out. . . .**

Xcode will present a window that lists some repositories it already knows about, plus a text field for the URL of any other. Xcode knows about some repositories because you registered them in the **Accounts** panel of the Preferences window. And, of course, it knows about remotes you added to other projects.

But User B is a stranger to all of that. She'll have to enter the URL for the passer-rating repository and click **Next**. The checkout window shows progress bars as it goes through the process of gaining access to the remote, and then offers a get-file sheet for her to select a directory to receive the project folder.

> **Note**
>
> Or, User B might be given a window telling her that whatever is at the other end of the URL she entered "doesn't appear to be a git repository," which could mean anything. It covers bad credentials, bad connection, bad URL. . . but the usual explanation is a bad URL. Consult whoever gave you the URL and a Git tutorial for the formats Git expects for remote URLs.

With that, User B has a complete copy of the master branch of the passer-rating directory, including the complete revision history. The remote from which she checked out is linked to the local repo as `origin`, and pushes and pulls go through it by default.

User A

User A has definite ideas about code style. In particular, he doesn't like the long identifiers in `rating.c` for the components of the passer rating. He does a search-and-replace to change all instances of *Component* to *Comp*.

Change: Replace All in File

He did this by selecting **Find** →**Find. . .** (⌘F), and typing `Component` into the text field that slides down into the editor. As he typed, the editor highlighted its contents to show the matching text. He has a choice of options from a popover window he can summon by clicking the magnifying-glass icon in the search field and selecting **Edit Find Options. . .** from the drop-down menu (Figure 7.6). He can search by literal text or regular expression, whether the match must be at the beginning, at the end, anywhere in, or all of a word. He can make the search case sensitive, and let it wrap around to the start of the document when it reaches the end.

He definitely wants to make the search case sensitive, so as not to disturb the `component` parameter to `pinPassingComponent`.

If he wants more flexibility, but doesn't want to bother with regular expressions, he can stick with a text search, set the insertion point in the search field, and select **Insert Pattern** (^⌥⌘P). This will show a drop-down with common wildcard patterns, like word characters, various kinds of whitespace, and even email, IP, and web addresses. Selecting one adds it to the search text.

> **Note**
>
> You'll wish it did more. The great thing about wildcard patterns in regular-expression searches is that you can pick out the actual content the wildcard matched and use that to refine the search or build the replacement. When you use the simplified find patterns, once the pattern matches, you have no access to the details.

To replace, he clicks the popup menu at the left end of the search bar, and changes it from **Find** to **Replace**. (Or he could have selected **Find** →**Find and Replace. . .**, ⌥⌘F, in the first place.) Another field appears to receive the replacement text; he enters

Figure 7.6   Selecting **Edit Find Options. . .** from the drop-down menu attached to the search badge brings up a popover box to adapt in-file searches to your needs.

`Comp`. The Replace field offers three actions: **Replace** substitutes the field contents for the single highlighted search result in the document. **All** does the replacement for every instance of the match. And if he holds down the Option key, **All** will become **All in Selection**. He wanted to cover the whole file, so he released the Option key and clicked **All**.

> **Note**
>
> If User A wanted to do a replace-in-selection, he'd have to do a dance that other editors don't require. The usual way is to make your selection, enter the find and replace strings, and call for in-selection replacement. It can't work that way for Xcode because in-file searches are incremental: You can't set up a search-and-replace without losing your selection in favor of the search results. So User A would have had to enter his search and replacement text first, then select the range he wanted to operate on.

Change and Conflict: The Copyright Claim

Also, he's noticed that Xcode has copyrighted all the files to Fritz Anderson (see the sidebar). User A is greedy; he wants the riches to be had from `passer-rating` for himself. He uses the Find navigator to replace every instance with "User A." I'll show you how User B did the same thing later in this chapter.

Selective Commits

Ideally, Git revisions represent coordinated changes to the project. Each commit serves a discrete purpose, even if more than one file is changed. User A has made edits for two purposes—pilfering the copyright and cleaning up the variable names. If you followed the ideal of conceptual revisions, that's now a problem because `rating.c` embodies both. On the other hand, it's against human nature to expect a programmer to edit a file, accomplish one task, commit it, and only then make changes for the other task.

Git accommodates this with a "cherrypicking" option to its `add` command, and Xcode's Commit editor takes it further. The marker between the last-committed and current versions of a group of lines has two controls (Figure 7.7). The right end of the marker drops down a menu allowing you to exclude the change from the planned commit or to remove the change from the uncommitted file entirely. The left end of the marker is a toggle: If it is a checkmark, the change will be checked in; if it's a prohibition mark, the change ribbon will turn gray, and this commit won't include that change. This is another example of how Xcode's version-control support puts a wrapper on the technical details of the underlying system.

User A does two commits: The first is to be for the coding-style changes, so he unchecks the copyright changes, leaving them for the second commit. Eventually, he'll push his accumulated commits into the shared repository.

Whose Project Is It?

Xcode's templates for source files include a standard comment at the beginning showing the name of the file (which it knows because it created and named the file), the date it was

Figure 7.7 (top) Xcode's Commit sheet offers two ways to manage multiple changes to a file. The drop-down menu disclosed from the right end of the change marker lets you withhold a change from this commit, or even abandon the change for good. (bottom) The check/prohibit toggle button is a more convenient way to withhold a change. The second range of lines has turned gray, showing they will not be committed.

created (because it knows when it created it), the name of the person who created the file, and a copyright notice (the year of which it knows from when it created the file). The names of the creator and copyright holder may surprise you. How did it get those?

Like any modern operating system, OS X has user accounts under which all user applications run. When you set up your Mac on its first run, you gave a short user name and longer natural name to the first, administrative user of the computer. If you added accounts, you provided natural names for those users, too. Xcode fills in the "Created by" line of the comment from that natural name.

The copyright claim includes a copyright holder and a year, as by law it must. Xcode *could* fill this in from the user's natural name, but that's almost never necessary. When you create a project or target, Xcode asks you for an **Organization Name**, which it uses for the copyright holder. For your own work, you'd enter your name (Fritz Anderson), but if it's work for hire, you'd enter the name of the owner of the project (The University of Chicago).

Failing that, Xcode will use the company name on the "Me" card in the Contacts application. Failing *that*, it will use the full name on the "Me" card.

If you don't set an organization name at the start, you can always select the project itself in the Project navigator (top item in the list), open the File inspector (expose the Utility area on the right, and select the first tab, which looks like a sheet of paper), and edit the **Organization** field.

User B

User B has opinions of her own about copyright—she assumes (mistakenly) that the claim is good only if made in the full legal name of the author. She replaces all of the claims by "Fritz Anderson" in her copy with "Frederic F. Anderson." Also, she sets the **Organization** name in the Project inspector, so the problem won't come up again.

She makes her changes to the copyright notice using a global search-and-replace. She starts by selecting the Find navigator (third tab), or **Find → Find in Project. . .** (⇧⌘F).

The Find navigator contains a search field and some options (Figure 7.8).

We'll get back to the options in detail, but what she sees is the following:

- At the top, a path control cascading from the action (**Find**) through the search type and word-boundary selections (**Text** and **Containing** by default). She wants to do a replace, not just a find, so she clicks the first segment and changes it to **Replace**.

- A button (it shows itself to be a button only when the mouse cursor hovers over it) that says **In Project**, to select the file set the search is to cover. She clicks it to see the options, and the provision for creating her own, then clicks it again; an in-project search is just what she wants.

- A popup menu to choose case sensitivity. It doesn't matter now, but she should remember to look, or she'll get more or less than she expects.

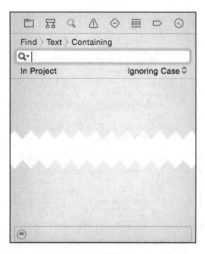

Figure 7.8 The Find navigator presents a search field and affordances for configuring the search.

- The magnifying-glass drop-down in the search field itself, giving a history of recent searches, and the same character-pattern palette the in-file search field offers.

User B types `Fritz Anderson` in the search field and presses Return. The list below it fills with all the matches, organized by file, showing each match in context. It's only a single line, but it's better than nothing, and it's not much trouble to click an entry to get the whole story. See Figure 7.9.

> **Note**
>
> The buttons that execute a global replace won't be active until a search has been done. You're not allowed to fly blind.

User B has a problem: She wants to correct the copyright claim, but the files should still identify *Fritz* Anderson as the creator. She has more matches than she wants. She has two ways to deal with this.

- She can command-click on each instance she wants to replace, and then click **Replace** (which is now active, because there would be a difference between replacing just the selections and doing a **Replace All**, which would replace all instances, selected or not).

- She can click **Preview**.

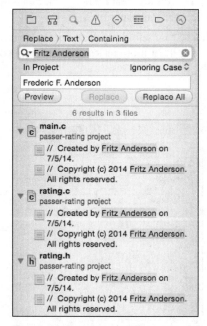

Figure 7.9   The results of a find-in-project come in the form of a table grouped by file, showing the matches in a one-line context. The Find navigator has been switched over to Replace mode and is ready to replace all instances of "Xcode User" with "Fritz Anderson."

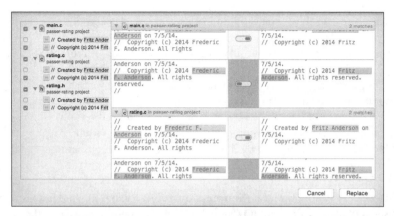

Figure 7.10   Clicking the **Preview** button in the multi-file replace view displays a comparison of each match, after and before the replacement. A toggle at each match lets you accept or reject the changes.

If she opts for a preview, a variant of the familiar Comparison editor drops (Figure 7.10) containing a source list of all the matches, and the after-and-before contents at each match. Click the toggles to accept or reject each replacement. She rejects the creator credits, and clicks **Replace**.

This being the first time she issues a command with project-wide effects, Xcode will drop a sheet offering to take a *snapshot* of the project (Figure 7.11). A snapshot is an archive of the whole project that provides a last-resort way to revert to the state of the project before the change.

You can recover the snapshot through the **Projects** panel of the Organizer window (⇧ ⌘ 2); select your project and a snapshot, and a button below the snapshot list will offer to **Export Snapshot**. Xcode uses the word "export" advisedly—the result will be a

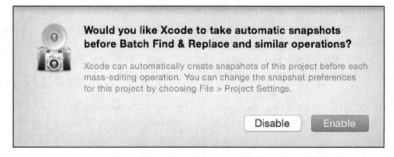

Figure 7.11   The first time you attempt a project-wide change, Xcode offers to create a snapshot that preserves the current state of the project.

separate directory with the contents of the snapshot, not a reversion of the project you're working on.

You can change your mind about snapshots by selecting **File** → **Project Settings. . .** and editing the **Snapshots** tab.

Snapshots mimic the habits of developers who don't practice version control, but they aren't a replacement. It's awkward to do them frequently, there is no way to segregate changes by their purpose, and there is no way to browse the back versions. Think of snapshots as disaster recovery if version control goes completely wrong.

User B commits her changes to the local repository, and then pushes it.

Back to User A

This is where User A does his push (**Source Control** → **Push. . .**). And it doesn't work. An alert sheet slides down to tell him that his copy of the repository, even without his changes, had fallen behind the one he's trying to push to. ("Behind" in the colloquial sense is a difficult word to apply to a network of developers whose files, as here, are actually newer than the remote repository reflects. In version control, a local copy is behind the remote if the remote has changes that the local hasn't seen yet.)

He has to pull the remote's contents into his local set before he can push his own changes. He chooses **Source Control** → **Pull. . .** (⌥⌘X); he selects **origin/master** from the popup (it should be the only choice) and clicks **Pull**. An activity indicator spins while Git retrieves the remote's content, and then a progress pie says Xcode is "detecting conflicts" in what it found.

And it found some, in all three of the files he was trying to push. If this were command-line Git, this would be tedious, because you'd have to refer to the list of conflicts, then hunt down the markup Git adds to the conflicted files, remember which versions of the conflicted lines you want to keep, save your decisions, and use `git add` to put them in the staging list.

Merging Revisions

Xcode reduces this to the point where your only headache is in deciding what version is to prevail. Immediately upon detecting the conflicts, it tells you that you can't proceed with your push until you've examined them all and made your choices. The source list at the left side of the comparison sheet that appears lists every file that would be altered by the pull (Figure 7.12). Some of these are benign—Git could figure out how to merge the changes line by line—but if there is a line that was changed by the two contributors after their versions split from their common ancestor, Git can't make a choice. You have to resolve it.

`rating.c` is the most interesting file—it contains a conflicted line, but also some lines Git had no trouble choosing. User A's local version is more or less on the left, and the version that would be pulled is on the right. A control at the bottom of the editor (Figure 7.13) lets him pick which version he wants of each group of lines.

> **Note**
>
> I say "more or less" because there are three things to show—your version, the remote's version, and the result of your choices between them—and Xcode makes do with only two

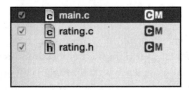
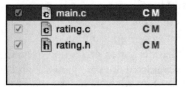

Figure 7.12   (left) When you pull a version of the working files that conflicts with your own, Xcode's Merge editor lists the conflicted files with a red **C** marker. (right) Once the conflicts are resolved, the **C** markers turn gray, and you can complete the pull.

Figure 7.13   The control at the bottom of the Merge editor gives you four choices for resolving differences between the local and remote versions of a group of lines: the local version followed by the remote; the local version; the remote version; or the remote followed by the local. The options to use both versions are available only for conflicts.

views. The view on the left shows the result of your choices. You can see your lines, but only if you opt to use them in the final merge. The control implies you'd be choosing the version "on the left," but it's not visible on the left until you choose it.

Lines without Conflicts

Let's start with the easy part: the lines that don't conflict. By default, command-line Git does unconflicted merges automatically: If only one version has changed a line since the common ancestor of the two, the change wins.

Xcode gives you more control. The Merge editor draws blue ribbons to highlight each group of changed lines, with a marker in the middle that looks like a sliding switch. The local version is on the left, and the remote is on the right. The slider points to the version that wins. You can't use the marker directly. Instead, select the ribbon for a change group (look for the outline a selected group picks up—it's easy to miss), and use the control at the bottom of the editor sheet to make your choice (see Figure 7.14). The options to use both versions, one after the other, aren't available for unconflicted lines.

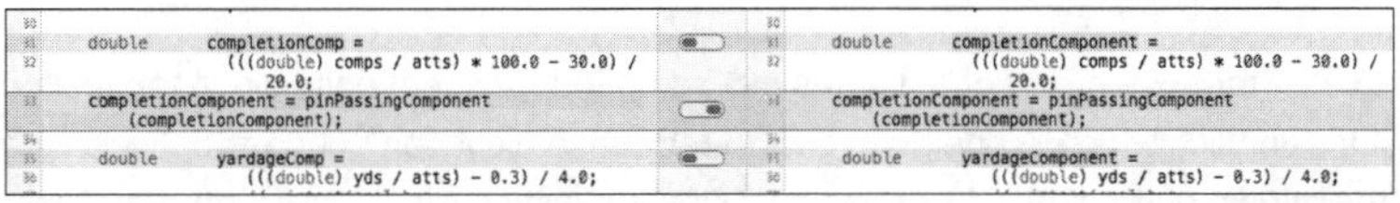

Figure 7.14   Git doesn't let you pick and choose groups of lines to be merged from a pull, but Xcode displays all the potential changes and lets you choose whether to accept them.

Conflicted Lines

That leaves the conflicts. User A and User B started with a common version that claimed copyright for Fritz Anderson. Independently, they changed the claims, using different names. Git has no way to prefer one over the other, so it reports a conflict and forces you to decide. Conflicted lines are joined by red ribbons, again with a lozenge in the middle. But this time, there is no slider: With no way to choose, the lozenge contains a question mark (Figure 7.15, top).

It's up to User A to resolve the conflict, using the control at the bottom of the sheet. In this case, he'll concede User B's use of "Frederic F. Anderson" and select the third segment (use remote) of the control. For the rest, the no-conflict lines, he's adamant about those shortened variable names. He picks the second segment (use local) to keep his changes.

With all the conflicts cleared (see the source list on the right side of Figure 7.12), Xcode enables the **Pull** button, and only then does User A's working set reflect the results.

Committing the Choices

Deconflicting edits are no different from any other kind of edit. They're present on disk, but not in any repository. As with any other modified files, the Project navigator flags them with **M** badges. User A must commit the merged files to his local repository (providing a commit message explaining the merge), and then push the state of his repo out to the remote. Assuming the remote hasn't picked up any more changes from User B, the push goes through.

He can send an email to User B to let her know there are changes for her to pull. Or he could just let her discover them for herself, but that says something worrisome about how A and B are getting along.

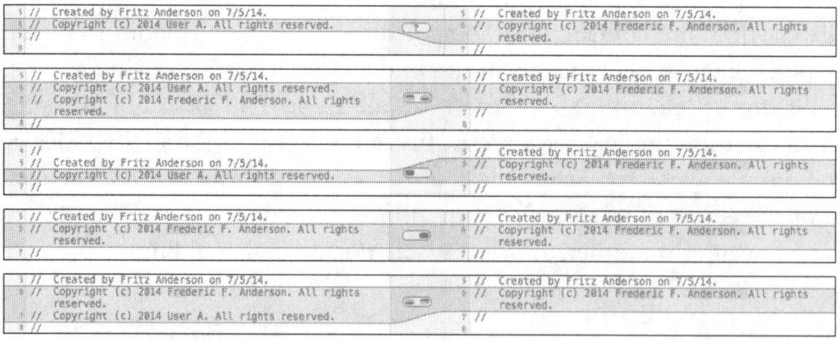

Figure 7.15   (top) When part of a file has picked up independent edits since the last common revision, it's a conflict, which Xcode highlights in red. Because it can't choose between them, the marker in the middle of the highlight ribbon contains a question mark. The control at the bottom of the Merge sheet lets you choose among (second through last) local-before-remote, local, remote, and remote-before-local.

The Version Editor

Checking files into version control, or even merging them, is not much use if you can't see what you changed. Xcode's Version editor (third segment of the **Editor** control in the toolbar) lets you do just that. Click the Version editor segment and hold the mouse button down (Figure 7.16). The Version editor has three views:

- You'll use the **Comparison** editor most frequently; you've already seen it, in specialized forms, whenever refactoring or version-control actions require a side-by-side display of changes.
- **Blame** displays files broken up to reflect which commit was responsible for the current version of a line.
- The **Log** view lists all commits that affected the current file.

I'll cover each, starting with the Comparison view.

Comparison

If you've been following along, the passer-rating project has accumulated a few revisions by a couple of authors. Select one of your source files and switch the editor to the Version view. It splits into two panels: The left side shows your file in its current state, saved or not. The right side shows what it looked like the last time you committed it. See Figure 7.17.

Just now, they're probably identical, but try editing the current copy of the file. A blue band appears across the editor, stretching from your changes to the equivalent position in the committed version. If you made changes within a line, the differences are highlighted in a muted yellow.

The editor panes are real editors: You can make any changes you want, though any changes you make to a committed version won't stick. Between the columns, in each of the change ribbons, is a numbered marker. Clicking it selects that change; once a change ribbon is selected, you can move rapidly among them with the Up- and Down-Arrow keys. The triangle at the right end of the marker signals a drop-down menu with the single command **Discard Change**, letting you wind those lines back to their form in the earlier revision.

Figure 7.16   The right segment of the **Editor** control anchors a drop-down menu to select the three version-control editing styles.

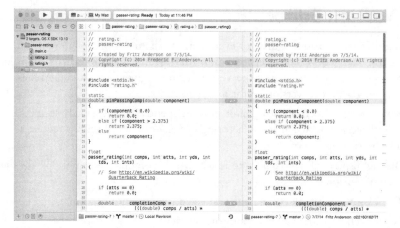

Figure 7.17   The Comparison view of the Version editor puts two versions of a file side by side, with a highlight connecting the changes you made between the two versions. The jump bar at the bottom lets you select among versions and branches.

> **Note**
>
> If you just want to abandon all the changes you made to a file since the last revision, there's no need to do it piecemeal. Right-click the file in the Project navigator and select **Source Control →Discard Changes...** from the contextual menu. If you expose the File inspector in the Utility area, a section will give the full details of the file's version-control status, including a **Discard...** button. If you want to abandon the changes to all your files, there's **Source Control →Discard All Changes....**

The editor isn't confined to the last two versions. You'll find a jump bar at the bottom of each pane, with segments representing the repository, branch, and revision the pane displays. Each segment is a popup menu; you can set the halves of the editor to any revision you like, and you'll be shown the differences between them.

There's an even easier way to select revisions. Click the clock icon at the bottom of the gutter between the panes. You'll be rewarded with a timeline, a black bar with hash marks; the shorter marks represent the revisions that affect this file, the longer ones dates (see Figure 7.18). Move your mouse pointer over the timeline; Xcode displays a popover showing the date, the revision ID, the committer, and the description for that version.

There are arrowheads on either side of the timeline. Clicking the timeline moves the arrow on that side to the click location, and that side of the editor is filled with that revision of the file.

The graphical Comparison editor is a great way to visualize the changes in your code, but it's not usable if you want to communicate the differences to others. You could give them full access to your repositories, urge them to buy Macs, sign up as Apple developers, and install Xcode; or you could select **Editor →Copy Source Changes**, which will put a listing of the differences, in the style of the `diff` command-line tool, onto the clipboard.

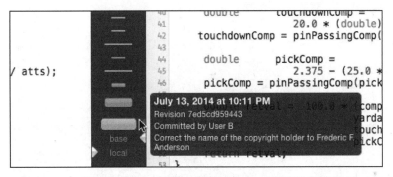

Figure 7.18   Clicking the clock icon at the bottom of the center column of the Comparison editor reveals a timeline of revisions for the current file. Hovering the mouse pointer over a tick displays information about that revision. Clicking to either side of a tick will display the corresponding version in the editor view on that side.

Blame

The Comparison view shows your revisions along one axis, the accumulated changes between two revisions. The Blame view lets you see another: who wrote what parts of your current file, when, and why. Choose **Blame** from the Version-editor segment in the toolbar to expose the Blame view.

> **Note**
>
> "Blame" is the technical name for this perspective on a version-control system and probably reflects the mood of developers as they track down the perpetrator of this or that change. Subversion tactfully offers "credit" as a synonym.

The right-hand panel in the editor goes away, to be replaced by a column of annotations. Each note matches up to lines in your code. At minimum, it shows the author and date of the last commit that changed those lines; if room permits, the annotation will include the commit message. See Figure 7.19. You can get the full details of any commit by clicking the information button in the annotation box.

As always, you can select any revision from the jump bar at the bottom of the editor to see how contributions arrived and were overwritten over the history of the file.

Log

The Log view gives a third perspective on the history of a file. Select **Log** from the Version editor's drop-down menu in the toolbar. This is a single view of the file, as of the revision you select from the jump bar. The column to the right shows the full information for every revision that affected that file, and only those revisions.

Revisions that have files uniquely associated with them (merges don't) include a notation like **Show 2 modified files**. Clicking the notation drops a comparison-browser sheet with a source list containing every file in that revision and a side-by-side comparison of the selected file after and before the commit.

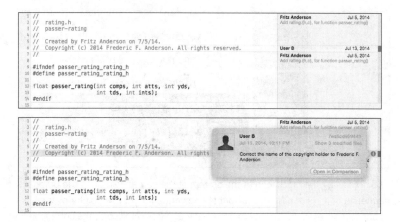

Figure 7.19 (top) The Blame column annotates each group of lines in a file with the details of the commit that was responsible for them. Bigger blocks of lines permit more information to be shown. The bars at the right margin are more intense for more recent revisions. (bottom) Clicking the information button in an annotation pops up the full details of the commit, including address-book information about the person responsible, so you can render your compliments at the click of a mouse.

> **Note**
>
> The `git` command-line tool will give you something similar that might suit you better: `git log --name-only` will print every revision in the current history, with the commit messages and a list of the files that were changed in each.

Branching

One more thing. Programming is not a linear activity. I've gone through the revision process as though it were a unitary march of progress with every step leading surely to a bigger, better program. That's not real life. In real life, you have ideas that may or may not be useful in your product, and you shouldn't pollute the often-parallel progress of your "good" revisions while you play with them.

You do this with *branching*, which lets you accumulate revisions along separate lines (branches) of development and merge them as you need. passer-rating (so far) is too simple to provide a good example, so I'll just explain how it works; you can follow along with Figure 7.20.

Every project in Git or Subversion starts with one branch, which Git calls `master`. This example begins with just the one branch. Our developer comes up with a good idea and creates a branch she calls `good-idea` (the quality of her ideas doesn't extend to the names she makes up). She does this by selecting **New Branch. . .** from her working copy's submenu in the **Source Control** menu. A sheet appears so she can give the branch

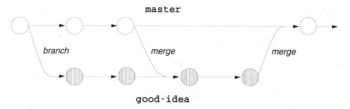

Figure 7.20   The main line of development of this project goes along the revisions in the `master` branch. A developer has an idea she wants to try out, so she creates the `good-idea` branch, occasionally merging in the improvements from `master`. When she's done, the `good-idea` changes can be folded back into `master`.

its name, and she clicks **Create**. The sheet shows an activity spinner, reports success, and goes away. The local repository is now focused on `good-idea`.

She then does the normal work of revising and testing her program. In the meantime, she also needs to maintain the program on the `master` branch, which reflects what has gone out to users, and which other developers are using as the common meeting point for their own revisions. She switches back to the `master` branch using the **Source Control →working copy →Switch to Branch...** command. The command summons a sheet displaying all branches, local and remote, that are available to her; she selects `master`, clicks **Switch**, and gets busy. See Figure 7.21.

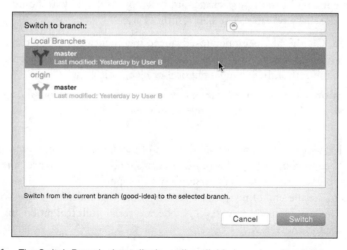

Figure 7.21   The Switch-Branch sheet displays all available branches, local and remote. (Remote branches may take a few seconds to appear if getting a list entails a network transaction.) Selecting a branch and clicking **Switch** checks the files on that branch out into the working copy.

In Figure 7.20, both branches progress by a couple of revisions, and she decides her work on good-idea can't proceed without taking account of changes made to master. She can do this by selecting **Source Control →working copy →Merge from Branch...** if she is on the good-idea branch; she selects the source branch (master) from the picker sheet, and clicks **Merge**. Or, if she is on the master branch, she selects **Merge into Branch...** and selects good-idea.

Either way, she'll be presented with the merge-comparison sheet so she can review the changes and approve them one by one.

She makes a few more revisions to good-idea before she is satisfied that her idea really was good and it's ready to go into the main branch. She selects **Merge into Branch...**, chooses the master branch, and completes the final merge.

Summary

This was a long chapter, but there's a lot to version control, and the benefits of mastering it are immense. When you created your first project, Xcode provided a Git repository for you, just by your checking a box. If you had registered an account on an Xcode server, you could even have Xcode hook you up with a fresh remote repository. In this chapter, you began to use it, committing your work step by step. Then you were able to compare versions of your work to see what was done when, and to get a measure of forgiveness, of which there is not enough in this world.

Xcode's support for Git and Subversion is good enough for day-to-day work, but it's not comprehensive. You dipped into the command line to round out repository management. There is much more to Subversion and Git than I can cover in one chapter. The command-line interfaces to those packages are very powerful, and you should at least look at them to learn what's available. The best resources are:

- **Git**—*Pro Git*, the best beginner-to-advanced treatment of Git. You can read it online for free at http://git-scm.com/book, but consider supporting Scott Chacon, the author, by buying a physical or electronic copy.

- **Subversion**—*Version Control with Subversion*, written by (some of) the authors of Subversion and revised with each release of the tool. Find it at http://svnbook.red-bean.com/.

In particular, seek out and understand the idea of tagging a revision, which allows you to mark the place in your project's history that corresponds to (for instance) a release. Tagging is the biggest gap in Xcode's version-control support.

This takes me to the end of my generic introduction to Xcode. Now that you have a background, you can proceed to the tasks Xcode was really built for: producing graphical applications for iOS and OS X.

Part II

The Life Cycle of an iOS Application

## 8

Starting an iOS Application

Now that you have the basic skills down, let's move on to a real project. You'll build an iPhone application that manages a list of quarterbacks and displays their game and career statistics.

Planning the App

Before coding, it's best (though not customary) to know what you're doing. Specifically, what are you going to present to the app's user, what data do you need to keep to make that presentation, and how do you translate between the data and the presentation?

Model-View-Controller

The Model-View-Controller (MVC) design pattern formalizes those questions into an architecture for graphical applications. The Cocoa Touch application framework is designed to implement applications that follow the MVC pattern. If you don't follow it, you will find yourself "fighting the framework": Winning through to a finished application would be difficult, and maintaining it would be miraculous. The Xcode development tools are designed to support Cocoa programming and therefore the MVC pattern. MVC divides the functionality of an application into three parts, and each class in the application must fall into one of them:

- Model objects embody the data and logic of a particular problem domain. Models tend to be unique to each application. You can create your own subclasses of NSObject or NSManagedObject to give life to your models.

- View objects handle user interaction, presenting information and enabling the user to manipulate data or otherwise influence the behavior of the program. Views are usually drawn from a repertoire of standard elements, such as buttons, tables, scrollers, and text fields. Views ideally know nothing about any problem domain: A button can display itself and report taps without needing to know what tapping means to your application. In iOS, views are instances of UIView or its many subclasses.

- Controller objects mediate between the pure logic of the model and the pure mechanics of the views. A controller object decides how views display and how user actions translate into model events. In iOS, controllers are almost always instances of subclasses of `UIViewController`.

Okay, in practice some classes won't fall exactly into model, view, or controller. If you have a view custom-built to display your particular data, making that view completely independent of your data model makes no sense. Still, MVC is an important discipline: If you fudge on it, you should be aware that you're fudging and consider whether you can restore the MVC separation.

The Model

From the nature of a passer rating, all you need is one model class: a `Passer` to carry one passer's name, and the total attempts, completions, yards, touchdowns, and interceptions. Let's make this a little more interesting: Ratings can be calculated over as many attempts as you like and are usually calculated per-game as well as in a career aggregate. So `Passer` should "own" any number of `Game` objects, with details of the game (who played, what date, and so on) as well as the passing statistics for that game.

The model then looks like the diagram presented in Figure 8.1.

What about a passer's aggregate statistics—the career yards, touchdowns, and rating? Those can be pulled out of his `Games`—it will turn out not to be hard at all.

The Views

iOS applications don't usually have a concept of documents, but even simple ones acquire many screens' worth of views. You'll deal in passers and their games, and you need to view and edit both.

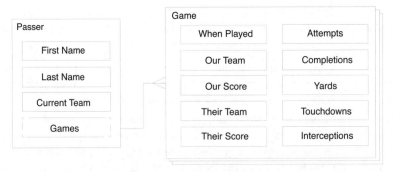

Figure 8.1   The summary description of what data a passer-rating app would need leads to the plan shown in this diagram: A `Passer` object serves only to identify a single player; his career statistics are in a set of `Game` objects that `Passer` "owns."

You need a list of passers, who can be created or edited in a separate view; and a view devoted to a selected passer, with a list of games that need a view of their own to create or edit them. A sketch of the flow appears in Figure 8.2.

> **Note**
>
> That's what a full version of Passer Rating should look like, and getting it down on paper is an essential step. Alas, this book will run out of Xcode examples before we complete the app.

Typically, each phase of an iOS application displays a view object—a `UIView`—that fills the screen. That main view usually contains a hierarchy of other views. For instance, the `Passer` editor at the lower-left corner of the sketch (refer to Figure 8.2) consists of a

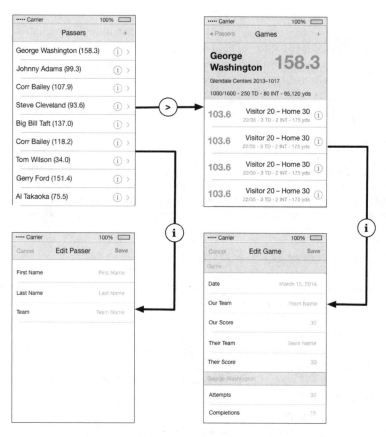

Figure 8.2   A rough sketch shows how we'd like the iOS Passer Rating app to look and flow. It starts (top left) with a list of passers. Tapping a row shows the detailed record for that passer (top right). The user can add or edit passers (bottom left) and games (bottom right).

wrapper `UIView`; it contains a navigation bar (`UINavigationItem`, at the top), which in turn contains two buttons (`UIBarButtonItem`, at either end). It also contains a table (`UITableView`) with three rows (`UITableViewCell`), each containing a label (`UILabel`) and a text-entry field (`UITextField`).

The Controllers

iOS applications are organized around a sequence of view controllers, objects derived from `UIViewController`. Each view controller mediates between model objects and the views that fill the device's screen. For each full-screen view you see in the sketch, you must provide a `UIViewController` subclass to link the data in the model to the views on the screen; you may need to provide more if the visible views require it. In the life cycle of a view, the controller comes first; when it is initialized, it creates or loads the view objects and sets them up to reflect the model.

Now, even a simple application like this slides four main views onto and off of the screen, according to a precise hierarchy. Managing the relationships between them—which to slide in, which to slide back to—would seem to be an involved task, and it is. But, thankfully, it is not a task you need to worry much about. UIKit, the user-facing part of iOS, provides umbrella view controllers (such as `UINavigationController`) that manage the navigation tasks for you by taking ownership of your controller objects. All you need to do is request a transition between the views, and the umbrella takes care of the rest.

> **Note**
>
> The screen of the iPhone 6 Plus is midway between those of iPad and the non-plus iPhones. In iOS 8, Apple introduced a way to present an iPad side-by-side view for master and detail displays that reverts to the screen-by-screen hierarchy on smaller screens. It's an impressive feature, but it doesn't have much effect on the Xcode workflow.

Starting a New iOS Project

Start by creating a new Xcode project, selecting **File → New → Project...** (⇧⌘N). Select **Application** under **iOS**, and from the array of application types, select Master-Detail Application. Passer Rating follows the common pattern of presenting a progression of lists and detail views, under a navigation bar that provides a "breadcrumb" trail back up the tree. The Master-Detail Application template is a skeleton for such an app. Click **Next**.

The next panel in the New Project assistant lets you name the project **Passer Rating**. That much is obvious.

The next item is **Organization Name**; whenever Xcode creates a new text file, it includes a copyright notice, and this is to be the name of the holder.

Organization Identifier is the next field. Every application in the iOS (and OS X) universe has a string that uniquely identifies it. The Passer Rating app needs one. The customary way to produce a unique identifier is to reverse the order of your domain name,

add a dot, and then give the application name, suitably encoded for the OS. I own the
wt9t.com domain, so I'd fill in **com.wt9t**.

> **Note**
>
> You don't have a domain name of your own? Next you'll be telling me you don't have a
> T-shirt for the project. Get one (a domain name). They're cheap, and you don't have to do
> anything else with them.

Xcode generates an identifier for you and displays it just under the company ID:
com.wt9t.Passer-Rating.

The **Language** popup allows you to choose Swift or Objective-C as the primary
language for the application code. It's possible to mix the two in a single project—see
Apple's guide on the subject—but this project will be pure Swift.

Devices determines whether the template should include UI setups for iPhone, iPad,
or both. Select **iPhone**; Passer Rating presents so little information that spreading it across
an iPad screen would be absurd.

Last of all, check the **Use Core Data** box. Core Data is Cocoa's object-persistence and
relational framework, and will be very handy for keeping the database organized. The
project template will add a number of convenient housekeeping methods for getting a
Core Data–based application running.

Click **Next**, and you'll be shown a get-folder sheet like the one you first saw in
Chapter 2, "Kicking the Tires." Pick a spot, and be sure to set **Source Control** to create a
local (**My Mac**) Git repository.

Clicking **Create** unmasks the project window as before, and once again, you see the
Target editor.

> **Note**
>
> If this project were to include Objective-C classes, you'd also have to specify a **Class Prefix**
> in the Project Document section of the File inspector. This would be three letters (two is
> no longer recommended) for Xcode's class templates to prepend to the names of your new
> classes. Objective-C has no namespaces; if you chose an "obvious" name for a class, you'd
> likely be sharing it with another in Cocoa or a third-party library. The collision might halt
> your build in the link phase, or it might lead to bugs that could be very difficult to track
> down. Prefixing the class names with something you hope is unique cuts down on the risk.

Target Editor

The Passer Rating project consists of two targets: "Passer Rating," which produces the
app, and "Passer RatingTests," which will contain the application test suite. Xcode will
initially show you the **General** editor for the Passer Rating target. (Click the Passer
Rating project item at the top of the Project navigator to bring it up yourself.) It provides
an interface for the basic settings that identify your project—its identifier, target
environment, orientations, and where it can find the images that are the face UIKit puts
on your app. It also keeps a list of the libraries the target will link to.

Take note of the **Deployment Target** field in the "Deployment Info" section: This is
where you designate the *minimum* version of the operating system your app will accept. It

won't run on anything less, and you can be assured that you can use all of that OS's features freely. The project template set this to the latest version (8.2 as I write this). We'll be exploring features unique to iOS 8, so leave the setting alone.

There is another concept, the *SDK*, which you can find in the **Build Settings** tab. In Xcode's parlance, an SDK is a tree of headers, libraries, and other resources that let your app use the features of a particular version of an OS. In the past, Xcode came with a library of development kits for back versions of OS X, but now you'll get only the latest iOS and the one or two versions of OS X that the Xcode can run on.

Even though you no longer have a choice of SDKs, you should remember the rule: The target version is the *earliest version on which you will run*, and the SDK version is the *latest version from which you can draw functionality*. If you want to be compatible back to iOS 5.1, set the target to 5.1, use the current SDK, and be careful not to use any features from later OSes. The build system will link your app so it does not require the newer API in order to run.

> **Note**
>
> Also, if you target an OS that is earlier than the SDK, the build system will give you the behavior of the older OS, even if the later one fixes bugs and adds features—you'll be given the behavior you developed for and expected.

What's in the Project

The project template you chose for Passer Rating includes a lot:

> **Note**
>
> If you don't see the Navigator area, highlight the button near the right end of the toolbar that shows a bar at the left side of the window rectangle; the Project navigator is the first tab.

- **Class `AppDelegate`:** The application itself is represented by an object of class `UIApplication`, which you should never have to subclass or replace. True to the delegation pattern used throughout Cocoa, all of the unique behavior of the application comes through the methods of a delegate object, which the application object calls into. `AppDelegate` is declared as a subclass of `UIResponder`, and an implementor of the `UIApplicationDelegate` protocol (it promises to include the methods `UIApplication` needs from its delegate). The template for the `.swift` file contains a good starter for managing the application life cycle, including setting up the Core Data database.

- **`Main.storyboard`:** A storyboard is a graphical representation of the layout of your user interface, plus the top-level flow between the screens in your program. We'll be living with this one throughout this project.

- **Class `MasterViewController`:** This is, as the name says, the controller for the master (root-level) view of Passer Rating, which the design says will be a table of passer names and ratings. Because navigation-based applications almost always start with a table, the template makes `MasterViewController` a subclass of `UITableViewController`, which is suited for running a table view. The implementation file includes skeletons of the methods you'll need to fill in the table. It also provides an instance of `NSFetchedResultsController`, which does a lot to bridge Core Data data stores with tables.

- **Class `DetailViewController`:** The controller for the next layer of Passer Rating is the one that will be seen when the user taps a passer's name. The template declares it a simple subclass of the generic `UIViewController`.

- **`Images.xcassets`** is a catalog of the minimum set of images iOS will require in order to run an application. It starts with AppIcon, which is what you'd think it is. As screen sizes, UI conventions, and resolutions have proliferated, and human nature being what it is, Xcode projects accumulated a large number of such images, many of them long-since obsolete. The media-assets catalogs wrap them all up in a single project entry, with a slot for each variant. Applications seeking an asset need only ask for it by name, and the asset-catalog mechanism will provide the best fit for the environment.

  If you want your app to run on iOS 7 or earlier, you should also have a LaunchImage, for the image—don't call it a splash screen—that displays in the ideally tiny period between launch and being ready for work. Click the **+** button below the image-set list, name it **`LaunchImage`**, fill in the (now huge) variety of image slots, and register the name of the set in the **General** tab of the Target editor.

- **LaunchScreenxib** replaces the `LaunchImage` file and image set. This is an Interface Builder screen layout to be displayed at launch. Because the layout in interface files can (should) adapt to any screen size, orientation, and resolution, you won't have to provide a multiplicity of PNGs for every possible combination—current or future. The template gives you a generic layout including the app's name and copyright information; you should adapt it to the actual initial appearance of your app. If you *don't* provide a launch layout, iOS use the next-best launch image, and if necessary, "zoom" your existing UI to fit the screen. See Chapters 11 and 12, "Building a New View" and "Auto Layout in a New View," for extensive details on Interface Builder and layout.

- **`Passer_Rating.xcdatamodeld`:** Core Data isn't a full-service database, but if you have a background in SQL, there are helpful analogies. The Data Model file is the equivalent of an SQL schema. It defines the entities (think "tables") that will hold the data, and the attributes (think "columns") those entities will have. It also sets up one-to-many and many-to-many relationships between entities (think "never having to look at a join table again"). Xcode provides a graphical editor for data models.

- In the Supporting Files group, **`Passer Rating-Info.plist`**: This is the source file that yields an `Info.plist` file to be embedded in the application. It provides basic information on what the application can do, what data it can handle, and how it is presented to the user in the Home screen. Some of that information is presented

to the user as text, so its content is merged with the application's `InfoPlist-`
`.strings` for the user's language. (Chapter 21, "Localization," covers localization
in OS X, but most of the concepts apply to iOS, as well.)

> **Note**
>
> An Objective-C project would also contain a `main.m` file for the executable file's
> entry point, and `Passer Rating-Prefix.pch` to set up the symbols for compiling
> the ObjC class files. Neither is needed for Swift.

- The "Passer RatingTests" target has a class file and `Info.plist` support similar to
  the app target's.

> **Note**
>
> An older Objective-C project would include a Frameworks group to display system and
> third-party libraries to be linked dynamically into the application. That's rarely necessary
> any more. Both Swift and Objective-C rely on importing modules, which take care of
> precompiled symbols and linkage automatically.

Xcode's template for the project also includes a panoply of build settings, specifying
how Passer Rating is to be compiled, linked, and organized.

The project is fully functional, as far as it goes. Run it: **Product → Run (⌘R)**. Xcode
builds the app, and in a few seconds, the iOS Simulator starts up and launches Passer
Rating. Out of the box, the app is the iOS/Core Data equivalent to "Hello World": It
shows an empty table under a navigation bar with **Edit** and **+** buttons. Tapping the **+**
button adds a row with the current date and time; tapping the new entry pushes the
"detail" view into view; the **Edit** button in the root list (or swiping across a row) lets you
delete rows. You can close and reopen the app to find that the rows you added are still
there. See Figure 8.3.

Summary

In this chapter, you began work on an iOS application. Before doing anything in Xcode,
we decided what the app would do and what it would look like.

Once that was done, you knew enough to have Xcode create the project. You explored
the Project editor and saw how it managed the configuration of the application itself.
Then you explored the files Xcode's template provided.

The "empty" application Xcode provided was runnable; you found that running it
launched the iOS Simulator, which allowed you to use the app.

Now you're ready to make the empty app your own, to start implementing the design
we put together in this chapter. We'll start with the model.

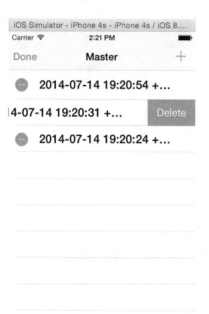

Figure 8.3   The skeletal code that comes with the Core Data + Master-Detail Application project template is enough to produce an app that will run in the iOS Simulator. It will add rows to its table, and, as shown here, it will respond to the **Edit** button by offering to delete rows.

## 9

An iOS Application: Model

It's time to put some flesh on Passer Rating's data design. The Core Data framework for iOS and OS X provides a powerful system for managing object-relational graphs and persisting them in an SQLite database.

> **Note**
>
> SQLite (you will make it a gentler world if you tolerate both "ess-cue-light" and "see-kwel-light") is the full-featured SQL database library and command-line tool at the foundation of Core Data. The Core Data API is agnostic about its bottom layer (on OS X, there are two alternatives) and affords no direct access to the underlying database. The library is a standard component of both iOS and OS X. See `http://sqlite.org`.

Xcode includes essential support for Core Data. In this chapter, you'll see how to use Xcode's graphical editor to turn a data design into an executable data model.

Implementing the Model

Core Data is going to store the model objects for you and track their relationships to each other. To do that it needs a *managed-object model*, which specifies what *entities* are in the data store, and what *properties* and *relationships* they have. In the completed application, this is kept in a `.mom` file, which is efficient but not human-readable. For development, you will be editing an Xcode data–model file (`.xcdatamodel`) that displays all this information graphically, in a format not too different from the model sketch in Figure 8.1.

> **Note**
>
> As your application evolves, so will your data model. Data files created with one managed-object model are not compatible with another. Core Data provides techniques for migrating data stores to later models, if it has the full sequence of models available to it. The aggregated versions are kept in directories—`.momd` for use at run time, and `.xcdatamodeld` in Xcode.

Entities

Select `Passer_Rating.xcdatamodeld` in the Project navigator. The Data Model editor comes in two parts. The column on the left lists the top-level contents of the model, the main ones being entities. Entities describe individual records in the Core Data database. If you're familiar with SQL databases, these are roughly like tables.

The model supplied from the template is very simple: There is one entity, `Event`. If you select it in the editor, you'll see its properties in three tables. (If you don't see tables, make sure the **Editor Style** control at the lower right has the first segment selected, for the tabular layout.)

- **Attributes** hold simple data like strings, dates, or numbers. `Event` has one attribute, `timeStamp`; you see in the top table that this attribute is of type `Date`.
- **Relationships** link entities one-to-one, one-to-many, or many-to-many. Core Data maintains relationships without your having to deal with keys or joins.
- **Fetched Properties** define fetch requests (queries for objects matching search criteria). These amount to relationships that are not continually updated as the database changes; to get a current object set, you'd have to refire the fetch yourself. Fetched properties have their uses, but you won't have any of those uses in this project.

Click the right half of the **Editor Style** control to have a look at the other view of the model. This gives you a diagram of the whole model, in which each entity is represented by a box that contains its attributes and relationships. With only one entity, having only one attribute, the diagram is unprepossessing.

Let's make something to see of it. Switch back to the Table style. Select the `Event` entity and press the Delete key. You want to add entities of your own. Going by Figure 8.1, you need two: `Game` and `Passer`. `Game` has some interesting content, so let's start with that.

1. The bar at the bottom of the editor has two circled **+** buttons, and if you look carefully, you'll see the tiny triangle that tells you it is an anchor for a drop-down menu; each can add more than one kind of thing. The thing you want to add is an entity for games.
   Hold the mouse button down on the **+** button on the left and select **Add Entity**. An entity named `Entity` appears in the entities section of the editor. Double-click the entity's name in the list to make it editable; name it **Game**.
2. `Game` will refer to `Passer`, so it should be in the model even if we don't fill it in right away. Click **Add Entity** again (the most recent use of the button sticks), and name the resulting entity **Passer**.

Attributes

So now you have `Game` and `Passer` entities, but they don't hold any data. Entities are aggregates of simple data; these are *attributes*.

3. With `Game` still selected, click the **+** button at the bottom of the Attributes list. A new attribute appears in the table with its name ready for editing.

4. Name the new attribute **whenPlayed**. You'll notice that the Type column for whenPlayed says it is of **Undefined** type. That's undesirable, but you'll take care of that soon.

5. Instead, create some more attributes: `attempts`, `completions`, `interceptions`, `ourScore`, `ourTeam`, `theirScore`, `theirTeam`, `touchdowns`, and `yards`.

> **Note**
>
> Remember to press Return when you're finished editing a name; if you add another attribute before doing so (depending on how you do it), Xcode will abandon the edit and leave the name as `attribute`.

6. You're running up the score on the errors reported in the status area in the toolbar, because none of those attributes have types. Let's take care of that. Start with whenPlayed: Select **Date** from the popup in the Type column.

7. "Scalar type" is not everything there is to say about an attribute. Click the right end of the **View** control (rightmost in the toolbar) to expose the Utility area. The Utility area is divided into an upper section, the Inspector, and a lower one, the Library. Drag the bar at the top of the Library down to make the Inspector as large as possible, and click the third tab to show the Data Model inspector.

8. Select `yards` in the Attributes list; this loads the properties of that attribute into the inspector (see Figure 9.1).

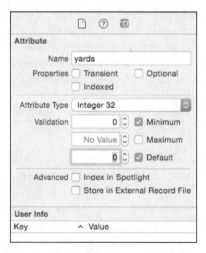

Figure 9.1   The Data Model inspector, focused on `Game`'s `yards` attribute. This is another way to set the type of the attribute, and it allows you to set detailed information on how Core Data is to treat it.

The inspector has three sections, the first of which, **Attribute**, is the most interesting. The name, yards, is right. The **Properties** checkboxes reflect how Core Data stores the attribute. Leave **Transient** (the attribute would be in the model, but not persisted) and **Indexed** (Core Data would efficiently retrieve Game objects by yards) unchecked. Uncheck Optional: The record of the game isn't complete unless it counts the yards gained.

In the second half of the section, set the **Attribute Type** to **Integer 32**—an integer in the range of plus-or-minus two billion. When you do that, **Validation** fields appear to receive a **Minimum**, **Maximum**, and **Default** for the attribute. Core Data will refuse to save an object with an attribute out of range; and if you make an attribute mandatory, it's wise to have Core Data initialize it to something legal. Zero is a good choice for a new record. To enable a default (which we want for this project) or a validation (which we don't), check the respective checkboxes.

> **Note**
>
> There is an argument to be made that you shouldn't make an attribute mandatory, or set validation conditions, until late in the development process. Core Data will raise an error if you try to save an object in which a mandatory attribute isn't set or any attribute isn't in range. If your code isn't finished, you might not have gotten around to setting everything.

The third section, **Advanced**, has to do with the system-wide Spotlight search feature. The **Spotlight** box exposes the attribute for indexing. **Store in External Record File** is for Mac applications like Mail, which keeps messages in a Core Data store for its own use, but wants to link those records to files (one per record) that Spotlight can search.

The **User Info** part lets you add any information you like, in key-value form, to the description of this attribute. You won't be introspecting the database's metadata, so you can ignore this section. **Versioning** gives hints to Core Data if you revise the schema for your database—it will migrate your data to the new schema *if it can*. Ignore it.

That's yards taken care of, and six more integer attributes to go. This looks tedious. There's a better way. Click attempts; then hold the Command key down and click completions, interceptions, ourScore, theirScore, and touchdowns. Now all six to-be-integer attributes are selected.

Turn your attention to the Data Model inspector, and change the properties as before: not optional, integer 32, default, and minimum zero. You've just set the properties of all six attributes.

ourTeam and theirTeam should be non-optional strings; check the **Min Length** box and set a minimum-length validation of ten characters or more.

And that sets up the attributes for Game. Do the same for Passer, with three mandatory string attributes, firstName, lastName, and currentTeam. Use your judgment on defaults and validations.

Relationships

The data model so far is not very useful. You can store and enumerate Passers, and you can do the same with Games, but quarterbacks participate in games, and Game is the only thing that holds a quarterback's actual performance. Core Data calls the link between two entities a *relationship*.

9. Make sure the `Passer` entity is selected. A passer may start with no games played but will eventually play in many. Choose **Add Relationship** from the drop-down on the right-hand **+** button; click the **+** button under the Relationships table; or select **Editor** → **Add Relationship**. A new entry appears in the Relationships list.

> **Note**
>
> If you don't see the new relationship, make sure the disclosure triangle next to the "Relationships" label is open.

> **Note**
>
> Whenever you're in doubt about what you can do in an editor, check the **Editor** menu. It shows different commands depending on the type of editor you are using, so it changes a lot. What's available now may be very different from what you saw the last time you opened that menu.

10. Name it **games** (it's a good idea to name a relationship the same as the related entity, plural if the relationship is to be to-many).

11. Select **Game** from the popup in the Destination column of the Relationships table. `Game` doesn't have any relationships yet, so there's nothing to do yet with the Inverse column.

12. Turn to the Data Model inspector, which now shows options for a relationship. The items at the top reflect your choices from the table, so you can leave them alone. **Optional** is checked, which is right, because the passer may not have played at all.

13. For the **Type**, select **To Many**, because a passer may play in more than one game. (Note that Core Data will take care of record IDs and foreign keys silently.)

14. There is an **Ordered** checkbox. Normally, an object's to-many relationship is represented as a *set*, an unordered collection of unique objects. Checking **Ordered** makes the relationship an *ordered set*; like an array, its elements have an inherent order; like a set, no element can appear more than once.
    This example has no inherent or preferred ordering for related objects, and ordered relationships come with a performance penalty, so we won't be using them.

15. Don't bother with setting a minimum or maximum: The relationship is optional, so a minimum is irrelevant, and we're okay with however many `Games` may be linked to this `Passer`.

16. The **Delete Rule** is important. What happens if the `Passer` is removed from the database? You wouldn't want its `Games` to remain; there's no point in having statistics that aren't related to any `Passers`. You have four choices:

    - **No Action** does nothing when the `Passer` is deleted; the `Games` will be orphaned *and* they will have dangling references to the now-deleted `Passer`. You don't want that.

- **Nullify** is scarcely better; the Games remain in the database, but at least their back-references to the Passer are closed off.

- **Deny** goes too far, as it would prevent a Passer from being deleted so long as it had any Games. You'd have to unlink all of them before you could delete.

- What you want is **Cascade**. Deleting a Passer would pursue the relationship and delete all of the objects it reaches: No Passer, no Games.

17. The rest of the inspector covers the global-search, metadata, and versioning attributes I showed you for attributes. Again, you don't care.

At this point, you can ask a Passer for all of its Games, and it can give them to you. But you can't ask a Game for its Passer. You need to establish an *inverse relationship*. Select the Game entity, and create a relationship named passer. The destination is Passer; the inverse is games.

> **Note**
>
> In fact, it's so rare not to want an inverse for a relationship that momc, the compiler that translates .xcdatamodels into .moms, will warn if you don't specify one.

Now that you have both ends of the one-to-many relationship, you can specify an inverse: In the Inverse column, specify games. In the Data Model inspector, the relationship is *not* optional: A Game without a Passer makes no sense, and we'd like Core Data to enforce that. Setting the **Type** to **To One** lets Core Data know to treat passer as a direct link to one Passer, and not to a set of many. And for this relationship, the **Delete Rule** should be **Nullify**—you want the Passer to live, with its relationship to this Game removed.

The data model is complete. Click the Graph (right-hand) side of the **Editor Style** control at the bottom to see all the entities laid out in a diagram (Figure 9.2) that looks a lot like the original design in Figure 8.1. (You'll have to drag the two entity blocks apart if they overlap.)

You can edit—even create—the data model in the Graph view if you wish; it's just a matter of using the **Add** buttons and the Data Model inspector.

> **Note**
>
> This data model would not pass muster as a design for a "real" database. The name Game is a misnomer, as it implies a particular event held at a particular place and time, at which at least two quarterbacks make passes; but you're using Game to refer to one passer's performance at that event. A more sophisticated model would make the Game entity describe the event and use a join to link between Passers and Games and hold one quarterback's performance at that game. Further, a quarterback may play for many teams during his career, and it would be interesting to list all the games a team played; the model should normalize a Team entity out of Passer and Game. Noted. It's just an example.

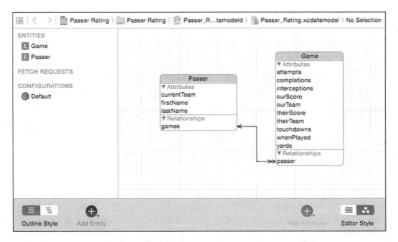

Figure 9.2   The Graph style of the Data Model editor shows all the entities in the model laid out in a block diagram. The one-to-many relationship between `Passer` and `Game` is shown by an arrow with one head at the `Passer` end and many on the `Game` end.

Managed-Object Classes

You could begin using the data model right away. You could ask Core Data to instantiate a `Game` as a generic object of class `NSManagedObject` that can set, store, and return its attributes when you pass it a name: `aGame.setValue(aDate, forKey: "whenPlayed")`. You could instantiate a `Passer` the same way, and it would be an `NSManagedObject` that handled those attributes. It would work. It worked for the dummy `Event` entity when you ran the project template unaltered.

But...

You'll have noticed a lot that isn't in the data model. There is no passer-rating attribute—the point of the whole application—anywhere. `Passer` has no attributes for career attempts, completions, yards.... What are you going to do about that?

What you're going to do is to calculate passer rating and other stats while the application is running, rather than storing them. Those statistics are derived from the numbers you do store. In order to do those calculations, you'll need Swift methods that draw on the attributes of `Passer` and `Game`. And to have those methods, you'll need classes (subclasses of `NSManagedObject`, as it happens) that implement them. You need `.swift` files for each.

> **Note**
>
> For safety's sake, if you're following along, commit your project *now*. Remember the "Your First Commit" section of Chapter 7, "Version Control."

Creating the Classes—the Wrong Way

Here's the way Xcode provides for creating NSManagedObject subclasses, and it is wrong. If you want to follow along anyway, make sure you did that commit I just told you to do, and then start a new branch for just this experiment (**Source Control → Working Copy → New Branch. . .**)—call it `native-mo-classes`. Once we're done with the exercise, you can jump back to the master branch, and carry on from where you left off.

Select **File → File. . .** (⌘N). Navigate the New File assistant to **iOS → Core Data → NSManagedObject subclass**. The description says that this is "An NSManagedObject subclass," but that undersells it. Click **Next**.

> **Note**
>
> You can get to the same place without the template picker by selecting **Editor → Create NSManagedObject Subclass. . .** while the Data Model editor is visible, so long as at least one entity is selected.

The next two pages are unique to creating NSManagedObjects. The first shows you a list of the data models in your project (only one in this case). Check the boxes next to each one from which you want to draw classes. The next page lists all of the entities defined in those models; check those off to select the classes you want to generate. You want to create custom classes for Passer and Game, so check both and Click **Next**.

A get-file sheet appears for you to select a directory to receive the source files. To be tidy, create a directory just for the model objects: With the Passer Rating source directory selected, click **New Folder**, and name it **Model**. Make sure the new directory is selected in the file browser by clicking on it.

In addition to the pickers for the Project-navigator group (put it into the group for the Passer Rating target) and targets (just the app target, not the tests), the get-folder sheet presents a **Language** popup (choose Swift), and a checkbox labeled **Use scalar properties for primitive data types**. NSManagedObject is a container for object values—numbers like completions must be wrapped in NSNumber objects.

This is true to the way Core Data works, so this exercise will leave the box unchecked; but boxing and unboxing the numbers is more work for you. If you check this box, your new subclasses will expose numbers in their native forms, doing the translation for you.

Click **Create**. You'll see two new files in the Project navigator for the Passer and Game code. They should have **A** badges to show they have been added to the local repository, but have not yet been committed. Because you want to keep the Project navigator tidy, select the new files (shift- or command-clicking as necessary) and then **File → New → Group from Selection**. They'll be wrapped in a group named "New Group," which you can rename (for instance, to **Data Model**) by clicking on it and pressing Return.

The project and data-model files pick up **M** badges, to reflect the addition of the files, and the assignment of classes to the Passer and Game entities.

> **Note**
>
> The Project navigator represents groups by yellow folders, and you probably associate folder icons with filesystem directories. That isn't so in this case. At the first approximation, Xcode's yellow group folders are simply a convenient way to organize your files. Files stored in the same directory can be in different groups; moving a file to another group doesn't move it on disk.

You're on a speculative branch for this experiment, and it's time to go back to the master branch. Xcode (and Git) will complain if you do that without committing your changes, so do that, and select **Switch to Branch. . .** from your project's submenu under **Source Control**.

> **Note**
>
> If you didn't create a branch, select **Source Control → Discard All Changes. . .** to wind back to a version created before you generated the class files.

Why Doing It Xcode's Way Is a Mistake

Now, a thought experiment: You created the Passer and Game classes because you want to go beyond the simple accessors Core Data provides you. You'd want to add methods like this:

```
/// Fetch an array of all games played on a certain date.
/// :bug: As implemented, the games must have been played
///       at the same instant.
class func gamesOnDate(date: NSDate,
                       inContext context: NSManagedObjectContext)
                 -> [Event]?
{
    // Ask for all Games...
    let req = NSFetchRequest(entityName: "Game")
    // ... played on a certain date
    req.predicate = NSPredicate(format: "whenPlayed = %@", date)
    // Do the fetch:
    var error: NSError?
    let result: [AnyObject]? = context.executeFetchRequest(req,
                                                error: &error)
    if result == nil {
        // If it were no-matches, result would be [].
        // A nil means there was an error; log it.
        NSLog("gamesOnDate fetch failed; error = %@",
            error!)
    }
    return result as? [Event]
}
```

All is well. Next, add a string property, weather, to the Game entity. And. . . now what?

If you want a reliable way to keep `Game` up with changes in your data model—and some day they will be a lot more complex than this—you'd want to repeat the process of generating it from the data model. When you try this, Xcode will do. . . nothing. The change remains in the data model, but `Game.swift` won't have changed.

> **Note**
>
> If the generated class files were an Objective-C `.h` and `.m` pair, Xcode would warn you that they were to be overwritten. It is likely that by the time this book sees print, the same will happen for Swift class files.

You're in a corner. It's not so hard now—just add another `@NSManaged var` declaration—but as the model becomes more complex, changes like this become error-prone at best.

The Right Way—`mogenerator`

Xcode's treatment of Core Data isn't history's first instance of the problem of enhancing automatically generated code. In object-oriented programming, the solution is almost always to let the generator have sole control over the class it creates, and subclass that for your customizations. Unfortunately, Xcode's managed-object class generator isn't quite flexible enough to do this for you—you're left to cobble the subclasses by hand.

Jon "Wolf" Rentzsch has created `mogenerator`, a command-line tool that does exactly that. Download and install the tool from `http://rentzsch.github.io/mogenerator/`; the installer will put `mogenerator` into `/usr/local/bin`, which makes it available from the command line.

> **Note**
>
> Tools like `mogenerator` have to adapt to developments like Swift, and while they adapt, they can change rapidly. Your best strategy to keep up is to pull in the latest version from GitHib: `https://github.com/rentzsch/mogenerator`.

This time, you will be using the "live" copy of the project, which you've already restored. Xcode's generator fills in the class names itself, but `mogenerator` needs you to set them yourself. Expose the Data Model inspector in the Utility area. Select `Game` and set **Class** to `Game`, and for `Passer`, `Passer`.

`mogenerator` is a command-line tool, with many options. You only need to use a select few with the same parameters every time. This is a job for a shell script you can run from the terminal:

```
#! /bin/bash

echo $(which mogenerator)

# Conjure a name for the generated files
OUT_DIR="`dirname "$1"`/mogenerated"
```

```
mogenerator --model "$1.xcdatamodeld" \
  --swift \
  --output-dir "$OUT_DIR"

ls "$OUT_DIR"
```

> **Note**
>
> The options for generating Swift managed-object classes are concise; Objective-C output requires a little more caretaking. Run `mogenerator --help` to see what's available.

You'll find this script as `run_mogenerator.sh` in the sample code. Copy it into your project directory, or just above, so entering paths won't be so tedious, open the Terminal application, and start it up:

```
$ #    Make the script containing the script current.
$ cd parent-directory
$ #    In this example, this directory contains the project directory
$ ls Passer\ Rating
AppDelegate.swift         Info.plist
Base.lproj                MasterViewController.swift
DetailViewController.swift  Passer_Rating.xcdatamodeld
Images.xcassets
$ #    Make sure the script is executable
$ chmod +x run_mogenerator.sh
$ ./run_mogenerator.sh Passer\ Rating/Passer_Rating
/usr/local/bin/mogenerator
2 machine files and 2 human files generated.
Game.swift  Passer.swift    _Game.swift _Passer.swift
$
```

With this, the project directory contains a new directory named `mogenerated`, containing `.swift` files for the `Game` and `Passer` classes you'll be using, and `_Game.swift` and `_Passer.swift` classes that are directly connected to those entities. When you change your data model, just run `mogenerator` again: It will regenerate the underscore files (which of course you've left untouched) to reflect the changes, while leaving your work undisturbed.

> **Note**
>
> `mogenerator`, Swift, and the Swift interface to Core Data may take some time to settle down. You're not supposed to edit the machine (underscore) files, but from time to time, you may have to fix compiler warnings and even crashes. See Chapter 17, "An iOS Extension," where `mogenerator`'s default code has to be edited to make it usable in libraries.

The new files have to be part of the project before you can use them. One way to do this is to open a Finder window to display their icons, and drag them (one-by-one, or together, or in their enclosing folder) into the Project navigator. Be sure to clear the filters at the bottom of the navigator—it will accept new files only if you can see where in the whole project you are dropping them.

The other way is to select **File → Add Files to "Passer Rating"...** (⌥⌘A). A get-file sheet descends for you to choose the files (if they're in the same directory, command-clicking will add to the selection) or their enclosing directory.

Identifying the files is not enough. Xcode needs some more information, which it collects in a drop-down sheet in the case of a drag, or in an extension to the get-file sheet. The options are:

- **Destination: Copy items if needed**—In this case, the new files are in the directory tree rooted at the project file. That's not always the case; you may be importing source or resources from another project. You might want Passer Rating simply to refer to shared files, but more often you want your project directory to be a self-contained package of everything the project needs. In that case, check this box; Xcode will copy the added files to your project directory.

- **Added folders:**—If you add a directory to your project, you could mean one of two things: In this case, adding the `mogenerated` directory is simply a convenient way to add each of the files it contains. Selecting **Create groups** creates a yellow group folder in the Project navigator that contains the files in the directory. But imagine an app that contains portraits of presidents of the United States, and you want to be free to change or add portraits in the years to come. The directory itself is a resource to be copied into the finished app, with everything it contains. If that's your plan, select **Create folder references**. The folder reference will be shown in the Project navigator with a blue icon.

- **Add to targets:**—This is a table showing every target in the project; in this case, just Passer Rating and Passer RatingTests. You're familiar with targets and memberships from Chapter 6, "Adding a Library Target." This table is a convenient way to take care of all the new files at once. If C-family source is among them, don't worry about the header files; Xcode is smart enough to keep them out of targets. (Adding an `.h` file to a target makes it a resource to be copied into the app product, which you'd rarely want to do.)

In this case, be sure **Added folders:** is set to **Create groups for any added folders**; and select Passer Rating as the sole target. The files are in the project directory tree already, so there's no need to copy them.

Click **Finish** if you've dragged the files, or **Add** if you're using the add-files sheet.

Preparation

Previous versions of this book stuck closely to the code Xcode generated from the project template. My idea was that you should see only what was crucial to the workflow. This time it's different.

Passer Rating has requirements all its own—every application does. The template code does too little, and too much, because it is built to provide as much guidance as possible on how to proceed. In some cases, what it does to produce a generic app structure is too clever to make a good example.

This time, I'll be aggressive about revising the template code to make the process clearer. The first targets will be infrastructure in the form of utilities and extensions. I'll build these up as the need occurs, but here is where we start. I'm keeping it short here, but you can learn more from the comments in the sample code.

Utilities

`Utilities.swift` will build up conversions and common facilities like string formatting, file handling, and—for this chapter—the same pinning function we saw in Chapter 5, "Compilation."

```
/************* Pinning functions ***************/
/// Pin a `Comparable` between two limit `Comparable`s of the
/// same type.

func pinComparables<T:Comparable> (
    value: T, lower: T, upper: T) -> T
{
    if value < lower { return lower }
    else if value > upper { return upper }
    else { return value }
}

/// Given a lower and upper bounds, return a function that
/// will pin a `Comparable` between them.

func limitPinner<T: Comparable>
     (lower: T, upper: T) -> (T -> T)
{ return { value in pinComparables(value, lower, upper) } }
```

Extensions

`Extensions.swift` will add functions and properties to existing classes.

The first is for `NSFetchedResultsController`, which apps use to manage the retrieval of Core Data objects. Given an entity, selection criteria, a sort order, and a way to group the data, `NSFetchedResultsController` handles the details of loading the data, and presents it to the app neatly packaged up as sections and rows.

iOS applications typically use fetched-results controllers to fill the sections and rows of `UITableViews`: You select the object by converting the section and row into a two-level index path and passing it to the results controller through `objectAtIndexPath`.

This sounds like a subscript: You shouldn't have to do the paperwork to convert two numbers into a path and put it into a long-winded function call. Fortunately, Swift lets you define subscripts:

```
/****************** NSFetchedResultsController ******************/

/** Add subscripts to NSFetchedResultsController. */
extension NSFetchedResultsController {

    /** Return a managed object given an index path. */
    subscript (indexPath: NSIndexPath) -> NSManagedObject {
        return self.objectAtIndexPath(indexPath) as! NSManagedObject
    }

    /** Return a managed object given section and row numbers. */
    subscript (section: Int, row: Int) -> NSManagedObject {
        let indexPath = NSIndexPath(forRow: row, inSection: section)
        return self[indexPath]
    }
}
```

UITableView also retrieves objects—cells—by path or section-and-row, via the
cellForRowAtIndexPath function. Turn it into an instance function of the table view:

```
/****************** UITableView ******************/

/** Add subscripts to retrieve a table-view cell by path or section+row.
*/
extension UITableView {

    /** Return a table-view cell given an index path.

        :bug: Should check the arity (2) of the path.
        :bug: Does not handle the exception raised for indices
            out of range.
    */
    subscript (indexPath: NSIndexPath) -> UITableViewCell {
        return self.cellForRowAtIndexPath(indexPath)
    }

    /** Return a table-view cell given section and row.
        Implemented through self.cellForRowAtIndexPath.

        :bug: Could bounds-check the section and row, but does
            not.
    */
    subscript (section: Int, row: Int) -> UITableViewCell {
        let indexPath = NSIndexPath(forRow: row, inSection: section)
        return self.cellForRowAtIndexPath(indexPath)
    }
}
```

passer_rating

We wrote a C function for calculating passer ratings in Chapter 3, "Simple Workflow and Passive Debugging." This time we do it in Swift, taking advantage of the generic pinner functions in Utilities.swift:

```
/// Define a function that pins a Double to the range for
/// a component of an NFL/CFL passer rating.
let ratingPinner = limitPinner(0.0, 2.375)


/// Calculate the NFL/CFL passer rating, given performance
/// statistics for a game (or any other time period).
func passer_rating(#completions: Int, #attempts: Int,
                   #yards: Int, #touchdowns: Int,
                   #interceptions: Int)
                   -> Double
{
    //  See http://en.wikipedia.org/wiki/Quarterback_Rating

    if (attempts <= 0) { return 0.0 }

    //  Statistic-per-attempt, with both converted to Double,
    //  recurs in all four components. Make the definitions
    //  easier to read and understand by encapsulating it.
    func perAttempt(stat:Int) -> Double {
        return Double(stat) / Double(attempts)
    }

    //  Compute the components to sum into the rating
    let components = [
        (100.0 * perAttempt(       completions) - 30.0) / 20.0,
        (perAttempt(               yards) - 3.0) / 4.0,
        20.0 * perAttempt(         touchdowns),
        2.375 - (25.0 * perAttempt( interceptions))
    ]

    //  Pin the components and add them up
    let retval = components.map(ratingPinner).reduce(0.0, +)
    return 100.0 * retval / 6.0
}
```

The Swift way to write this function is very different from the C:

- It creates the pinning function (ratingPinner) by specializing the generic pinner.
- passer_rating defines an *internal function* (perAttempt) to simplify code that had cluttered and obscured the C version.
- Instead of each value being tucked into its own local variable, the components are treated as items in an array. The variables were necessary only because there was no

better way to keep the values around for further processing, not because we needed
to identify them anymore.

- The pinner applies to all the component values; you can *map* a function over an
  array with the `components.map(ratingPinner)`, which applies
  `ratingPinner` to each item and returns an array with each result.

- We then want the sum of the pinned components. They're all going into the same
  number, and we don't have to identify each of them—which C forced us to do. The
  `Array` method `reduce` takes a starting point, and applies a function of your
  choosing to accumulate a result. "Plus" is a function, and if you're calculating a
  grand total, you'd start from zero. `anArray.reduce(0.0, +)` yields a `Double`
  with the total.

Using concepts like dynamically defined functions and array processing lets us express
the top-level meaning of `passer_rating` without burying it in the bottom-level
management of the lifetime of a numeric value. It is also about three-fourths the line
count of the C version, despite being more generously commented.

Specializing the Core Data Classes

We've made a start on the plumbing, and now we can start on using the `Game` and
`Passer` classes to make sense of what's in the database. `mogenerator` gave us
underscore-named classes to take care of the "dumb" end of managing games and passers
as database records; the plain classes will put them to work in Passer Rating.

Putting `Game` to Work

`mogenerator` put a number of convenience properties and methods into the
machine-owned classes. In `_Game`, for instance, you find this:

```
@NSManaged var attempts: Int32
@NSManaged var ourTeam: String
```

`@NSManaged` instructs Swift to treat these properties not as code or fronts for in-memory
data, but as portals to the Core Data storage for the values.

We have `Game.swift` all to ourselves. Let's add our first extension to the stored
data—what the app is supposed to be all about:

```
@objc(Game)
class Game: _Game {
    var passerRating: Double {
    return passer_rating(
        completions:    Int(self.completions),
        attempts:       Int(self.attempts),
        yards:          Int(self.yards),
```

```
        touchdowns:      Int(self.touchdowns),
        interceptions:   Int(self.interceptions)
        )
    }
}
```

We put # marks on the arguments for passer_rating, so we have to include the
argument labels in the call; not a bad thing, because there's no inherent reason the
parameters should be in the order they are, and the labels protect against putting values in
the wrong places.

passerRating is a Double-valued property of Game. It's computed (not stored), and
because there's only one body of code associated with it, it can only be read, not set.

Putting Passer to Work

Passers should have passer ratings, too, but Passer doesn't include the underlying totals to
compute them; those all come through the games at the other end of the to-many games
relationship. So we must add code that exposes the totals as computed properties, and
derive the career rating from that:

```
/// The passer's career passer rating
var passerRating: Double {
return passer_rating(
    completions:     self.completions,
    attempts:        self.attempts,
    yards:           self.yards,
    touchdowns:      self.touchdowns,
    interceptions:   self.interceptions)
}

/** Helper function to get the sum of a career statistic
    @param attribute the name of a key for an integer attribute of Game
*/
func sumOfGameAttribute(attribute: String) -> Int
{
    let keyPath = "@sum.\(attribute)"
    return self.games.valueForKeyPath(keyPath) as Int!
}

var attempts:Int { return sumOfGameAttribute("attempts") }

var completions:Int { return sumOfGameAttribute("completions") }

var yards:Int { return sumOfGameAttribute("yards") }

var touchdowns:Int { return sumOfGameAttribute("touchdowns") }

var interceptions:Int { return sumOfGameAttribute("interceptions") }
```

We've taken advantage of the key-value coding method `valueForKeyPath:` to pull (for instance) the `attempts` of each game from the `games` set, and then to sum (`@sum`) the results.

You can use aggregate keypaths to derive some other interesting facts about a passer—for instance:

```
var firstPlayed: NSDate {
    return self.games.valueForKeyPath("@min.whenPlayed") as! NSDate
}

var lastPlayed: NSDate {
    return self.games.valueForKeyPath("@max.whenPlayed") as! NSDate
}

var teams: [ String ]
{
let theGames: AnyObject =
    self.games.valueForKeyPath(
        "@distinctUnionOfObjects.ourTeam")
    return theGames.allObjects as [ String ]
}
```

Some Test Data

Passer Rating won't work without data. In a finished product, that would be easy: The user provides his own data. But we can't wait for a full suite of editors in the app to see how it works. You need some test data to preload into the app.

This can take the form of a CSV file. I have a script, `generate-games.rb`, that will produce a good-enough data set:

```
firstName,lastName,attempts,completions,interceptions, ...
Jimmy,Carter,37,11,1,0,56,2010-03-24,Boise Bearcats,2, ...
Andy,Jackson,33,8,1,1,30,2010-03-24,Modesto Misanthropes,9, ...
James,Madison,20,15,0,4,241,2010-04-14,San Bernardino Stalkers,47, ...
Quinn,Adams,9,3,1,1,17,2010-04-14,San Bernardino Stalkers,47, ...
...
```

> **Note**
>
> The script runs to nearly 300 lines, so look for it in the sample code. The output is flawed—team A is recorded as playing at team B on the same day that team B is at team C, and Big Bill Taft turns out to be a much better quarterback than you'd expect. Those aren't relevant to exercising what the app does; for further information, check the Wikipedia entry for "YAGNI."

If the sample data doesn't exist, or doesn't reflect the latest version of `generate-games.rb`, it should be (re)built. Can Xcode take care of this?

Yes. First, add `generate-games.rb` to the project by the add–files command you saw before, or simply by dragging it in from the Finder. Don't include it in any target; it's just a tool, not in itself a component in the built application.

Now open the Project editor (click the top row of the Project navigator), and select the Passer Rating target. Click the **Build Phases** tab to reveal the agenda for building it. We want that agenda to include running `generate-games.rb`. Do this by selecting **Editor →Add Build Phase →Add Run Script Build Phase**. A new phase, labeled "Run Script," appears at the bottom. It's no good running `generate-games.rb` *after* the "Copy Bundle Resources" phase moves the sample data into the application, so drag the new phase up so it comes before. Double-click on the phase's title and change it to **Generate Test Data**.

The Run Script editor (click the disclosure triangle if it isn't visible) comes in three parts:

- At top, you provide the script to be run. This won't be `generate-games.rb`: The script works by writing to standard output, which you'll have to redirect to a file. So for the **Shell**, specify the vanilla **/bin/sh**, and for the script, the one–liner

```
/usr/bin/ruby "${SRCROOT}/Passer Rating"/generate-games.rb \
            > "${SRCROOT}/Passer Rating"/sample-data.csv
```

(I've broken the line with a \ for readability, but you should put it all on one line.) The quotes are necessary. The SRCROOT shell variable will expand to a path to your Passer Rating directory, and the space there and in the rest of the path will confuse the sh interpreter.
Be very careful: It's not always clear when a build variable or path will pass through a shell; assume you don't have to escape unless the context makes it obvious that you will.

I arrived at the quoting you see here by trial and error. The Generate Test Data phase failed because the interpreter couldn't find paths cut off at spaces. I tinkered with placement until the errors stopped.

- Next comes a table of input files. If Xcode knows what files go into and out of a phase, its build system can skip the phase if the inputs haven't changed since the last run. Click the **+** button below the **Input Files** table and enter `"$(SRCROOT)/Passer Rating"/generate-games.rb`.

- For an output file, enter `"$(SRCROOT)/Passer Rating"/sample-data.csv`. In both cases, include the quotes.

Note

Experienced UNIX shell programmers will be disturbed to see variable references of the form `$(VAR)`, using parentheses instead of braces. In a shell script, this would evaluate the variable and then attempt to execute it. The Xcode build system is different: It treats parenthesized variable references the same as braced, and always requires that you delimit the variable names one way or another. **But:** your code for other interpreters, such as the body of this script phase, has to conform to the practice for those interpreters.

This run-script phase says, "Run the Ruby script `generate-games.rb`, sending the output to `sample-data.csv` in the project root directory. If the output file is already there and is newer than the script, don't bother."

> **Note**
>
> At least that's how it's supposed to be. For this purpose at least, every Xcode in the last ten years has run the script regardless.

Now all you have to do is make sure `sample-data.csv` is part of the Copy Bundle Resources build phase, so it will make its way inside the Passer Rating app. Click the disclosure triangle to expose the table of files to be included, click the **+** button to add the CSV file and...

There are a couple of problems. The first is that, not knowing what to do with an `.rb` file when you added it to the project, Xcode dumped it into the copy-resources phase. You don't want `generate-games.rb` to be in the product. Easy enough: Select its entry in the table and click **−**.

The bigger problem is a chicken-and-egg thing: `sample-data.csv` doesn't exist, so there's no way to put it into the table. The solution is to do a build (**Product → Build**, ⌘ **B**). That runs `generate-games.rb` and puts `sample-data.csv` in the project directory. Now you can click the **+** button, then the **Add Other...** button to find the CSV file. Xcode offers to add the file to the project, which is just what you want.

When they're all set up, the script and resources build phases should look like Figure 9.3.

Xcode marks both the Ruby and the CSV file for inclusion in the source-control repository, as evidenced by the **A** badges next to their names in the Project navigator.

Source Control and Product Files

Strictly speaking, `sample-data.csv` is a product file, completely reproducible from `generate-games.rb`, and there should be no point in treating every hit on the script as a significant source-control event. It shouldn't go into a repository...

...but we're going to include it anyway to demonstrate integration builds in Chapter 15, "Unit Testing."

If you were to do it the right way, you'd look around in the Xcode menu commands, and the File inspector, and the Commit editor... and find there is no way to do that from within Xcode. You'd have to break out the Terminal.

The first thing to do is to prevent Xcode from including `sample-data.csv` in the next commit. Tell Git to remove the file from the staging area:

```
$ git status
# On branch master
# Changes to be committed:
#    (use "git rm --cached <file>..." to unstage)
...
#  new file:    sample-data.csv
...
```

Figure 9.3   The Generate Test Data and Copy Bundle Resources build phases, set up to run the `generate-games.rb` script and produce `sample-data.csv`, which is then copied into the Passer Rating product. `Main.storyboard` is shown in red because Xcode has never been able to keep track of storyboard files. It's harmless.

```
$#    The offending file is there
$#    and Git gives a hint on how to remove it:

$ git rm --cached sample-data.csv

$#    That took care of it for now:
# On branch VersionControl
# Changes to be committed:
#    (use "git rm <file>..." to unstage)
...
... sample-data.csv isn't there ...
... but it is here: ...

# Untracked files:
#    (use "git add <file>..." to include in what will be committed)
#        sample-data.csv
#        ../Passer Rating.xcodeproj/project.xcworkspace/xcuserdata/
...
```

Git may be subtle, but it is not malicious. When you ask for the status of your working directory, it shows you what files will be in the next commit, but it also tells you how to withdraw a file. Once you do, Xcode badges `sample-data.csv` with a **?**, which at least means it won't commit it, and Git calls it "untracked."

That's all you really need, but such files accumulate in the sidebar in the Commit editor, as though Xcode hoped you might relent. Clutter hides significant information, so you'd prefer never to see that file, or any `.csv` file, in source-control listings again. You saw the `.gitignore` file in Chapter 7, "Version Control," and here it is one more time:

```
$ #   Make sure you're in the same directory as
$ #   the .git local-repository directory
$ ls -a
.                       Passer Rating
..                      Passer Rating.xcodeproj
.DS_Store               Passer RatingTests
.git                    run_mogenerator.sh
.gitignore
$ #   append something to the .gitignore file
$ #   (which will be created if it isn't there)
$ cat >> .gitignore *.csv xcuserdata/ <^D>
```

What this does is tell Git (and Xcode) not to mention any `.csv` files when they report on the state of source control. I added the `xcuserdata/` directory as well. It preserves information particular to your use of the project, from schemes and breakpoint lists to the file you last selected in the Project navigator. You can mark the important things as "shared" if you need them to be visible to all users; and Xcode won't treat every tab selection as a significant source-control event.

Did it work?

```
$ git status
# On branch master
# Changes to be committed:
... still no sample-data.csv ...
# Untracked files:
#   (use "git add <file>..." to include in what will be committed)
#
#   .gitignore
... none here, either ...
$#   (Let's make sure the .gitignore file sticks around:)
$ git add .gitignore
```

I won't go into the details of the simple CSV parser (`SimpleCSVFile`) I built, and the code I added to `Passer` and `Game` to make them clients of the parser. If you need the details, they're in the sample code. The application delegate is set up so that when the app starts up, it loads its Core Data store from the CSV.

Making the Model Easier to Debug

You've already run Passer Rating with the dummy data model from the template. This has stored a `Passer_Rating.sqlite` file in the app's documents directory. If the contents of that file don't match up with the current managed-object model (`.mom`), Core Data will report an error and your application will be crippled. (The code that comes with the template actually crashes the app.)

But you've changed the model to add `Passer` and `Game`. You'll probably change it again.

What I do in the early stages of development is to delete the `.sqlite` data file at the start of every run. Eventually, of course, you'll want your persistent data to persist, but this is a quick, easy way to save yourself some headaches.

Find `var persistentStoreCoordinator` in `AppDelegate.swift`. Add some code after the declaration of `storeURL`:

```
if _persistentStoreCoordinator == nil {
    let storeURL = self.applicationDocumentsDirectory
        .URLByAppendingPathComponent("Passer_Rating.sqlite")
#if ALWAYS_DELETE_STORE
    //  For ease in debugging, always start with a fresh data store.
    NSFileManager.defaultManager().removeItemAtURL(storeURL, error: nil)
#endif
```

Swift does not have a preprocessor such as you might be used to from C-family languages. There are no macros, and what had been `#defined` symbols in the Objective-C API are converted to names for Swift constants. There is one exception: You can guard blocks of code with `#if ... #end` directives.

But you can't do it as casually as you can in C: No `#if 0` blocks to temporarily (worse, permanently) disable code while still keeping it in the source file. The `#if`'s argument has no value; there are no comparisons or arithmetic; the argument is either defined (exposing the contents of the `#if` block) or not (hiding them from the compiler). And, the only way you can define it is as a build setting (or a command-line argument to the `swiftc` tool).

Open the **Build Phases** tab of the Target editor, and search for **Other Swift Flags**. Usually, this will be empty. Double-click the field for the setting in the Passer Rating target, and enter **-D ALWAYS_DELETE_STORE**. That will admit the `removeItemAtURL` statement to the program code.

Summary

You've started building an iOS application in earnest. You learned how to use the Data Model editor to construct a Core Data managed-object model that embodies your design, making entities that describe the data types, and endowing them with attributes that have suitable types and constraints. You also traced relationships among the entities to express the fact that `Passer`s play `Game`s.

You went one step further into the model by writing its first actual code. You had Xcode build `NSManagedObject` subclasses from the entities, and made first-class objects out of the database records.

Finally, the need for test data drove you to your first encounter with the **Build Phases** tab in the Target editor. You added a script phase that generates test data, and set the phase up so that it produces it on demand.

## 10

An iOS Application: Controller

If I were smart, I'd start unit-testing the model as soon as the first draft was done, before adding the complexity of a human-interface layer. But I'm not smart; I'm going to put testing off until Chapter 15, "Unit Testing."

Instead, let's go ahead with the first cut at a real app. Xcode's Master-Detail Application template provides a working version of the first table. Let's convert that into a table of quarterbacks and their ratings.

You remember from the "The Controllers" section of Chapter 8, "Starting an iOS Application," that the view comprising a full-screen stage in an iOS application is managed by a *view controller*, a subclass of `UIViewController`. iOS services view controllers with a defined repertoire of method calls throughout the life cycle of the view: loading, response to events, and teardown. It is your responsibility to provide a `UIViewController` that supplies these methods. In this chapter, I'll fill out the initial controller, `MasterViewController`.

> **Note**
>
> Again, I can't supply complete listings for the files you'll be working on. The project template will provide much of what I don't show, so you'll have that in front of you already. For the rest, see the sample code you can get by following the instructions in the Introduction. Note that the sample code folders *do not* include Git repositories; use them for reference only. Switching from your own version-controlled directory to a sample will lose your repo.

Renaming Symbols in Objective-C

Just for this section, I'm going to back off to the Objective-C version of Passer Rating I showed in *Xcode 5 Start to Finish*. The reason is that Xcode provides powerful tools for *refactoring*, using Xcode's insight into your code to make intelligent edits to your source. The problem is that for now, the tools are ObjC *only*. In time they will surely support Swift, but not yet. Let's pretend we're working with `Passer.h`, `Passer.m`, and the Objective-C classes that use them.

In the first version of the `Passer` class, I have a convenience constructor, a class method named `quarterbackWithFirstName:last:inContext:`. This is wrong. By Cocoa conventions, a convenience constructor should begin with the name of the class, and I think it's bad style to say `last:` when the argument sets a property named `lastName:` it should be `passerWithFirstName:lastName:inContext:`.

Refactoring the Name of an Objective-C Method

You've done a global search-and-replace before, in Chapter 7, "Version Control;" this is just a matter of finding every instance of `quarterbackWithFirstName:last:in-Context:` and substituting `passerWithFirstName:lastName:inContext:`, right?

Not so fast. You'll have to take care of the second part of the selector, and that means examining every instance of `last:` to make sure it's part of the `quarterbackWith-FirstName:last:inContext:` selector. To be correct, a search would have to involve a regular expression that captures all, and only, the uses of those strings that are the selector for that method. That means accounting for the arguments that come between the parts; the possibility that a call might be spread across more than one line; interpolation of line and delimited comments; uses of the bare selector in `@selector` expressions; and preventing changes to a possible method named `quarterbackWithFirstName:last:-team:inContext:`.

If you're a regular-expression hobbyist, you might be able to come up with search-and-replace expressions that work. But they would take more time to formulate and verify than it would to do all the changes by hand. Refactoring does it right the first time.

`quarterbackWithFirstName:last:inContext:` was declared in `PRPasser.h` and defined in `PRPasser.m`. Open either file, and click anywhere in the name of the method. Select **Edit → Refactor → Rename. . . .**

A sheet appears, with just the original selector shown. As you edit the selector, you'll find that Xcode will not accept a new name—it will display an error message—unless it has the same number of colons as in the original selector. That makes sense; if the number of arguments differs, there's no way to redistribute them.

Click **Preview**, and examine the changes in the comparison sheet. (Xcode will probably offer to make a snapshot of your project, as it did in Chapter 7, "Version Control.") Every use of the symbol—the declaration, the definition, and calls, whether on one line or three—are changed. Xcode can do this because refactoring doesn't rely on searching at all: It has an index of all uses of the symbol, so it can differentiate it from near-misses and ignore issues of spacing and parameters.

Click **Save**, and commit the change to version control. (Yes, really. You should commit every time you have a group of modified files that represent a single, logical change to your project. If you commit frequently, your commit log will reflect your intentions, and not be just a list of mini-backups.)

Refactoring a Class Name

There was another naming problem, this time with the `MasterViewController` class. The name, provided by the project template, is descriptive in its way, but it described the class's *role*, but not what it *did*. It's a list of passers, and the name ought to reflect it: `PasserListController`. This is another case for the name-refactoring tool.

Surely this *can* be done with a search-and-replace? That doesn't quite work. For one thing, though it isn't the case here, `MasterViewController` might appear as a substring of some other symbol.

For another, the name of `MasterViewController` isn't just in text files. iOS apps are laid out in `.nib` and `.storyboardc` files—object archives—which refer to classes by name. `.xib` files, from which Xcode compiles NIBs, and `.storyboard` files, from which `.storyboardc`s are derived, are ultimately XML, but the XML is emphatically not human-editable. You'd have to go into a special editor, Interface Builder, and ferret out all the references.

You'd find the class name `MasterViewController` in either the `.m` or `.h` file, and click on it. Then select **Edit →Refactor →Rename. . .**, as before. Enter `Passer-ListController`, and make sure you check the **Rename related files** box. Click **Preview**, and have a look at the changes:

- Wherever `MasterViewController` had appeared in the source files, Xcode substituted `PasserListController`. You've seen this already.

- The files whose base names had been `MasterViewController` now have the base name `PasserListController`.

- In the `.m` files for `PasserListController` and `AppDelegate`,

  `#import "MasterViewController.h"`

  has been changed to

  `#import "PasserListController.h"`

  so the renaming of the files carried over into the `#import` directives.

- `Main.storyboard` is included in the list of changed files. Look at the comparisons: You'll see some complex XML, and the class-name references are changed. You'd also see that this wasn't a simple search-and-replace in the XML source; the refactoring made structural edits to the files that would not have been safe for you to do by hand.

- The names of the files in the header comments wouldn't change. Refactoring renames only the symbols, not the contents of comments or strings. Xcode can't be sure which occurrences of a string in human-readable content are literal and not symbolic.

Save and commit the changes. The Commit editor flagged the `Passer-ListController` files as **A+**, to indicate that they've been "added" under their new names. Behind the scenes, Git will record a deletion of the files with the old names, and the addition of them under the new names; and it will bridge the old histories into the new entries. Xcode spares you the messy details.

That's what Xcode can do for you in Objective-C. Now back to Swift. . .

Renaming a Class in Swift

Xcode's master-detail application template seeded your project with two view controller classes, `MasterViewController` and `DetailViewController`. These are okay for placeholders, but they don't tell you what the classes are for.

We know what they are for: One lists passers, and the other lists games. They should be `PasserListController` and `GameListController`.

Fortunately, though we don't have the refactoring tools, Swift is a simpler language, and Xcode's Find navigator is now powerful enough for this job. So long as you are careful, all you need is a global find-and-replace, and a change in the name of one file.

You saw the Find navigator at work in Chapter 7, "Version Control," so this shouldn't be hard for you: Click the third tab in the Navigator area, and use the chain of popup menus to select **Replace** → **Text** → **Matching**. The string to search for is **MasterViewController**, and the replacement is **PasserListController**. Press Return in the find field to fill the navigator's list with all occurrences of the class name—you'll see that it even catches the name of the master-controller scene in `Main.storyboard`. Perfect. Click **Replace All**, and you're done.

Repeat the process to change `DetailViewController` to `GameListController`.

Now rename the files: Click the file's name in the Project navigator (first tab), and move the mouse pointer a little bit; or simply press Return with the file selected. Either way, the file's name is selected for editing. Enter the base names **PasserListController** and **GameListController**. The project file acquires an **M** version-control badge to show its file roster has changed, and the renamed files are marked with **A+**. Now would be an excellent time to commit the changes.

Editing the View Controller

The new `PasserListController` method is still set up to display the placeholder `Event` entity from the template. That's long gone, and you'll have to substitute your own code to show `Passers`. The template code is set up to use `NSFetchedResults-Controller`, an auxiliary class that provides many services for listing, grouping, sorting, and editing a list of Core Data objects.

`NSFetchedResultsController` is a very powerful facility, but it's daunting unless you are comfortable with the underlying Core Data technology. Cocoa books rightly treat Core Data as an advanced topic, and the fetched-results controller is one step above that.

However, we can clean up the worst of it. The template Xcode gave us for the master (now passer-list) controller is too simple (the `Event` entity has just one attribute) and too clever (it employs a number of tricks to make itself generic) at the same time. We can cut it down.

We took the first step in Chapter 9, "An iOS Application: Model," by adding subscripts to `NSFetchedResultsController`: The template contains a number of calls to `objectAtIndexPath()`, which is verbose and requires a cast of the result:

```
let object = fetchedResultsController.objectAtIndexPath(indexPath)
                    as! NSManagedObject
```

Swift needs to qualify property names with `self` only in the presence of a function argument in the same name, and the `subscript` definition is not only more terse, it takes care of casting the result to `NSManagedObject`:

```
let object = fetchedResultsController[indexPath]
```

The template pulls the Core Data managed object context through the initialized `fetchedResultsController`, even though `PasserListController` has a `managedObjectContext` property of its own. Here is how that property is defined:

```
var managedObjectContext: NSManagedObjectContext?
```

... which is to say, the variable is an optional `NSManagedObjectContext`, because it must start out as nil and wait for the `AppController` to initialize it. Later references to the property will have to be unwrapped with the `!` operator: `managedObjectContext!`.

That's not necessary, because we can see (or are at least willing to bet) that the property will always be initialized before it is used. Change the declaration to

```
var managedObjectContext: NSManagedObjectContext!
```

and you never have to remember to unwrap it yourself. Code with unnecessary optional-value handling is much harder to read. This allows you to turn

```
let context = fetchedResultsController.managedObjectContext
```

into

```
let context = managedObjectContext
```

and eliminate even that, because there's no need to use a `context` variable to "simplify" the long retrieval of the value from the fetched-results controller.

The Table View

`PasserListController` is a subclass of `UITableViewController`, itself a subclass of `UIViewController` that takes care of some of the details of screens that consist solely of tables. Table views fill themselves in through the *Delegate* design pattern: The table provides almost all of the user-side behavior, and calls back to the controller (or other object)—the delegate—to provide the details that make a particular use of the table special. A `UITableView` doesn't keep any data itself; it pulls it from the data-source delegate.

> **Note**
>
> In fact `UITableView`s have two delegates: One named `dataSource` to supply the content, and another, `delegate`, to handle table-wide operations like inserting and deleting cells.

Data sources serve up the *cells* that make up the rows of the table; they create `UITableViewCell`s and fill them in with data. Typically, this is done only when the table asks for a row (in the method `tableView(_, cellForRowAtIndexPath:)`). The controller you get from the template factors the task of populating the cell into the custom `configureCell(cell:,atIndexPath:)` method. Find that method, and substitute this:

```
func configureCell(cell: UITableViewCell,
    atIndexPath indexPath: NSIndexPath) {
    let passer = fetchedResultsController[indexPath] as! Passer
    cell.textLabel.text = "\(passer.firstName) " +
                          "\(passer.lastName) " +
                          "\(passer.passerRating))"
}
```

The `indexPath` carries the section (always zero for this simple list) and row for the cell; the `NSFetchedResultsController` subscript method we created makes it simple to pull out the matching `Passer`. The method sets the text content of the cell with the passer's name and rating.

Setting Up the Passer List

The `fetchedResultsController` method sets up a fetch request (think of it as a SELECT, if you're SQL-minded) that describes and sorts the objects for presentation to the view controller. The template gives you code that is "clever," to make it as generic as possible; knowing what we know about Passer, and using the shortcuts we created, we can cut it down:

```
var fetchedResultsController: NSFetchedResultsController {
    //  Already there? Return it.
    if let existing = _fetchedResultsController { return existing }

    //  Set up the fetch request (think SELECT in SQL) for
    //  the contents of the table.
    let fetchRequest = NSFetchRequest(entityName: "Passer")
    fetchRequest.fetchBatchSize = 20

    //  Order by last name, then first.
    fetchRequest.sortDescriptors = [
        NSSortDescriptor(key: "lastName", ascending: true),
        NSSortDescriptor(key: "firstName", ascending: true)
    ]

    //  Create the fetched-results controller.
    _fetchedResultsController = NSFetchedResultsController(
            //  Passer, ordered last name, first
            fetchRequest: fetchRequest,
            //  In my context
            managedObjectContext: managedObjectContext,
```

```
            //  No sections
            sectionNameKeyPath: nil,
            //  Generic name for the cache
            cacheName: "Master")
    _fetchedResultsController!.delegate = self

    //  The fetch doesn't work? Bail. Don't try this at home.
    var error: NSError? = nil
    if !_fetchedResultsController!.performFetch(&error) {
        abort()
    }

    return _fetchedResultsController!
}
var _fetchedResultsController: NSFetchedResultsController? = nil
```

Creating a New Passer

The insertNewObject method gets called when the user taps the **+** button in the navigation bar; the link is made in viewDidLoad. The code in the middle inserts an Event in the database and sets its timeStamp. As supplied in the template, insert-NewObject pulls the entity (table) type from the fetchedResultsController, and instantiates the new object from that.

That's clever, but you already have a generator for Passer instances that avoids all the filibuster. Replace the body of the method with:

```
func insertNewObject(sender: AnyObject) {
    //  Create using mogenerator's convenience initializer
    let newPasser = Passer(
        moc: managedObjectContext)

    //  We added a default-value dictionary and
    //  a way to initialize a Passer from it:
    newPasser.setValuesForKeysWithDictionary(
                        newPasser.defaultDictionary)

    // Save the context.
    var error: NSError? = nil
    if !managedObjectContext.save(&error) {
        abort()
    }
}
```

Giving every new Passer the same name and team isn't ideal, but it lets us move on and get back to it later.

Live Issues and Fix-it

I've made some substantial changes, and I'd like to see whether the compiler will accept them. In a traditional workflow—and if you followed my advice in the "Quieting Xcode Down" section of Chapter 2, "Kicking the Tires," you're in a traditional workflow—you'd run the file through a check compilation.

Xcode 6 has a command to do just that: **Product →Perform Action →Compile** will compile just the file in the current editor, without rebuilding the whole project. The command is buried two layers deep, but you could always use the **Key Bindings** panel of the Preferences window to assign a convenient key equivalent.

If you select the command, and you and I are in sync (go to the sample code if we aren't), there won't be any errors, but there will be an error flag in `insertNew-Object`—"Incorrect argument label in call (have 'moc:', expected 'managedObjectContext:')." Easy enough; replace `moc` with `managedObjectContext`, just like it says.

There's another way to do this, which most people prefer; it's a matter of taste. Back in Chapter 2, I had you go into the Preferences window, **General** panel, and uncheck **Show live issues**. Go back and check it.

What happens now? With no errors, nothing much. Try undoing that change from `moc` to `managedObjectContext`. The error flag returns instantly—you no longer have to ask Xcode to recompile. Now you notice something: The red badge in the margin for errors usually contains a "!". This badge has a white dot.

Click the badge. A *Fix-it* popover appears, offering a change in your source that would clear the error (or at least put it off till later in your code). See Figure 10.1. In this case it contains only one option, but it's the right one: Change `moc` to `managedObject-Context`. If there were more than one possibility, you'd be offered them. Highlighting

```
49    func insertNewObject(sender: AnyObject) {
50        // Create using mogenerator's convenience initailizer
51        let newPasser = Passer(    ⊙ Incorrect argument label in call (have 'moc:', ex...
52            moc: managedObjectContext)
53
54        // We added a default-value dictionary and
55        // a way to initialize a Passer from it:
56        newPasser.dictionaryRepresentation =
```

```
49    func insertNewObject(sender: AnyObject) {
50        // Create using mogenerator's convenience initailizer
51        let newPasser = Passer(    ⊙ Incorrect argument label in call (have 'moc:', ex...
52            managedObjectConte t: managedObjectContext)
53    Issue ⊙ Incorrect argument label in call (have 'moc:', expected 'managedObjectContext:')
54    Fix-it  Replace "moc" with "managedObjectContext"
55
56        newPasser.dictionaryRepresentation =
```

Figure 10.1   (top) The red badge for some Swift errors contains a dot instead of an exclamation point. (bottom) Clicking the dot brings up a Fix-it popover that suggests a correction for the error. The suggested correction is shown temporarily in your code.

one will show what your code would look like if the change were carried through. Press Return or double-click the highlighted suggestion to accept the change.

For C-family languages, Fix-it uses the llvm library to gain insights into your code and to check what it finds against questionable coding practices. For instance, this sort of loop is idiomatic in C programming:

```
int     ch;
while (ch = getchar())
    putchar(ch);
```

but using an assignment (=) in a Boolean context like the condition of a while loop smells. Meaning an equality test (==) and doing an assignment is a very common error. When the missing-braces-and-parentheses warning is enabled, Xcode will detect that you could mean either assignment or comparison, and the Fix-it popover will offer corrections that suit either interpretation. See Figure 10.2.

The Real Passer Rating

If all has gone well, you no longer have a boilerplate application: You have an app that calculates and displays passer ratings. Let's try it out. Select **Product →Run (⌘R)**.

Another Bug

By now you know that when I say something like "if all has gone well," the app will crash. And so it has: The Debug navigator shows a trace back through an exception handler, and the console says

```
Terminating app due to uncaught exception 'NSInvalidArgumentException',
    reason: '*** -[NSDictionary initWithObjects:forKeys:]:
    count of objects (1) differs from count of keys (12)'
```

followed by a stack trace that last touched your code at. . . a very long symbol. You can pick it out as yours only by the familiar-looking substring SimpleCSVFile. Like C++,

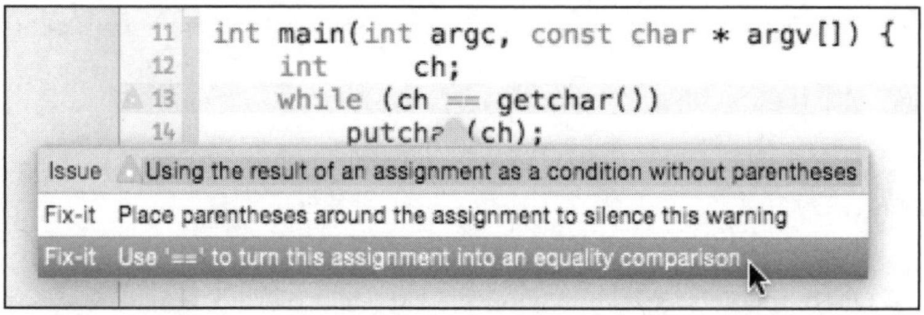

Figure 10.2   When more than one solution is possible (as in this assignment in the condition of a while loop), Fix-it will offer the alternatives and demonstrate what the corrected code would look like.

Swift keeps track of functions through "mangled" names that identify their host classes, parameter types, and return types. These are not human-readable.

Fortunately, the Xcode toolchain carries a demangling tool you can run from the command line (lines backslash-broken to fit the page, and indented for readability):

```
$ xcrun swift-demangle _TFC13Passer_Rating13SimpleCSVFile3runfS0_\
        FFGVSs10DictionarySSSS_GSqCSo7NSError_GSqOS_8CSVError_

_TFC13Passer_Rating13SimpleCSVFile3runfS0_FFGVSs10DictionarySSSS_\
        GSqCSo7NSError_GSqOS_8CSVError_ --->

Passer_Rating.SimpleCSVFile.run (Passer_Rating.SimpleCSVFile)
        (([Swift.String : Swift.String]) -> ObjectiveC.NSError?)
        -> Passer_Rating.CSVError?
```

It would be nice to see what was going on in `SimpleCSVFile.run(block:)`, but after the app ran through the exception handler, that information was lost. It would be nice if it weren't.

> **Note**
>
> An *exception* is a signal by program code—your own or in the system—that something has gone wrong. When an exception is raised, execution resumes at the nearest caller that has registered to handle it. If nothing does handle it, the last-resort handler kills the application. That's what happened here. Coders in other languages often use exceptions as routine control structures. Cocoa avoids them for reasons of performance and stability, and Swift makes them effectively inaccessible. In Cocoa/Objective-C/Swift, exceptions are reserved for conditions severe enough to threaten the integrity of the app and its data.

There is a way to do that. Open the Breakpoint navigator, which shows you a list of all the breakpoints you set in your project. It isn't confined to what you created by clicking in the margins of your source; in particular, you can set an *exception breakpoint*, which will halt execution whenever an exception is raised.

You'll find a **+** button at the bottom-left corner of the Breakpoint navigator. If you click it, you'll be shown a popup menu, from which you can select **Add Exception Breakpoint. . . .** An "All Exceptions" breakpoint appears in the list. You can configure it (right-click it, or Option-Command-click to see a popover), but the default behavior is good enough.

> **Note**
>
> One case for editing the breakpoint is to cut off C++ exceptions, which some OS libraries use routinely.

With the exception breakpoint set, run Passer Rating one more time. Now when the exception is raised, the debugger shows you the last point of contact with your code:

```
let values = NSDictionary(objects: fields,
                          forKeys: headers)
            as! [String: String]
```

and the stack trace in the Debug navigator shows you the backtrace you got in the console message before. Almost.

The main part of the Debug navigator is taken up by the stack trace, showing all of the pending functions from the crashed/breakpointed function at the top, to the root `start` function at the bottom. Your functions are highlighted in two ways: First, their names are shown in black instead of gray, to show that Xcode can display their source code.

Second, they are marked with a blue icon with the head-and-shoulders badge that Apple customarily uses for "user." The icon indicates the framework the function came from. Other examples are a purple mug for the Cocoa frameworks, an olive series of dotted lines (which may represent layers of bricks) for Foundation and Core Foundation, a dark-pink briefcase for the event-servicing frameworks, and a tan circle for the runtime library.

Not many of these are interesting. There is a lot that goes on inside Cocoa, and beyond knowing what called you, what you called, and what crashed, there's not much profit in watching Cocoa crawl around inside itself. Xcode understands. In the bottom-left corner of the Debug navigator is a button (Figure 10.3) that filters the stack trace. When it is highlighted, you see only frames for which there are debugging symbols, or at which control passed between libraries. When it is not, you see everything.

The debugger, especially the description of the exception, tells you what you need: The last of our lines to be executed was, you remember,

```
let values = NSDictionary(objects: fields,
                          forKeys: headers)
            as! [String: String]
```

The exception message said that there was only 1 object for 12 keys, so immediately you're interested in `fields` and `headers`. Have a look at the variables pane at the left of the Debug area. Click the disclosure triangles in the left margin. Sure enough, the `fields` variable holds an `NSArray` (which is the public, abstract class—what's shown is the concrete subclass `_NSArrayI`) with one element, an empty string. `_headers`, the instance variable backing the `headers` property, points to an array of 12 elements.

So the question is, what would cause a line to present a single empty element? Well, if the file ends with a newline character, the "last" line, as delimited by the last newline, will be empty. Disclosing the contents of `self` in the variable display confirms this: `_lineCount` is exactly the number of lines in `sample-data.csv`.

> **Note**
>
> I'm guessing. I haven't tested. I'm wrong.

The solution is to add one test before the assignment to `values`:

```
//  Blank line; go to the next one
if fields.count <= 1 { continue }
```

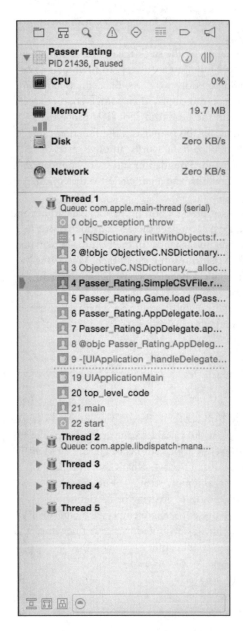

Figure 10.3   (left) By default, frames that are probably irrelevant to your code are redacted from the stack trace in the Debug navigator. Their place is taken by lines across the display. (right) Clicking the button at the bottom-left of the navigator expands the list to show all frames.

And, because the CSV parser ought to catch some errors:

```
if fields.count != headers.count {
    //  There should be as many fields as headers
    return .LineFormat(path, lineCount,
                       headers.count, fields.count)
}
```

... where `.LineFormat` is an enumerated value of the `CSVError` enum. `CSVError` defines four error types, each with its own combination of data for the details. You can find the whole thing in the sample code, but here is a taste:

```
enum CSVError {
    case LineFormat(String, Int, Int, Int)
    case EmptyFile(String)
    case NoSuchFile(String)
    case ClientError(String, Int, NSError)

    func code() -> Int {
        switch self {
        case .LineFormat:    return -3
...
        }
    }

    //  Representing the SimpleCSVFile-side error
    //  conditions is easy; translating them into
    //  NSErrors, a little more involved:
    var nsError: NSError {
        var userDict:[NSString:AnyObject] = [:]

        switch self {
        case let .NoSuchFile(fileName):
...
        case let .EmptyFile(fileName):
...
        case let .LineFormat(fileName, lineNumber, expected, actual):
            userDict = [
                NSFilePathErrorKey              : fileName,
                NSLocalizedDescriptionKey    :
                    "File \(fileName):\(lineNumber) has " +
                    "\(actual) items, should have \(expected)",
                CSVErrorKeys.ExpectedFields.toRaw() : expected,
                CSVErrorKeys.ActualFields.toRaw()   : actual
            ]
        case let .ClientError(fileName, lineNumber, error):
...
        }
```

```
        return NSError(domain: WT9TErrorDomain,
                       code: code(),
                       userInfo: userDict)
    }
}
```

Running Passer Rating

Everything is fixed now, I promise. Run the app. The iOS Simulator starts, and after a
delay, you see the first cut at Passer Rating (Figure 10.4). It required a little focused effort
on the controller end, but the data model seems to be holding up with some
reasonable-looking results. When you swipe across a row in the table, or tap the **Edit**
button, the app offers to delete a passer, and when you tap **Delete**, the passer collapses out
of sight. The **+** button creates one passer with the name "FirstName LastName," but that's
all you asked for. As far as it goes, the app works (until you tap one of the passer's entries
in the list; the app will crash when it can't find the `timeStamp` attribute in `Passer`).

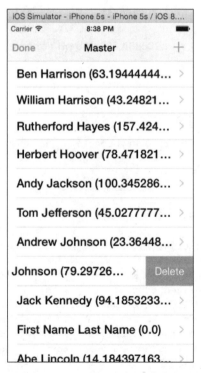

Figure 10.4   The first real version of Passer Rating, at last. It reads the sample data, lists the
passers and their ratings, and responds to commands to add and delete passers. The format of the
ratings themselves can be cleaned up later.

> **Note**
>
> Deleting passers in the running app is a little frightening because you can do that only so many times—at most 43, from this data set. However, you're not going to run out because I've rigged `AppDelegate` to reload the sample data set every time the app is run.

When you're done, click the Home button at the bottom of the simulated iPhone (or **Hardware** → **Home**, ⇧ ⌘ H, if your screen can't accommodate the simulated devices at a one-for-one scale), and return to Xcode. But wait: The **Stop** button in the Workspace window's toolbar is still enabled. What's going on?

Remember that iOS apps don't halt when the Home button is pressed; they go into suspension in the background, and can resume their run at any time. The **Stop** button is still active, and the debugger is still running, because Passer Rating hasn't quit. Tapping its icon on the home screen will bring it to the foreground again, still running.

This is the right thing to do, but not always what you want. If you want your app to stop, click the **Stop** button. Or, simply go on with your work, and issue the **Run** command. Xcode will present a sheet offering to stop the incumbent.

> **Warning**
>
> The alert that offers to stop the incumbent process offers to suppress this warning in the future. *Don't check that box.* Suppose you are engaged in a long debugging session, and you are at a breakpoint. You want to resume running. You're concentrating on your work, not the tool. Which button, labeled with a triangle, will you reach for? The tiny **Continue** button tucked into the lower middle of the window? Or the large, friendly **Run** button at the top left, which would ruin your debugging history if that alert didn't save you?

Summary

In this chapter, I proved the data model by turning it into a real iPhone application. On the way, I showed you how to change class and file names from what Xcode's template gave you into something practical and informative.

You came across Fix-it, which offers automatic fixes of syntax errors and warnings, and Live Issues, which exposes errors and warnings as you type. The combination, made possible by the nimble `llvm` library, won't be enough to remove "check compilation" from your vocabulary, but you'll find that the moment-to-moment support will keep you working with fewer breaks in your flow.

A bug in Passer Rating's CSV parser gave you a chance to get better acquainted with the Debug navigator, and to see how it can do a little data mining to make debugging easier. And, you used the debugger console to get a better idea of what's going on.

Building a New View

The passer list works well enough now. It's not fancy, but it very nearly matches the wireframe in Figure 8.2. One thing it is lacking is a transition from a list of passers to a passer summary and a list of games. For this, you will create a new view controller and make the acquaintance of Interface Builder.

The Next View Controller

The thing to remember is that unless you are doing some custom drawing or event handling, there's little reason to create a new subclass of `UIView`. The standard views are so generic, versatile, and easy to combine that making a new one is rare. What isn't rare is the need to set the content of views and respond to the events they capture. You know already that this is the business of the controller layer of the MVC design pattern, for which you'll need a subclass `UIViewController`.

If You Want to Add a View Controller

This time around, it wasn't necessary to add a view controller. The master-detail project template provided a detail view, and all you had to do was a little renaming and repurposing. What would you have to do to create a new view controller?

It's not hard. First, you need `.swift` source files for a subclass of `UIView-Controller`. Select **File** → **New** → **File...** (⌘N), and pick the iOS → Cocoa Touch template. You'd name the class, select `UIViewController` as the superclass, find that Xcode had appended `ViewController` to the class name you'd just typed, and change your class name back. Select **Swift** for the **Language**. This being a view controller, there will be a checkbox, **Also create XIB file**, that I'll discuss shortly.

> **Note**
>
> Xcode's revision of the name you chose for your class is annoying, but the principle is sound: Pick a name that describes the role. It seems obvious, but the temptation to call a controller for editing passers either `PasserEditor` or `PasserEditorView` is strong.

Click **Next**, and use the get-folder sheet as you have before, to pick a place for the files on-disk, select a project group to display them, and assign them to one or more targets.

In principle, you're done. Your controller could build its entire view tree in code by implementing the `.loadView()` method.

In practice, you'd rarely do that. You would instead embody the controller's view in a layout created in an Interface Builder document—usually a storyboard so you can integrate it into the flow of your application design. If you need a stand-alone design—for instance, if you intend to use the same layout repeatedly in different contexts—you'd isolate the view in its own XIB file.

That's the purpose of the checkbox, **Also create XIB file** that became active when you elected `UIViewController` as the superclass. If you check it, Xcode will create a XIB linked to the new class.

If you want to add your controller to the storyboard flow, you'd add it and its view to the canvas as a scene. Create the scene by looking for **View Controller** in the Object library in the Utility area, and dragging it into the canvas, where it will bloom to the size of a screen. Click the bar above the scene to select the controller, and use the **Custom Class** field in the Identity inspector (third tab) to identify your new class as the controller.

Storyboards, Scenes, and Segues

Superficially, Interface Builder looks like a tool for drawing UI layouts. And that is *part* of what it does: More accurately, Interface Builder is a visual editor for the relationships between objects in your application. What-goes-where is just one kind of relationship.

> **Note**
>
> From the 1990s through Xcode 3, Interface Builder was a separate application. There are other editors in Xcode that are also radically different from the main code editor, but because of its long history of being a stand-alone application, people still speak of IB as a thing apart.

You've seen UI-layout editors before, on many other platforms: Most of them emit executable code that constructs the view hierarchy described in the editor; or they work on files that the build process turns into executable code; or at least they construct data streams that script the creation of UI objects. IB is similar in that the files it works on are compiled and installed at build time for use in the target application.

That's where the similarity ends. Remember this: *There is no code. There is no script.* Interface Builder products are not executable; instead they are archives of Cocoa objects. The archives include links between objects and methods both within themselves and externally. Many newcomers who are used to other systems want code so they can "see how it's really done." The IB products *are* how it's really done. Except in trivial cases, it's hard to produce code that mimics NIB loading correctly; and in some cases (particularly on OS X) it isn't possible.

> **Note**
>
> That is at least where you should start your thinking. On iOS, it's often useful to instantiate, arrange, and link views dynamically—it's how many project templates start out—but code should not be the first technique you try. Interface Builder can be intimidating because it feels magical. As with most of Cocoa, it does things you may be used to controlling yourself. Relax. In the long run, if you learn to use Interface Builder effectively, you'll spend much less of your life fighting the operating system.

A storyboard goes beyond even that: It provides a *canvas* that holds *scenes*, each representing a controller that runs (roughly) a whole screen at a time; linked by *segues* running from individual controls to the next scene to be presented. When tapping a button in the running app triggers a segue, the tap goes directly to UIKit, which creates the next scene and its controller, gives the outgoing controller a chance to touch up the new one's configuration, and moves the scene onto the screen. Again: The storyboard product makes a lot happen that you may be accustomed to controlling yourself. If you can adjust your thinking to take advantage of the flow, you'll find you can do almost anything, and much more easily.

Arranging Your Tools

Interface Builder has peculiar needs for its editing space. A completed storyboard is very large. You can zoom in or out using the **Editor → Canvas → Zoom** submenu, or by pinch gestures with a trackpad, but even if you are working on a single scene in your app, every pixel in the canvas view is precious. A Mac screen that is otherwise respectable for development probably won't show all of an iPad layout at once.

> **Note**
>
> At the maximum, zoomed-in scale, the canvas displays the layout to match the screen point-for-point. This is the only scale at which Interface Builder allows you to lay out views. However, you can add scenes and link outlets, actions, and segues in zoomed-out views.

At the left edge, IB has a document outline view that you'll rarely want to close, and on the right, you need the Utility area open to create and adjust the views you insert. If you use an Assistant editor (and sometimes you must), things get tighter still. What you don't need are the Navigator area, because you'll spend most of your time on one IB document, or the Debug area.

This is a job for tabs. You probably already have your workspace window set up as you prefer for editing source files. Start from there. Select **File → New → Tab** (⌘ T). This is where you'll do all your IB work, so double-click on the tab's name and change it to `Interface Builder`.

Now configure the tab: Use the Project navigator to select `Main.storyboard`. With the **View** control in the toolbar (three rectangles with portions highlighted), close the Navigator and Debug areas and open the Utility area. The bottom part of the Utility area is called the Library; select the Object library tab (the third one, with the cube) to show the repertoire of objects you can put into the canvas or a scene.

With the Project navigator gone, how will you get to other files? That's not a problem in this project: Passer Rating has one storyboard, and that's all it will ever need. But sooner or later you'll have a project with more than one file that needs attention from Interface Builder. How do you switch among them without shoving the Navigator area back into the window?

You've probably already noticed the bar that spans the top of the Editor area. This is the *jump bar*. It presents a number of controls for navigating your project directly. What interests you at the moment is the path control, spanning most of the bar. It takes the form of a series of arrow-shaped segments. Each segment is a link in the chain that starts with the project and goes down through the project's groups, to the file on which the editor is focused. (In the case of structured documents, it will go on through the hierarchy of functions or IB objects.) If the current file has a selection, one last link identifies the selection by name. See Figure 11.1.

Clicking a segment displays a popup menu offering a choice of the projects, groups, files, and selections available at that level in the hierarchy. The popup is itself hierarchical, so you can trace a new path for the editor. If one level of the jump bar has too many items to search by eye, you can narrow it incrementally by typing a search string—the search key isn't consecutive, so `alcon` will turn up the `PasserListController` and `GameListController` Swift files.

This suggests a strategy if you have many XIBs and storyboards, and want to work on them in a dedicated **Interface Builder** tab. Open the Project navigator again. In the search field at the bottom, type `.xib` to narrow the list down to the project's XIBs.

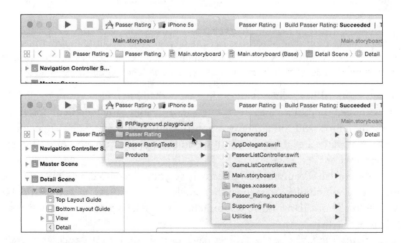

Figure 11.1   (top) The jump bar runs across the Editor area between the tabs and the editor itself. The main part of it is a path control tracing from the project through your groups to the current file and its selection. (bottom) Each level of the path control is a hierarchical popup menu that lets you set the path.

Figure 11.2   Interface Builder is easier to use if you give it its own tab, configured for the purpose.

Command-click each so they are all selected. Then select **File → New → Group from Selection**. All of your XIBs are now in a common group, which means that they are all at the same level in your jump bar. You can move your storyboard files to the same group. The file segment of the path control will switch you among the design files directly. You can close the Project navigator for good. Your workspace should look like Figure 11.2.

Building a View

The Master-Detail Application template provides a detail controller class (the one we've renamed to `GameListController`) and realizes it in `Main.storyboard` as the third scene in the canvas (Figure 11.3). The first scene, marked with the single arrow that shows it is the initial scene in the storyboard, is for a `UINavigationController`. It is joined

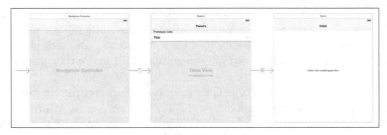

Figure 11.3   The master-detail project template fills `Main.storyboard` with three scenes: a navigation controller that contains a master scene (Passer List Controller), which cascades to a detail scene (Game List Controller).

by a *root view controller* segue to its initial content, the `PasserListController` that presents the roster of passers. In turn, a *push* segue links it to the next step, the game list.

The navigation controller is a wrapper on the other two; it manages a stack of views that slide into and out of the screen as the user navigates a hierarchy, such as from a passer in a list to the passer's detailed record. It also maintains a navigation bar at the top of the screen to display the current view's title and a back button so the user can step back through the hierarchy (from passer to passer list). The first scene linked to it is the *root view*, the first view the navigation controller will display.

The succeeding views in the controller stack all display navigation bars, but those controllers don't actually manage those bars: The bars are there so you can allow for the space as you work the layout out.

The last view in the chain, the "detail" view that we've renamed `GameList-Controller`, comes from the template as a plain view, empty but for a single label; the template simply filled the label with the time-of-day held by the dummy `Event` entity. That's not what we want, but before we get rid of it, there's something to notice.

> **Note**
>
> All `UIViewController`s have a `title` property that `UINavigationController` uses to fill in the title in the navigation bar. The Master-Detail template has filled these with "Master" and "Detail," which is beginning to get tedious. Select each scene with the canvas zoomed in to 100 percent. The active scene will show three icons in the bar at the top; the first represents the view-controller object. Click it, and then select the Attributes inspector (fourth tab at the top of the Utility area). Set **View Controller—Title** to `Passers` and `Games`, respectively. Then, select the navigation bars in each scene, and set the titles there, too.

Outlets and Assistants, in Passing

Click the middle item in the **Editor** group in the toolbar—it looks like two linked rings, to suggest the display of two related things. This adds an *Assistant editor* to the Editor area. This probably ruins the window layout you worked so hard to construct, so make adjustments until you have something like Figure 11.4.

At base, the Assistant editor is just another editor, allowing you to see more than one file as you work on them. And that is one way you can use it. What makes the Assistant editor special is that it can automate its choice of content, adapting itself to what you do in the main editor. The jump bar in the assistant determines the relationship it will pursue. Use the first segment as a menu to set the assistant to **Automatic**, and click on the various objects in the IB canvas. You'll see that the assistant shows the source code that backs each object.

Click the white bar above the Game Controller scene. As fits the pattern, the Assistant editor fills with `GameListController.swift`. If more than one file met the need, the control at the right end of the jump bar would show how many matched, and would present arrowheads on either side to switch between them.

The template has added this line to the class declaration:

```
@IBOutlet var detailDescriptionLabel: UILabel!
```

Figure 11.4   Adding the Assistant editor by clicking the middle button in the **Editor** group (the one that looks like linked rings) requires some adjustments to the project layout.

So: One of the properties of the controller is a reference to the label in the middle of the view. There's something more—notice the `@IBOutlet` attribute. It is merely a signal to Interface Builder that this property of the view controller is eligible to receive a pointer to something in the scene.

> **Note**
>
> The `UILabel` type carries an exclamation point, which you saw earlier in the "Editing the View Controller" section of Chapter 10, "An iOS Application: Controller." It guarantees that although the value will start as `nil`, Swift can assume it will be non-`nil` before your first use of it.

For your first look at what this means, hover the mouse cursor over the dot you see in the gutter next to the line (Figure 11.5). That dot shows that a link has been made between an IB object and that outlet. Interface Builder demonstrates the link by highlighting the label in the canvas when the mouse hovers over the linkage dot.

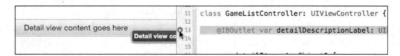

Figure 11.5   `@IBOutlet` properties are meant to be filled with pointers to objects that will be realized when a scene is loaded. Hovering the mouse cursor over the linkage bubble next to an outlet property highlights the corresponding object in the controller's scene.

That's all there is to see this time around; there will be much more later. For now, we don't need that label. Select it in the game-controller scene, and press Delete. After taking note that the connection bubble next to the property `var` is now empty, select the line and delete that, too. Now that the outlet property is no longer defined, Xcode will flag an error on the reference to it in `configureView()`; delete those lines, too.

> **Warning**
>
> If you go the other way around, and forget to delete the label, you're heading for a crash: When the scene loads, the storyboard still calls for linking the label. UIKit will look for the outlet property in the controller, and will throw an exception when it doesn't find it. The error message will be only vaguely helpful, and you're on your own finding the dangling reference. Make sure you clean up both ends.

The Billboard View

Now you can add content of your own. The design calls for two elements: a billboard containing overall statistics for the passer, and a table with the details of each game. Start with the billboard.

The billboard will contain labels of various sizes and styles. First, add the container itself. Click in the search field at the bottom of the Object library (third tab, bottom part of the Utility area), and type **UIView**. You'll see an entry labeled "View." Drag it out of the library and into the scene in the editor. As you drag it, it transforms into a rectangle that sizes itself to the available space in the scene. Let it go.

You don't want the billboard to take up the whole space. Click on it to display resizing "handles" at the sides and corners. Given how large the new view is, this may not help you much—it's white-on-white, and there's no way to identify which corner or side you're dealing with. Select **Editor** → **Canvas** → **Show Bounds Rectangles** to show the edges of the view. Better.

Drag the bottom edge up until the view takes up about the top quarter of the available space (168 points). This may be a bit tricky—IB clips the handles to the edge of the superview. It may be easier to grab the top handle, size it down, then drag the resized view up until it abuts the navigation bar.

The billboard view is supposed to be light gray, to match the navigation bar. In the Attributes inspector, there's a **Background** control, which has two parts: The left part is a color well, which you can click to get a color palette to edit the color. The right part is a drop-down menu containing standard colors. Click the color well to bring up the color-picker palette; click the magnifying-glass button and then the navigation bar that's already in the scene. The inspector should look like Figure 11.6.

Pretty nice, eh? Use the first segment of the Assistant editor's jump bar to display a **Preview** of the layout. (Select the `GameListController` scene if it isn't already selected.) You'll see something like Figure 11.7, with the scene rendered as it will be on screen.

The Preview view includes a **+** button in the lower-left corner to add device layouts to the display, such as the various sizes of iPhones and iPads. Each preview has a white bar at

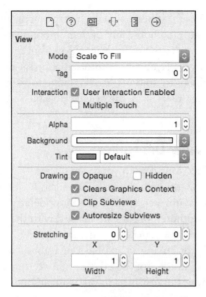

Figure 11.6   The Attributes inspector for the passer billboard view should look like this when you're done.

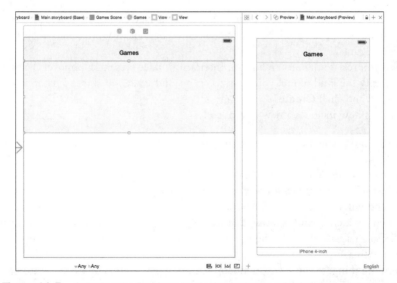

Figure 11.7   Selecting the **Preview** view in the Assistant editor's jump bar displays a straightforward rendering of the selected scene. Controls at the lower left change the presentation of the view for different screen sizes, orientations, and idioms.

the bottom naming the format ("iPhone 4-inch," for instance), and providing a button that will rotate the view. You can choose any of them more than once: The second time you add a layout, it will appear in the other orientation from the existing one, allowing you to monitor changes in your layouts in both orientations at once.

There are a couple of fixups to do. First, we'll arrange to make the billboard visible to GameListController, and then make the briefest possible acquaintance of Auto Layout.

Linking Views to a View Controller

View controllers exist to link your data to your views. GameListController needs direct access to its main view (through the view property, which is linked automatically in Storyboard scenes) and to its subviews (which you must identify and link yourself). The instance variables containing those pointers are marked with the @IBOutlet attribute. @IBOutlet has no effect on the generated code. It is merely a signal to Interface Builder that the property is eligible for linking to an object in a storyboard or NIB.

Select the game list scene in the storyboard canvas; make sure it is visible while the Assistant editor is open. From the first item in the assistant's jump bar, select **Automatic →GameListController.swift**. Experiment: Click another scene or view, and see that the assistant tracks the selection and displays the corresponding controller's source code. Get back to the GameListController scene.

Hold the Control key down and drag from the billboard view into the controller's class block. It doesn't matter where, so long as it isn't in content blocks like enums or funcs. A horizontal insertion bar appears in the code, labeled to show that if you release the mouse button there, you'll be creating an outlet or an action method (which I'll get to later). See Figure 11.8.

When you release the mouse button, Interface Builder presents a popover dialog for you to specify the kind of link you want to create, and what you want to name it. Call it **billboard** and click **Create**.

Your class now includes a new line of code:

```
@IBOutlet weak var billboard: UIView!
```

This shows an outlet for a UIView named billboard. weak means that the controller doesn't "own" the view, *and*, if every other owner (such as the view tree) relinquishes it, billboard will become nil. You've seen the ! before—the var is "implicitly unwrapped," which is your promise that by the time your code starts using it, billboard will refer to an actual object, so Swift will free you from having to decorate every reference with a !.

One more thing: If you have the document outline expanded (click the button at the lower-left corner of the canvas, if not), and you expand the outline under "Games Scene," you'll find a UIView containing a UIView. This means that the root view that comes with the scene contains another view, which we know is the billboard. As this scene becomes more complex, the generic names won't be useful.

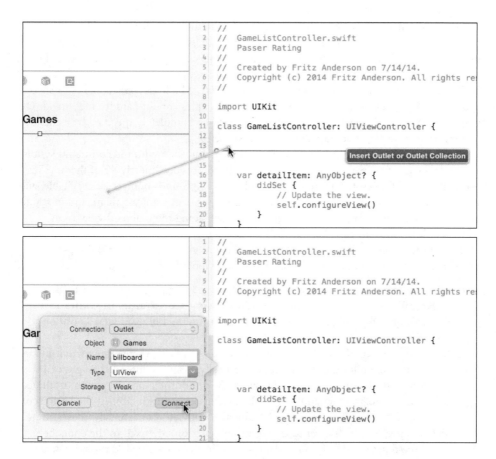

Figure 11.8   (top) Control-dragging from a view in a storyboard scene into the code for the scene's controller shows an insertion bar for an outlet or an action. (bottom) Releasing the mouse button brings up a popover for you to specify the kind of link, its type, and its name. Clicking **Connect** inserts an @IBOutlet for the view.

With the billboard view still selected, go to the Identity inspector (third tab in the Inspector panel) and type **Billboard** in the **Label** field in the Document section. Tab out of the field, and find that the billboard now appears in the outline under that name.

Auto Layout for the Nonce

Next, Auto Layout. Auto Layout is a technique for ensuring that your views are always placed and sized as you intend them, no matter the size or orientation of the screen—this view spaced 8 points below that, centers aligned, and so on. Expressing "intention" is a hard thing to do right, and Apple was at pains to do it right. Unfortunately, that requires you to take pains, too.

For the moment, we will do the very least we have to do to make the billboard display correctly on the screen (or at all; Auto Layout's best guess at what we want crushes the billboard to zero height in landscape orientation). This chapter is quick-and-dirty. I'll go into depth in Chapter 12, "Auto Layout in a New View."

You express your intentions as a system of *constraints*, which Cocoa reconciles to lay out your views. It is versatile and effective. The core principles are not hard to understand: Every view's size and placement on both axes should be completely specified by a chain of constraints that must not contain contradictions. Simple.

Simple to understand, but not to get right. I wasn't satisfied with the constraints system for the billboard view we're about to build until I had produced nearly 40 of them. (This was with Xcode 5; Xcode 6 represents a lot of progress.) Some conflicts are inevitable, and you have to give Auto Layout a way out by assigning priorities among them, and in a long chain of dependencies, there's a lot of trial and error. Doing the billboard view right would consume most of this chapter.

This chapter will be all about building the billboard view. There are five things you must do to get over the immediate problem of the billboard disappearing:

1. Click the white bar above the `GameListController` scene, and select **Editor →Resolve Auto Layout Issues →Add Missing Constraints in Game List Controller**. This will put best-guess constraints on the billboard view's position relative to its nearest neighbors.

2. If you still have the Preview assistant open to show a 4-inch screen in portrait mode, you see that the billboard is compressed vertically, from the intended height of 168 points to 106. If you rotate the preview, the height of the billboard goes to nothing.

3. Select the billboard view, and look at the Size inspector (fifth tab): At the bottom of the panel is a list of the constraints IB added to the view. Horizontally, the "leading" and "trailing" spaces (I'll get to that terminology soon) are fixed to the container, and those don't seem to be a problem; you want the sides glued to the sides of the screen.

   The top and bottom edges are placed relative to the respective *layout guides*, notional lines in the screen view that represent the extent to which upper and lower bars (navigation, tab, status, toolbar) compress the usable vertical space. As I placed and sized the billboard, the top edge is at the upper guide, and 368 from the lower. The upper guide, allowing for the status and navigation bars, is 134 points from the top of the screen. So when the device is turned to landscape, the billboard's available height is $320 - (0 + 64)$ `(bars)` $- 368$ `(bottom margin)` $= -112$ points. The "missing constraints" did not serve us well.

   On reflection, we care about the billboard's being just below the upper bars (we have a constraint for that), we don't care about its keeping a consistent distance from the bottom (but IB gave us a constraint for that); for now, we do care about its having a consistent height (but we don't have a constraint for that).

4. Select the billboard view itself. An i-beam line extends from its bottom edge to the bottom of the view, representing the bottom-edge constraint. Click to select it. (It's

hard to catch, but IB gives you a hint by highlighting it when the mouse cursor is over it.) Press Delete to get rid of it.

5. At the lower-right corner of the editor, you see a palette of button groups. The one with four segments governs Auto Layout. With the billboard view still selected, click the **Pin** button (⊢口⊣). A popover view appears in which you check the box marked **Height**. Click **Add 1 Constraint** at the bottom of the popover.

That's it; the billboard behaves as intended on all screen sizes and orientations, in the preview and the simulator. There will be one more step once you've populated the billboard.

Lots of Labels

The billboard view consists of 14 instances of the UIKit class `UILabel`. Some of them are labels in the colloquial sense—static text that identifies something else on the screen. Others are "labels" because even though the application will change their content, the user can't. They'll be placed in three groups:

- The *name label*, across the top
- The *left-side* group, consisting of labels and values for cumulative statistics like total attempts
- The *right-side* group, with summary information like the overall passer rating, the passer's most recent team, and the span of his career

> **Note**
>
> The cries of horror you will be hearing will be those of professional graphic designers. Ignore them. They're used to it.

The Name Label

This is only one label, extending across the top of the view.

Type `label` into the Library search field to turn up the label (`UILabel`) view. Drag it into the top of the billboard view. The Attributes inspector will have a **Text** field; fill it with **FirstName LastName** as a placeholder, and discover that most of what you typed was truncated (with an ellipsis) because the label was too narrow. `UILabels` adjust their text size (down to a limit you can set) to fit the content to the bounds of the label; if that's not enough, they truncate. Stretch the label across the top of the detail view so no shrinkage is necessary.

The passer's name is pretty important, so let's give it some emphasis. The **Font** element in the inspector shows the text to be "System 17.0." Click the boxed-T button to open the **Font** popover (Figure 11.9). Make it **System Bold** and 18 points.

The Right-Side Group

Now a label for the passer rating, on the right side, just under the name. This is really, really important, and I have no taste, so make it big, bold, and red. Fill it with 158.3 and set the font to System Bold, 52 points (you'll need to stretch the bounds). For

Figure 11.9   (left) Clicking the **T** button in the **Font** field in the Attributes inspector displays a popover to specify the font, style, and size for the text in a view. (middle) The **Font** popup menu offers you the "System" fonts, plus the dynamic-typography categories. (right) Selecting **Custom** from the **Font** popup enables the **Family** popup, which offers every font family available in iOS 8.

Alignment, choose right-aligned (the third segment), so numbers less than 100 will line up. Click the color well at the left end of the **Text Color** control in the inspector; that gets you the Colors palette. Use the fifth tab in the palette, and select the "Maraschino" crayon. The passer rating is now really, really red. Experiment with **Shadow** and **Shadow Offset**, if you like.

A label for a team name, System Bold, 14 points, right justified, should go under the big rating label. Set its text to `Tacoma Touchdown-Scorers`, the longest team name in the data set, so you can be sure it will fit. In the Attributes inspector, there's a stepper for **Lines**; if you set it to **2**, the team name can wrap to two lines. Resize the label so the whole name is visible.

And this is the last one, I promise: A label to show the start and end dates of the passer's career: Below the team name, System, 12, right justified. Fill with the widest plausible content, `10/29/2015-10/29/2015`.

> **Note**
>
> If your curiosity led you to the Preview assistant, you probably found the results of the layout so far discouraging—the right column is partly or wholly beyond the right end of the billboard. We'll fix it soon.

The Left-Side Group

The statistics come next. Start with one label, `Attempts`, System, 14-point, regular, sized to fit, and positioned under the left end of the name label. You need four more captions, and you can save some effort by duplicating the one you just set up: **Edit → Duplicate** (⌘D), or hold down the Option key and drag. Line those up under the original, then edit each so that they read `Attempts`, `Completions`, `Yards`, `Touchdowns`, and `Interceptions`.

> **Note**
>
> You can set the text style of multiple items by selecting them all and setting the style in the Attributes inspector.

Next, the labels for the statistics themselves. Insert five `UILabels` next to the stat-name labels. Throughout the process, Interface Builder will snap your views to blue guide lines that show standard spacing and alignment with their neighbors. In the case of views with text content, you'll also be given a dotted line when the view's baseline is aligned with its neighbors. When in doubt, align baselines.

I suggest filling the value labels with `00,000` as a guide to the minimum necessary width. The identical content won't help in listings, so select each, and in the Identity inspector, set its Xcode label to correspond to the statistic it is to display. The statistic-name labels will show up in listings with their content, so distinguish the numeric labels with a `#`: `#Attempts`, `#Completions`, and so on.

Make their text style the same as the stat-name labels, only right-justified.

Just for fun, make sure the Game List Controller scene is selected, and select the **Editor →Resolve Auto Layout Issues →Update Frames** command, which you can also find in the third button (⊢△⊣) of the Auto Layout group in the canvas.

No. All the labels were moved out of sight. If you select them in the document outline, you'll see that they've all been moved to a Y position of –64, which would be the top edge of the scene, relative to the top of the billboard. With nothing to guide it, Auto Layout resolves the (absent) constraint network by putting everything in the same place. You have to add some constraints so it won't wreck your display. Undo (**Edit →Undo**, ⌘ Z, did I need to tell you?) the layout.

Again making sure the game list scene is selected, select **Editor →Resolve Auto Layout Issues →Add Missing Constraints**. Once again, Interface Builder will take its best guesses at what you intend for the layout and create constraints accordingly.

If you click around among the labels, you'll see blue i-beams and alignment strokes representing the constraints. The network of constraints is complete and consistent, so the **Update Frames** command is disabled.

It looks good enough for now. See Figure 11.10.

Cleaning Up

But it isn't. Because Auto Layout is the result of a mathematical solution to a complex network of constraints that may be contradictory or insufficient, you can't always predict how it will go wrong when it does. What follows is the story of what I saw when I ran

Figure 11.10   The billboard view as it comes from the hard work of filling in the constituent labels. The lines around the labels are their layout rectangles, which are the criteria Auto Layout uses to calculate layout.

this layout through the Preview assistant and the iPhone 5 simulator. You will see something different—I saw different things between the preview and the simulator—but we should come out the same by the end.

The Columns Collide

Figure 11.11 shows the first problem, apparent even in the Preview assistant.

The statistics in the left column run into the rating, team name, and dates on the right. By default, Interface Builder has you edit scenes in a generic form factor that might adapt itself to any size or shape of screen, and the generic width didn't tip us off that a 320-point screen wouldn't allow the room our layout needed.

If you look again at the layout, you'll see that the bounds of the number labels are much wider than necessary—above 70 points. *In my layout*—I almost guarantee yours will be different—Interface Builder set a fixed width for the #Attempts label, and aligned the leading and trailing edges of the other four to it; the effect being to make all five the same width. If we resize the #Attempts label, the other four will follow.

Figure 11.11   The Preview assistant's guess at the billboard layout has the views in the left half overrunning the ones on the right.

Select #Attempts, and expose the Size inspector. Find the numerical width constraint in the list, and click the **Edit** button for it. A popover will appear showing that the constraint is set to be equal to 72 (or the like). Change the number to 48 (that's what worked for me) and tab out of the field. All the integer-stats labels will narrow (the other four are tied to #Attempts, remember), and the Preview assistant shows that the columns no longer overlap. It doesn't look perfect, but it's good enough; we're going to replace all of it in the next chapter.

The Billboard Collapses

The simulator tells a different story. The billboard view is there, but it occupies only a 20-point-wide swath in the middle of the view. The right column goes left from the right edge, the left column from the left edge, so the two seem to be exchanged on the screen.

Obviously, something was wrong with the constraints on the edges of the billboard. I looked closely at the Size inspector for the billboard and found that the leading and trailing edges were fixed to the leading and trailing edges of the top layout guide. And, it appears, the breadth of the guide line might be 20 points, or 320 points beginning 160 points to the left of the view…

That's just wrong. If I'd done the layout myself, I would have fixed the edges to the edges of the root view, the one that contains the billboard. Double-click those leading and trailing constraints and press Delete to get rid of them.

Then, with the billboard selected, click the Pin (⊢□⊣) button to bring up a popover for adding constraints to a view (Figure 11.12). Uncheck **Prefer Margin Relative**, make sure the left- and right-neighbor boxes show **0**, and make the struts between them and the center solid (and therefore effective) by clicking them.

The **Update Frames** popup should be set to **Items of New Constraints** so the billboard will move to its newly constrained position (which shouldn't be different in this case). The alternative is **All Frames in Container**, but I'm never bold enough to expose myself to a total rearrangement after adding only a couple of constraints.

Then click **Add 2 Constraints** to install them. Two things to remember:

- You have to click the **Add … Constraints** button to install the new constraints. Clicking away, or bringing another window forward, will make the popover disappear, but it won't add the constraints.

- The constraints will be *added*. The popover does not edit existing constraints. Whatever you create with the Pin button will be added to the constraint set, even if another such constraint is already there.

Figure 11.12　The Pin (⊢□⊣) button displays a popover window for adding constraints to a view. In this case, you want to set the leading and trailing edges to be zero points from the nearest neighbor (the sides of the main view). Clicking the struts next to the fields so they become solid indicates you want to add those constraints. Note that the **Prefer Margin Relative** button is unchecked.

The Table View

It's almost an afterthought—we don't yet have a table view to hold the individual game performances, taking the form of a `UITableView`. Typing **table** in the Library search field should show you a "Table View." Drag it into the lower part of the main view. (Take care not to use the "Table View Controller" instead.) You'll have to expand it to fit the available space. This isn't too hard at the sides and bottom, because Interface Builder "snaps" the edges to the bounds of the main view, but it won't give you any help with the top edge.

This is something that Auto Layout actually makes easier. Place the table view in the lower part of the scene, and size it so it is clear of all neighbors. Click the ⊢□⊣ button in the Auto Layout group at the bottom right of the canvas to expose the **Pin** popover. Set all four spacing fields to 0, making sure the drop-down menu for the upper spacing makes it relative to the billboard view.

> **Note**
> IB prefers side margins to be inset by a standard amount (16 pixels), and by default calculates edges relative to that inset. Uncheck **Prefer margin relative** to ensure that the sides stick to the sides of the root view itself.

Set the **Update Frames** menu in the popover to **Items of New Constraints**, and click the acceptance button at the bottom, which now has the label **Add 4 Constraints**. The table view will snap to exactly the position and size you want, with the added benefit that it will resize in sync with the rest of the scene.

Outlets

We just added 14 labels to the billboard view, and nine of them display names, dates, and statistics taken from the Passer Rating data store. You know how to do this: Control-drag into the class declaration in `GameListController.swift` to create `@IBOutlets` linking the labels to the controller.

Every NIB, and every Storyboard scene, has an owner. This is an object that is external to the scene (or NIB); the loading mechanism then fills the `@IBOutlet` properties with pointers to objects in the scene. Storyboards and XIBs have different treatments for owners:

- Interface Builder's editor for XIBs includes an "object" in the document outline named "File's Owner." This object does not literally exist in the XIB; Interface Builder shows it in a section of the document outline for placeholders. It stands in for the owner object that will load the XIB (actually its NIB product) at run time.

- In a storyboard, each scene belongs to a `UIViewController` subclass. The controller's placeholder appears in the document outline, and in the top bar when the scene is selected, as a yellow circle with a "view" in the middle.

When you create a subclass of `UIViewController`, `UITableViewController`, `NSWindowController`, or `NSViewController`, Xcode enables a checkbox marked **Also create XIB file** (OS X projects will add "**for user interface**"). If you check it, Xcode will create a XIB in addition to the new class's `.swift` file. Xcode knows what the owner class will be, so it sets the class of File's Owner accordingly.

If you create a XIB alone, Xcode would not know what the class of File's Owner should be, and you would have to set it yourself: You'd select the File's Owner icon in the document outline and open the Identity inspector (third tab in the Inspector view in the Utility area). The first field will be a combo box to enter the name of the owner's class. The box will autocomplete as you type.

It's the same with view controllers in a storyboard: After you drag a view controller into the canvas to create a scene, the owner is identified as a plain `UIViewController`. You must edit the class name in the Identity inspector to point the scene at the right controller.

> Note
>
> There are other kinds of controller in the object library, some of which you'd subclass (`UITableViewController` always), some not. Use those, not the plain view controller, and set the controller class as needed.

Back to the specifics of `GameListController`. We have to hook the controller's `@IBOutlets` to objects in its scene. You could type in `var` declarations for all the labels you'll be using. Try it: Display the Assistant editor and select **Automatic** from its jump bar to show GameListController.swift.

Somewhere inside the declaration of class GameListController, declare the outlet for the "dates" label:

```
class GameListController: UIViewController {
    @IBOutlet weak var datesLabel: UILabel!
```

Go back to the document outline sidebar at the left edge of the canvas (click the button in the lower-left corner if it isn't visible), and right-click on "Games," the Englished name of the scene's owner. A small black heads-up display (HUD) window appears, containing a table of outlets, among them datesLabel. There's a bubble at the right end of that row in the table. Drag from it to the label you set up with a range of dates, and release; the adjoining column in the HUD fills with a reference to the label (Figure 11.13).

Now, when the scene is loaded, the owning GameListController's datesLabel property will contain a pointer to that label.

> **Note**
>
> The first icon in the white bar above the scene represents the same controller object; the right-click method works there, too. Also, the bubble next to the outlet declaration in GameListController.swift contains a black dot—you can drag from there to an element in the storyboard and make the link that way.

This is a great way to link views to outlets—if the outlet properties are already defined, as they might be if you were reusing an existing File's Owner object and dropping it into a scene.

In this case, it would be tedious, because the outlet vars haven't been declared. The control-drag-into-source is the better option.

Figure 11.13   Right-clicking the "GameListController" entry in the document outline opens a heads-up display window that includes the controller's outlets. Drag from an outlet's linkage bubble to a view in the controller's scene, and the outlet's @property will be filled with a pointer to that view.

Hooking Up the Outlets

Before you go on a spree of making outlet connections, taking a little care will pay off: There is a **+** button next to the right end of the assistant's jump bar. Click it. The Assistant area is now divided into two editors. Use the lower editor's jump bar, starting at the **Manual** category, to navigate to `Passer.swift`. You want the names of the new outlets to match up with the names of the `Passer` properties they display, and the new editor will give you a reference for the property names.

Now control-drag from the variable labels to make new properties in `GameList-Controller`. Use this convention in naming the outlets: Take the name of a Passer property, and add **Label** to it. The team name label goes into the controller interface as **currentTeamLabel**, attempts as **attemptsLabel**, and so on.

> **Note**
>
> Interface Builder can also link controls to action methods, declared with the `IBAction` tag in the class `@interface`. When you trigger a control that you've linked to an `IBAction`, the action method is executed. See the "Wiring a Menu" section of Chapter 19, "Starting an OS X Application," for an example.

`GameListController` needs to know about the table view, as well. Control-drag a link from the table into `GameListController`, and name the new outlet `tableView`.

Checking Connections

Do one last pass to verify that everything is connected to what it's supposed to connect to: With the storyboard in the main editor, and the `@IBOutlet` declarations for `GameList-Controller` showing in an Assistant editor, run your mouse down the connection dots, and make sure every view gets highlighted in turn.

If an outlet isn't connected, or is connected to the wrong view, drag from the connection bubble to the correct view. An `@IBOutlet` can refer to at most one view—it's just a single pointer. A view can be connected to many outlets because it has no reference back to the outlets. Checking the outlets, one by one, and reconnecting them as needed will be enough to get you out of any tangles.

There is an exception to the one-view-per-outlet rule: You can have an *outlet collection*. So far as the Swift code goes, a collection is little different from a single-object connection; the only new thing is that the type of the outlet is an array of the views in the collection:

```
@IBOutlet var numericLabels: [UILabel]!
```

The billboard contains five labels that display integers. We may want to clear all of them out simultaneously. The naïve approach would be to keep an array var, and fill it with all the outlet variables:

```
var numericLabels:[UILabel]!
...
numericLabels = [attemptsLabel, completionsLabel,
                yardsLabel, touchdownsLabel,
                interceptionsLabel]
```

But that's accident prone: Some day, you will add, drop, or rename labels in that list, and it's not always clear when in the life cycle of the view controller you should initialize the array that is after the label outlets are initialized, but before any possible use of numericLabels.

This is why there are outlet collections. Start by control-dragging from one of the integer labels (such as the one marked "Attempts") into GameListController.swift, as before. But this time, when the outlet popover appears, choose **Outlet Collection** for the **Connection** type, not **Outlet**. Name the collection (**numericLabels** is fine), and accept **UILabel** as the **Type**.

The collection starts with one member, the one you created the collection from. Drag from the bubble in the gutter next to the collection outlet var to each of the other integer-valued labels. Each will be added to the collection.

> **Note**
>
> If you add a label by mistake, control-click on it to bring up a heads-up display, find the link to numericLabels, and click the small **x** next to it.

The function to empty all the labels becomes very simple:

```
func emptyIntegerLabels() {
    for label in numericLabels {
        label.text = ""
    }
}
```

> **Note**
>
> Outlet collections do not guarantee the order of the views in their arrays. If the order is important, select each of the views in Interface Builder and set the **Tag** value of each to a distinct number (it's well down in the Attributes inspector, in the "View" category); then check the tag property of the view to confirm its identity.

Connecting GameListController

Interface Builder is great, but you still have to write code to get data from the model into the view. You'll make some changes to GameListController.

The template provides a setter for detailItem, setDetailItem:, that calls through to a configureView method. That's where you'll move the statistics in Passer to the labels in the view.

The template Xcode gave you had to be generic, but you know what kind of object the detail item will be. Rewrite the declaration of the property:

```
var detailItem: Passer? {
    didSet {
        // Update the view.
        self.configureView()
    }
}
```

The `configureView` Method

Here's `configureView`. It's a little long, but there's a point I want to make:

```swift
let integerProperties = [
    "attempts", "completions", "yards",
    "touchdowns", "interceptions"
]

func configureView() {
    if detailItem == nil { return }
    let passer = detailItem!

    for name in integerProperties {
        let stat = passer.valueForKey(name) as! Int
        let label = self.valueForKey("\(name)Label") as! UILabel
        label.text = "\(stat)"
    }

    // ratingFormatter is defined in Utilities.swift
    // It formats a number into a decimal string
    // with a mandatory single digit after the
    // decimal point.
    let ratingString =
        ratingFormatter.stringFromNumber(
                        passer.passerRating)
    passerRatingLabel.text = ratingString

    currentTeamLabel.text = passer.currentTeam

    // shortDateFormatter is defined in Utilities.swift
    // It formats a date into a short string according
    // to the user's locale. In US English, this would
    // be mm/dd/yyyy.
    let startDate = shortDateFormatter.stringFromDate(
                                    passer.firstPlayed)
    let endDate = shortDateFormatter.stringFromDate(
                                    passer.lastPlayed)
    datesLabel.text = "\(startDate) { \(endDate)"

    fullNameLabel.text = passer.fullName
    title = passer.fullName
}
```

How `configureView` Works

Here's where the care in naming the label outlets pays off:

1. Loop through the integer property names in `integerProperties`.

2. Get the corresponding integer from the passer by key-value coding (an Objective-C technique that gives access to object properties through string paths—the same feature is available in Swift for all objects that descend from Objective-C classes, or are tagged with the @objc attribute). In this case the name of the attribute is the key string.

3. Append "Label" to the property name, and use that as the KVC key to get the corresponding UILabel outlet from the controller itself.

4. Format the integer value as a string and put it in the label's text property.

Consolidating the names of the Passer properties in an array, and making the names of the outlet vars a simple variant on the property names, relieves the need to repeat the same assignment pattern for each property-label pair. Changes in the number or names of the properties can be handled simply by editing the property-name array.

Code Completion and Snippets

You probably fumbled a bit as you filled in all this code. Cocoa Touch is a huge API, and nobody remembers every symbol and method name. NSString has more than 130 methods in its Objective-C interface. If you don't have a crib, you might be pausing to look up spellings all the time. Here is where you turn on another feature I had you turn off in the "Quieting Xcode Down" section of Chapter 2, "Kicking the Tires."

Open the Preferences window (**Xcode → Preferences. . . , ⌘ comma**), and turn to the **Editing** tab of the **Text Editing** panel. Check **Suggest completions while typing**.

Now try the line let startDate = shortDateFormatter.stringFrom-Date(passer.firstPlayed) again, typing **sho**. Xcode pops up a window offering to complete the symbol and shows the proposed completion in gray in the editor (Figure 11.14). There are about a dozen symbols beginning with sho, so you can scroll the popup through all of them. Pressing the Up- or Down-Arrow key lets you choose.

Automatic completion is surprisingly good. It's context sensitive, and I've found that when I've recently used one symbol from an enum list,or even if I'm typing in a context in

Figure 11.14   With autocompletion on, typing a partial symbol will yield a list of possible completions, including a brief description of each. Select one and press Return to accept a completion.

which that enum type is expected, the next suggestions prefer other members of the same enum.

Continue typing to refine the completion list. When the selected completion shares a prefix with other suggestions, pressing the Tab key will advance the cursor through the common prefix, narrowing the completion list. If you're satisfied with the current suggestion, press Return and continue editing.

Completion is sometimes perverse, offering suggestions that have nothing to do with what you want. This is particularly painful when you want to type a symbol (e.g., **completion**) that shares letters, but not case, with another (e.g., **COMPLETION**). You can type to the end of your desired spelling, but Xcode will insist on the other one. If this happens to you (or if you simply want to suppress the popup), press Escape, and the completions will go away.

> **Note**
>
> Don't like automatic completion at all? If **Escape key shows code completions** is checked, you can summon the code-completion window whenever you want it. Even with escape-completion turned off, you can still invoke completion with **^Space**.

Code Snippets

Code completion doesn't stop at spelling. Xcode supports *code snippets* (see the second tab, marked with braces, in the Library section of the Utility area), which are blocks of code you can insert and edit for your purposes.

Passer Rating calls for saving the app's managed-object context whenever a `Passer` or `Game` object changes. An example is at the end of `PasserListController.insert-NewObject(sender:)`. The pattern

```
// Save the context.
var error: NSError? = nil
if !managedObjectContext.save(&error) {
    abort()
}
```

is a stereotype that comes up in the app repeatedly. If the code were easier to enter, it might even be possible to do something better than that foolish `abort()` call.

Comment-out the existing code for reference, and paste a copy of it in the same place; you could use the code as a snippet unchanged, but let's include some placeholders so it can be customized:

```
var error: NSError? = nil
if !managedObjectContext.save(&error) {
    NSLog("In %@: could not save %@",
        "<#method name#>",
        "<#how failed#>")
```

```
    //  MOCSaveException is defined in Utilites.swift
    NSException.raise(MOCSaveException,
            format: "Context: %@",
            arguments: getVaList(["<#how failed#>"]))
}
```

The placeholders are bracketed in <# #> pairs, with some text to cue the coder on the sort of thing that should replace them. You might want to shift the placeholder code to the left margin (**Editor** → **Structure** → **Shift Left**, ⌘[), so the leading whitespace won't appear when the snippet is expanded.

Select the snippet text, and drop it into the Snippet library pane (bottom of the Utility area, second tab). The border of the area will highlight, and you can release the mouse button. See Figure 11.15.

The new snippet will appear at the bottom of the list, with a generic name like "User Snippet." Double-click it to expand a popover displaying the snippet's content. Click **Edit**, and the popover allows you to label it, select the scope (language, context) in which it should be available, and—most important for the moment—the completion shortcut. Enter **savemoc** for the shortcut, and see Figure 11.16 for the rest. Click **Done**.

Go back to the main editor and delete your work on the snippet. Type **sav**; the resulting completion popup will show you the name of your snippet, and the description you supplied. Press Return to insert the snippet text, with the placeholders highlighted. The Tab key will step you through them, and when you're finished, this is what you'll have:

```
var error: NSError? = nil
if !managedObjectContext.save(&error) {
    NSLog("In %@: could not save %@",
        "PasserListController.insertNewObject",
        "the new Passer")
```

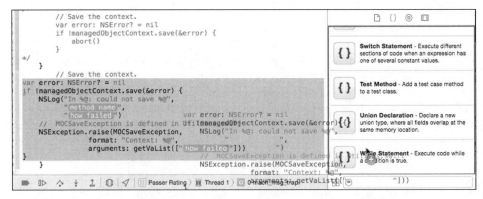

Figure 11.15   After building up a code snippet, select it and drag it into the Clipping library in the second tab at the bottom of the Utility area.

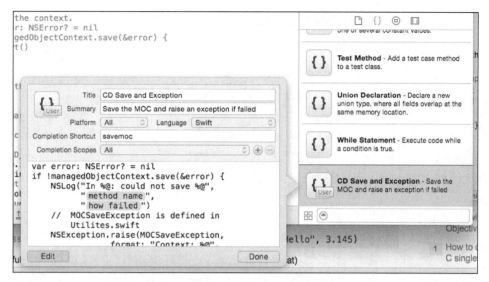

Figure 11.16   Find the snippet you dragged in (as "User Snippet"), double-click it, click **Edit**, and fill in the labels, context, and completion shortcut.

```
//  MOCSaveException is defined in Utilites.swift
NSException.raise(MOCSaveException,
          format: "Context: %@",
          arguments: getVaList(["Trying to save a new passer"]))
}
```

With a template to work from, you can produce better-performing and more consistent code without tedium.

Testing the Billboard View

Everything should be in place now. Run Passer Rating. Xcode builds the app and installs it in the iOS Simulator, which launches it. (The app takes a long time to load that CSV file—long enough that you might worry that iOS would kill it for being nonresponsive, but there are things you can do about that. See Chapter 16, "Measurement and Analysis.")

Select a passer from the initial view. Something like the view in Figure 11.17 should appear. All of the labels are filled in. It works. The game table is still empty, but you've made progress in making the data available to the user.

Figure 11.17   Running Passer Rating and selecting a passer shows that the passer-detail view works.

Summary

This was a long chapter, but you got a lot done. The passer table at the root of the application came almost fully implemented from the project template; all you had to do was change some formats and data-table names. This time, you took a view from practically nothing to a display of the unique data Passer Rating manages.

You provisioned the screen with a table and a container view for the summary billboard. After that, it was all labels, but you learned how to lay them out and how to use the Attributes editor to fit them to their purposes. And, I showed you how to finesse the problem of Auto Layout, at least for a while.

Data displays need data, and controller objects move data from the model to the views. Using Interface Builder with an Assistant editor, you gave GameListController direct access to the data labels and filled them in from the Passer object.

And, at least through the billboard display, it works. The rest, the table of games, will come in Chapter 13, "Adding Table Cells," later on. But first I will (and you should) take a closer look at laying out that billboard view.

## 12

Auto Layout in a New View

Chapter 11, "Building a New View," was about creating scenes in Passer Rating. To preserve that focus, I finessed the issue of Auto Layout with a quick workaround. For the purpose of an exercise, you don't need to do more solely for a screen the size and shape of a 4.7-inch iPhone; Passer Rating is not a professional-grade product.

You'll need to know more sooner or later, and this chapter is a closer look at Auto Layout. You can put it off, or even skip it. I won't know.

> **Note**
>
> If you attempted Auto Layout in Xcode 4, you found it was a nightmare, and I wouldn't blame you if you were a bit phobic on the subject. It got better in Xcode 5, and much better in Xcode 6. However, the new workflow is available only if you select at least **Xcode 5.0** in the **Opens in** popup in the File inspector. If you choose **Xcode 4.6** compatibility—maybe you or a coworker have to open the file in Xcode 4 for legacy—you're back to the horrible old workflow.

Why Auto Layout?

For decades, NeXTStep, Cocoa, and Cocoa Touch used *autoresizing* to adapt the layout of views to changes in geometry—the resizing of a window or the rotation of a device. Autoresizing was very simple: Notionally, each view had "springs," which would permit it to be resized on one or both axes, and "struts," which governed whether an edge of the view would maintain its distance from the corresponding edge of its container. As the superview resized, the subviews would adjust according to the spring-and-strut rules.

Limitations of Autoresizing

This worked. Mostly. But there were some things it couldn't do, things that would have been common had they been easy. Application code would have to intervene for special cases, and some requirements had to be met by trial and error.

Layout can't be a matter of the window pushing or pulling on its contents, which push or pull on theirs, and so on down the line. Suppose you have a label that absolutely must be readable in full, and it's three layers down in the containment hierarchy. Its container must not become so small that the full label can't be shown; so the container above must not become small enough for that to happen; and so on to the container above that, up to the root view of the window. The only place to enforce that must-not-shrink requirement is in the size limits for the window itself: Experiment, see how small the window can get without pressuring the label, write that dimension down, and set it in the parameters for the window.

Now translate the label from English to German: Pour your translations into a duplicate XIB file, see how the widths work out, and repeat the experiments to determine how to constrain the window.

You have ten international markets. And there's another label that must be readable at all times, and its content is determined in code. This entails some arithmetic.

We have computers to do arithmetic. In the real world, constraints on size and layout propagate up and down—and even across—the containment hierarchy. There have to be compromises and priorities: "I want this label to be centered and wide enough to show its contents (I don't need it wider), but it has to be at least 8 points away from the controls on either side, and to preserve that distance, respond first by moving it off-center, and if you must, by narrowing the label. Stop the window (three layers up) from resizing if it means making the label any narrower than 120 points. As for the next ten views. . ."

Auto Layout

Auto Layout can express all of this. And while Auto Layout has a reputation for complexity, it's a lot simpler than writing code to implement that description.

Internally (meaning: don't think too hard about this), any two views can be related to each other by *constraints*. A constraint applies to a specific property in each view (such as location of edge, center, or baseline; height, width) and specifies gaps and alignments by an offset, a multiplier, and a priority. Views may have "inherent" sizes, and some views (usually ones containing text) can resist being drawn wider or narrower than their contents. Auto Layout takes all of these constraints and reconciles them to produce an overall layout that satisfies as many as possible, sacrificing lower-priority ones to meet higher priorities.

The Thing to Remember

"Satisfying all constraints" imposes a duty on you: For each view, on each axis, the chain of constraints should fully specify the view's location and size (*sufficiency*). And, the constraints must not contradict (*consistency*). If those conditions are not met, Auto Layout will raise exceptions, and Interface Builder will post warnings.

The Player Billboard, Revisited

In Chapter 11, "Building a New View," I had you put together the billboard view at the top of the `PRGameListController` view with little thought of declarative layout. You switched a couple of constraints to get a bug out of the way, and asked Interface Builder to do the rest.

Why You Should Do More

It's good enough for a start, but there are flaws. Unless you were very careful about alignments, the generated constraints were a little off of your intention, and when you turned the billboard to landscape, your narrow elements wasted most of the available space (Figure 12.1).

> **Note**
>
> What I show in Figure 12.1 shows how *my* constraint network played out. Your own may look different, but probably no better.

Start by examining the constraint system you have now. There are a few ways to explore: If you select a view in the canvas editor, it will display lines to show the constraints that apply to it; the Size (fifth) inspector will include a list of those constraints, and double-clicking an item will select that constraint. The constraint objects themselves stand alone in **Constraints** categories you'll find throughout the document outline. (You may have to dig; it helps if you enter the name or type of the view you're looking for.) Selecting one will highlight it in the editor. Selecting one in the editor canvas itself requires some dexterity, but Interface Builder helps by highlighting the bar when you're pointing to it, and providing a slightly wider hit area than is visible.

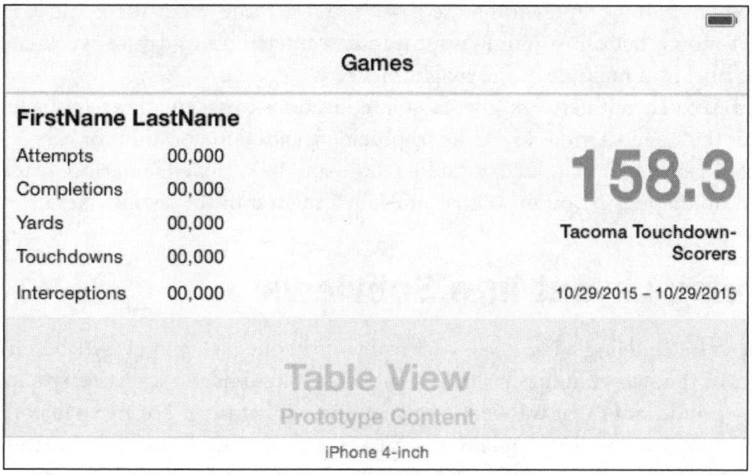

Figure 12.1   The automatically generated constraint system you can get from Interface Builder is workable, but it doesn't make the best use of the area available in landscape orientation.

Whose Constraint Is It, Anyway?

The way Interface Builder displays constraints makes it tempting to say that a view that is subject to a constraint "owns" it. In the sense you're probably thinking about, that isn't so. A constraint is an independent object—you can even point an @IBOutlet at it. Except for size constraints, they link to two views; neither view is privileged, neither is an owner. That you can get at a constraint through one of its views is a convenience.

However, each constraint *is* owned by a view. A constraint between two views is held by their first common container.

Once a constraint is selected, you can delete it or use the Attributes (fourth) inspector to edit it.

> **Note**
>
> The **Editor →Canvas** menu contains a number of options for what information Interface Builder will show, particularly as relates to constraints. What interests us now are **Show Bounds/Layout Rectangles**, which frame views according to either the .frame property of the UIViews, or, what may be different, the bounds that Auto Layout uses to measure spacing and alignment. Also, there are options that expose constraint relationships—some essential, and some useful as debugging aids.

One thing to notice: When you ask Interface Builder to add missing constraints, it can only guess at your intentions, but the guesses aren't too bad. One thing is particularly good: Most of the constraints cascade. Usually, the most important thing about the layout of a view is not its absolute location, but how it lines up with another.

Consider a partial calendar view that consists of a row of day-of-week labels, and below it a few rows of buttons representing the days. You don't care about the x-and-y location of a day-of-month button; you only want it to be centered on its day-of-week label, and below the label by a multiple of the height of a row.

A good Auto Layout network gives absolute locations to as few views as possible. The strategy for the calendar view would be to provide an absolute location for *one* day-of-week label—the first, last, or middle day—and let relative (centering, spacing) constraints do the rest. If you move that one label, the rest of the layout takes care of itself.

Factoring Layout into Subviews

In Chapter 11, "Building a New View," I had you lay out each and every label in the billboard. For the stats column on the left, that meant a subnetwork of size, spacing, and alignment specifications that was very fragile and very confusing. For five pairs of labels, identical but for the text they contain, that makes no sense. In this section, we're going to factor that complexity out by defining a custom view that wraps both the name and the value of the integer statistics. On the way, I'll show you how to create custom views that you can configure directly in Interface Builder.

What should such a `UIView` subclass—call it `StatView`—look like? Nothing exciting: Just a rectangle with two text areas, one for the name, one for the value. See Figure 12.2.

The process of laying out the name and total will be up to a new `UIView` subclass, `StatView`, to be defined in its own source file `StatView.swift`. Don't create the file yet. A `StatView` may be simple, but some things have to be tweaked before they look right. How does it lay out its contents? (It's going to be a single view object, so it can't use Auto Layout.) What fonts look good? How does it determine its "fitting" size (minimal needed to fully present its content)? Events like layout generate a cascade of callbacks into a view—how do you sort out which callback should trigger a `StatView`'s internal layout?

The Playground

One of the blessings of Swift is that it is complete enough that it can be executed interactively (or nearly so) in a Run-Edit-Print Loop (REPL): You enter your code, the REPL interprets it, and you see the results. There is a command-line REPL (type **swift**, or **xcrun swift** in Mavericks), but Xcode 6 includes a visual edit-and-display environment, the *playground*, that makes it easy to develop even moderately complex software, even if it produces graphical output—such as the contents of a view.

That's the skeleton. Where do we put it?

Select **File → New → File...** (⌘ **N**). In the template chooser that drops down, select iOS → Source → Playground, then go through the usual steps to save the new file and associate it with your project. You shouldn't place it in any target.

> **Warning**
>
> iOS and OS X playgrounds are different environments, depending on different frameworks. If your playground doesn't behave as you expect, look to the top of the file and see whether the first `import` is for Cocoa or UIKit.

The only executable line in the new playground will be an assignment to a `String` variable (Swift knows it's a `String` because its initial value is one): `var str = "Hello, playground"`. There is a gray column on the right side of the editor pane, containing one line, next to the assignment statement: `"Hello, playground"`.

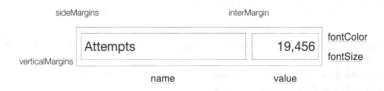

Figure 12.2   A wireframe for a simple view that displays a label and an integer. `StatView` will have inspectable properties for the label, the value, and the color and size of its text.

Let's start with a simple example: Extracting a square root by Newton's Method. Replace the contents of the playground with this:

```
import UIKit

func newton_sqrt(square:  Double,
                 epsilon: Double = 0.001)
     -> Double
{
    func close_enough(one: Double,
                      two: Double)
        -> Bool {
        println("close_enough(\(one), " +
            "\(two), \(epsilon))")

        let   diff = abs(one - two),
              denom = max(abs(one), abs(two))
        if denom == 0 { return true }
        return (diff / denom) <= epsilon
    }

    var lag = square
    var guess = square / 2.0

    while !close_enough(guess, lag) {
        lag = guess
        guess -= (guess * guess - square) / (2.0 * guess)
    }

    return guess
}

// newton_sqrt(200, epsilon: 0.0001)
```

Xcode colors and error-checks playground code just as it would in any other editor. So far, nothing impressive: It just sits there.

Now un-comment the call to newton_sqrt. The gray column comes alive as the function executes: The inital assignments to guess and lag are tagged with 100.0 and 200.0, respectively; loop contents get counts: (8 times).

> **Note**
>
> A converging algorithm like this depends on getting the terminal condition right; you're likelier than not to get it wrong on the first try and find yourself in an infinite loop. If that happens, press ⌘ **period** to stop the loop. You will have a few seconds to edit the code to hard-code a break into the loop.

What about that `println()` call in the embedded `close_enough` function? You don't want to know that it printed something eight times, you want to see what was printed.

Open the Assistant editor (the paired-ring item in the toolbar). If the root of its jump bar isn't set to **Timeline**, switch it over. The timeline includes a white box, **Console Output**, showing the output.

That's not all. The heart of `newton_sqrt` is the last computation in the loop:

```
guess -= (guess * guess - square) / (2.0 * guess)
```

If you hover the mouse pointer over the gray margin of the playground, you'll see two symbols appear, a QuickLook eye and a bubble. In a simple case like this, the QuickLook popover won't tell you anything you didn't see in the margin, but for more complex data types, QuickLook will show you array contents, `struct` members, and so on.

Click the bubble on that line. This is new: Another box appears in the timeline, this time containing a line chart showing the value computed on that line at each iteration. That's going to be useful. See Figure 12.3.

StatView

Now we're ready to clear out this playground and attack `StatView`. There are obvious properties we'd like to see—they're the API it shows its clients:

- A `String` for the name of the statistic
- An `Int` for the value

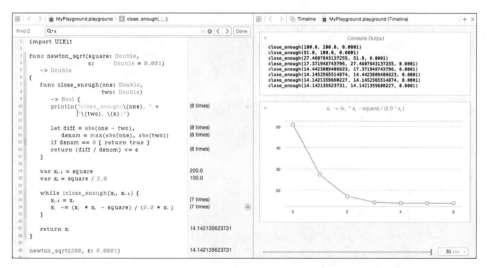

Figure 12.3   Playgrounds allow you to write entire classes, monitor their execution, and refine them in real time. The Timeline assistant displays compiler errors, console output, and expression results over time. Swift syntax gives Unicode characters first-class treatment, so some variables can have "real" mathematical names.

- A font size
- A font color

That gets us a start on the class:

```
import UIKit
import QuartzCore

internal let defaultFontSize:Double = 17.0
internal let verticalMargins:CGFloat = 2.0
internal let sideMargins:CGFloat = 2.0
internal let interMargin:CGFloat = 4.0

@IBDesignable
public
class StatView: UIView {
    /// Set the label string to be displayed
    /// at the left side of the view
    @IBInspectable public
    var name: String = "" {
        didSet {
            nameLayer.string = name
            setNeedsLayout()
        }
    }


    /// Set the integer value to be displayed
    /// at the right side of the view
    @IBInspectable public
    var value: Int = 0 {
        didSet {
            statLayer.string = "\(value)"
            setNeedsLayout()
        }
    }


    /// Set the size of the font to be used
    @IBInspectable public
    var fontSize: Double = defaultFontSize {
        didSet {
            textFont = UIFont.systemFontOfSize(
                            CGFloat(fontSize))
            setUpLayers()
            setNeedsLayout()
        }
    }
```

```
    @IBInspectable public
    var fontColor: UIColor = UIColor.blackColor() {
        didSet {
            nameLayer.foregroundColor = fontColor.CGColor
            statLayer.foregroundColor = fontColor.CGColor
        }
    }
    // More to come
}
```

`@IBDesignable` and `@IBInspectable`—what are those?

Up through Xcode 3, and in Project Builder before it, it was possible to create linkable frameworks that included the resources and code that could draw and operate a view (`NSView`). The IB plugins could provide their own attribute-inspector forms to set the unique properties of the included views.

Plugins disappeared in Xcode 4, an all but total rewrite. Experience had shown that injecting arbitrary code into privileged software is a very bad idea. Developers had to fall back on inserting blank `UIView` placeholders into their layouts, changing the classes in the Identity inspector, and waiting for the simulator to show them what the outcome was.

As of Xcode 6, Interface Builder accepts *designable* views for *Live Rendering*. IB uses the code and resources of custom views in the layout scenes, and offers controls to set their properties. You designate a view as designable by declaring it `@IBDesignable public`. You expose properties for editing in IB by declaring them `@IBInspectable public`.

`StatView` lays itself out as two Core Animation text layer objects (`CATextLayer`). Text layers have their limitations, but for this application, they offer the right mix of features and convenience. The contents and font size are all marked `@IBInspectable`.

The layout and measurement of the contents has to be flexible in response to changes in the view's frame; those come from outside as the view is placed in its superview and managed by Auto Layout. Here are the highlights—the sample code tells the whole story:

```
@IBDesignable
public
class StatView: UIView {

    // ...

    public required override init(frame: CGRect) {
        fontColor = UIColor.blackColor()
        super.init(frame: frame)
        setUpLayers()
        setNeedsLayout()
    }

    public required init(coder aDecoder: NSCoder) {
        // ...
    }
```

```
private let nameLayer = CATextLayer()

private let statLayer = CATextLayer()

private var textFont =
    UIFont.systemFontOfSize(CGFloat(defaultFontSize))

private var idealSize = CGSize(width: 100, height: 22)

private
func setUpLayers()
{
    let layerFont = UIFont.systemFontOfSize(CGFloat(fontSize))
    for subLayer in [nameLayer, statLayer] {
        subLayer.fontSize = CGFloat(fontSize)
        subLayer.font = layerFont

        subLayer.foregroundColor = fontColor.CGColor
        subLayer.backgroundColor = UIColor.clearColor().CGColor
        subLayer.contentsScale = UIScreen.mainScreen().scale
    }
    nameLayer.truncationMode = "end"

    layer.backgroundColor = UIColor.clearColor().CGColor
    layer.addSublayer(nameLayer)
    layer.addSublayer(statLayer)
}

override
public func layoutSubviews()
{
    // Minimum bounding boxes of the element
    let stringAttrs = [NSFontAttributeName: textFont]
    let statString = "\(value)"
    var statSize:CGSize = statString.sizeWithAttributes(stringAttrs)
    statSize.width += 3.0
    let nameSize: CGSize = name.sizeWithAttributes(stringAttrs)

    // Minimum bounding box of the content
    idealSize = // ...

    // Frame for the statistic in the current bounds
    let statFrame = // ...

    // Frame for the name in the current bounds
    var nameFrame = // ...
```

```
        //  Set the respective frames
        nameLayer.frame = CGRectIntegral(nameFrame)
        statLayer.frame = CGRectIntegral(statFrame)
    }

    public
    override func intrinsicContentSize() -> CGSize {
        return idealSize
    }
}
```

We saw how Playground lets you monitor the execution of simple numeric code while
you worked; how about graphical output?

Add this after the class definition:

```
var statBounds = CGRect(x: 0, y: 0, width: 200, height: 20)
let theView = StatView(frame: statBounds)
theView.name = "Interceptions"
theView.value = 123
```

Already there's something to notice: You don't have a view hierarchy to hold it, but you
can create a StatView and set its properties. The margin indicates some activity,
including some internal structure names out of the lldb debugger, but nothing
helpful—but notice that the "value" of the assignments is the StatView itself.

Click the inspection bubble on that last line, the assignment to value. What you see in
the timeline is this:

	theView.value = 123
✕	
	Interceptions 123

... a rendering of the StatView.

Drop the font size and adjust the bounds to fit:

	theView.frame = adjusted
✕	
	Interceptions 123

Keep the frame, but increase the font size so the content will no longer fit the width:

	theView.fontSize = 16.0
✕	
	Interce... 123

Looks ready for the real world. Use **File → New → File. . .** (⌘ N), create an empty Swift
file named StatView.swift (you don't need a class template), remove the import

Foundation line, and paste in the StatView definition. Make sure it's part of the Passer Rating target.

Installing StatView

Now for the experiment. Return to Main.storyboard, and remove all the integer-stat name and value labels. (You've done a version-control commit, so this isn't scary.) On my storyboard, that takes the number of constraints in the billboard from 56 to 13.

Find UIView in the Library pane of the Utilities area, and drag it into the billboard where the **Attempts** name and number had been. Adjust it to a reasonable size and change its class (Identity inspector, third tab) to StatView. While you're in that inspector, set its Document: **Label** to **Attempts**. Interface Builder knows how to identify UILabels by their content, but not StatViews.

Watch the status view in the middle of the toolbar: Xcode compiles inspectable views just for the purpose of rendering them in Interface builder. When that finishes, there's no apparent change in the view—the class as written has no default values. But the Attributes inspector has a new "Stat View" section, with **Name**, **Value**, and **Font Size** fields. The numeric fields even have steppers to nudge the values up and down. See Figure 12.4. Set these to **Attempts**, **11230** (just as a placeholder), and **14**. Adjust the location and size accordingly.

> **Note**
>
> The first time Interface Builder sees a live-editable view (including after a cleaning of the derived-products cache that contains code for IB's use), it will render the view's frame with no contents. Further, if, as with StatView, the layout relies on the preferred size of the view, IB will complain that the constraint set is ambiguous—there are no constraints defining the size of those views. The size constraints will appear only when the view classes have been compiled for display. Wait a minute or so, and you should see the error flags disappear.

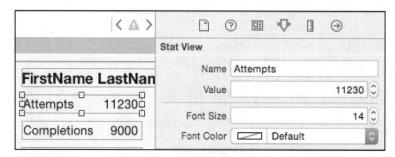

Figure 12.4 Designating StatView as @IBDesignable and its content and font size as @IBInspectable allows StatViews to appear as they would at run time, and brings the inspectable properties through to the Attributes inspector.

> **Note**
>
> Because a designable view is code that runs in Interface Builder as well as in your app, you can debug it in IB, too: Select the view and then **Editor → Debug Selected Views**.

Now we can go to town. We could repeat the drag/drop/new class/resize process, but the **Attempts** `StatView` is right for most of it, so duplicate it four times, either by **Edit →Duplicate (⌘ D)**, or simply by option-dragging from the original into a new position.

> **Note**
>
> Don't confuse the editing **Duplicate** with the **File →Duplicate...** (⇧⌘ S) command, which is for saving a copy of the active file under a new name.

Change the names of the new `StatView`s to **Completions**, **Yards**, **Touchdowns**, and **Interceptions**; you might need to adjust the widths to match that of the widest view. Hand-align the leading and trailing edges.

Do not set any constraints.

Planning Constraints

In Chapter 11, "Building a New View," I had you trust Interface Builder's guesses on the intended layout, with just a few tweaks to relieve the biggest errors. We won't do that here. To do Auto Layout right requires a detailed, thoughtful plan.

One thing to consider is that a classic iPhone screen is only 320 points on its smaller axis. The billboard we drew is 168 points tall on my storyboard (yours may vary, it doesn't matter). In portrait, accounting for the status and navigation bars, on a 4-inch screen, about half of the screen is available to the game table—enough to be useful.

Not so in landscape orientation (Figure 12.1). The billboard, plus navigation bar, plus status bar approach three-quarters of the available height. At the minimal row height of 44 points, there is room for two rows, and taller custom rows are out of the question. The billboard should have a separate, shorter layout for landscape.

Before iOS 8 and Xcode 6, this was bad news. If you wanted layouts that were not just tweaked, but qualitatively different, you had to keep separate constraint networks in code, and respond to orientation changes by swapping them. Layouts for large-screen devices such as iPad have the same problems, though iOS alleviates the problem by accommodating parallel resources for the two screen sizes. That's not practical any more.

iOS 8 responds with *size classes*. The details are sophisticated, but so far as Interface Builder is concerned, all you need to know is that each axis is either *compact* (narrow, like an iPhone in portrait orientation, or short, like an iPhone in landscape), or *regular* (like iPads in either axis). Interface Builder allows you to identify any constraint as being for compact or regular environments, or to say it is for *any* environment, compact or regular.

Three classes on two axes make nine environments; some constraints are inactive in some environments; and some are active in more than one (but not all) environments. No graphical presentation can express it fully and well. If you try to do it by eyeball and on the fly, you will be lost.

Back off and consider the goals.

The main thing is to make the billboard shorter. There's much more room on the horizontal axis, so if we can move some of the information into a third column, that's a win. Figure 12.5 shows the goal, which can be summarized as follows:

- The five-row stack of StatViews can be broken into two stacks of three and two.

- The passer rating can be shifted up close to the top of the billboard, because the passer's name is unlikely to span the width of a "regular" screen.

- Accordingly, the trailing edge of the passer's name can be pulled back to an offset from the rating label, not the trailing edge of the billboard.

- There will usually be no need to allow vertical space for the team name to span two lines.

On my layout, the billboard that had been 168 points tall in portrait becomes 107 points in landscape; enough for one-and-a-half extra table rows of standard height. Worth doing.

That's the goal. Now the strategy. The first thing to remember is that every view should have *some* kind of complete constraint set for every combination of size classes, even if the set isn't ideal for all of them. Doing this silences Interface Builder's warnings (there could be dozens) of faulty constraint sets, and ensures that if you miss something, or Apple introduces yet more screen sizes, Auto Layout won't punish you with grossly inappropriate layouts.

The plan for regular-height screens in Figure 12.5 is the most conservative; it's a good fallback for any combination of width and height you hadn't provided for explicitly. So the any-width, any-height (**wAny/hAny**) layout should hold what our plan shows as any-width, regular-height (**wAny/hRegular**).

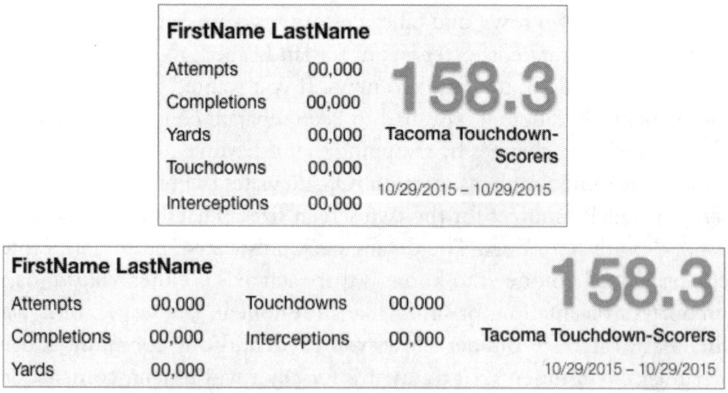

Figure 12.5   The original layout of the billboard view (top) used two columns to put as much information as possible into the restricted width of a classic iPhone screen. Having a wider screen (bottom) adds room for a middle column to hold elements that had been at the bottom of the first.

- **Any Layout (including hRegular)**
  Here, then, is the fallback layout:
  - The passer-name label is anchored to the top and left of the billboard.
  - The passer name spans the full width of the view.
  - The name and the **Attempts**, **Completions**, and **Yards** StatViews are left-aligned with each other.
  - The **Touchdowns** and **Interceptions** StatViews are left-aligned with each other.
  - The **Touchdowns** StatView is aligned with **Yards**.
  - All StatViews, and the passer-name label, have the same fixed vertical space between them.
  - All StatViews are the same width, at least wide enough for the widest content, plus a little padding. Experimenting shows this should be about 140 points minimum.
  - The rating label is anchored to the trailing edge of the billboard, and wide enough to fit its content.
  - The top of the rating label is aligned with the top of the **Attempts** StatView, and therefore clears the bottom of the name label.
  - The trailing edges of the rating, team, and date-range labels are aligned.
  - The bottom of the billboard is a fixed distance below the **Interceptions** StatView; the StatView column is the taller of the two, and should determine the height of the billboard.
  - The team name label's leading edge observes a distance of *at least* 4 points from the trailing edge of the **Yards** StatView.
  - The team name label is tall enough to accommodate two lines.
- **Compact Height (such as classic iPhone landscape)**
  The three-column-wide layout is a different story:
  - The top of the rating label lines up with the top of the passer-name label.
  - The name label ought to be the width of its content, but it's more important that it keep a fixed distance from the leading edge of the rating.
  - The top of the **Touchdowns** StatView is aligned with the top of **Attempts**.
  - The team name label's height is reduced to accommodate one line. It's important that it be wide enough to show all its content.
  - The center of the **Touchdowns** StatView is lined up with the center of the billboard. This, and changing its top to line up with **Attempts**, moves it and **Interceptions** to the middle column.
  - *However*, centering is less important than giving full width to the team name. If the name is wide, the middle column should be pushed off-center.

That's a lot, but once you've learned how to think about layout, it's not really hard, just painstaking. You're a programmer. You know the difference.

Two Line Counts, Two Labels

Forcing a two-line label to lay itself out in a single line is close to impossible. The label will force its single-line width, or truncate, or wrap, and there's no good way to guarantee it will do something that is both consistent and desirable.

The solution is to have *two* team-name labels, one for a single line, and one for two. Select the existing team-name label, and press Delete to get rid of it.

> **Note**
> You did a version-control commit before doing this, right?

We're interested in two cases:

- Short ("compact height") screens should have a one-line label, regardless of width.
- Any other screen height can afford a two-line label; in fact, needs one, because the billboard will likely be narrow enough to require a line break.

You've noticed that the bottom of the Interface Builder canvas has a bar labeled **wAny hAny**. This indicates that the layout you do will apply to any size or orientation of the device screen. The choice of labels is for specific sizes. Click on the bar; you'll see a size-class picker (Figure 12.6) that responds to mouse movements by highlighting rectangles. The left column and top row represents "compact" screens on those axes; the

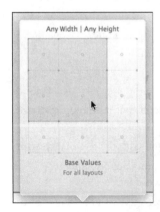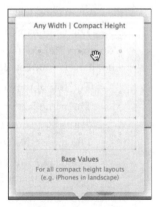

Figure 12.6   (left) By default, the Interface Builder canvas is set up for creating generic (**wAny**/**hAny**) layouts. (middle) Classic iPhones need **wCompact**/**hRegular**. (right) Interface Builder recommends that landscape orientation for classic iPhones be set up with **wAny**/**hAny**. Dots appear among the nine cells to show which configurations will be affected by the selected classes.

right and bottom "regular," and the middle column and row, "any," or don't-care dimensions. The default class, **wAny/hAny**, is right in the middle.

Select **wAny hCompact**. The size-class bar changes from white to blue to indicate that everything you do will apply only to that combination of size classes.

> **Note**
>
> Don't kid yourself with these abstract size classes. For 2015, at least, you're designing for 320-point iPhones. Click the GameListController icon (the first one) above the game-list scene, and in the Attributes inspector, select a non-Plus iPhone from the **Size** popup, and the **Orientation** corresponding to your target size class.

Drag a UILabel from the object library into the proper place for a team name, and format it as before. Set it to have one line; fill in the **Label Text** with something unreasonably long like **one-liner with place and team name**. Constrain it to a single-line height (like 20 points). See the "for both" paragraph below, for common constraints.

Look at the bottom of the label's Attributes inspector. There will be two checkboxes: The first will be simply **Installed**. If the view were to be displayed in all circumstances, this would be checked, but we don't want that; make sure it's cleared. Below it is a box labeled **wAny hC – Installed**. That *is* checked: The view will be in the billboard on any compact-height layout.

> **Note**
>
> If your ideas about layout are more intricate, click the **+** button next to the plain **Installed** button, and select any combination of size classes to add a new **Installed** switch.

Switch the canvas's view classes to **wAny/hAny**. The one-line team label will disappear (it's not installed for any but compact height). Drag in the two-line UILabel; format it the same as the other, but make it narrower, two lines tall, and set **Label Lines** to **2**. Give it the text **two-liner with place and team name**; not only will it challenge the layout, it will make the label easier to find in the document outline. Constrain this label to a two-line height (36 points). If you look at the bottom of its Attributes inspector, you'll find that it is **Installed** for **wAny hAny**, making it the default.

For both, set the trailing (right) edge to that of the rating label (158.3); that fixes their horizontal position, because the rating has a defined margin into the billboard. Set the top edge to a distance of 8 points from the rating label, which will fix its vertical position. Set the bottom edge to a distance of 8 points from the date-range level; given that the date label has a fixed margin from the bottom of the billboard when the height is compact, this completely defines the height of a short billboard.

GameListController will have to set both labels when it sets up the billboard. Control-drag from one of them into GameListController.swift, and create an *outlet collection*; I named it **teamLabels**. The outlet will be declared as an @IBOutlet for [UILabel]!, and a connection bubble will appear next to the declaration. Drag from the bubble to the other label, thus adding that label to the collection. Now, when the storyboard loads, `teamLabels` will be an array containing references to both labels. Change

```
currentTeamLabel.text = passer.currentTeam
```

to

```
for label in teamLabels {
    label.text = passer.currentTeam
}
```

I just got you through the hard part—you had to place two labels, and their constraint sets, and at least one of them is invisible at any time. The rest is tedium. Do a version-control commit *now*.

Constraints for Real

As for the constraints on the permanent views, the plan forces us to start from scratch. I repeat: If you start from a complete set of constraints and try to adapt them to other size classes by cut-and-try, you will get yourself into serious trouble.

Focus Interface Builder on the game-list scene, open the document outline at the left side of the canvas, and expand every view within the billboard view. The views that have constraints will have blue subcategories that contain them. Select everything in those blue folders (except for the constraints on the team-name labels) and press Delete to remove them.

Delete only the constraints under the billboard view *itself*, *not* the ones at the top level of the scene. They hold the billboard and table views in place, and there's no need to risk losing track of them if we accidentally update the view frames.

Try not to hit anything in the **Resolve Auto Layout Issues** menu, whether in the **Editor** menu or the ⊦△⊣ widget in the canvas. If you trigger a layout before you're ready for it, views *will* fly beyond the bounds of their containers, and one or both dimensions will go to zero.

Default (Any/Any)

Start with the default—**wAny hAny**. Run through the "Any Layout" checklist above. You can do most of these with the ⊦□⊣ popover (or the **Editor** → **Pin** submenu, depending on which makes more sense to you). Here are some more hints:

- Don't set any absolute constraints—point insets, sizes or spacing—you don't have to. If you want a column of `StatViews` down the left edge of the billboard, set the leading edge of the passer-name label to a fixed distance (8 points) from the billboard's leading edge; then align all the `StatViews` to that. Change the indent of the name label, and all the `StatView` go with it.

- Pay close attention to the division between the **hAny** and **hCompact** layouts. The first three `StatViews` (Attempts, Completions, Yards) line up with each other; and the last two (Touchdowns, Interceptions) line up. How the two groups align with each other depends on whether the height class is Compact.

- You can set the `StatViews` to have equal widths by command-clicking on each and selecting **Editor → Pin → Widths Equally**. Do the same for **Heights Equally**.

- You can rely on the rating label to be wide enough, because text containers "know" the minimum width they need to display their content. By default, Interface Builder sets this constraint (**Content Compression Resistance**) to have a priority of 750—important, but if the layout doesn't work with the natural width, this will be sacrificed to fulfill constraints with higher priority.

Any Height (not Compact)

If you're careful, and you're *certain* that you've competed the full constraint set for a view in the currently selected size class, you can have Interface Builder trigger those constraints; this would be useful when you pin the name label to the right edge of the billboard and want to see whether it lays out as expected. Select that view (only) and then **Editor → Resolve Auto Layout Issues → (Selected Views) Update Frames** (⌥⌘ =, or the equivalent in the ⊦△⊦ popover). If it doesn't work out, you can always undo.

The critical thing to remember is that in this two-column layout, all five `StatViews` line up, but you don't do that directly. You've set the defaults that the **Attempts/Completions/Yards** group aligns at the leading edges, and the **Touchdowns/Interceptions** group aligns at their leading edges. To get the effect of the whole column lining up, just align the leading edges of **Touchdowns** and **Attempts**; the default alignments will take care of the rest.

Landscape (wAny/hCompact)

Switch to **wAny/hCompact**, and follow the checklist. The main difference is that **Touchdowns** and **Interceptions** move to the center column. Break the leading-edge alignment between **Touchdowns** and **Attempts**, and add top-edge alignment to those two `StatViews`. That, and center-aligning **Touchdowns** in the billboard, completely specify the layout of the center column.

Chasing Issues

All along, you've been selecting individual views and triggering **Selected Views: Update Frames** (⌥⌘=) in either **Editor → Resolve Auto Layout Issues** or the ⊦△⊦ popup. When you're sure of your placements for the entire view, select the view-controller placeholder icon (rightmost in the scene's upper bar) and choose **All Views in Game-ListController: Update Frames**. Undo and repair as needed.

When things are mostly under control, take note of the red or yellow badge next to the controller's name in the document outline. Click it; a list of Auto Layout issues appear. The red badges show cardinal sins: The constraints on the horizontal or vertical placement of a view are either insufficient or contradictory. Click one of these; the problem view will be highlighted.

In the case of insufficient constraints, you will be given a moderately informative tooltip describing the problem. In the case of conflicting constraints, a popover will appear showing them, and you can check off the ones you can sacrifice.

The yellow badges note views that are merely misplaced. If you highlight such a view, you'll see a dotted outline where Interface Builder thinks the view *should* go if its constraints were fired. Clicking the badge on a warning affords a popover giving you the choice of moving the view to conform to the constraints; changing the constraints to conform to the view; or allowing Interface Builder to replace the view's constraint set with its best guess of what the intended placement should be. You'll have the option of applying your chosen solution to all the views in the container.

A Tweak

It *almost* works (Figure 12.7, top). On an iPhone 5 in landscape orientation, the unreasonably long one-line team name runs into the middle column, and is forced to truncate itself. This is a shame, because this may be the only place to see the full name of the team, and while it's nice to have the middle column centered, there is empty space to its left.

What's happening is that new constraints come in with the highest priority—1,000. Auto Layout *must* enforce those constraints. As for the label (and some other views, mostly text containers), it "knows" what width it has to be to display its contents in full. This is the **Content Compression Resistance Priority (Horizontal)** constraint. By default, this has a priority of 750. The centering of the **Touchdowns** and **Interceptions**

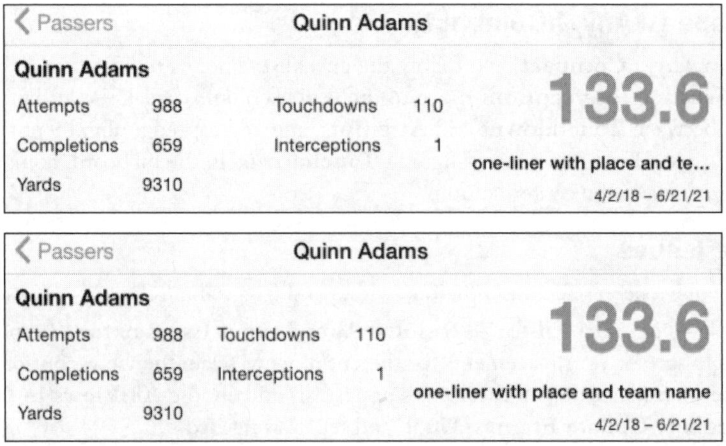

Figure 12.7   (top) By default, the centering of the middle column trumps the "desire" of the team-name label to display its full contents. (bottom) Changing the priority of the centering constraint to below the full-contents constraint allows the team-name label to push the middle column off-center if necessary.

`StatViews` trumps the preferred width of the team name label, which then has to truncate its contents.

Find the centering constraint—it's in the Size inspector for the **Touchdowns** `StatView`, where you can click **Edit**; or you can find it in the document outline by typing **Touch** in the search field, and double-click it. Either way, you'll be able to edit the priority of the constraint. All you need is for centering to be lower than 750; 749 will do.

Now when you run Passer Rating, the long contents of the team-name label push the **Touchdowns** column off center if necessary. See Figure 12.7, bottom.

Summary

That was a lot of work. You can understand why many developers avoided Auto Layout as long as they could, especially if they walked away from Xcode 4's. . . unsatisfactory support for it. There are now four iPhone formats in two orientations each. "As long as possible" has come to an end. Apple had been hinting, then warning, of this for more than two years before the introduction of the iPhone 6.

Auto Layout *can* be very complex, but with a few habits, it can be brought down to mostly only tedious:

- Remember the One Rule: Every view, for both axes, must have constraints that specify the locations of its edges, completely and without inconsistency. Look at everything through that lens.

- Plan! Make a sketch. Study it. Decide what you want to accomplish, and the minimal set of constraints you need to do it. If you can clearly state what you want, you're not far from a specification.

- Make as few absolute constraints—spacing, size, alignment offsets—as you can. If you have a grid, identify the one element you can anchor to an absolute position and size, and make all the other members of the group aligned, or equal-sized, or centered. That way, changing just the anchored views will bring the rest of the layout along for free.

- Interface Builder's "suggested" constraints aren't that bad for a start—they even observe the anchor-and-align rule when possible. If your requirements are simple, you may be able to get by with just a tweak from the suggested set; if nothing else, the suggestions may be useful to keep your views from flying away or collapsing as you bring in your planned constraints.

- **Most important**, do not add constraints off the top of your head. Without a plan, you will inevitably violate the One Rule, and from there you'll thrash to the point where a working layout system will be impossible.

## 13

Adding Table Cells

Y ou've filled the game-list view with everything but...a list of games. In this chapter, you'll hook up the game table, produce a custom view for the table cells, and pick up some techniques along the way.

The Game Table

The master-detail project template provided the root-controller class that became `PasserListController`. That was a subclass of `UITableViewController`. It was preconnected to its table, and was provided with an `NSFetchedResultsController` that needed little modification to deliver `Passers` to the table.

`GameListController` is not a table-view controller; it's just a `UIViewController` for a view that happens to include a table. Table-view controllers are already connected to their tables; you'll have to do the connecting yourself.

The first thing to do is to modify the declaration of `GameListController` to promise that it will implement the methods the table needs to display cells and respond to events:

```
class GameListController: UIViewController,
                 UITableViewDataSource,
                 UITableViewDelegate
```

Outlets in the Table View

You have to connect the table view to the controller. That's been done at the controller's end—you set the `tableView` property when you built the view in Interface Builder. But the table view has to know where it can get its data (its `dataSource` property) and what will handle its events (the `delegate` property). Return to the storyboard, focus on the Game List Controller scene, and control-drag connections from the table to the yellow controller icon in the bar below the scene. Select `dataSource` from the heads-up menu that will appear; repeat the process for `delegate`.

> **Note**
>
> Earlier, you created and linked @IBOutlets in GameListController from views in its scene; this time you're linking a view outlet to the controller.

> **Warning**
>
> It's common for UIKit objects to rely on delegates and data sources. Unless they are connected, they do nothing. Despite their importance, Interface Builder doesn't make it obvious that you should connect them. Forgetting to do so is one of the most common causes of bugs, no matter how experienced you are.

Adding Required Protocol Methods

Once the parser catches up to the change, the activity view in the middle of the toolbar will flag an error. This is Swift calling out your failure to implement the data-source methods you promised.

In the Issues (fourth) navigator, the red-badged error message is annotated, "…/GameListController.swift:12:1: Type 'GameListController' does not conform to protocol 'UITableViewDataSource'." Open the disclosure triangle, and you will find the specific methods you're missing: tableView(_, numberOfRowsInSection:) in one case, tableView(_, cellForRowAtIndexPath:) in the other.

Go to the bottom of the declaration of class GameListController, and add this function:

```
// MARK: - UITableViewDataSource

func tableView(tableView: UITableView,
            numberOfRowsInSection section: Int)
    -> Int {
    if let passer = detailItem {
        return passer.gameArray.count
    }
    else { return 0 }
}
```

> **Note**
>
> The // MARK: directive puts the text in the rest of the line into the function popup in the last segment of the jump bar. If you prefix it with a hyphen, the label will be preceded by a dividing line.

It would be nice if Xcode could help with autocompletion—it knows about the UITableViewDataSource API. You can start typing **tableView(**, but then you get to the end of the main function name; autocompletion puts you at the first parameter name, and there's no way to get to the rest of the signature from the keyboard. The best you can do is to scroll through the completion list to find the declaration you need. We can hope this will be fixed by the time you read this.

```
enum CellType: String {
    case Basic = "Basic Game Cell"
    case Tall = "Tall Game Cell"
    case Fancy = "Fancy Game Cell"
}

let gameCellType = CellType.Basic

func tableView(tableView: UITableView,
               cellForRowAtIndexPath indexPath: NSIndexPath)
    -> UITableViewCell {
    // ...

    let cell = tableView.dequeueReusableCellWithIdentifier(
                    gameCellType.rawValue)
                    as! UITableViewCell
    let passer = self.detailItem!
    let game = arrangedGames![indexPath.row]

    switch gameCellType {
    case .Basic:
        let playedStr =
            shortDateFormatter.stringFromDate(game.whenPlayed!)
        let ratingStr =
            ratingFormatter.stringFromNumber(game.passerRating)!
        let content =
            "vs \(game.theirTeam) \(playedStr) - \(ratingStr)"
        cell.textLabel?.text = content

    case .Tall:
        // ...

    case .Fancy:
        // ...
    }

    return cell
}
```

> **Note**
>
> I'll lead you through three variants on the layout of the game cell in this chapter. The variant in use is selected by the `gameCellType` instance variable, which is either `.Basic`, `.Tall`, or `.Fancy`. `tableView(_, cellForRowAtIndexPath:)` switches among them to initialize each cell type as needed. Later, when I get to the other variants, I'll show only the new code (mostly whatever goes in the `case` clauses); the rest will stay the same. The table in `Main.storyboard` contains a prototype for each variant.

Adding Model-to-View Support

arrangedGames is a property of GameListController that caches the games relationship in the Passer being displayed.

The Passer.gameArray property is an array of Games, derived from the games relationship from Passer, and sorted by date into an array. Whenever a new passer is assigned to detailItem, the cached game list is dropped; if the list is wanted later, arrangedGames fetches it.

```
var detailItem: Passer? {
  didSet {
    // Drop the game cache
    _arrangedGames = nil

    // Update the billboard.
    if billboard != nil {
      self.configureView()
    }
    // Update the table
    if tableView != nil {
      tableView!.reloadData()
    }
  }
}

// ...

// MARK: - Game cache

var arrangedGames: [Game]? {
  if let passer = detailItem {
    if _arrangedGames == nil {
      //  The game array isn't known, and there's
      //  a Passer to supply one. Get the array
      //  and remember it.
      let gameSet = passer.games as NSSet
      let dateSort = NSSortDescriptor(key: "whenPlayed",
                        ascending: true)
      _arrangedGames =
        gameSet.sortedArrayUsingDescriptors([dateSort])
        as? [Game]
    }
  }
  return _arrangedGames
}
// Games cache; reload if nil
var _arrangedGames: [Game]? = nil
```

A Prototype Cell

You've noticed that the placeholder for `UITableView` is labeled "Table View / Prototype Content." Prototype cells allow you to create and lay out custom cells in the table itself; when UIKit calls your `tableView(_, cellForRowAtIndexPath:)` method, you ask the table to instantiate a cell.

> **Note**
>
> If a table in a stand-alone view has a custom cell, you have to create the cell yourself, loading a separate NIB for just that cell.

Search the Object library (at the bottom of the Utility area, third tab) for **cell** to find "Table View Cell," and drag it into the table, where it becomes a prototype instance of `UITableViewCell`. For the first pass at the game table, we're sticking to a simple, single-string format: Use the **Style** popup in the Attributes inspector, and select **Basic**.

The `tableView(_, cellForRowAtIndexPath:)` method we have for the `.Basic` case asks the table view for a cell with the identifier "Basic Game Cell". Enter that in the **Identifier** field.

We don't yet have an editor for game instances, but let's be prepared: Select **Detail** from the **Accessory** popup to put a circled-i button in the cell, which will eventually lead to the editor. The finished cell should look like Figure 13.1.

The Game Table: First Run

Now go back to your code-editing view, because you're about to run the app.

Run it, and select a passer. So far, so good. The table fills with cells for each game the passer played. The detail button is there as expected. The strings overrun the width of the cells, but it's just a prototype to see whether the table works at all (Figure 13.2).

Have a look at the Debug navigator. The application isn't halted, so the area for the stack trace is empty, but at the top of the navigator you'll find four bar graphs, labeled CPU, Memory, Disk, and Network (Figure 13.3).

Xcode comes with Instruments, a sophisticated tool for capturing event-by-event performance data and displaying it on a time scale. It's a powerful debugging tool, but it requires a special build, and then some setup. (Hold the mouse button down on the toolbar's **Run** button to see that there is a **Profile** action that runs your app under Instruments.)

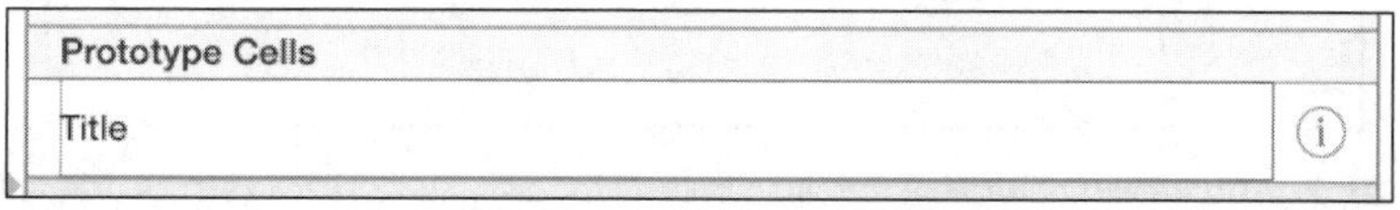

Figure 13.1   The prototype for the simple "starter" cell for display in the game table.

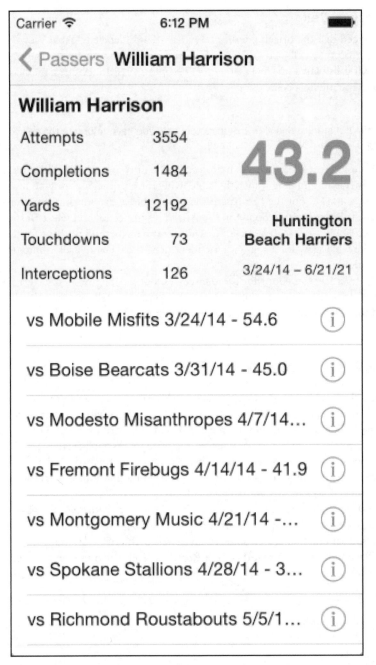

Figure 13.2   The new mechanism for filling in cells for a `Passer` record works on the first try.

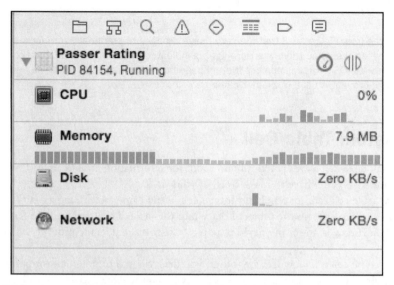

Figure 13.3   Bar graphs at the top of the Debug navigator show trends in the processor, memory, storage, and network usage of your application. Clicking the round gauge button above the graphs toggles their presence in the navigator.

> **Note**
>
> You'll learn more about Instruments in Chapters 16, "Measurement and Analysis," and 26, "Instruments."

For most developers, the incentives work out that profiling with Instruments is a special occasion—special enough that some developers never run it at all until their applications get into obvious performance trouble. That kind of trouble is the effect of performance bugs that accumulated, unobserved, over the whole development process.

There's another reason performance bugs don't become obvious: The iOS Simulator is not an emulator. It is an OS X application that floats on top of hardware that is ten times as fast as an actual device, and, with paged memory, has practically unlimited memory, not a hard gigabyte. Bugs that would be serious on an actual device may not be noticeable in the Simulator.

The debug-time graphs provide a continuous reminder of performance issues. They aren't high-precision, but you can see trends. Even if your app doesn't run into visible trouble on a Mac, the absolute numbers in the graphs will warn you when you approach the actual limits of a device.

In this case, the only appreciable hit on the CPU comes when you scroll the game table, as the app fetches new data and fills in recycled cells for display. It's not a big hit, and you don't see any persistent demand. The same goes for memory: Usage escalates as the data is loaded, and a little more when you first scroll the list and cause OS caches to fill, but in my case, it settled in around 22 MiB. In a 1-GiB machine, that's nothing. No worries so far.

> **Note**
>
> You'll see from Figure 13.3 that memory usage dropped to practically zero for a while, to return when the game table was scrolled (as indicated by the burst in CPU usage). Evidently the OS X virtual-memory system paged the game data out while the app was idle, and brought it back in when it came back into use.

A Custom Table Cell

The default table cell leaves practically no room for information about games. If you want to see your data, you'll have to make a cell of your own.

A new table cell calls for a new prototype cell in the game table. Drag a new `UITableViewCell` from the Object library into the table. This time we'll go far beyond UIKit's standard cells, so set the **Style** popup to **Custom**, and its identifier to `Tall Game Cell`.

A prototype cell is a view like any other; you drag views into it and customize them as you need. It's a standard-size table-view cell, as wide as the table and 44 points high (the recommended minimum size of a tappable object). That's not tall enough to accommodate what we want to do. We need a custom cell. Drag the top or bottom edge of the cell (or use the Size [fifth] inspector) to make it taller; my experiment left me with a cell 85 points high.

Now you go through much the same drudgery as for the passer-detail view in Chapter 11. Remember to set the **Accessory** view to **Detail**:

- A large label for the game rating. I used `158.3` (the maximum rating), System Bold, 30 points, blue, left justified. Put it in the upper-left corner. The initial size of the label is too small to accommodate the content, but dragging a resizing handle will make it snap to a large-enough size. Use the ⊢□⊣ popover to anchor it 8 points from top and left, and lock in the height and width.

  > **Note**
  >
  > For the leading and trailing edge spacing, the ⊢□⊣ popover will offer to **Constrain to margins**, which are a standard inset from the sides of a superview. In this case, it's easiest to uncheck the option.

- At the top right, a label for the teams, scores, and the date of the match. For size, fill it with

  ```
  Tacoma Touchdown-Scorers 88
  Tacoma Touchdown-Scorers 88
  12/12/12
  ```

  Use the **Lines** stepper/field to make the field accommodate three lines; the easiest way to enter multi-line text is to use the **Text** field and use Option-Return for line breaks. Make it System Italic, 10 points, right justified. Use ⊢□⊣ to lock in the size, and pin it to top 8 points, left 8 points.

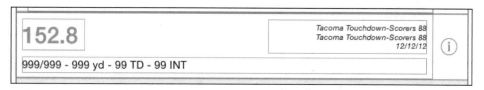

Figure 13.4   The finished layout of the game-list cell.

- Across the bottom, a label in System 14 points, left justified. Size it with **999/999 - 999 yd - 99 TD - 99 INT**; as before, use ├□┤ to lock it down.

When you're done, you should have something like Figure 13.4.

Note

I also added Auto Layout constraints to the labels, but let's not revisit that process.

What about connecting the cell to `GameListController`? For the passer-detail view, you used @`IBOutlets` for the connections, but the controller manages only one of those views at a time. For the game cell, it will be reloading the prototype cell over and over again. There can't be a single outlet for the cell or its labels. What the controller *will* have at any moment is a pointer to the cell it is working on right then. It can pull pointers to the labels from that.

This is done by setting the *tags* of the labels. Every `UIView`—cells and labels included—can have an integer associated with it. You can retrieve the view from its hierarchy if its tag is unique by sending `viewWithTag()` to any ancestor view with the subview's tag.

By default, the tag is **0**. Use the Attributes inspector to set the rating label's tag to **1**, the scoring label to **2**, and the statistics label to 3. You'll find the **Tag** field low in the inspector, in the "View" section.

Finally, with the cell selected, expose the Size inspector. Take note of the height (85 points in my case). `UITableView` normally doesn't measure the rows it presents; there's one height for all of them, and by default it's 44 points. Select the game table in the `GameListController` scene. Tables put a "Table View Size" section at the top of the Size inspector. Set **Row Height** to the height of your cell (85). The basic cell will also grow to 85 points, but that doesn't matter anymore.

Save all your work, and check it in.

Now modify `tableView(_, cellForRowAtIndexPath:)` in `GameList-Controller.swift` to load the compiled `GameTableCell` NIB whenever it needs a fresh cell. The method can then find the labels, and format the game data into each.

```
let gameCellType = CellType.Tall

enum TallCellTag: Int {
    case RatingLabel = 1
    case ScoreLabel = 2
```

```
    case StatsLabel = 3
    // More on this later:
    case ReactionImage = 4
}

func tableView(tableView: UITableView,
            cellForRowAtIndexPath indexPath: NSIndexPath)
    -> UITableViewCell {
    // Internal function to translate between the label enum
    // and the actual UILabel for which it stands.
    func labelWithTag(tag: TallCellTag) -> UILabel
        { return cell.viewWithTag(tag.rawValue) as! UILabel! }

    // ...
    switch gameCellType {
    case .Basic:
        // ...

    case .Tall:
        labelWithTag(.RatingLabel).text =
            ratingFormatter.stringFromNumber(game.passerRating)!

        labelWithTag(.ScoreLabel).text =
            "\(game.ourTeam) \(game.ourScore!)\n" +
            "\(game.theirTeam) \(game.theirScore!)\n" +
            shortDateFormatter.stringFromDate(game.whenPlayed!)

        labelWithTag(.StatsLabel).text =
            "\(game.completions!)/\(game.attempts!) - " +
            "\(game.yards!) yd - \(game.touchdowns!) TD - " +
            "\(game.interceptions!) INT"

    case .Fancy:
        // ...
    }

    return cell
}
```

Run Passer Rating one more time. When you tap a passer, his full record appears, including the complete statistics on every game. The display portions of the app behave as specified, as you can see in Figure 13.5.

> **Note**
>
> The tagged-label approach worked well for this simple case. However, if your needs were more complex—more intricate data, or even custom drawing—tagged subviews won't be enough. You'd need to create a new subclass of UITableViewCell. Such a subclass

Figure 13.5   The text-based custom cell displays complete game-by-game information in a readable form.

would have outlets of its own for its labels and would expose a property that would accept a `Game` object as its represented object. Setting the `Game` would cause the custom cell class to fill its labels from it. `tableView(_, cellForRowAtIndexPath:)` could simply set the game property and not worry about the details of the cell view.

Adding Some Graphics

I'm never satisfied. Football is an emotional sport, its fans alternating jubilation with despair. The game list should reflect this. There should be a graphic in each row expressing how the passer's performance feels.

A Cell with an Image in It

This calls for yet another custom cell. Fortunately, all the contents of the previous cell can carry over with little change. Select the custom game cell in Interface Builder, and duplicate it (by **Edit → Duplicate**, ⌘D—don't choose **Duplicate. . .** in the **File** menu).

1. In the Attributes inspector, change the new cell's **Identifier** to `Fancy Game Cell`.
2. Resize the cell to a height of 96 points. This should also change the table's general row height.
3. Change the statistical-summary label to two lines, and use Option-Return to put a line break between "yd" and the number of "TD"s.
4. Search the Object library for `Image`, which will show you an image view (`UIImageView`). Drag it in, put it into the lower-left corner of the cell, and resize it to 30 × 30 points.
5. Constrain its bottom edge to 8 points above the bottom of the cell, set its leading edge to align with that of the rating label, and fix its height and width to 30.
6. Give the image view a tag of **4**.

The result should be like Figure 13.6.

Hooking the Image View to the Images

You have to finish `tableView(_, cellForRowAtIndexPath:)` (excerpts):

```
let gameCellType = CellType.Fancy

// ...

func tableView(tableView: UITableView,
        cellForRowAtIndexPath indexPath: NSIndexPath)
  -> UITableViewCell {
// func labelWithTag(), cell, passer, game...

  switch gameCellType {
  case .Basic:
    // ...

  case .Tall:
    // ...
```

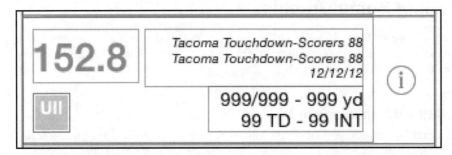

Figure 13.6   The last iteration of the game cell adds a `UIImageView` to the lower-left corner.

```
case .Fancy:
  labelWithTag(.RatingLabel).text =
    ratingFormatter.stringFromNumber(game.passerRating)!

  labelWithTag(.ScoreLabel).text =
    "\(game.ourTeam) \(game.ourScore!)\n" +
    "\(game.theirTeam) \(game.theirScore!)\n" +
    shortDateFormatter.stringFromDate(game.whenPlayed!)

  labelWithTag(.StatsLabel).text =
    "\(game.completions!)/\(game.attempts!) - " +
    "\(game.yards!) yd\n\(game.touchdowns!) TD - " +
    "\(game.interceptions!) INT"

  let reactionView = cell.viewWithTag(TallCellTag.ReactionImage
                                      .rawValue)
             as! UIImageView
  // Fetch the reaction image for the rating
  let reactionImage = (game.passerRating < 122.0) ?
           UIImage(named: "Despondent"):
           UIImage(named: "Elated")
  // Set the image.
  reactionView.image = reactionImage;
}

return cell
}
```

The Assets Catalog

That leaves the images themselves. I drew up a couple of badge images (PNG, with transparency) and produced single-resolution and double-resolution (60 × 60 pixels) versions (find these in the `icons` and `images` folder in the sample code):

- `Despondent.png` – 30 × 30 pixels
- `Despondent@2x.png` – 60 × 60 pixels
- `Elated.png` – 30 × 30 pixels
- `Elated@2x.png` – 60 × 60 pixels

Note

If you can, draw up at least your simple images in a vector-drawing application, and let it take care of scaling the images for single- and multiple-resolution sizes.

Image Sets

Before Xcode 5, if you had images to embed in your application, you simply dragged them into the Project navigator and did the usual negotiation about whether it should be copied, its target memberships, and its place in the group hierarchy. Keeping a rigorous group hierarchy, giving each functional group its own folder in the navigator so you know what images are being used for each purpose, would keep the image zoo under control.

Few humans do such things. I've seen projects that evolved through adding, replacing, and discarding images to the point where dozens of the .pngs in the project navigator were orphans. Clearing out the deadwood is nearly impossible, because there's no way to be certain which are still in use.

That's gone. You no longer have to keep references to image files in the Project navigator. When you create a new iOS application target, the template includes an *asset catalog*, a container with the .xcassets extension. Its entry in the Project navigator looks like a folder, but it doesn't open in the navigator. Instead, it presents an editor for the catalog—select Images.xcassets.

An asset catalog contains *image sets*, each of which contains representations of what is notionally a single image, adapted for the resolutions and devices on which they will be displayed. Images in image sets can be retrieved by the name of the set; UIKit will do the work of selecting the suitable representation without your having to specify it.

The sets keep the many representations out of the Project navigator, and group them by function. When you have to replace an image, there's only one place you have to go, and the catalog editor will take care of cleaning up the obsolete representations.

By default, the catalog includes an AppIcon set for the application's icon. If you intend your app to run on iOS 7 or earlier, you should provide a LaunchImage set for the static image that iOS would display while your app is launching.

> **Note**
>
> An OS X application can keep its icon set in an asset catalog, as well.

The editor is divided into a "Set list," a source list of image sets on the left side, and the "Set viewer," the main view. Select a set from the source list, and the Set viewer will show all the representations in that set. The Utilities area adds an Attributes inspector (third tab) for each image and image set.

Adding Images to the Assets Catalog

Drag the six image files into the Set list of the assets catalog. That's it. Xcode will infer the set grouping and resolutions from the names and the actual sizes of the images (Figure 13.7).

The new code for tableView(_, cellForRowAtIndexPath:) already uses UIImage(named:) to retrieve images by name from the asset catalog. Run Passer Rating again; the build process compiles the catalog into a single binary file that UIKit can efficiently use, and the app launches. (You can still use asset catalogs in projects targeted for iOS versions earlier than 6. For compatibility, catalogs are not compiled; their contents are placed separately in the application's bundle.)

Figure 13.7   Dragging image files at single-, double-, and treble-resolution into the Set list of an assets catalog sorts them by name into image sets and displays each resolution of each set. Setting **Render As Template Image** prepares the images for tinting when UIKit displays them.

> **Note**
>
> The first time Xcode 6 opens an older project, it adds an asset-catalog file. This is harmless—you don't have to use it—but the **General** tab of the Target editor will help you migrate your icons and launch images into the catalog. That's harmless, too, and a very good idea.

Select a passer and scroll through the game list. Games in which the passer earned a rating of 122 or above are greeted with elation; lesser performances, with despondency (Figure 13.8).

> **Note**
>
> Class `UIImage` provides an extremely useful tool for handling resizable images. Consider a button for an OS X dialog. The button's shape and background are provided by a template image. The template is no more than the left end cap (with its rounded corners), a one-pixel column demonstrating how to color the body of the button, and the right end cap. Applying `-[UIImage resizableImageWithCapInsets:]` to the template yields a special `UIImage` that, when rendered in a wider rectangle, fills the space by preserving the proportions of the end caps, and stretching that single pixel across the width between them. The Image Set editor lets you slice a managed image into three or nine segments. Expose the feature with **Editor →Show Slicing**. There isn't room in this book for a full discussion, but it's well worth your time to look into it.

Icons and Launch Displays

While we're here, it's time to fill in the icons and—if you need them for iOS 7 or earlier—launch images. In the asset catalog, select the AppIcon image set. If you've dealt with icons for iOS applications before, what you see may come as a pleasant surprise: the set carries wells for double- and treble-resolution images for iPhone Spotlight, Settings (29 points—58 pixels—on a side), and the Home-screen app icon.

The repetition of "iPhone" and "iOS 7,8" should be a clue: The Passer Rating application is an iPhone-only app targeted at iOS 8. The Attributes inspector for an icon image set carries checkboxes for iPhone and iPad icons for iOS 6 through 8, plus a box for Mac icons.

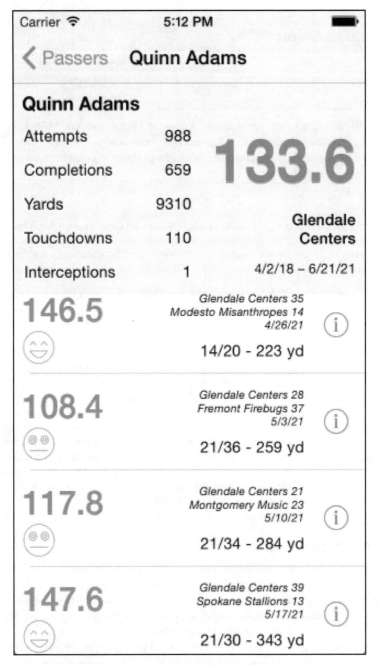

Figure 13.8   The final incarnation of the game cells includes a graphical assessment of the passer's performance in that game.

The checkbox labeled **iOS icon is pre-rendered** is a convenience for setting the flag in the app's `Info.plist` file that tells iOS that the "gloss" effect iOS put on application icons in versions 6 and earlier is not wanted.

Adding iOS 6 slots for iPhone gives you three more images to fill for the smaller application icon at two resolutions and a single-resolution Spotlight/Settings icon.

> **Note**
>
> Note that the icon wells are labeled in *points*, not pixels. An iPhone application icon, pre-iOS 7, is 57 points on a side, and that's how it's labeled. That's 57 *pixels* at single resolution, but at 2×, it's 114; and so on for 3× images. You're expected to do that math yourself.

Check all the iOS boxes. To cover every icon style for two devices running two operating systems, you'd have to provide 16 icon images. If you were building a Mac icon set instead, you'd have to fill 10 spaces.

> **Note**
>
> A long-standing bug in the image set editor has the icon slots running off the right side of the editor canvas. You can get around this by hiding the side navigators and narrowing the set list.

Let's not get crazy; uncheck all but the iPhone/iOS 7 and 8 options; that's three icons, at 2× and 3×, respectively. I've drawn Passer Rating's icon in the six sizes required, and I dropped each image file into its respective slot. Done (Figure 13.9).

Now launch the image, which is necessary if you can't use the launch XIB or storyboard the application template provides for iOS 8 or later. (I'll come to the reasons you should provide a XIB/storyboard soon.) Assuming it isn't running already, an application launches when the user taps its icon on the Home screen. The launch process concludes when the app is ready to respond to user actions. Both the OS and the app do some work before the app is ready for service. This can take some time even now—it took more on the iPhone as it was in 2007.

Apple resorted to some stagecraft. In the period before an application is running, iOS pulls a *launch image* (or launch screen XIB or storyboard) from the app's bundle and displays it until the app can present its first active screen and respond to user actions. This is a user-experience trick: Showing the user something that *looks* like the app's main screen

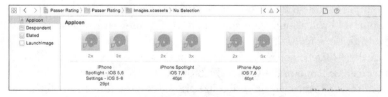

Figure 13.9   The complete repertoire of application icons can be covered in six images if you set the Attributes inspector's checkboxes to limit the set to iOS 7 and 8 on iPhone.

assures the user she's running the app she intends and gives her the impression that the device is responding to her more quickly than it really can.

> **Note**
>
> This isn't a "splash screen." A real splash screen blocks the user's access to her data for a certain amount of time. A launch image (or XIB) goes away as soon as the app is ready for use. Ideally, the interval between tapping your application's icon and its being ready for service is zero, and the launch display should never appear at all. That ideal will be tested in Chapter 16, "Measurement and Analysis."

Launch images come first in this history, so I'll start with those.

Select the LaunchImage image set. In the Attributes inspector, select **Portrait** orientation for all sizes of iPhone for **iOS 8 and Later**, **iOS 7 and Later**, and **iOS 6 and Earlier**, covering the status bar or not. (For a commercial product, we'd include a landscape image for iOS 8.) The Attributes inspector offers many more options for iPad (portrait and landscape), and the same for iOS 6 and earlier (including iPad images that don't cover the status bar).

Taking into account the single-resolution variants supported by iOS 6, there are 20 possible images (the status-bar variants mean that the practical maximum is 18). You begin to see the appeal of a launch XIB.

Back off and uncheck everything but the iPhone **Portrait** orientations for iOS 7 and 8, and give thanks: It's only four images. I used the **File → Save Screen Shot** (⌘ S) command to capture screen shots of the passer-list screen. I masked all text out with my favorite graphics editor. Launch images should not have anything that looks like data or reflects the locale. There is only one set of launch images for all locales. A transition from an image of an English-language button to the live button is smooth; but if you're using a German localization, the appearance of foreign-language text that is replaced by the local text is jarring.

> **Note**
>
> When you take screen shots for purposes like this, make sure the iOS Simulator's screen is shown full size: **Window → Scale → 100%** (⌘ 1).

That's the historical context. iOS 8 introduces *launch storyboards* (which include XIBs). You can provide an Interface Builder product for a stand-alone view; the new-app template gives you one to start from. This gives the system something to present that doesn't depend on the shape or resolution of the device's screen—the large, treble-resolution iPhone 6 Plus is obviously just the beginning. If you *don't* provide a launch layout, iOS will assume your app isn't ready for modern screen sizes, and will "zoom" it to fit the screen.

If it isn't there (maybe you're working with an existing project), create the storyboard and register its base name in the **General** tab of the Target editor. Because the launch files are arranged through Auto Layout, using size classes, one file can reliably fill any screen the app launches into. Remember that the NIB (compiled XIB) will be drawn before any of your code has executed—there's no view controller backing the display. It's just for show, as a way to use one file to show your initial screen on any iOS screen, current or future.

Summary

This chapter told the story of how Passer Rating fills its game table from a `Passer`'s `games` set. This took us to another feature of Storyboard, the ability to specify prototype cells for a table. We advanced through three stages:

- A simple text-only cell as provided by iOS, just to test the mechanism
- A cell with a custom layout that can display the full information about a game in a compact and interesting (or you could make it interesting) format
- A development of the full-information cell that supplemented the contents with a `UIImageView`

The image was silly, but it yielded an in-depth look at the asset-catalog feature, which makes it much easier than before to manage the explosion of system images an iOS application might have to carry.

14

Adding an Editor

The last substantive change we'll make to Passer Rating is to add an editor for passers. The task itself will be very quick—you know how to add a scene, and the concepts of the editor are not difficult. But it'll give us the chance to take a deeper look at Storyboard.

The Plan

We already know roughly what we want to do—the layout is already there in Figure 8.2 in Chapter 8, "Starting an iOS Application." It's a modal view (it slides up from the bottom), containing a table with rows for editing a passer's first and last names and the name of his current team. **Save** and **Cancel** buttons allow the user to exit the editor one way or another.

Adding a Modal Scene

Bring `Main.storyboard` into the editor, and use **Editor** → **Canvas** → **Zoom** → **Zoom Out** (⌥⌘() to zoom out to give you room to drag in a new view. Find "View Controller" (`UIViewController`) in the Library portion of the Utility area (make sure the third tab, for the Object library, is selected), and drag it in just below the game-list controller (the segue arrow will be easier to follow that way).

Key Equivalents

The deeply buried commands to zoom the Interface Builder canvas in and out have little to recommend them, especially on the U.S. keyboard. **Zoom Out** (⌥⌘() is effectively ⌥⇧⌘[, which is awkward in itself, and because it involves holding the Shift key at the start of an animation, the transition runs at less than half speed.

The solution is to open the **Key Bindings** panel of the Preferences window and type `Zoom` in the search field. There are a lot of commands with that word in them, so look for the items marked "Editor Menu for Interface Builder...." (The full text of the description is never visible, because the column in which it appears is not resizable.)

The second column contains the key equivalent for each command; click a cell, and any key combination you press will be assigned to the menu item; click away from the field to make the change permanent. The equivalents I chose were ⌘= for **Zoom to 100%**; ⌥⌘[for **Zoom Out**; and ⌥⌘] for **Zoom In**.

Any (maybe all) of these will conflict with keys assigned to other commands. If Xcode flags the assignment in yellow, this isn't a problem—the two commands are active in different contexts, such as in a debugger view and Interface Builder, and the context determines the command. If the combination is flagged red, the conflict is between two commands that may be active in the same context. Click the **Conflicts** filter in the key list to expose all the issues, and decide how you want to resolve the clashes.

The search field in the **Key Bindings** tab has a popup menu at the left margin that lets you filter your search by description, keys used in the equivalents, or both.

> **Note**
>
> The Apple terminology for invoking a command from the keyboard has always been "equivalents," in recognition of research showing that while the user isn't aware of it, remembering the key combination and shifting the hands to enter it is *slower* than using a mouse to pick the command from a Mac-style top-of-screen menu. On a Mac, such key combinations are not "shortcuts," nor do they "accelerate" anything. Nobody believes that, but the point lives on in Cocoa UI terms.

Select the new scene, and the Identity inspector (third tab, top of the Utility area). Name the **Class PasserEditController**. Make a mental note to build such a class.

The scene consists of two parts: A toolbar at the top, and a table below it. It would be tempting to control this scene with a UITableViewController, but if you do that, the whole scene must be a UITableView. We don't want that.

Contrariwise, we don't want to just drop a UITableView into the scene, either. We're going to take advantage of *static table cells* for the editing form, and you can't have those without a UITableViewController. It seems we're stuck.

While pondering this, drag a UIToolbar in, and put it at the top of the scene—you'll have to zoom to a scale of 100 percent. Set the constraints to be zero from the leading and trailing edges of the superview, and zero from the Top Layout Guide (the imaginary line below any bars at the top of the screen—you may have to start the top well below any top bars before you get the top guide as an option).

The toolbar already contains a button labeled **Item**. Toolbars don't have any vertical layout, and they take care of their own horizontal layouts: Drag in a "Flexible Space Bar Button Item" (it's inert, but yes, it's technically a button) to the right of it, and another UIBarButtonItem to the right of that.

Now you have two buttons labeled **Item**. There is a time to be enigmatic, but human-interface design is not it. Select the button on the left. If this were a UIButton, you'd edit a **Title** field in the Attributes inspector. Bar-button items are different, because very often they have standard titles or icons. Look at the "Bar Button Item" section of the Attributes inspector.

- Set the **Style** popup to **Bordered**. Putting borders around buttons went out of style with iOS 7, but that's the historic name for what we want, and if you run on iOS 6, you'll get the dark-gray sunken appearance.

- Have a look at the **Identifier** popup. It starts at **Custom**, which allows you to set the title, as you'd expect. But there are many items offering standard button types. Some of them correspond to icons—a **Stop** button carries a large saltire—but some get rendered as strings, like **Save**. What's the good in that? iOS renders "acceptance" buttons in a heavier font, and because the title is standard, it will localize the title. Choose **Save** from the **Identifier** popup.

- Select the left-hand button in the bar and set its identifier to **Cancel**.

These buttons should do something. They will, soon.

Toolbars don't have a way to label themselves the way navigation bars can. Cheat: Drag in a `UILabel`, title it `Edit Passer`, set it in System Bold, 17. Select the label and the bar (you can't put the label *in* the bar), and use the alignment control to align it horizontally with the center of the outer view (IB doesn't recognize subviews of toolbars); and the pin control to fix the distance from the top edge. The content will run off the end of the label, but if you have the **Resolve Auto Layout Issues** menu redo the layout for the scene, the label's content will push it out so the full text is visible.

An Embedded View Controller

To review: We can't have a `UITableViewController`, because we need that toolbar. But if we simply drop a `UITableView` in, we can't have the static table cells that will make our lives so much easier.

> **Note**
>
> Other developers might solve this by putting the editor in the same `UINavigation-Controller` chain as the other scenes; or wrap the editor's table-view controller in an additional navigation controller stack just to get a top bar. I'm having you do it this way so I can show how you can break out of the navigation-controller stack and still have control; and how you don't have to fall prey to dilemmas like this.

So we're going to have our `UITableViewController`. And our toolbar. Without compromise. The trick is the *embedded view controller*, in which the editor view cedes a container for another controller to run.

Type **contai** into the search field at the bottom of the Library panel, to find and place "Container View" into the Passer Edit scene. This doesn't look good. It's too small, but some constraints will take care of that (zero to bottom, leading, and right edges of the container; zero to the bottom of the toolbar).

The container seems to have brought another view controller with it. Probably Interface Builder has placed it inconveniently, but that, too, is easy to deal with: Zoom the canvas out so you can drag the child scene to the right of the editor. You find that the new scene has sized itself to match the container. Good. You also find that the new scene has assigned itself a `UIViewController`. Bad. See Figure 14.1.

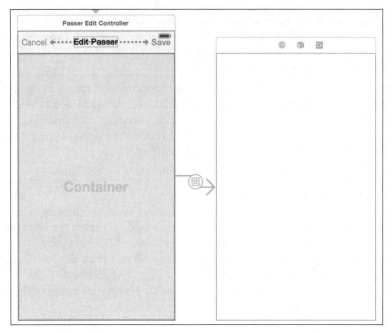

Figure 14.1   The editor view has its toolbar and a container for its table, but the container view brought in a plain `UIViewController`, when we need a `UITableViewController`.

The reason it's bad is that we need a `UITableViewController`. That's ultimately a subclass of `UIViewController`, but if you simply set the class of the existing controller, Interface Builder won't correct its presentation to include the tools for building a table. This is the wrong scene for the wrong controller.

Bring in the right controller. Find the Table View Controller object and drag it into the canvas. As far as Interface Builder knows, this is a stand-alone scene, so it is shown at the screen size you're currently using for the storyboard. Not a problem.

Control-drag from the container view in the editor scene to the new table-controller scene. A heads-up window will appear so you can set the type of segue you want. Click **embed**, which is the only choice you have. The container can have only one embedded controller, so the embed segue to the interloping `UIViewController` is broken. Select its scene and press Delete.

Select the new table controller, and use the Identity inspector to set its class name to `PasserEditTableController`. It's unwieldy, but a stranger (including you, next month) will need every part of the name to understand what the class does.

> **Note**
>
> Setting the controller class name should be all you need to produce a storyboard with the proper connection to the controller. Sometimes not. In such cases—as I write this,

embedded controllers are—you have to set the name of the module in which the class is to be found. In the Identity inspector, set **Module** to the application's main module `Passer_Rating`. The application module takes the alphanumerics in the name of the application with underscores replacing anything else.

Segues should always have names. Select the embed segue and use the Attributes inspector to set the **Identifier** to something like `Passer Edit Embed`.

Linking the Editor to the Passer List

We need a way to get from the root list of passers to the editor. This is complicated—but only slightly—by the fact that there will be two uses for the editor: to work on the content of an existing `Passer`, and to populate a new one.

We can do most of the jump from an existing `Passer` in Interface Builder. `PasserListController.viewDidLoad()` hasn't changed since the project template gave it to us. Part of what that method does is to set the right button of its navigation item to the standard **Add** button. We need to use that button as the root of a segue, and code isn't the way to do it.

Drag a bar button from the Library into the right end of the navigation bar in the passer-list controller scene. Select the standard **Add** identifier in the Attributes inspector. Control-drag from the new **Add** button to the passer–editor scene.

> **Note**
>
> I bet your editor scene and the **Add** button can't fit on the screen at the same time. Good news: You can't do much with the zoomed-out view of the canvas, but you *can* drag segues.

You'll be offered a menu of segue types; choose **Present Modally**. The segue is to be triggered by a tap on the accessory, and it should present the editor modally (sliding up from the bottom over the `Passer` list).

> **Note**
>
> With its bigger screen, the iPad offers other ways to present modal views. Consult the documentation for `modalPresentationStyle`.

Provide an identifier for the new segue: **Edit passer**. The Attributes inspector for the segue offers other **Transition** styles, but let's not get fancy; experiment with them yourself.

> **Note**
>
> It's an identifier, not a coding symbol. There's no compiler to tell you the identifier should be uncomfortable for a human to read.

Now for editing an existing `Passer`. `UITableViewCells` can display one of five standard accessories at the right end of the row:

- Disclosure, a right-facing caret to indicate that tapping the cell will disclose the next-lower layer of the hierarchy.

- Detail, a circled **i**, which will summon an editor for the object the cell represents. You have to tap the accessory itself to get the editor. (In iOS 6 and earlier, this was a chevron in a blue circle.)

- Detail Disclosure, which shows both the caret and the circled **i** to show that tapping the detail button will show an editor, and tapping anywhere else in the row will navigate to another screen.

- A checkmark.

- No accessory at all.

The passer table's prototype cell has the disclosure accessory because we've been using the cell to advance to a display of one passer's record. Now that we want to edit it, we need a detail-disclosure accessory. Select the cell in the Passer List Controller table, and use the Attributes inspector to set **Accessory** to **Detail Disclosure**.

The detail-disclosure accessory is a button. As such, it can trigger a segue. You will be tempted to drag an additional segue from it to the editor controller. That will work, as far as it goes, but there is a problem: In order to edit an existing passer, the `prepareFor-Segue (_, sender:)` method has to know which passer it is. By the time control gets to that method, that information is lost; one accessory tap looks like any other.

Leave the question aside for the moment.

Static Table Cells

Now we can build the editing form from the table embedded in the Passer Editor scene. Zoom in on the table in that scene and select it. You will make these changes:

- Change **Content** from **Dynamic Prototypes** to **Static Cells**.

- Notice that **Sections** is set to **1**. That's what we want.

- Change **Style** to **Grouped**. **Plain** style is better for sectioned data—it keeps the section header on screen even when you scroll far down in the section—but a grouped table is better for a static presentation.

- **Selection** should be **No Selection**.

Now move on to that one section. To select the section, either find it in the document outline, which you can expand with the arrowhead button at the lower-left corner of the canvas, or by control-shift-clicking on the section in the scene, and picking the section.

You'll make two changes: Set **Rows** to **1**, and set **Header** to **Passer**. (IB will force it to all-caps, but that's okay.) The form will have three rows, but if you lay out one, and duplicate it twice, you'll have three identical layouts without more trouble.

You're down to one cell. Drag a label into it (vertically centered in container; fixed leading margin; no width specified—let the intrinsic text-content constraint take over), and set the title to **First Name**. Drag in a UITextField and put it at the right end of the cell (fixed trailing edge, width 190 points at priority 751, baseline aligned with the label, leading space to the label greater than or equal to 4 points). Scroll the Attributes inspector down a little to find some popups that set the behavior of the keyboard for the field; Set **Capitalization** to **Words** (which fits proper names better), and turn **Correction** and **Spell Checking** off.

Select the section again, and set it to have three rows; as I promised, the three have the same layout. Set the label titles to `First Name`, `Last Name`, and `Current Team`. Just to be stylish, set the **Placeholder Text** in the text fields to `First`, `Last`, and `Team`.

The Editor View Controllers

We've worked up quite a debt in unimplemented code, and now we must pay off.

Create the promised classes, `PasserEditController` (a subclass of `UIViewController`) and `PasserEditTableController` (subclass of `UITableViewController`).

The last two statements in `viewDidLoad()` in `PasserListController` set up an **Add** button for the passer list's navigation bar. Remove them. This obsoletes `insertNewObject`, but it's harmless, and it would be a distraction to remove it.

The Editor Table

The editor table doesn't have to do much. It must keep track of its text fields and their contents; and it has to accept and return the strings the fields edit. If we carefully choose the names of the fields and the properties that back them, we can automate much of the task of shuttling data between the fields and the `Passer` properties. The `Passer` values are `firstName`, `lastName`, and `currentTeam`. The names of everything else will be, or be derived from, those names.

Now that we have class files, we can link the fields to `PasserEditTableController`. Rig your Interface Builder tab so the Assistant editor is visible and the first segment of its jump bar set to **Automatic**; and the Navigator and Utility areas are hidden to make room. The assistant will show the controller's source files when its scene is selected. Control-drag from each field into the top of the definition of `PasserEditTableController` in `PasserEditTableController.swift`.

Add one more `var` property, making the top of the class definition look like this:

```
class PasserEditTableController: UITableViewController {
    @IBOutlet weak var firstNameField: UITextField!
    @IBOutlet weak var lastNameField: UITextField!
    @IBOutlet weak var currentTeamField: UITextField!

    weak var parent: PasserEditController!
    // ...
```

The controller's API uses a dictionary to pass the editor's values in and out. One might think the best way to get the values into and out of the editor would be to call out each in a `String` property, but this technique has the advantage of removing the structure of the data from the API, and providing a single way to pass the data back and forth regardless of whether it's for an existing or new record. Also, there are Key-Value Coding (KVC) methods that make it easy to get and set object properties through dictionaries. The dictionary keys will be firstName, lastName, and currentTeam.

Here's how you'd move the field values into and out of the editor table:

```
let propertyNames = ["firstName", "lastName", "currentTeam"]
var     values:[String:String] {
    get {
        var retval: [String:String] = [:]
        for name in propertyNames {
            let field = valueForKey("\(name)Field") as! UITextField
            retval[name] = field.text ?? ""
        }
        return retval
    }
    set {
        for name in propertyNames {
            let field = valueForKey("\(name)Field") as! UITextField
            field.text = newValue[name] ?? ""
        }
    }
}


override func viewDidLoad() {
    super.viewDidLoad()
    // prepareForSegue comes before the view is populated with its
    // text fields. There are other ways to solve this, but in this
    // case, we call out to the wrapper view for the values now that
    // the table is ready for them.
    parent.childReadyForValues()
}
```

If the editor table is simple, the container does practically nothing:

```
class PasserEditController: UIViewController {
    override func prepareForSegue(segue: UIStoryboardSegue,
                                  sender: AnyObject?) {
        if segue.identifier! == "Passer edit embed" {
            childEditor = segue.destinationViewController as!
                                  PasserEditTableController
            childEditor.parent = self
        }
    }

    // As a convenience to the client, hold a reference to whatever
    // we're editing. PasserEditController doesn't do anything with it.
    var representedObject: Passer?

    // MARK: - Child editor support
```

```
    var childEditor: PasserEditTableController!
    var editValues: [String:String] {
        get {
            return childEditor.values
        }
        set {
            _savedValues = newValue
            childEditor?.values = newValue
        }
    }
    var _savedValues: [String:String]?

    func childReadyForValues() {
        childEditor.values = _savedValues!
    }
}
```

The embed segue is like any other: It has a source controller and a destination controller. When it is triggered (by loading the edit controller from the storyboard), it gets a `prepareForSegue(_, sender:)` message, as it would for any other segue. From that, it can get a pointer to the embedded controller (there's no way to link an outlet to the child in Interface Builder).

> **Note**
>
> `prepareForSegue(_, sender:)` depends on the embed segue having an identifier (Passer edit embed). Be sure to select the embed segue between the edit controller and its table sub-controller and set its name in the Attributes inspector.

However, at that moment, the views haven't been instantiated in either the parent or the child; and while the parent can rely on its own views' existence when `viewDid-Load()` is called, it can't be sure about the child. Therefore, the transaction of handing the values to be edited off to the child has to wait until it is ready. `PasserEditController` takes care of this by publishing a `childReadyForValues()` method to receive the signal.

Passing the Data to the Editor

First, let's get the data into the editor. We have an entry to the editor in the form of the `Edit passer` segue, but we have two uses for it. One of them, adding a `Passer`, is straightforward: Have the **Add** button trigger a segue; there's only one **Add** button.

The other use, for editing an existing passer, is trickier. There is no one origin; you have to know which passer triggered the transition. If you hooked up the detail button directly to the segue, that information would be lost. So you have to do some processing ahead of time, while you still can identify the passer.

The most straightforward way to do this is to add an old-fashioned `UITableView-Delegate` method to `PasserListController`:

```
//  Remove the in-code setup for the add button so
//  the one connected to the editor segue is used:
override func viewDidLoad() {
  super.viewDidLoad()
  self.navigationItem.leftBarButtonItem = self.editButtonItem()
}

...

//  Handle the new Edit passer segue:
override func prepareForSegue(segue: UIStoryboardSegue,
                             sender: AnyObject?) {
  switch segue.identifier! {
  case "showDetail":
    let indexPath = self.tableView.indexPathForSelectedRow()!
    let object = (fetchedResultsController[indexPath] as Passer)
    (segue.destinationViewController as GameListController).detailItem = object

  case "Edit passer":
    let editor = segue.destinationViewController as PasserEditController
    if let passer = _passerToEdit {
      //  The accessory button was tapped; capture the selected
      //  Passer and its values
      editor.editValues = passer.dictionaryWithValuesForKeys(
        ["firstName", "lastName", "currentTeam"])
      editor.representedObject = _passerToEdit
    }
    else {
      //  The Add button was tapped; there is no existing
      //  Passer, and all the values are blank.
      editor.editValues = ["firstName":"", "lastName":"", "currentTeam":""]
      editor.representedObject = nil
    }

  default:
    println("Unhandled segue in PasserListController (\(segue.identifier))")
  }
}

...

//  Respond to a tap on the accessory button for a Passer
override
func tableView(tableView: UITableView,
  accessoryButtonTappedForRowWithIndexPath
             indexPath: NSIndexPath) {
  _passerToEdit = (fetchedResultsController[indexPath] as Passer)
```

```
performSegueWithIdentifier("Edit passer",
                          sender: _passerToEdit)
}
```

It's been a long time since we've run Passer Rating. Do it now; tap on the detail-disclosure button on one of the rows, or on the **Add** button. The new editor slides up from the bottom, populated correctly. You can edit the fields (see Figure 14.2).

Getting the Data Back

What you can't do is close the editor, nor get your work back into the model. Up through iOS 5, the most straightforward way to get this done was to declare a `protocol` that `PasserListController` could implement. When the **Cancel** or **Save** button is pressed, the editor would use the delegate methods to signal the results to the list controller, its delegate.

But why do this, when Storyboard can eliminate the editor-side code, and free the client from setting a delegate outlet and conforming to a strict API?

You can't dig out of a view controller with an ordinary segue. If you control-dragged a segue from the **Cancel** button back to the `PasserListController,`you'd get a segue

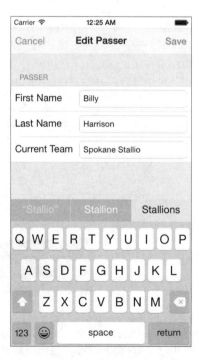

Figure 14.2   The new editor fills itself from exiting `Passer`s as hoped. You just can't close it.

that creates a new passer-list controller. That's what most segues do—they create view controllers.

What you want is an *unwind* segue. An unwind (or exit) segue shops itself up the chain of view controllers until it finds one that can handle the transition. (If you think of that chain as the sequence of modal and navigation presentations that arrived at the scene where the segue was triggered, you've got a workable idea, but it's a bit more complex, and you can modify it in code.)

A view controller declares its readiness to handle an unwind segue by implementing an @IBAction method with one argument of type UIStoryboardSegue. The Swift compiler and the runtime don't care about those properties—the information is lost by then. Interface Builder *does* care about them. Even as @IBAction in a method declaration tells IB that a method is a candidate to handle control events, the combination of @IBAction and the argument type adds the method to IB's candidates for unwind handlers.

By its nature, the target for an unwind segue is undefined. The undefined target of a control action is represented by the First Responder placeholder. The undefined handler for an unwind is represented by the red **Exit** icon (the last) in the bar above the scene containing the sender. You always start an exit segue from the placeholder (the opposite from the way you create other segues), by control-clicking on the placeholder. This brings up a heads-up list of all unwind @IBActions defined in the project. Drag from the bubble for the handler to the control that should trigger that unwind. See Figure 14.3.

Before you can do that, you have to provide the handlers. There are two exits from the editor: **Cancel** and **Save**. PasserListController needs a handler for each:

```
// MARK: - Editor completion
@IBAction func editorDidSave(segue: UIStoryboardSegue) {
    let editor = segue.sourceViewController as! PasserEditController
    //  representedObject is set if the editor comes from an
    //  accessory button. If it's nil, it's from the + button.
    let passer = editor.representedObject ??
        Passer(managedObjectContext: managedObjectContext)
```

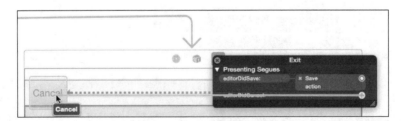

Figure 14.3   Control-clicking on the **Exit** placeholder opens a list of all unwind handlers in the project. Drag from the bubble next to the desired handler to the control that will trigger the segue. Existing triggers are labeled with the handler name. Dragging from an already-filled handler entry will add another control as a potential trigger.

```
passer.setValuesForKeysWithDictionary(editor.editValues)

    //  From the "savemoc" snippet:
    var error: NSError? = nil
    if !managedObjectContext.save(&error) {
        NSLog("In %@: could not save %@",
            "editorDidSave()",
            "Could not update from edited values")
        //  MOCSaveException is defined in Utilites.swift
        NSException.raise(MOCSaveException,
            format: "Context: %@",
            arguments: getVaList(["Could not update from edited values"]))
    }
    NSLog("Hit didSave: \(segue.identifier)")
}

@IBAction func editorDidCancel(segue: UIStoryboardSegue) {
    //  If the edit was canceled, there's nothing to do.
    NSLog("Hit didCancel: \(segue.identifier)")
}
```

That works. You can create a new passer (albeit without a link to any games, and therefore no career dates or ratings), or edit an existing one, and the changes show up in the passer list and in the passer-detail view. If you cancel, nothing happens. That's how it's supposed to be.

Segues

By now we've seen four kinds of connection that can appear on the storyboard canvas: Show Detail (to advance through a navigation controller); Present Modally (to slide up a view for a one-screen sidetrack for something like an editor); Embed (container-child relationship); and Relationship, which is not an actual segue but a connection between a controller that presents a series of views (such as a navigation controller) and the first of that series (the *root view controller*).

There are three others: Present As Popover (presents the destination controller in an iPad popover view); Show Detail (the destination controller becomes the detail part of a split view); and Custom (your own `UIStoryboardSegue` subclass). See Figure 14.4.

> **Note**
>
> Unwind segues don't appear on the canvas at all—by their nature, they don't have predetermined endpoints, and therefore no graphical representation.

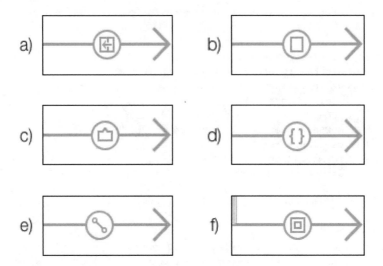

Figure 14.4   The Storyboard editor represents segues by seven types of arrows: a) Show, or Show Detail, for pushing the next controller onto a navigation stack. b) Present Modally, to present the next controller as a modal view. c) Present As Popover, a `UIStoryboardPopoverSegue` to present the destination controller as an iPad popover. d) Custom, representing a `UIStoryboardSegue` class you write yourself. e) Relationship, which shows that the container view on the left, such as a navigation-controller scene, dynamically manages content scenes, of which the scene on the right is the first. f) Embed, showing that the controller on the left sets a portion of its view aside for the single controller on the right.

Summary

In the course of adding a modal editor for Passer Rating, we decided we wanted a presentation like that of an ordinary `UIViewController`, but with a `UITableView` showing static cells. If you want static cells, you have to use a `UITableViewController`, which we didn't want.

We solved the problem by employing the embed segue, to set aside a portion of the editor controller's view to be run by a table-view controller.

With the table view in hand, we added static cells to create the form we needed for the editor. You saw how to take advantage of the Key-Value Coding technique to move the edited data between three controllers and the model with the minimum of fuss.

You arranged a modal segue to get into the editor; on the way, I showed you how to solve the problem of a segue that might come from a source that could be lost by the time you saw it.

Having gotten the data in, we had to get it out. This was an opportunity to set unwind segues by creating handlers for the transitions we needed and linking the **Cancel** and **Save** buttons to an **Exit** placeholder attached to their scene.

And last, you saw a gallery of the kinds of segues you'll see in your work with Storyboard.

You also learned something that you may have to explain to your managers: Storyboard saves a lot of effort, and cuts your exposure to errors, but it's not magical. You can't build an application "just by drawing." Every scene has to be backed by a controller object you provide, at least as a skeleton, in advance. The demos that look magical (and seduce nontechnical managers) hand-wave the significant coding effort you'll still have to put in.

With three of the four views we planned in Figure 8.2 squared away, the Passer Rating app looks to be well in hand. There's one thing, though.

I don't trust those ratings.

15

Unit Testing

All of your development so far on the passer-rating projects has left out one essential consideration:

How do you know it works?

Yes, you know generally what to expect, and you've used the Xcode debugger to verify that what the application does makes sense, but you don't have the time, and most people don't have the discipline, to monitor for every possible error. Ideally, for every change to your application, you'd verify that nothing broke. With a prompt warning, you can isolate the problem to the last thing you did.

This discipline of verifying each little part of your application is called *unit testing*. The meticulous search for errors is the sort of mind-numbing, repetitive, perfectionist task you bought a computer to do.

This is a well-enough understood problem that solutions have been devised in the form of testing frameworks. Such frameworks make it easy to take your code, more or less in the actual context in which you use it, present it with known inputs, and compare the results with what you expect. If everything is as expected, the test succeeds; otherwise it fails. The framework provides a way to run all the tests, record the results, and report on them.

Unit testing is a first-class part of Xcode. Any product template you choose will include a target for the product, and a parallel target constitutes a *test suite*, linked against the XCTest framework.

The suite consists of subclasses of XCTestCase, which implement tests as methods whose selectors begin with test. The code in the test methods exercises a small, manageable part of the product's functionality and challenges the results with *assertions*. An XCTest assertion macro checks the results against its criterion—Boolean true or false, equality, and the like—and if the criterion fails, it records the failure and a message you provide to describe it.

Although the test suite is a separate target, it can't be run independently. It is bound to the product target and is treated as the implementation of the product's Test build action. You remember that Xcode recognizes five goals for a build: Run, Test, Profile, Analyze, and Archive. You're already familiar with Run—it's how you execute an application for debugging—and Analyze. We'll get to Profile in Chapter 16, "Measurement and Analysis," and Archive in Chapter 18, "Provisioning." This chapter is about Test.

Selecting the Test action (**Product** → **Test**, ⌘U):

- Builds the product
- Builds the test target
- Launches the product
- Injects the test suite into the project, runs the tests, and collects the results
- Closes the product

If any test failed, the failure message is attached to your code and the Issue navigator in the same way that syntax errors are.

> **Note**
>
> Xcode's project templates come with test targets, but that was not always the case; in Xcode 4, test targets were optional, and before that, you had to add them yourself. If your project doesn't have a test target, select the project file, which is the top line in the Project navigator, to display the Project/Target editor. Click the **+** button below the source list, or select **Editor** →**Add Target...**. (A small button at the left end of the Project editor's tab bar opens and closes the source list.) Xcode will drop the familiar New Target assistant sheet. You'll find a "Cocoa Touch (or Cocoa) Testing Bundle" target in the Other category. *Be very sure* that you select the target from the list for the platform you intend; if your product is iOS, and the test is OS X, things become confusing very quickly. In addition to the usual details, you'll be allowed to choose a **Target to be Tested**.

The Test Navigator

Xcode 6 confers its highest honor on unit testing by giving it its own navigator (Figure 15.1). The navigator lists every test case (`XCUnitTest` subclass) in the project, and every test method in those classes. The status of the last run of a test is shown by a green-checkmark or red-X diamond badge next to it.

Those badges are not merely informative: Clicking a test or a whole test case runs just those tests. If you are working on just one test, you don't have to run the entire test suite just to get the results you need.

Those badges also show up in the margins of the test code (see Figure 15.2). Clicking the badge repeats just that test. If a test has never been run (or never run since the project was open), there will be no mark, but if you hover the mouse over the row, a "play" button will appear.

> **Note**
>
> The Test navigator makes it easy to manage and run tests, but there is another list of tests in the Scheme editor. The **Info** tab for the Test action lists all test suites and their tests, from which you can select the ones you wish to run. The Test navigator is for running a test or a test class as you work on bugs. The list in the Scheme editor governs the tests and classes that will be run when you select the full-up Test action. This is important for your own day-to-day work, but you can also share those settings with others by checking the **Shared** box at the bottom of the sheet. Shared schemes are available not just to your partners, but to drive the automated build and test process in Xcode Server. See Figure 15.3.

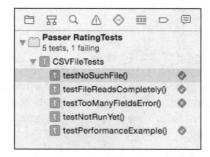

Figure 15.1   The Test navigator lists every `XCUnitTest` class in the test target, and every test method in those classes. Flags in the right column indicate the result of the last run of those tests: a red-X diamond for failures, a green-checkmark diamond for successes. Tests that haven't been run have no mark at all, but hovering the mouse pointer over their names gives you a "Play" button to click.

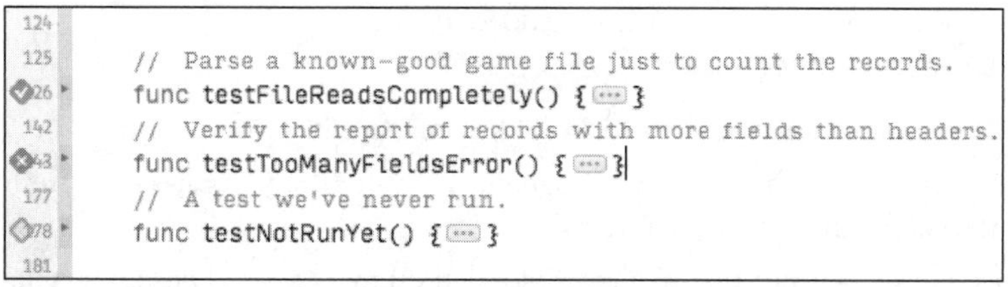

```
124
125        // Parse a known-good game file just to count the records.
26  ▶      func testFileReadsCompletely() { ⋯ }
142        // Verify the report of records with more fields than headers.
43  ▶      func testTooManyFieldsError() { ⋯ }|
177        // A test we've never run.
78  ▶      func testNotRunYet() { ⋯ }
181
```

Figure 15.2   The success and failure flags are repeated in the margin next to the code for test methods. Clicking a badge reruns just the one test.

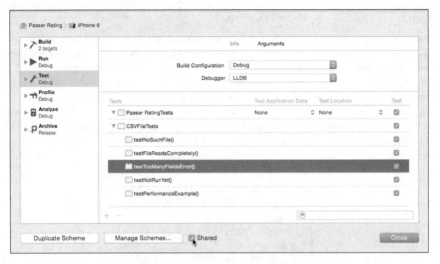

Figure 15.3   The Test panel of the Scheme editor lets you select which tests will be run in the next run of the Test action. By checking the **Shared** box at the bottom of the sheet, you can make the current scheme available to all users of the project, and not just private to your own workspace.

Testing the CSV Reader

Let's see how this works by constructing some tests of SimpleCSVFile, the rudimentary parser for .csv data files. We already have a Passer_RatingTests.swift file; change the test class to CSVFileTests, and rename the file accordingly: the class, by doing a search-and-replace in the Swift file; and the file itself by selecting it in the Project navigator, pressing return, and typing the new name. Press Return to commit the name change—the file will pick up the **A+** source-control badge to show it has been re-"added" to the local repository under its new name.

The file comes with four methods.

- setUp is run before each test (selector beginning with test) method.
- tearDown is run after each test. Together with setUp, you can create fresh, consistent conditions for each test.
- testExample is just that: An example method that's a test, because its selector begins with test, containing only an XCTAssert(true, ...). Running the Test action without doing anything else will show this test as passing.
- testPerformanceExample is a skeleton for a test that calls measureBlock() to measure the performance of your code. For now, the only metric measure-Block() collects is elapsed "wall" (as in clock-on-the-wall, not processor clock) time, but the API has room for more metrics in the future. We'll see more of performance measurements in Chapter 16, "Measurement and Analysis."

> **Note**
>
> Remember that you can't rely on the order in which tests will be run. If a test needs a specific starting condition that isn't covered by `setUp`, the test will have to configure the conditions itself. If you really need a test to use the end-state of a previous test, your best bet is simply to put both tests in the same method.

The CSV Test Code

We can do more with our tests than reflect cheery acceptance. Replace `testExample` with something better, as well as some housekeeping code (these are excerpts, with some of the existing code left in for context):

```swift
import Foundation
import UIKit
import XCTest
import Passer_Rating

class CSVFileTests: XCTestCase {
  enum TestFiles: String {
    case GoodFile = "2010-data-calculated.csv";
    case TooManyFields = "too-many-fields.csv";
    case NotEnoughFields = "not-enough-fields.csv";
  }

  // The SimpleCSVFile object to investigate (set in each test)
  var csvFile : SimpleCSVFile? = nil
  // An array of the dictionaries SimpleCSVFile presents while parsing.
  var records : [[String:String]] = []

  // When the file name is set, load up a parser
  var csvFileName: String? = nil {
    didSet {
      if let fileName = csvFileName {
        let bundle = NSBundle(forClass: CSVFileTests.self)
        let csvPath = bundle.pathForResource(fileName, ofType: "")

        // Yes, assert that the test bundle contains what you
        // think it does. Do you really want to scour your code
        // for a test "failure" that came from a bug in the
        // test itself?
        XCTAssertNotNil(csvPath,
                "Finding \(fileName) in the test bundle.")

        csvFile = SimpleCSVFile(path: csvPath!)
        XCTAssertNotNil(csvFile,
                "Loading \(fileName) from the test bundle.")
      }
```

```
    else {
      csvFile = nil
    }
  }
}

override func setUp() {
  super.setUp()
  records = []
}

override func tearDown() {
  super.tearDown()
}

// MARK: - Error handling

//  Utility method to verify the NSError object from the
//  CSVError item is as expected.

func checkNSErrorContent(error: CSVError,
        requiredDict: [NSObject:AnyObject],
        domain: String = WT9TErrorDomain) {
  let nsError = error.nsError
  XCTAssertEqual(nsError.domain, domain,
          "CSVError object had the wrong domain.")

  if let csvErrorDict = nsError.userInfo {
    //  If the NSError had a userInfo dictionary,
    //  compare it against the keys and values passed in
    //  through requiredDict.
    for (key, requiredValue) in requiredDict {
      if let csvValue: AnyObject = csvErrorDict[key] {
        let csvStrValue = "\(csvValue)"
        let requiredStrValue = "\(requiredValue)"
        XCTAssertEqual(csvStrValue, requiredStrValue,
            "CSVError.nsError wrong value for required key \(key)")
      }
      else {
        XCTFail("CSVError.nsError lacked required key \(key)")
      }
    }
  }
  else {
    XCTFail("CSVError objects are supposed to have dictionaries")
  }
}
```

```
func testNoSuchFile() {
  // The parser gets a path that doesn't resolve to a file.
  let noSuchFile = "no-such-file.csv"
  csvFile = SimpleCSVFile(path: noSuchFile)

  // Run the parser. It should not pass any data back.
  let result = csvFile?.run{ _ in
    XCTFail("Nonexistent file should never present a record.")
    return nil
  }

  // It should return a .NoSuchFile error.
  switch result! {
  case let .NoSuchFile(fileName):
    // The file in the error should match the given path.
    XCTAssert(fileName.hasSuffix(noSuchFile),
      "Nonexistent file path should come back through the error")

    // The NSError from the error object should identify the
    // file and explain the error.
    checkNSErrorContent(result!, requiredDict: [
      NSFilePathErrorKey: noSuchFile,
      NSLocalizedDescriptionKey: "No such file \(noSuchFile)"
      ]
    )

  default:
    XCTFail("Wrong return for no-such-file.")
  }
}


func testFileReadsCompletely() {
  // Parse a known-good game file
  // just to see if the record count is right.
  csvFileName = TestFiles.GoodFile.rawValue
  let result = csvFile!.run { record in
    self.records.append(record)
    return nil
  }

  if let realResult = result {
    // You can't XCTAssertNotNil and refer to `result!` in the
    // message string. XCT evaluates the message before testing
    // the not-nil condition. When `result` _is_ nil, the string
    // interpolation will crash on the attempt to unwrap it.
```

```
        XCTFail(
            "The good file should produce no errors; got \(realResult).")
        }
    XCTAssertEqual(328, records.count,
                "Wrong number of records from \(csvFileName).")
    }
}
```

As I said, it's mostly housekeeping. What's most interesting are the functions whose names begin with XCT. These come from XCTest. Here, they verify that the requested test file exists and can be read (XCTAssertNotNil), that it could be parsed (XCTAssert on the success of run()), and that the number of records matched the count I made in advance (XCTAssertEqual). A full list will come later in this chapter.

You can see the obsessiveness that goes into a good test; in fact, these tests are probably not obsessive enough. It's tedious, but once it's written, the test harness does the hard work, and you won't be single-stepping through every line of the parser as it plows through hundreds of records.

Xcode will be pelting you with undefined-symbol errors by now. None of the Passer Rating classes or methods are recognized in your test target. Swift symbols—naming classes, functions, and types—are organized into *modules*, having roughly the same scope as each library or executable unit. SimpleCSVFile is part of the application module, Passer_Rating; for the Passer_RatingTests module to see it,

- The Swift file that refers to SimpleCSVFile must include the statement "import Passer_Rating." The SimpleCSVFile.swift file shown above does this already.

- SimpleCSVFile.swift must attach the public attribute to every function and type to be used from other modules.

Add public attribute wherever it's needed in SimpleCSVFile.swift:

```
public
enum CSVErrorKeys: String {

// ...

public
enum CSVError: Printable {
    case LineFormat(String, Int, Int, Int)

// ...

// While we're at it, make it easier to print out error objects.
// Defining a `description` property makes a type comply
// with `Printable`, so it can be interpolated into a string
// with `\()`.
```

```
    public var description: String {
        var retval = "CSVError."
        switch self {
        case let .NoSuchFile(fileName):
            retval += "NoSuchFile(\(fileName))"
        case let .EmptyFile(fileName):
            retval += "EmptyFile(\(fileName))"
        case let .LineFormat(fileName, lineNumber, expected, actual):
            retval += "LineFormat(\(fileName):\(lineNumber), " +
                      "expected \(expected), got \(actual))"
        case let .ClientError(path, line, error):
            retval += "ClientError(\(path):\(line), " +
                      "NSError = \(error))"
        }

        return retval
    }

    public
    var nsError: NSError {
        var userDict:[NSString:AnyObject] = [:]
// ...

}

public
let WT9TErrorDomain =        "com.wt9t.error"

// ...

public
class SimpleCSVFile {
// ...

    public
    init(path: String) {

// ...

    public
    func run(block: ([String: String]) -> NSError?
        ) -> CSVError?
    {
```

Now that the SimpleCSVFile class and its associated types and data are visible to other modules, the undefined-symbol errors should go away.

Test Data

The CSVFileTests class relies on three data files, listed in enum TestFiles: 2010-data-calculated.csv, a known-good data file; too-many-fields.csv, which has more record fields than headers; and not-enough-fields.csv, which doesn't have enough. The last two were constructed for the sole purpose of verifying that SimpleCSVFile catches the error and refuses to continue work.

Later in this chapter, we'll be testing the accuracy of the passer_rating function, and we'll need a typical game-data file and another file of ratings independently calculated from the same records.

For that, you'll need a data set that is fixed, not the one that periodically regenerates itself as a part of Passer Rating's build process, so take the current edition of sample-data.csv, and copy a year's worth of games—328 in the toy league I created, covering 32 passers—into a separate file (2010-data.csv in my tests). 2010-data-calculated.csv is the "gold standard" version of the file, an input for the test methods, containing known-correct results for all of the calculations. 2010-data.csv is the "normal" data file to be used by Passer Rating as it makes those calculations for itself.

Drag the test data files into the Project navigator under the test-target group or use **File → Add Files to...** (⌥⌘A) to select them from the get-file sheet. In either case, make sure they go into the test target only.

> **Note**
>
> To ensure that the tests are reproducible, the test data should be checked into source control.

Running the Tests

Let's execute the test by holding the mouse button down on the **Action** button at the left end of the toolbar and selecting **Test**, or by selecting **Product → Test** (⌘U). Xcode builds Passer Rating and then the test bundle. The first thing that happens is that Xcode reports the build succeeded (if it didn't, clean it up; I'll wait).

When the build finishes, you'll see the iOS Simulator launches and opens Passer Rating. This is normal: XCTest works by injecting your test code into your running application. Your tests will run under actual operating conditions, not in an isolated test-bench environment. That's why it was not necessary to link SimpleCSVFile.swift into the test target.

Passer Rating closes as swiftly as it appeared (net of how long it takes to reload the game data every time), and the next thing you see is the Issues navigator, which (if you've been keeping up) has one red flag. See Figure 15.4. Except for the red badge being a diamond instead of an octagon, test failures are no different from the errors you'd get from a compilation: Click one, and you'll be shown the assertion's message spread in a banner in your test code.

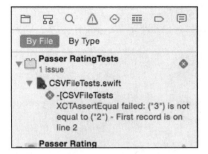

Figure 15.4   One of the tests of `SimpleCSVFile` failed. The locations and messages from the failures appear in the Issues navigator.

One of the failures comes in `testTooManyFieldsError()`, where `SimpleCSVFile` is deliberately fed a file with more record fields than headers. The parser refuses the file, which is good, and returns a `CSVError` object with all the expected information...

```
func testTooManyFieldsError() {
  csvFileName = TestFiles.TooManyFields.rawValue
  let result = csvFile!.run { record in
    XCTFail("CSV file with the first data line bad should not call out")
    return nil
  }

  if let realResult = result {
    switch realResult {
    case let .LineFormat(file, line, expect, actual):
      //  Verify the associated values
      XCTAssert(file.hasSuffix(csvFileName!),
        "File name reported in the LineFormat error")
      XCTAssertEqual(expect, 16, "Expected fields")
      XCTAssertEqual(actual, 17, "Actual fields")

      /**************** Failed ****************/
      XCTAssertEqual(line, 2, "First record is on line 2")
      /*****************************************/

      //  Verify the NSError conversion
      checkNSErrorContent(realResult, requiredDict: [
        NSFilePathErrorKey                  : file,
        NSLocalizedDescriptionKey           :
                    "File \(file):\(line) has " +
                    "\(actual) items, should have \(expect)",
        CSVErrorKeys.ExpectedFields.rawValue  : expect,
        CSVErrorKeys.ActualFields.rawValue    : actual
        ])
```

```
    default:
      XCTFail("Expected a LineFormat error, got \(realResult)")
    }
  }
  else {
    XCTFail(
      "File with too many fields in the first record " +
      "should yield an error.")
  }
}
```

. . . except for that one about the line number where the error was found. The error should have occurred at line 2, the line after the header, containing the first game data; that's where the mismatch should become apparent. The associated `Int` value in the `CSVError` `LineFormat` case should say so. Instead, the test reports it occurred at line 3. That's wrong.

Testing and the Debugger

What's going on? You need to see what the parser is doing on those lines. Fortunately, the debugger works in unit tests. Set a breakpoint at the start of `SimpleCSVFile.run()`, and run just `testTooManyFieldsError()` by clicking the red diamond next to its name in the Test navigator or as it appears in the margin of the definition of the method.

The breakpoint at `run()` fires, but look at the stack trace in the Debug navigator: The call came from `AppDelegate` via `Game`. This isn't the test run; because you're running the test in the full context of Passer Rating, you're seeing the parsing run from the initialization of the app. Click the **Continue** button in the debugger bar, and wait for the second call to `run()`.

Now you're at the test run, and you can step into `prepareToRun()`. It reads the file into a string, then bursts it into an array of lines:

```
linesFromFile = realContents.componentsSeparatedByCharactersInSet(
              NSCharacterSet.newlineCharacterSet())
```

When `prepareToRun()` returns, `run()` uses a `for` loop to step through `linesFromFile`, bursting each line at the commas to get fields.

If you're watching the variables display in the Debug area, you see something on the second pass through the loop that you'd expect should be the first line of the data: The string for that line is empty! The first line of data doesn't come through until the *third* pass through the loop, and the method reports the error line as number three.

With a little thought, it should come to you: This is the CSV file that was exported from the spreadsheet of precalculated statistics. CSV has its origins in Microsoft Excel, and as codified in the Internet Engineering Task Force's RFC 4180, CSV is supposed to have Windows-style line endings—carriage-return, line-feed. The `componentsSeparated-ByCharactersInSet()` method burst the file at each occurrence of a character in the `newlineCharacterSet()`, not caring that in this file, the CRLF pair represents a single line separator.

> **Note**
>
> In practice, almost nobody observes RFC 4180. Every implementor has his own ideas about quoting, escaping, treatment of numerics, and line endings. This is an instance of write conservatively, read liberally: Make sure your CSV files are strictly compliant with the standard, but tolerate flaws in others'.

Fight down the temptation to simply open the file in a text editor that will convert the line endings. `SimpleCSVFile` is supposed to work with real CSV files (so long as they don't have any commas or quotes in the fields); it may have a life beyond this one project; and it really ought to handle a line delimiter that will probably appear in most of the files it sees.

It so happens that `Extensions.swift` has an extension on `String` that does just what we need:

```swift
extension String {
    /// Break the receiver at line endings and return
    /// the lines in an array of String.
    func brokenByLines() -> [ String ]
    {
        let scanner = NSScanner(string: self)
        let lineEnders = NSCharacterSet.newlineCharacterSet()
        var retval = [String]()

        scanner.charactersToBeSkipped = nil
        while !scanner.atEnd {
            //  Alternate between skipping line breaks and
            //  reading line content.
            var token: NSString? = ""
            scanner.scanCharactersFromSet(lineEnders,
                                     intoString: nil)
            var success: Bool
            success = scanner.scanUpToCharactersFromSet(lineEnders,
                                          intoString: &token)
            if success {
                retval.append(token! as! String)
            }
        }
        return retval
    }
}
```

In `prepareToRun()`, replace

```swift
linesFromFile = realContents.componentsSeparatedByCharactersInSet(
            NSCharacterSet.newlineCharacterSet())
```

with

```
linesFromFile = realContents.brokenByLines()
```

This time all of the methods in `CSVFileTests` come through clean.

Adding a Test Class

Now that you're sure the data is coming in as you expect it, you can build a `RatingTest` class to read the CSV that contains the precalculated values for the rating and its completion, yardage, touchdown, and interception components, and compare their presumably correct (or at least independently calculated) values against the values the `passer_rating` function produces.

Those numbers never leave `passer_rating` as originally written, so let's make them easier to test by breaking them out:

```
// Note that the function is now declared `public`.
public
func passer_rating(#completions: Int, #attempts: Int,
                   #yards: Int, #touchdowns: Int,
                   #interceptions: Int)
                   -> Double
{
    //  See http://en.wikipedia.org/wiki/Quarterback_Rating

    if (attempts <= 0) { return 0.0 }

    //  Compute the components to sum into the rating
    //  CHANGED: Break the component calculations into a separate func.
    let components = rating_components(completions: completions,
                      attempts: attempts, yards: yards,
                      touchdowns: touchdowns,
                      interceptions: interceptions)

    //  Add the components up
    let retval = components.reduce(0.0, +)
    return 100.0 * retval / 6.0
}


public
func rating_components(#completions: Int, #attempts: Int,
                       #yards: Int, #touchdowns: Int,
                       #interceptions: Int)
                       -> [Double]
{
```

```
//  Statistic-per-attempt, with both converted to Double,
//  recurs in all four components. Make the definitions
//  easier to read and understand by encapsulating it.
func perAttempt(stat:Int) -> Double {
    return Double(stat) / Double (attempts)
}

return [
    (100.0 * perAttempt(      completions) - 30.0) / 20.0,
    (perAttempt(              yards) - 0.3) / 4.0,
    20.0 * perAttempt(        touchdowns),
    2.375 - (25.0 * perAttempt( interceptions))
].map(ratingPinner)
}
```

Now create the test class: **File → New → File...** (⌘N) and select an iOS Test Case Class. The sheet that Xcode presents allows you to enter a name (**RatingTest**), and a superclass, defaulted to XCTestCase.

But for the class name, the new RatingTest.swift file is identical to the one that came with the project template. The complete listing of the test must be left to the sample code—there's just too much of it to print in full. Here are the main points:

1. setUp() uses SimpleCSVFile to read 2010-data-calculated.csv, which contains the "golden" calculations, generated independently from a spreadsheet. It loads the data, as Dictionarys, into an array named games.
2. testCalculation() loops through games, runs the passer-rating calculations on the statistics, and compares the results against the golden values.

The testCalculation() loop does its real work in the XCTest... assertions:

```
//  This is inside the record-by-record loop
//  For each record, define a function that
//  yields the integer value corresponding to
//  a key string:
func i(key: String) -> Int {
    return record[key]?.toInt() ?? 0

    //  lhs ?? rhs evaluates to lhs! if non-nil,
    //  to rhs if lhs is nil.
    //
    //  Therefore:
    //  If there is no value for `key` in `record`,
    //  that's nil, the lhs expression short-circuits
    //  to nil, so return zero.
    //  If the value for `key` in `record` can't be
    //  interpreted as an integer, that's nil, so
    //  return zero.
```

```
    //  Otherwise, return the value for `key` in
    //  `record`, as an integer.
    //
    //  Swift can be terse, but it is ruthless.
}


//  Compare the two component sets, within epsilon
var  allComponentsGood = true
for i in 0 ..< gcValues.count {
    allComponentsGood = false
    XCTAssertEqualWithAccuracy(components[i], gcValues[i], epsilon,
        "\(componentNames[i]) does not match at line \(lineNumber)")
}

//  If the components checked out, compare the passer ratings,
if allComponentsGood {
    let goldenRating = self.componentFormatter.numberFromString(
                            record["rating"]!)
                            as Double
    let myRating = passer_rating(
        completions:    i("completions"),
        attempts:       i("attempts"),
        yards:          i("yards"),
        touchdowns:     i("touchdowns"),
        interceptions:  i("interceptions")
    )
    XCTAssertEqualWithAccuracy(myRating, goldenRating, epsilon,
        "Passer ratings don't match at line \(lineNumber)")
}
```

... and if you looked up the passer-rating formula on Wikipedia, you wouldn't be surprised that the three assertions you see here—that the yardage component and the rating, calculated two ways, should match the "right" answers—generated 292 test failures. See Figure 15.5 for the results in the Report navigator.

> **Note**
>
> In the sample code, you'll see the error-tolerance variable's name is not `epsilon`, but ϵ. If you have Unicode, why settle for second-best?

The assertion errors are variants on a single theme (line broken to fit the page):

```
RatingTest.swift:88: error:
    -[Passer_RatingTests.RatingTest testCalculation] :
    XCTAssertEqualWithAccuracy failed:
    ("2.375") is not equal to ("1.9") +/- ("0.001")
    - Yards does not match at line 1
```

Figure 15.5   The Report navigator chronicles all major events in a project since the project was opened. Selecting a Test run displays every failed assertion in the run. Fortunately, the descriptive strings attached to the assertions make it easy to determine exactly which value went wrong.

The assertion `XCTAssertEqualWithAcuracy` checks whether two floating-point values are close enough to be called equal. The yardage component from the in-app calculation, 2.375, doesn't match the precalculated value of 1.9. This points straight at this line in `rating.swift`:

```
(perAttempt(                       yards) - 0.3) / 4.0,
```

That should be 3.0, not 0.3. That's the bug. Select **Product → Test** (⌘ U), or the **Test** action from the leftmost button in the toolbar, to run all the tests for the Passer Rating project. The Report navigator shows green checkmark badges on all tests. This is what you want to see (Figure 15.6).

My unease about the ratings I was seeing was right, and now I have a test of 328 games to make sure that if it ever goes wrong again, I'll know right away.

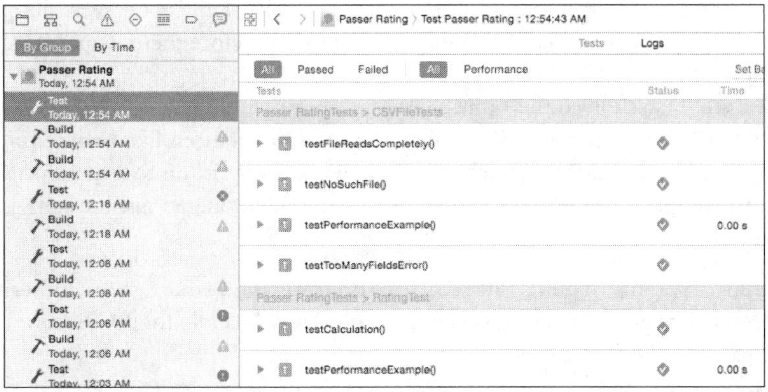

Figure 15.6   Running all tests in a project creates an entry in the Report navigator that details the results of every test case.

> **Note**
>
> When you program a Cocoa application, you get used to referring to embedded files through `NSBundle.mainBundle()` (`[NSBundle mainBundle]`). This doesn't work for test classes because the main bundle for testing is the application, not the test suite. The right frame of reference is to the bundle containing the class itself: `NSBundle(forClass: RatingTest.self)`.

Asynchronous Tests

In earlier versions of Xcode, Apple emphasized a distinction between *logic tests*, in which elements of an application are linked into the test bundle and exercised on their own, and *application tests*, which are run in the context of the application. Now, all testing is done in the application context.

It's not hard to gain insight into an application's state: Because Passer Rating is completely initialized before it's turned over to your tests, you can ask the `UIApplication` singleton for the application delegate (`AppDelegate`), get the application's `managedObjectContext`, and have complete access to the game database. Your code can edit the store, and, for instance, delete a `Passer` and verify that the deletion cascades to its `Games`. If you're ingenious, you can send `Passer-ListController` (the top item in the `UINavigationController` that is the root controller for the app delegate's `window` property) a message indicating that a passer editor (coming soon) has returned with new data.

Testing Asynchronous Code

But that takes you only so far. The things that most need reproducible tests in an application are the human interactions and network transactions, and those depend on delayed returns from the run loop or completion callbacks. This isn't easy at all; on the simple model we've seen so far, test cases will have exited before there would be any results to examine.

Xcode 6 still hasn't solved the human-interface testing problem—probably no automated test framework could. But for asynchronous operations like networking, `XCTest` adds an "expectations" mechanism that lets a test wait (up to a timeout) for an operation to complete. Passer Rating doesn't have any such operations, but here is the general outline:

- Use the `expectationWithDescription()` method your test case inherits from `XCTestCase` to create an "expectation" object as a handle for XCTest to manage the pause in the test.
- Create an asynchronous operation, something that incorporates a callback block. The networking API in Cocoa consists almost exclusively of such high-level operations.

- In the callback block, send `fulfill()` to the expectation object, effectively waking up the testing mechanism. Now you can put all the assertions you need to the callback data.

- After you've set up the operation and given it its callback block, trigger (`resume`, `start...`) the operation.

- Keep your test case from exiting by calling `waitForExpectationsWithTimeout(_, handler:)`, giving it a time limit on how long it should wait, and a block to execute when all expectations have been `fulfill()`ed. If there was no timeout, and no failures, the `NSError` parameter to the block will be `nil`; otherwise, it will describe the outcome.

Documentation of Last Resort

It can be frustratingly hard to find definitive documentation for new API like this. If you know the symbol you're looking for, or something closely related, you can get to the interface declarations for the XCTest framework. One way to do this is to type an assertion name and command-click on it. Xcode will display what look like documented stubs for the XCTest classes. This file does not literally exist—Xcode is showing you a translation it generated on-the-fly from the Objective-C header files.

This gets us to the other approach: Select **File → Open Quickly...** (⇧⌘O) and start typing something—anything—that might seem related to what you are looking for. The Open Quickly viewer will show a list filtered by what you typed, matching even strings that don't include your input consecutively. For instance, typing **xctexpe** turns up `XCTestExpectation` and `XCNotificationExpectationHandler`. Double-clicking (or selecting and pressing Return) on either one will take you to the Objective-C header that declares (and in the case of XCTest, documents) the symbol.

For more on looking up API, see Chapter 24, "Documentation in Xcode."

XCTest Assertions

Assertions—statements that test for expected conditions—are the core of unit testing. If the condition is not met, `XCTest` logs it as a failure. In Objective-C, assertions are implemented as macros that wrap more primitive methods. One purpose of the macros is to hide some ugly code that validates the types of the values being tested as the tests are being run.

That kind of run-time testing isn't necessary in Swift—the compiler is plenty strict on data types on its own. In practice, this means that for every type of data to be tested, there should be a separately declared assertion `func`. Generic typing cuts the variants down to a handful; and overloading of function names means that even though Swift needs five different generics to assert inequality, you see only the one `XCTAssertNotEqual ()` function. Command-click on `XCTAssertNotEqual` in your code to draw back the curtain.

Assertion function names begin (with one exception) with `XCTAssert`. The initial parameters vary as necessary, but you are always allowed a description `String`. The description is optional. (Objective-C assertions end with a format string and however many additional parameters will satisfy the format.) Hence:

```
XCTAssertEqualWithAccuracy(components[i], gcValues[i], epsilon,
         "\(componentNames[i]) does not match at line \(lineNumber)")
```

Notice that your annotation only has to describe the circumstances of the test; `XCTest` will print out the particulars of any mismatch.

Here are the available assertions. See the Swift or Objective-C interfaces for the exact details of how to call them and what they do.

Simple Tests

These are the simplest assertions—true or false, nil or not.

- `XCTFail`—This is the simplest of them all. `XCTest` logs a failure, plus your formatted message.
- `XCTAssertTrue` / `XCTAssert`—Fails if the Boolean expression you test is `false`. Use this or `XCTAssertFalse` if you have complex conditions that the more specific assertions don't handle. For Objective-C tests, the usual rules for Boolean tests apply: zero or `nil` values are false, anything else is true.
- `XCTAssertFalse`—Fails if the Boolean expression you test is `true`.
- `XCTAssertNil`—Fails if the object pointer you test is not `nil`.
- `XCTAssertNotNil`—Fails if the object pointer you test is `nil`.

Equality

Equality assertions test for whether two things are equal. They have to be of the same type, to start with. Swift will enforce this, and the requirement that they implement the `Equatable` protocol, at compile time; Objective-C won't let you know until the mismatch—even so minor as using a signed-integer constant to check the `count` of an `NSArray`—makes the test fail.

- `XCTAssertEqual`—Fails if the values you test are not equal.
- `XCTAssertNotEqual`—The complement of `XCTAssertEqual`.
- `XCTAssertEqualWithAccuracy`—Never test floating-point values for exact equality; you have to assume there will be rounding errors with anything but trivial calculations on trivial values. Instead, decide on an *epsilon* value—how close the two can be for you to call them equal—and test whether the values are within that margin. Pass the two values and your epsilon to the macro; it will fail if they differ by more than that.
- `XCTAssertNotEqualWithAccuracy`—The complement of `XCTAssertEqualWithAccuracy`.

- XCTAssertEqualObjects (*Objective-C only*)—Fails unless [value1 isEqual: value2]. This is equality of the values of two objects, and not just their pointers (for which you'd use XCTAssertEqual). Take care for the order of the objects, as isEqual: doesn't have to be reflexive. Objective-C needs this variant because its scalars can be compared with plain-old-data operations like ==, but objects can't. Swift doesn't make the distinction.

- XCTAssertNotEqualObjects (*Objective-C only*)—The complement of XCTAssertEqualObjects.

- XCTAssertGreaterThan

- XCTAssertGreaterThanOrEqual

- XCTAssertLessThan

- XCTAssertLessThanOrEqual (*Swift only*)—These tests are exposed in the autogenerated Swift interface, but not in the corresponding Objective-C header.

Exceptions

These assertions are available to Objective-C tests only. Older Cocoa API may throw exceptions if called under improper conditions, like being on the wrong thread or receiving illegal parameters. You might throw some exceptions of your own—but not in Swift. Apple has always discouraged the use of exceptions for routine flow control, and has gone so far as to drop direct support for them in Swift.

> **Note**
>
> The original reason was that Objective-C exception handling imposed too much of a performance penalty, even when no exceptions are thrown. This is no longer the case, but current thinking is that modern, heavily concurrent and interdependent applications simply cannot piece themselves or their data back into working order after a catastrophic failure.

Exception assertions deal with expressions that have two effects: some sort of calculation plus the presence or absence of a throw. The expression parameter to the macros will usually be more elaborate than single values. Bear in mind that assignments and comma expressions are legal, so you can still capture values while you test for exceptions. You can encapsulate complex expressions in helper methods; exceptions thrown inside them will propagate up to the assertion macro.

The XCTest macros evaluate the expressions only once.

- XCTAssertThrows—Fails if the expression you submit does not raise an exception.

- XCTAssertNoThrow—Fails if the expression you submit raises an exception.

- XCTAssertThrowsSpecific and XCTAssertNoThrowSpecific—Fails if an exception of a specific class is not (or is) thrown. This way you can test that your code is doing what you expect with your own subclass of NSException, while distinguishing different exceptions thrown by other libraries.

- `XCTAssertThrowsSpecificNamed` and `XCTAssertNoThrowSpecific-Named`—Some exceptions (usually `NSExceptions`) aren't distinguished by class, but by a subtype indicated by the exception's name. These assertions fail upon the absence or presence of an exception of the given class and name.

Summary

Automated testing is a liberating discipline for a programmer. Any change you make *probably* doesn't have any effect on anything else, but most bugs live in the space between "probably" and "actually." A good testing régime relieves you of obsessive audits that never answer the question: Does it all still work? You'll know; and with that confidence, you'll be free to make bold changes to your application.

In this chapter, you learned about `XCTest`, the Xcode framework for unit-testing applications, and how to build tests from the `XCTestCase` class. I walked you through part of the exhaustive task of producing a test suite that would verify that the process of reading a CSV and pulling accurate statistics from it works correctly. In the course of it, you found a couple of bugs that would be at least tedious to discover by checking the whole application by hand. Now that you have this test, you won't have to worry that something you do in the future will bring those bugs back.

Finally, I ran through the assertions that `XCTest` makes available to verify that what you expect is what actually happens.

Now, let's move on from *whether* Passer Rating works, to *how well*.

16

Measurement and Analysis

Passer Rating has quite a way to go before it's useful for the general public, but you've run it several times, and begun a testing régime, and you're pretty confident that to the naked eye, it works.

As usual, the qualifier ("to the naked eye") outweighs "it works." There are issues in Passer Rating of speed and memory performance. Before you can act, you have to know what's going on—you have to profile the app. The Instruments application is the tool for profiling applications.

> **Note**
>
> If you follow along with me—I recommend starting from the sample code for the end of the previous chapter—your statistics won't match mine. You and I have different computers, different devices, different operating systems, background loads, free RAM and storage... all of which can have big effects on how a measurement run will turn out. In this chapter, I'll stick to two significant figures, which is the limit of what's meaningful.

Speed

The sample code has been changed so that `generate-games.rb` produces a league history from 2014 to 2053—13,054 games, 1.1 MB in size. You'll find the product, `sample-data.csv`, in the same directory. Substitute them into your project, and run the app in the simulator.

Passer Rating takes an appreciable amount of time to start up; with the enlarged data set, if you ran the app on a device, it wouldn't start at all: When you launch, the screen shows the startup image for 21 seconds, and then you're back to the home screen. It takes too long: If your app doesn't respond to user actions for more than 20 seconds, the system watchdog timer kills it. It has to be faster.

> **Note**
>
> In crash dumps, you'll know that the watchdog killed the app if the exception code is `0x8badf00d`.

To analyze speed, I'll be working with Passer Rating on an iPhone 6. The iOS Simulator provides a lot of insight into how an app will work, but it is only a simulator: It has multiples of the RAM available to a device, and if it should run out, it can page memory to disk. It exposes the OS X API, and the shared API is optimized for a different processor. And, especially, the simulator has a much faster CPU.

To install Passer Rating on a device for testing, you have to be a paid member of the iOS Developer Program, register the device, and obtain a signing certificate.

> **Note**
>
> You may have a different device to test on, or if you aren't an iOS Developer Program member, you won't be able to test on a device at all. If you can't participate, just read along. You can find the details of getting permission to load an app into an iOS device, and how to do so, in Chapter 18, "Provisioning."

The **Code Signing Identity** that authorizes Xcode to install your app on a device can be set on a per-configuration basis. Typically the "Debug" configuration would use your developer certificate and "Release," the distribution certificate. But we're not at the point of distribution, so set the identity to **iOS Developer** for both.

Plug in the device, and use the second segment of the scheme control (next to the **Run** and **Stop** buttons) to direct the next build to it. If you've already enabled the device for development, Xcode will have arranged for a development profile that includes Passer Rating and your device. (See the Provisioning chapter if this isn't clear.)

> **Note**
>
> Xcode's iPhone SDKs come with symbol tables for the current Mac and iOS operating systems, but these aren't updated for bug-fix releases; instead, when Xcode runs into a device with an OS minor version it hasn't seen before, it loads the new table from the device itself. The Devices window (**Window → Devices**,⇧⌘ **2**) will explain. It should take only a minute or two.

The Debug Navigator

Click the **Run** button; Xcode will do a fresh build targeted at a device and install the product in your phone. When that's done, it launches Passer Rating.

> **Note**
>
> If the phone is locked with a passcode, you'll have to unlock it before Xcode will let you proceed.

The Debug navigator gives us the first clue: During initialization, the performance bar graphs show the app comes close to saturating one of the cores in the device—90 percent of CPU, sometimes less, sometimes 100 percent or more. See Figure 16.1. (Modern devices have two or three processor cores, so a process could take 200 or even 300 percent, but the major work in Passer Rating isn't threaded yet, so it uses one core at a time.)

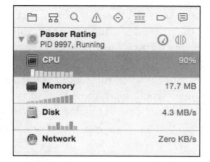

Figure 16.1   The first clue that something is wrong with Passer Rating's performance at startup is the CPU bar graph in the Debug navigator, which shows it taking around 100 percent of the time on one of the device's processor cores.

Click on the CPU bar graph in the Debug navigator, and you'll see more of the story: a detailed running history of how much processor time Passer Rating is soaking up currently, over time, and as a proportion of the available resources (Figure 16.2).

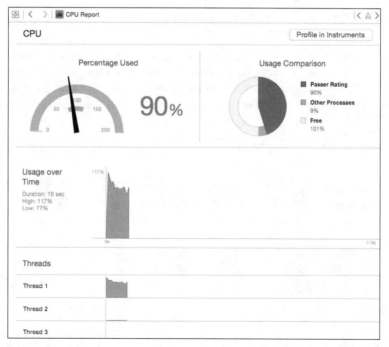

Figure 16.2   Clicking one of the bar graphs at the top of the running Debug navigator presents the details of the Passer Rating's resource usage currently, over time, and as a percentage of available resources.

My first guess was that `SimpleCSVFile` was so simple that it was inefficient. My temptation was to dive into the parser code, audit it, tinker with the works, introduce "speed optimizations" maybe duck into Objective-C or even `asm` blocks in the C code, and try again.

Don't do this. Don't guess. Instruments will tell you *exactly* where your app is spending its time. That's the "low-hanging fruit"; make those parts of your code faster, and you've done more to solve the problem than if you'd nibbled around the periphery.

Use the **Stop** button to halt the app.

Instruments

Profiling an application is easy, or at least easy to start. Xcode provides an action for it. Select **Product** → **Profile** (⌘ I), or the **Profile** option in the Action button in the toolbar. (You probably think of it as the Run button, but if you hold the mouse down on it, it offers all four of the routine actions.)

The profiling application, Instruments, will launch and offer you a choice of what kind of profiling you want to do. See Figure 16.3. This chapter will show you the basics of what Instruments can do; Chapter 26, "Instruments," goes into much more depth.

> **Note**
>
> On later runs, Instruments will use the same trace template. Or, you can use the Scheme editor to preselect the template you want.

Pick the Time Profiler template, and click **Choose**. A window for a new *trace document* appears, containing a track for **Time Profiler**. Instruments comes with 22 document templates, each containing a selection from a repertoire of profiling modules. Alas, these modules are called *instruments*. Be on the lookout, and I'll try to be clear on which I mean.

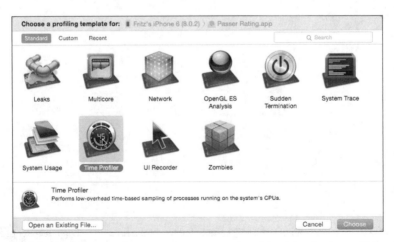

Figure 16.3   When Instruments starts, it presents a template picker for the profiling suites it offers.

Trace documents can be customized: Select **Window → Library** (⌘ L) to reveal a library of the available instruments. Drag your choices into the track view at the top of the document window. (If an instrument won't work with the platform you're working on, a yellow caution flag will appear in the lower-right corner. You won't need the flag; it seems that if an instrument is exactly what you need, it won't work for your app.)

If you selected **Profile** in Xcode, Instruments stands ready to profile your app. If Passer Rating doesn't launch immediately, click the **Record** button at the left end of the toolbar to launch it and start recording. In this case, Time Profiler examines Passer Rating every millisecond to see what code is executing, and the call chain that led to it.

As with many instruments, Time Profile reports statistical data: Over a long enough run, moment-to-moment samples will build up an overall picture of the "hotspots" where the app is spending its time. This is the low-hanging fruit: If a single method is responsible for most of the time spent in the app, any improvement will make the whole app noticeably faster.

iOS and Instruments give you some grace when you're measuring performance: The watchdog timer does not fire, and Passer Rating is allowed to run as long as you need, even though it is unresponsive. In my setup, It took about 50 seconds to present the initial passer list—more than twice the limit. Embarrassing. See Figure 16.4.

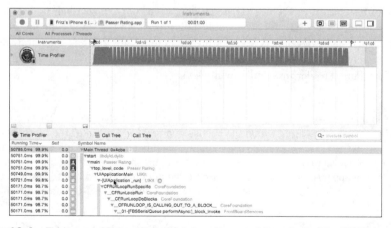

Figure 16.4   This trace of Passer Rating paints a discouraging portrait of the CPU being nearly saturated for more than a minute. The top part of the window is the Trace area, with a track showing CPU usage over time. Below it is the Detail area, for cumulative stack traces of the code that was executing.

An Honest Profile

It's worse than that. I cheated. Look at the top of `Passer.swift`:

```
var allPassers: [String: AnyObject] = [:]

enum PasserFetchStrategy {
    case HorribleKludge;
    case StraightCoreData;
}


let fetchStrategy:PasserFetchStrategy = .HorribleKludge
```

When `Game .loadGames()` reads a record from the sample file, it calls `Passer-.existingPasserByName (_, last:, context:)` to check for an existing `Passer` object to link to the `Game` object. If there is no existing `Passer`, it creates one.

That lookup eats up a lot of time, which would have distracted from the other points I had to make. The horrible kludge is this: When it's asked for a `Passer`, `existing-PasserByName (_, last:, contect:)` doesn't do a Core Data fetch at all. It looks the object up in an in-memory dictionary, `allPassers`.

Let's pretend we don't know about that. Unmask the *real* Core Data code by changing `fetchStrategy` from `.HorribleKludge` to `.StraightCoreData`. Run the profile again.

This is not good. On my iPhone 6, the data set loads in 59 seconds. Three times the watchdog timeout. A fresh-faced programmer will blame the code optimizer: By default, the project templates set the build configuration for profiling to **Debug**, in which the Swift compiler is set to `-Onone`—no optimization at all. Open the Scheme editor (**Product → Scheme → Edit Scheme. . .**, ⌘ <), select the Profile action, and change **Build Configuration** to **Debug**. That gets you `-Ofast`. Does that help?

Profile again. 46 seconds. It's better, only a bit more than twice the timeout limit.

More experienced developers learned this lesson long ago: Turning the knobs all the way up is rarely good enough. We have to think about what Passer Rating is actually doing. The Time Profiler instrument will tell us.

> **Note**
>
> There is another setting, `-Ounchecked`, which removes all the runtime safety checks on dereferencing `nil`, staying within the bounds of arrays, and the like. The better of opinion is that this is a bad idea, even if you've tested comprehensively and are sure the checks aren't needed. No test is comprehensive. Better to crash at the spot of the error rather than let the app walk dead and crash far from the critical spot. I'd like to give you the run time with an unchecked build, but the Swift compiler in Xcode 6.1.0 crashed when I tried.

The Time Profile

The key is in the timeline at the top of the window. You see an area graph of how much of the device's processing capacity the app used at each moment. From just after launch to the moment the passer list appears, the CPU (at least one core of the two) is saturated,

100 percent or close to it. There is a solid block for a short period, and then occasional notches, when the app waited for data to be written out to store. That part of the app takes up 90 percent or more of the startup time, and is where we start.

> **Note**
>
> If the high-load part of the track is crowded into the left end of the display, you can zoom in. First, make sure the app has stopped; the track will accumulate time even if the app is paused. You're done collecting data, so click the **Stop** button (which had been the **Record** button). There are three ways to zoom in: **View → Snap Track to Fit** (**^ ⌘ Z**) will expand the display so that the entire record will fill the timeline view. Control-dragging across a span that interests you expands the display to show just that span. Finally, below the label area at the left end of the timeline is a strip with a small knob in it. Dragging it right will zoom in, and dragging left will zoom out. It's like a spring-loaded audio shuttle—the farther you drag, the faster you zoom, so be gentle.

Drag the mouse across that latter part of the track. When you select a part of a trace, the statistics in the detail area at the bottom of the window are filtered to just that time period. (If you don't see a detail area, click the next-to-last button in the toolbar, the one that looks like a window with its bottom edge highlighted.)

Time Profiler displays the processing load as a tree of functions and the functions they call. The first line of the display is labeled "Main Thread." The Running Time column shows Passer Rating spent all its time in that thread; not surprising. As you click the disclosure triangles next to the labels, you see the functions that were called from that level—the OS launch function `start`, then the runtime root `main`, and eventually something you care about, `Game.loadGames(_, context:, error:)`. Below that, the trace splits into separate calls, among them the chain through the process of reading the CSV file and converting it into `Passer` and `Game` objects down through `SimpleCSVFile.run(_)`. As the call tree branches, the percentages show what proportion of the total run time went into each.

The tree is intricate; it contains a lot of functions you can't do anything about, because they're in the operating system. You can cut it down: Open the Extended Detail view (to the right of the call-tree detail, click the last button in the toolbar if you don't see it) and select the Display Settings inspector (middle tab). This inspector filters the display. Check **Hide Missing Symbols** and **Hide System Libraries**. Now you see just your application code (most of which you, and not the compiler, wrote) and how much time it took up. You can now chase down the tree, searching for the biggest time sinks.

This is informative, but not the best perspective. You can display the time sinks without having to chase them down. Click **Invert Call Tree**. What this shows is every function that was a time sink; the tree below each is every call chain that led to it. This can be crucial.

For example: `objc_msgSend`, which dispatches Objective-C method invocations, is called whenever you use an Objective-C object. That's everywhere. With **Invert Call Tree** and **Hide System Libraries** off, use the search field to find `objc_`. Option-click on the disclosure triangle for the main-thread entry, expanding its call tree completely.

objc_msgSend appears everywhere, a millisecond here, a millisecond there. Set **Invert Call Tree**, and you can see the function takes up more than 9 percent of the app's time. How an expensive function was called does not matter as much as how expensive it is.

> **Note**
>
> As a system function—and an unavoidable one—you can't do anything about objc_msgSend. That's why you set **Hide System Libraries** to narrow the list down to your own code. You can do something about your code.

First Attempt—Batching Saves

The filtered tree fingers Game.loadGames(_, context:, error:) as the main culprit, at 41 percent of the loading process. Double-click the line for that function. Instruments reads Game.swift, and shows the loadGames function, with highlights on the most time-consuming lines (see Figure 16.5). In this case, the save of each new Game,

```
if !context.save(&savingError) {
```

consumes more than half the time spent in the function. save(_) is part of Core Data; so long as that's our persistence method, there's nothing we can do about it. However, we can call it less often, saving only every ten games rather than every one:

```
// in loadGames()
var batchingCount = 10
let batchSize = 1

// ...
```

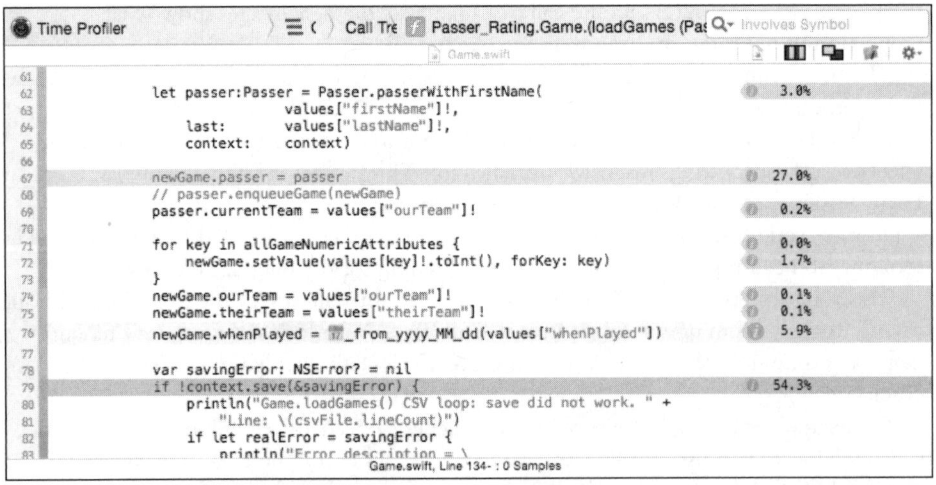

Figure 16.5 shows a Time Profiler call tree with source code. The source code visible:

```
61
62          let passer:Passer = Passer.passerWithFirstName(          3.0%
63                      values["firstName"]!,
64          last:       values["lastName"]!,
65          context:    context)
66
67          newGame.passer = passer                                  27.0%
68          // passer.enqueueGame(newGame)
69          passer.currentTeam = values["ourTeam"]!                  0.2%
70
71          for key in allGameNumericAttributes {                    0.0%
72              newGame.setValue(values[key]!.toInt(), forKey: key)  1.7%
73          }
74          newGame.ourTeam = values["ourTeam"]!                     0.1%
75          newGame.theirTeam = values["theirTeam"]!                 0.1%
76          newGame.whenPlayed = _from_yyyy_MM_dd(values["whenPlayed"])  5.9%
77
78          var savingError: NSError? = nil
79          if !context.save(&savingError) {                         54.3%
80              println("Game.loadGames() CSV loop: save did not work. " +
81                  "Line: \(csvFile.lineCount)")
82              if let realError = savingError {
83                  println("Error description = \
```

Game.swift, Line 134- : 0 Samples

Figure 16.5   Double-clicking on a line in a Time Profiler call tree displays that function's source code, highlighting the most time-consuming statements.

```
parsingError = csvFile.run { (values) in
    // Initialize a new Game, connect it to a Passer...

    if ++batchingCount % batchSize == 0 {
        var savingError: NSError? = nil
        if !context.save(&savingError) {
            println("Game.loadGames() CSV loop: save did not work. " +
                "Line: \(csvFile.lineCount)")
            if let realError = savingError {
                println("Error description = "+
                        "\(realError.localizedDescription)")
            }
            else {
                println("But the error came back nil!")
            }
            return savingError!
        }
    }
    return nil
}

// ... respond to parsing errors...

// One more save in case the last objects
// didn't make it into the looped save:
var savingError: NSError? = nil
if !context.save(&savingError) {
    println("Game.loadGames() CSV loop: save did not work. " +
        "Line: \(csvFile.lineCount)")
    return false
}
// ... on to the rest of the function
```

The next profiling run shows many fewer pauses for saving the changes—a tenth as many, in fact. From launch to passer list, 33 seconds. Just over twice as fast as the First run. This is progress; make it another 50 percent faster, and the app will actually launch on a user's phone.

Second Attempt—Batching Game Assignments

The top consumer of processor time is `SimpleCSVFile.run(_)`. Double-click that line of the call tree to find that it spends 63 percent of its time here:

```
if let userErr = block(values) {
```

That doesn't make a lot of sense. This is a call into the block passed to run by `Game.loadGames(_, context:, error:)`; that block is our own code. It turns out that setting **Hide Missing Symbols** obscures block code. Uncheck it to reveal the tree as it descends into the block. The new champion is _Passer.addGamesObject(_) at 23 percent. This comes from the loadGames loop, as the new Game is linked to its Passer object.

Let's repeat the batching strategy. This time it's a little trickier: Instead of adding a new Game to the Passer's games relationship right away, each Passer should accumulate the new games and add them as a group every so often. Here's an excerpt from Passer:

```
let queueCapacity = 20
var gameQueue: NSMutableSet = NSMutableSet()

//  Put a game into the gameQueue bag;
//  put the accumulated games into this Passer
//  once enough have come in.
func enqueueGame(aGame: Game) {
    gameQueue.addObject(aGame)
    if gameQueue.count >= queueCapacity {
        flushGameQueue()
    }
}

//  Add the accumulated games all at once
func flushGameQueue() {
    self.addGames(gameQueue)
    gameQueue.removeAllObjects()
}

class func forAllPassersInContext(
    context: NSManagedObjectContext,
    body:(Passer) -> () ) {
    //  ... fetch all Passers from the context and
    //  pass each to the closure the caller provides...
}

//  Flush the game caches of all Passer objects
class func flushGameQueues(#context: NSManagedObjectContext) {
    forAllPassersInContext(context) { $0.flushGameQueue() }
}
```

In the loadGames loop, Game replaces

```
parsingError = csvFile.run { (values) in
    // ...
    newGame.passer = passer
    // ...
}
```

with calls that accumulate new games into their Passers:

```
parsingError = csvFile.run { (values) in
    // ...
    passer.enqueueGame(newGame)
    // ...
}
// ...
Passer.flushGameQueues(context: context)
```

26 seconds. Getting closer.

Third Attempt—The Horrible Kludge

Now the biggest consumer is `Passer.existingPasserByName(_, last:, context:)`, at 24 percent of the total during the `loadGames` loop. This is where we started, with my guess that the `.HorribleKludge` option was the best thing I could do to make Passer Rating tolerable for testing. I'd guessed wrong, but now it's our last, best option.

Change

```
let fetchStrategy:PasserFetchStrategy = .StraightCoreData
```

to

```
let fetchStrategy:PasserFetchStrategy = .HorribleKludge
```

One last time through the profiler: 20.1 seconds. On the latest-model iPhones (as I write this), Passer Rating, loading the 16,000-line sample file, has a sporting chance of surviving long enough to display data. There's more work to be done, but trebling the performance of a critical stretch of code is a good day's work.

> **Note**
>
> Now that we've sacrificed our principles, we can move on to rationalizing it. In the data set we have, there are fewer than 50 passers. Keeping 50 keys and object records—or even hundreds—is not a great demand on memory, and is a big win for speed. However: The keys I've used assume the full name of every quarterback is different, and the table indexes only one database, one `NSManagedObjectContext`. If we move on to a data model with more than one league (as we will when we get to the Mac application), we can't have a global dictionary. Last: This doesn't solve the problem, it just delays the problem until you reach 16,000 records. The right solution is to free up the main thread to serve user events immediately by putting the loading process on a background thread.

There's always something more you can do, subject to how comfortable you'd be with the tradeoff between performance and code complexity. The division of CPU time is flat enough now that algorithmic tweaks are harder to find. What you'd do next, instead, is to experiment with the constants that determine how often games are flushed into passers, and the data flushed into the store. You're no longer interested in analyzing the call tree, just the total clock time for loading the data.

Fortunately, there's a tool that fits this task.

XCTest and Performance

Xcode 6 brings another way to gauge the performance of your app. The bar graphs in the Debug navigator give you approximate, whole-app hints that you might want to investigate further, and Instruments will give you particulars down to processor instructions, if you wish. There's room for something in between.

The biggest problem is that you have to *pay attention*. The bar graphs have to be visible, and you have to look away from the device's screen. Instruments works well if you focus on problem areas you might even know about. There's no practical way to check whether your latest work has inadvertently harmed performance; it's not realistic to expect you to be careful enough with more than one host device, or to keep long-term records to see trends; and anything that requires eyeballs can't be automated, either as a part of your routine, or for integration builds.

You've read Chapter 15. You know this is a perfect case for unit testing. Xcode 6 introduces performance metrics to the XCTest framework.

The template for a unit-testing subclass includes a sample performance test, `testPerformanceExample ()`, that contains only a call to `measureBlock ()`. `measureBlock` is very simple: it puts a timer on the code in the closure you supply. It runs the block ten times, and records the average and standard deviation for the run.

When you look at the results of a performance test, you'll appreciate those ten runs. Performance depends on factors you can't control or reproduce, such as network bandwidth, or CPU time and memory claimed by other processes. Even jiggling the phone might trigger motion events that wake background apps registered with Core Motion. An average and margin are the best you can do.

There is a downside: If you're investigating a very time-consuming operation, the ten iterations mean that the performance test will take ten-times-forever. In the case of Passer Rating, you might want to cut the sample-data file down to eight seasons or so. That shouldn't matter if the issue is with the read-Game loop, and not with the accumulation.

Each time you run a performance test, Xcode shows the results in the margin of the test, and more informatively in the Results navigator. See Figure 16.6. Clicking on the test results, whether in the navigator or in the source code, produces a popover showing the timing for each of the ten runs.

If you need to run code that shouldn't contribute to the timing, you can exempt it by fencing it with `stopMeasuring ()` and `startMeasuring ()`.

You're usually interested in the effect your changes have on performance. The report on a performance run offers to make that run the baseline (**Set Baseline**) for comparison with later ones. Those reports will be based against the baseline performance.

Performance measurements can vary, but if the error margin in the average within a single test exceeds 10 percent, Xcode will suggest that the data is too scattered for a meaningful average. By default, it will report the test as failed, and won't make a permanent record of it; you can click the **Set Baseline** button (or **Edit** in later runs) to force Xcode to accept the average.

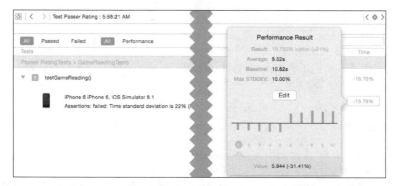

Figure 16.6 The Results navigator displays cumulative results for performance tests. Clicking the timing at the left end of the log entry opens a popover showing the ten runs from the last test, and a comparison to the earlier test you've designated as a baseline.

The only thing XCTest measures for now is the real-world duration of the code in a `measureBlock` call. If you call up the interface for XCTest (see the "Documentation of Last Resort" section of Chapter 15, "Unit Testing") to see hints of a future in which other metrics will be available for you to control through the `measureMetrics` method.

In the case of Passer Rating, your performance-test method should set up a Core Data stack of its own in the `setUp()` function, and tear it down in `tearDown()`. Look at `AppDelegate.swift` for the `managedObjectContext` property and the properties it calls upon.

Memory

In earlier editions of this book, I spent half of this chapter describing the memory instruments—Allocations and Leaks. Until the last couple of years, memory-management bugs were of far greater concern than time performance: One way or another, by losing memory to orphaned objects (leaks) or attempting to give back memory you don't own (over-releasing), mismanaging memory crashes apps.

That's still the case, but Cocoa has developed to the point where it proved too hard to demonstrate memory bugs in an app as simple as Passer Rating. Automatic Reference Counting, which automatically pairs claims on memory with releases, and Swift, which closes off most of the remaining openings to errors, have all but eliminated memory bugs. All but: These are conveniences, not total solutions. Cocoa developers still have to understand Cocoa's reference-counted memory management.

In particular, you should understand *retain cycles,* in which object A claims to own object B, and vice versa. A can't be returned to the memory pool because B claims it; B can't be released because A claims it. There are a number of solutions: `weak`, `unowned`, and `unsafe/undretained` references. If B's hold on A is weak, A can be released, because a weak reference can't save it. A still has a strong reference to B, and with the dissolution of that link, B will be released as well.

Apple's documentation, including a chapter in *The Swift Programming Language,* explains these issues in depth. I'm glad, but regretful, that there's no good way to illustrate them in an overview chapter like this.

Summary

In this chapter, I showed you three tools for testing performance and memory bugs in Cocoa applications: the summary graphs and displays in the Xcode Debug navigator; the time-based profiling application, Instruments; and the `measureBlock` method in the XCTest unit-testing framework.

Instruments served well in tracking down a fatal performance bug in Passer Rating. It relieved you of trial-and-error fixes to code that wasn't the problem, by pointing you to the exact parts that were the problem. It provided the tools to measure what you did, and the courage to take radical steps when they were needed.

There is a *lot* more to Instruments, both the details of the application itself, which I'll cover in depth in Chapter 26, "Instruments," and the techniques for applying each instrument.

## 17

An iOS Extension

Frameworks have been part of Cocoa since the days of NeXTStep. A framework is a kind of *bundle*, a directory that is meant to be treated as a single, indivisible unit (see Chapter 22, "Bundles and Packages," for details). In the case of a framework, the directory contains a dynamic library, plus the resources—NIBs, image files, etc.—the library needs to provide an integrated, shareable, reusable package of services.

Frameworks are in wide use in OS X not just as open or commercial projects to pass among themselves, but as units of the operating system itself. Look in /System/Library and /Library to find Frameworks/ directories for every function in OS X that isn't at the level of the Unix kernel.

As an offshoot of the Darwin operating system, iOS, too, is built around system frameworks for Foundation, UIKit, and much more. However, Apple had a strict rule: All the executable code in an app had to be compiled into a single binary sealed into the application package. The exceptions were scripts that provide program logic (like Lua in Corona SDK), so long as they were not changeable; or JavaScript loaded into UIWebView.

And, there were to be no dynamic libraries, and therefore no frameworks. If you wanted to add prepackaged code to your iOS application, you had to incorporate it as a static library or build it from source.

iOS 8 changes this. One of the features is that apps can now offer system-wide services such as activities (handlers for data from any other app), notifications, and "today" widgets. These could be done simply by running the whole provider app in the background, but that's expensive in memory and performance. The only reasonable way to do it is to factor those services into single-purpose packages—frameworks.

In this chapter, we're going to add a widget for the user to see when she drags the Notification Center down from the top of the screen. It's not going to be ambitious, nor particularly useful; but neither is Passer Rating. "Passer of the Day" (POTD) will display a summary of the career of the last passer selected in the app.

Adding the Today Target

The first step will be to add the Passer of the Day target to the project—nothing more, there will be other work to do, but the target has to exist before you can do it. Select **File** →**New** →**Target. . .**, or click the **+** button at the bottom of the source list in the Project editor.

> **Note**
>
> Don't see the source list? Try clicking the toggle button in the top-left corner of the editor.

This gets you the New Target assistant sheet that has become so familiar to you. Select **iOS** →**Application Extension** →**Today Extension** and click **Next**.

> **Note**
>
> Be sure you've selected the category in the iOS section; selecting OS X for iOS, or vice versa, is a frequent source of confusion.

The Options sheet is unremarkable, but for two things.

- The **Organization Identifier** is not editable. The extension's identifier must be derived from that of the application in which it is to be embedded.
- There is an additional popup, **Embed in Application:**. An extension must be packaged in a containing app. You are given a choice of all application targets in the project; in this case, Passer Rating is your only choice.

Clicking **Finish** will produce one more sheet, an alert asking whether you want to "activate" the scheme for the Passer of the Day target. This is a bit dramatic—you have a new target to work on, of course you want to select its running environment—but there is a purpose: Extensions must be *contained* in one of your applications, but when they run, they are *hosted* in the context of other applications. Today widgets execute in the Notification Center, for which the iOS Simulator provides a host pseudo-application.

The new target adds a reference to `NotificationCenter.framework` to the project and to the "Link Binary With Libraries" build phase of the widget. It adds an "Embed App Extensions" build phase to the Passer Rating target. This is no different from any other Copy Files build phase, but it is preset to move POTD into the app's `Frameworks` directory, and it has a descriptive name.

There will be a new `Passer Rating.entitlements` file, a property list with the key `com.apple.security.application-groups`; the value is an empty array, which Xcode will soon fill in for us.

The target itself consists of `TodayViewController.swift` for a `UIView-Controller` that may include methods from `NCWidgetProviding`; `MainInterface-.storyboard` for the widget layout; `PasseroftheDay.entitlements`; and a Supporting Files group containing the widget's `Passer Rating-Info.plist`.

That's a start.

Designing the Widget

The layout of the widget itself is nothing remarkable—just a slight variation on the billboard view in GameListController, based on the landscape (wAny/hCompact) layout, because vertical space is at a premium in the Notification Center. The interesting part is the design of the executable components. See Figure 17.1.

Passer Rating and Passer of the Day are not stand-alone entities.

- POTD needs to know which passer was last selected in Passer Rating.
- Both use StatView, which simplifies data management and makes Auto Layout much easier.
- They need common access to a single database.
- Both use a core data stack and NSManagedObject subclasses to process the objects in the database.

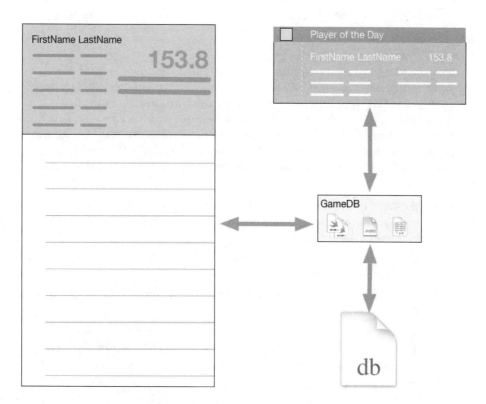

Figure 17.1   Creating GameDB.framework gives Passer Rating and Passer of the Day a single code base for data access and the common StatView.

You *could* do most of this by compiling _Game.swift, StatView.swift, and the Code Data-related properties that are already in AppDelegate directly into the two; when developers shared "libraries" among themselves, the easiest way to do it was to simply dump the library source into their projects. There would be a common source-code base, but no common object code. All that would remain would be data access.

Data Access

Ordinarily, an app's data is isolated in its *sandbox*; other applications—including extensions—have no access unless the user affirmatively shares them with document-sharing, access to resources like the photo library, or through the clipboard. Extensions are no different.

iOS makes an exception: Applications and applets can claim an entitlement to access common data by declaring that they subscribe to an *application group*. This can't be done arbitrarily—you can't stick the Pages group into your application .entitlements file and read the user's documents. Application groups must be registered with Apple; any claim one of your apps or extensions makes on a group is checked against the group identifiers for your developer-programs team.

Registering an App Group

Here's how you connect apps with a group:

Open the Project editor by selecting the top entry in the Project navigator, then select the Passer Rating target. Click the **Capabilities** tab. Find App Groups, and click the switch to turn it **ON**. (Apple still sees the need for labels in a switch, for itself.)

The section expands to display a table of **App Groups**, which is empty for now. Click the **+** button below the table, and type **group.com.wt9t.Passer-Rating.widget**. (Apple will reject it if you aren't registered with the iOS Developer Program as me—make your own ID.) Press Return or Tab to complete the entry. The checklist below the table summarizes what Xcode will do:

- Add the "App Groups" entitlement to your entitlements file (this adds the group ID to the array value of com.apple.security.application-groups in Passer Rating.entitlements)

- Add the "App Groups" entitlement to your App ID (by which it means adding it to your app's registration with Apple)

- Add the "App Groups containers" entitlement to your App ID (again, adding it to the app's registration)

Xcode will negotiate the latter two with Apple Developer Programs online. If the ID belongs to someone else, or there is some other problem, you'll be alerted. Sometimes the problem can be worked out by having Xcode repeat the negotiation—there will be a button for that.

See Figure 17.2.

Next, do the same for Passer of the Day in the **Capabilities** tab of its Target editor. The process is identical, but now that Xcode knows about your group ID, it will offer to

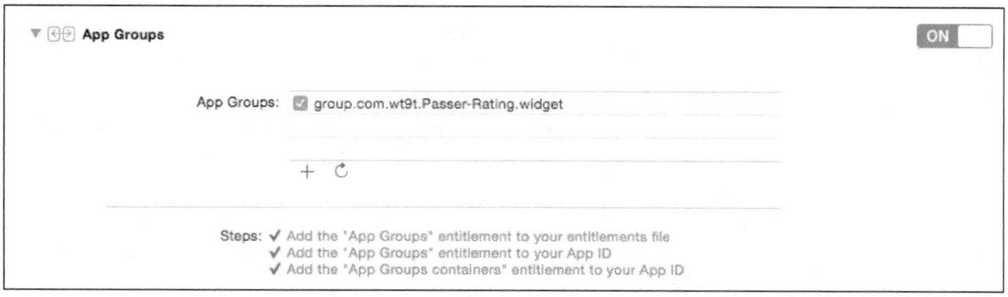

Figure 17.2   Once Apple accepts your group registration, the **Capabilities** tab of the Target editor will show all the automated steps as complete.

autofill it. Now the group has been registered with Apple for both Passer Rating and POTD.

Sharing Defaults

What did all of this do? Applications and extensions that share a group can make selected data available to each other—the identical files and user defaults (preferences).

When the user selects a passer from the `PasserListController` view, Passer Rating can put the passer's first and last names (which are, pathetically, the only keys we use for the `Passer` entity) into a shared `NSUserDefaults` domain, one having the same name as the app group:

```
public
let GameDBContainerKey = "group.com.wt9t.Passer-Rating.widget"
public
let GameDBPasserFirstKey = "GameDB.lastPasser.firstName"
public
let GameDBPasserLastKey = "GameDB.lastPasser.lastName"

/* ... */

override func prepareForSegue(segue: UIStoryboardSegue,
            sender: AnyObject?) {
    //  Work with the shared defaults repository,
    //  not the single-app one

    let defaults = NSUserDefaults(suiteName: GameDBContainerKey)!

    if let segueID = segue.identifier {
        switch segueID {
        case "showDetail":
            let indexPath = self.tableView.indexPathForSelectedRow()!
            let object = (fetchedResultsController[indexPath] as! Passer)
            defaults.setObject(object.firstName,
                        forKey: GameDBPasserFirstKey)
```

```
        defaults.setObject(object.lastName,
                            forKey: GameDBPasserLastKey)
        (segue.destinationViewController as!
                    GameListController).detailItem = object

    case "Edit passer":
        /* ... */
    }
}
defaults.synchronize()
}
```

When Passer of the Day fills in its view, it can recover the first and last names from the shared defaults:

```
func fillViewContents() -> NCUpdateResult {
    let defaults = NSUserDefaults(suiteName: GameDBContainerKey)!
    let selectedFirstName = defaults.stringForKey(GameDBPasserFirstKey)
    let selectedLastName = defaults.stringForKey(GameDBPasserLastKey)
    /* ... */
}
```

The shared defaults store is one part of what Apple calls the shared "container."

Sharing Files

Group containers can also share file storage, such as the Core Data store of Game and Passer objects. Both Passer Rating and Passer of the Day can reach that file through a URL into the container directory:

```
/// A URL to the App Group container directory.

var sharedDocumentsDirectory: NSURL {
    let fm = NSFileManager.defaultManager()
    return
        fm.containerURLForSecurityApplicationGroupIdentifier(
                                    GameDBContainerKey)!
}

/// The URL for the Passer Rating data store.

var storeURL: NSURL {
    return self.sharedDocumentsDirectory
            .URLByAppendingPathComponent("Passer_Rating.sqlite")
}

/// The app's NSPersistentStoreCoordinator, nearly unchanged
/// from the template code.
```

```
var persistentStoreCoordinator: NSPersistentStoreCoordinator {
    if _persistentStoreCoordinator == nil {
        var error: NSError? = nil
        _persistentStoreCoordinator =
            NSPersistentStoreCoordinator(
                    managedObjectModel: self.managedObjectModel)
        if _persistentStoreCoordinator.addPersistentStoreWithType(
            NSSQLiteStoreType,
            configuration: nil,
            URL: storeURL,
            options: nil,
            error: &error) == nil {
                // Again: Never abort() out of production code.
                abort()
        }
    }
    return _persistentStoreCoordinator
}
var _persistentStoreCoordinator: NSPersistentStoreCoordinator!
```

Then, both apps can edit and access the same Core Data file. In the real world, we'd have to take exquisite care to ensure that neither app will change the data store while the other is using it. That one client—POTD—will only be reading the database mitigates the problem, but doesn't eliminate it. In this example, my solution to the problem will be to ignore it.

> **Note**
>
> Until now, our strategy for the data-store file had been to delete it and rebuild at every run of Passer Rating. It was useful while the data model was under development, and we needed a performance challenge. It's untenable now that a second client must refer to the same data—never mind that iOS won't tolerate a Today widget that won't be ready for display for 20 seconds. The sample code will show you how the Core Data stack initialization and the managed-object classes were changed so the database would be built only if it is absent.

A Shared Library in a Framework

I still won't have you fill in the workings of the Passer of the Day extension. The unique parts shouldn't be particularly interesting by now—it's just a view controller and a storyboard. What is interesting is how POTD and Passer Rating can do more to share resources.

We've concentrated on sharing data through app groups, which is essential to the work of POTD, and handwaved the issue of shared resources and shared function. The two apps have a lot in common.

- They need to set up a Core Data stack based on the common data store.
- They read (and Passer Rating writes) `Games` and `Passers`.
- They both use `StatViews` for the detailed statistics.
- They use the same date and number formatters.
- Only Passer Rating uses the `sample-data.csv` file, but if something outside the app is to handle the rest of the Core Data business, it makes no sense to keep that one part inside.
- If that's the case, it doesn't make sense to keep `SimpleCSVFile` away from the workings of the data store—it's used nowhere else.
- Passer ratings belong to `Games` and `Passers`; the app doesn't compute them anywhere else, and if it did, then so might POTD. There goes `rating.swift`.

Why duplicate all this? The code belongs in a shared library; shared code plus resource files makes a framework. A framework can manage a single data store and isolate it from the specialized workings of the app and the widget.

Factoring the shared code out of Passer Rating begins with adding a framework target: **File → New → Target. . .**, and select **iOS → Framework & Library → Cocoa Touch Framework**. Click **Next**, and name the framework **GameDB**, and set the **Language** to **Swift**. Once again, the Options page offers **Embed in Application:**, with **Passer Rating** the only available option. In OS X, you can distribute a framework that could go into a `Library/` directory and be shared across all processes. iOS restricts third-party frameworks to the context of single applications.

Because you designated Passer Rating as the container for the framework, Xcode takes the liberty of adding `GameDB.framework` to the app's "Link Binary With Libraries" build phase, *and* to its "Target Dependencies"—see that section of the **Build Phases** tab in the app's Target editor, joining Passer of the Day. Whenever you build Passer Rating, Xcode makes sure the other two have been built first.

Xcode gives you just a few files: `GameDBTests.swift` for the unit-test target that tags along, and `Passer Rating-Info.plists` for both the framework and the tests. One thing might surprise you: `GameDB.h`. No need to look back—you did specify the language as Swift. However, shared libraries are shareable to Objective-C code, and can be written in Objective-C as well. `GameDB.h` is an umbrella header, which should `#include` headers for Objective-C classes you want to expose to clients.

> **Note**
>
> Xcode takes care of exposing your Swift API to Objective-C by generating a `module-name-Swift.h` file that contains `@interfaces` for all symbols you define as `public`. Find *Using Swift with Cocoa and Objective-C* in iBooks for full details; it's free.

Another surprise: There is no source file. You have to create one of your own. Frameworks are built around a single root class that initializes the library; they can expose other classes, but you have to create the root class and identify it in the framework's `Passer Rating-Info.plist`.

Do that: Create a new class, **GameDB** (⌘ **N**, **iOS** → **Source** → **Cocoa Touch Class**). GameDB will contain an `initialize()` class function to set up the library, and hold the `loadSampleData()` function that had been a part of `AppDelegate` in Passer Rating.

```swift
private var _gameDB: GameDB? = nil
public
func sharedGameDB() -> GameDB {
    if _gameDB != nil { return _gameDB! }

    _gameDB = GameDB()
    return _gameDB!
}


public
class GameDB: NSObject {

    override public class func initialize() {
        initUtilities()
    }

    /// The bundle that contains this class (the framework),
    /// where resource files are to be found.
    var gameDBBundle = NSBundle(forClass: GameDB.self)

/**
    Create and initialize the data store.

    :param: baseName the base name of the .csv file containing
                the initial data.
    :param: createIfAbsent whether the file should be created
                if it isn't there. The app, which has time to do this,
                should pass true; the widget, false.
    :param: error a by-reference pointer to an NSError, valid
                only if the function returns false
    :returns: true if, one way or another, the data store is
                present and loaded.
    :returns: false if the data store is absent, and could/should
                not be created.
*/
    public
    func loadSampleData(baseName: String,
                        createIfAbsent: Bool,
                        error: NSErrorPointer)
        -> Bool
    {
        //  Is the store file there? If so, the work is done.
        if storeExists { return true }
```

```
        // By here there is no store. Can we create one?
        createStore = createIfAbsent
        if !createStore { return false }

        // Yes, create it.
        if let csvPath = gameDBBundle.pathForResource(
                         baseName, ofType: "csv") {
            // .loadGames will call through to
            // sharedGameDB().managedObjectContext,
            // which in turn will create the Core Data stack.
            let success = Game.loadGames(csvPath, error: error)
            return success
        }
        return false
    }


    public
    var managedObjectContext: NSManagedObjectContext {
        if _managedObjectContext == nil {
            let coordinator = self.persistentStoreCoordinator
            _managedObjectContext = NSManagedObjectContext()
            _managedObjectContext.persistentStoreCoordinator =
                                                       coordinator
        }
        return _managedObjectContext
    }
    var _managedObjectContext: NSManagedObjectContext!

    /* ... and so on through the rest of the Core Data stack.
       See the original code in AppDelegate.swift.
       ... */
}
```

Now transfer the managed-object classes to GameDB, and the supporting utilities, by selecting them all in the Project navigator, and using the File inspector checkboxes to reassign them from Passer Rating to GameDB:

- Passer_Rating.xcdatamodeld
- rating.swift
- SimpleCSVFile.swift
- StatView.swift
- Utilities.swift
- _Game.swift
- Game.swift
- _Passer.swift

- `Passer.swift`

- `sample-data.csv`

Passer Rating uses almost all of the extensions in `Extensions.swift` exclusively. The one exception is the `brokenByLines()` extension to `String`; copy that over into `GameDB.swift`.

> ### Note
>
> Swift classes can't be used in other modules—clients of frameworks, or unit tests—unless they and the methods you want to publish are marked in Swift as `public`. Those APIs, in turn, can't be made public unless their superclasses are public. This bites in the case of `_Game` and `_Passer`. Those are created by `mogenerator`, and the whole point is that you shouldn't edit them. The version of `mogenerator` that was current when I wrote this didn't declare the machine classes and their `@NSManaged` attributes `public`; they had to be edited. A pull request has gone in to add those tags; check your machine-side code, and edit it as necessary.

Now that we've committed the managed-object classes to a single store, we can simplify them by having them refer to a global `NSManagedObjectContext`. See the sample code for the details.

With everything wrapped up, select **GameDB** in the Scheme popup in the toolbar, and then **Product → Analyze** (⇧⌘B). There will build errors, for this is a world of sin and pain. Sort them out.

Next, switch to the Passer Rating scheme, and analyze, correcting errors as you go. You'll have dozens, from `AppDelegate`, `GameListController`, `PasserEdit-Controller`, and `PasserListController`: The Core Data and other symbols that went into `GameDB.framework` are no longer visible in the `Passer_Rating` module; you have to add `import GameDB` to bring those objects back into scope.

`AppDelegate` becomes much simpler. The functions and properties that handled Core Data are gone. Most of the other functions from the template can be left empty. The exceptions are here:

```
@UIApplicationMain
public
class AppDelegate: UIResponder, UIApplicationDelegate {

  override public class
  func initialize() {
    //  Initialize the shared defaults store with
    //  empty first and last names.
    let groupDefaults = NSUserDefaults(
          suiteName: GameDBContainerKey)
    groupDefaults?.registerDefaults([
          GameDBPasserFirstKey: "",
          GameDBPasserLastKey: ""])
  }
}
```

```
var window: UIWindow!

func application(application: UIApplication!,
    didFinishLaunchingWithOptions launchOptions: NSDictionary!)
  -> Bool {
  let navigationController =
    self.window!.rootViewController as! UINavigationController
  let controller =
    navigationController.topViewController as! PasserListController

  var error: NSError? = nil
  return sharedGameDB().loadSampleData("sample-data",
    createIfAbsent: true, error: &error)
}

func applicationWillResignActive(application: UIApplication!) {
  //  Update the store for the widget to read
  sharedGameDB().saveContext()
}

func applicationWillTerminate(application: UIApplication!) {
  sharedGameDB().saveContext()
}

//  ... plus application{Did/Will}Enter{Back/Fore}ground,
//  and applicationDidBecomeActive, which are empty.
}
```

Run Passer Rating and satisfy yourself that it works with all the data functions factored out into the library. (Having trouble? That's what the sample code is for.) You'll be pleased at how much more tolerable the app is now that it no longer has to rebuild its database every time.

The Today Extension

With everything else stable, you can afford to concentrate on the Passer of the Day extension.

MainInterface.storyboard starts you with a 320-point-wide scene with a UILabel in the middle. Xcode knows this is a Notification Center widget, so it gives the view a dark-gray background to simulate the dark-vibrant NC view. See Figure 17.3.

The task will be easier than the exhaustive process I put you through in Chapter 12, "Auto Layout in a New View." Complex Today widgets can benefit from size classes: iPad will run iPhone-only apps in an iPhone-sized emulator, but the Notification Center will be full-width regardless. The layout should look good on any screen, and you might want

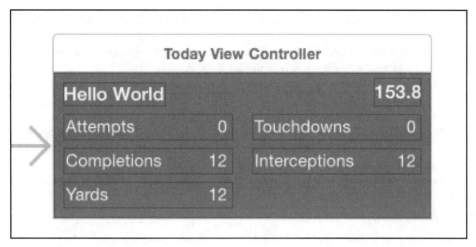

Figure 17.3   The Passer of the Day widget consists of two labels, for name and rating, plus five StatViews. All should be control-dragged into @IBOutlet vars in TodayViewController.

to take advantage of the extra space to show more information. Fine. We won't be doing that.

Put labels at the top of the view for the passer's name and rating. Set them in the dynamic Headline font, aligned leading for the name and trailing for the rating, **Color** white, **Background Default**, which is clear. Pin them 8 points from the top and nearest edge of the view and align their baselines.

> **Note**
>
> Interface Builder will encourage you to use offsets from abstract margins and layout guides. Resist—you may have to use the popups in the top and bottom fields to force the offsets to use the near edge of the view, but I've found the absolute offsets more reliable than the "intelligent" ones.

For the StatViews: Vertically, 8 points to the nearest neighbor—sides of the superview, offsets from the view above. All heights and widths equal. Align the top edges of the ones in the left column with the ones in the right.

Here's a trick for getting the widths right: In the document outline at the left side of the canvas, control-drag from the **Attempts** StatView to the widget's superview, and select any X-offset constraint—you're going to change it. Select the **Attempts** view, find the new constraint in the Size inspector, double-click on it. Change the constraint so that

```
(center of the view) = (trailing edge of Attempts) + 8
    or
(trailing edge of Attempts) = (center of the view) - 8
```

The equal widths and side-edge offsets do the rest: The near-center edges of the StatViews all keep a distance of 8 points from the center; therefore, the distance between the left and right columns is always 16 points. The effect is sparse on a wide screen, but the look is consistent.

The distance between the **Yards** item and the bottom of the wrapper view ensures that the widget will always be tall enough to display its contents.

Make the **Font Color** white, and the **Font Size** 14. If you have to use a scaled-down window in the iOS Simulator, the strokes will be attenuated and hard to read, but if you set **Window → Scale → 100%**, you'll find the lettering clear.

The StatViews will all show up in the document outline and constraint descriptions as "Stat View," with no way to tell them apart unless you click on them and see which view highlights in the canvas. Use the **Document:Label** field in the Identity inspector to set usable names. Another thing to check in the Identity Inspector: **Module** should be **GameDB**; that's where the definition of the view is.

> **Note**
>
> @UIDesignable views rely on Interface Builder's building and executing their classes to render them. The Xcodes available as I write this are not reliable at getting this done; it's common that the compilation of StatView.swift isn't quick enough to survive IB's timeout. The best you can do is to select one of them and then **Editor → Debug Selected Views**.

You may be way ahead of me: Control-drag from the view elements into TodayViewController so it can set their contents:

```swift
import UIKit
import NotificationCenter
import GameDB

class TodayViewController: UIViewController, NCWidgetProviding {

  @IBOutlet weak var passerNameLabel: UILabel!
  @IBOutlet weak var ratingLabel: UILabel!
  @IBOutlet weak var attemptsStat: StatView!
  @IBOutlet weak var completionsStat: StatView!
  @IBOutlet weak var yardsStat: StatView!
  @IBOutlet weak var touchdownsStat: StatView!
  @IBOutlet weak var interceptionsStat: StatView!

  var laggingFirstName = ""
  var laggingLastName = ""

  override func viewDidLoad() {
    super.viewDidLoad()
    fillViewContents()
  }

  override func didReceiveMemoryWarning() {
```

```
  super.didReceiveMemoryWarning()
  // Dispose of any resources that can be recreated.
  // You must take this more seriously than you might
}

func widgetPerformUpdateWithCompletionHandler
    completionHandler: ((NCUpdateResult) -> Void)!) {
  completionHandler(fillViewContents())
}

func fillViewContents() -> NCUpdateResult {
 // Pull Passer Rating's passer selection in from
 // the common preferences. The keys are defined in
 // GameDB.swift.

  let defaults = NSUserDefaults(suiteName: GameDBContainerKey)!
  let selectedFirstName = defaults.stringForKey(GameDBPasserFirstKey)
  let selectedLastName = defaults.stringForKey(GameDBPasserLastKey)

  if selectedLastName == nil || selectedLastName == nil {
    return .Failed
  }

  if selectedFirstName == laggingFirstName &&
      selectedLastName == laggingLastName {
    return .NoData
  }

  laggingLastName = selectedLastName!
  laggingFirstName = selectedFirstName!

  let passer = Passer.passerWithFirstName(selectedFirstName,
                                    last: selectedLastName)

  passerNameLabel.text = passer.fullName

  // ratingFormatter is an NSNumberFormatter that came in when
  // you transferred Utilities.swift to GameDB.
  ratingLabel.text =
               ratingFormatter.stringFromNumber(passer.passerRating)!

  attemptsStat.value = passer.attempts
  completionsStat.value = passer.completions
  yardsStat.value = passer.yards
  touchdownsStat.value = passer.touchdowns
  interceptionsStat.value = passer.interceptions
```

```
        return .NewData
    }
}
```

iOS installs extensions that are embedded in *container apps*, but they run in the context of *hosting apps*. That's easy to see in the case of action or export extensions: Any app can present them, and the apps must configure the extensions and transfer data to them. When you **Product →Run** them, you have to designate the host app with the **Executable** popup in the Scheme editor, or declare you want Xcode to **Ask on Launch**.

Today widgets execute in the Notification Center, a single system-wide facility. The Simulator uses a special process, Today, to host them. Today doesn't appear in the **Executable** menu, so select **Ask on Launch** (making sure the Passer of the Day target is selected). When you run the widget, the Simulator displays the Notification Center, with your widget in place (you hope).

You can set breakpoints and debug Passer of the Day just as you would any other program. Because lldb (and therefore the Xcode debugger) can target more than one process for debugging, you can go back to Xcode, select the Passer Rating scheme, and run that, too. The jump bar in the Debug area lets you switch between the contexts.

There's more: If you have a library (static or dynamic) in the same project as an app that uses it, you can break into its code and debug it, too. You don't have to specially "launch" the library (the concept makes no sense) or designate it for debugging at all.

Build Dependencies

Chances are, you haven't found it so easy to build and run Passer Rating and the Passer of the Day widget all together. You may be seeing a lot of compilation errors that say neither app recognizes GameDB symbols, even after you've taken care to import GameDB in every source file that refers to them. Changes to the library might not show up in one or the other.

Here's the problem.

- When you created both the POTD and the GameDB targets, you designated Passer Rating as the containing application.
- Xcode modified the build phases for Passer Rating to show that the app depends on both the extension and the framework. You can see this in the first section of the **Build Phases** tab for the app's Target editor. That's good.
- It also added GameDB.framework to Passer Rating's "Link Binary With Libraries" phase. That's not necessary, but good.
- Xcode never asked whether Passer of the Day depends on GameDB.framework, so it doesn't appear in POTD's link-with-libraries phase, but if you import a module, the build system silently adds it to the link phase. That's good.

- What Xcode doesn't figure out is that POTD *depends* on GameDB.framework. It doesn't register that changing the framework should force a rebuild of the extension. That's a problem.

- Passer Rating does depend on both, but the build system does not guarantee the order in which dependencies are processed—Xcode is even free to build dependent targets concurrently. Even if the app build does update both targets, it's likely neither will use the current version of the other. That's bad.

You have to tell Xcode about the dependency: Select Passer of the Day's Target editor and the **Build Phases** tab. Click the disclosure button on the "Target Dependencies" phase, and the **+** button under the table. A sheet will drop that lists all the targets in the project. Select **GameDB** and click **Add**.

> **Note**
>
> Do not add Passer of the Day as a dependency of GameDB.framework. First, it's not true. Second, you'll have set it up so that Passer of the Day must be built after GameDB.framework, which must be built after Passer of the Day.... Xcode will detect the circular dependency and refuse to go through with the build. Think through the actual dependencies. If you really do have a circular dependency, refactor your libraries; this isn't just a technicality, it's defective design.

The Result

With everything in place, select the Passer of the Day scheme and one of the iOS Simulator targets, select **Product → Run (⌘ R)**, and choose the Today process as the host. The Simulator should display the Notification Center's **Today** tab, including POTD. See Figure 17.4.

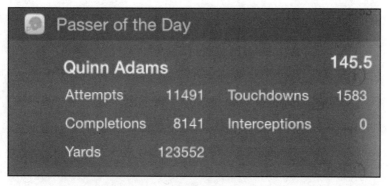

Figure 17.4   The complete Passer of the Day widget summarizes the career of the past-selected quarterback from the Passer Rating app, whether it is running or not.

Drag up from the bottom of the screen to dismiss the Center, launch Passer Rating (you'll have to have built it recently enough to be compatible with the widget), and tap a passer in the initial screen. Drag from the top to expose the Notification Center again. The POTD widget should show the passer you selected, and his statistics.

Summary

Frameworks are an essential part of Cocoa development. Making them available for iOS development gives every app the ability to extend the system and other apps with its unique services.

In this chapter, you saw how to build a Today widget, the simplest kind of extension. We went through how extensions can share data with their applications through App Group containers. We went further by factoring the shared functions of the two apps into a common shared library—a framework—that incorporates both executable code and data resources.

Next: How to put your apps out into the world.

18

Provisioning

Here's the short of it: Apple does not want any app running on any iOS device that isn't written by someone it trusts. It doesn't want any apps in general circulation that it doesn't curate through its App Store. At each stage of the life cycle of your app—from testing on your desktop, to circulating it among beta testers, to final distribution—you have to jump through some hoops.

For the first several years, the process was straight out of Lovecraft: You had to manage two signing certificates by generating requests on your Mac; upload them to Apple's provisioning portal; wait for the portal to issue the certificates; download, and install them in your keychain. You had to log in to register a unique identifier for every product. You had to log in to register every device you wanted to debug on. For each application, you had to log in to request a "provisioning profile" for each purpose of debugging, beta testing, and shipment to the App Store, and install them into Xcode. Change any of the certificates or devices? Log in, and reissue the profiles.

The potential for error was enormous. Nobody got it right.

As Xcode has developed, more and more of the burden has shifted from the portal web site to Xcode itself. Today, the process is *almost* transparent. You'll still need to understand the underlying principles, but until it comes time to circulate your app, Xcode does it all for you.

This chapter will show you the triangle of identities—signing, application, and device—that go into provisioning an iOS app for installation on a device, and how to turn those identities into provisioning profiles. I'll start with the process for iOS applications, then explain the differences for OS X.

Apple Developer Programs

To get your app onto a device, Apple has to trust you (or if it can't, it at least has to be able to identify you and track you down). It needs your name and address, your assent to the licensing terms, and a payment that both defrays its costs and verifies you are who you say you are. Early on, you'll have to pony up for a paid iOS developer program ($99 in the United States for the past eight years).

To join, visit `http://developer.apple.com/`, click the large image for the iOS (or Mac) Developer Program, and proceed from there. A shortcut to the same process is to open the **Accounts** panel of Xcode's Preferences window, hold down on the **+** button, and select **Add Apple ID. . . .** A sheet will drop down asking for the Apple ID and password associated with your developer registration, but it will also have a **Join a Program. . .** button that takes your browser straight into the application process.

General (App Store) Program

There are two kinds of registration for the general iOS and Mac developer programs.

Organizations

Organizations (companies) are entities with credentials like a DUNS number from the Dun & Bradstreet credit-rating organization. Apple allows them to have more than one developer working on the company account; these are organized into a hierarchy of actors, with different levels of privilege.

- **Team Members** may install apps for development purposes, subject to the authorization of senior members of the team. Members can't authorize anything; they can only post requests to Admins or the Agent.

- **Team Admins** can invite others to the Organization account, approve devices for use in development, manage signing identities, issue distribution profiles, approve requests from Team Members, and do all the things Team Members can do.

- There can be only one **Team Agent** because the Agent represents the legal authority and identity of the Organization. She is responsible for keeping the program membership in good standing and reviewing and accepting contracts.

Individuals

The story is much simpler for developers registered in the Individual program: Access is available to only one person, who acts as Team Agent. No permissions, no restrictions.

Enterprise Program

Apple has a separate "Enterprise" developer program for organizations wishing to develop apps for in-house use. Member organizations can distribute apps, like expense trackers, strictly within themselves, without having to publish them through the App Store. The apps can be installed on an unlimited number of devices, subject to a provisioning profile that must be renewed every three years. Enterprises have Members, Admins, and Agents, as with the Organization account.

Apple's B2B program offers another way to distribute an application, even a custom version of an application, to an organization. The organization doesn't have to qualify for or maintain an Enterprise membership, and there is no awkwardness about allowing outside developers access to Enterprise credentials. A B2B release is distributed through the App Store, but it is not visible to the general public. The organization makes a bulk purchase of the custom app for its employees, who are given claim codes for use on their

App Store accounts. That's only a snapshot of the B2B program; see `http://developer`
`.apple.com` for the current details.

Provisioning for iOS

Here is what happens in the iOS provisioning process—the process of getting an
application from Xcode to a device. Xcode (usually) hides the details from you, but there
are always corner cases that will be hard to deal with if you don't know what's really going
on.

> **Note**
>
> The process for OS X provisioning is closely analogous, except that you must apply both a
> distribution certificate and an installation certificate when you submit applications to the
> Mac App Store.

Authorization to install an app *always* consists of three identities.

- A **signature**—The app must be cryptographically signed by a developer (or in the
  case of general distribution, a Team Admin or Agent) to identify it with the
  developer-program membership. The certificate represents a *signing identity*. Apple
  issues the signing certificates.

- An **application ID**—This identifies the particular app. It's a simple string, made
  unique through the reverse-domain convention, that you register to your program
  membership through Apple. This is the same as the bundle ID set in the
  application's `Info.plist`. For Passer Rating, this is `com.wt9t.Passer-Rating`.

- An **authorized device**—App Store and Enterprise applications can be installed on
  any iOS device in the world. For development and beta, the device has to be
  registered with Apple for your program membership. Your program has 100
  registrations, and each lasts a year; you can unregister a device, but its slot won't be
  available to you until the anniversary of your membership.

On the basis of these, Apple will issue a *provisioning profile*. It binds your app ID, one or
more authorized signers, and one or more devices together into a cryptographic bundle
that assures your iOS device that it's permitted to accept the app. There are development
profiles for tethered debugging, ad hoc profiles for beta testing, and distribution profiles
for forwarding to the App Store.

> **Note**
>
> Ad hoc (beta) distribution may pose a political problem if you develop for an organization.
> The 100-device registry is a finite resource of the organization and must be managed. You
> can't develop if you can't register new devices, but there will be pressure to authorize
> copies for the CEO, your boss's boss, your boss's boss's committees...all of whom will
> "test" your app by running it once to show to their friends. Before the question arises,
> make sure your organization establishes a policy that conserves the device registry for
> testing and development.

What You'll See

Xcode 6 does almost all of this itself. The portal site, renamed "Certificates, Identifiers & Profiles," is still there, but it mostly serves as a dashboard for your provisioning information, as an additional interface for performing registrations, and as the only interface for obtaining distribution profiles and certificates. You can reach it by logging into `http://developer.apple.com/membercenter/`.

> **Note**
>
> "Certificates, Identifiers & Profiles" is a cumbersome name, so I'll keep calling it the "portal."

Registering Your Team Membership

Before you do any developer-program-related work, open the Preferences window and select the **Accounts** panel.

The **Accounts** panel gathers the addresses and credentials for three kinds of network services: Source-code repositories; Xcode Server accounts; and, what interests us here, the Apple IDs for a registered developer. My own setup is varied enough to make a good example—see Figure 18.1.

To add an Apple ID, hold the mouse down on the **+** button at the bottom left of the source list, and select **Add Apple ID. . .** from the menu that drops down. You'll be asked for the Apple ID you use for development, the account password, and a description of the account so you can identify it in the list.

With the credentials in hand, Xcode logs into your developer account, identifies all the teams you belong to, and downloads all of the provisioning profiles associated with your team memberships. If you don't have all of the signing certificates you're entitled to, Xcode will apply for them and install them. If you don't have Apple's intermediate signing-authority certificates, Xcode installs them. Figure 18.1 shows what my entry looks like.

If you find you still lack a signing certificate you need, click the **+** under the certificate list in your team-member detail sheet (Figure 18.1, bottom), and select the type of certificate you need. Xcode will apply for the certificate, download it, and install it.

Registering Your App

When you create an iOS project, the **General** tab of the Target editor will protest that Xcode doesn't know of any provisioning profiles for the product. To get a profile, you have to be on the team of a developer-program member. You'll be invited to select one of your team memberships from a popup menu. You can also decline to select a team (**None**), possibly because you don't have a membership, nor do you work for anyone who does. Or, Xcode may not be aware of your registration as a developer with Apple. **Add an Account. . .** will open the **Accounts** panel of the Preferences window to take care of that.

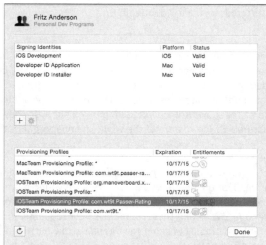

Figure 18.1   When an Apple ID account is added to the **Accounts** panel of the Preferences window, (top) Xcode fetches all developer-program teams that ID is associated with. (bottom) Selecting a team membership and clicking **View Details...** displays all certificates and provisioning profiles available to that team member.

> **Note**
>
> The terminology can get a bit tangled. A *program member* is a person or organization that has paid $99 to have access to the App Store, provisioning profiles, prerelease software, and the like. Each program member has a *team*. Individual-program members have themselves as a one-person team. Organizations can have the hierarchy of team members I discussed at the beginning of this chapter. A *registered developer* hasn't paid a dime to Apple; he's merely clicked the **Register** link tucked into the corner of the `developer .apple.com` web page. Apple collected an Apple ID from him and got his assent to a terms-of-service agreement. A mere registered developer doesn't belong to any team, but organizational program members can invite him.

Selecting the team gives Xcode another opportunity to serve. Now that it knows which program membership owns the product, it joins the company identifier and product name you gave when you created the target into a Bundle Identifier, which it registers with Apple. Xcode and Apple know the signing identities for all the team members, the application ID, and your team's roster of registered devices. That's all three of the prerequisites to issuing a provisioning profile: Xcode asks Apple for a *Team Provisioning Profile* for the app—one that recognizes the developer certificates of everyone on your team—and installs it. By the end of all this, your whole team is authorized to load your app into any registered device for debugging.

> **Note**
>
> There are two kinds of team provisioning profile. The *generic* one has an application ID of *, meaning it will authorize any application. For a while, that was the one-and-only team profile. In the modern era, access to Apple's cloud services is granted per-application identifier; apps that use those services have to have profiles specifically for their respective identifiers. These are still called team profiles because they carry the developer identities and registered-device rosters of the whole member organization.

> **Note**
>
> You remember that if you're a mere Member of a team, you don't have the authority to register devices or application identifiers, or even to issue yourself a development signing certificate. Instead of delivering them to you immediately, the provisioning system will email the Admins and Agent asking them to approve your requests. When they do, have Xcode refresh your information by clicking the circular-arrow button in the team-member details sheet (Figure 18.1, bottom).

You say your device isn't registered? Plug it in, assure it that it can trust your computer, and find it in the Devices browser, **Window** → **Devices** (⇧ ⌘ 2). Select the top line of the device's entry, and click the **Enable for Development** button in the main view. Xcode will ask you which of your teams should register the device (you can choose more than one). Xcode installs (or exposes) some performance–debugging facilities on the device itself (**Settings** → **Developer**, just above the panels for applications); downloads the symbols for your device's version of iOS, if Xcode hadn't seen that version before; and registers the device with the teams you selected. A change in the authorized-device list means a change in the provisioning profiles, so Xcode repeats the download of all of the affected profiles.

> **Note**
>
> In some cases—for beta (ad hoc) users particularly—it's not practical or desirable to plug the device into Xcode. Those devices have to be hand-entered in the portal. Enter the site, select the iOS section (if you have a choice), and select the **Devices** section from the source list on the left. Click the **+** button and enter a convenient name for the device, and its *UDID*. This is a 40-character hexadecimal string that uniquely identifies the device. The Devices organizer displays the UDID prominently; nontechnical users should plug the device into iTunes, select it, and click the serial number to reveal the UDID. The text is not selectable, but the usual **Copy** gesture will put the string onto the clipboard so the user can mail it to you.

Protecting Your Assets

This is a lot of work, even if you didn't have to do much of it yourself. You can get most of it back, or retrieve it on another machine, just by adding the same accounts to the **Accounts** panel and reentering your credentials.

But there is one part Apple and Xcode can't restore for you: Your signing identities rely on public/private key cryptography. Xcode generates a private key for each certificate it applies for. As the name says, it's private. Apple never sees it. It exists only in your keychain: Look for it in the **login → Certificates** section of the Keychain Access application; if a certificate has a disclosure triangle next to it, opening it will reveal the private key—in fact, this is a good way to diagnose a missing private key, which is a common cause of code-signing problems.

If it's lost, it's gone. Irrecoverable. The only remedy is to revoke that certificate and apply for a new one, which makes all applications that rely on it, and aren't already in the App Store, stop working.

So back it up. You can preserve just the key pairs by selecting the certificates in Keychain Access and selecting **File → Export Items. . .** (⇧⌘E), but Xcode can do better for you. In the **Accounts** panel, select **Export Accounts. . .** from the menu attached to the gear button at the bottom of the source list. Xcode will lead you to a password-protected archive of all your assets. Keep it somewhere safe, away from your development machine.

> **Note**
>
> If you distribute signing certificates to support a consortium of developers on an "open" project, expect Apple to revoke the certificates and ban you from its developer programs. Personal accountability for the use of developer credentials is part of the deal.

Prerelease Distributions

Apple draws a line between installations of applications on an iOS device.

Development is the process of loading an app for debugging. It's an interaction between the device, the developer, and the debugger. It requires a development signing certificate for the developer personally.

Distribution refers to any dissemination of an application for nontethered use by other devices; the app can be installed over the air without the need for a desktop computer.

> **Note**
>
> The word "distribution" has picked up synonyms over the years in serial attempts to make the purpose clear. The signing identity for the purpose has the common name "iPhone Distribution." The portal refers to those certificates as "Production." The build configuration for the purpose (actually, you'd probably have more than one) is "Release." The usual way to create a distribution package is with the Archive build action, the result of which is an archive, so the process may be called "archiving."

In-House Betas

When your app has progressed enough to need testers who don't use Xcode, you can create an *Ad hoc* package. An ad hoc distribution may be installed on any device, one of up to a hundred, registered to your team.

They can install through iTunes, but more commonly, they accept an over-the-air (OTA) installation. Using their devices, they follow an `itms-services:` URL. The URL leads to a manifest file, which in turn contains the URL for the application package (`.ipa`) itself, plus resources like descriptions and download icons. These assets can be hosted on any HTTPS server.

Enterprise distribution is closely related. The differences are that the app can be installed on any device, not just registered ones; and your license requires you to restrict access to members of your organization.

Earlier versions of Xcode helped you make ad hoc and Enterprise distributions by collecting the URLs and text for the manifest when you saved the distribution `.ipa`. Xcode no longer does this. However, the manifest is just a property-list (`.plist`, see Chapter 23, "Property Lists") file, and the specifications can be found on the Internet or in older Apple documentation.

Apple's current emphasis is on Mobile-Device Management (MDM) systems for distributing ad hoc and Enterprise applications. MDM for iOS has many advantages, including an App Store–like catalog of the apps you need to distribute, and push notification for updates. There are commercial firms that will provide MDM services to you, or what may be easiest, you can use the Profile Manager in Xcode Server to handle the registrations, hosting, cataloguing, and pushes.

Apple promises that developers who use ad hoc distribution for purposes other than testing, or in-house distribution for use outside of the licensed organization, will be terminated. Bear it in mind.

TestFlight Beta Distribution

Beta distribution is new. Apple now provides a service, TestFlight, that uses the App Store distribution system to send your beta software out to as many as 1,000 testers. All you have to do is give the email addresses for the invitations, and all they have to do is to install TestFlight on their devices. The app will manage the download, and keep them up with new betas as you release them.

Apple still needs some control: One of the reasons for App Store curation is that Apple must assure its customers that they won't be exposing themselves to malware. You can imagine what an opportunity it would be for a criminal to invite a thousand people to try out his fun game, a hidden part of which is a password logger.

So you must submit public betas to Apple just as you would for a published app. The differences are

- You register the app with iTunes Connect as new (if it is new) or as a newer version of an existing app, but you designate it as a prerelease. Prerelease registrations are quick because they need none of the metadata specific to the App Store, and submitting the test version directs the app to TestFlight, not the store. The version currently in the store is untouched.

- The registration adds a beta-testing entitlement to the prerelease version, prompting the iOS runtime to connect it to logging, reporting, and update services.

- You need a new copy of the app's distribution profile, one that reflects the beta entitlement. Refreshing your profiles in the Accounts preference panel will fetch it for you.

- You build and archive the app as before. You apply the **Validate...** and **Submit...** actions to the archive as you would for a product release (see "The Build" later in this chapter).

- Apple will review the app for signs of malice or other gross offensiveness. If it finds none, it posts the test version and sends out your invitations.

The TestFlight app takes care of downloads and update pushes, and harvests logs and user comments to return to you.

> **Note**
>
> Apple provides another, "internal" service under the TestFlight name. It will distribute over the air to as many as 25 testers, with as many as 10 devices each, so long as they are registered with iTunes Connect as part of your organization, and have enough privileges to deter you from using anyone you wouldn't trust implicitly.

TestFlight is not the single answer to every testing need. It is set up for apps that are "beta" in the strict sense of the word: Feature-complete, and usable by people who understand the purpose of the app more than how it's built.

It isn't suited to releases that have gaps, stubbed-in functions, known bugs, or other things that developers and product managers can work around, but "civilians" shouldn't be expected to. For those purposes, distribute ad hoc. Even if you're a solo developer, you can still register your friends' devices so they can test for you.

The Capabilities Editor

What I've described covers the bare minimum of the registrations and certifications you'll need to distribute an application. There are additional capabilities that need some combination of additional credentials and continuing support from Apple; or advertising in the app's Info.plist file (see "Bundles and Packages"); or claims in its *entitlements* file; or linkage to additional system frameworks.

Xcode 6 provides a unified editor for the most common capabilities in the Target editor's **Capabilities** tab. Each facility has an on/off switch. Clicking the disclosure triangle describes what the facility is and what Xcode will do to enable it for your product. Some capabilities have further options.

OS X-only Capability

All of the capabilities available to OS X are also available to iOS, except for one: **App Sandbox**. It's a long story, which I'll tell later in "OS X Sandboxing."

Capabilities for Both iOS and OS X

The remaining six OS X capabilities are also available to iOS:

- **iCloud** is the shared-storage service for a user's Apple devices. Turning on the capability will register the requirement with Apple and put the store identifier into your entitlements file.

- **Game Center** is the Apple-hosted mediator for leaderboards and player challenges. Xcode will register your app as using Game Center; note the need for GameKit in your Info.plist, and link GameKit.framework to the app. iOS apps are automatically registered for Game Center, but you must still turn the capability on to use it. Additionally, you must log into iTunes Connect (itunesconnect .apple.com) to obtain the necessary credentials for your app.

- **In-App Purchase** lets you sell application services from your app. There are restrictions on what you can sell—see the review guidelines and the IAP documentation for details. Flipping the switch links StoreKit.framework and adds IAP to the app's registration with Apple. You will still have to register your IAP products with iTunes Connect.

- **Keychain Sharing** lets your applications share credentials through a common keychain. Each app must list each shared keychain's identifier in its entitlements file. This option lets you manage that list.

- The **Maps** capability is slightly different between the two platforms. On OS X, it links the MapKit framework and claims privileges for displaying maps. All iOS apps are privileged to display maps; this capability advertises that your app can provide routing information for specific areas of the world, and specific combinations of transportation, so you can specialize in streetcars and ferries in Atlantic City.

- **App Groups** must be registered with Apple under your application ID. Apps that share a group identifier can have access to common files, and communicate with each other, as a relaxation of the normal app-sandboxing policies. You add container IDs in reverse-DNS form, beginning with `group:` `group.com.wt9t.football`. Containers are registered with Apple, and your team's group IDs can be refreshed from Developer Relations just as team provisioning profiles are.

iOS Capabilities

- **Passbook** is the system for putting bar-coded tickets and coupons on the user's screen. Publishers of Passbook-enabled apps manage the passes centrally and push changes out to users through Apple's push server (think of an airline selling a ticket weeks before a flight, and pushing a seat assignment into an on-screen boarding pass shortly before boarding). The capability registers the app's claim with Apple and in the entitlements file; `PassKit.framework` is added to the link phase.

- **Apple Pay** claims the right to accept payments for physical goods and services through Apple's payment-clearance system. The claim and the necessary identifiers are registered with Apple and in the entitlements file.

- **Personal VPN** permits the app to configure and provide an on-device VPN service. It is registered with Apple and claimed in the entitlements file; selecting the capability links `NetworkExtension.framework`.

- **Inter-App Audio** is a specialized service that allows one app to exchange MIDI commands and audio streams with another. Activating it registers the entitlement with Apple, adds it to the application entitlements file, and links `AudioToolbox.framework`, with which you are about to share a long adventure.

- **Background Modes** exposes checkboxes for your app to claim the privilege of running periodically while it is not the frontmost application. iOS permits only limited operation in the background, and your app must declare the services you want in its `Info.plist`. Apple's reviewers will check to see that your app is doing what you claim with its background privileges.

- **Associated Domains** An iOS app may claim a special relationship with an HTTP/HTTPS server by listing the server's domain name as an associated domain. One use for this would be with Handoff: The user of a Mac is browsing a page at `apple.com`; there's nothing special about that host, so a handoff of the browsing task would simply open Safari to the same URL.
  Suppose you had a weather-radar service, available as a web site and an iOS app. Your app could claim an association with your site's domain name, and be launched to show the same radar display as was on the browser. (There are safeguards against apps' hijacking others' pages.)
  This capability lists the associated domains, prefixed by a keyword of your choosing to describe the kind of activity your app would be willing to take over.

- **HomeKit** is Apple's framework for linking apps to home-automation systems that control heating, cooling, lighting, and the like. HomeKit takes care of registering the home's "users," and cataloguing rooms and areas within the house. It can then present users with all the controls available to particular rooms, or group actions provided by different apps. HomeKit apps can be controlled through Siri.

  All of this requires interapplication communications and cross-device administration through iCloud. Turning on the capability claims the entitlement, registers your app, and links the HomeKit framework.

- **Data Protection** indicates that all document-file access by the app should be encrypted to one degree or another. The protection levels are Complete (locking the device cuts off all access to a file, even if you had it open); Complete Unless Open (your app can keep access to a file if the file was open when the device was locked); or Complete Until First Login (the file becomes readable the first time the user unlocks the device after startup).

  However, you can only specify those levels in the portal's listing of your app's privileges. You can always specify encryption options on individual files and data blocks in your code.

- **HealthKit** is a secure database shared by apps on a device. They can exchange information, so one app can track walking distance; another, meals; and a third, total calories gained and expended. The iOS Health app provides a shared control panel for collecting, displaying, and securing the contents of the database.

  The capability claims the relevant entitlement, registers the capability to Apple, and advertises it to the device itself.

- **Wireless Accessory Configuration**. Apple calls its system for communicating between iOS devices and accessories (including AirPlay and some HomeKit devices) MiFi. Accessory makers can get specifications and support by registering with Apple at `https://developer.apple.com/programs/mfi/`. On the device side, the Wireless Accessory Configuration entitlement allows the app to communicate with a particular MiFi device for setup.

OS X Sandboxing

iOS has a strict security régime that keeps each app in a "sandbox," an environment in which an app has no access to files outside the application package or that it did not create, nor to device services except as permitted by the OS.

OS X 10.7 Lion introduced sandboxing to the Mac as an opt-in for most applications, and mandatory for all apps sold through the Mac App Store. You can't get access to Apple services like iCloud or Game Center without selling through the App Store, and you can't get into the App Store without sandboxing.

The idea is to make it harder to attack the user's Mac by having the operating system block any service the developer didn't declare. If you didn't say you need to operate a socket for incoming network connections, and your app suddenly attempts to do that, the change must (the theory goes) have come from malware that exploited a weakness in your app.

By default, the sandbox is completely closed to everything but direct interaction with the user. It can't even read or write files. Everything else is an exception, which you must claim through the app's entitlements file. You must sign (and, for the App Store, Apple must countersign) the app to seal it against alteration. You declare your requested entitlements in an `.entitlements` file (in the property list format; see Chapter 23, "Property Lists"). The build process embeds them in the signed application binary.

The **Capabilities** tab of the Target editor gives you checkbox access to the most common entitlements. When you turn sandboxing on, Xcode adds a `your-app-name` `.entitlements` file to the application target. The repertoire is:

- Network
    - Incoming connections (Server)
    - Outgoing connections (Client)

- Hardware
    - Camera
    - Microphone
    - USB
    - Printing

- Apps
    - Contacts
    - Location
    - Calendar

- **No Access**, **Read Access**, or **Read/Write Access** to
    - User-selected file
    - Downloads folder
    - Pictures folder
    - Music folder
    - Movies folder

> **Note**
>
> There are many more possible sandbox entitlements. Some are obscure (deservedly or not), such as access to AppleScript, shared preferences, or files that have the same base names as files the user had authorized in the same directory. Some are *temporary exceptions*, which could mean that Apple is still working out how to implement the privileges they represent; or it could mean that Apple means eventually to close off those privileges, and is giving developers time to figure out workarounds. And some you may have to invent for yourself, in the (usually forlorn) hope that Apple's reviewer will open the sandbox to some privilege that your app absolutely needs. Search the Documentation organizer for the *Entitlement Key Reference*, ask around in the developer forums at `http://devforums.apple.com/`, and comb through WWDC videos. This is one of the few instances where the forums are of more use than Stack Overflow.

Take special note that if you want to read and write files outside your app's sandbox directory, you must ask for the privilege. Even then, you will gain access only to files that your user has explicitly designated. These could be dragged and dropped onto your app's icon in the Finder or the Dock, or into one of your windows (if you handle file drops); or through PowerBox (so named because it's...like a box), the secure OS X process that replaces the open-file and save-file sheets.

If you submit your app for App-Store review, be sure to include a justification for every entitlement you claim—common, uncommon, or exceptional—in the review notes. For example, "MyEditor is an editor for document files and must have read and write access to user-identified files. It needs to make outgoing network connections to download templates and to validate user-entered URLs."

Why Sandbox?

The most powerful incentive for adopting sandboxing is that you can sell your app through the App Store. This isn't just a matter of having a convenient way to distribute your work and collect payments. App Store access enables your app to use a number of OS X features that require the use of Apple servers:

- iCloud
- In-app purchase
- Push notifications
- Game Center

But there is another reason. Sandboxing is intended to prevent an application from being an attack vector. Even if the app gets pwned, it can't erase a user's files, send her contacts to an identity thief, or operate a spam SMTP server (always granting that the latter two could still happen if the app originally asked for the necessary privileges). A sandbox error that crashes your product is embarrassing, but embarrassments happen, and people will wait (briefly) for a fix. A breach that ransacks the user's system will ruin you.

Why Not Sandbox?

If sandboxing doesn't fit your application's needs, don't use it. The only costs are that you won't be able to sell through the Mac App Store, and thus make use of Apple-served features.

What needs would interfere with sandboxing? Basically, if you want general-purpose access to resources that belong to the system or other applications, you can expect sandboxing to pinch. Common trouble spots are

- Gaining privileged access to system resources or access-restricted files. If you've written an editor for system-configuration files, you're out of luck.

- Writing an assistive application. The sandbox will let you expose your UI through the accessibility API, but if you want to send accessibility events *to* another application—a technique that many developers use as poor-man's inter-application communication—the sandbox will stop you.

- You can receive and respond to Apple events (most commonly from AppleScript), but you can send them only to applications you list in a temporary exception entitlement. An Open Scripting Architecture script editor won't work in the sandbox.

- You can't access other apps' preferences unless, under a temporary exception, you list the domains you want to access. Also, you can share data among apps in a suite by having each declare themselves to belong to an "application suite" keyed to your development team ID.

- You can't load kernel extensions. Are you surprised?

These are all useful, reasonable things to do; you just can't do them and work in the sandbox.

Gatekeeper and Developer ID

OS X 10.8 Mountain Lion introduced Gatekeeper, another way to reassure your users about the safety of your apps, without the limits the sandbox imposes. When Gatekeeper is in effect, all downloaded applications (or executable documents like scripts) are on a blacklist, and users will not be permitted to open them. Only apps that come from "identified" developers are on the whitelist.

You become "identified" by obtaining a *Developer ID* cryptographic signing identity from Apple and applying it to your app. Signing with a DevID clears it for execution, with only a one-time warning that it had been downloaded from the Internet.

Getting a Developer ID

Developer ID is available to any member of the $99 Mac Developer Program. In fact, once you're in the program, DevID is almost impossible to avoid: When you enter your developer account in the **Accounts** panel, the DevID certificate is created and installed. This is another public/private key pair, so secure it either by creating a developer-account archive or exporting it from Keychain Access.

As a paid member of Apple's Mac Developer Program, you will have five signing identities; be careful to keep them straight in your mind and in your keychain.

- **Developer ID Application** is the certificate you'll apply to get your app past Gatekeeper. Don't bother to set any certificate in the "Code Signing Identity" build setting; Xcode asks you to choose your Developer ID certificate when you click the **Export. . .** button in the Archives organizer.

- **Developer ID Installer** is used to assure Gatekeeper about non-application products like installer packages and `.xip` archives. Xcode never touches the DevID installer certificate; you use it with the `productsign` and `xip` command-line tools.

> **Note**
> `xip` is pronounced "chip."

- **3rd Party Mac Developer Application** sounds similar to the Developer ID Application certificate, but the closer analogue is the "iPhone Distribution" identity on the iOS side: In a build to be uploaded to the Mac App Store, you select this identity in the "Code Signing Identity" build setting. As with the iOS distribution certificate, the certificate has to match up with the application's ID through a provisioning profile you get from Apple.

- **3rd Party Mac Developer Installer** is *not* an analogue to the Developer ID Installer certificate. Unlike with iOS packaging, you use separate signing identities to prepare an application for validation and submission to the Mac App Store. The Developer Application certificate is used in the build process. The Developer Installer certificate is applied when you click **Validate. . .** or **Export. . .** in the Archives organizer. You'll be presented with a choice of installer certificates; choose the default Xcode offers you unless you are *positive* you need something else.

- The **Mac Developer** certificate is different from the two "3rd Party Mac Developer" certificates, for all that it has nearly the same name. The concept is most similar to the "iPhone Developer" identity you use for iOS development. It is the build-time signing identity you apply to debug builds when you're testing identity-sensitive features like sandboxing, Developer ID, and access to Apple cloud services. This, too, matches to a provisioning profile, in this case a *development* profile.

Using Developer ID

Open an Xcode project containing a Mac application target, and select **Product →Archive**. All going well, Xcode will show you the Archives organizer with your application archive displayed. Click **Export. . . .** A sheet drops down presenting your options (Figure 18.2). The top choice, **Export Developer ID-signed Application**, is the one you want. Click **Next**.

Once you've chosen the distribution method, Xcode examines the archive, the provisioning profile, and your keychain. It then gives you a popup menu to select the signing identity you want to apply—the one it selects is usually correct.

An activity spinner turns for a while as the cryptographic signatures are assembled, and at last you are given a put-file sheet so you can save the completed application.

That's it. Xcode gets you a certificate, it signs your app with it, it puts the app on disk. It's actually more trouble to save an unsigned application. You're free to distribute the app however you like; any method—`.zip` archives, disk images, CD-ROMs, email attachments, paper tape—that a Mac application can survive. The only difference is that when a user of Gatekeeper downloads it, OS X will let her run it.

> Note
>
> Once you start embedding frameworks or helper tools in your app, things get complicated; each needs its own signature independent of the application's. This should be easier than it is, and it may have become so by the time you read this. Until then, have a look at Jerry Krinock's solution on GitHub at `https://github.com/jerrykrinock/DeveloperScripts/blob/master/SSYShipProduct.pl`.

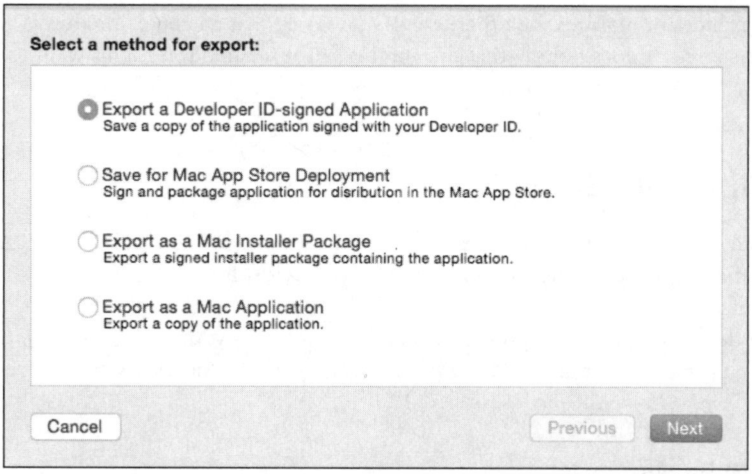

Select a method for export:

○ Export a Developer ID-signed Application
Save a copy of the application signed with your Developer ID.

○ Save for Mac App Store Deployment
Sign and package application for disribution in the Mac App Store.

○ Export as a Mac Installer Package
Export a signed installer package containing the application.

○ Export as a Mac Application
Export a copy of the application.

Cancel   Previous   Next

Figure 18.2   The sheet that appears when you click **Export...** on a Mac archive offers the choice of creating a Developer ID–signed application package.

Limitations

Developer ID is not a panacea. It doesn't guarantee that the application is secure. It does not prevent an app from doing something malicious. It detects the app's signature only the first time it is launched from download quarantine; if something injects malicious code at run time, the OS won't detect it. It doesn't apply to any file that wasn't downloaded or was downloaded by means other than the usual browsers or mail applications. Unlike App Store products, it does not attest that someone has reviewed the app for security or quality.

> **Note**
>
> Gatekeeper will restrict downloaded documents, as well, if they are of a "dangerous" type, like scripts or installer packages. The `productsign` tool can apply your "Installer" Developer ID to packages, and `xip` can produce archives of "dangerous" files that can be expanded safely by double-clicking them. See the respective `man` pages.

The only assurance that Gatekeeper gives—and the UI is careful to say so—is that the developer of an app is "identified." When you signed up for the Mac Developer Program, you gave enough information that Apple can find you. If it discovers you've been distributing malware, it can revoke your Developer ID, and your applications won't run any more. Want to continue distributing malware? Come up with another identity and bank account, and pay another $99. Cheap if you're an evil mastermind, but most scammers won't bother.

Which is why you can't get a Developer ID without paying for the Mac Developer Program.

Developer ID and sandboxing are separate concepts. If you want your app to be in the Mac App Store, sandboxing is mandatory and DevID is pointless. Outside the App Store, neither excludes or requires the other. DevID says only that an app came from a (so far) reputable source. It does not say that the app is safe, or secure. You might want to consider sandboxing as a backstop to your secure-coding practices.

Distribution Builds

Once your project goes from development to distribution (you remember this is any dissemination of an app to be run untethered), Xcode is still friendly, but higher maintenance.

If Xcode has a distribution profile on-hand that matches your application ID, it will match the profile to your app, and the profile will specify the necessary signing certificate. Good.

Basic Build Settings

The build settings for your product are the key to the selection of the profile and the signing identity.

The (INFOPLIST_FILE) setting is the name of the precursor for your product's Info.plist file. The precursor you see in the Project navigator is almost a complete Info.plist, but it has some build-setting references that have to be resolved, and it's missing some keys. The build process finishes up the file and installs it in the app bundle as Info.plist.

> **Note**
>
> Info.plist is at the core of most OS X and iOS products; learn more about property list files in Chapter 23, "Property Lists," and the content of Info.plist in the "The Info.plist File" section of Chapter 22, "Bundles and Packages."

Info.plist is where your app specifies its application ID (CFBundleIdentifier), which is how the build system can identify the matching provisioning profile.

At least that is how it could go, and did until recently. Now, it has been recognized that release builds could be ad hoc or for publication, and provisioning profiles may be issued with wildcard application IDs. So the build settings now include a key, PROVISIONING_PROFILE, that you set to precisely identify the profile you mean; the popup list will include every profile Xcode knows about. It's optional now, but Apple warns that it will be required soon.

The profile knows what signing identity it requires. If you leave the signing identity build setting (CODE_SIGN_IDENTITY) to accept a generic "iPhone Developer" or "iPhone Distribution" identity, the build system will pick the right one. You *can* select a different identity, but if it's one that Xcode doesn't match to your app, it's probably the wrong one.

> **Note**
>
> In Chapter 25, "The Xcode Build System," we'll get into the way Xcode classifies build settings by purpose and destination platform. For now, notice that the project template

puts profiles and identities for iOS devices in device-only special cases. This is because if you are running a Debug build, you may want to run it on your iPhone (which would require an iOS developer signature) or the iOS Simulator application (which should not have any signature). Don't change the scope of a setting unless you know why you're doing it; tidiness is not enough.

If all those ducks are in a row, you're ready to do an Archive build. Barring special circumstances.

Adjusting the Build Settings

It may not be so simple. In my work, we've had to work on the same basic product, using three means of distribution:

- A straightforward article that's headed for the App Store, as I showed you. It needs development profiles, and a final App Store distribution profile. When we test though TestFlight, we use the same target—the only difference is that the beta is registered in the **Prerelease** tab in iTunes Connect.

- A beta version for ad hoc distribution among devices registered in the developer portal, perhaps of the current App-Store product, perhaps of the next generation. It needs an ad hoc distribution profile.

- An in-house version, distributed under our Enterprise license. It *must* have its own application ID, because it has to be provisioned out of our Enterprise account, and Apple won't let us reuse the App Store version's ID. It needs a distribution profile of its own, issued under that program membership.

Let's tease out the Enterprise-versus-App Store issue first: Two developer-program memberships means two different teams, each with its own distribution signing certificate and its own source for provisioning profiles. Xcode's integration with the provisioning process weds each target to a single team membership. Our product must have two targets, one for App Store–related builds, and one for Enterprise. There are two products, each following an independent path to distribution, and we don't have to worry about both at once.

Note

Projects, of course, can have many targets, each with its own team membership. There's nothing wrong with keeping the App Store and Enterprise targets in the same project.

Let's proceed with the other two products: the App Store article and its beta counterpart.

We don't *have* to treat the beta as a separate product. It can share its application ID, icons, and versioning progression with the release article. If so, the two can share an Info.plist. It's easy; all you have to do is clone a "beta" build configuration from the Release configuration that simply selects the "ad hoc" (beta) distribution profile.

> **Note**
>
> Chapter 25, "The Xcode Build System," covers build configurations in exhaustive detail, but here's the short of it: The process of building an application invokes many separate tools, each with many options to configure its behavior and identify its inputs and outputs. A build configuration is a package of those settings. You can have more than one—by default, you get Debug and Release—to tailor the process to the purpose of a build.

Generating the beta product then becomes a simple matter of choosing the configuration. If you duplicate the App Store target's scheme and name it something like **MyApp beta**, and select the beta configuration for the Archive action, you can switch between the release methods just by selecting a scheme from the popup menu in the toolbar.

Apple doesn't recommend this for serious development. If your product is already in the App Store, your beta product is going to be an early version of the next release. If the beta and the released version share application IDs, the beta will overwrite the public release app on your testers' devices. Few people will volunteer to beta-test software if it means losing the working version. So CFBundleIdentifier, the app ID, has to be different.

CFBundleVersion, what Apple is calling the "build number," will probably be different, too. You'll have many betas for *MyApp 1.1*, all of them with the same "marketing" CFBundleShortVersionString (1.1). If the CFBundleVersion is also 1.1, you'll find that iOS (and the OS X installer) won't replace the beta app with new betas—the OS refuses to install an application package that has the same CFBundle-Version as the incumbent. For an example of a build number, select **Xcode → About Xcode** to see the difference between a "marketing" version number (6.1) and a "build" number (6A1052c).

If the identifier and the bundle version have to be different, then the beta and final products must each have their own Info.plist, the file that sets those properties (and others) for an application bundle. Your project does not contain a literal Info.plist; instead, it contains precursors named Info.plist that must be processed into the Info.plist to be installed in the application package.

Select your product's precursor file in the Project navigator, and then select **File → Duplicate...** (⇧⌘S). Give the new file a suitable name reflecting the target name and its purpose as a beta. Edit the new file:

- Give the file its own CFBundleIdentifier (bundle ID), because you don't want to overwrite the release article on your testers' devices. You'll have to register the ID with the portal, and (for a beta product) have Apple issue an "ad hoc" provisioning profile for that ID.

- Create names for the betas' own icon files—your testers would like to be able to tell the beta apart from the production app. You'll have to add the icon keys by hand: The build system creates the icon records from your settings in the target editor, but for a custom plist, you'll have to do it yourself. See Chapter 22, "Bundles and Packages," for the keys and their meaning.

- Set CFBundleVersion to conform to the build-versioning scheme you've chosen.

- You'd want a beta to have a distinctive name, but leave **Bundle name** (CFBundleName) alone. By default, it's set to ${PRODUCT_NAME}, which is taken from the **Build Settings** for the current configuration.

Create such a configuration: Create an "Ad Hoc" build configuration by cloning the Release configuration in the Project editor. That will add an Ad Hoc variant to all of the settings in the Target editor's **Build Settings** tab. Adjust the settings for the Ad Hoc variant as needed by clicking the setting's line and clicking the disclosure triangle to expose the Ad Hoc configuration: At least, select your cloned Info.plist precursor file, set **Product Name** to something that distinguishes the beta version, and select the ad hoc provisioning profile.

Then create a new scheme for building the beta version: Use **Product →Scheme →Manage Schemes...** to reveal the list of the project's build schemes. Duplicate the default scheme for your product, give it a name (**My App Ad Hoc**) and click **Edit....** For the Archive action, set the **Build Configuration** to your custom ad hoc configuration. The scheme will appear in the popup menu in the project window's toolbar. You can switch between the beta and final releases instantly.

Eventually, your new version will be good enough that its replacing the old one is no loss. That's the point at which you can move on to a TestFlight public beta, using the scheme you set for App Store releases.

The Build

The goal is to produce an archive from which you can generate a distributable product. To produce an archive you must have

- The necessary distribution (and in the case of OS X, installation) identities, with both the public and private keys, in your keychain.
- A provisioning profile that authorizes the kind of distribution you intend.
- A build configuration that selects the proper profile, and an Info.plist that declares a matching bundle ID.
- A scheme, the Archive action of which designates the correct build configuration.
- The scheme, and a target-device (not simulator) destination, selected in the scheme popups at the left end of the project window's toolbar.

Select **Product →Archive**. Wait. Assuming there are no build errors, the Archives organizer will appear with your product selected.

> **Note**
>
> This is another of those "if all goes well" situations. If there's a regular compilation, linkage, or resource error, you know what to do. If it's a provisioning problem—the profile, the identifier, the certificates—every unhappy build is different. In the Documentation browser, look up the Troubleshooting chapter of the App Distribution Guide, and work from there.

If you're headed for an App Store, you'll have to have registered the app with iTunes Connect, providing all the necessary marketing, legal, and technical information—including your application ID. And you must have told iTC that the app is "Ready for Upload." (It's up to you to get the application ready.)

With that done, you can click the **Validate. . .** button to subject your app to some automated tests. Then you can click **Submit. . .**, and tell Xcode to submit the binary to the App Store.

And that takes you into review and, we hope, to release.

Summary

Provisioning applications for development and release has always been intricate, but it's gotten better. Xcode and Apple Developer Programs do what they can to make the process as painless as possible for as many developers as possible.

But you should understand the underlying principles—what the provisioning system expects, and how Xcode wraps the process—in case your needs are atypical or if something just goes wrong. I reviewed the three prerequisites to installing an app on an iOS device: signature, application ID, authorized device. Everything else is a variation on the common theme.

With that in mind, the magic Xcode performs with your developer privileges should have been clearer to you. You saw the interplay of identities, entitlements, and permissions come together to produce an application you can distribute, whether through an App Store, or (in the case of OS X applications) by your own means, with at least some assurance to your users that you are doing no harm.

Part III

Xcode for Mac OS X

## 19

Starting an OS X Application

Now you can advance to Xcode skills that apply to OS X development. If you're a Mac developer, I hope you haven't skipped Part II, "The Life Cycle of an iOS Application." Most of what I showed you in the iOS part of this book applies to Mac projects as well, and I won't be repeating them in these chapters.

By the same token, if your interest is in iOS, *don't stop reading*. You aren't done yet! Bundles and property lists aren't the priority for you that they are in OS X, but you have to know about them and their place in Cocoa development. In particular, have a look at the section on `Info.plist` in Chapter 22, "Bundles and Packages."

What you're going to do now is to port the Passer Rating iPhone app to OS X. Because you kept a good separation in the Model-View-Controller design, the model layer of the application could come through unchanged (though you're going to expand it a bit). The view and controller layers will be all new; the human-interface layers for the two platforms, UIKit on iOS and AppKit on the Mac, share some concepts but are very different.

> **Warning**
>
> This chapter builds upon the work in the iOS Passer Rating application. The narrative concentrates on the workflow of setting up an OS X application, at the expense of complete transparency about everything that was needed for the adaptation. After you have Xcode instantiate the project template, you *must* download the sample code (if you haven't already), or you won't be able to follow along. The tradeoff was not easy for me to make, but the alternative was to drown the Xcode techniques (the subject of this book) in code listings and diffs. I'll guide you through the process, but have the finished code for this chapter handy so you can fill in the gaps.

The Goal

A desktop application is a different sort of thing from a mobile app. Desktop apps present their information in windows, and users expect data-handling windows to represent *documents*, each of which stores its data in its own file. Mac Passer Rating *could* present only one window for only one data set, but as you'll see, it's not much more trouble to work with documents. That way, the user can organize passer statistics into leagues, which he can exchange with others.

The top level of the iOS Passer Rating app was a list of passers. Does that make sense if you have more than one document? If you have documents for discrete leagues, it may be better if you take *teams* as the root of the data set. This will entail a slight rework of the data model, which I'll get to presently.

So a league (the document) has a list of teams. Each team has a list of passers that have (at least for a time) played for it. Each passer has a list of game performances. When you were working on the iPhone screen, you were restricted to showing only one level of the hierarchy at a time. On the desktop, you can make it all visible. Something like Figure 19.1 is what you'll be shooting for.

Getting Started

Starting a Cocoa application project is scarcely different from what you saw in Chapter 2, "Kicking the Tires": Select **File → New → Project...** (⇧⌘N), which will give you an empty workspace window and a New Project assistant sheet. Select **OS X → Application** from the master list at the left, and the Cocoa Application icon from the array at the right. Click **Next**.

Now you come to the panel of project options, and there are quite a few of them.

- **Product Name** will be `Mac Passer Rating`. It's a dumb name for an application—the user knows she's using a Mac, and doesn't care that there are other versions—but it helps you keep track of things if the project has a distinctive name. You can rename the product later by seeking out "Product Name" in the **Build Settings** tab of the Target editor.

- The **Organization Name**—the copyright holder—your name (Fritz Anderson).

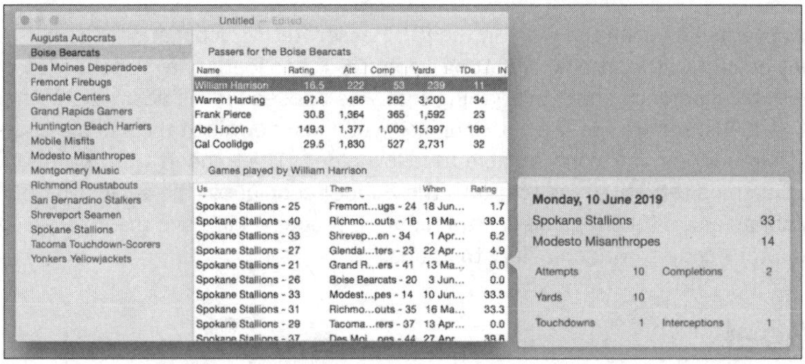

Figure 19.1   Mac Passer Rating as we want it to look, at least for the purpose of this example. A document represents a "league" composed of teams (left table). Selecting a team fills the upper table with the passers who have played on it. Selecting a passer lists all of his game performances in the lower table. Clicking on a game brings up a popover window with the details.

- **Company Identifier** forms the prefix for the application ID. For my purposes, this is `com.wt9t`. Enter your own.

- The **Bundle Identifier** concatenates the company identifier and the product name. This is how the application will be identified to the system and (if you intend to sell through the Mac App Store) to Apple. The field isn't editable; it's just for your information.

- The choices for **Language** are **Objective-C** and **Swift**. We are Modern, so select **Swift**.

- Yosemite and Xcode 6 bring storyboards to Mac development; we want one. Check **Use Storyboards**.

- Check **Create Document-Based Application** because the app will produce documents. The document options in this panel have big effects on the boilerplate code Xcode's template will produce for you.

- OS X relies on filename extensions to regulate which files go with which applications. Mac Passer Rating won't be sharing any common document types, so fill **Document Extension** with something distinctive like `leaguedoc`—you shouldn't include a dot. Don't feel you have to restrict yourself to three or four characters: The people who use Mac Passer Rating won't ever have to type the extension.

- You used Core Data for iOS Passer Rating, and you'll use it here. Check **Use Core Data**.

Now click **Next**, which drops a select-directory sheet for you to place the project directory (which will be named `Mac Passer Rating`, like it or not). Make your choice, check **Create git repository on**, select an Xcode server if you have one, **My Mac** if not, and click **Create**. The Workspace window now fills with the skeleton of the application.

- `Document.swift` defines the class that loads and stores the league data, and presents it for display and editing. `Document` is the controller class in the Model-View-Controller pattern. AppKit, the Cocoa framework for Mac applications, encompasses a sophisticated scheme for managing documents, centered on the `NSDocument` class. `NSDocument` responds to requests to read, save, present, or edit its data; your document subclass merely customizes the standard behavior.
  Because you asked for a document that uses Core Data, `Document` is a subclass of `NSPersistentDocument`, which does even more for you. It takes care of loading and saving data, and it handles undo and redo events.
  Let's start now on renaming classes and files so they make sense for their roles in the application: Do a global replace to change `Document` to `LeagueDocument`; `WindowController` to `LeagueWindowController`; and `ViewController` to `LeagueViewController`. Remember to set the last segment of the **Find** popover to **Matching** to find only the exact words, and to update the file names.

> **Warning**
>
> This doesn't do the whole job. The Find navigator promises to change the class names in the storyboard, but you will have to select each of these objects, and change their class names with the Identity inspector.

You'll also want to rename the window-controller scene (Identity inspector, **Storyboard ID** "League Window Controller").

- `Document.xcdatamodeld` is an empty data model for the original `Document` class. We'll be deleting it—we have a nearly complete model from Passer Rating—but not yet.

- `Images.xcassets` is a container for icons and the images you will use in your application. Image sets relieve the burden of tracking the ever-proliferating gaggle of images in various sizes and resolutions that go into a modern application. See the "Image Sets" section of Chapter 13, "Adding Table Cells," for the details.

- `Info.plist`, in the Supporting Files group, is a precursor to the `Info.plist` file that describes the properties and behavior of the application to the Finder and Launch Services. The **General** and **Info** tabs of the Target editor provide a (relatively) simple way to customize this file. Remember, the "Bundles and Packages" and "Property Lists" chapters will tell you more about `Info.plist`. `InfoPlist.strings` provides a dictionary that matches `Info.plist` entries to translated versions.

- Were this an Objective-C project, Supporting Files would include `Mac Passer Rating-Prefix.pch`, the source for the project's precompiled header. Review the "Precompilation" section of Chapter 5, "Compilation," for a review.

- `Main.storyboard` will be compiled into the human interface for the application.

- `AppDelegate.swift` defines `AppDelegate`, the application-delegate class. It is rare that you'd have to subclass `NSApplication`, AppKit's fundamental application class; every customization you'd routinely need can be done through the delegate. Mac Passer Rating doesn't need even that: we won't touch the file.

As with the iOS template, Mac Passer Rating is runnable as is. Select **Product → Run** (⌘ R). In a moment, you'll be running the application, which won't look like much—just a menu bar with **Mac Passer Rating** in it. Select **File → New → File. . .** (⌘ N), and you'll see a document window that you can close, resize, and even save to a file that will reopen if you double-click it in the Finder. See Figure 19.2.

> **Note**
>
> If you save a document file at this stage, be sure to delete it. You'll be changing the data model for Mac Passer Rating. Once upon a time, Core Data would simply crash and leave you guessing, but now it throws an exception with the description, "The autosaved document. . . could not be reopened. The managed object model version used to open the persistent store is incompatible with the one that was used to create the persistent store." Watch the debugger console.

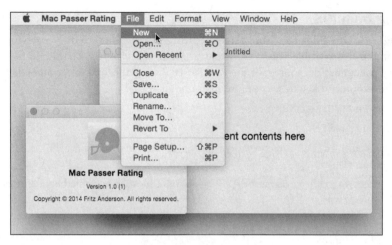

Figure 19.2   The document-application template is runnable as is. You can create a new document and save it to a file that you can reopen in the Finder. I got eager, and filled in the AppIcon set in `Images.xcassets`, to be picked up by the standard About box.

> **Warning**
>
> `NSPersistentDocument` is supposed to handle all of the standard behaviors of an OS X document: Creating, reading, editing, and saving. You need only add the specifics for your application. However: If you select **File → Duplicate...**, ⇧⌘S, and save the new file, AppKit will write what appears to be a document file, plus files of the same name with `-wal` and `-shm` appended. Without these, the document file will be rejected as corrupt. This has been the case through two major revisions of OS X. The best solution as I write this is the open-source `BSManagedDocument` class, from Mike Abdullah.

Once the novelty has worn off, you'll want to turn this application into something about football.

Model

As I said, adding a third level to the hierarchy—the team—requires a rework of the model. The data model and supporting classes from the iOS Passer Rating app are a good place to start.

Now we can throw `Document.xcdatamodeld` away in favor of the existing one. Select it in the Project navigator and press Delete; when Xcode asks what you want to do with it, click **Delete**. The name of the model file doesn't matter, so don't worry about the replacement's having another; by default `NSPersistentDocument` loads all the compiled `.mom` files and merges them into a single model.

Porting from iOS

Select **File** → **Add Files to "Mac Passer Rating"...** (⌥ ⌘ A) to drop a get-file sheet. (The command is available only if the Project navigator is visible.) Navigate to the directory containing the source for the iOS Passer Rating app, and select these files (hold down the Command key to select more than one file):

- `SimpleCSVFile.swift`
- `rating.swift`
- The `mogenerated` directory, or whatever container you had for the `Game` and `Passer` classes
- `Passer_Rating.xcdatamodel` (Data-model files are portable between OS X and iOS projects.)
- `Extensions.swift`
- `Utilities.swift`

You'll have to adapt some of the files to OS X—some `import UIKit`, and `Extensions.swift` should lose the extensions to `UITableView` and `NSFetchedResultsController`.

> **Note**
>
> If you didn't follow along in the iOS part of this book, you can recover these files from the sample code. If you arranged your iOS source directory so that some files are in different subdirectories, you'll have to make a different add-files pass for each directory.

Check **Copy items into destination group's folder (if needed)**; select **Create groups for any added folders** so the `mogenerated` class files come in individually, and not as whatever their directory happens to contain when you build; and make sure **Mac Passer Rating** is checked in the **Add to Targets** table. Click **Add**. The files appear in the Project navigator; you'll want to select them all, issue **File** → **New** → **Group from Selection**, and rename the resulting group something like `Model`.

> **Note**
>
> This would be a good time to commit the project to the local repository.

Adding an Entity

The next step is to factor (database-savvy developers would say *normalize*) `ourTeam` out of `Game` and into a new entity, `Team`. Click on `Passer_Rating.xcdatamodel`, and (using the skills you picked up in Chapter 9, "An iOS Application: Model") create the `Team` entity, with one attribute, `teamName`. `teamName` should be a string, indexed, not optional, and with an obviously invalid default name like **UNASSIGNED_NAME**. Add a relationship, `games`, tracing to many of the `Game` entity; deletion should cascade.

Game can lose the `ourTeam` string attribute, and gain `team`, a to-one relationship to `Team`, nullifying on delete. Be sure to set up this relationship as the inverse of `Team`'s games. When you're done, the diagram view of the data model should look like Figure 19.3.

As with `Passer` and `Game`, you will want to add a convenience method that will generate a `Team`; that will require an `NSManagedObject` subclass to wrap the `Team` entity.

You'll still have to create the `Team` class, and you'll need to bring the existing machine classes up-to-date with the changed model. Select the `Team` entity in the Data Model editor, expose the Core Data inspector (third tab at the top of the Utility area), and set **Class** to `Team`.

Now open Terminal, and regenerate the class files:

```
$ # cd to the same directory that includes Passer_Rating.xcdatamodeld.
$ cd 'whatever/Mac Passer Rating'
$ # Run mogenerator.
$ mogenerator --model Passer_Rating.xcdatamodeld \
    --output-dir mogenerated \
    --swift

3 machine files and 1 human files generated.
$
```

> **Note**
>
> `mogenerator` will preserve the human-editable `Game.swift` and `Passer.swift` files, so there's no danger in running it on this new project. If you haven't kept the old code around, you can find the directory in the sample code for the end of this chapter. **Note well** that Part III will rely on `Passer.swift` and `Game.swift` as they were *before* Chapter 17, "An iOS Extension." This project won't include any extensions, and there will be no app-group container or system-wide store.

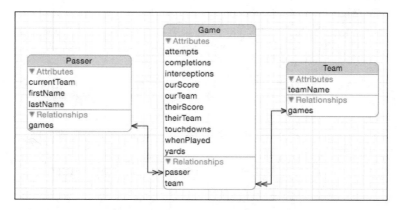

Figure 19.3   For the Mac, the Passer Rating model adds a `Team` entity. Each `Team` relates to many `Games`. `Game`'s `ourTeam` string attribute goes away, as its purpose is served by `team.teamName`.

Use **File → Add Files to "Mac Passer Rating"...** (⌥ ⌘ A) to add the mogenerated directory to the project. It should go into the Mac Passer Rating target and be added as a group of files, and not a reference to a living folder.

We were going to add a convenience method to Team so we can find and create Teams. Turn to Team.swift, and create the method and a couple of derived properties:

```swift
import Foundation
import CoreData


@objc(Team)
class Team: _Team {

  class func teamWithName(name: String,
                          context: NSManagedObjectContext,
                          create: Bool)
    -> Team?
  {
    var retval: Team? = nil

    let fetch = NSFetchRequest(entityName: "Team")
    fetch.predicate = NSPredicate(
      format: "teamName = %@", name)
    var error: NSError? = nil
    let result = context.executeFetchRequest(fetch,
      error: &error)
    if let records = result {
      if records.count > 0 {
        retval = (records[0] as! Team)
      }
      else if create {
        retval = Team(managedObjectContext: context)
        retval?.teamName = name
      }
    }
    else {
      NSLog("\(__FUNCTION__): Could not execute a fetch of \(name)")
    }
    return retval
  }

  var ownTotalScore: Int {
    return self.games.valueForKeyPath("@sum.ourScore") as! Int
  }

  var oppTotalScore: Int {
    return self.games.valueForKeyPath("@sum.theirScore") as! Int
  }
```

```
  var passers: [Passer] {
    let unionOfPassers =
      self.games.valueForKeyPath("@distinctUnionOfObjects.passer")
      as! NSSet?

    if let passerSet = unionOfPassers {
      return passerSet.allObjects as [Passer]
    }
    else {
      return []
    }
  }
}
```

The model has changed, and `Passer` and `Game` should change. Where you create a new `Game`, in `csvFile:readValues:error:`, use `teamWithName(_, context:, create:)` to link up to a `Team` rather than recording the `ourTeam` string directly:

```
newGame.team =
    Team.teamWithName(values["ourTeam"]!,
    context: context, create: true)!
```

Elsewhere, wherever a team name was referenced through `ourTeam` in `Game`, refer to `team.teamName`. For instance, in `Passer.swift`:

```
var teams: [ String ]
{
    let theGames: AnyObject =
        self.games.valueForKeyPath(
            "@distinctUnionOfObjects.ourTeam")!
    return theGames.allObjects as! [ String ]
}
```

becomes

```
var teams: [ String ] {
    let theGames: AnyObject =
        self.games.valueForKeyPath(
            "@distinctUnionOfObjects.team.teamName")!
    return theGames.allObjects as! [ String ]
}
```

And remember to revert `existingPasserByName(_, last:, context:)` to the version that looked up `Passer`s in a particular `NSManagedObjectContext`, instead of keeping one in-memory table for the whole app:

```
class func existingPasserByName(first: String!,
                                last:String!,
```

```
        context: NSManagedObjectContext!
    -> [Passer]
{
    . . .
```

And make sure existingPasserByName(_, last:, context:) uses Core Data—the passers have to be found in the specified context, not pulled in from a global dictionary:

```
let fetchStrategy:PasserFetchStrategy = .StraightCoreData
```

Note

You'll want to refer to the sample code for the end of this chapter for all the details.

Wiring a Menu

Let's get this thing doing *something* before we go much further. Will LeagueDocument load up some sample data (yes, the same .csv sample you labored with on iOS) and display at least some team names?

The first thing to do is to add a menu item to Mac Passer Rating's **Edit** menu to load up a document. Select Main.storyboard in the Project navigator; Interface Builder will appear with three scenes in the canvas: the Application scene, the Window Controller scene, and the View Controller scene. We're interested in the Application scene, which consists of placeholders for the App Delegate and First Responder, plus the Main Menu.

Main Menu embodies the application menu bar. The OS X project template starts you with a loaded-out menu bar ready for grammar-checking, rich-text tables, and more. Click the **Edit** label in the Application scene to drop the **Edit** menu down. The lower half of the menu contains a lot of items having to do with searching and speech that don't fit Mac Passer Rating. Click on each, and press Delete.

While you're at it, delete the **Format** and **View** menus, too; but take care to close the menus before pressing Delete: In the peculiar hierarchy of AppKit menus, the menu bar is a menu; it contains menu *items*, whose contents may themselves be menus. If you try to delete an open **Format** menu (for instance), Xcode will delete the *menu*, but not the menu *item* that contained it. You can tell by the fact that a gap remains in the menu bar where the menu was. Select that and delete it; or close the menu so the Delete key will kill both the item and the menu it contains.

You add a menu item by dragging it from the Object library (in the lower part of the Utility area, third tab) into the menu. Type **menu** into the library's search field. Find "Menu Item," and drag it to the bottom of the open **Edit** menu. See Figure 19.4.

Double-click in the **Item** label, and replace the name with **Fill with Test Data**; and in the blank area at the right end of the menu item, double-click, hold down the Command key, and press **t** to make the key equivalent ⌘ **T**.

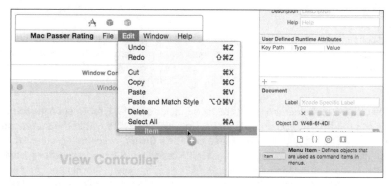

Figure 19.4   Dragging a new menu item into a menu.

Note

When I did this, I held down the Shift key to get what I thought would be a capital T. This resulted in a key equivalent of ⇧⌘**T**; not what I wanted. I reselected the field and hit Delete; this made the key equivalent **Delete**. This is a good time to make friends with the Attributes inspector, the fourth tab in the upper part of the Utility area. When you have a menu item selected, the top two fields are **Title** and **Key Equivalent**, and the latter has an **x** button to clear it.

Target/Action

Now you want the menu item to do something. As in the iOS app, user-interface elements direct a message (an *action*) at an object (the *target*) when they are triggered. You haven't written the action method yet, but you can make up a name for it: fillWithData:.

What about the target? You'll search Main.storyboard in vain for a reference to LeagueDocument—that's a class that's associated with individual documents, not the application as a whole. To what Cocoa object will you assign the task of responding to fillWithData:? *I don't know,* says a stubborn part of your subconscious, *anything that wants to respond to it, I guess.*

This turns out not to be a stupid answer in Cocoa. AppKit keeps a continually updated *responder chain,* a series of potential responders to user actions. The chain begins at the "first responder," which may be the selected view in the front window, and then proceeds to the front window, the window's document, and finally to the application itself. You may have noticed that each scene in the storyboard has in its title bar (when the scene is selected), and in its listing in the document outline, a red cube, which represents the **First Responder**. A user interface control can designate the **First Responder**, whatever it may be at the time, as the target of its action, and AppKit will shop the action up the responder chain until it finds an object that can handle it.

> **Note**
>
> The responder chain is a little more complicated than that. For more information, consult Apple's documentation for NSApplication, NSResponder, and the related Programming Topics articles.

> **Note**
>
> Like the other placeholder icons in Interface Builder scenes, First Responder does not literally exist in the storyboard. It is a *proxy*, a way for objects within the storyboard to make reference to outside objects. These are **File's Owner**, which is the object that caused the compiled storyboard to load; **First Responder**, the current starting point for the responder chain; and **Application**, the NSApplication object that embodies the application as a whole. If you don't see a Placeholders section, click the boxed-triangle button next to the bottom of the sidebar to expand it to labeled icons.

First Responder

If you try control-dragging an action link from the new menu item to the **First Responder** icon, you're balked. Interface Builder presents a HUD for the link, asking you to choose the method selector for the desired action. The list it presents does not include fillWithData: because you just made that up. Before you can make the link, you have to tell Interface Builder that fillWithData: is a possible action.

Interface Builder allows you to do this by selecting the **First Responder** object in the top bar of a scene, or in the document outline, and exposing the Attributes inspector (fourth tab). The inspector shows an empty table for user-defined actions that a responder might answer to. Click the **+** button, click the new row to put focus on the table, press Return to make the **Action** label editable, and type **fillWithData:**. The "Type" column presents a combo field of possible control types that might send that action; you can leave it as id, the generic object type, unless you want IB to offer to originate the action from senders of that type only. We don't care. Interface Builder now knows that in this storyboard, fillWithData: is one of the actions a responder might perform.

> **Note**
>
> In AppKit, action methods must take one argument: fillWithData:, with a colon, not fillWithData, without—the names are distinct. If you leave the colon off, IB will supply it.

Now you can control-drag from the new menu item to First Responder, and the HUD will contain fillWithData:. The display will even be scrolled close to it, as a rough match for the item's label. Make the connection. See Figure 19.5.

> **Note**
>
> The Connection inspector (sixth tab in the inspector portion of the Utility area) affords another way to make the connection—and to break it. Select First Responder and the Connection inspector. The "Received Actions" section fills with the same long list of actions you saw in the connection HUD when you control-dragged to the FR icon, but it's larger and easier to scroll. Next to each selector is a bubble; dragging from it to the menu

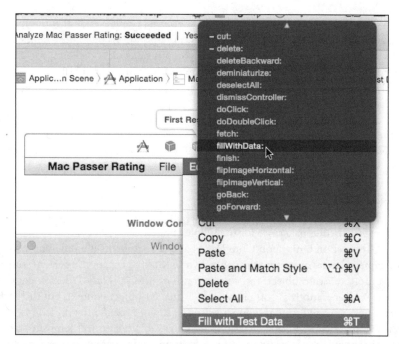

Figure 19.5 Control-dragging from a menu item to First Responder produces a heads-up window that includes `fillWithData:`, the method we had added to the First Responder's repertoire of action methods.

item would make the connection, and a label would appear showing where the connection went to. An **x** button next to the connection label lets you break the connection.

Loading Data into `LeagueDocument`

Importing the `.csv` file is simple—most of the work was done on the iOS side. Add `sample-data.csv` to the project, then edit `fillWithData(_)` into `LeagueDocument.swift`:

```
@IBAction
func fillWithData(sender: AnyObject) {
    let mainBundle = NSBundle.mainBundle()
    if let csvPath = mainBundle.pathForResource(
                    "sample-data", ofType: "csv") {
        var error: NSError? = nil
        let success = Game.loadGames(csvPath,
            context: self.managedObjectContext,
            error: &error)
    }
}
```

Attaching the @IBAction directive to fillWithData() tells Xcode that the function is eligible to receive commands from UI elements; in response, Xcode puts a connection bubble in the gutter next to the declaration. If you put LeagueDocument.swift in the assistant editor for Main.storyboard, you could drag from the bubble to any element that could send a command—a menu item, a button—and from then, triggering the control would trigger the action.

In this case, the connection bubble is not filled. **Edit → Fill with Test Data (⌘ T)** gets sent to First Responder, not the document itself. It would not be accurate to show the connection on that particular function, because for all Xcode knows, the responder chain might hit another object implementing fillWithData() first.

Adapting to a Managed Document

For Passer Rating, we set up the Core Data stack in the application delegate. This makes sense: There is only one data store for the whole application.

A OS X application built upon Core Data–backed documents is a different matter. Every document has its own store, managed by the NSPersistentDocument superclass of the LeagueDocument object. NSPersistentDocument is lazy: You can perform as many Core Data operations as you please in its managed-object context, but the backing data store is never created until the document itself is saved for the first time.

When will that first save happen? You don't know. Xcode's project template starts you on an app that adopts the autosaving, state-restoration, and versioning behavior expected of modern apps. The user can *request* a save to mark progress or to choose the name and location of a document, but before that happens, the system will save the contents even of an "untitled" document deep within the user's Library/ directory.

And until that first autosave happens, the Core Data context will have no store, and calling save() to write into it will cause an exception. Passer Rating, having a data file from the start, could save the managed-object context periodically in the run of Game.loadGames(); Mac Passer Rating can't.

Edit loadGames() to get it out of the business of writing to the data store:

```
public
class func loadGames(csvFilePath:    String,
                     context:         NSManagedObjectContext,
                     error:           NSErrorPointer)
    -> Bool
{
    let csvFile = SimpleCSVFile(path: csvFilePath)
    var parsingError: CSVError? = nil

    parsingError = csvFile.run { (values) in
        let newGame: Game! = Game(managedObjectContext: context)
        assert(newGame != nil, "Could not create a Game")

        let passer:Passer = Passer.passerWithFirstName(
                    values["firstName"]!,
```

```
            last:       values["lastName"]!,
            context:    context)

        passer.enqueueGame(newGame)
        passer.currentTeam = values["ourTeam"]!

        for key in allGameNumericAttributes {
            newGame.setValue(values[key]!.toInt(),
                            forKey: key)
        }
        newGame.team =
            Team.teamWithName(values["ourTeam"]!,
            context: context, create: true)!
        newGame.theirTeam = values["theirTeam"]!
        newGame.whenPlayed = DATE_from_yyyy_MM_dd
                                    (values["whenPlayed"])
        return nil
    }

    if let pError = parsingError {
        if error != nil { error.memory = pError.nsError }
        return false
    }

    Passer.flushGameQueues(context: context)
    return true
}
```

Also, I cut `sample-data.csv` down to just 8 seasons, from the 40 we had in Chapter 16, "Measurement and Analysis." We're through with torture tests.

> **Note**
>
> The "DATE" in the listing is not what you'll find in the sample code. The name of that function, defined in `Utilities.swift`, begins with the Unicode emoji for a calendar leaf. I have too much fun.

Testing the Command

This is enough for you to see whether the menu command works. Set a breakpoint at the beginning of `fillWithData:`. Run Mac Passer Rating. With Yosemite's state-restoration feature in place (you can turn it off in the **Options** tab of the Scheme editor's **Run** panel), you may see the document window from your first run; if not, make a new one with ⌘ N. Save the document (anywhere, any name). Then select **Edit → Fill with Test Data** (⌘ T).

> **Note**
>
> If the command is dimmed (inactive) check `Main.storyboard` to see whether it's connected to First Responder. AppKit will activate a menu item only if something in the responder chain implements its action method.

Two things will happen. First, the breakpoint you set at the beginning of `fillWithData:` will trigger, so you know the menu item worked. Second, if you continue, the title bar will add the gray **Edited** flag, to show that the command resulted in a change of the document's contents—even if you can't see it.

Now save the document—**File → Save...** (⌘ S). This gets you the save-file sheet you expect, but you might not have expected the **File Format** popup menu it contains. On iOS, Core Data stores are SQLite database files. On OS X, where Core Data originated, there are three types of stores: SQLite, Binary, and XML.

- **SQLite** is the most useful for most purposes. It's fast, and can handle data with hundreds of thousands of records. The SQL layer gives you more sophisticated search predicates and statistical fetches (like the `@sum` of all the `completions` in all of a `Passer`'s `Games`).

- But for smaller data sets, SQLite files are bulky, and aren't big enough for the efficiencies of a true database to be apparent. The **Binary** format provides a compact format that is faster for small data sets. It does not, however, give you the sophisticated queries and calculations a relational database provides.

- **XML** stores are adequate for small data sets, but the real purpose is for debugging: The format is human-readable, so you can write out just enough records and relationships to exercise the feature you're investigating, and see how the store reflects it.

Saving in the respective formats will get you files with the extensions `.sqlite`, `.binary`, and `.xml`. Descriptive, but they don't associate the files with your app, and affording all three types of storage isn't an attractive feature for most users.

Identifying a Type for League Data

Matching an application to its file types is one of the many functions of `Info.plist`. The Target editor (click the top row of the Project navigator, and make sure the Mac Passer Rating target is selected) provides a special editor for `Info.plist` in the **Info** tab. The categories we're interested in are **Document Types**, which describes how a document file relates to the application, and **Exported UTIs**, which describes how such files are to be treated by the system in general.

Click the disclosure triangles for both; we're going to add a Uniform Type Identifier (UTI) for League data, and pare the document type down to a reference to the UTI. See Figure 19.6.

Start with the UTI. We're going to define the type ID `com.wt9t.league` for the content of League files. A League file has

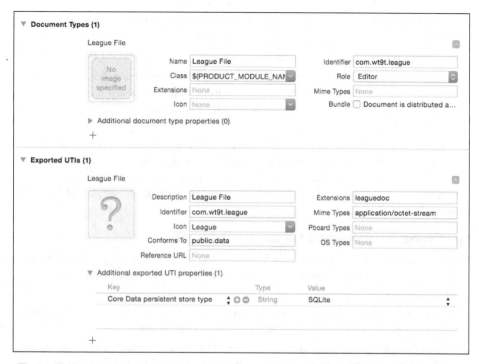

Figure 19.6 The template for a Core Data document–based application defines the document file only in terms of the app. It's cleaner to separate the type definition (which you define for a Uniform Type Identifier) from the document definition (which declares what Mac Passer Rating, in particular, does with League files).

- A **Description** of `League File`, which is what will be shown as the file type in the Finder.
- The **Identifier** `com.wt9t.league`.
- An **Icon** named `League`, which we will add to `Images.xcassets` soon.
- The type **Conforms To `public.data`**. UTIs are defined as refinements of well-known types. For instance, a system that doesn't know how to handle an XML property list might be able to fall back to `com.apple.property-list`, `public.xml`, `public.data` (a byte stream), or `public.item` ("something-or-other").
  The most useful references to UTIs are in `UTType.h` and `UTCoreTypes.h`. The command line `open -h UTType.h` will find a header file and open it in the default editor for C headers; if you prefer a different application, add `-a applicationName`.

- **Extensions**—you have only one, `leaguedoc`. Don't include the dot. Strangely, the template for application targets asks for an extension, but never records it anywhere.
- **Mime Types**—use the most generic, `application/octet-stream`.
- You won't be publishing a reference for the type as a **Reference URL**; you don't want to put the data on the clipboard, so you don't need **Pboard Types**; and sadly, the pre-OS X document-type identifiers (**OS Types**) are all but unsupported. Leave them all blank.

A League file will be an SQL Core Data store, and as you've seen, that's a special case for documents. Open the **Additional exported UTI properties** subview, and click in the table that appears. Type `Core` in the Key column; you should be offered the completion "Core Data persistent store type;" make it a **String**, and select **SQLite** as the Value.

Specifying How the App Handles League Files

The **Document Types** entry can now be reduced to a description of how Mac Passer Rating handles League documents, plus a reference to the `com.wt9t.league` for the system-wide details.

- Remove all the "Additional document type properties" by clicking the **x** buttons at the top-right of each. The UTI supplies that information.
- The **Name** is, once again, `League File`. The Finder, through Launch Services, would use this string to display the file type if there were no UTI definition, but the name is still used within the `NSDocument` system as an in-app label for the document type.
- The Uniform Type **Identifier** is `com.wt9t.league`.
- **Class** tells AppKit which of your `NSDocument` classes handles this type of document. You rarely have to write a dispatcher of your own; this item tells the loader, `NSDocumentController`, the name of the class, which is enough to instantiate (in our case) a `LeagueDocument` object, which can take care of reading, display, and writing from there.
  This used to be simply the name of the class, but Yosemite introduces modules, which segregate class names among the libraries in an application. The full name of `LeagueDocument` is `Mac_Passer_Rating.LeagueDocument`. The module name, before the dot, identifies the class as being a part of the application's main module, which is named after the app, with non-alphanumerics replaced by underscores.
  The app product's name is apt to change over the course of development, so Xcode fills this in as `$(PRODUCT_MODULE_NAME).LeagueDocument`. The build variable `PRODUCT_MODULE_NAME` will be filled in with the correct name when `Info.plist` is copied to the application package.
- Mac Passer Rating's **Role** for League files is as an **Editor**. This cues Launch Services about what happens when the user double-clicks a file icon, or selects the Finder's

File → **Open With** menu. A "viewer" app can read the file, and possibly convert the contents into a document it can save; an "editor" can open, save, and create the file; and a role of "none" means that while the file is *associated* with the app—the app may define the file's icon and type—it isn't a document, and the Finder should not open the app when the file's icon is double-clicked.

- You have to provide a UTI, or an **Extensions** list, or **Mime Types** for a document type. We have a UTI, so the other two fields should be left blank.

- There's no need to define an **Icon**; the UTI does that.

- Keep **Bundle: Document is distributed as a bundle** unchecked. A bundle document looks like a single, indivisible icon in the Finder, but is in fact a directory containing the components of the document. That isn't the case here. Chapter 22, "Bundles and Packages" will tell you more.

Application and Document Icons

I had you set the icon for com.wt9t.league to "League." As part of my preparation for this chapter, I put together a set of icon images for both the application and the document. See Figure 19.7. When you select **Editor → New OS X Icon** while editing Images.xcassets, you are given an image set with five point sizes (16, 32, 128, 256, and 512), in single and double resolutions. These get compiled into an icon-set .icns archive, and when the Finder needs to render the icon, it can pick the image that fits best.

Ideally, each image would be crafted to its purpose, showing richer detail in the larger sizes, and clear, assertive shapes in the smaller. Those choices would be reflected in the two resolutions for each size: ten images in total.

In practice, when the 2x image for one size has the same pixel count as the 1x image for the next, people copy the same image over. They create the bitmaps from the same vector drawing. If you are just meatballing it, you can get away with a 128×128 image, and accept the way it gets fuzzy as the OS scales it up and down.

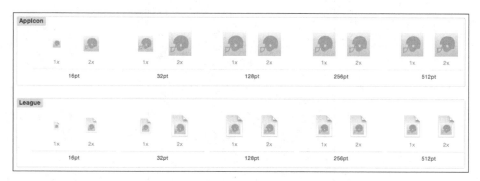

Figure 19.7   A full icon suite for OS X comprises up to ten images. In practice, some sizes can be omitted, and the double-resolution image for one size can be duplicated to serve as the single-resolution image for the next larger.

> **Note**
>
> If you can get a PDF vector rendering of an image, you have a better option: One of the options in the Attributes inspector for an image set is **Image Set: Types**. Choosing **Vectors** from the popup reduces the set to a single "Universal" slot. Drop the PDF into it, and `NSImage` or `UIImage` will render it in any size you need. The result is as sharp as any bitmap you could provide. Be aware that the rendering will scale lines as well, so a three-point line in a large view may become a hairline in a small one. Sometimes you want this, sometimes not.

One of the image sets contains the Passer Rating logo superimposed on a generic document icon. I named the set **League**. When it builds Mac Passer Rating, Xcode generates `League.icns` from the image set, and includes it in the application bundle.

However, the `.icns` archive exists only in the finished application; it's nowhere to be found in the project directory. When you type `League` in the **Icon** field, Xcode renders it as a gray question mark. If, on the other hand, you composed the `.icns` yourself (there is an Icon Composer app for it in the add-on Graphics Tools for Xcode package), you could drop it into the image well, and Xcode would add the archive to the project.

The file specification, cut down and tailored to Mac Passer Rating, should look like Figure 19.6, bottom. Now, when you save a League file, Finder will recognize its relation to the app, and display it accordingly (Figure 19.8).

Figure 19.8   Filling in the specs for the document-file type provides a name and icon for the file type.

Summary

This chapter started you off on some new Xcode skills, against the background of an OS X version of the passer-rating project. To do this, you had to go through some conversions: You created a document-based Core Data application, and you imported existing code.

You saw that modern Mac applications are built from a storyboard with at least two root scenes: the Application scene, which contains the main menu bar and the application delegate; and the controller for the app's document windows. This posed a conundrum when an app-wide facility—a menu command—had to communicate with a document-specific facility: editing the content of a specific document when the screen might contain many. You learned how the First Responder proxy in Interface Builder, and the responder chain, bridge the gap.

Finally, we adapted the way Mac Passer Rating must cooperate with OS X's policies for saving and displaying files: Because the OS will save the file autonomously, we let go of our own Core Data saves. We also committed to a choice of file formats, and identified Mac Passer Rating's league files as belonging to the application, and carrying a distinctive icon.

## 20

Bindings: Wiring an OS X Application

If you have another look at Figure 19.1, you'll see that even in the abbreviated form Mac Passer Rating will take, there will be more than 20 pieces of information distributed across 4 displays, to be filled in, edited (in some cases), and coordinated across updates. This is going to involve some tedious, repetitive code and a lot of communications infrastructure through the network of objects, isn't it?

Not as much as you'd think. AppKit (the Mac-specific part of Cocoa) offers a facility called *bindings*, supplemented by NSController classes, which are subtle when you first encounter them, but once you master them, can cut your coding burden by an order of magnitude.

> **Note**
>
> Experienced Mac programmers—and Apple itself—will warn you: Bindings are an advanced topic. If this were a book about AppKit, I'd be taking you through an initial round of doing it the "easy," though verbose, way. My purpose in this book is to show you how to take advantage of Interface Builder's support of bindings, which is a major feature.

Storyboard Segues in OS X

Apple made storyboards available to OS X applications in Yosemite and Xcode 5. The relationship among controllers in a desktop application is much more complex than in a mobile one: Most segues among iOS view controllers replace one full-screen controller with another. You *can* embed a controller within another's scene, but it's a matter of convenience more than necessity.

It's different in OS X. Application windows typically depict the whole content of documents; they contain discrete and largely independent displays of that content. Yosemite expects that nontrivial windows will be tiled with several view controllers, and each may in turn contain others. Containment is a feature in an iOS scene; it is the essence of an OS X scene. Named segues link child scenes to parents, just as the transition segues do in iOS.

Let's take a moment for the strategy behind putting a nested chain of all-but-independent view controllers on the screen at once. I want to talk about the structure of the league window *as it will be* when we're done, because it's important to understand from the start how to reconcile the quasi-independent nature of OS X view controllers with their need to share focus on one set of data. This chapter tells the story of how, precisely, to approach that problem. We're on a journey. What's the reward?

Not every relationship among storyboard scenes *is* a segue; you saw it in iOS, where a `UINavigationController`'s root-controller relationship doesn't trigger a `prepare-ForSegue(_, sender:)` anywhere: It's more like filling the navigation controller's `rootViewController` property as if it were an `@IBOutlet`.

You see much more of the segue-that-isn't in OS X storyboards, because it's so common that multiple view controllers will coexist in a single window. In the league window you see in Figure 19.1, there will be three: The window controller's window contains a split-view controller—Interface Builder will draw a line from the window to the split-view scene. In turn the two halves of the split view will link to the separate view controllers for the league list and the team detail.

The relationships those lines represent do not trigger a `prepareForSegue(_, sender:)` message to the parent controllers. You can't name them. In fact, they have no configuration at all—the Attributes inspector is blank when you select one.

There's a second factor: `NSDocument`, and therefore `LeagueDocument`, loads the window controllers that will present its content from the storyboard and binds the controllers to itself with `addWindowController`. But it has no control over when the controllers will be ready to receive its contents: Window controllers load their windows *lazily*. The document can pass the data itself to the controllers, but they won't yet be able to render it because the windows and their constituent views don't exist. Only when some application event calls for putting them on the screen, or some `func` asks for the controller's `window` property, will AppKit instantiate them, their view hierarchies, and if needed, their chain of sub-view controllers.

> **Note**
>
> It's common that developers will exercise a bit more control over window instantiation by calling `window` and throwing the actual value away: `windowController.window`.

Once the window exists, a controller can receive data for it without having to make a special case of accepting it but waiting to push it to the view layer. When both controller and view are ready, the document object will receive `windowControllerDid-LoadNib(_)`. The parameter will point to the controller, so the document can push its data into it. The controller, in turn, parcels the data out to its subcontrollers and views.

> **Note**
>
> It's a tempting thought that Interface Builder should be able to connect a document or window controller directly to its subcontrollers by way of `@IBOutlet`s. It's so simple, so

> direct, that you'll spend hours trying to figure out how to do this one little thing (as I did), and why the documentation won't tell you how. I'll save you the trouble: IB won't let you do it. You remember from iOS that you can't string outlets between view controllers. It's the same here; that the controllers will all be on-screen at the same time doesn't change it. You have to sew up all the relationships at run time. It's not obvious, but once you accept it, it's not that hard.

We're going to do it the other way around. All `LeagueWindowController` needs to access all the document contents is the `NSManagedObjectContext` that every `NSPersistentDocument` has. Everything else can be a fetch against the context. The window can reach the managed-object context because its `document` property was set when it was added to the doc's controller list. On the other side, it can get the league and team subcontrollers by asking the split-view controller for them.

Building the Document Window

Because we know that each layer of the controller hierarchy can always see at least its own views and the controllers it contains, we have all the control we need over loading the view controllers; instantiating their windows (or views); and passing the data they need down the chain from the document.

Loading the Window

The original `makeWindowControllers()` method in `LeagueDocument.swift` is as straightforward as can be: It instantiates the controller identified as "League Window Controller" and adds it to its list of window controllers:

```
var windowController: LeagueWindowController!
override func makeWindowControllers() {
    let storyboard = NSStoryboard(name: "Main", bundle: nil)!
    windowController = storyboard
        .instantiateControllerWithIdentifier("LeagueWindow")
        as! LeagueWindowController
    addWindowController(windowController)
}
```

The `instantiateController...` method loads the window controller and its window from the storyboard. The before that method returns, `LeagueWindowController` gets its `windowDidLoad` message. It takes that opportunity to capture the view controllers it contains, and to set a watch on something named `teamArrayController` in the league view controller—we'll find out more about that soon.

```
//  Use this as an ID tag for notices that a Team has been selected.
//  It's passed as part of the addObserver(...) call,
//  which will be explained later.
```

```
typealias  KVOContext = UInt16
var teamSelectionChange = KVOContext(12)

//  For the first part of this chapter, the league window will be
//  relatively simple. windowDidLoad() will have to do more once
//  the content of the window develops. When needed, change
//  usingSplitView to `true` to unmask the full functionality.
private let  usingSplitView = false

var splitViewController: NSSplitViewController!
var leagueViewController: LeagueViewController!

//  Uncomment this line when the split view and the team-detail
//  view are added to the window:
// var teamDetailController: TeamDetailController!

// ...

override func windowDidLoad() {

    if usingSplitView {
        //  Top-level controller in the window is the split controller
        splitViewController = contentViewController
                        as! NSSplitViewController

        //  First item in the split controller is the team list
        var splitItem = splitViewController.splitViewItems[0]
                    as! NSSplitViewItem
        leagueViewController = splitItem.viewController
                            as! LeagueViewController
    }
    else {
        leagueViewController = contentViewController
                            as! LeagueViewController
    }

    //  Watch the Team table for changes to the selection.
    //  More on this later.
    leagueViewController.teamArrayController.addObserver(
                        self, forKeyPath: "selectedObjects",
                        options: NSKeyValueObservingOptions(0),
                        context: &teamSelectionChange)
```

```
    if usingSplitView {
        // The second item in the split controller is the team details
        splitItem = splitViewController.splitViewItems[1]
                    as! NSSplitViewItem
        teamDetailController = splitItem.viewController
                            as! TeamDetailController
    }
}
```

After `LeagueWindowController` hooks up with its components, control returns to `LeagueDocument`, which calls `addWindowController` to complete its link to the window controller. That process includes setting the `document` property of the window controller. Now that `LeagueWindowController` knows about its document, it can capture the document's managed-object context, and pass it down to the `LeagueViewController`—it will need the MOC so it can pull the team records from the soup that is `LeagueDocument`'s Core Data store:

```
override var document: AnyObject? {
    didSet {
        if let document = document as? LeagueDocument {
            leagueViewController.managedObjectContext
                            = document.managedObjectContext
        }
    }
}
```

A Table View

Mac Passer Rating should have something that can display some data—a simple table to display the names of teams and the total points they and their opponents have scored. That's the job of the `LeagueViewController`.

The view's scene in `Main.storyboard` includes a label, "Your document contents," so it won't be blank. Delete the label. Open the Object library at the bottom of the Utility area (third tab, a square-in-circle), and search for **table**. Drag the Table View into the `LeagueViewController` scene. The view you dropped into the scene looks as simple as the `UITableView` in iOS. It isn't. `UITableView` is a subclass of `UIScrollView`; it manages every aspect of the table that isn't specific to your application.

The AppKit table you dragged into the scene appears to be as simple, but if you look at it in the document outline, you find it is a tree of views up to seven layers deep. See Figure 20.1. The root is a scroll view, which contains scroll bars, a "clip view" that manages the panning of the table itself as it scrolls, plus the table headers, which are in the "scroll view" because they are exempt from scrolling.

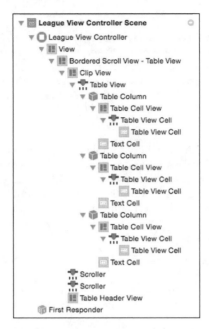

Figure 20.1   The apparently simple table view from the object library is actually a scroll view containing a tree of views and cells.

Okay?

Table views are one of the components of Cocoa that have decades of history behind them. The distinct subviews imply that you can select the behavior you want by omitting some—for instance, getting a static grid view by removing the actual NSTableView from the scroll view. That may have been true once; it isn't now. Everything you see is mandatory; if you don't want a feature, you must turn it off, not delete it.

It used to be worse: Table views were based on cells, subclassed from NSCell. These are not views; think of them as subroutines: Tell a cell to draw itself at a location on screen, and it will do so. If you want to present the same thing (possibly with different data), use the same cell and tell it to draw there. NSTableViews usually had only one NSCell per column, re-used to draw each row. Cells are much less resource-intensive than views. Most of AppKit's control views, such as text fields and buttons, rely on NSCells to draw their contents and respond to events.

This is an ingenious solution to the problem of putting a lot of structured elements on the screen of a computer that is a hundred times slower than a modern one, with a hundredth the memory. In the 21st century, we can afford to use views. From OS X 10.7 (Lion), NSTableView provides a view-based mode.

Let's start slow, with just a single table showing team names, the number of points they scored, and the number of points scored against them. Select the table view; it's hard to do in the deep stack of views, but the document outline and the shift-control-click popup are your friends (Figure 20.2). In the Attributes inspector, set the table for three columns.

Pick your method and go one level down from the scroll view to select the table.

The Attributes inspector gives you three levels of settings, for each level in NSTableView's place in the class hierarchy: first as a table view, then as a control view, and finally just as a view. Make these changes to the "Table View" section.

- Verify that the **Content Mode** is **View Based**.
- For **Columns**, set **3**.

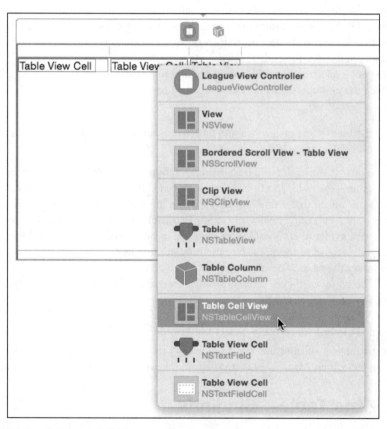

Figure 20.2 Shift-control-clicking on an Interface Builder view summons a popup window that lets you select any view among the layers drawn at that point. The alternatives of selecting the view you want from the document outline or tracing it through the jump bar work well; pumping the mouse button until the view you want is selected does not.

- You want columns to have **Headers**, **Resizing** (you can adjust the width by dragging the edge of a header), and **Reordering** (moving columns left and right through the display). Check them all.

- For **Column Sizing**, set **Sequential**. That way, when resizing the table makes it wider, the first column will grow wider until it reaches the limit you set, and then the second up to its maximum, and then the third.

Everything else can remain as it is.

So you've set three columns—where's the third? When you resized the table to fill the window, the second (and then last) column resized to fill the available space. The third column was added to the right, out of sight. Select the second column: Graphical handles will appear to either side, which you can drag to narrow the column enough to bring the third column into sight.

But you shouldn't have to do this by eye. Select each column in turn, and use the Size inspector to set the initial, minimum, and maximum widths. As with other settings in Interface Builder, you can select more than one view (such as the total-score columns) and set the width and limits for both at once.

While you're selecting columns, you'll see that the Attributes inspector offers a **Title** field. Name the columns `Team Name`, `Own`, and `Opp`.

> **Note**
>
> I made the Team Name column's width 240, with limits of 64 and 400. The two score columns are 64...64...120.

Let's see how it works so far. The **Simulate Document** command from earlier Xcodes is gone—the transition to windows composed from independent view controllers in a storyboard means that a simulation of a layout amounts to running the whole application. So... run the whole application: **Product → Run (⌘ R)**. The document window appears (Figure 20.3, top) with the table in place. You can drag the edges of the column headers to resize them, or drag them by the middle to reorder them. If resizing the columns makes the table wider than the window, you can scroll it. This is progress.

Resize the window (Figure 20.3, bottom). It seems layout issues will follow you wherever you go in Cocoa.

We've done Auto Layout before; it's not much different with AppKit than UIKit. By now you don't even have to think: Select the "Bordered Scroll View," which is the outermost container of the table, and use the ⊢□⊣ to stick the edges to the edges of the containing view. Run Mac Passer Rating again; the table resizes. Breathe. Commit.

Filling the Table—Bindings

The league table is in place, and AppKit has provided some useful services for it, but that does nothing for the actual display. `NSTableView` supports delegate and data-source methods much like those of `UITableView`, and for an application like this, we should prefer to use those methods.

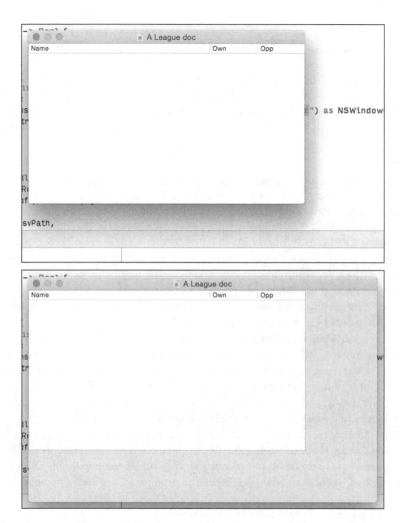

Figure 20.3   (top) The new table looks well enough until (bottom) you resize the window. This is yet another layout problem.

But *Xcode 6 Start to Finish* has never let good sense stand in the way of demonstrating an Xcode feature, and it's not beginning now. We're going to use *bindings*, a merger of Key-Value Coding (KVC), Key-Value Observing (KVO), and subclasses of NSController, which will track changes in the model and the view, and propagate the changes between them.

Object Controllers

You're still editing `Main.storyboard`, and focusing on the `LeagueViewController`. Type **array** in the Object library's search field, which should narrow the list down to "Array Controller," an instance of `NSArrayController`, which is a kind of `NSController` that provides automated access to groups of objects. Drag the icon into the view-controller scene. The controller won't show up in the view, but it will appear in the bar at the top of the scene, and as a member of the scene in the document outline.

> **Note**
>
> We've seen icons in Interface Builder that were mere placeholders. "First Responder" and "File's Owner" do not literally exist in a scene or a XIB; they just stand in for outside objects that will be resolved while the application is running. The `NSArrayController` icon isn't a placeholder—it is an object that *does* literally exist in the NIB archive, to be reconstituted when the NIB (the compiled product of a XIB or a scene) is loaded.

Make sure the array controller is selected, and use the Attributes inspector to set **Mode** to **Entity Name**, and the **Entity Name** field to `Team`. Don't check any of the items; you just need to examine the teams, so they shouldn't be **Editable**; memory and speed won't be a consideration, so **Uses Lazy Fetching** won't be useful.

And, make sure **Prepares Content** is unchecked. If an `NSController` object is told to prepare its content, and it doesn't already have an instance of the kind of object it manages, it will create one. This is usually what you want: If you're editing something, you want your editor to have something ready to edit from the start.

In this case, you're at the mercy of the loading process: An object controller that manages Core Data objects needs a managed-object context to work with. If you look closely at `makeWindowControllers()` in "Loading the Window," earlier in this chapter, you can see that `LeagueWindowController` and its view controller don't even see the document's Core Data context until after they have been initialized. Object controllers throw exceptions when you ask them to prepare Core Data content without a managed-object context to prepare it in. If **Prepares Content** isn't checked, the array controller won't touch Core Data until you let it.

Complete the setup of the array controller by switching to the Identity inspector and setting the Xcode **Label** in the Document section to **Team Array**. This will be the first of four object controllers, and you'll want to be able to tell them apart in lists and popups.

The table view and the "Team Array" array controller belong to the `LeagueViewController`; tie them to it by opening the Assistant editor so it shows `LeagueViewController.swift`, and control drag from each into the `class` definition to create outlets:

```
@IBOutlet var teamArrayController: NSArrayController!
@IBOutlet weak var tableView: NSTableView!
```

Now we start getting into bindings. Bindings rely on the KVO protocol. Any object can ask to be notified when any specified property of another object changes. There are many details, conditions, and caveats to that—look up KVO in the Documentation browser for the whole story—but the short of it is that properties of objects, and attributes of Core Data objects, can be observed for changes.

NSController and its specializations, like NSArrayController, use KVO to link the values of the objects they manage to user-interface elements. The links go both ways—a model object's values get propagated to the screen as they change, and editing a value on the screen updates the model, automatically. These links are called *bindings*. (This is a gross oversimplification, but it's enough to get you through Interface Builder's support for them.)

You've set up what is now the Team Array controller so that it observes objects of the Team entity. Where are those objects to be found? In the managed-object context (NSManagedObjectContext) of the current document. The document and the array controller are at opposite ends of a chain.

- The LeagueDocument, being a Core Data-based NSPersistentDocument, has the NSManagedObjectContext that manages the document's storage.

- The document sees only its neighbor in the chain, the LeagueWindow-Controller. It passes the context down into the window controller's managedObjectContext property.

- The window controller knows about the LeagueViewController it loads from the storyboard; the view controller has a managedObjectContext property for the window controller to fill.

- The view controller comes in from the storyboard with the Team Array NSArrayController, which needs the object context to retrieve the data. It sets the array controller's managedObjectContext property.

- The Team Array controller stands alone. Watch as this chapter progresses: The array controller is the *only* direct user of the document's Core Data content. Cocoa initialized the document object by creating the context, but so far as the code of Mac Passer Rating is concerned, everything but the array controller is a mere custodian for this one consumer.

The last step is reached when the view controller receives the managedObject-Context. It can then trigger the fetch of the Team roster:

```
var managedObjectContext: NSManagedObjectContext! {
    didSet {
        // Pass the MOC to the array controller.
        teamArrayController.managedObjectContext = managedObjectContext
        // Ask the array controller for alphabetical order.
        teamArrayController.sortDescriptors = [
                        NSSortDescriptor( key: "teamName",
                                        ascending: true)]
        // Have the team controller ask for the team roster.
```

```
teamArrayController.fetchWithRequest(nil,
                              merge: false
                              error: nil)
    }
}
```

Binding the Table to the Teams

Each row of the team table represents one instance of the `Team` class. In a view-based table, the table itself distributes the instances among its rows, and has to know how to pull them in. Without an `NSArrayController`, we'd set up the view controller or some other object to implement `NSTableViewDelegate` and `NSViewTableView-DataSource`, just as we would for `UITableView` in iOS. The table would ask for the number of records, and pull them in as needed.

`NSObjectController` and its subclasses take care of all that, at the expense of a steep learning curve, with no code. The two are linked by a binding. Select the table view and select the Bindings inspector (seventh tab). The inspector shows more than a dozen properties that can be linked into the table. The one we want is **Content**, in the Table Content section.

Click the disclosure triangle. What you'll see is a basic binding editor; the editors for all other bindings build on these elements.

- The **Bind to** checkbox determines whether a binding is active at all. Check it.

- The popup next to it gives you a choice of sources for bindings. This will include **File's Owner**, the **Shared User Defaults Controller** (so you can control preferences directly), and any `NSController` objects in the scene. The `NSArrayController` we call Team Array manages the `Team` objects, so select **Team Array**.

- Array controllers take care of selecting and sorting the objects they serve out; the results come through their `arrangedObjects` property. The **Controller Key** to access them is **arrangedObjects**, which Interface Builder should have filled in for you.

- **Model Key Path** will be important later, when the table's cells need specific properties of each `Team`, such as names and statistics. This binding is for the whole array, so leave it blank.

- **Value Transformer** is used for user-interface bindings. A value transformer is like an adapter between one form of data (e.g., whether a property is nil) to another (whether a button should be enabled). It saves having to create additional properties in model objects just to accommodate particular views. You want the objects as they are, so leave the field blank.

- Check **Raises For Not Applicable Keys**. If it is checked, and the property (model key path) you bind to can't be accessed through Key-Value Coding, AppKit will raise an exception at run time. It's imaginable that you wouldn't want that condition flagged, but usually it's an error, and you'll want to halt when it happens.

Binding the Columns to Team Properties

The table now knows the records it is to display—the objects from the application's Model layer—but not what to display from them. If you ran Mac Passer Rating, you could select rows, but there would be nothing in them. Each cell in a row must be told what to display.

The cells have a deeper hierarchy than you'd think; they are not the single views UITableViews deal in. Look again at Figure 20.1.

- Each column has an NSTableViewCell (or subclass) view, one-to-one.
- Each cell view is the root view for the control views that provide displayable, clickable, and editable contents of the cell.
- In AppKit, controls usually depend on NSCell subclasses to run them.
- Cells may have attachments that modify their behavior.

NSTableView assigns a reference to the object a row represents to each NSTableViewCell, through the cell's objectValue property. It's up to the cell and its subviews to link their content to the content of the model object.

To start, use the document outline to select **League View Controller** → **View** → **Bordered Scroll View** → **Clip View** → **TableView** → **Name** (the column) → **Table Cell View** (NSTableViewCell) → **Table View Cell** (an NSTextField that confusingly has that default text).

This time we use the Bindings inspector to set the Value binding in the **Value** section. This editor is more complicated. Bind the value to **Table Cell View** (named, alas, NSTableViewCell), and use the key path objectValue.ownTotalScore (objectValue is the Team object, ownTotalScore is the property of the object we want to display).

- **Allows Editing Multiple Values Selection**: If this is set, and the user selects more than one object (such as when we selected all the integer attributes of Game in Chapter 9, "An iOS Application: Model"), editing this one control would set the given property in all the selected objects. The team name isn't editable, and editing multiple selections in one selected row makes no sense; leave it unchecked.

- **Always Presents Application Modal Alerts**: If a control fails to validate, the usual behavior is to present the validation alert as a sheet attached to the window in which the error occurred. If you want a free-floating alert, check this box.

- **Conditionally Sets Editable**, **Enabled**, or **Hidden**: You set these properties of this text field (making it uneditable turns it into a label) in the Attributes inspector, but if the field is bound, you can override them case by case—maybe you want to dim the contents, but only for certain records. Don't set these unless you know you'll need them. **Conditionally Sets Editable**, in particular, can lead to surprises, if not crashes, if Cocoa spontaneously allows the user to edit values that shouldn't change.

- **Continuously Updates Value**: Usually, the model doesn't want to learn of new values for data until the user is finished entering them; the values in progress might trigger expensive actions or validation alerts. There are reasons, however, to want the in-progress content.

    - The model, or a custom `NSObjectController` you write, should evaluate the in-progress values to intervene in the editing to (for instance) display a red flag while the value is incomplete.

    - You may have noticed this in many Mac applications: If you edit a text field, the edited contents take effect when you press Tab or Return to formally close your edit. If the value isn't continuously updated, this is when it is reported to the controller and the model. If you *click elsewhere* instead of pressing a "completion" key, the new content is *not* reported. If the value is continuously updated, the controller and model can catch the final value no matter how editing stops.

    We won't be editing the team name, so don't check the box.

- **Raises For Not Applicable Keys**: We saw this in the table-content binding: A guaranteed crash if the property you name doesn't exist. Leave it checked.

- **Validates Immediately**: Whether the cell's content should be checked for validity as soon as you move on to another control, or should wait until the whole record is finished. We aren't editing the team name; skip it.

- **Multiple Values Placeholder**: If you do select more than one object, but the relevant property is different among them, this is what the control should display until the user supplies a common value. It's a placeholder; it never gets into the model.

- **No Selection Placeholder**: What to display when the `NSArrayController` has no selection. For instance, a label that describes the selected objects ("3 teams selected") could substitute "Select a Team."

- **Not Applicable Placeholder**: Your `NSObjectController` subclass may decide to characterize a property's value as "not applicable." If `Team` had a property for the brand of the artificial turf in its stadium, and a team plays on grass, the property would not be applicable.

- **Null Placeholder**: Another way for a property to be inapplicable or unspecified is for it simply to be `nil`, which controls usually represent as "(null)." This is what you display instead.

Do the same for `ownTotalScore` and `oppTotalScore`. These are numbers. The binding mechanism doesn't care that they are, and `NSTextField` will apply a reasonable format to display them, so there's no need to worry. Using the Attributes inspector to set the text-field views to right justification would be a nice touch.

All going well, the team table should be all wired up. Run Mac Passer Rating. If you don't have a previous League document open already, create one (⌘N) and fill it with the

Name	Own	Opp
Augusta Autocrats	1,934	3,905
Boise Bearcats	1,944	3,444
Des Moines Desperadoes	3,443	3,566
Fremont Firebugs	1,979	3,462
Glendale Centers	7,369	3,598
Grand Rapids Gamers	2,208	3,327
Huntington Beach Harriers	2,944	3,505
Mobile Misfits	2,204	3,411
Modesto Misanthropes	4,298	3,389
Montgomery Music	3,907	3,610
Richmond Roustabouts	3,394	4,013
San Bernardino Stalkers	5,387	3,593
Shreveport Seamen	4,185	3,551

Figure 20.4   The first version of Mac Passer Rating shows a sorted list of teams with their total scores. `NSArrayController` made it possible to do this with almost no code, even if it involved more effort in this trivial application. The less trivial your app, the more work you can save by using bindings.

sample data (**⌘T**). This time, all does go well. The document window shows the teams and the total scores, for and against. See Figure 20.4.

Commit.

The Arc of League Document Data

This gets us only a short way toward the goal set by Figure 19.1 in Chapter 19, "Starting an OS X Application." The team table should be reduced to a source list that selects a team and its passers.

From League Table to Source List

The first thing is to remove the last two columns of the League table. Such is the price of Progress. Select the "Own" and "Opp" columns and press Delete. Select the table view and remove the header by unchecking the **Headers** box in the Attributes inspector. (*Do not* try to delete the header view; remember that `NSTableView` needs its stereotyped view hierarchy.) Change the **Highlight** to **Source List**, which gets you the distinctive background color and selection style for a Mac-style source list.

The design calls for a *split view*, dividing the source list on the left from the detail view on the right. One way to accomplish this would be to add an NSView to hold the detail views on the right-hand side of the `LeagueViewController` scene, adjust the Auto Layout constraints on the source and detail views so they abut and together fill the scene, select both, and then **Editor** →**Embed in** →**Split View**. This would insert an `NSSplitView` that would contain the views in its halves. There would be some tweaking to do, but most of the work would simply be to connect the new labels and tables to the model, either by way of additonal `NSControllers` or directly from the `LeagueView-Controller`.

Instead, we'll adopt the Yosemite pattern of controlling each functional area of a window with its own `NSViewController` object. Instead of putting the master (Team) table and the detail view in a split view, all under the control of the `LeagueView-Controller`, we will add an `NSSplitViewController`, and make the two views its contents.

Keep your eye on the distinction: `LeagueViewController` will no longer be the sole controller in the window. Its scene will no longer constitute the whole content in the window. That whole-window role will now belong to the `NSSplitViewController` provided by AppKit. `LeagueViewController` will control just one of the two sides of the split, with the other managed by what we can call `TeamDetailController`.

Go to the Object library (bottom of the Utility area, third tab) and search for **split**, uncovering the "Vertical Split View Controller." Drag it into the canvas. (Be sure you grab the controller, not the bare view.) The controller scene comes with a two-way split and two view-controller scenes attached. There is almost nothing you can edit in an `NSSplitViewController`; it's there for bookkeeping and layout.

> **Note**
>
> In point of fact, `NSSplitViewController` isn't so simple; it takes care of things that would be tedious and repetitive for you to do yourself; and having access to the internals of AppKit, it can, for instance, not load one of its subcontrollers at all if its part of the split is hidden.

Delete the scenes that came with the split controller; they're not magic, and we can't put a controller in first place if there are any there already. Control-drag from the split-controller scene to the `LeagueViewController`, making it the first, and so far only, element in the split.

Next, drag an `NSViewController` into the canvas, and control-drag a connection to it from the split-view scene. The split view shows a two-way split between the master and detail views. Make the new view controller your own: Select it, and in the Identity inspector, name the class **TeamDetailController**.

Xcode will start pestering us about there being no such class as `TeamDetail-Controller`, so make an empty one: **File → New → File...** (⌘ N) to create a Swift class definition for `TeamDetailController` as a subclass of `NSViewController`. Just enough to give us some peace.

Complete the new hierarchy by control-dragging from the `LeagueWindow-Controller`'s icon in the window scene's title bar down into the split-view controller, making the split view the content view for the window. The line that appears between the two, and the lines that run from the `NSSplitViewController` and the two view controllers, are "relationships," not segues. No existing controller will get a call to `prepareForSegue(_, sender:)` to initialize the incoming scene.

This isn't really a problem, though: `NSSplitViewController` keeps a list of its `NSSplitViewItems`, which hold the respective view controllers. As an `NSWindow-`

`Controller`, `LeagueWindowController` has a `contentViewController` property that points to the split-view controller. There's a seamless path from the document, to the window, through the split view, down to the view controllers.

You saw in the "Building the Document Window" section above that the code for traversing the split view was already in `windowDidLoad`, but blocked off by the `usingSplitView` flag. Set it to `true` to enable the full process. (The sample code shows only the full-process version of `windowDidLoad`.)

Change `usingSplitView` to `true`, and uncomment the line declaring the `team-DetailController` property. It might be a good idea to flip back to "Building the Document Window" to review the way `windowDidLoad` works now.

Capturing the Team Selection

Think about what happens when you use the document window: You select a team from the source list (the `LeagueViewController` half of the split), and the detail view (the `TeamDetailController` half) responds to the selection by displaying the team's information. The change in selection, and which object was selected, has to be passed from the master to the detail, and being in different scenes, they can't communicate directly. The window controller, which has direct access to both, has to mediate.

You can see the complete arc of the process in Figure 20.5.

- You've already done the first part: `LeagueViewController` pulls `Teams` from the document's Core Data store, and fills its table with them.

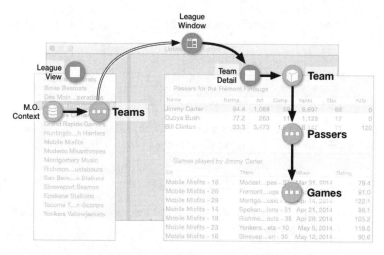

Figure 20.5   The contents of the league document window follow a path from the table of `Teams` drawn from the document's Core Data store, through a sequence of selections of `Team`, `Passer`, and `Game`. Each step is mediated by an `NSObjectController` or `NSArrayController`.

- You've probably clicked on some of the rows in the list of teams; the next thing we'll do is to make your selection of a team into an event that carries through to the team-detail view in the other half of the window.

- That "event" leaves the `LeagueViewController` to be captured by the `LeagueWindowController`.

- The event identifies the `Team` that the user selected; the window controller passes the `Team` down into the `TeamDetailController`.

... and we'll leave the rest for later.

I called the user's click on a team in the league-view table an "event." Cocoa has many mechanisms for objects to communicate with each other. This time, I'm going with *Key-Value Observing.*

> **Note**
>
> When any object starts observing a property of class X, the Objective-C runtime library (it's still there in Swift applications) creates a *new* subclass of X that has its own setter method for the property under observation. When any code sets the observed property, the wrapper method first takes note of the original value, calls through to the "real" setter method in X, and when the setting is done, triggers the observation methods of all objects that are observing the property.

Knowing this makes a bit more sense of the `addObserver` statement in `League-WindowController`'s `windowDidLoad` method. The call tells the `LeagueView-Controller`'s Team Array controller...

```
leagueViewController.teamArrayController.addObserver(
```

to register `self`, the `LeagueWindowController`,

```
        self,
```

as an observer of the `selectedObjects` property.

```
        forKeyPath: "selectedObjects",
```

There is no need for any special reporting on the before-and-after values of the property, and here's a tag value to make it easier to identify the event when it comes in:

```
        options: NSKeyValueObservingOptions(0),
        context: &teamSelectionChange)
```

`LeagueWindowController` defines the standard `observeValue...` method that catches all the property-changed events.

```
override func observeValueForKeyPath(keyPath: String,
            ofObject object: AnyObject,
            change: [NSObject : AnyObject],
            context: UnsafeMutablePointer<Void>) {
```

```
if context == &teamSelectionChange {
    if let selection = object.valueForKeyPath("selectedObjects")
            as? [Team] {
        teamDetailController?.representedObject =
            (selection.count > 0) ? selection[0] : nil
    }
}
}
```

> **Note**
>
> It's an `override` function because `NSObject`—and therefore every class in Cocoa—already implements it, and you have to add the `override` attribute to claim the function's place in the inheritance path. Swift has many such qualifiers, and it is particular that you should supply every attribute necessary, and only those. The easiest way to do this for an inherited or protocol function is to type the function's name—just the name, no keywords—and trigger code completion. If Xcode comes up with the function signature you want, it will also provide all the adornments.

The function checks the `context` parameter to verify that it matches the arbitrary tag we passed in, thus proving the event is a change in the set of selected objects in the Team Array controller. It treats the `selectedObjects` as an array of `Team` objects (`[Team]`).

If there are any selected `Teams` (there should be at most one), the function takes the first one and passes it down to the `TeamDetailController` as its `represented-Object`. If no `Teams` are selected, the `representedObject` is set to `nil`.

Which completes the top arc in Figure 20.5.

From Team to Tables

Bindings are built on Key-Value Observing. They extend KVO by linking model and view objects by having them observe each other. The binding editors you've seen in the Bindings inspector are presented once for every property of a view; you identify the object and its property that will exchange observations with the property of the view that the editor controls.

> **Note**
>
> You *can* bind properties of any two Cocoa objects in code, whether the pair are model and view or not. Few developers are happy to do so: The support for mutual bindings built into Interface Builder and the standard Cocoa objects is (believe it or not) easy to work with; getting the necessary behavior right to make your all-new classes bind properly can be difficult.

The `TeamDetailController` view consists of two tables, one of `Passers`, the other of `Games`. You've bound up a table before; you know we'll need an `NSArrayController` for each, one for `Passers`, the other for `Games`. These controllers need a source. In the case of the League table of `Teams`, that source was a direct fetch of all `Team` objects in the document's store.

Once the user selects a team, and the `Team` object finds its way to `TeamDetail-Controller`, it no longer matters that the objects are Core Data managed objects. The detail controller doesn't have to hit the database to find the passers on a team; it has the team itself, which can provide the list of passers directly.

This leads to the following definition of `TeamDetailController`:

```swift
class TeamDetailController: NSViewController {

    var currentTeamName: String? {
        let team = representedObject as? Team
        return team?.teamName
    }

    class func keyPathsForValuesAffectingCurrentTeamName()
                    -> NSSet {
        //  There is no setter method that KVO could use to trigger a
        //  changed-value observation for currentTeamName.
        //  currentTeamName is computed, never assigned; the
        //  computed value changes only when representedValue changes.

        //  keyPathsForValuesAffecting<PropertyName>() lets a class
        //  say, "send out an observation whenever any of the properties
        //  in this list change."

        //  Changing representedObject would change the computed value
        //  of currentTeamName, so return an NSSet containing
        //  "representedObject".
        return NSSet(array: ["representedObject"])
    }

    @IBOutlet var gameArrayController: NSArrayController!
    @IBOutlet var passerArrayController: NSArrayController!
    @IBOutlet var teamObjectController: NSObjectController!

    override
    var representedObject: AnyObject? {
        didSet {
            teamObjectController.content = representedObject
        }
    }
}
```

Bindings are hard to get your mind around, but give them credit: `TeamDetail-Controller` consists of four assignments, a constant object, and a data access. We're going to have a system of labels and tables that respond to the user's selection of 3 variables, each filtering the next, including string formatting and sourcing data to the tables, in 19 parsable lines of generously formatted code.

Let's complete the arc I began in "Capturing the Team Selection." I left off where the window controller passes the selected `Team` object into `TeamDetailController`:

- The `TeamDetailController` maintains an `NSObjectController` to "manage" the `Team` that is to be the focus of the view. In principle, this isn't necessary—binding editors do provide for binding directly to a property of the view controller itself; in practice, the notifications of changes work better if you leave as much of the chain as possible to `NSController` objects. When its `represented-Object` property is set, `TeamDetailController` makes it the content object for the object controller.

- An `NSArrayController` provides the content for the upper table, a table of `Passers`. Tables are usually run by `NSArrayControllers`; this one is set for **Mode Class** (not **Entity**—there's no contact with the main Core Data store), **Class Name `Passer`**.

The Passer Section

The upper half of the Team Detail view shows the `Passers` associated with the selected `Team`. It is a label, controlled by the Team Object controller, and a table controlled by an `NSArrayController` that manages a list of `Passer` objects.

Passer Array Controller

The big differences between the `NSArrayController` in the `LeagueViewController` scene are that the controlled objects are of **Class** (not **Entity**) **`Passer`**, and the source of the "Content Array" in the Bindings inspector is taken from the **`passers`** array from the Team Object's **`selection`**. Even though the Team Object controller, is an `NSObject-Controller`, with only one object to select, it has a `selection` property, and that's what you should draw from.

Do not prepare content, do not make the content editable. In the Identity inspector, name it *Passer Array*; there will be another array controller, and you'll need to tell them apart.

This binding draws from a `passers` property of `Game`, which we don't have yet: The Core Data schema links `Teams` only to `Games`; the game list has to be drawn by tracing through the `Passers` to their `Games`.

Add this property to `Team`:

```
var passers: [Passer] {
    //  Team doesn't have a relationship to Passer, except
    //  by way of .games. Have .games list the Passers
    //  in all Games, with the duplicates filtered
    //  out (a "distinct union" of Passers).

    let unionOfPassers = self.games.valueForKeyPath(
                    "@distinctUnionOfObjects.passer")
        as NSSet?
```

```
    if let passerSet = unionOfPassers {
        return passerSet.allObjects as! [Passer]
    }
    else { return [] }
}
```

> **Note**
>
> The Content Array binding for the Passer Array controller could have used **@distinct-UnionOfObjects.passer**, but let's keep the relationship in code—binding parameters are hard to debug.

Passer-Table Label

Drag a label into the scene, allowing Interface Builder to guide you on the standard margins from the top and sides of the root view. Stretch it out to the standard margin from the right edge of the root view, and select **Editor →Resolve Auto Layout Issues →Add Missing Constraints**. The Team Detail view doesn't need any adaptive layout; just place the views where you want them, and let IB add the constraints.

The contents of the label should adjust to the selected `Team`, which means binding to the Team Object `NSObjectController`. The label will have two bindings you haven't seen before:

- The label should describe the passer table using the name of the team, as in "Passers for the Birmingham Bearcats." You'd expect formatted text to come from application code, but the **Value With Pattern** binding can often put simple formatted text into UI elements without having to resort to code.

  Open the **Value With Pattern →Display Pattern Value1** editor and bind it to **Team Object**, **selection**, **teamName**—so far, what you'd expect. With-pattern editors add a field, **Display Pattern**. This field has a simple syntax: Write out the literal text, and add a placeholder for the bound value, as in **Passers for the %{value1}@**. It's always `value` plus a numeral. You'll see the reason for the numeral soon.

  The editor includes the special-case placeholder fields. The next step shows why we don't care what those are.

- We're also going to set the **Hidden** binding. If there is no team name to display, there's no way to fill the phrase "Passers for the..." that isn't awkward. Better to make the phrase go away. The binding is **Team Object**, **selection**, **self**. Every `NSObject` has the `self` property; it returns the object itself, which is convenient for cases like this, where you must specify a property, but want the object itself instead.

  The next field is **Value Transformer**. Enter `NSIsNil`—autocompletion will finish it for you. Descendants of `NSValueTransformer` bridge values of one type to another; a more sophisticated example would be if an object had an RGB `color` property that should be displayed by name, such as "green" or "magenta."

We want to hide the label when the selection is nil, because there is no Team to display. That's a yes-or-no Boolean question, and nil isn't a Boolean value. NSIsNil takes any pointer and returns whether the pointer is nil. If selection.self is nil, the transformer yields true (or YES in Objective-C), signaling that the label should be hidden.

Passer Table

This is yet another table view; except for the content being Passers, there isn't much new.

Find the Table View in the Object library, and drag it into the view. **View Based**; standard margin from the label, flush against the sides of the superview; **Add Missing Constraints** to lock those in; minimum width of 400 to keep it readable and constrain the width of the window; height fixed at 120 points.

Use the Identity inspector to set the enclosing NSScrollView's **Document Label** to **Passer roster**, so you can tell it apart from the game table that will come later.

Seven columns with headers, labeled **Name, Rating, Att, Comp, Yards, TDs, INTs.**

Select each column in turn. The Attributes inspector has a section for the default sort order for a column. For the numeric columns, set sorting to:

- **Sort Key**, the name of the PasserClass property that corresponds to the column.
- **Selector**. The field will default to **compare:**, a method of both NSString and NSNumber, which is what you need. The notation is Objective-C, so remember to include the trailing colon.
- **Order**: **Ascending**, initially. Clicking the column header will toggle the order between ascending and descending.

Note

By now, you'll be getting yellow warnings from Interface Builder about incorrect frames for views in the TeamDetailController scene. Some of these are genuine problems for you to solve by working on constraints and placements. However, in the version of Xcode I'm using, there are warnings about the clip views that surround the table views. I wasn't able to clear those warnings, but I saw no ill effects from them. Even Xcode has trouble getting Auto Layout right. As with any warnings, take Auto Layout warnings seriously, but if you've made a serious effort, and there are no visible problems, just let them go.

Set the **Sort Key** for the Name column to lastName, so we can stick to a simple compare: of strings. In a better app, Passer would have its own comparison method to yield **lastName**, firstName ordering, but let's keep it simple.

These are the *default* sort orders; we want the user to be able to change the order of the table by clicking a header. The table will use the Passer Array NSArrayController's arrangedObjects array. Array controllers can change the order and content of the arrangedObjects by applying its own sort descriptors and selection predicates.

When a column header is clicked, we want the array controller to change the sort descriptors it uses to produce the arrangedObjects. This entails yet another binding. Select the table view, the Bindings inspector, and the **Sort Descriptors** binding. Bind the table's sort descriptors to **Passer Array**, `sortDescriptors`. Any change to the table's sort order (as determined by clicks on the headers) will change the array controller's, and vice versa.

Users should be able to select `Passer`s from the table. Doing so should tell the Passer Array controller to update its selected object. Yet another binding. Edit **Selection Indexes**, and bind to **Passer Array**, `selectionIndexes`.

> **Note**
>
> Don't let the plural bother you. It's the only binding available, and because the **Selection →Multiple** box is unchecked, there will always be *at most* one selected `Passer`.

Finally, and most familiar: Bind the table's **Content** to **Passer Array**, `arrangedObjects`. That array will reflect the `NSArrayController`'s sorting and filtering properties.

For the cells, again, this is just as before (with one exception): Dig down into the table, the column, the table cell view, to the view that renders the relevant property of the `Passer` for the row. Bind to **Table Cell View**, **Model Key Path** `objectValue .attempts` (or whatever the `Passer` property the cell is to display; see Table 20.1). Remember to uncheck **Conditionally Sets Editable** so the application doesn't spontaneously turn the data labels into editable text fields. (What we've been treating as "labels" are in fact just `NSTextField`s with the **Editable** boxes unchecked.)

Table 20.1   Property Names for the Numeric Columns in the Passer Table

Column Head	Property
Rating	`passerRating`
Att	`attempts`
Comp	`completions`
Yards	`yards`
TDs	`touchdowns`
INTs	`interceptions`

> **Note**
>
> Interface Builder knows it is managing objects of class `Passer`; the autcompletion feature of the **Model Key Path** field *should* be able to suggest the names of `Passer` properties. This feature has always been spotty, and on the version of Xcode I'm using, there's no autocompletion; the field is tagged with a gray exclamation-mark flag. So long as the cell shows the right number when you run the app, you don't need to worry.

The Name column is a small exception: `Passer` does have a `.fullName` property, but we're not going to use it. Instead, let's use **Value With Pattern** again, but for two values, `lastName` and `firstName`. The first step is obvious: Disclose the **Display Pattern Value1** editor, and bind it to the **Table Cell View** with **Model Key Path** `obectValue.firstName`.

What now? That editor doesn't afford a way to use two values.

But the next one does. Binding **Display Pattern Value1** adds an additonal binding editor, **Display Pattern Value2** (and so on). It's just the same, except the **Model Key Path** is objectValue.lastName.

The trick is in the **Display Pattern** field: Make that **%{value1}@ %{value2}@**.

The Document Window so Far

It's been a while since Mac Passer Rating has been in runnable shape, so let's have a look: **Product → Run (⌘ R)**, Figure 20.6.

It's *almost* what we want. The problem is in the Rating column. The passer ratings go on for an unlimited number of significant figures, until they are truncated with ellipses when they run into the margin of the cells. The custom is to cut ratings off at the first digit of the fraction. Must we add a property to Passer that yields a properly formatted string?

No. Select the Team Detail scene in Interface Builder. Type **formatter** in the search field of the Object library to find green icons representing a repertoire of automatic formatters for numbers, dates, and even byte counts. Drag a number formatter into the rating cell. IB will place the formatter where it belongs in the hierarchy—the NSCell inside the NSTextField that displays the rating. (If it attaches to the NSTextField instead, that's not a problem.) The cell will look no different in the canvas, but the formatter is there.

Run Mac Passer Rating again... no, we overshot. The ratings now have *no* fractions. We'll have to customize the formatter. It's not visible in the storyboard canvas, and it doesn't show up in the jump bar or when you control-shift-click on the cell. You *can* find it in the document outline. Select it and turn your attention to the Attributes editor.

What you got was a formatter with **Behavior OS X 10.4 Default** (avoid **10.0+**; it's there for backward compatibility), **Style None**. We know that won't do, and neither will the other preset styles (though the **Spell Out** style could be fun); experiment with the

Name	Rating	Att	Comp	Yards	TDs	INTs
Warren Harding	97.7623...	486	262	3,200	34	0
William Harrison	16.5165...	222	53	239	11	36
Frank Pierce	30.8467...	1,364	365	1,592	23	47
Abe Lincoln	149.319...	1,377	1,009	15,397	196	0
Cal Coolidge	29.4740...	1,830	527	2,731	32	70

Figure 20.6   The passer table turned out well, with one exception.

Unformatted sample field, and see the result in the **Formatted** view. You'll have to switch to **OS X 10.4 Custom**.

This yields you many, many formatting options, for positive and negative values, padding, prefix and suffix strings, rounding strategies. . . . We need only a couple of settings (Figure 20.7).

All we want is to have at least one digit before and after the decimal place: 153.8, 14.0, 0.3, and so on. Those controls are near the bottom of the Attributes inspector. For **Integer Digits**, set the **Minimum** to **1**; the **Maximum** will be **3** in practice, but you don't need the formatter to enforce it. For the **Fraction Digits**, the **Minimum** and **Maximum** should both be **1**.

Run the app again; so far, so good.

> **Note**
>
> Let's begin to think about localization: You may have noticed that unless you set explicit formatting strings at the top of the inspector, you don't have any control over the grouping separator (thousands, a comma in the U.S.) or the decimal separator (a period in the U.S.). That is because these marks are locale-dependent: Some regions use space or period for grouping, and comma to mark fractions. These are controlled by the system-wide locale settings from the Language & Region panel of the System Preferences utility. If you, an

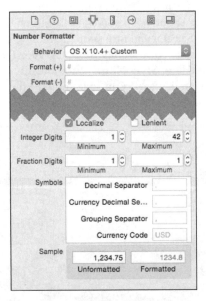

Figure 20.7   The customization options for an NSNumberFormatter are many, but if you just want the number to be shown with at least one digit on either side of the decimal point, you need only two fields.

American, display 1.345 to a German user, she will read it as what you would call "one thousand three hundred forty-five," which could be disastrous. Having a system-wide setting removes the possibility. iOS and OS X provide many formatting utilities that will apply the proper formats; don't just plow ahead with something like the `printf()` family.

Game-Table Label

Finishing up with the lower part of the Team Detail view, for the game table, is no great departure from what we've seen before, so I'll rush you through.

The label below the passer table will include the name of the selected passer. Because the selection in the passer table is bound to the `selectionIndexes` of the Passer Array controller, a click in the table will point the controller's `selection` key to the `Passer` for that row.

Place a new label below the passer table, left and right edges aligned to those of the "Passers for" label. Have IB add the missing constraints. The **Display Pattern** should be `Games played by %{value1}@`. Save time by using the `fullName` property this time: Bind to **Passer Array**, `selection`, `fullName`.

Game Array Controller

This is a reprise of what you did with the Passer Array controller: The controlled objects (Identity inspector) are of **Class Game**; the content array (Bindings inspector) is the `gameArray` of the `selection` of the **Passer Array** controller.

> **Note**
>
> This strategy is too simple: It pulls in *all* of the passer's games, not just the ones played for the selected Game. Let's make up a reason for doing that and save the trouble.

Game Table

Drag another table view in. Flush with the bottom and sides, standard margin from the game-table label. Unlike the other views, the game table has no constraint (explicit or content-based) on its height. This flexibility allows the document window to change height.

The columns should be Us (the Game's `teamName` property and `ourScore`, formatted as `%{value1}@ - %{value2}@`; Them (the same, except for the use of `theirTeam` as the name); When (`whenPlayed`); and Rating (the Game's calculated `passerRating` property).

Run Mac Passer Rating. Figure 20.8 shows the miserable record of Herbert Hoover as he was traded around the league. His skills are not the only problem here.

Almost all of the team names and scores in the second column run off the left end of the column, with ellipses showing the truncation. This was acceptable for numbers, whose digits are less significant the farther right they are. In this case, the user can make out the team names, even if truncated, but not the scores, which are essential information.

Also, all of the dates are "Monday". They, too are truncated, and the full format including the day of the week isn't useful.

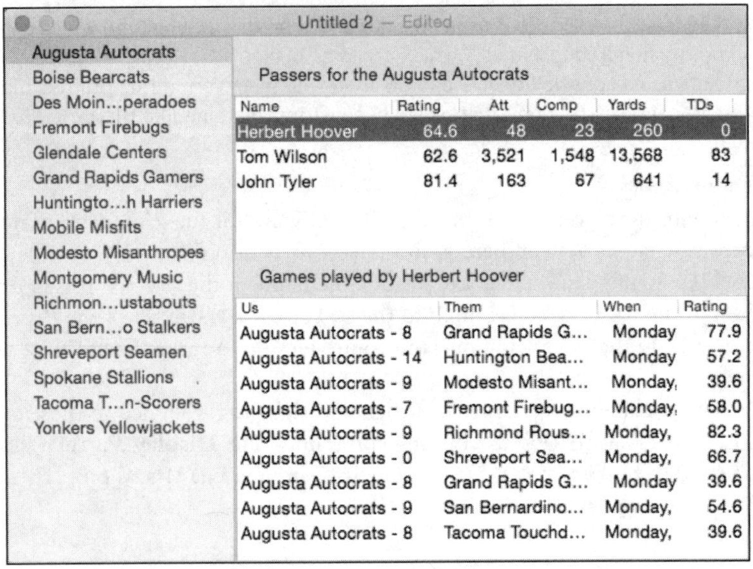

Figure 20.8   The game table needs some work on formatting.

I'm sure you noticed that in addition to a number formatter, Interface Builder lets you bring in a date formatter. Drop one on the When cell, and in the Attributes inspector, set it for

- **Behavior**: **OS X 10.4+ Default**
- **Date Style**: **Medium**—watch the **Sample** view to see the effect.
- **Relative Date**: No. You want the calendar date, even if it could also be called "Yesterday."
- **Time Style**: **No Time Style**. Football teams never play more than one game a day, so the time doesn't matter. Besides, showing the time will give away that the data set cheats, and sets each game for midnight.

As for the Them column, you can control the truncation policy of NSTextFields (which includes labels). Select the Them cell's text field content, and use the Attributes inspector to set **Layout** to **Truncates** (rather than attempt to wrap to an additional line, or making the content scrollable) and **Line Break Truncate Middle**. This will put the ellipses in the middle of the team-and-score cells, to show both enough of the team names to identify them, and the scores.

Do the same in the Us column.

Now that you have both the table (with its headers) and the Game Array controller, you can bind the sort descriptors as you like. For the Us and Them columns, I recommend sorting on the respective team names.

And that brings us to the document window we wanted from Figure 19.1.

Summary

Bindings are a tremendous convenience in OS X programming, and even this long chapter can't cover everything. In this chapter, I gave you an introduction to what bindings can do for you, but more to the point, I showed what Xcode can do to support them. It is *possible* to set up bindings in code, but Interface Builder is indispensable to getting them right, easily (comparatively) and quickly.

I showed you how bindings and formatters can render your data in forms that your model classes don't directly support, saving you from having to alter your model to accommodate per-view variations in presentation.

You used number and date formatters, and truncation controls, to control how information is presented in table cells and labels.

21

Localization

I'm pretty satisfied with Mac Passer Rating, at least as an example, but what would make it perfect would be if I could see it in French (they play football in Québec)—an application named Quart-Efficacité. Users of OS X specify what languages they understand by setting a list of available languages in order of preference in the **Language** tab of the **Language & Region** panel of the System Preferences application. When a user's list sets French at a higher priority than English, I'd like MPR to present menus, alerts, and labels in the French language.

> **Note**
>
> The localization techniques I'll show you are identical to the ones you'd use for an iOS app.

My plan for this chapter is a bit involved: First, I'll show you the core concepts behind localization in Cocoa. Next, I'll show you "how it's really done," the techniques Cocoa uses to find and use translations and adaptive layouts; I'll show how Xcode helps you create the files Cocoa localization needs to get the job done. You'll know what the result is supposed to be.

And then, very briefly, I'll tell you why you don't have to do it that way, and why you shouldn't.

How Localization Works

Cocoa applications load resources through the NSBundle class. When asked for a resource, NSBundle first searches the subdirectories of the application bundle's Resources directory in the order of the user's preferences for language. Language subdirectories are given such names as English.lproj, fr.lproj, or en-GB.lproj; plain-text language names are deprecated; you should use ISO-standard language abbreviations, optionally suffixed with a code to identify a regional variant.

If a directory that matches the user's language and region (such as fr-CA.lproj for Canadian French) can't be found, OS X falls back to the language-only variant (fr.lproj); then so on, down the list of the user's preferred languages; then to the *base localization* (in `Base.lproj`); and finally to strings and layouts in unlocalized resources, not in any `.lproj` directory.

If you look at the Mac Passer Rating target directory in the Finder, you'll see a `Base.lproj` directory containing `Main.storyboard`.

Bring up `Main.storyboard` in Interface Builder, and look at the jump bar above the Editor area. As you expect, it progresses from the project, through the enclosing groups, to the file itself. But there's one more level: It has the same name as the file, with `(Base)` appended. So far as Xcode is concerned, what you're seeing is only one of many possible variants on that file—the one that appears in `Base.lproj`.

> **Note**
>
> If you create an unlocalized resource of your own, Xcode won't initially track it for localization. *Do not* try moving it to an `lproj` yourself. At the very least, the file's name in the Project navigator will turn red, meaning Xcode can no longer find it; solve that by clicking the tiny folder button in the File inspector when the red label is selected. Worse, you may confuse the localization mechanism. Experience has shown that Xcode can be fragile when resources are localized behind its back. It is getting better all the time, but don't tempt fate.

Adding a Localization

Earlier versions of Xcode (up through version 3) treated localization on a file-by-file basis: You could put files of the same name—`Main.storyboard`, `Credits.rtf`—into separate `lproj` folders, but that was your business. Xcode took no notice of their being related.

This falls short of what a project needs on two counts. First, it's just inconvenient: If you're working on the English version of a resource, you'll want to work on the French version in parallel. Second, the point of internationalization is to produce a product that conforms to the user's locale; conceptually, you don't internationalize a file, you internationalize the whole project. Xcode now organizes the process of localization as a property of the whole project, not just file by file.

Base Localization

Xcode starts from a *base localization*. The idea is that base localization files embody the fundamental structure of the localizable resources, whereas the language/region-specific files fill in the details: `Base.lproj` contains `Main.storyboard`, which specifies the layout of the whole app, except for the document window itself.

> **Note**
>
> The strings in the storyboard are all in English, but that's incidental; it is in the Base localization because it is the authoritative layout.

The French localization will use the same layout, from the same storyboard. You do not have to redo the layout. Instead, you supply a `.strings` file, a dictionary that provides the French text that Cocoa will substitute for French-speaking users.

> **Note**
>
> If you're working from an older project, you won't have a Base localization. Xcode will start you on the process if you check **Use Base Internationalization** in the **Info** tab of the Project editor. It will present you with every file it understands to be localizable, and it asks whether you want to keep it in the English locale or move it to Base; and if you do move it to Base, whether you want to create a `.strings` file to separate the English-language content from the Base content—which in principle isn't in any language.

Why Base Localization?

Base localization works from the principle that, as much as possible, you should have one set of assets—storyboards and XIBs most prominent among them—that is authoritative for the application, and supply only enough information to cover the differences for each localization. This is much easier than duplicating those assets for each language and locale.

There are reasons you might want to keep a duplicate layout for another language—the cultural differences I mentioned earlier are good ones—but usually you don't need to do this, and you shouldn't. Take it to the extreme: You are supporting a dozen languages in three or four scripts. (This isn't uncommon, and you want to be rich enough to have this problem.) That's 12 layouts. Now add a row of buttons to one of them. And then to all the rest. Remember you have to link outlets and actions for each.

No. You'd rather not do that.

The classic justification for multiple layouts was that the same idea may be expressed in only two characters in a CJK script, but require...a lot in German. Some developers solve this by laying out for German, and if that means the Japanese get tiny islands of kanji in an expanse of dialog sheet, it can't be helped. Most developers would rather not do that, either.

And in the case of right-to-left scripts (Arabic, Hebrew), the need for duplicate layouts seems inescapable. The **OK** button has to be at the lower left, not the lower right as it is in L-T-R layouts.

You remember the pain I put you through in Chapter 12, "Auto Layout in a New View," admittedly an extreme case; for Mac Passer Rating, the default constraints offered by Interface Builder were enough. Here is where it pays off: Just as iOS size classes allow you to use the same storyboard for radically different layouts, the same storyboard can produce correct layout for kanji, Arabic, and German: Remember the compression resistance of text-containing views? The longer German label will push out the enclosing view (cascading out to the bounds of the window, if necessary) to make room.

If you get Auto Layout right, your views will accommodate even absurdly large content. See Figure 21.1.

What about Hebrew? Remember how all the horizontal spacing constraints were described as "leading" and "trailing," not "left" and "right"? Auto Layout knows that in

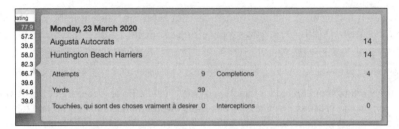

Figure 21.1   With proper Auto Layout, the game-view popover will present an orderly appearance even if one of its labels is pushed out by an absurdly long title.

Hebrew, the leading side of controls and text is on the right. If you did it right, Auto Layout will flop the layout for right-to-left scripts.

Something Worth Localizing

I've sold you once again (haven't I?) on the benefits of Auto Layout. Mac Passer Rating as it stands doesn't make much use of Auto Layout: It's just there to make sure everything sticks to each other; there's hardly any text at all to challenge the layout.

Game Detail View: Layout

Fortunately (for the purposes of demonstration), there is one piece missing from the plan · in Figure 19.1: A popover showing the details of a game selected from the lower table in the team detail view.

This entails yet another view controller. Drop a View Controller scene into the `Main.storyboard` canvas. Use the Identity inspector to set the controller **Class** to *GameDetailController*. The class file will come shortly.

> **Note**
>
> Notice that the field below, **Module**, is empty but for a placeholder saying "None." That will come back to us.

Size the scene's root view at 360 width, 220 height. Drop labels into the top half as shown in Figure 21.2, and `MacStatViews` in the bottom. It would be nice to attach `NSNumberFormatters`, in the **Decimal** style to the score labels; you *must* attach an `NSDateFormatter` in the **Full** date style (no time style) to the date label, in order to demonstrate localized layout.

Once again, I'll cut down on the network of constraints by creating an OS X version of the `StatView` label-and-number view class, `MacStatView`. Aside from adaptations to fit AppKit instead of UIKit, there's not much to be learned from it; you can find `MacStatView.swift` in the sample code for this chapter.

Figure 21.2   The Game Detail scene is not elaborate; the top half are labels, the bottom, `MacStatViews`.

Let's see how fast we can run through the constraints:

- Make the date label, at the top, observe the standard spacing from the top and sides of the enclosing view.
- For every view below the date, on the left side of the view, align the leading edges to the leading edge of the date, and their trailing edges to each other.
- For the views on the right, align their trailing edges to the trailing edge of the date, and their leading edges to each other.
- Make all the stat views of equal height and width.
- Put a minimum width on any one of the stat views of something like 110 points, and minimum height 25. Do this by setting a size constraint in the ⊢□⊣ popover. That will be an absolute constraint; turn it into an at-least constraint by selecting the constraint, and changing the **Relation** popup to **Greater Than or Equal** in the Attributes inspector.
- The views on the left side will determine the vertical placement of everything else:
    - Pin the vertical spacings between the date and the team names at 8 points.
    - Align the baselines of the team-name labels with their respective scores.
    - Align the tops of the left-hand `MacStatViews` with their neighbors to the right.
    - Pin the bottom of the **Touchdowns** stat view to the standard distance from the bottom of the view.

- Interface Builder is still complaining that the width or horizontal placement of the stat views is ambiguous. Here's a trick:

  - Drag a constraint *from* the **Attempts** stat view *to* the containing view. It doesn't matter what the relationship is, because you're going to change it.

  - Select the new constraint, and in the Attributes inspector change it to **First Item: Mac Stat View.Trailing**; **Relation: Equal**; **Second Item: Superview.Center X**; **Constant: –8**. (Select **Reverse First and Second Item** from one of the item popups if the views aren't in the right order.) The meaning is clear if you just read it off: "The trailing edge of the stat view is equal to the center of the container minus eight."

  - Pin the horizontal spacing between **Attempts** and **Completions** at 16, which ensures that **Completions** will align 8 points to the right of center.

  - The edges of the other stat views being pinned to **Attempts** or **Completions**, their placement becomes unambiguous, too.

  - The equal-width constraint on all the stat views ensures that owing to the compression-resistance constraint they carry (select one of them and look in the Size inspector), they will all be as wide as the one with the widest content; that, in turn, pushes the outer view to the width that accommodates all the views.

Finally, control-drag from the Team Detail scene to the new Game Detail scene, and accept the **Popover** style for the resulting segue. Select the segue and give it the name **Show game popover** in the Attributes inspector.

Also, set the **Anchor View** by dragging from the connection bubble in that field to the game table in the Team Detail scene. This sets the table as the place from which the popover is to be placed. Because we want the popover to appear to the right of the table, set **Preferred Edge** to **Right**.

Game Detail View: Code

We have the game-detail layout, but not the code behind it. Create a new class, `GameDetailController`, a subclass of `NSViewController`. Start it off with one property, and one modifier on the existing `NSViewController` property `representedObject`:

```
var game: Game!
override var representedObject: AnyObject? {
    didSet {
        game = representedObject as? Game
        //  loadStatViews()
    }
}
```

Having a `game` property, with an implicitly unwrapped type of `Game` already attached, is more than just a convenience.

But first, add @IBOutlets for the MacStatViews. This should be easy for you by now: Open the assistant editor and focus it on the new GameDetailController .Swift (it should be one of the **Automatic** options in the jump bar). Control-drag from each stat view into the class definition, and name each:

```
@IBOutlet weak var attemptsView: MacStatView!
@IBOutlet weak var yardsView: MacStatView!
@IBOutlet weak var touchdownsView: MacStatView!
@IBOutlet weak var completionsView: MacStatView!
@IBOutlet weak var interceptionsView: MacStatView!
```

What about the labels in the upper half? Try this: Control-drag from the date label at the top onto the declaration of the game property of GameDetailController. The property definition itself should highlight—see Figure 21.3, top.

Interface Builder offers to bind the label to the game property. Grab onto this with both hands: Leave **Bind** as **Value** (you can choose any of the bindable properties of the view); **self** in GameDetailController; and the **Key Path game.whenPlayed** for the value. Click **Connect**.

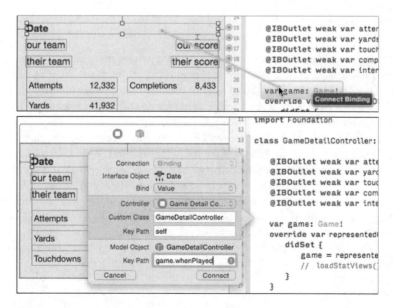

Figure 21.3   Control-dragging from a view that exposes key-value bindings to a key-value observable property in a controller class lets you bind the two, even though the controller class is not a subclass of NSController.

> **Note**
>
> Why didn't I tell you about this in Chapter 20, "Bindings: Wiring an OS X Application"? In that chapter, we were linking up a chain of selected objects, and collections subject to sorting and filtering into `arrangedObjects`. `NSController` classes are built to handle those concepts, not just direct access between two objects.

Do the same for the team names and scores: **`game.team.teamName`**, **`game.our-Score`**, **`game.theirTeam`**, and **`game.theirScore`**.

The stat views have to be filled in in the usual way. Add `loadStatViews` to `GameDetailController`, uncomment the call to it in the `didSet` block for `representedObject`, and add a call to `viewDidLoad`:

```
func loadStatViews() {
    if attemptsView == nil || game == nil { return }

    attemptsView.numericValue = game.attempts as! Int
    yardsView.numericValue = game.yards as! Int
    touchdownsView.numericValue = game.touchdowns as! Int
    completionsView.numericValue = game.completions as! Int
    interceptionsView.numericValue = game.interceptions as! Int
}


override func viewDidLoad() {
    super.viewDidLoad()
    loadStatViews()
}
```

Also, add a way to trigger the popover. Yosemite adds gesture recognizers, long a feature of iOS. A gesture recognizer detects mouse and trackpad gestures in the view to which it is attached. There is a repertoire of recognizers in the Interface Builder object library; type **gest** in the search field, and drag a click recognizer into the game table in the Team Detail Controller scene.

Interface Builder selects the new recognizer; in the Attributes inspector, mate it to the **Primary** button, require **2** clicks, and make sure it is **Enabled**. A double-click recognizer would have no way to tell the difference between a double click (which should trigger the recognizer) and a single click (which should go through to the view); it has to delay the delivery of the single click until the time runs out for the second click. That's not an issue for this case—this will be the only recognizer, and it wants the single click itself—so ignore the **Delays Events** checkboxes.

The easiest way to make a gesture do something is to treat it as if it were a control event, like the click of a button. Control-drag from the recognizer to `TeamDetailController.swift`, and have IB create an `IBAction` named gameTableClicked.

```
private let kGamePopoverSegue = "Show game popover"

@IBOutlet weak var gameTable: NSTableView!
```

```
@IBAction func gameTableClicked(sender: NSClickGestureRecognizer) {
    // What row was clicked? (If < 0, none was.)
    let location = sender.locationInView(sender.view!)
    let row = gameTable.rowAtPoint(location)

    if row >= 0 {
        //  Get the game for that row and trigger the popover segue.
        let game = gameArrayController.arrangedObjects[row] as? Game
        if let theGame = game {
            self.performSegueWithIdentifier(kGamePopoverSegue,
                sender: theGame)
        }
    }
}
```

I also added an outlet for the game table, since gameTableClicked needs to refer to it. If the click corresponds to a Game, gameTableClicked triggers the "Show game popover" segue, which means there should be a prepareForSegue method to set the details of the transition:

```
override
func prepareForSegue(segue: NSStoryboardSegue,
                     sender: AnyObject?) {
    if let segueID = segue.identifier {
        switch segueID {
        case kGamePopoverSegue:
            let popoverController = segue.destinationController
                as GameDetailController
            popoverController.representedObject = sender as! Game
        default:
            println("Unrecognized segue identifier \"\(segueID)\"")
        }
    }
}
```

> **Note**
>
> A reminder: If you type **prepareForSegue** and trigger autocompletion, Xcode will give you the full interface for the function, including override, func, and the parameter labels. Given how hard it can be to keep track of the modifiers for scope, overriding, and so on, this is a big help. Conversely, remember not to type func or the modifiers yourself: Xcode will insert duplicates anyway, and pepper you with syntax errors until you straighten it out.

Run Mac Passer Rating. Load the document with test data if necessary (**Edit → Fill with Test Data, ⌘ T**). Select a team and passer, and click on a game.

Modules and Namespaces

It crashes. The console says,

```
Unknown class GameDetailController in Interface Builder file
    at path /Users/fritza/Library/Developer/Xcode/DerivedData/...
```

This brings up a class of bugs that are hard to track down if you don't know where to look. How can `GameDetailController` be unknown? You're probably looking at `GameDetailController.swift` in the same window as this message.

Objective-C has the problem that every class goes into the same name space. That's why you avoid generic class names like `Shape`: If you create a class with that name, it's likely your app will link into some other library that uses the same name for a different class. The time-honored solution is to prefix all of your class names with letters that you can hope will avoid collisions. Foundation and AppKit use `NS`, and UIKit uses `UI`. Apple has taken to recommending that developers use *three* letters to prefix their own classes, this giving them a sporting chance (but no better) of staying clear of each other.

Swift is name-spaced. Every class belongs to some *module*; class names must still be distinct within a module, but classes with the same name in different modules won't interfere with each other. If you need access to the contents of another module, you `import` it into the Swift file in which you need access, as in "`import Cocoa.`" You can access objects in other modules only if they are declared `public`; if the object's symbol might conflict with one of your own, you have to prepend the module name and a dot to the name.

Your application has a default module, which normally has the name of the target, with non-alphanumerics replaced by underscores. In the case of Mac Passer Rating, the application module is `Mac_Passer_Rating`.

And there's your problem: We created the `GameDetailController` scene before we defined the class. When we told Interface Builder that the class was `GameDetail-Controller`, there was no such class, and IB had no idea where it might be found. So—as we noticed—the **Module** field in the Identity inspector was blank.

`GameDetailController` is in the `Mac_Passer_Rating` module; type the name into the **Module** field, or reenter the class name, which will prompt Interface Builder to complete the module name.

Run it again, and select a game. The popover appears, looking as you'd hope.

Localizing for French

This section will walk you through the process of localizing the Mac Passer Rating itself; we'll get to how it's treated by the Finder (or the iOS home-screen springboard) later. We'll start by adding another language to the project structure, and then how to approach storyboards, file resources, and in-app code.

Adding a Locale

Localization begins in earnest when you open the Project editor (select the top item in the Project navigator, and choose the whole-project icon at the top), then click the **+** button under the **Localizations** table. **Editor → Add Localization** will give you the same: A choice from a few common languages, and a further choice for an astonishing variety of languages and regions in which they are spoken (Figure 21.4).

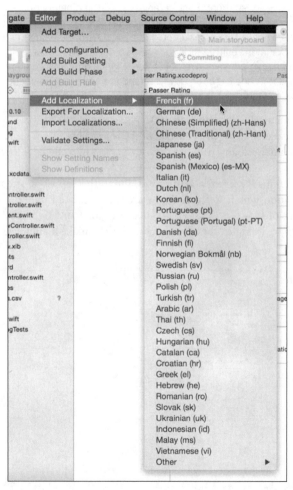

Figure 21.4   Add a localization to a project by clicking the **+** button below the **Localizations** table in the Project editor, or by selecting **Editor → Add Localization** and taking your pick. There are a lot to pick from.

> **Note**
>
> The project I've started you with has only one file—Main.storyboard—in the
> Base.lproj directory, and therefore only one resource it will recognize as localizable. To
> add variety, I've added Credits.rtf to the Base.lproj directory of the sample code.
> (Previous versions of Xcode included this very file as part of the application template.)
> The app template wires the **About...** menu item to the application method orderFront-
> StandardAboutPanel:, which tries by various means to put an About box together. If it
> finds a Credits.rtf, or .rtfd, or .html, its contents are added to the box.

> **Note**
>
> What you're looking at isn't just a list of languages—the dialects of French in Burkina
> Faso and Chad are not much different. But there is more to localization than just
> language. This is a list of *locales*. You could get away with the same English text
> throughout the Commonwealth; but if you want to depict an animal (some areas that use
> Commonwealth English are sensitive about some kinds of animals), or center a map on the
> capital city, the difference between New Zealand and India is significant, even if both treat
> corporate nouns as plural.

By whichever method, select **French (fr)**.

Xcode drops a sheet (Figure 21.5) listing all the localizable files it found in the Base
directory. You can uncheck any you don't want to bring into the new locale, but we want
them all.

The second column, **Reference Language**, shows the version of the file from which
the French localization will be derived. These are the Interface Builder resources to be
scanned for strings, or files that should be copied over for translation. If Mac Passer Rating
had developed a more complex set of resources, it might make a difference whether your

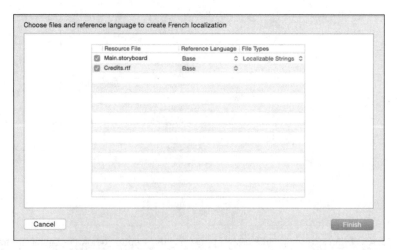

Figure 21.5   When you select the French localization, Xcode shows you the resources it found in
the lproj directories, and how it proposes to generate the localization resources.

new locale's main storyboard should be derived from the broad-layout copy you made for German, or the compact one you have for Simplified Chinese. But we're just starting out, we have only one version of each file, so the popup menus in this column have one choice each.

The third column, **File Types**, lets you choose the form the localized resource will take. In particular, for Interface Builder layouts, you have a choice of a **Localizable Strings** file (the default); or **Interface Builder** *document type*, a complete duplicate of the "reference" layout.

Click **Finish**. The obvious change is that the **Localizations** table now has a row for "French." The real change is in the Project navigator. Type **fr** in the search field at the bottom of the navigator; you will see that some files aren't "files" any more, but groups with disclosure triangles. Each contains a resource of some kind tagged "(French)." `Credits.rtf`, is simply a duplicate but for the added tag; the file attached to `Main.storyboard` is a `.strings` file. (Figure 21.6, top).

Starting Simple: `Credits.rtf`

Let's start simple, with the straightforward replacement of the contents of `Credits.rtf`. The file I'm using—it used to come with the application template—contains a brief, humorous list of credits (like **With special thanks to:** Mom). See Figure 21.7. Brevity and humor are virtues, so I'll just translate it.

Select `Credits.rtf` in the Project navigator. Take the Base version (with the "(Base)" tag attached) or the container (the one with the disclosure triangle), which will give you the reference version, which happens to be in English. It's important that we be in sync here—the French version starts out with the identical content, and it's easy to find that you're working on the wrong version.

Xcode has an RTF editor, so the credits appear in the editor as they would in the About box. (It's the standard AppKit rich-text editor, so if you want one of your own, it's about 30 lines of code.) If you look in the jump bar, you'll see the progression from the project, down the enclosing groups to `Credits.rtf`, and then `Credits.rtf (Base)`.

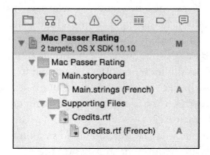

Figure 21.6   When the "French" localization was added, the localizable resources picked up counterparts that were either modifiers or outright replacements for the originals.

Figure 21.7   AppKit generates an About box for your application if you don't supply your own. If the `Credits.rtf` file is present, it goes into a scrolling display in the middle of the window.

The last segment will jump you between the localizations. You can jump to the other localization from that segment of the bar.

The File inspector for each version of a file includes a common **Localization** table, listing all the locales in the project. You can remove a localization for a file by unchecking the locale in the table. Or, if you visit another version of the file, you can add a localized version by checking its entry in the table (Figure 21.8).

Have a glance at the project tree in the Finder. `en.lproj` and `Base.lproj` have been joined by `fr.lproj`. `Main.storyboard` in the Base folder has been matched in the French folder with `Main.strings`.

What about `Credits.rtf`? Despite its starting out in `Base.lproj`, Xcode puts its French counterpart in a `fr.lproj` folder in the *project* directory, not the Mac Passer Rating target directory. This may be a bug, and you won't see it in a future version. Xcode still finds the file, and includes it in the application package where it belongs.

The idea of localization in Xcode is that you are given a copy of a "reference" version of a resource (usually the Base version, but you can choose another when you add the localization) for you to edit as the locale requires. It's getting to the point where, if you can imagine a way two files in a project might relate to each other, Apple can say, "There's an assistant for that." Select `Credits.rtf`, activate the Assistant editor, and from the root of the jump bar, select **Localizations**.

If there were more than one localization, you could step through them with the arrowheads at the right end of the jump bar, or by pressing ⌃ ⌘ **Left Arrow** or **Right Arrow**, but there's only one alternative this time. By now, you should have the English version in the main (left) editor and the French version in the Assistant (right) editor.

Figure 21.8   The File inspector for all versions of the `Credits.rtf` file includes a **Localization** table to enable or disable localization of the file for a locale.

Replace the contents of each line of the French file with:

- **Les ingénieurs:** Certains gens
- **Conception d'interface humaine:** D'autres gens
- **Test:** On espère que ce n'est pas personne
- **Documentation:** N'importe qui
- **Nous remercions particulièrement:** Maman

The obvious way to test this localization is to shuffle your language preferences in the System Preferences application, launch Mac Passer Rating, and see whether the About box contains the new text. This would, however, also make any other application you launch use the French localization until you switch the preference back. This is inconvenient unless you prefer to work in French.

> **Note**
>
> Changing the system-wide language preference *will* be necessary when you edit `InfoPlist.strings` to localize things like the display name of the application. You'll have to build the app, change the preference, and relaunch the Finder using ⌥⌘ **Escape**.

You can change the language preference for an Xcode target with the Scheme editor (**Product →Scheme →Edit Scheme...**, ⌘ <). Select the Run action, and the

Options tab. The **Application Language** popup will include every language for which the app is localized, plus:

- **System Language**, which uses the priority list from the **Language & Region** panel of System Preferences.

- **Double Length Pseudolanguage**, which renders all the strings from the Base localization twice, to challenge the layout.

- **Right to Left Pseudolanguage**, which makes Auto Layout's layout solutions assume a right-to-left language like Hebrew or Arabic.
  This is why horizontal constraints refer to "leading" and "trailing" edges, and not "left" and "right." (Even when the label is **Left** or **Right**, you usually get leading-and-trailing constraints.) You can request an explicit left-or-right constraint by selecting it in Interface Builder, and in the Attributes inspector unchecking **Respect language direction** either item; the menu items for the edges then become **Left** and **Right**.

Switch the language to **French** and run the app. Not much has changed—we've done nothing with the menu and window contents, though system-supplied strings like number and date formats and automatically generated menu titles have switched over. Select **Mac Passer Rating** →**À propos de Mac Passer Rating**. Where once the credit text was in English, it now is in French (Figure 21.9). It's a start.

Figure 21.9 Providing a French version of `Credits.rtf` and setting the **Application Language** in the Scheme editor to **French** lead AppKit to use the localized version of the credits in the automatically generated About box.

Localizing `Main.storyboard`

Before Xcode 5, and OS X Mavericks (10.9), this was not a pleasant section to read, nor to write. Localizing a XIB (storyboards weren't available) entailed going to the command line to analyze the original, extract all the strings, generate a `.strings` file, then synthesize the original and the translated strings into a new, localized XIB for you to maintain for the rest of your life.

Things are better now. When you choose to localize an Interface Builder resource, Xcode takes care of extracting the strings, and AppKit reads the `.strings` file when it loads the resource and substitutes the translations. Select `MPRGameViewController.xib` from the Project navigator. As before, it's shown as a group, and clicking it displays the primary version—in this case, the one and only copy of the XIB in the Base localization—and, if you select **Localizations** in the Assistant editor's jump bar, you'll see not a duplicate of the XIB, but the extracted `.strings` file.

As provided, the file is simply a restatement of the base strings:

```
/* Class = "NSTableColumn"; headerCell.title = "When"; ... */
"v8C-L2-cIW.headerCell.title" = "When";

/* Class = "NSMenuItem"; title = "Clear Menu"; ... */
"vNY-rz-j42.title" = "Clear Menu";

/* Class = "NSTableColumn"; headerCell.title = "Us"; ... */
"vcc-ie-bqj.headerCell.title" = "Us";

/* Class = "NSMenuItem"; title = "Help"; ... */
"wpr-3q-Mcd.title" = "Help";

/* Class = "NSMenuItem"; title = "Copy"; ... */
"x3v-GG-iWU.title" = "Copy";

/* Class = "NSTableColumn"; headerCell.title = "Yards"; ... */
"xIc-Wa-jK0.headerCell.title" = "Yards";

...
```

It's a series of key-value pairs. The keys are Interface Builder's internal identifiers for the elements, and each is commented with the class and original content. To get a French rendering of a label, edit the strings. They're in the `fr.lproj` directory, AppKit sees from its name that it matches the storyboard in `Base.lproj`, and it merges them.

> **Note**
>
> It's not likely you would, but don't give a `.strings` file the same base name as an Interface Builder document if you don't intend to localize them.

The technical task is easy, though tedious in a large project: Replace "Touchdowns" with "Touchés," "Attempts" with "Tentées," and so on. In my experience, the social task of getting a domain expert to come up with translations is the hard part.

The preceding excerpt becomes:

```
/* Class = "NSTableColumn"; headerCell.title = "When"; ... */
"v8C-L2-cIW.headerCell.title" = "Quand";

/* Class = "NSMenuItem"; title = "Clear Menu"; ... */
"vNY-rz-j42.title" = "Effacer le menu";

/* Class = "NSTableColumn"; headerCell.title = "Us"; ... */
"vcc-ie-bqj.headerCell.title" = "Nous";

/* Class = "NSMenuItem"; title = "Help"; ... */
"wpr-3q-Mcd.title" = "Aider";

/* Class = "NSMenuItem"; title = "Copy"; ... */
"x3v-GG-iWU.title" = "Copier";

/* Class = "NSTableColumn"; headerCell.title = "Yards"; ... */
"xIc-Wa-jK0.headerCell.title" = "Verges";
```

The equivalents that are specific to Mac Passer Rating are

Touchdowns	Touchés
Attempts	Tentées
Yards	Verges
Interceptions	Interceptées
Completions	Captées
Rating	Efficacité
Quarterback	Quart
Fill with Test Data	Remplissez avec les données de test

AppKit does *not* give you translations of standard menu items like **Cut** or **Quit**. You have to fill in the .strings file yourself.

Apple can give you a little help here. It has a localization-support page at https://developer.apple.com/internationalization/, where you can download tools (developer registration required). Look for "AppleGlot" in the Downloads section. The AppleGlot tool itself hasn't gotten much attention, but the real trove is in the glossary files that Apple used to translate its applications and system software. They're in many languages, among them French. I won't fill up more pages with the full translation of the menus and other items; see fr.lproj/Main.strings in the sample code.

You've finished the translation; now run the application. Figure 21.10 shows a League document window under the three localized options. The top window uses the doubled

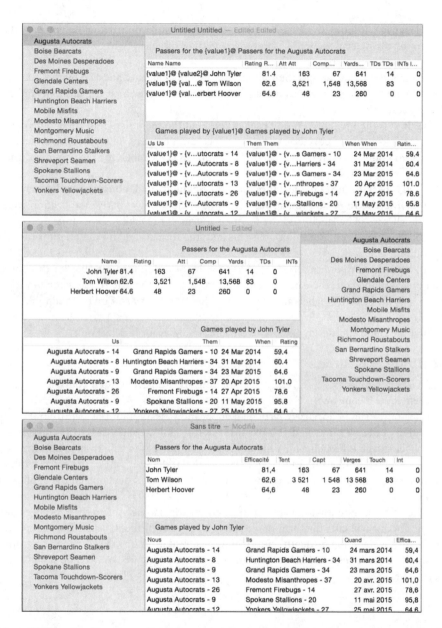

Figure 21.10   The Mac Passer Rating League document window, running under three application languages set in the Scheme editor. (top) The **Double Length Pseudolanguage** duplicates every string in the layout. (middle) **Right to Left Pseudolanguage** flops the layout, putting the source list at the left, and rejustifying most of the data. (bottom) The **French** language adopts the localized formats and strings—except for the labels above the passer and game tables.

pseudolanguage. It looks about as you'd hope, except that if you narrow the window, the labels in the team detail view don't prevent its getting too narrow to display them fully. You've learned something.

The second window adopts the right-to-left pseudolanguage. Sticking by the default leading/trailing constraints got us quite a lot, but the justification on the numeric and date columns bears attention.

The third is the French. You don't see it here, but the menus are translated. The date and number formats are correct, and so are the column headers. The proper names are supposed to come through untranslated. The problem is the labels for the passer and game tables. They're still in English.

If you go back to the Scheme editor, check **Localization Debugging: Show non-localized strings**, and run again; any strings that don't yet have a localization will be shown in all-caps. The labels (and the format patterns in the tables) show up as un-localized. I localized them; I double-checked; the formats are still the ones for the Base localization.

This is a bug in Yosemite. I hope it's fixed by the time you read this, but for this book, it's an opportunity. So is the game-detail popover. It shows the date of the game in proper French, but the stat-view labels are still in English—`MacStatView` isn't a localizable control.

These are opportunities to explore two more strategies for localization.

Localizing Resources

AppKit won't localize the `MacStatViews` for you, so you have to do it yourself. But it hasn't left you on your own:

Any resource can be localized. When an application asks `NSBundle.mainBundle()` for a path to a file, `NSBundle` first looks for it in the app's `.lproj` directories first. If the preferred language is French, and a file of the desired name is in `fr.lproj`, `NSBundle` will return a path to that file. Failing that, it goes down the user's list of preferred locales; then to `Base.lproj`; and finally to the common `Resources` directory in the application package.

So we'll add an English-language list of labels for the stat views, and then localize it for French. The list will take the form of a *property list* (`.plist`) file. Chapter 23, "Property Lists," explains the topic in-depth, but for now, just pull in `stat-labels.plist` from the sample code. It's been added to the Project navigator; feel free to click on it and see what's there.

The English version, in Table 21.1, is trivial.

Table 21.1   The English Mapping between the Stat View Labels in the Storyboard and the Ones for Display in an English Locale Is Trivial

Attempts	Attempts
Completions	Completions
Yards	Yards
Touchdowns	Touchdowns
Interceptions	Interceptions

If you're playing along, you can find the Property List template in the new-file assistant under "Resources." Name it `stat-labels.plist` and put it in the `Base.lproj` directory. Make the root element a dictionary, and fill in the keys and values as shown. (See Chapter 23 for the technique.)

Next, use the File inspector to add a French localization by checking the **French** box under Localizations. Use the **Localizations** view in the Assistant editor, or simply click the (`French`) version in the Project navigator, to edit the French version (Table 21.2) like this:

Table 21.2   The French Mapping for the Stat View Labels Makes Some Changes

Attempts	Tentées
Completions	Captées
Yards	Verges
Touchdowns	Touchés
Interceptions	Interceptées

Then, when the popover loads, edit the names of the stat views:

```
override func viewDidLoad() {
  super.viewDidLoad()

  // Read the home-grown localization dictionary for the stat views
  let mainBundle = NSBundle.mainBundle()
```

```
    if let statLabelURL:NSURL = mainBundle.URLForResource(
                "stat-labels", withExtension: "plist") {
        if let labelMap = NSDictionary(contentsOfURL: statLabelURL)
                    as? [String:String] {
            // Use the IB-provided names to look up the localized ones.
            for statView in [attemptsView, yardsView, touchdownsView,
                    completionsView, interceptionsView] {
                statView.name = labelMap[statView.name]!
            }
        }
    }
    // Fill in the numbers.
    loadStatViews()
}
```

Running Mac Passer Rating in both English and French shows the labels adjust to the
current locale—the URLForResource(_, withExtension:) call directed the URL
for stat-labels.plist to the file in the proper .lproj.

Localizing Program Strings

Sticking with bindings to format the "Passers for..." and "Games played..." labels will
be tricky at best. There is API for establishing and modifying bindings, but there is a
reason most people avoid it. This is our chance to look at the third case for localization:
strings generated in code.

Putting switch statements or per-language formatting objects, or other piecemeal
locals-management into code is exactly what AppKit has allowed us to avoid so far. It
helps us here, too: Your code can refer to localizable strings by key, and the localized
strings will be pulled out of the .lproj at run time.

The process starts with the code that uses the string. We'll have Team and Passer
generate the label strings themselves. This is a need peculiar to TeamDetail-
Controller, so it makes the most sense to put the code into extensions in Team-
DetailController.swift:

```
extension
Passer {
  func passerGameHeader() -> String {
    let format = NSLocalizedString("Games played by %@",
      comment: "Format string for the label over the games table")
    let retval = NSString(format: format, fullName)
    return retval as! String
  }
}


extension
Team {
  func teamPasserHeader() -> String {
```

```
    let format = NSLocalizedString("Passers for the %@",
      comment: "Format string for the label over the passers table")
    let retval = NSString(format: format, teamName)
    return retval as! String
  }
}
```

Where you'd otherwise use a string literal, you invoke `NSLocalizedString(_, comment:)`. The first argument is a key for looking up the localized version of the string, and the second (`comment:`) provides the context a translator might need to determine the correct phrasing for the particular use.

> **Note**
>
> `NSLocalizedString(_, comment:)`, as shown here, is actually an invocation of NSLocalizedStringfull, with three of the arguments defaulted so the search takes place in `Localizable.strings` in the search path within the main bundle. In Objective-C, the optional arguments are taken care of by wrapping the big function invocation in C preprocessor macros.

Now all you need is a strings file—`Localizable.strings`—for each `.lproj`, to fill in the correct string at run time. There are two ways to do this.

genstrings

The first sends you to the command line to run the `genstrings` command. At its simplest, here is all you have to do:

```
$ # Focus on the target directory
$ cd 'Desktop/Mac Passer Rating/Mac Passer Rating/'
$ # This is the directory containing your source files.
$ genstrings *.swift
$ ls
...
Localizable.strings
...
$
```

The new `Localizable.strings` file contains a dictionary of all the invocations of `NSLocalizedString(_, comment:)`, with both keys and values equal to the key string, and the comment you gave appearing in a comment line:

```
/* Format string for the label over the games table */
"Games played by %@" = "Games played by %@";

/* Format string for the label over the games table */
"Passers for the %@" = "Passers for the %@";
```

That's the Base version. Add it to the project, display it in the editor, and use the File inspector to add a French localization: When you click the **Localize...** button, Xcode tells you it will have to move the file into an `.lproj` folder, and asks which one. Move it to Base. The table of locales is now open to you; click French, and you know the routine from here:

```
/* Format string for the label over the games table */
"Games played by %@" = "Jeux de %@";


/* Format string for the label over the games table */
"Passers for the %@" = "Quart-arrières des %@";
```

All that's left is to drop the Display Pattern bindings for the labels and replace them with plain Value bindings, thus working around the bug. For each label, uncheck the pattern binding, and check the Value binding.

- The label on the upper table, for passers, is bound to **Team Object**, `selection`, `teamPasserHeader`.

- The one on the lower, for passers' games, is **Passer Array**, `selection`, `passerGameHeader`.

Important: The failed localizations for the pattern bindings are still in `Main.strings`. Edit `Main.strings` to delete them or comment them out.

Run Mac Passer Rating one more time: The labels appear in the proper languages.

`xliff` Files

I took you through all of this because you can't analyze your localizations and dig out the corner cases without getting your hands on the way Cocoa has localized applications for decades, and still does. You have to know these techniques. But you don't have to use them.

Xcode 6 introduces support for the `.xliff` XML schema for exchanging translation dictionaries. At any time in your localization efforts, you can display the Project editor (Project navigator, top item, select the project itself), and select **Editor → Export for Localization. . . .** Xcode will ask you whether you want to export just the development strings (that is, in Base, `Info.plist`, and in-code), or the strings for the locales you've added. Pick one, give the export a name, and place it on-disk.

The result will be a directory with the name you picked, containing `.xliff` files for each locale (elided and line-wrapped for space):

```
<xliff ...>
<file original="Mac Passer Rating/Base.lproj/Main.storyboard"
    source-language="en" datatype="plaintext" target-language="fr">
    <header>
        ...
    </header>
    <body>
        ...
        <trans-unit id="aTl-1u-JFS.title">
            <source>Print...</source>
            <target>Imprimer...</target>
```

```
            <note>Class = "NSMenuItem"; title = "Print..."...</note>
        </trans-unit>
        <trans-unit id="aUF-d1-5bR.title">
            <source>Window</source>
            <target>Fenêtre</target>
            <note>Class = "NSMenuItem"; title = "Window"...</note>
        </trans-unit>
        <trans-unit id="bib-Uj-vzu.title">
            <source>File</source>
            <target>Fichier</target>
            <note>Class = "NSMenu"; title = "File"...</note>
        </trans-unit>
        ...
    </body>
</file>
</xliff>
```

The top-level `<file>` elements identify each source file; one nice feature is that even if you have `.strings` files in place for an InterfaceBuilder document, the translations will be identified with the XIB or storyboard, not the `.strings`.

The initial content of the strings will be marked as `<source>` elements; you can add translations as `<target>` elements. This gives you a single file to pass on to your translator. When she's done, she can pass it back, and you can select **Editor → Import Localizations...** to integrate the changes.

This solves one big problem with `.strings` files: What happens when you change a storyboard, adding a scene, or, what turns out to be worse, adding and removing labels or controls? The answer with `.strings` is that because the changes occurred only in the base-language file, you'd have to save a copy of the localization files, remove the localization from the storyboard, and add it back. The resulting `.strings` file would contain only the English-language content, and you'd be left to merge the translations you'd done into it.

When you export an `.xliff`, you get a listing of existing translations, and the structure of the base storyboard. It's already merged, and all you have to do is fill in the gaps.

The Rest

Edit the French `.strings` file and check your work so far by running Mac Passer Rating. Most strings will still be in English, but if you trace down to the game popover, you should see results...

... except you don't. The labels, for which the `.strings` file did provide translations, are all overwritten by the application with numbers, proper names, or a date. The first two shouldn't be translated, and the date relies on the system-wide date formatter provided by OS X, and your system as a whole is still set for English formats.

The stat views are another matter: They aren't standard AppKit elements, so AppKit doesn't know how to apply a `.strings` file to them. You'll have to set their labels in-code.

Localizing System Strings

You saw earlier that localizing `Main.storyboard` didn't take care of the application menu (**Mac Passer Rating**). There are other gaps, as well: The default About box contains the English application name and copyright notice; if you viewed MPR's icon on a French localization of the Finder, it would have the English name, and its documents would be labeled in English.

All of these strings come from `Info.plist`, which I cover in Chapter 22, "Bundles and Packages," and Chapter 23, "Property Lists." There has to be only one `Info.plist` in a bundle directory (such as an `.app` bundle), but you can change how its contents are presented through a `.strings` file in the `.lproj` directory corresponding to the user's locale.

You localize `Info.plist` just as you would any other resource—by adding a `.strings` file, in this case `InfoPlist.strings`. When you start, there is no such file in the project, because the only locale is the Base one, and by definition, there's no localization to do. When you added the French language, again there was no `InfoPlist.strings`, because there were no translations yet.

There are two kinds of keys by which `InfoPlist.strings` can pick the strings to be localized: If you want to set a value corresponding one-to-one with an `Info.plist` key, use that key as the key for the translation. Otherwise, use the string that appears in the base `Info.plist`.

To do what Mac Passer Rating needs, you first have to add two keys to the base source file for `Info.plist`. Select that file in the Project navigator, and add two rows:

- **Bundle display name** (`CFBundleDisplayName`). As a placeholder, set this to the string `${PRODUCT_NAME}`; the actual string will be pulled from the localization files.

- **Application has localized display name** (`LSHasLocalizedDisplayName`) tells Launch Services and the Finder that they must take the extra trouble of looking up the localized version of the app's name.

Next, the localized values of the `Info.plist` keys for French. Ordinarily, you'd create an `InfoPlist.strings` file in `fr.lproj`, and write the key-value pairs for `CFBundleName` (**Quart-Efficacité**), `CFBundleDisplayName` (also **Quart-Efficacité**), and `NSHumanReadableCopyright` (**Copyright... Toutes droits reservées.**).

> **Note**
>
> You might think that you could use the File inspector to add a French localization to the `Info.plist` file, just as you did for `Main.storyboard`, and get an `InfoPlist.Strings` file. That doesn't work: Xcode follows the strategy it uses for other resource files, and duplicates the base `Info.plist` into the `fr.lproj` directory. You have to create the `InfoPlist.strings` yourself.

This is all `fr.lproj/InfoPlist.strings` need contain (some lengthy strings are elided, and line breaks added):

```
/* One-to-one values for Info.plist keys */
"NSHumanReadableCopyright" =
        "Copyright ... Toutes droits reservées.";
"CFBundleDisplayName" = "Quart-Efficacité";
"CFBundleName" = "Quart-Efficacité";

/* The file-type string is inside an array, and a single plist key
   doesn't correspond to it. Use the untranslated value as the key: */
"League File" = "Fichier de Ligue";
```

Testing the `Info.plist` localization comes in two parts. The first is easy: Run Mac Passer Rating and verify that the application menu and About box are as you expect.

Finder behavior is trickier, because you have to set your preferred language in the **Language & Text** panel of System Preferences, and then relaunch the Finder so it will pull the localized strings. System Preferences tells you to log out and log back in to see the results of the change. There's another way: Press ⌥⌘**Escape**, select Finder, and click **Relaunch**. Finder will reappear in your selected language.

> **Note**
>
> While you're in **Language & Text**, visit the **Formats** tab to be sure that the **Region:** matches the language you chose. The switch should be done automatically, but if you created a custom format set, it will stick. If it does, you won't see localized date and time formats in your applications.

If all went well with the `InfoPlist.strings` modification, Finder should present Mac Passer Rating as Quart-Efficacité. See Figure 21.11.

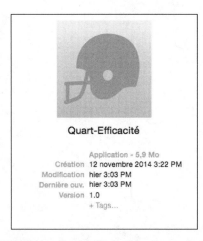

Figure 21.11   When displayed in a French Finder, Mac Passer Rating should be displayed as Quart-Efficacité.

Summary

In this chapter, I gave you an overview of the tasks that go into localizing a Mac application; the same techniques apply to iOS.

You saw how to add a localization to a file that the application template put into the default `Base.lproj` directory, as well as how to add localizations to the project and to an unlocalized file.

I then went on to techniques for translating menus (easy) and UI layouts. Once upon a time, if you wanted localized layouts, you had to produce separate XIB files, one way or another. The `ibtool` command-line tool made it possible to extract strings from one XIB and inject them into another, but it was an easy process to get wrong. Modern Xcodes, and the application frameworks' acceptance of `.strings` files at run time, have made it a matter of a few clicks (and several calls to your translator's voicemail).

Then came techniques to apply `.strings` files to the application code itself—`InfoPlist.strings` for Finder strings, and `Localizable.strings` for strings that would otherwise be hard-coded in your source.

We started caring about how Mac Passer Rating presented itself in the Finder, so we walked through the intricate process of adding icons and file types to the application package.

And, I covered how to test your localization at run time and in the Finder.

## 22

Bundles and Packages

Many of Xcode's products take the form of *packages*, directory trees that the Finder presents as single files. Let's pause to consider the problem of resources. Resources are the sorts of data that are integral to an application, but for one reason or another aren't suitable to incorporate into source code: strings, lookup tables, images, human-interface layouts, sounds, and the like.

In the original Mac OS, applications kept resources in *resource forks*, mini-databases kept in parallel with the data stream one normally thinks of as a file. The problem with the Resource Manager was that it did not scale well to sets of many, large, or changeable resources. The catalog written into each resource file was fragile, and any corruption resulted in the loss of every resource in the file. Modern apps use many more and much larger resources, and the tasks involved in managing them become indistinguishable from the tasks of a filesystem. Filesystems are a solved problem; they are as efficient and robust as decades of experience can make them. Why not use the filesystem for storing and retrieving resources?

One reason to avoid shipping application resources as separate files is that an application that relies on them becomes a swarm of files and directories, all more or less critical to the correct working of the application, and all exposed to relocation, deletion, and general abuse by the application's user. Meanwhile, the user, who just wants one thing that does the application's work, is presented with a swarm of files and directories.

OS X provides a way to have the flexibility of separating resources into their own files while steering clear of the swarming problem. The Finder can treat directories, called *packages*, as though they were single documents.

A Simple Package: RTFD

A package can be as simple as a directory with a handful of files in it. The application that creates and reads the package determines how it is structured: what files are required, the names of the content files, and what sort of subdirectory structure is used.

A common example of an application-defined package is the RTFD, or rich text file directory. The Apple-supplied application TextEdit, in its `Info.plist` file, specifies what kinds of documents TextEdit can handle; among these is NSRTFDPboardType, which is listed as having suffix rtfd and is designated as a package file type. When it catalogs TextEdit, the Finder notes that directories with the .rtfd extension are supposed to be packages and so treats them as if they were single files, without displaying the files within.

It is sometimes useful to look inside a package, however, and the Finder provides a way to do that. Right-clicking on a package file produces a popup menu containing the command **Show Package Contents** (see Figure 22.1). Selecting that command opens a new window showing the contents of the package directory, which can be further navigated as in a normal Finder window.

In the case of RTFD, the package directory contains one plain RTF file, TXT.rtf. The RTF file incorporates custom markup, such as

```
The icon looks like this:\
\
\pard\tx560\tx1120\tx1680\tx2240\tx2800\tx3360\tx3920\tx4480
\tx5040\tx5600\tx6160\tx6720\pardirnatural
\cf0 {{\NeXTGraphic icon60@2x.png \width2400 \height2400
}}\
```

Here, the markup refers to a graphics file—in this case, icon60@2x.png—that is also in the RTFD directory.

> **Note**
>
> Cocoa's AppKit application framework provides support for package-directory documents. NSDocument subclasses handle package reading and writing by overriding readFromFileWrapper(_,ofType:,error:) and fileWrapperOfType(_,error:). The NSFileWrapper class provides methods that assist in creating and managing complex file packages.

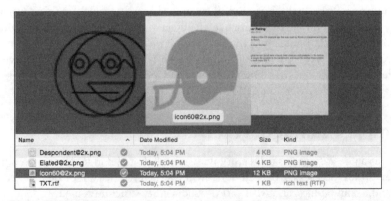

Figure 22.1   Right-clicking a package document in the Finder presents a menu that includes the command **Show Package Contents**, which shows the files within the package.

Bundles

A *bundle* is a particular kind of *structured* directory tree. Often, bundles are shipped as packages—the most familiar type of bundle, the application, is an example—but the concepts are separate. A directory can be a bundle without being a package, or a package without being a bundle, or it can be both. Table 22.1 has examples.

Table 22.1 Examples of Directories That Are Bundles or Packages or Both

	Not Bundle	Bundle
Not Package	Other directories	Frameworks
Package	Complex documents	Applications

There are two kinds of bundles in OS X: *versioned bundles*, which are used for frameworks—structured packages of dynamic libraries, headers, and the resource files that support them—and *modern bundles*, which are used for applications and most other executable products.

Note

"Modern" is a relative term; modern packages were in NeXTStep long before Cocoa.

At the minimum, a modern Mac bundle encloses one directory, named `Contents`, which in turn contains all the directories and files composing the bundle. The `Contents` directory contains an `Info.plist` file, which specifies how the bundle is to be displayed in the Finder and, depending on the type of the bundle, may provide configuration data for loading and running the bundle's contents. Beyond that, what the `Contents` folder contains depends on the type of the bundle.

Application Bundles

OS X applications are the most common type of bundle (see Figure 22.2). An application directory has a name with the suffix `.app`. The `.app` directory is a file package; even though it is a directory, the Finder treats it as a single entity. This allows the author of the application to place auxiliary files for the application in a known place—inside the application bundle itself—with little fear that they will be misplaced or deleted.

The `Contents` directory of an OS X application bundle most commonly contains

- `Info.plist`, an XML property list file that describes such application details as the principal class, the document types handled, and the application version. More on this file in the next section.

- `Resources`, a directory containing the application icon file, images, sounds, human-interface layouts, and other parameterized content for the application. Common content, such as button images, may be found in the `Resources` directory itself; localizable files are kept in `.lproj` directories. There will typically be a `Base.lproj` directory for the default layouts and strings, with additional

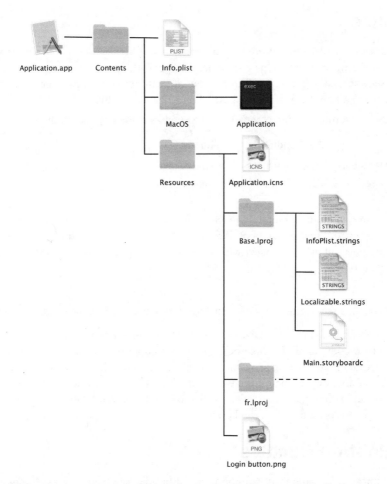

Figure 22.2   The structure of a typical application bundle. The executable file is at `Contents /MacOS/Application`. The default structure of the application's human interface is specified in a compiled storyboard, `Contents/Resources/Base.lproj/Main.storyboardc`; presumably, a French `.strings` file is inside `Contents/Resources/fr.lproj`. The custom image for a button, `Login button.png`, is common to all languages and therefore appears in the `Resources` directory itself.

`.lproj` directories to supply customizations for specific locales. When an application seeks a resource, the Cocoa or Core Foundation bundle managers will look first in the `.lproj` directory that corresponds to the current language and locale.

- `MacOS`, a directory containing the executable binary for the application, along with any other executables.

- `Frameworks`, a directory of frameworks that are themselves versioned bundles, containing a dynamic library, resources needed by the library, and header files needed by users of the library. An application typically includes a framework because it links to the framework's library.

The `Info.plist` File

The `Info.plist` file, found in the `Contents` directory of any modern bundle and at the root of the `.app` bundle for iOS applications, is the locus of much of the information OS X and iOS need to make sense of a bundle. This file provides icon and naming information to the Finder/Home screen, flags and environment variables to Launch Services, "default" screen images in various sizes and orientations for iOS apps, and specifications for the basic structure of applications and plugins. It's a property list (`.plist`) dictionary file, a format I'll cover in Chapter 23, "Property Lists."

The Target editor's **General** and **Info** tabs form a specialized editor for the target's `Info.plist`. They'll give you at least a first cut at the settings you need without much trouble.

You can also edit the `Info.plist` file directly, using the Property List editor (see Chapter 23, "Property Lists"). Sort of. The `Info.plist` you will be editing is a precursor of the file that will go into the product package.

What you're seeing is a source file that Xcode will process to generate the final property list. It's this processing phase that allows you to use build-variable references instead of literal values for some of the keys. The handling of the target-specific `Info.plist`s is special: They are *not* to be included in any build phase of your target—that will just copy the unprocessed source file into the application's `Resources` directory. Instead, the name of the file is specified in the `INFOPLIST_FILE` build variable. The build system picks it up from there.

> **Note**
>
> Most targets need their own `Info.plist`s. A project with more than one target has more than one `Info.plist` file to manage. Versions of Xcode before 6 handled the potential collision by prefixing the target's name to the precursor file's: `my framework-Info.plist`. Xcode 6 insists on segregating target files in their own directories, and has dropped the target-prefix convention, but you may run into it in older projects.

Localizing `Info.plist`

Some `Info.plist` properties are localizable. A file named `InfoPlist.strings` should be in the `.lproj` directory for each localization of your application. Localizable keys can then be assigned per-locale values. For instance, `InfoPlist.strings` in the `English.lproj` directory might include the pair:

```
CFBundleName = "PasserRating";
CFBundleDisplayName = "Passer Rating";
```

The same file in the `fr.lproj` directory might include

```
CFBundleName = "Q-Effic";
CFBundleDisplayName = "Quart-Efficacité";
```

For users whose language preferences place French above English, the Mac `Passer Rating` icon will be labeled `Quart-Efficacité`. The name of the bundle directory, however, will still be `PasserRating.app`, even if the casual user doesn't see it.

The Xcode Property List editor customizes itself for `Info.plist`s. When the name of a file ends in `Info.plist`, it will fill the dictionary key column with popup menus offering the keys peculiar to that kind of property list. This means that you should avoid using Xcode to edit property lists whose names end that way (like the `DirectoryInfo` `.plist` file you're setting up for some names and addresses) but aren't actual `Info.plist`s.

`Info.plist` **Keys for Applications**

`Info.plist` keys have proliferated as more and more OS services need to characterize the needs and capabilities of applications. In earlier editions of this book, I was able to list almost every key—even a couple whose names appeared *nowhere* on the Internet. That's not possible any more.

What you'll see here are the most frequently used keys for application `Info.plist`s. I've itemized the dictionary keys, followed by the plain-English labels used by the Property List editor.

Keys for Both iOS and OS X

The keys in this section apply to application bundles on both OS X and iOS.

- **Structure**

  - `CFBundleExecutable` (Executable file), the name of the executable file, which may be an application binary, a library, or plugin code. It corresponds to the `EXECUTABLE_NAME` build setting, which in turn is derived from `PRODUCT_NAME` (plus an optional prefix and suffix, which you'd rarely use). A bundle that mismatches this entry with the actual name of the executable file will not run. Applications must specify this key.

  - `CFBundleIdentifier` (Bundle identifier), a unique identifier string for the bundle, in the form of a Java-style reverse domain package name, such as `com.wt9t.Passer-Rating`. Xcode initializes this to the company ID you supplied when you chose the project template, followed by `${PRODUCT-_NAME:rfc1034identifier}`, and you can expect to leave it alone. All bundles must specify this key.

  - `CFBundleInfoDictionaryVersion` (InfoDictionary version), a compatibility-check version number for the `Info.plist` format. Xcode injects this version number when it builds bundles. I've never seen a version number other than 6.0. All `Info.plist` files should include this key.

  - `CFBundlePackageType` (Bundle OS Type code), **optional on iOS**, the four-character type code for the bundle. Applications are type `APPL`, frameworks are `FMWK`, plugins are `BNDL` or a code of your choosing. See also `CFBundleSignature`. OS X applications must specify this key.

  - `CFBundleSignature` (Bundle creator OS Type code), **optional on iOS**, the four-character creator code associated with the bundle. OS X applications must specify this key, but it's rare for it to be anything other than `????`.

  - `NSPrincipalClass` (Principal class), the name of the bundle's main class. In an OS X application, this would normally be `NSApplication`; in iOS, `UIApplication`.

  - `NSMainNibFile` (Main nib file base name), the base (no extension) name of the application's main NIB file, almost always `MainMenu` on OS X, and `MainWindow` on iOS (when a main NIB is used at all). Use `NSMainNib-File-ipad` (Main nib file base name (iPad)) to specify a separate NIB for your app when it's launched on an iPad.

  - `NSMainStoryboardFile` (Main storyboard file base name), the base (no extension) name of the application's main Storyboard file, usually `Main` on OS X. The iOS equivalent is `UIMainStoryboardFile`; see below.

- **User Information**

  - `CFBundleGetInfoString` (Get Info string), **Mac only**, a string that supplements the version information supplied by `CFBundleShortVersion-`

String and CFBundleVersion. Formerly, this key was used for copyright strings, but that is now handled by NSHumanReadableCopyright.

- CFBundleIconFile (Icon file), the name of the file in the Resources directory that contains the bundle's custom icon, a file in .icns format for Mac, .png for iOS. You can omit the extension. An iOS application would prefer CFBundleIconFiles, an array of standardized names for the various rendering sizes of the application icon.

  All of this is moot in Xcode 6. The **General** tab of the Target editor lets you specify images for icons, either file by file or through an asset catalog. From that, the build system will inject the necessary icon references into Info.plist.

- CFBundleShortVersionString (Bundle versions string, short), a short string with the product version, such as **4.3.4**, of the bundle, suitable for display in an About box or by the App Store. See also CFBundleGetInfo-String. This key may be localized in InfoPlist.strings. Applications must specify this key.

- CFBundleVersion (Bundle version), the build version of the bundle's executable. In the past, this string was nearly identical to the short version string, with maybe a suffix like b2 to mark prerelease versions, or a serial number of the build that produced this binary: **2.1b4 (2133)**. The current practice is to use just the build serial number. iOS will refuse to install a new binary over an existing application unless the bundle version of the new binary is greater than the previous one. An integer serial number is easiest for you to generate, and for iOS to parse.

- CFBundleDisplayName (Bundle display name), the name for the Finder or Home screen to display for this bundle. The value in Info.plist should be identical to the name of the application bundle; localized names can then be put in InfoPlist.strings files for various languages. The OS will display the localized name *only* if the name of the application package in the filesystem matches the value of this key. That way, if a Mac user renames your application, the name he intended—and not the localized name—will be displayed. Project templates will initialize this key to ${PRODUCT_NAME}. See also CFBundleName. Applications must specify this key.

- CFBundleName (Bundle name), the short—16-character maximum—name for the application, to be shown in the About box and the **Application** menu. See also CFBundleDisplayName. This key may be localized in InfoPlist.strings; Xcode initializes it to ${PRODUCT_NAME}. Applications must specify this key.

- **Localization**
  - CFBundleDevelopmentRegion (Localization native development region), the native human language, and variant thereof, of the bundle, like fr-CA for

Canadian French. If the user's preferred language is not available as a localization, this is the language that will be used.

- **Documents and URLs**

  - CFBundleDocumentTypes (Document types), an array of dictionaries specifying every document type associated with the application. Use the **Info** tab of the Target editor for the application target to edit these; you'll save yourself some headaches.

  - CFBundleURLTypes (URL types), an array of dictionaries defining URL schemes, such as http:, ftp:, or x-com-wt9t-custom-scheme:, for which the application is a handler. Use common schemes with care; if you're a web browser, you support http:, but if you just happen to pull some resources from an HTTP server, don't advertise yourself to the whole system as being able to service http URLs. This tag is much more useful in iOS, where your application's custom scheme can provide a handy interapplication communications method for other applications, email, and the web. See Apple's documentation, and the **Info** tab of the Target editor, for details.

  - UTExportedTypeDeclarations (Exported Type UTIs), an array of dictionaries that describe the types of documents your application can write, and which you want Launch Services to know about. The entries center on declaring a UTI and the chain of UTIs the principal UTI conforms to. This key is used by Spotlight to build its list of document types. UTIs take precedence over the declarations in CFBundleDocumentTypes as of OS X 10.5. Again, it's easier to manage this list through the **Info** tab of the Target editor. See Apple's documentation for the format of the dictionaries.

  - UTImportedTypeDeclarations (Imported Type UTIs), an array of dictionaries that describe the types of documents your application can *read,* and which you want Launch Services to know about. The entries are the same format as used in UTExportedTypeDeclarations. The **Info** tab of the Target editor provides an easy editor for this.

Keys for OS X

These keys apply only to OS X applications and cover launch configurations, help facilities, and information on the documents and URLs the application handles. The Info.plist structure antedates OS X, so many keys have fallen into obsolescence, but the OS has to support them for backward compatibility. The template you instantiate for a new application target will give you everything you need to start, and the **Info** tab will help you with *almost* everything you'd ever need to fit what you want to do, but there's no substitute for following the OS release notes.

- **Structure**
  - `CSResourcesFileMapped` (Resources should be file-mapped), if `YES` or `<true/>`, Core Foundation will memory-map the bundle resources rather than read the files into memory.
  - `ATSApplicationFontsPath` (Application fonts resource path), a string. If your application contains fonts for its own use, it contains the path, relative to the application's `Resources` directory, to the directory containing the fonts.
- **User Information**
  - `NSHumanReadableCopyright` (Copyright (human-readable)), a copyright string suitable for display in an About box. This key may be localized in `InfoPlist.strings`. Applications must specify this key.
  - `LSApplicationCategoryType` (Application Category). This is a string containing an Apple-defined UTI that describes for the Mac App Store what kind of application this is—Business, Lifestyle, Video, etc. Ordinarily, you'd set this in the **General** tab of the application's Target editor, so you don't have to bother with the UTIs. When you submit your app through iTunes Connect, you will be allowed two categories for your listing; make sure the primary one is the same as your `LSApplicationCategoryType`.
- **Help**
  - `CFAppleHelpAnchor` (Help file), the base name, without extension, of the initial help file for the application.
  - `CFBundleHelpBookFolder` (Help Book directory name), the folder—in either the `Resources` subdirectory or a localization subdirectory—containing the application's help book.
  - `CFBundleHelpBookName` (Help Book identifier), the name of the application's help book. This name should match the name set in a `<meta>` tag in the help book's root file.
- **Launch Behavior** These keys control how Launch Services launches and configures a Mac application. iOS has a "Launch Services" framework, but there is no public interface for it.
  - `LSBackgroundOnly` (Application is background only), if it's the string 1, the application will be run in the background only and will not be visible to the user.
  - `LSEnvironment` (Environment variables), a dictionary, the keys of which are environment-variable names, defining environment variables to be passed to the application upon launch.
  - `LSGetAppDiedEvents` (Application should get App Died events), indicates, if `YES` or `<true/>`, that the application will get the `kAEApplicationDied` Apple event when any of its child processes terminate.

- `NSSupportsSuddenTermination` (Application can be killed immediately after launch). When you log out, restart, or shut down, OS X takes care that all running applications will be given the chance to clean up, ask the user to save files, and so on. If this key is `<true/>`, the system will shut down your application with a BSD kill signal instead. You can still use `NSProcessInfo` methods to restore the ask-first policy (such as when you are in the middle of writing a file), but the kill policy makes shutdowns much quicker.

- `LSMinimumSystemVersion` (Minimum system version), a string in the form 10.x.x, specifying the earliest version of OS X or iOS this application will run under. Under OS X, if the current OS is earlier (back through 10.4), it will post an alert explaining that the app could not be run.

- `LSMinimumSystemVersionByArchitecture` (Minimum system versions, per-architecture), a dictionary. The possible keys are `i386` and `x86_64`. For each key, the value is a string containing the three-revision version number (e.g., 10.9.3) representing the minimum version of OS X the application supports for that architecture.

- `LSMultipleInstancesProhibited` (Application prohibits multiple instances), indicating that, if `<true/>`, only one copy of this application can be run at a time. Different users, for instance, would not be able to use the application simultaneously.

- `LSUIElement` (Application is agent [UIElement]), if set to the string 1, identifies this application as an *agent application*, a background application that has no presence in the Dock but that can present user interface elements, if necessary.

- `LSUIPresentationMode` (Application UI Presentation Mode), an integer between 0 and 4, representing progressively greater amounts of the OS X UI—Dock and menu bar—to be hidden when the application is running. See Apple's documentation for details.

- **Other Services**
  - `LSFileQuarantineEnabled` (File quarantine enabled): If `<true/>`, Launch Services will regard the files your application creates as though they had been downloaded from the Internet and warn the user of the possible risk in opening them. You can exempt files from quarantine with `LSFileQuarantineExcludedPathPatterns`.
  - `LSFileQuarantineExcludedPathPatterns` (no editor equivalent) is an array of glob wildcard patterns for files (locations, extensions, etc.) that will be exempt from quarantining even if `LSFileQuarantineEnabled` is set.
  - `NSAppleScriptEnabled` (Scriptable), indicating that, if `YES` or `<true/>`, this application is scriptable. Applications must specify this key.

- `OSAScriptingDefinition` (Scripting definition file name), the name of the `.sdef` file, to be found in the application's `Resources` directory, containing its AppleScript scripting dictionary.

- `NSServices` (Services), an array of dictionaries declaring the OS X services this application performs, which will appear in the **Services** submenu of every application's application menu, subject to the **Keyboard Shortcuts** tab in the **Keyboard** panel of System Preferences. The dictionaries specify the pasteboard input and output formats, the name of the service, and the name of the method that implements the service. See Apple's documentation for details.

Keys for iOS

These tags are unique to iOS applications. *In general*, if you want to customize any `Info.plist` key for a particular device, create a custom key composed of the base name, followed by a hyphen, then `iphoneos`, a tilde, and a device specifier (one of `iphone`, `ipod`, or `ipad`). For example: `UIStatusBarStyle-iphoneos~ipad`. In practice, you can omit the `-iphoneos` part: `UIStatusBarStyle~ipad`.

- **Structure**
    - `UIMainStoryboardFile`, the base name of the storyboard package that is the root of the application. Use this, or `NSMainNibFile`, but never both. If you have a separate storyboard for iPhone or iPad only, add the base name to `UIMainStoryboardFile~ipad` or `~iphone`. (`ipad` and `iphone` are all-lowercase.)
    - `UILaunchStoryboardName` (Launch screen interface file base name), the base name of a storyboard that iOS will display instead of a default screen image while your application is launching. With the proliferation of screen sizes, the use of a storyboard, which can adapt to many sizes, makes more sense than having a bitmap image for each size. You'll find a discussion in the section "Icons and Launch Displays" in Chapter 13, "Adding Table Cells."
      Note well that if you do not have a launch XIB or storyboard, iOS takes that as a sign that your app is not prepared to run on a screen like the iPhone 6 or 6 Plus. If there are only images, your app will run "zoomed" to fit the larger screen.
    - `LSRequiresIPhoneOS` (Application requires iOS environment), whether Launch Services will refuse to launch the application except on an iOS device. The tag is optional, because it should go without saying.
    - `CFBundleIconFiles` (Icon files), an array of filenames for the application icons. These are expected to be the same icon in the various sizes needed by different iOS platforms; the system will look through the files themselves to pick the proper one. If you omit the file extensions, the system will find

"@2x" and "@3x" Retina Display variants automatically. Overrides `CFBundleIconFile`. (optional)

- `UIAppFonts` (Fonts provided by application), an array of paths within the application bundle for application-supplied font files.

- `UIRequiredDeviceCapabilities` (Required device capabilities), an array of strings, like `telephony`, `wifi`, or `video-camera`, that describe what device features your application cannot run without. This is used by iTunes and the App Store to save users who don't have those features from buying and installing your app.

- `UIRequiresPersistentWiFi` (Application uses Wi-Fi). The Property List editor's summary is a little misleading. By default, iOS will shut down the Wi-Fi connection if you haven't used it for half an hour. If this key is present and `YES`, the Wi-Fi transceiver will be turned on as soon as your application is launched, and it will stay on as long as it is running.

- `UISupportedExternalAccessoryProtocols` (Supported external accessory protocols), for an array of strings naming all the external-device protocols your application supports. The protocol names are specified by the manufacturers of the accessories.

- **User Presentation**

  - `UIStatusBarStyle` (Status bar style), the style (gray, translucent, or opaque black) of the initial status bar. The names of the styles used in the iOS API are used, the default being `UIStatusBarStyleDefault`.

  - `UIStatusBarHidden` (Status bar is initially hidden), if `YES`, the status bar is hidden when your application is launched. Before coveting those 20 extra pixels, please consider whether you want your customers to shut down your app whenever they need to check the time or see whether they're running out of power.

  - `UIInterfaceOrientation` (Initial interface orientation), indicating the screen orientation the application starts up in. Look up enum `UIInterfaceOrientation` in the UIKit headers for the available values; the `Info.plist` entries are supposed to be the *names* of those orientations. The default is `UIInterfaceOrientationPortrait`.

  - `UISupportedInterfaceOrientations` (Supported interface orientations, Supported interface orientations [iPad], and Supported interface orientations [iPhone]), an array naming the orientations your app will support on the iOS or iPad. If you don't specify `UIInterfaceOrientation`, iOS will use the device's orientation if it is in the list; if not, it will default to one that is. `~ipad` and `~iphone` variants are permitted.

- `UIPrerenderedIcon` (Icon already includes gloss and bevel effects), if `YES`, iOS will not add a shine effect to it. This setting is obsolete as of iOS 7, which never puts a shine effect on icons.

- `UIViewEdgeAntialiasing` (Renders with edge antialiasing). If you draw a Core Animation layer aligned to fractional-pixel coordinates, it normally isn't anti-aliased. You can set this key to `YES` if you draw that way and want to take the performance hit of making it look nice.

- `UIViewGroupOpacity` (Renders with group opacity), if `YES`, allows Core Animation sublayers to inherit the opacity of their superlayers. Cooler appearance, slower performance.

- `UILaunchImageFile` (Launch image), `UILaunchImageFile~ipad` (Launch image [iPad]), and `UILaunchImageFile~iphone` (Launch image [iPhone]), the name of the file that is shown between the time the user selects your app in the Home screen and the time when it can render its content. This worked well when there were three combinations of size, resolution, and orientation to support. Use `UILaunchStoryboardName` instead; a simple storyboard will do a much better job.
  Besides, this key has been made obsolete by. . .

- `UILaunchImages` (set through Target editor/assets catalog only), an array of dictionaries describing the launch images iOS may display when launching the app. Each dictionary specifies a filename, minimum OS version (so your launch image can match the iOS 7 appearance of your app), size, and orientation.

- **Behavior**

  - `UIApplicationExitsOnSuspend` (Application does not run in background), if true, tapping the Home button on the iOS device will shut down your app, rather than putting it into the background. Think hard before publishing an app that does this.

  - `UIBackgroundModes` (Required background modes). iOS gives apps a grace period of no more than ten minutes to perform tasks from the background if they ask for it. An app can claim ongoing exceptions such as media playback, VoIP, location updates, server checks, and more. The easiest way to make the claims is by turning on **Background Modes** in the **Capabilities** tab of the Target editor. Be prepared to defend your claim in the App Store review process.

  - `UIFileSharingEnabled` (Application supports iTunes file sharing), if `YES`, the contents of the app's `Documents/` directory will be visible while the device is plugged into iTunes. This allows your users to move files between their devices and their computers.

  - `UINewsstandApp` (Application presents content in Newsstand), if `<true/>`, the app claims it is a downloader and renderer for Newsstand subscription content. iOS will present it as a title in the Newsstand group, rather than as a stand-alone application. If you are offering a Newsstand app, you must fill in other keys, such as `UINewsstandIcon`.

- `NS*UsageDescription` (Privacy - * Usage Description) "*" is one of eleven privacy-related keys such as `Camera`, `HealthShare`, `Location`, or `PhotoLibrary`. The list will grow as Apple adds features to its products that have privacy implications. For each such feature your application might use, iOS will ask whether the user grants access to it. These keys are for your explanations for why you want access.

- `MKDirectionsApplicationSupportedModes` (Maps routing app supported modes). For an application that gives routing direction, this is an array of modes of travel, indicating, for instance, that the app provides routes for road travel, foot, and subways. Use the **Maps** section of the **Capabilities** tab in the Target editor to check off the services you provide.

- **Localization**
There are a number of `Info.plist` keys that advertise the app's ability to conform its text and appearance to the user's locale. Chapter 21, "Localization," covers them.

Summary

This chapter explored bundles and package directories, important concepts in both OS X and iOS development. Most of Xcode's product types are bundles. I reviewed the structure of simple packages and application bundles and examined the `Info.plist` file, which communicates a bundle's metadata to the operating system.

## 23

Property Lists

Cocoa uses *property lists* (also called *plists*, after the common extension for property-list files) everywhere. They are the all-purpose storage medium for structured data, both for application resources and even application documents. Though I've put this chapter into the OS X section of this book, property lists are important to iOS developers, as well.

- Many of Apple's standard formats for configuration files are simply specifications of keys and trees for property lists. If you want a configuration file of your own, you could do much worse than a specialized plist file.

- In particular, applications on iOS and OS X alike include an `Info.plist` file that tells the system how the app is to be presented and what kinds of data it handles. See Chapter 22, "Bundles and Packages," for details.

- The property-list format is very mature—older than OS X itself. Cocoa can parse plist files in one line of code, directly into Foundation data types.

> **Note**
>
> A confession: Property lists are central to Cocoa development. If you want to write software for iOS or OS X, you have to be able to read them by eye, create them by hand, and use them programmatically. They aren't going away. But see the "JSON" part of the "Other Formats" section near the end of this chapter. More and more products need to exchange data with servers and devices running other operating systems. For broad data interchange, JSON is a better choice.

Property List Data Types

A property list is an archive for the fundamental data types provided by the Objective-C Foundation framework. It consists of one item of data, expressed in one of seven data types. Five property list types are scalar—number (including integer and real), Boolean, string, date, and data—and two are compound—ordered list and dictionary. An ordered list can contain zero or more objects of any property list type. A dictionary contains zero or more pairs, consisting of a key string and a value object of any property list type.

A property list can express most collections of data quite easily. A passer's performance in a single game could be represented as a dictionary of numbers with the keys `attempts`, `completions`, `interceptions`, `touchdowns`, and `yards`. A game could be a dictionary containing the date, team names, scores, and the performance dictionary.

Both Core Foundation and Cocoa provide reference-counted object types that correspond to the property list types (see Table 23.1).

Table 23.1   Property-List Types in Cocoa and Core Foundation

Data Type	Cocoa	Core Foundation	Markup
Number	NSNumber	CFNumber	`<integer>` `<float>`
Boolean	NSNumber	CFBoolean	`<true/>` `<false/>`
Text	NSString NSMutableString	CFString CFMutableString	`<string>`
Date	NSDate	CFDate	`<date>`
Binary Data	NSData NSMutableData	CFData CFMutableData	`<data>`
List	NSArray NSMutableArray	CFArray CFMutableArray	`<array>`

Associative Array	NSDictionary
	NSMutableDictionary
		CFDictionary
		CFMutableDictionary
			`<dict>`
			`<key>`...
			plist type ...
			`</dict>`

In fact, you can pass a Cocoa property list pointer to a Core Foundation routine for the corresponding type; you can also use a `CFTypeRef` for a property list type as though it were a pointer to the corresponding Cocoa object. (Crossing the border between Foundation's Objective-C world and Core Foundation's pure-C world raises some memory-management issues that Automatic Reference Counting can't work out for itself. Search for "Transitioning to ARC Release Notes" in the Documentation organizer for the details of the `__bridge` family of type casts that give ARC the hints it needs.)

Beyond that, Swift's Array, Dictionary, and scalar types bridge seamlessly with the Foundation data types. Almost: First, at this early state of the language, the bridging can run into bugs. Second, at the boundary between Swift and property-list API, all `Dictionary`s are `[String:AnyObject]`, and all `Array`s are `[AnyObject]`, `AnyObject` being the Swift type that encompasses Objective-C objects such as the contents of property lists. Converting between the data you want to represent and the data types Swift can accept can be challenging.

> **Note**
>
> The dictionary data type in Cocoa requires only that the keys in a dictionary be objects of an immutable, hashable type; Core Foundation dictionaries can be even more permissive. However, if you want to use a Cocoa or Core Foundation dictionary in a property list, all keys have to be strings.

Editing Property Lists

When you started the Passer Rating iPhone app, the first thing Xcode showed was the Target editor for the application. The third tab, **Info**, is a specialization of the Property List editor for `Info.plist`, which contains a dictionary describing to the OS how the application is to be presented. Each line of the top section represents one key-value pair at the top level of the dictionary; the **Info** editor refines the experience by wrapping some of the top-level keys (such as document and data types) into distinct lists of convenient graphical editors. See Figure 23.1.

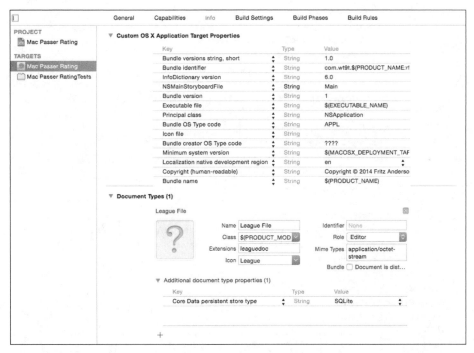

Figure 23.1   As soon as an application project is created, Xcode presents a Target editor to edit its `Info.plist` file. The first and third tabs, **General** and **Info** (shown here), are specialized editors to set the application's presentation and behavior.

Still, it's just an editor for a particular kind of property list. Let's have a look at the real thing. Use the search field at the bottom of the Project navigator to search for **plist**. The only file surviving in the navigator should be Info.plist. Click on it.

Not much to see. It's Xcode's generic Property List editor, which is just a little simpler than the Target editor's **Info** tab. What's the big deal? Do this: Right-click on the file's name in the Project navigator, and select **Open As → Source Code**. Now the Editor area fills with something like this:

```
<?xml version="1.0" encoding="UTF-8"?>
<!DOCTYPE plist PUBLIC "-//Apple//DTD PLIST 1.0//EN"
    "http://www.apple.com/DTDs/PropertyList-1.0.dtd">
<plist version="1.0">
<dict>
    <key>CFBundleDevelopmentRegion</key>
    <string>en</string>
    <key>CFBundleDocumentTypes</key>
    <array>
        <dict>
            <key>CFBundleTypeExtensions</key>
            <array>
                <string>leaguedoc</string>
            </array>
            <key>CFBundleTypeIconFile</key>
            <string>League</string>
            <key>CFBundleTypeMIMETypes</key>
            <array>
                <string>application/octet-stream</string>
            </array>
            <key>CFBundleTypeName</key>
            <string>League File</string>
            <key>CFBundleTypeRole</key>
            <string>Editor</string>
            <key>LSTypeIsPackage</key>
            <false/>
            <key>NSDocumentClass</key>
            <string>$(PRODUCT_MODULE_NAME).LeagueDocument</string>
            <key>NSPersistentStoreTypeKey</key>
            <string>SQLite</string>
        </dict>
    </array>
    <key>CFBundleExecutable</key>
    <string>$(EXECUTABLE_NAME)</string>
    <key>CFBundleIconFile</key>
    <string></string>
    <key>CFBundleIdentifier</key>
    <string>com.wt9t.$(PRODUCT_NAME:rfc1034identifier)</string>
    <key>CFBundleInfoDictionaryVersion</key>
```

```
        <string>6.0</string>
        <key>CFBundleName</key>
        <string>$(PRODUCT_NAME)</string>
        <key>CFBundlePackageType</key>
        <string>APPL</string>
        <key>CFBundleShortVersionString</key>
        <string>1.0</string>
        <key>CFBundleSignature</key>
        <string>????</string>
        <key>CFBundleVersion</key>
        <string>1</string>
        <key>LSMinimumSystemVersion</key>
        <string>$(MACOSX_DEPLOYMENT_TARGET)</string>
        <key>NSHumanReadableCopyright</key>
        <string>Copyright © 2014 Fritz Anderson. All rights reserved.</string>
        <key>NSMainStoryboardFile</key>
        <string>Main</string>
        <key>NSPrincipalClass</key>
        <string>NSApplication</string>
</dict>
</plist>
```

You likely are relieved to see that the property-list format is XML and that Cocoa's built-in writer for .plist files indents it nicely. The top-level element is <plist>, which must contain one property list element—in this case, <dict>, for the Info.plist dictionary. A <dict> element's contents alternate between <key> string elements and property list value elements. One of the keys, CFBundleDocumentTypes, has an <array> value. An <array> may contain zero or more property list elements, of any type—in this case, only one <dict> describing Mac Passer Rating's document type. I covered Info.plist keys at length in Chapter 22, "Bundles and Packages."

> **Note**
>
> I'm indulging in two cheats here. First, what you're looking at is not the Info.plist that will be inserted into the application bundle. It's a source file for a compiler that the build system uses to fill in variables and insert some invariant keys—you see variable names like ${PRODUCT_NAME}. Second, the Info.plist in the app bundle won't be an XML file; it will be a *binary plist,* as I show later in this chapter.

What's good about XML is that it is standard: Correct XML will be accepted by any consumer of a document type definition, regardless of the source. A .plist file generated by any Cocoa application will be treated the same as one generated by a text editor.

What's bad about XML is that it must be correct. If you forget to close an element or miss the strict alternation of <key> and values in <dict> lists, you will get nothing out of Apple's parser.

Usually, you don't have to worry about this sort of thing because you'll be using the Property List editor in its graphical form. You don't see the opening and closing tags, so you can't omit them. The editor forces you to put a key on every element in a dictionary and restricts you to the legal data types. Simple.

However, sometimes it's not practical to use the Property List editor to create or maintain property lists. Let's have a look at how the editor works, and then I can develop why it's not for every task.

The Property List Editor

We're going to create a property list that describes how to make an omelet. I'll leave to you what the file would be good for. Bring Xcode forward. Select **File** → **New** → **File...** (⌘ N), and navigate the New File assistant thus: OS X → Resource → Property List. (You can get the same thing from the iOS part of the assistant.) If you have a project window open, you'll be shown the usual put-file sheet. Call it **Omelet**. (Xcode will add .plist for you.) The other controls for disposing the new file in the project are now long-familiar to you.

You'll be presented with the same kind of Property List editor that you saw for the Info.plist file, only it's empty, but for a single line at the top, labeled Root. The Property List editor lets you generate <dict> or <array> plists, and the popup menu in the second column lets you choose which. Make sure it's a **Dictionary**.

But there's no obvious control for adding any content. What to do? There are two approaches.

Look at the **Editor** menu. It's dynamic, adjusting its content to the type of the active editor. Now that it's a Property List editor, you'll find the command **Add Item**. Select it, and a new row appears in the editor.

Or, hover the mouse cursor over the Root row. A + button will appear in the first column. Clicking it will add a row. See Figure 23.2, top.

The new row will be a key-value pair for the dictionary, with a *key*, represented as a text field that is open for editing; a *type*, represented as a popup listing the possible plist types; and a *value*, which is editable if the type is a scalar.

The omelet recipe will have three sections, named Ingredients, Material, and Method. Ingredients should be a dictionary, with the keys naming the ingredients; the values should be dictionaries themselves, keyed quantity and unit. So name the first new row **Ingredients**, and set its type to **Dictionary**, as in Figure 23.2, top.

You want more items in the recipe. You want the Material and Method elements to be siblings of Ingredients, and you want to add ingredient dictionaries as children of Ingredients. That's two styles of adding rows to the editor.

Select the Ingredients row, and press the Return key (or, click the + button at the right of the Key cell, or select **Editor** → **Add Item**). This produces a new sibling row, which you can name **Material** and make a dictionary. See Figure 23.2, middle.

Select the Ingredients row again. At the left margin of the row, there is a disclosure triangle that is turned to the right, indicating that the container is closed. Click the triangle to open the container, which doesn't make much difference because a new dictionary doesn't have any contents to show.

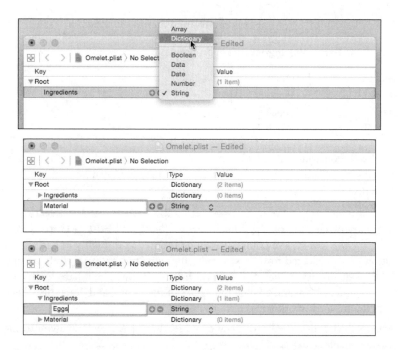

Figure 23.2   (top) Selecting **Editor → Add Item** inserts the first element in a new property list. Select from a popup menu in the Type column to indicate the data type the element represents. (middle) Pressing the Return key or clicking the **+** button when a container element is closed inserts a new element that is a sibling of the selected container. (bottom) If the container is open, pressing Return or clicking **+** inserts the new element as a child of the container.

Now press Return. A new row appears, but this time it is indented to show that the new element is *inside* the Ingredients dictionary (Figure 23.2, bottom). The difference is whether the disclosure triangle points closed or open. If closed, you get a sibling at the same level. If open, you get a child, enclosed in the container.

So now you have an element inside Ingredients. Name it **Eggs**, and make it a dictionary. Open Eggs, press Return (or click the **+** button) twice to create new elements named **quantity** (type **Number**, value **3**—it's a generous omelet) and **unit** (type **String**, value **count**). You've completed your first ingredient.

> **Note**
>
> Make a mistake? Undo works as normal. If you want to get rid of an item, select it and press Delete, or click the **–** button in its Key column. Deleting a container deletes all of its contents as well.

Add more siblings to Eggs—or children to Ingredients—as shown in Table 23.2.

Table 23.2   The Remaining Ingredients in an Omelet

Mushrooms	Count	2
Salt	Pinch	1
Butter	Ounce	2

Doing this the obvious way, clicking new-sibling and new-child buttons at each step, and setting the same unit and quantity keys for each new dictionary, is tedious. There are some shortcuts.

- Once you have one dictionary (Eggs) set up the way you want it, select that dictionary by clicking on the container row (Eggs), and **Edit → Copy** (⌘ C). When you paste the row you've copied, it will be inserted as though you had clicked the **+** button on the selected row. So select the Ingredients dictionary while it's open, or the Eggs dictionary while it's *closed*, and **Edit → Paste**. You'll have to change the pasted element's key and change the values of the "unit" and "quantity" keys, but that's the minimal work you'd have to do anyway.

- When you've finished editing a key or value, the Tab key will take you to the next visible editable string.

- The Return key will close a text-field cell if one is open. Pressing it again will create a new element (sibling or child) as though you'd clicked the **+** button on the selected row. The new row will have the key string (if it's in a dictionary) or the value string (if it's not) ready for editing. The initial type will be for a string, which is probably the type you'd want if you're motoring through several new rows at a time.

The `Material` dictionary should be simple key/string pairs, as shown in Table 23.3.

Table 23.3   Materials for Making an Omelet

Bowl	Small
Fork	Table fork or small whisk
Crêpe pan	10" nonstick
Spatula	Silicone, high-heat
Egg slicer	Optional, for slicing mushrooms

The Method array should contain strings, as shown in Table 23.4.

Table 23.4   Instructions for Making an Omelet

Heat pan to medium (butter foams but doesn't burn)

Warm eggs in water to room temperature

Slice mushrooms

Sauté in 1/4 of the butter until limp, set aside

Break eggs into bowl, add salt

Whisk eggs until color begins to change

Coat pan with 1/2 the butter

Pour eggs into pan, and tilt to spread uniformly

When edges set, use spatula to separate from pan, then tilt liquid into gaps

Leave undisturbed for 30 seconds

Loosen from pan, and flip (using spatula to help) 1/3 over

Top with mushrooms

Slide onto plate, flipping remaining 1/3 over

Spread remaining butter on top

It's important that Method's strings appear in order, so it has to be an array. If it's not in the order you want, you can drag items into the order you want. See Figure 23.3.

When you've done it all, your Property List editor should look like the one in Figure 23.4.

Search-and-replace works in property lists as it does in regular text files. If you click **Find →Find. . .** (⌘F), the find bar appears. If you type **butter**, the containers open to show and highlight all instances of the string. Clicking the left- and right-arrow buttons in the find bar (or pressing ⇧⌘G or ⌘G) navigates among the found rows, but it doesn't enable them for editing.

If you want to replace butter with margarine, **Find →Find and Replace. . .** (⌥⌘F) will add a replacement row to the find bar. (Or, use the popup at the left end of the find bar to select **Replace** instead of **Find**.) Put **margarine** in the second field, and click the **All** button, thus confirming your standing as a barbarian.

Find →Find in Workspace/Project. . . (⇧⌘F) works, too. The Find navigator appears, you enter **butter**, and the plist appears in the list of matches.

Egg Slicer	String	Optional, for slicing mushrooms
▼ Method	Array (14 items)	
Item 0	String	Heat pan to medium (butter foams but doesn't burn)
Item 1	String	Warm eggs in water to room temperature
Item 2	String	Slice mushrooms
Item 3	String	Sauté in 1/4 of the butter until limp, set aside

Figure 23.3   You can reorder array elements by dragging them where you want them.

Key	Type	Value
▼ Root	Dictionary	(3 items)
▼ Ingredients	Dictionary	(5 items)
▼ Eggs	Dictionary	(2 items)
unit	String	count
quantity	Number	3
▼ Mushrooms	Dictionary	(2 items)
unit	String	count
quantity	Number	2
▼ Salt	Dictionary	(2 items)
unit	String	pinch
quantity	Number	1
▼ Butter	Dictionary	(2 items)
unit	String	ounce
quantity	Number	2
▼ Parsley	Dictionary	(2 items)
quantity	Number	1
unit	String	sprig
▼ Material	Dictionary	(5 items)
Bowl	String	Small
Fork	String	Table fork or small whisk
Crêpe Pan	String	10" nonstick
Spatula	String	Silicone, high-heat
Egg Slicer	String	Optional, for slicing mushrooms
▼ Method	Array	(14 items)
Item 0	String	Warm eggs in water to room temperature
Item 1	String	Heat pan to medium (butter foams but doesn't burn)
Item 2	String	Slice mushrooms
Item 3	String	Sauté in 1/4 of the butter until limp, set aside
Item 4	String	Break eggs into bowl, add salt
Item 5	String	Whisk eggs until color begins to change
Item 6	String	Coat pan with 1/2 the butter
Item 7	String	Pour eggs into pan, and tilt to spread uniformly
Item 8	String	When edges set, use spatula to separate from pan, then tilt liquid into gaps
Item 9	String	Leave undisturbed for 30 seconds
Item 10	String	Loosen from pan, and flip (using spatula to help) 1/3 over
Item 11	String	Top with mushrooms
Item 12	String	Slide onto plate, flipping remaining 1/3 over
Item 13	String	Spread remaining butter on top

Figure 23.4   The Property List editor showing the finished `Omelet.plist`. You can open or close all of the subelements in a dictionary or array by holding the Option key when you click the disclosure triangle.

Why Not the Property List Editor?

The Property List editor generated a correct property list with all the data in what seems to be the most direct way possible. What more is there to say?

It isn't perfect. Right-click on the file in the Project navigator, and select **Open As** →**Source Code** from the contextual menu. Once again, you'll see the plist in the XML format in which it is stored.

You have doubts about your recipe. Maybe a little garnish would be nice, but you can't decide. So you add an XML comment to the `Methods` array:

```
<key>Method</key>
<array>
    .
    .
    .

    <string>Slide onto plate, flipping remaining 1/3 over</string>
    <string>Spread remaining butter on top</string>
    <!-- Should I add parsley? -->
</array>
```

Using the contextual menu, select **Open As** →**Property List** again. Make a tentative advance in presentation by adding Parsley (sprig, 1) to the `Ingredients` dictionary. (You'll have to open the dictionary; Xcode saves open/collapsed state, but reverts to all-collapsed if you change editors.) Switch back to **Source Code**.

The comment you added is gone. If you use the Property List editor to change a property list, it will destroy any content that isn't property-list data. Similarly, if you take advantage of the build option to apply a preprocessor pass to the compilation of `Info.plist`, so you can have `#includes` and conditional content, those directives will be lost if they pass through the Property List editor.

> **Warning**
>
> If you intend to treat property lists as normal source files, using comments for notes or to comment content out, you must *never* edit them with the graphical editor. Viewing them is okay—in fact, it's unavoidable, because Xcode puts you back in the graphical editor every time you return to the file—but don't change them.

Commenting and preprocessing aside, a text editor can just be the best tool for the job. Large and repetitive structures are a bit easier to handle in XML text, it's easier to handle programmatically generated files, and maybe you just like to work with source.

There's a way you can do this without forcing the Source Code editor every time. Select your property-list file in the Project navigator, and open the Utilities area (using the right-hand button in the **View** control in the toolbar). Make sure the File inspector tab (the first one) is selected. You'll see various information about the file and its status in your project (Figure 23.5, left); the one you're interested in is the setting in the **Type** popup menu.

It starts with **Default – Property List XML**. Scroll through the menu (it will be quite a ways down) until you find the **Property List / XML** group, and select **XML**.

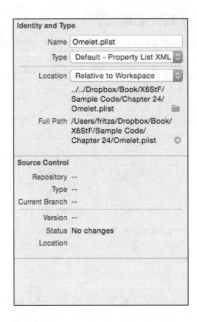

Figure 23.5   The popup under the filename in the File inspector chooses the editor and syntax that Xcode will apply to that file. You can force Xcode always to use the XML editor for a particular `.plist` file by selecting **XML** in the **Property List / XML** group, instead of **Property List XML**.

Nothing happens to the editor. Select a different file in the Project navigator, then go back to `Omelet.plist`. Now it appears as an XML file, and always will, without your having to tell Xcode to switch.

> **Note**
>
> That Xcode labels **Property List XML** as a default suggests that you might be able to change the default, and get the plain-XML editor all the time, without setting it for each file. In Xcode 3, you could do that. The feature disappeared with Xcode 4.

If you commit to creating and editing property lists in XML, you lose the safety of the Property List editor in keeping the syntax correct. There are a couple of ways to reduce the risk.

First, you can start your own `.plist` files by editing a known-good `.plist` file. It's difficult to omit the processing instruction or the `<plist>` skeleton if they are already in the file.

Second, you can use the macro or glossary facilities of your text editor to create a document skeleton and wrap your entries in proper tags. Bare Bones Software's BBEdit comes with a `.plist` glossary for just this purpose.

Once you have your property-list file, you'll need to know whether it is syntactically correct—if it isn't, you can't use it. The best way is to use the `plutil` tool. In the

Terminal, type **plutil** *pathToPropertyList*. You will see either *pathTo-PropertyList*: OK, or a diagnostic message pointing to the first line that confused the parser. See man plutil for details.

> **Note**
>
> One of the commonest errors is forgetting that the text portions of the property list XML are parsed character data, which means that < and & must be represented by < and &.

Other Formats

If you stick to editing property lists as text, you'll find that text editors can display and edit only *most* property-list files. There are two other formats a plist file may use. One is also text, the other is binary.

Text Property Lists

Property lists came to Cocoa's architecture from its ancestor framework, NeXTStep. In NeXTStep, property lists were encoded in what Apple calls a legacy format, but it is used often enough that you should be familiar with it. defaults, the command-line interface to the preferences system, the bundle specifications for the editor TextMate, and many of the internal Xcode configuration files use the text format.

> **Note**
>
> I have worked on projects to produce apps for presenting the work of non-technical scholars. Someone will tempt you to offer the scholar a "simple" XML schema to make her content machine-readable. Assume the data really is complex enough to make XML a sensible option, and nevermind the technical issues. Hand-coding non-trivial XML is hard enough for you and me; I have *never* seen even PhDs consistently produce usable XML. Structured text formats, like classic plist or JSON, are the way to go.

Text property lists have only two primitive types: string and data (Table 23.5).

Table 23.5   Encoding for Text-style Property Lists

Type	Coding
String	"Two or more words" *or* oneWord
Data	< 466f6f 626172 >
List	(Shirley, "Goodness and Mercy", 1066)
Associative array	{ key = value; "key 2" = < 332e3134313539 >; }

Strings are surrounded by double-quote characters, which may be omitted if there are no spaces in the string. Number, date, and Boolean values must be stored as string representations, and the application that reads them is on its own for converting them to their respective types. The convention for Boolean values is to use the strings YES and NO.

Data elements are delimited by angle brackets and contain pairs of hexadecimal digits, representing the bytes in the data. Any whitespace in the digit stream will be ignored.

Arrays are surrounded by parentheses, and the elements are separated by commas. Dictionaries are surrounded by braces, and the `key` = `value` pairs are *followed by* semicolons, which means that the last element must be closed off with a semicolon.

Binary Property Lists

With OS X 10.2 (Jaguar), Apple introduced a binary property-list format. Binary plists are smaller and load faster. Programmatically generated plists are binary by default; Xcode, for instance, writes `Info.plist`s in binary. Property lists can be converted between XML and binary format in place using the `plutil` command-line utility in the form

```
plutil -convert format pathToFile
```

where `format` is either `binary1`, for conversion to the binary format, or `xml1` for the XML format; and `pathToFile` is the path to the file to convert.

> **Note**
>
> Both Xcode and BBEdit will translate binary property-list files into XML for editing.

The build settings `INFOPLIST_OUTPUT_FORMAT` and `PLIST_FILE_OUTPUT_FORMAT` influence how Xcode writes `Info.plist` and other plist files, respectively, into your product. By default, these are `binary`, but you can set them to `XML`.

JSON

JSON is not an alternate property-list format, but it is more and more an alternative solution. It, too, organizes data primitives into arrays and dictionaries.

Property lists have some advantages, or at least little cost:

- The root object doesn't have to be an array or dictionary.
- There is a way to express infinite or not-a-number numeric values.
- There is a way to distinguish integer, real, and Boolean value types.
- Property lists can contain `NSDate`s; end of story. There is no standard representation for dates in JSON; most developers agree on the ISO8601 text format, but writing and parsing even standard date formats is surprisingly hard to get right in every case.
- Property lists can contain binary data as part of the binary stream, or XML `CDATA`, or angle-bracketed base64 code. There is no standard format for binary data in JSON. You can base64-encode your data into a string and insert that, but that's another application-specific convention you have to agree on.
- With decades of tuning behind the software, Apple's plist codecs are as fast as they can be. Most implementations of JSON (for the moment) are a little slower, with JSONKit a notable exception.
- The size of binary plist files is in the neighborhood of JSON. (If download speed is a concern, however, most servers will zip-compress outgoing data, which is a bigger win for text than binaries.)

Apple's plists fall short of the ideal one way or another:

- XML is verbose; XML plists are significantly bigger than the equivalent JSON.
- The text format has fewer distinct data types, and is restricted to ASCII (or an 8-bit character set, if both sides agree on one).
- The binary format does better than either, and doesn't have the parsing overhead, but humans can't read it, and so can't debug it without converting to one of the other formats.
- There are libraries that scripting software can use to create and consume plists, but add-ons, especially niche add-ons, can have performance and reliability problems.
- JSON has a `null` data value, equivalent to an Objective-C or Swift `nil`. The problem is that `nil` isn't an object—if you want to indicate a null value in an `NSArray` or `NSDictionary`, you have to use the singleton `NSNull()` object. But `NSNull` is not a permissible type in a property list.
- There are Internet standards for the JSON format.
- Property lists cannot natively represent cross-references among objects. (The `NSCoder` archiving family uses a plist schema that handles object references, but that's an application of the format, not part of the format itself.)
- As a practical matter, **plists are readable only by Apple devices**. That's unacceptable in a cross-platform application, which means essentially any client-server system.

Cocoa has the `NSJSONSerialization` class to bridge JSON to the Foundation data types, similarly to `NSPropertyListSerialization` for property lists. Neither representation fully supports all the data types you might have put in your data; there are only so many property list types, and so many JSON types. Both classes have methods that will check your object trees to verify that they can be formatted.

I've gone most of the way through the chapter explaining how you can use property lists to store and transmit data. And that's what I should do: The format is key to Cocoa development, and it's not going away. But:

If you're going to exchange data with other platforms, use JSON.

Specialized Property Lists

Many of Cocoa's standard "file formats" are simply property lists with stereotyped keys and enumerated values. Xcode knows about these stereotypes; you can assign a type to a plist by opening it, and right-clicking in the editor view. The contextual menu includes a **Property List Type** submenu. If Xcode encounters a stereotyped plist, such as `Info.plist` or an iOS Settings bundle, it will choose the repertoire of common keys and values.

Once a property list type is established, the Key column in the Property List editor assumes a much more active role. Xcode now knows what keys this particular plist supports and what types are appropriate to those keys.

For example: An iOS application `Info.plist` will include the key `UTExported-TypeDeclarations`. If you add a row to the plist, the key field is no longer a simple text field, but a combo field (a text field with a scrollable list of choices) in which "Exported Type UTIs" is an option. If you select it, Xcode changes the type of the row to array—because the `UTExportedTypeDeclarations` element must have an array value.

If you open that array, and add a row to it, Xcode will create a dictionary—`UTExportedTypeDeclarations` must contain dictionaries—prepopulated with the three keys (and types) required of those dictionaries.

For a key that has a restricted set of scalar values, Xcode will set the element to the proper type, and instead of an editable value field, the value column will contain a popup of English-language names for the legal values.

> **Note**
>
> The values are still editable text, and if you click in most of their area, you'll get an editing field. For the popup menu, click on the arrowheads at the right end of the row.

Remember that combo fields are text fields, not menus. Xcode offers them wherever it's legal to enter a custom value. Treat that key or value as editable text, and ignore the attached list. The list isn't comprehensive or restrictive; if something you need isn't there, type it in yourself.

The combo fields' lists scroll to offer presets that match what you've typed. This is handy, but the matching is case sensitive. If you aren't finding what you expect, try typing with an initial cap.

Having English-language equivalents for all of your keys and values cuts you off from the actual content of those elements; even if XML editing isn't to your taste, you may want to audit what's going into your file. There are two strategies for this:

- Open the Utility (right) area, select Quick Help (the second tab), and click in a row. Quick Help will show the English name and the "declaration," the actual encoded key. You're out of luck for English-language values.

- Select **Editor** → **Show Raw Values & Keys** (or the same command from the contextual menu). The Property List editor will switch over to its "normal" behavior, displaying the uninterpreted keys and values.

Summary

This chapter introduced property lists, a ubiquitous data-storage format in Cocoa. You've seen how to use the Property List editor and text tools to manage them. I showed you the other ways property lists can appear on OS X and iOS, and how Xcode adapts itself to the stereotyped formats of well-known specializations of the plist format. By now, you should be pretty comfortable with the concept.

Part IV

Xcode Tasks

Documentation in Xcode

The combined documentation for developer tools and the current versions of OS X and iOS run to about a gigabyte and a half, and Apple updates it continually. Xcode incorporates an extensive help and documentation system to give you quick access to the documents while you are coding, and a browser for when you need to go into more depth. In this chapter, I'll show you how to make the most of the facilities Xcode provides, and how you can add your own documentation.

Quick Help

Quick Help is Xcode's facility for getting you information about the API with as little interruption as possible. The presentation is lightweight but thorough, and if you need to go deeper, the links are there.

Inspector

Quick Help is available on permanent view in almost every editor. Simply expose the Utility area (third segment of the **View** control at the right end of the toolbar) and select the Quick Help inspector (second tab).

- If you're editing source, and the editing cursor is in a symbol for which Apple has documentation, Quick Help will show you a summary of how a method (for instance) is invoked, a description of what it does, the types and purposes of its parameters, and what it returns. It will tell you the earliest version of the OS that supports it, and it will offer you cross-references to overview documentation, related API, and the header file in which the symbol is declared. The information is drawn from the docset corresponding to the SDK you're using, and formatted to match the language. See Figure 24.1, left.
  Quick Help works on your own symbols, too, but all you will get is a reference to the declaration—unless you provide documentation of your own. More on that later.

- When you select an object in Interface Builder, Quick Help provides documentation for the object's class.

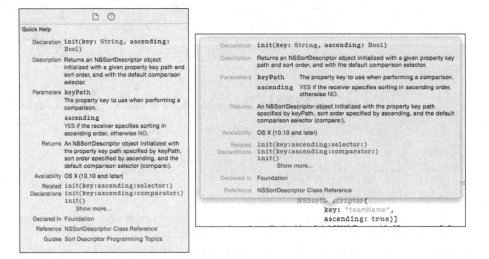

Figure 24.1   (left) When the Quick Help inspector is open, and the text cursor is in any documented symbol, the inspector displays a summary of the symbol, parameters, and other information. It includes clickable cross-references. (right) If you hold down the Option key and click on a documented symbol, Xcode displays a popover window with the same information.

- In the Project/Target editor's **Build Settings** tab, selecting a row will fill Quick Help with what will usually be the most complete documentation you can find of the setting. The description includes how the setting might get a default value, the build variable underlying the setting (see Appendix A, "Some Build Variables"), and the compiler flag, if any, the setting sets.
- In property list editors, and the **Info** tab of the Target editor, if Xcode displays an English-language equivalent of a key in the editor, Quick Help will show you the underlying key.

Popover

Holding down the Option key and mousing into a symbol will put a dotted line under it and highlight it in blue. If you click, a popover appears with most of the content you'd see in the Quick Help inspector. See Figure 24.1, right. (You can do the same thing by selecting **Help → Quick Help for Selected Item**, ⌃ ⌘ ?.)

Option-double-clicking on a symbol brings up the Documentation browser and jumps to a catalog of documentation about the symbol. It's not a search—your search settings in the browser have no effect. The gesture takes you directly to the documentation without any searching.

```
if (okay) {
    [self.delegate cookieParse
}
else {
    NSError *    error = parse
    NSLog(@"%s: Parse failed
        __PRETTY_FUNCTIO
    [self.delegate cookieParserParseDidFail: self error: error];
```

Inside the popup:
- -[AudioTasksAppDelegate cookieParserDidFinish:]
- -[CookieParserDelegate cookieParserDidFinish:]
- Search for Definitions
- Show in Symbol Navigator

Figure 24.2   If there is more than one definition for a symbol, command-clicking will produce a popup listing all definitions, and offering to search the project for it or to reveal symbols that contain the string you command-clicked, in the Symbol navigator.

An abbreviated form of Quick Help is also available during code completion. When the completion popup is showing, click on one of the choices, and see a few words of the symbol's description, and a link to details, at the bottom of the popup.

Now is the time to mention command-clicking:

- Command-clicking on a symbol opens the file in which the symbol is defined and highlights the definition. The search is context sensitive: Often, more than one class will implement a method, but if the context makes the class of the receiving object clear, a command-click will take you directly to the definition of the method for that object. If the class can't be identified for certain—this is often the case for delegate-protocol methods—a popup menu offers you the choice. See Figure 24.2.

- Adding the Option key to a command-click shows the declaration in the Assistant editor; remember that adding the Option key to any navigational gesture directs the result to the Assistant editor.

Open Quickly

Most programmer's editors have some sort of open-quickly or open-selection command that lets you select a filename and have the editor find and open the file named in the selection. Xcode's **File → Open Quickly. . .** (⇧ ⌘ O) does the same. But that doesn't end it.

The Open Quickly dialog has a search field that does an incremental search of the names of the files, local and system, that your project can access. All of the possible matches, including directory paths, are listed in a table.

There's more: The search extends to symbols, not just filenames. Enter **brokenBy-Lines**, and you'll be shown the match and its location in `Extensions.swift`. This is not a simple incremental match. Apple anticipated that you might want to look up a symbol or file whose name you don't quite remember; just enter the parts you do remember: Enter **bblin**, and it will find (among others) **brokenByLines**. See Figure 24.3.

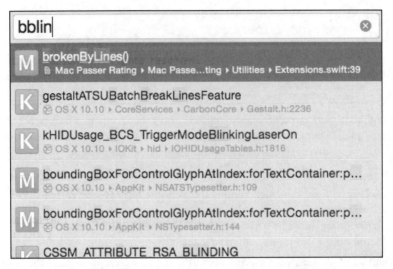

Figure 24.3   The Open Quickly dialog finds files and symbols accessible to your project based on an incremental search. It is not necessary to remember the whole name; any sequence you enter will be matched against any sequence of characters in the name, consecutive or not.

Help

Like every OS X application, Xcode has a **Help** menu. The first item in it is not a menu item at all, but an incremental search field. As you type, the contents of the menu are replaced with items in two sections:

- **Search** lists every menu item that contains the text you typed. Mousing over the listed items opens up the corresponding menu and places a pointer next to the item. Clicking on a listed item has the same effect as selecting the item itself. Some "hidden" items will be shown, and some will not. "Alternate" items that appear only when you hold down a modifier key (open the **Navigate** menu and press and release the Option key to see what I mean) will be found. You will not find menu items that Xcode has removed, in particular commands in the **Editor** menu that don't apply to the current editor.

- **Documentation and API Reference**, ⇧⌘0, opens the Documentation browser. More about that shortly.

- **Xcode Overview** opens the Documentation browser on a series of articles introducing Xcode and how to use it.

- **Release Notes** are version-by-version summaries of the changes and issues in Xcode. "Release notes" doesn't sound like much, but for most Apple technologies, the notes can be as important as the "real" documentation. Where the regular documentation has to tell you how Xcode is *meant* to work, the release notes will tell you what features have issues, and how to work around them.

- **What's New in Xcode** itemizes the new features and services of each release of Xcode 6, with links to details. There are also links to the new-features documents for releases back to Xcode 4.1.

- **Quick Help for Selected Item**, ∧ ⌘ **?**, is the same as option-clicking. It displays a popover with Quick Help for the selection.

- **Search Documentation for Selected Text**, ∧ ⌥ ⌘ **/**, is the equivalent to an option-double-click: It's a menu item and key combination to bring the Documentation browser up on the contents of the selection.

The Documentation Window

Quick Help is good for focused reference, but you also need simply to read the documentation. To do this, you use the Documentation browser (**Window →Documentation and API Reference**, ⇧ ⌘ **0**).

The Documentation browser consists of a large view for content, plus two sidebars you can open with buttons in the toolbar. See Figure 24.4.

The Navigator Sidebar

The Navigator sidebar has two tabs. The first presents an outline of the entire documentation library. This will eventually reach every page in the documentation sets, but there are thousands of pages, and the tree that leads to class references is five layers deep. The first layer or two have descriptive names like "Data Management," but unless you have a miraculous sense of how Apple thinks of such things, there doesn't *seem* to be much use in the Library navigator.

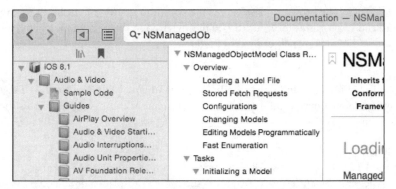

Figure 24.4   Buttons in the toolbar of the Help browser show two sidebars, a navigator that indexes the documentation library; and a table-of-contents list for the currently displayed document.

The second tab is the Bookmark navigator. It's straightforward: The documentation pages, and every indexable section within the pages, carry bookmark buttons; click one, and the name of the section and article appears in the bookmark list. Clicking a bookmark returns you to that location; you can reorder the list by dragging, and a contextual menu lets you delete bookmarks or open them in new tabs.

The Table of Contents Sidebar

The second column is for a table of contents. Apple's documentation is organized into "books," "articles," and "sections." The table of contents lays out the structure of a major division in an outline view.

If the document on display is an API reference, the outline makes good use of Apple's standard layout for class references, with major divisions for task-grouped method lists, class methods, and instance methods.

Class Info

Another feature of class references is a header section outlining a class's superclasses and implemented protocols, its framework, the OS releases in which the class is available, a declaration header, and links to related documents and sample code. See Figure 24.5.

And when you're looking at a class or reading an article, you may want to browse to other pages not directly cross-referenced, but on the same subject. This is the most useful feature of the Library navigator: Select **Editor → Reveal in Library** to see the Library navigator with the outline opened to the current document—and the related items around it.

Searching and Navigation

The Documentation browser follows the conventions of a web browser: It has a search bar, back and forward buttons, bookmarks, tabs, and ways to share the contents.

I've already covered bookmarks, and I shouldn't have to tell you about back and forward buttons. The browser doesn't offer the common gesture of scroll-left to navigate backward and scroll-right, forward. (If you're interested in the gesture in general, it's in the **Trackpad** and **Mouse** panels of System Preferences.)

Tabs

Command-clicking on a link opens the linked page in a new tab; the **New → Tab** (⌘ T) command gets you a new, blank browsing environment. You can drag tabs across the bar to reorder them.

Searching

The search bar is the main way you'll navigate the documentation. At the first level, it's simple: Type your search terms; as you type, the browser displays a drop-down list showing a selection of matching articles (Figure 24.6). Press Return to accept the leading result, or click in the drop-down to select another match. This is almost ideal.

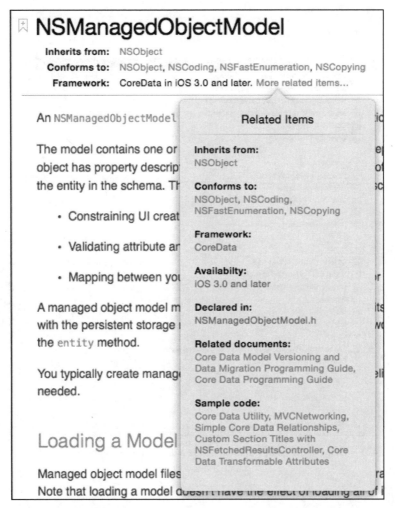

Figure 24.5   The class-summary frame at the top of class references shows the basic information for the class, including references to documentation and sample code.

If you decide you need to see another article—and this will happen frequently, because the "selected," and even the "best," matches are often not useful—the experience deteriorates. There is no way to recover the suggestion drop-down unless you back off the last character of the search field and type it again.

But returning to the search field and pressing Return again gets you the "Show All Results" page, which is the most useful result of a documentation search. (It's also available if you select **Show All Results** in the suggested-results drop-down.)

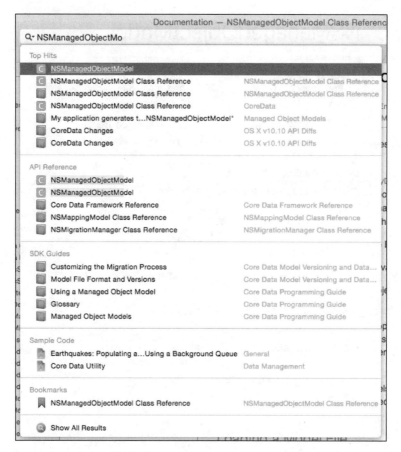

Figure 24.6   Typing in the search field produces a drop-down menu of some of the articles that match the search term.

The page shows all articles that match the search string, tabbed between API, SDK overviews, developer-tools topics, and sample code. The drop-down is one-way; the all-results page is a page with a place in the browser's history. If one result is unsatisfactory, you can go back to the results and try again. And, it contains *every* match for your search, not just a best-guess selection. The only advantage to the drop-down is that the entries display the title of the next-higher division of the documents. See Figure 24.7.

You can restrict the search by clicking the magnifying-glass button in the search field. This will produce a popover containing a choice of **OS X** and **iOS** to search documentation for those platforms only; **All SDKs** to force the browser to search all of the available docsets; and **Automatic**, to allow it to guess the scope of the search from context, such as the currently selected target in the front project window (Figure 24.8).

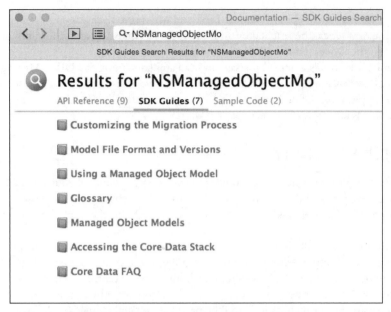

Figure 24.7 The most valuable product of a search is the all-results page, listing all matching articles by title, organized by the scope of the article.

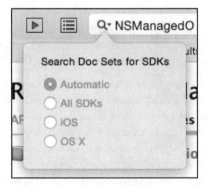

Figure 24.8 Clicking the magnifying-glass button in the search field produces a popover window for you to choose the scope of your documentation searches.

Export

The **Export** button, at the right end of the toolbar, gives you options for alternative views of the current documentation page and for sharing references to it. You can bookmark the page, view its underlying HTML in Safari, fetch the PDF document that includes the contents of the current page, or view it in iBooks. If a playground is attached to the page, the **Export** menu will open it.

There are two other options, **Email Link** and **Message**. Each page in the documentation set can be reached by an xcdoc URL. Following an xcdoc link opens Xcode and the Documentation browser and displays the page.

Email Link creates an email message in Mail.app containing the URL; **Message** pops up a window containing the URL and a field to receive a destination as understood by the Messages application. Click **Send**, and the recipient sees the link in Messages, a compatible instant-message service, or an SMS text.

Keeping Current

Xcode and Apple's documentation do not come out on the same schedule. They can't. Even if it were practical to halt one team while the other caught up to a release, the documents will still be extended and revised, and be ready for the public, at a much faster pace than a complex set of developer tools can.

When you first install Xcode, you don't have a complete local documentation library. What is packaged into ~/Library/Developer/Shared/Documentation/DocSets is a skeleton of a couple hundred megabytes with minimal content, filled in with references to content at developer.apple.com. The equivalent local library is an order of magnitude larger. Not including the full library makes downloading Xcode faster, and it frees Apple from providing an obsolete library (or having to rebuild the Xcode distribution every few weeks as documentation is revised).

> **Note**
>
> In earlier releases of Xcode, docsets were kept in an all-users library at
> /Library/Developer/Documentation/DocSets, and before that, inside the
> /Developer tree. Now, each user has a personal copy of the documentation.

So the first thing you're going to do when you install Xcode is to run it, need it or not. It will immediately compare its local document set with what's on Apple's servers, and it will commence a download of a gigabyte or more.

Documentation is provided in *documentation sets* (docsets), essentially large web sites plus the indexes that make Quick Help, the browsing outline, and full-text searching possible. Each docset is nearly self-contained, though it can have references out to the web.

The entries at the top level of the Documentation browser's Library navigator correspond to the current docsets. (Only the documentation for the current operating systems and developer tools is included, even if you still have older docsets installed.)

Docsets have to be downloaded and (on an irregular schedule) updated. Some, like current OSes and the developer tools, download automatically, but others, for older systems or "retired documents," are optional. You control the download process through the **Downloads** panel of the Preferences window (Figure 24.9).

Docsets (and additional development tools) are shown with checkmarks if they are present and up-to-date, and as download (circled-arrow) buttons plus estimated sizes if they are not. If you choose to download an item, its status is replaced by a progress bar showing how far the download has come.

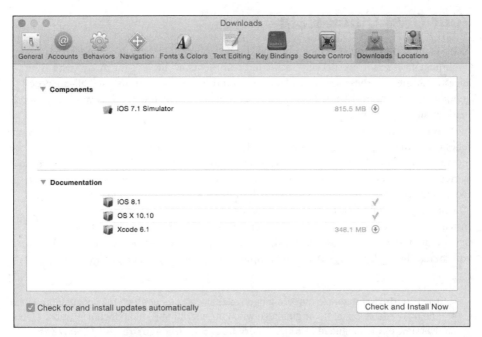

Figure 24.9   The **Downloads** panel of the Preferences window lists all of the documentation sets and other tools Xcode can install or update over the Net. Some are optional, shown with a circled down-arrow and their sizes.

By checking the **Check for and install updates automatically** box, you allow Xcode to download hundreds of megabytes of revised documentation at the most inconvenient moment possible—a consideration if your Internet connection is relatively slow. If you want better control over the process, there's a **Check and Install Now** button to start downloads on demand. (Remember to click this button whenever it's convenient; updates are rarely publicized.)

In previous versions of Xcode, the **Downloads** panel, or the documentation display itself, showed the location of the docset package, the version number, and other information. No longer. You needed the version number to report bugs, but the viewer now carries a floating **Provide Feedback** link, which includes the version in its report to Apple.

You still need to report the version if a docset won't load for you at all. You can find the version number by navigating to the docset in the Finder, right-clicking its icon to select **Show Package Contents**, and inspecting the `Info.plist` inside the **Contents** directory. You're looking for the `CFBundleVersion` key.

Your Own Quick Help

Xcode's documentation system is not closed. Development systems have generated documentation sets from specially formatted comments in the API for many years. The ancestor of most of these systems is JavaDoc, and the most commonly used all-purpose generator is Doxygen (`http://www.doxygen.org/`), which derives its vastly expanded markup language from that.

Xcode 5 introduced a way to add your own documentation to Quick Help. This system relies on a built-in parser for comments in the HeaderDoc format Apple has used since the introduction of OS X. The same markup can be used to feed third-party documentation aggregators, like Doxygen, to publish overall guides to your API and install them in the Documentation browser. This system is still in place for C-family languages in Xcode 6.

But not for Swift. Xcode does not recognize HeaderDoc comments in Swift source. Instead, it captures documentation comments written in a radical subset of reStructuredText (reST). Conversely, the C-family system does not recognize reST comments. There is no aggregator to compile stand-alone reference guides.

> **Note**
>
> reStructuredText is a simple markup language that can produce rich-text documents while still being readable as is. Its original use was for generating Python documentation. Find an overview of the language at `http://docutils.sourceforge.net/docs/user /rst/quickref.html`. The easiest way to play with reST is to install the `restview` package by way of the `pip` package manager for Python. (You'll have to install `pip` first, and remember to use `sudo`.)

That, at least, was the situation as of Xcode 6.2. To be fair, the only "documentation" for the feature has been one sentence in a release note and a casual conversation between a blogger and an Apple engineer. Even though the technique is good enough for purposes of Quick Help, Apple is not recommending it, nor claiming it is ready for use. That will surely be better by the time you read this.

> **Note**
>
> My "authoritative" source is the NSHipster blog at `http://nshipster.com/swift-documentation/`.

C-Family Documentation

This is one time I'll fall back on techniques for C-family code, if only to prepare you for the features you can hope for in the new reST-based system.

How to Generate Quick Help

If you know how to write documentation comments (you'll learn in the next section), getting Xcode to incorporate them in Quick Help is trivial: It just does it.

Here is the in-code declaration for `-[SimpleCSVFile run:error:]`, the only `SimpleCSVFile` method accessible to client code:

```
/**
Parse the CSV file.
Loops through the lines of the input file, interpreting the first line
as unique keys for the data fields contained in the remaining lines.

The keys and values for each line are gathered into an NSDictionary,
which is presented line-by-line through the supplied block.

It is an error for the file to have a line with a different number of
fields than specified in the header line.

@bug The parser does not handle quoted or escaped fields at all.

@param      block   A block the caller supplies to accept
                    record-by-record data from the receiver.
@param[out] error   A pointer to an `NSError` object pointer, or nil.
                    If non-nil, and an error occurs (signified by a
                    return value of `NO`), `*error` will describe the
                    problem.
@return     `YES` if parsing succeeded.
@return     `NO` if it did not. If an `NSError**` parameter
            was supplied, `*error` will describe the problem.
*/
- (BOOL) run: (SimpleCSVRecordBlock) block
       error: (NSError **) error;
```

The comment begins with /** to signal that this is for documentation, followed by a
one-sentence summary that will show up in high-level indexes of the API. Then comes a
lengthier description, and specially marked-up annotations of -[SimpleCSVFile
run:error:]'s parameters and return value.

You don't have to do anything else. Option-click any occurrence of -[SimpleCSV-
File run:error:], and you'll get a popover containing the same formatted Quick
Help as you'd get for any symbol in an Apple SDK; simply clicking on a symbol fills the
QuickHelp inspector (Figure 24.10).

The **Build Settings** tab in the Target editor includes a setting for "Documentation
Comments" warnings. When the switch is on, clang will give you a running assessment
of the validity of your comments, such as whether the parameter names you specify
correspond to the names in the declaration.

Documentation Comment Syntax

Xcode's help parser recognizes a concise set of markup symbols to give meaning to parts of
the comment—such as for parameters, return types, and special notes. The markup
keywords are prefixed with either @ or \.

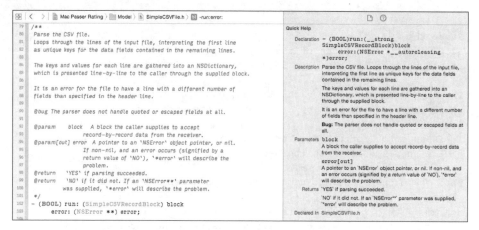

Figure 24.10 Click any symbol that has a documentation comment where it is declared, and you will see a popover with the formatted documentation. Xcode does not interpret style markup in the documentation. Compare to the documentation recovered from the reStructuredText comments attached to the same method in Swift in Figure 24.14.

- @param—The first word is the parameter name; everything thereafter is a description. There can be more than one @param directive. If you follow the @param with [in], [out], or [inout], the rendered documentation will annotate it as being input-only, output-only (as it would be for pointers to NSError*), or both.

- @return—Describes the return value of a function/method.

- @exception—The first word is the name of an exception a function/method could raise; the rest is a description. There can be more than one @exception. *Doxygen only.*

- @bug—Commentary on a bug in the API.

- @todo—Commentary on work yet to be done for the API.

- @warning—Text that will be presented with a red bar in the margin.

- @deprecated—Flags and indexes an API as deprecated, with your notation.

- @see—An external URL or an internal symbol that Doxygen will link to.

- @author—The name, URL, or email address of the author of the annotated code. If you provide an email address, remember to escape the @ with a \.

- @c, @p—One word of "code" or "parameter" text that will be set in a monofont. Stretches of more than one word should be set out in the corresponding HTML markup.

- @em, @e, @i—One word to be set in italics.

- @b—One word to be set in boldface.

The character-style tokens are awkward to write and read. Doxygen supports Markdown style markup, so code symbols could be rendered as `` `symbol` `` and not `@c symbol`. Further, Markdown tokens can apply to phrases, not single words. When not using Markdown, Doxygen accepts HTML markup for phrases; Xcode ignores HTML.

Xcode doesn't interpret Markdown for Quick Help, so you have to choose between a faithful rendering and an annotation that's easier to read and write in the source, and not too bad in the rendered text, versus having Quick Help render your notes as you intend. For my part, I prefer to use Markdown.

Doxygen

Doxygen (`http://www.doxygen.org/`) is a much more powerful system. It has an enormous repertoire of tags to generate detailed help systems, with clickable dependency and inheritance diagrams, indexes, and search. It can target languages as diverse as Objective-C, Java, and FORTRAN (but not yet Swift). It can generate HTML, LATEX, Docbook, Xcode docsets, and many more. The variety of tags and configuration options can be confusing, but once you've settled on the subset you'll use, you don't need to think of anything more than writing your docs. The results are worth the effort; see Figure 24.11.

This book can't cover all the variants of markup and options Doxygen affords. If you need to know more, browse the manual at `http://www.doxygen.org/`, or download the PDF of the current edition.

Preparation

Getting a basic installation of Doxygen is simple: Go to the web site, select **Downloads →Sources & Binaries**, and find the `.dmg` containing the latest version. Download it, mount the disk image, and drag the Doxygen app into the `/Applications` directory.

I recommend you install the GraphViz package of command-line graphics tools, so Doxygen can generate class and dependency diagrams. The Homebrew package manager makes this very easy:

- Install Homebrew if you haven't already. Go to `http://brew.sh`, copy the `ruby` command on that page, and paste it into the Terminal. The documentation there will help you with troubleshooting—if you've installed anything in `/usr/local` on your own, `brew` may ask you to think twice about what you've already installed. You should not need to use the `sudo` command; if a permissions-related error occurs, go back to the Homebrew site and look for troubleshooting advice.

- Enter `brew update` to ensure you have all the current "recipes" for downloading and building packages.

- Enter `brew install graphviz`. The Graphviz tools will be installed in `/usr/local/Cellar/graphviz/version/bin/`. Enter `ls /usr/local/Cellar/graphviz` to discover the actual version number.

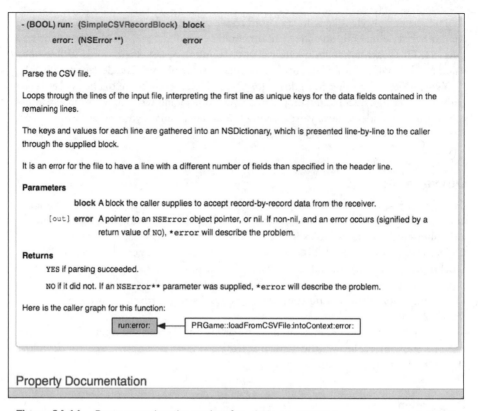

Figure 24.11   Doxygen renders the markup for - [`SimpleCSVFile run:error:`] shown earlier in this chapter into cross-referenced and indexed HTML.

Configuring Doxygen: Basic Settings

doxygen proper is a command-line tool that processes your source code under the direction of a configuration file. The Doxygen app for OS X is mostly an editor for the configuration. Double-click Doxygen to run it.

> **Warning**
>
> Three years after the introduction of Gatekeeper, the security provision that by default refuses to launch applications that had not been signed by Mac Developer Program members, Doxygen isn't signed. If you are using Gatekeeper (you should), Finder will block you. To get around this, right-click on the Doxygen application icon, select **Open**, and click **Open** in the warning alert that ensues.

What you'll see is a "wizard" window with a list of views at the left, and a form at the right. See Figure 24.12.

doxygen being a Unix command-line tool, it needs a working directory. The first thing you'll do is set it, using the affordance at the top of the window. There's a text field

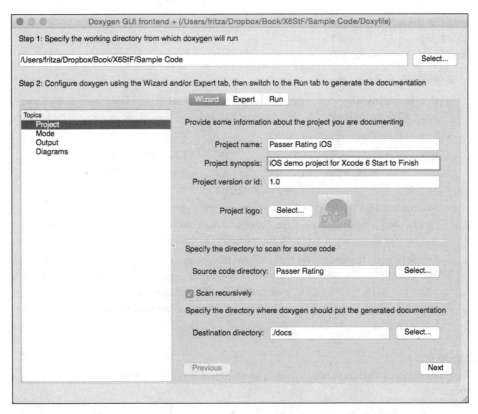

Figure 24.12   The `doxygen` command-line tool is wrapped in a graphical "wizard" for editing the configuration file for your project.

there to enter the path directly, but use the **Select...** button to pick the `Passer Rating` project directory—that's the directory that contains the project file, not the one that contains the source.

Now it's time to fill out the configuration. You do this in two stages; the **Wizard** tab presents a simplified English-language interface that you can use for most of the setup. Then you round it out in the **Expert** tab, which is just a structured editor for the configuration file.

> **Warning**
>
> Doxygen (for the moment) works with a remarkable number of languages, but (for the moment) Swift is not among them. These steps are for the Objective-C version of the iOS Passer Rating as it existed in *Xcode 5 Start to Finish*.

Project Panel

The **Project** panel points Doxygen at its source and destination directories and accepts project-wide settings like the title and logo.

- **Project name**—`Passer Rating iOS`
- **Project synopsis**—Something brief to explain what Passer Rating is: `iOS demo project for Xcode 6 Start to Finish`
- **Project version or id**—`1.0`
- If you supply a logo image, bear in mind that it will be rendered full-size on every page of the documentation. If the image is huge, the page headers will be huge. I used the 60 × 60 icon for Passer Rating.
- **Source code directory**—Doxygen works by going through your source files, parsing and indexing them. Use **Select...** to choose the source directory within the project directory. Check **Scan recursively** to search subdirectories as well.
- **Destination directory**—This is where the generated documentation goes. *Do not* put it in the source directory; the version-control implications could be nightmarish. Click the **Select...** button, and in the select-file dialog, select the project directory, and click **New Folder**. Enter a name like **docs**. Select that new directory and click **Choose**.

Mode Panel

The **Mode** panel determines, at a rough level, how Doxygen is to interpret your source files.

- For the desired extraction mode, pick **All Entities**. Doxygen will generate documentation for all methods, constants, functions, etc., even if you haven't yet put documentation comments on them. In a production project, you might want to filter out things you've decided not to document, but for this demo, it will be fun to see what Doxygen can turn up.
- You are also asked to "optimize" for the language the project is written in. Objective-C is not on offer, but this is a radio group, so you have to pick one. Leave this option alone; you'll take care of it in the **Expert** tab.

Output Panel

Doxygen can produce documents in any or all of five different formats. Check only **HTML, with navigation panel**, and **With search function**. The **Change color...** button gives you hue, saturation, and value sliders to dress up the emitted pages; suit yourself.

Diagrams Panel

Select **Use dot tool from the GraphViz package**, and have fun: Check all of the available graph types.

Expert Settings

If you want, you can go to the **Run** tab, run Doxygen, and have it show you the results (but you haven't told it where to find GraphViz yet, so go back to the **Diagrams** panel and choose some other option). But you can get better results if you use the **Expert** tab.

To serve a multitude of needs and tastes, Doxygen has a multitude of options. They are all documented in the manual you can download from the web site. They are all in the **Expert** tab. You will need to touch very few, but it's not going to be easy: The expert settings fall into 17 panels, some of them very long. The options have been put into some order of related elements, but it's not always easy to see what that order is. You will have to pick through the items to track down the ones you need.

The **Expert** tab labels each setting with the name it has in the key-value pairs in the configuration file. If you hover your mouse over a name, an explanation will appear in the text area at the bottom left. Each setting has an editor appropriate to its data type. Settings labeled in black haven't changed from their defaults; if you change one, it will be labeled in red.

Project Panel

Check JAVADOC_AUTOBRIEF (just above halfway through the list) to emulate JavaDoc's feature in which the first sentence of a documentation block is harvested as a short description in summary tables. Otherwise, you'd have to call out brief descriptions with @brief.

In the **Mode** panel of the **Wizard** tab, you were forced to "optimize" the output to present the API for a particular language, none of them Objective-C. You get to undo this by locating all the OPTIMIZE_OUTPUT_FOR_ ... items near the bottom of the list, and unchecking them.

Doxygen infers the language of a source file from its extension, so when it parses your .m files, it will recognize them as Objective-C. .h files remain ambiguous, which is the right thing for many projects. Relieve the ambiguity by adding a line to the EXTENSION_MAPPING table that follows the optimization checkboxes: Enter **h=Objective-C** in the text field, and click the **+** button.

HTML Panel

The HTML panel controls the formatting of the HTML Doxygen produces. This is where you set up Doxygen to index your documentation as an Xcode docset. The settings come about a third of the way down the list.

- GENERATE_DOCSET is the master setting. Check it.
- DOCSET_FEEDNAME sets a name for a grouping of documentation sets. The set you're building now is for the iOS Passer Rating app, but it might be part of a suite of docsets for *Xcode 6 Start to Finish*. Set it to **Xcode 6 Start to Finish**.
- DOCSET_BUNDLE_ID is a unique identifier for this set; it sets the bundle identifier in the docset's Info.plist. I used **com.wt9t.x6stf.docs.ios**.

- DOCSET_PUBLISHER_ID, by contrast, uniquely identifies you as the source of this and other docsets. I used **com.wt9t.x6stf.docs**.

- DOCSET_PUBLISHER_NAME is your name as presented to humans. I'm **Fritz Anderson**.

Dot Panel

Set DOT_PATH to the same **/usr/local/Cellar/graphviz/version/bin** path you collected when you had Homebrew install GraphViz.

> **Warning**
>
> If you still have a legacy GraphViz and Doxygen setup, you'll find that dot will want to draw on tools from the X11 package. Because Doxygen will run dot once or twice for every @interface and file in your project, it will spawn dozens of instances of the X11 app. Because you likely don't have the X11 infrastructure installed on your Mac, each instance will wait for you to authorize it to install the X11 libraries. This is undesirable. The tools from the current GraphViz won't do this, so be sure to enter the bin/ from your latest installation.

Running Doxygen

You've been creating a reusable configuration file, and you should save it. Select **File → Save** (⌘ S). The default name for the file is Doxyfile, and there's no reason to change it. I recommend placing it in the proposed working directory, which is the directory that contains Passer Rating.xcodeproj.

At last you are ready to produce some documents. Select the **Run** tab and click **Run doxygen**. The text area fills with the run log, which is intimidatingly long. If you elected dot as the graphics generator, and a lot of graph types, some of the dot processing may take a while.

The doxygen tool will not halt with formatting errors, nor even call them out conspicuously. Be sure at least to skim the log for error messages. The first run may take a couple of minutes, but doxygen has the grace not to regenerate graphs for structures that have not changed.

When processing is done, click **Show HTML output**. Your preferred web browser will open the root page of the generated documentation (which will be index.html in the html subdirectory of your designated documentation folder).

This will be the designated "main," or overview, page, and if you don't specify one, it will be blank but for a navigation bar at the top. Clicking in the bar shows you more: indexes of classes and their members; files and their contents; to-dos and bugs. If you asked Doxygen for a client-side search interface, every page will include a search field that will do an incremental search of the docset.

Installing a Docset

When you set `GENERATE_DOCSET`, Doxygen adds a `Makefile` that will direct `make` to install the docset into `~/Library/Developer/Shared/Documentation/DocSets`, where Xcode can find it. In Terminal, set the working directory to the generated HTML directory, and run `make`:

```
$ # Assuming you're in the project directory:
$ cd docs/html
$ make install
    ...
Output from make
    ...
$
```

Quit and reopen Xcode, and open the Documentation browser. Your docset should show up in the Library navigator's outline. The outline will trace through all the indexes in the set. Click on one, and the browser will display the corresponding page. The table of contents sidebar will *almost* work—it will fill in as you'd hope when you arrive at a class reference page, but clicking an item clears the table out after taking you to your selection. See Figure 24.13.

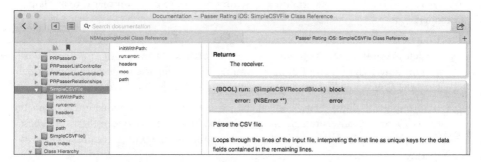

Figure 24.13   A makefile in the `http` directory Doxygen produces installs your documentation for use by the Xcode Documentation browser.

> **Note**
>
> Doxygen has the annoyance that its terminology and formatting aren't tailored to Objective-C; it's hard to minimize its C++ conventions. There are other options, and they have the advantage of matching the style of Apple's own docs. Apple's HeaderDoc is supplied with the Xcode tools—look for `HeaderDoc` in the Documentation browser. It is simple to generate a suite of HTML documentation—all that's involved are a couple of command-line tools and customizing some template files. However, things rapidly become difficult when you try to generate a docset; you're left to hand-code some of the indexes. Search the tools documentation for `HeaderDoc` for more information. appledoc, `http://gentlebytes.com/appledoc/`, is an open-source generator that will produce docsets. It's not as mature as Doxygen, and while appledoc's narrower focus makes the configuration system less complex conceptually, the lack of a graphical editor hurts it.

Swift and reStructuredText

The story on user-generated documentation from Swift code is brief: As I write this—I expect it to change very quickly—Xcode's documentation system for Swift has no other purpose than to provide content for Quick Help. It does this fairly well, with a little room for growth, but there is no support for generating aggregated reference documents such as you would get from Doxygen or HeaderDoc.

> **Note**
>
> To be fair, this is no different from Apple's policy before Swift: Xcode itself has never taken responsibility for generating reference documents. (HeaderDoc is maintained, but it's a legacy from the days when NeXT was on its own for generating documentation.) The problem is not that Apple doesn't provide a documentation aggregator; it's that so far, nobody does.

Documentation comments for Swift are written in the reStructuredText markup language. They are set out with either a double-asterisk comment block (/** ... */) or line-by-line triple-slashes (///)

reStructuredText has a rich grammar for laying out text and applying styles and cross-references, but the Xcode grammar provides only the minimum that Quick Help can render:

- Body text, obviously. No style markup, URLs are plain text. Paragraphs must start at the left margin of the source text (see below for what "left margin" means), unless you mean to indent them. I don't recommend indenting them, because you'll usually keep the Quick Look inspector narrow enough to make indented text awkward.

- Itemized lists (bullets). Start a line at the left margin with an eligible bullet character such as * or -. Consecutive items do not need blank lines between them. A sublist should have a space before its items, but keep the limited width in mind and be sparing.

- Enumerated lists. Begin the item with a number or letter followed by a period (other delimiters are accepted). Changing the enumeration or bulleting style is supposed to have the effect of introducing a sublist, but that hasn't made it into the 6.2 interpreter. Regardless of the value of an enumerator, the items will be numbered consecutively. ("1. . . . 4." will show as "1. . . . 2.")

- Field lists. Begin the paragraph with a keyword bracketed by colons (e.g., `:returns:`), and the text will be formatted into a section of the help. Only two tags receive special treatment:

  - **`:param:`** indicates a parameter for a `func`. Use one for each parameter. The first word after the directive will be set in a monospaced font, and the following text will appear on the next line. All `:param:`s are consolidated into a single "Parameters" section.

  - **`:returns:`** indicates the return value of a `func`. There is no special treatment for any part of the text. You can have more than one, which is useful because you often want to call out special return values, as with

    Returns the index of the item in the Array
         nil of no item is found

    Multiple `:returns:` clauses are consolidated into a single "Returns" section.

Other field lists are recognized, but are not given the special treatment of getting their own sections in the Quick Help display. Writing

`:bug: The parser does not handle quoted field values.`

will place a labeled-and-indented paragraph in the body of the description. See Figure 24.14.

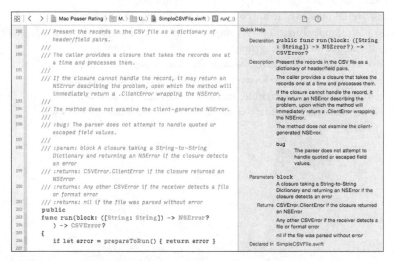

Figure 24.14 reStructuredText comments will attach Quick Help documentation for the Swift definition that follows that is about as good as that for HeaderDoc comments in Objective-C. This is the same `SimpleCSVFile` method as shown in Figure 24.10.

Quick Help's idea of the "left margin" of a document comment will leave half your documentation indented apparently at random, but makes sense once you catch on to the principle. The least-indented line of the comment block defines the "left margin." /// comments are easiest: If all text appears *two* (or one, or three...) spaces after the last slash on the line, the help text is rendered as flush-left. If any of the text appears one space more after the last slash, it will be indented; if one space less, it defines the left margin and everything else is indented.

The left margin in a block comment is counted from the beginning of each line. The least-indented comment line becomes the least-indented paragraph in the help text. If you have text on the same line as the /**, the space between it and the second asterisk counts as its margin.

More words won't help; experiment on your own.

Rich-text markup, as for italic or monospaced text, is passed through Quick Help as is. So are section titles, tables, images... if it's not on this list, it isn't there. This is no different from how C-family comments are treated.

Summary

This chapter took you on an in-depth tour of Xcode's documentation system. You saw how to use Quick Help to get on-the-spot guidance on APIs, Interface Builder objects, and build settings, and how to quickly access the declarations of methods and other symbols in your code.

I showed you the Documentation browser and how to navigate it and search for articles. You learned how to manage and update your document sets.

You discovered how easy it is to generate Quick Help for your own code: Add some comments with standard markup to your declarations, and you're done. `clang` will even warn you if you get the syntax wrong.

Finally, I introduced Doxygen, a system for generating thorough, indexed, and searchable documentation sets. Doxygen should be able to produce and install documentation sets you can examine in Xcode's Documentation browser, and I showed you how it *ought* to work. Unfortunately, it doesn't work with Xcode 6 yet.

25

The Xcode Build System

If you're used to building software with Unix tools like `make`, odds are you don't quite trust IDEs like Xcode. In a makefile, you can directly set compiler options, even file by file. You can designate build dependencies, so a change to a header file will force recompilations of the implementation files that depend on it—`clang` even has a mode that generates the dependency trees.

At first glance, Xcode doesn't give you that control. It's "magic," and while you're proud to make magic for your users, you don't trust it for yourself.

This chapter aims to take some of the magic out of the Xcode build system. Even if you aren't a veteran of `make`-based projects, you'll gain a better understanding of what Xcode does for you and how you can control it.

How Xcode Structures a Build

A makefile is organized around a hierarchy of goals. Some goals, such as the frequently used `clean` or `install` targets, are abstract, but most are files. Associated with each goal is a list of other goals that are antecedents—dependencies—of that goal and a script for turning the antecedents into something that satisfies the goal. Most commonly, the antecedents are input files for the programs that the script runs to produce a target file. The genius of `make` comes from the rule that if any target is more recently modified than all of its antecedents, it is presumed to embody their current state, and it is not necessary to run the script to produce it again. The combination of a tree of dependencies and this pruning rule make `make` a powerful and efficient tool for automating such tasks as building software products.

The organizing unit of a makefile is the target-dependency-action group. But in the case of application development, this group is often stereotyped to the extent that you don't even have to specify it; `make` provides a default rule that looks like this:

```
%.o    :   %.c
    $(CC) -c $(CPPFLAGS) $(CFLAGS) -o $@ $<
```

So all the programmer need do is list all the constituent .o files in the project, and the built-in rule will produce the .o files as needed. Often, the task of maintaining a makefile becomes less one of maintaining dependencies than one of keeping lists.

In the same way, Xcode makes dependency analysis a matter of list-keeping by taking advantage of the fact that projects are targeted at specific kinds of executable products, such as applications, libraries, tools, or plugins. Knowing how the build process ends, Xcode can do the right thing with the files that go into the project.

A file in an Xcode workspace belongs to three distinct lists.

Projects. A file appears once in the Project navigator for each project it belongs to. This has nothing to do with whether it has any effect on any product of a project. It might, for instance, be a document you're keeping handy for reference, or some notes you're taking. If you're working with a workspace, a file might be in the workspace without being in any project; the easiest way to do this is to make sure no project is selected (command-click to undo any selections) and select **File → Add Files to. . .** (⌥ ⌘ A).

> **Note**
>
> To be more precise, there are no files "in" a project or workspace. Projects and workspaces keep *references* to files. Xcode makes tracking files and building easier if a project's inputs are in a tree descending from the directory that holds the project file; but if the files are *in* anything, they're in the tree. The project just knows where they are.

Targets. A file may belong to zero or more *targets* in a project. A file is included in a target's file list because it is a part of that target's product, whether as a source file or as a resource to be copied literally into the product. When a file is added to a project, Xcode asks you which targets in the project should include the file. You can also add files to a target through the checkboxes in the File inspector, or by dragging them into a build phase in the Target editor.

A target is identified with the set of files that compose it. There is no concept of including or excluding files from a single target on the basis of its being built with a Release or Debug configuration. If you need disjoint sets of files, make a separate target for each set; a file can belong to more than one target, and you can set preprocessor macros per-target. This does mean that the two targets have to coordinate their settings; .xcconfig files, introduced later this chapter, make that very easy.

Build Phases. What role a file plays in a target depends on what *phase* of the target the file belongs to. When a file is added to a target, Xcode assigns it to a build phase based on the type of the file: Files with clang or Swift-compilable suffixes get assigned to the Compile Sources phase; libraries, to the Link Binary With Libraries phase, and most others to the Copy Bundle Resources phase. (See Figure 25.1.)

Build phases are executed in the order in which they appear in the Target editor. You'd almost always want the Compile Sources phase to complete before Link Binary With Libraries phase—that's the way they come—but you *can* drag them into any order you like.

When you create a target, either in the process of creating an Xcode project or by adding a target to an existing project, you specify the kind of product you want to produce, and you can't change it except by making another target. The target type forms

Figure 25.1   Build phases in a modest project. You gain access to build phases by selecting a project item in the Project navigator, clicking on a target, and then the **Build Phases** tab in the Target editor. The phases are represented by tables that can be expanded to reveal the files that belong to them. One of the ways to add a file to a phase is to drag it into the phase's table.

one anchor—the endpoint—in the Xcode build system's dependency analysis: It tells the build system what the product's desired structure (single file or package) is and how to link the executable.

The other anchor of the build system is the set of build-phase members for the target. The Compile Sources build phase, along with the sources you add to it, yield object files, which are the inputs to the linkage phase implicit in your choice of target type. The various file-copying phases and the files you supply for them yield the copy commands needed to populate the auxiliary structure of an application.

What a makefile developer does with explicit dependencies and the default rules, Xcode does by inference: It determines how new files are to be processed into a product, and how that processing is to be done. Even if you use the product of one target to build another, Xcode will detect the dependency and incorporate the build of the dependent target into the process for the composite target. All Xcode needs is for the two targets to be within the same workspace—they don't even have to be in the same project.

Build Variables

The action for the default make rule for .c files parameterizes almost the entire action. The command for the C compiler and the set of flags to pass are left to the makefile variables CC, CPPFLAGS, and CFLAGS. You set these flags at the head of the file to suitable values, and all the compilations in your build comply.

Xcode relies similarly on variables to organize build options, but at a much finer granularity. There is one variable for each of the most common settings. For instance, the variable GCC_ENABLE_CPP_RTTI controls whether clang's -fno-rtti will be added to suppress generation of runtime type information in C++. This variable is set by a popup ("Enable C++ Runtime Types") in the **Build Settings** tab of the Target editor. See Figure 25.2.

Let's have a good look at the **Build Settings** tab. Select a project in the Project navigator to fill the Editor area with the Project/Target editor, then select a target. Click the **Build Settings** tab. Right under the tab bar, you'll see two pairs of buttons: **Basic/All**, and **Combined/Levels**. **Basic** narrows the list down to a handful of essential elements; I'll get to the distinction between the combined and by-level presentations shortly. For now, the most straightforward presentation is **All** and **Combined**.

The list you see is a front end for most of the build variables Xcode maintains for this target. If you have the Utility area (right-hand area in the **View** control) visible, and the Quick Help (second) inspector selected, you can see a description of any setting you select. In brackets, at the end of the description, are the name of the build variable the item controls and what compiler option, if any, it affects. Both the label and the description are searchable: The list in Figure 25.2 was narrowed down to two entries by typing rtti into the search field at the top of the list.

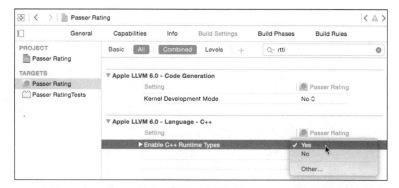

Figure 25.2   The list of settings in the **Build Settings** tab of the Target editor is extensive, but you can get it under control by typing something relevant to the setting in the search field. Typing `rtti` narrows the list down to a setting for C++ runtime type information, but also to a setting whose description merely refers to RTTI. The Quick Help inspector in the Utility area explains each setting, including the name of the associated build variable and the compiler flags it sets.

> **Note**
>
> It's common for closely crafted makefiles to customize the compiler flags for some of the source files. The Xcode build system allows for this. In the **Build Phase** tab, the table for the Compile Sources phase has a second column, "Compiler Flags." Double-click an entry in that column to get a popover editor for additional flags for that file. You won't get Quick Help for what you enter, but you can explore the **Build Settings** list to see what options are available. What you type will be *added* to the flags used in compiling the file—it's not possible to override the general settings, and it's not possible to make separate per-file settings for different configurations.

Settings Hierarchy

The "Combined" list of settings shown in the **Build Settings** tab is the authoritative list of what flags and directives will be applied in building the target. However, the Xcode build system provides richer control over those settings. What's in the combined list is a synthesis of settings that come from a hierarchy of up to six layers.

- BSD environment variables
- Xcode's own default values
- The current configuration set for the whole project
- The current configuration set for the current target
- Command-line arguments to the `xcodebuild` command-line tool, if you're using it
- Added per-file compiler options

Figure 25.3 illustrates how the hierarchy works.

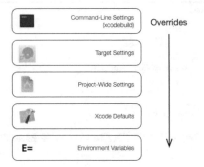

Figure 25.3   The hierarchy of build settings in Xcode and `xcodebuild`. A setting may be made at one or more of these layers, but the topmost setting in the hierarchy controls. Settings in higher layers may refer to settings from lower layers by the variable reference `$(inherited)`. The top layer, command-line settings, is present only in an `xcodebuild` invocation.

You'll deal most often with target and project settings; the others rarely arise. The project level allows you to set policies for every target in the project—things like the root SDK or warnings you always want to see—so a change in one place affects all. You can still exempt a product from the general policy by putting an alternate setting into its target: The target setting will override the project setting.

Levels

With this in mind, you can click the **Levels** button in the bar under the **Build Settings** tab (Figure 25.4). The Target editor now shows four columns for each setting, representing the default, project, and target values, and the net value that is actually effective for the target. You can edit only the middle two columns—target and project. The level that is responsible for the effective setting is highlighted in green.

> **Note**
>
> The same **Build Settings** tab is available in the Project editor, but without the target-level column.

Each level that sets (not just inherits) a value is shown in bold with a green background. The distinction between setting and inheritance is important: If, for instance, you set a string setting to empty at the target level, the effective setting will be an empty string, *not* the setting inherited from the project; if you change the project setting, the effective setting, through the target, will still be blank—watch for that green box. Likewise, setting a value to be the same as the value to the right isn't an acceptance of the inherited value; it's just an override that happens to repeat the inherited value.

If you want to remove an override from the hierarchy, select the line for that setting, and press the Delete key. The setting won't go away—it will just clear the value from the level (project or target) on which the editor is operating. You'll see the effect when you

Figure 25.4   With the **Levels** view selected, the Target editor shows how each level of the settings hierarchy contributes to the settings that will be used to build the target. The chain proceeds from right to left, starting with Xcode's default for the project type at the right, through the project and target levels, and to the net setting on the left. You can edit the settings at the project or target level. The place where the operative value for a setting is selected is highlighted in green.

see the current level's value lose its boldfacing, and the green box go down to the next-lower level. When you select a different row in the table, the cells that don't carry values will be blank.

Editing Build Variables

The **Build Settings** table is intelligent about what values you can put into it.

- Some values—such as the multiple flags you can put into the "Other C Flags" setting—are logically lists. Xcode lets you edit the items individually, in a table to which you can add and remove rows.

- Some settings, such as Booleans or code-signing identities, are constrained to the few values that make sense for them. The Value column shows a popup menu with the possible values.

- Any value can be edited free-form—if you click in the value and move the mouse pointer a little, you are in a text field.

- If you are editing a value at the target level and want to supplement, rather than replace, the inherited value, include $(inherited) where you want the original setting to appear.

The **Build Settings** table is filtered for your consumption. Underlying the descriptions in the Setting column are the names of variables Xcode uses to specify the build; and the Value column displays the settings as they *effectively* are, not as they *actually* are. You'll see this when editing the text of variables whose value depends on the content of other variables: The "Architectures" setting may look like "Standard" in the list, but if you edit it as text, you find it's $ (ARCHS_STANDARD).

> **Note**
>
> If you've done shell scripting, you're used to delimiting environment variable names in braces: ${VISUAL}. Strings in parentheses are replaced by the output of the commands they contain. This is *not so* when you use Xcode build variables. Use parentheses to refer to them: $(SDKROOT).

You can change the table to display the underlying variable names and values. The command **Show Setting Names** in the **Editor** menu will reveal the names of the build variables; **Show Definitions** shows the raw text of the settings.

Configurations

So far, I've treated build settings as the product of a simple hierarchy of defaults and overrides. But build settings can be varied on another axis: A target may have different settings based on your purpose in building it, such as debugging, release, or distribution. You encapsulate these settings in *build configurations*, which you can select for each action in your product's scheme.

When it generates a new project for you, Xcode provides two configurations, Debug and Release, which it sets up with reasonable values for those two purposes. In general, the Debug configuration generates more debugging information and turns off code optimization so your program will execute line by line in the debugger, as you'd expect. Both OS X and iOS run apps on two or more processor architectures, and the Debug configuration will save time by building the target for one architecture only.

Switching between configurations is easy: The **Info** tab for each action in the Scheme editor includes a **Build Configuration** popup that lets you choose the configuration you use for that action. You can make the switch and take an action in one step by holding down the Option key while invoking the action; the Scheme editor sheet will drop down, and you can make your changes before proceeding.

If your target depends on other targets, even in other projects, those other targets will be built with the configuration you set at build time, so long as they have a configuration of the same name; otherwise they will be built in their default configurations.

Adjusting Configurations

The point of a build configuration is to have alternate settings for each purpose. This is where you get into conditional settings. As you've browsed the **Build Settings** tab, you've noticed that some settings have disclosure triangles next to them (Figure 25.5), and their values are tagged with a grayed-out "<Multiple values>." These settings have different values depending on which configuration is being used. Click the triangle, and the row opens to show subrows for each available configuration. You can make your choices there.

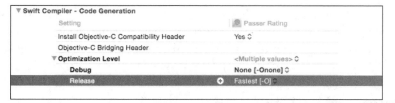

▼ Swift Compiler - Code Generation	
Setting	📷 Passer Rating
Install Objective-C Compatibility Header	Yes ⌄
Objective-C Bridging Header	
▼ Optimization Level	<Multiple values> ⌄
Debug	None [-Onone] ⌄
Release	⊕ Fastest [-O] ⌄

Figure 25.5 When a setting has different values for different configurations, its value is displayed as "<Multiple values>," and Xcode displays a disclosure triangle for the row. Opening the triangle shows the configurations and their values.

If you hover the mouse pointer over a row for which there are no per-configuration settings, a temporary disclosure triangle appears. Opening that row will again show the values (identical until you change them) assigned to the setting for each configuration.

Figure 25.6 ties it all together: It shows how settings can percolate up from the defaults, through the project and target settings, and finally to the values that will direct and condition the build process. You can add configurations of your own, if you need to. The **Info** tab of the Project editor includes the list of all the configurations available to the project. You start out with Debug and Release. To create your new configuration, click

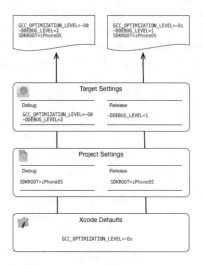

Figure 25.6 A complete example of the inheritance of build settings. By default, Xcode sets all compilations to optimize for size (bottom); that setting survives into Release builds, but for the Debug configuration, the target turns optimization off. The project sets the base SDK for all builds to iPhoneOS, meaning whatever iOS SDK is current (middle). The developer defines a DEBUG_LEVEL macro to different values depending on the configuration (top). The result is a set of build settings tailored to debugging (top left) and release (top right).

the **+** button; this will pop up a menu offering to duplicate one of the existing configurations—it doesn't make sense to offer a new, empty configuration, because the new configuration has to include *some* settings. Make your selection, enter a name, and you're done.

Configuration Files

Configurations, too, come with disclosure triangles. Open one, and you'll see a list of the targets the project contains. This lets you select a configuration file that adjusts the settings for each target.

What's a configuration file? Here's the rationale: Say you have several projects. Perhaps you have policies for settings you must have for all of them, and the defaults supplied by Xcode aren't appropriate for you. If you just use the Project/Target editor, you will have to make those settings by hand for each configuration in each project. If your requirements vary by target type, it gets that much worse.

Configuration (.xcconfig) files are the solution. These are text files that contain key-value pairs for any settings you want to enforce.

Creating a Configuration File

You start on an xcconfig file by selecting **File → New → File...** (⌘ N), and finding "Configuration Settings File" in the **Other** category (OS X or iOS, it doesn't matter) of the New File assistant. The assistant will then put you through the routine of naming and placing the file and assigning it to a project. It will offer to make the new file part of a target. You don't want your configuration file copied into your products, so make sure none of the targets are selected.

> **Note**
>
> An xcconfig file has to be included in a project—not a target—before the project can find and use it.

When you've done that, you find you have a text file that's empty but for a comment block with your name, copyright, and date at the top. What to do now? You can get one step closer from the command line: If you give the xcodebuild command the target, architecture, and configuration you're interested in, along with the -showBuild-Settings option, it will print all the environment variables that would prevail in the course of a build:

```
$ xcodebuild -showBuildSettings -configuration Release
Build settings for action build and target "Mac Passer Rating":
    ACTION = build
    ALTERNATE_GROUP = staff
    ALTERNATE_MODE = u+w,go-w,a+rX
    ALTERNATE_OWNER = fritza
    ALWAYS_SEARCH_USER_PATHS = NO
    ALWAYS_USE_SEPARATE_HEADERMAPS = YES
```

```
APPLE_INTERNAL_DEVELOPER_DIR = /AppleInternal/Developer
APPLE_INTERNAL_DIR = /AppleInternal
...
```

But there's a problem: Not every build setting carries through into the build-process environment. Xcode consumes GCC_ENABLE_CPP_RTTI, for instance, when it constructs the clang build commands it will issue. The symbol never makes it out of the build system to be visible in this list. Still, it's a start. Remember that you don't have to put every setting into a configuration file—in principle there is no defined, limited set of them—and if you intend to have different settings by SDK or architecture, you'll have to get xcodebuild to generate each settings list separately, and merge them as shown in the next section.

Once that is done, you can return to the Project editor's **Info** tab and use the popups in the "Based on Configuration File" column to select the xcconfig file.

SDK- and Architecture-Specific Settings

Cocoa development often involves targeting different SDKs and processor architectures with different binaries. You may have ARMv7 assembly in your iOS app that isn't runnable on ARMv6 devices or the simulator. You may want to use the OS X 10.6 SDK for 32-bit builds, but 10.7 for 64 bits. The xcconfig format allows for these. For instance, the file may contain

```
(1) GCC_VERSION = com.apple.compilers.llvm.clang.1_0
(2) GCC_VERSION[sdk=iphonesimulator4.3][arch=*] =
                        com.apple.compilers.llvmgcc42
(3) GCC_VERSION[sdk=iphoneos4.3][arch=armv6] = 4.2
```

1. Use clang for any builds, unless a condition overrides it.
2. If the build uses the iOS Simulator 4.3 SDK, use the gcc-fronted llvm compiler. (I broke the line for space; it should be all on one line.)
3. If the build is for iOS 4.3 on a device *and* for the ARMv6 architecture, use gcc 4.2. (This insane configuration—Xcode doesn't even come with gcc or llvmgcc, and gcc was terrible at generating ARM code—is only an example.)

The matching to SDK and architecture is done by glob expression, which means that if you have to express a range of matches, like "any iOS 8," you can match on iphoneos8*, as an override to an unconditional setting for other OSes.

> **Note**
>
> The graphical editor also allows you to set conditions. When you hover the mouse pointer over a configuration in a setting, a small **+** button appears; clicking it will add a condition row inside the configuration. The title of that row is a drop-down menu, in which you can select from the available conditions. See Figure 25.7. Because Xcode arranges conditional settings *within* configurations, you'll have to duplicate conditions for each configuration.

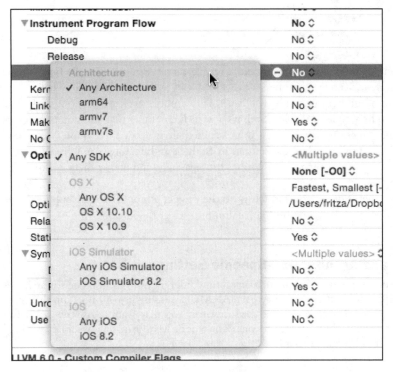

Figure 25.7   The **+** button next to the per-configuration label of a build setting lets you select a combination of architecture, OS, and platform to which a new conditional setting will apply.

Preprocessing `xcconfig` Files

As with C-family source files, you can insert the contents of one `xcconfig` file into another with an `#include` directive. That way, you can have a base configuration file containing settings common to all your targets and build configurations, and `#include` that in files that are specific to each of them.

This enables an interesting trick. Consider the following configuration file (call it `common.xcconfig`):

```
MY_LIBS_FOR_DEBUG = -lmystuff_debug
MY_LIBS_FOR_RELEASE = -lmystuff
OTHER_LDFLAGS = $(MY_LIBS_FOR_$(WHICH_LIB))
```

There may be a `Debugging.xcconfig` file that sets:

```
WHICH_LIB = DEBUG
#include "common.xcconfig"
```

... and a `Release.xcconfig` file that contains:

```
WHICH_LIB = RELEASE
#include "common.xcconfig"
```

The effect is that `OTHER_LDFLAGS` will be set to the value of `-lMY_LIBS_FOR_DEBUG` from `Debug.xcconfig`, and `-lMY_LIBS_FOR_RELEASE` from `Release.xcconfig`. In this simple case, it would have been easier just to set `OTHER_LDFLAGS` yourself, but quite sophisticated conditional configurations can be built up this way.

There are no header search paths for `xcconfig` files. If you `#include` a file, it has to be in the same directory.

Command-Line Tools

Sometimes there is no substitute for a command-line tool. The Unix command line presents a well-understood interface for scripting and controlling complex tools. Apple has provided a command-line interface to the Xcode build system and toolsets through three main commands: `xcodebuild`, `xcrun`, and `xcode-select`.

xcodebuild

Using `xcodebuild` is simple: Set the working directory to the directory containing an `.xcodeproj` project package, and invoke `xcodebuild`, specifying the project, target, configuration, and any build settings you wish to set. If only one `.xcodeproj` package is in the directory, all of these options can be defaulted by simply entering

```
$ xcodebuild
```

That command will build the first target in the current configuration of the only `.xcodeproj` package in the working directory. Apple's intention is that `xcodebuild` have the same role in a nightly build or routine-release script that `make` would have.

In building a target, specify one of seven actions for `xcodebuild`:

- **build**, the default, to build the specified target out of `SRCROOT` into `SYMROOT`. This is the same as the **Build** (for debugging) command in the Xcode application.

- **test** runs the test suite for the selected scheme. You can specify a destination to select an attached device or a simulator configuration.

- **analyze** has the same effect as selecting **Product → Analyze**. You should specify a target, and you must specify a scheme.

- **archive**, to do the equivalent of the **Product → Archive** command in Xcode. You must specify the workspace and scheme for the build.

- **clean**, to remove the product and any intermediate files from `SYMROOT`. This is the same as the **Clean** command in the Xcode application.

- **install**, to build the specified target and install it at `INSTALL_DIR` (usually `DSTROOT`). The Installation Preprocessing build variable is set. There is no direct equivalent to this action in Xcode because there is no way to elevate Xcode's privileges for setting ownership, permissions, and destination directory.

- **installsrc**, to copy the project directory to SRCROOT. In Project Builder, Xcode's ancestor, this action restricted itself to the project file package and the source files listed in it, but it now seems to do nothing a Finder copy or command-line `cp` wouldn't do.

> **Note**
>
> Settings like SRCROOT can be set for a run of xcodebuild by including assignment pairs (SETTING=value) among the parameters.

If more than one project or workspace package is in the current directory, you must specify which you are interested in, with the respective -project or -workspace option, followed by the name of the package. Not specifying a target is the same as if you had passed the name of the first target to the -target option; you can also specify -alltargets.

xcodebuild uses the configuration you specify in the Scheme editor panel for the build action, unless you pass a -configuration flag in the command. For the commands that require a scheme, you must name it with the -scheme option; setting a scheme is a good idea anyway.

As in the scheme selector in the toolbar of a project window, you may specify a -destination, such as a simulator configuration, operating system, attached device, architecture, or platform, all provided as key-value pairs. Find the details by typing **man xcodebuild** at a command line.

See man xcodebuild for full details.

xcode-select

It is perfectly legal to have more than one copy of Xcode on your computer. This most commonly happens shortly after WWDC in June of every year: Apple announces new versions of its operating systems, and seeds them to developers along with a prerelease version of Xcode that comes with the not-yet-final SDKs for those systems. In the meantime, those developers still need to develop and maintain their apps for systems in current release. They need both the current-release Xcode and the seeding version.

> **Warning**
>
> If you need to do this, *do not* accept updates from the Mac App Store; they will remove all previous versions of Xcode. See the "Downloading Xcode" section of Chapter 1, "Getting Xcode," for details.

Each version of Xcode comes with its own set of tools and SDKs—that's why you're interested in having two. If you're invoking xcodebuild or a tool like clang from the command line, how can you be sure you're getting the right one? For command-line tools, it is not enough to trust in the version in /usr/bin: The tools in that directory are not the tools themselves. If you inspect them, you'll see that no matter how massive they ought to be, they are all about 14 KB in size. That's because they are trampoline apps that refer to the "real" ones in the Xcode bundle (or the command-line tools download directory if you downloaded them without Xcode). So you have to make those trampolines bounce to the versions you want.

You can do this with xcode-select. At its simplest,

```
$ sudo xcode-select --print-path
```

will tell you which Xcode is current, and

```
$ sudo xcode-select --switch /Applications/Xcode-6.2.app
```

will make a particular version of Xcode (6.2, in this case) current. xcode-select keeps track of the Developer directory in the Xcode package, but it will let you get by with the full path to the application, including the .app suffix.

> **Note**
>
> When you download an Xcode beta, you'll find Apple has named it Xcode-beta, which is uninformative. I prefer to rename it with the version number, as shown here.

> **Note**
>
> xcode-select changes Xcode for all users on your machine and affects system assets, so you must prove administrative privileges, such as through sudo, to make the change.

xcrun

If you have different projects requiring different SDKs and toolsets, you have a problem. Not with Xcode itself—the IDE always finds its own versions—but with scripts and makefiles. Having the same makefile produce a different product depending on the admin's mood is no way to run a business.

xcrun lets you force the choice of an SDK and a toolset. If you need to find clang, for instance, you can run

```
$ # Find the currently-selected version of the Swift compiler:
$ xcrun --find swiftc
/Applications/Xcode-Beta.app/Contents/.../usr/bin/swiftc
$ # What SDKs are installed?
$ xcodebuild -showsdks
OS X SDKs:
OS X 10.9                       -sdk macosx10.9
OS X 10.10                      -sdk macosx10.10

iOS SDKs:
iOS 8.2                         -sdk iphoneos8.2

iOS Simulator SDKs:
Simulator - iOS 8.2             -sdk iphonesimulator8.2
$ # Run the Swift compiler for the 10.10 SDK:
$ xcrun --sdk macosx10.10 swiftc -print-ast SimpleCSVFile.swift
```

Custom Build Rules

Xcode's build system can be extended to new file types and processing tools. The default rules in the build system match file extensions to product types and process any source files that are newer than the products. You can add a custom rule that instructs the build system to look for files whose names match a pattern and apply a command to such files. See Figure 25.8, top.

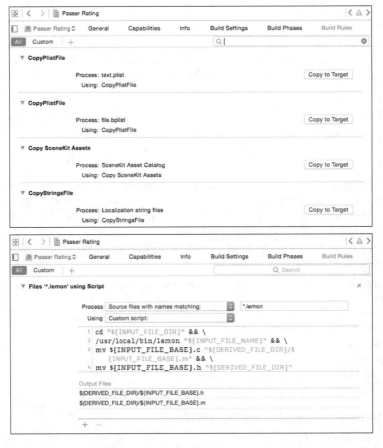

Figure 25.8 (top) The **Build Rules** tab of the Target editor lets you match up file types with the tools that will process them for a build. When you first examine the list, it contains the default suite of actions for the standard file types. (bottom) Selecting **Editor → Add Build Rule** adds a row to the table, in which you can specify a file type and the rule (possibly your own script) to process it.

Create a rule by selecting **Editor → Add Build Rule** while the **Build Rules** tab is visible, or by clicking the **+** button at the top of the view. A row appears at the top of the table, containing an editor for your new rule. The **Process** popup menu allows you to select from some of the types of source files that Xcode knows about and includes a **Source files with names matching:** item for you to specify source files with a glob expression (like `*.lemon`).

The **Using** popup shows all of Xcode's standard compilers, or you can select **Custom script:** to open an editor for your own script (see Figure 25.8, bottom). Don't worry about the size of this field; it will grow vertically as you type.

You may use any build variable you like in the shell command. Additionally, some variables are specific to custom rule invocations:

- `INPUT_FILE_PATH`, the full path to the source file (`/Users/xcodeuser/MyProject/grammar.lemon`)

- `INPUT_FILE_DIR`, the directory containing the source file (`/Users/xcodeuser/MyProject/`)

- `INPUT_FILE_NAME`, the name of the source file (`grammar.lemon`)

- `INPUT_FILE_BASE`, the base, unsuffixed, name of the source file (`grammar`)

Apple recommends that intermediate files, such as the source files output by parser generators, be put into the directory named in the `DERIVED_FILE_DIR` variable.

You can't delete or edit the defaults that are initially in the rules list, but any rule you add will override a corresponding rule that appears lower in the list. You can set priorities by dragging your rules higher or lower. You won't be able to drag a rule down among the standard rules, but that doesn't matter: Why would you add a custom rule, then specify that the standard one should override it?

Builds in the Report Navigator

You set the build system into motion by selecting an action or by issuing the **Build** (⌘B) command, or one of its relatives, from the **Product** menu. (**Build** is just an alias for **Product** →**Build For** →**Build For Running**, ⇧⌘R.)

> **Note**
>
> Once you've memorized the keyboard commands for actions like Run, Test, Profile, and Analyze, you can hold down the Shift key to do the corresponding build without going through with the action.

The result, if everything goes well, is a file or package embodying your product. If it doesn't, the now-familiar Issues navigator will list all the errors, warnings, and notes that turned up, and you can select an issue to jump to the place in your source that raised it.

But sometimes that isn't enough. You want to see how the build was done, right or wrong—perhaps you suspect that a step hadn't been taken. And, if you run into an error in linkage or code signing, the Issues navigator is of limited help because there is no corresponding source file. That's where the Report navigator comes in.

The Report navigator (the eighth tab in the Navigator area) contains an item for each major event in the life of your project, such as actions or source-control commands—anything that could generate text logs from tools that handle the events.

Do a build, select the Report navigator, and click the top item representing the results of the last action you took. What you'll see is a summary of the steps that went into the action (see Figure 25.9).

The buttons immediately below the tab bar offer the choices **All/Recent** and **All Messages/All Issues/Errors Only**. The latter group filters the list in order of importance: The all-messages setting lists everything that happened, good or not; the others eliminate the entries for successful steps and for steps that would not prevent the build from completing.

The **All** setting displays every step that contributed to the *current* state of the target. That's not the same as a list of what happened the last time you did a build: Your last build did not repeat compilations for source files that had not changed; the contributions for those files come from earlier builds. The **All** setting folds those older compilations into a complete history of the current target. If you want to restrict the list to what was done in the last build, select **Recent**.

A Simple Build Transcript

What follows is the build transcript for archiving Passer Rating, a simple app built from only 14 Swift files and a handful of resources.

I ran the project through an Archive build, which processed every element of the app, including both the `armv7` and `arm64` architectures. When the build was done, I selected it in the Report navigator, selected **All** of the history, and **All Messages**. I selected

Figure 25.9   The log for a build can be filtered to narrow it to the items you want to focus on. If you select **All Messages** (not shown), you'll get a list of every action taken in the build, including the steps that succeeded. If you select **Errors Only**, the list narrows down to error messages only.

Editor → Copy Transcript for Shown Results (All, All Messages) as Text, and pasted the results into a text editor.

The transcript is 96 KB of text in 590 lines. The commands that went into the build were in single lines that approached 6,000 characters, involving filesystem paths of around 270. What follows is less a "transcript" of that build process, and more a "schematic."

- Most of the build tools are run from directories deep inside the Xcode application package itself. The intermediate paths are elided to `Xcode.app`.

- The intermediate and final products are built in a complex tree inside `~/Library /Developer/Xcode/DerivedData`. Those are elided to `~/Library /Developer/Xcode/...` until the last element or two of the paths.

- `~/TargetDirectory` appeared in the transcript as a full pathname from `/Users` through the target directory within the project directory.

- I broke lines with backslashes. I indented lines that continued, or were contained by, other commands.

If you want the full, undiluted experience, just do what I did, and inspect the results. Here's the summary:

```
Build target Passer Rating

Write auxiliary files

/bin/mkdir -p ~/Library/Developer/.../Passer\ Rating.build
write-file ~/Library/Developer/.../Passer\ Rating.hmap
write-file ~/Library/Developer/.../Passer\ Rating-generated-files.hmap
/bin/mkdir -p ~/Library/Developer/.../arm64
write-file ~/Library/Developer/.../arm64/Passer\ Rating.LinkFileList
write-file ~/Library/Developer/.../swift-overrides.hmap
/bin/mkdir -p ~/Library/Developer/.../armv7
write-file ~/Library/Developer/.../armv7/Passer\ Rating.LinkFileList
write-file~/Library/Developer/.../Passer\ Rating-project-headers.hmap
...


Create product structure

/bin/mkdir -p ~/Library/Developer/Xcode/.../Passer\ Rating.app

SymLink ~/Library/Developer/Xcode/.../Passer\ Rating.app \
        ~/Library/Developer/Xcode/.../Applications/Passer\ Rating.app
    cd "~/projects/Passer Rating"
    export PATH="Xcode.app/.../usr/bin:/usr/bin:/bin:/usr/sbin:/sbin"
    /bin/ln -sfh ~/Library/Developer/Xcode/.../Passer\ Rating.app \
        ~/Library/Developer/Xcode/.../Applications/Passer\ Rating.app
```

The build system starts by creating the root build directory and the subdirectories for the arm64 and armv7 architectures, and initializes some scratch files. It creates the application package (remember it's just a directory with the .app extension), and makes an internal link.

Each stage of the build begins with the "invocation" of a pseudo-command that shows the intention of the block that follows, containing the actual command-line invocations that carry out the intention. You'll see that most of the build process works through external tools, rather than methods within the Xcode IDE itself.

In this case the pseudo-command is SymLink. Xcode performs the link with the standard ln command, but notice that before the build calls out to any command-line tool, it always sets the PATH environment variable to one that looks to /usr/bin within Xcode's current SDK before falling back on the standard system paths.

```
CompileSwiftSources normal arm64 com.apple.xcode.tools.swift.compiler
    cd "~/projects/Passer Rating"
    export PATH="Xcode.app/.../usr/bin:/usr/bin:/bin:/usr/sbin:/sbin"
    Xcode.app/.../swiftc -target arm64-apple-ios8.2 \
     -module-name Passer_Rating \
     -O -D ALWAYS_DELETE_STORE \
     -sdk Xcode.app/.../SDKs/iPhoneOS8.2.sdk -g \
     -module-cache-path ~/Library/Developer/DerivedData/ModuleCache \
     -I ~/Library/Developer/.../BuildProductsPath/Release-iphoneos \
     -F ~/Library/Developer/.../BuildProductsPath/Release-iphoneos -c \
     -j4 ~/Target-Folder/AppDelegate.swift \
     ~/Target-Folder/mogenerated/Game.swift \
     ~/Target-Folder/PasserEditController.swift \
     ~/Target-Folder/PasserListController.swift \
     ~/Target-Folder/SimpleCSVFile.swift ~/Target-Folder/StatView.swift \
     ~/Target-Folder/rating.swift \
     ~/Target-Folder/mogenerated/_Passer.swift \
     ~/Target-Folder/PasserEditTableController.swift \
     ~/Target-Folder/Extensions.swift \
     ~/Target-Folder/mogenerated/Passer.swift \
     ~/Target-Folder/Utilities.swift \
     ~/Target-Folder/mogenerated/_Game.swift \
     ~/Target-Folder/GameListController.swift \
     -output-file-map \
         ~/Library/Developer/.../Passer\ Rating-OutputFileMap.json \
     -parseable-output -serialize-diagnostics \
     -emit-dependencies -emit-module \
     -emit-module-path \
         ~/Library/Developer/.../Passer_Rating.swiftmodule \
     -Xcc -I~/Library/Developer/.../swift-overrides.hmap \
     -Xcc -iquote -Xcc \
         ~/Library/Developer/.../Passer\ Rating-generated-files.hmap \
     -Xcc -I~/Library/Developer/.../Passer\
       Rating-own-target-headers.hmap \
     -Xcc -I~/Library/Developer/.../Passer\
       Rating-all-target-headers.hmap \
     -Xcc -iquote \
         -Xcc ~/Library/Developer/.../Passer\
           Rating-project-headers.hmap \
     -Xcc -I~/Library/Developer/.../include \
     -Xcc -IXcode.app/.../usr/include \
     -Xcc -I~/Library/Developer/.../DerivedSources/arm64 \
     -Xcc -I~/Library/Developer/.../DerivedSources \
     -emit-objc-header -emit-objc-header-path \
         ~/Library/Developer/.../Passer_Rating-Swift.h
```

How does Swift know about all the Swift files in the project without your having to cross-reference them in your code? Simple: It compiles them all at once, from an invocation that passes every one of them to the compiler. In the course of the build, swiftc, the Swift compiler, emits hmap files; the extension stands for "header map," recalling its original purpose of recording dependencies within and across source files.

The last two switches in the swiftc invocation ask for an Objective-C header, PasserRatingSwift. This is an essential ingredient in making Swift code accessible from Objective-C: You get a -Swift.h header file for each of your modules for free; all your ObjC code has to do is to #include it, and you can carry on. Here's a sample:

```
SWIFT_CLASS("_TtC13Passer_Rating8StatView")
@interface StatView : UIView
@property (nonatomic, copy) NSString * name;
@property (nonatomic) NSInteger value;
@property (nonatomic) double fontSize;
- (instancetype)initWithFrame:(CGRect)frame OBJC_DESIGNATED_INITIALIZER;
- (instancetype)initWithCoder:(NSCoder *)aDecoder \
                OBJC_DESIGNATED_INITIALIZER;
- (void)layoutSubviews;
- (CGSize)intrinsicContentSize;
@end
```

The header redeclares every construct in your Swift modules that you mark as @objc and public. If some of your methods or data structures don't translate to the Objective-C model, they can't be bridged.

Notice that the @interface is prefaced with a declaration of the "mangled" class name, _TtC13Passer_Rating8StatView. Swift's source-code symbols are heavily overloaded between modules, generic types, and function signatures; and then they have to be pushed through linkers and other tools that are language-agnostic and need names that make the distinctions explicit. Like C++, Swift reduces all the qualifications to a string that encompasses the name and all its qualifiers. You can recover the human-readable name by passing it to the swift-demangle tool (available only by way of xcrun):

```
$ xcrun swift-demangle _TtC13Passer_Rating8StatView
_TtC13Passer_Rating8StatView ---> Passer_Rating.StatView
```

The next step is to do it all again:

```
CompileSwiftSources normal armv7 com.apple.xcode.tools.swift.compiler
    cd "~/projects/Passer Rating"
    export PATH="Xcode.app/.../usr/bin:/usr/bin:/bin:/usr/sbin:/sbin"
    Xcode.app/.../swiftc -target armv7-apple-ios8.2 \
    -module-name Passer_Rating
...
```

This seems gratuitous, until you notice the difference in the pseudo-command: The first invocation called for compiling the source down to instructions for the arm64 processor; this time, the target is armv7. Every target architecture needs a build of its own—one of the ways the Debug configuration speeds its builds is that it limits itself to the single architecture the product is about to run on.

```
Ditto ~/Library/Developer/.../DerivedSources/Passer_Rating-Swift.h \
        ~/Library/Developer/.../arm64/Passer_Rating-Swift.h
    cd "~/projects/Passer Rating"
    export PATH="Xcode.app/.../usr/bin:/usr/bin:/bin:/usr/sbin:/sbin"
    /usr/bin/ditto \
        -rsrc ~/Library/Developer/.../arm64/Passer_Rating-Swift.h \
        ~/Library/Developer/.../DerivedSources/Passer_Rating-Swift.h

Ditto ~/Library/Developer/.../DerivedSources/Passer_Rating-Swift.h  \
        ~/Library/Developer/.../armv7/Passer_Rating-Swift.h
...
```

The newly minted bridging headers are moved to more convenient directories. The ditto command is similar to the cp copy command, with options to exclude items like version-control directories, and to handle extended attributes compatibly.

```
DataModelVersionCompile \
        ~/Library/Developer/.../Passer\ Rating.app/Passer_Rating.momd \
        Passer\ Rating/Passer_Rating.xcdatamodeld
    cd "~/projects/Passer Rating"
    export PATH="Xcode.app/.../usr/bin:/usr/bin:/bin:/usr/sbin:/sbin"
    Xcode.app/Contents/Developer/usr/bin/momc \
     -XD_MOMC_SDKROOT=Xcode.app/.../SDKs/iPhoneOS8.2.sdk \
     -MOMC_PLATFORMS iphoneos ~/Target-Folder/Passer_Rating.xcdatamodeld \
     ~/Library/Developer/.../Passer\ Rating.app/Passer_Rating.momd
```

The .mom file Passer Rating uses at run time is compiled from your data-model design.

```
Ld ~/Library/Developer/.../Passer\ Rating normal armv7
    cd "~/projects/Passer Rating"
    export IPHONEOS_DEPLOYMENT_TARGET=8.2
    export PATH="Xcode.app/.../usr/bin:/usr/bin:/bin:/usr/sbin:/sbin"
    Xcode.app/.../clang -arch armv7 \
     -isysroot Xcode.app/.../SDKs/iPhoneOS8.2.sdk \
     -L~/Library/Developer/.../BuildProductsPath/Release-iphoneos \
     -F~/Library/Developer/.../BuildProductsPath/Release-iphoneos \
     -filelist ~/Library/Developer/...Passer\ Rating.LinkFileList \
     -Xlinker -rpath -Xlinker @executable_path/Frameworks -dead_strip \
     -LXcode.app/.../usr/lib/swift/iphoneos -Xlinker -add_ast_path \
     -Xlinker ~/Library/Developer/.../armv7/Passer_Rating.swiftmodule \
     -miphoneos-version-min=8.2 -framework MapKit \
     -framework NetworkExtension \
     -Xlinker -dependency_info \
     -Xlinker \
        ~/Library/Developer/.../Passer\ Rating_dependency_info.dat \
     -o ~/Library/Developer/.../Passer\ Rating
```

```
Ld ~/Library/Developer/.../Passer\ Rating normal arm64
    cd "~/projects/Passer Rating"
    export IPHONEOS_DEPLOYMENT_TARGET=8.2
    export PATH="Xcode.app/.../usr/bin:/usr/bin:/bin:/usr/sbin:/sbin"
    Xcode.app/.../clang -arch arm64 \
    -isysroot Xcode.app/.../SDKs/iPhoneOS8.2.sdk
...
```

Here's where the linker gets run to wire up (almost) all the unsatisfied references among your modules and the system frameworks. Note that this, too, has to be done once per target architecture.

The linker is the `clang` C-language compiler. By the time it reaches linkage, your code has lost all of its Swift-like attributes—it's just binary indexed by mangled symbols.

```
Ditto ~/Library/Developer/.../Passer_Rating.swiftmodule/arm.swiftmodule \
        ~/Library/Developer/.../Passer_Rating.swiftmodule
...

Ditto ~/Library/Developer/...Passer_Rating.swiftmodule/arm.swiftdoc  \
        ~/Library/Developer/.../Passer_Rating.swiftdoc
...
```

The interfaces for a Swift module go into `.swiftmodule` and `.swiftdoc` files in a `.swiftmodule` directory. `ditto` assembles them; there is one package per architecture.

```
CreateUniversalBinary \
        ~/Library/Developer/.../Passer\ Rating.app/Passer\ Rating  \
        normal armv7\ arm64
    cd "~/projects/Passer Rating"
    export PATH="Xcode.app/.../usr/bin:/usr/bin:/bin:/usr/sbin:/sbin"
    Xcode.app/.../lipo \
     -create ~/Library/Developer/.../Passer\ Rating  \
     ~/Library/Developer/.../Passer\ Rating  \
     -output ~/Library/Developer/.../Passer\ Rating.app/Passer\ Rating
```

The `lipo` tool was created when "universal"—multiple-architecture—binaries were called "fat" binaries. It takes libraries and executables that are identical but for their architectures, and archives them into single files from which the operating system can select the needed version. In this case, the universal carries the `armv7` and `arm64` binaries.

```
PhaseScriptExecution Generate\ Test\ Data  \
        ~/Library/Developer/.../Script-...990D.sh
    cd "~/projects/Passer Rating"
    /bin/sh -c \"~/Library/Developer/.../Script-...990D.sh\"

CpResource Passer\ Rating/sample-data.csv  \
        ~/Library/Developer/.../Passer\ Rating.app/sample-data.csv
```

```
cd "~/projects/Passer Rating"
export PATH="Xcode.app/.../usr/bin:/usr/bin:/bin:/usr/sbin:/sbin"
builtin-copy -exclude .DS_Store -exclude CVS -exclude .svn \
    -exclude .git -exclude .hg -strip-debug-symbols \
    -strip-tool Xcode.app/.../strip -resolve-src-symlinks \
    ~/Target-Folder/sample-data.csv \
    ~/Library/Developer/.../Passer\ Rating.app
```

These pseudo–commands execute the "Generate Test Data" script and copy the resulting sample-data.csv file into the application package. It's only one text file, but the builtin-copy "tool" takes care to strip out extraneous files, remove unnecessary symbol information, and ensure that symbolic links stay clean.

```
CompileStoryboard Passer\ Rating/Base.lproj/Main.storyboard
    cd "~/projects/Passer Rating"
    export PATH="Xcode.app/.../usr/bin:/usr/bin:/bin:/usr/sbin:/sbin"
    export XCODE_DEVELOPER_USR_PATH=Xcode.app/Contents/Developer/usr/bin/..
    Xcode.app/Contents/Developer/usr/bin/ibtool --target-device iphone  \
        --errors --warnings --notices --module Passer_Rating  \
        --minimum-deployment-target 8.2 --output-partial-info-plist  \
        ~/Library/Developer/Xcode/.../Main-SBPartialInfo.plist  \
        --auto-activate-custom-fonts --output-format human-readable-text  \
        --compilation-directory \
            ~/Library/Developer/Xcode/.../Passer\ Rating.app/Base.lproj  \
        ~/Target-Folder/Base.lproj/Main.storyboard

/* com.apple.ibtool.document.warnings */
~/Target-Folder/Base.lproj/Main.storyboard:aD1-LC-OKV:
    warning: Constraint referencing items turned off \
    in current configuration. \
    Turn off this constraint in the current configuration.
```

Storyboards get a compilation step, too. This step generated a warning, prefaced by the pathname of the source file and the object ID of the offending element. (If the source were textual code, this would be a line number.) The Xcode IDE turns these into a yellow badge, a link to the location of the problem, and the message.

```
CompileAssetCatalog ~/Library/Developer/Xcode/.../Passer\ Rating.app  \
        Passer\ Rating/Images.xcassets
    cd "~/projects/Passer Rating"
    export PATH="Xcode.app/.../usr/bin:/usr/bin:/bin:/usr/sbin:/sbin"
    Xcode.app/Contents/Developer/usr/bin/actool \
        --output-format human-readable-text --notices --warnings \
        --export-dependency-info \
        ~/Library/Developer/.../assetcatalog_dependencies.txt \
        --output-partial-info-plist  \
            ~/Library/Developer/.../assetcatalog_generated_info.plist \
        --app-icon AppIcon --launch-image LaunchImage \
```

```
    --platform iphoneos --minimum-deployment-target 8.2 \
    --target-device iphone --compress-pngs \
    --compile ~/Library/Developer/.../Passer\ Rating.app \
       ~/Target-Folder/Images.xcassets

2014-11-22 20:51:13.416 IBCocoaTouchImageCatalogTool[21763:1375516] \
    CoreUI(DEBUG): CSIGenerator using LZVN Compression coreui ...
/* com.apple.actool.document.notices */
~/Target-Folder/Images.xcassets: \
    ./LaunchImage.launchimage/[iphone][736h][3x][portrait]...: \
    notice: This launch image only applies to iOS 6.x and prior \
        but the minimum deployment is 7.0 or later.
/* com.apple.actool.compilation-results */
~/Library/Developer/.../Passer Rating.app/AppIcon29x29@2x.png
~/Library/Developer/.../Passer Rating.app/AppIcon29x29@3x.png
...
~/Library/Developer/.../Passer Rating.app/LaunchImage-800-667h@2x.png
...
~/Library/Developer/.../Passer Rating.app/Assets.car
```

Asset catalogs are picked apart and rearranged for efficient access at run time. This includes processing PNG files into a format that is perfectly legal, but not recognized by some graphics applications. If you poke around in your iOS .app packages, don't be alarmed if you can't examine the PNG files.

   The catalog compiler issues a couple of notices about images being present that won't be used with an app that will never run on iOS 6 or earlier; and a progress list of the assets it processed. The Xcode IDE doesn't pass those on for display, but you can see them in the full transcript, or by expanding the step in the log as displayed by the Report navigator.

```
ProcessInfoPlistFile \
  ~/Library/Developer/.../Passer\ Rating.app/Info.plist \
  Passer\ Rating/Info.plist
  cd "~/projects/Passer Rating"
    export PATH="Xcode.app/.../usr/bin:/usr/bin:/bin:/usr/sbin:/sbin"
    builtin-infoPlistUtility ~/Target-Folder/Info.plist  \
     -genpkginfo \
        ~/Library/Developer/.../Passer\ Rating.app/PkgInfo  \
     -expandbuildsettings -format binary -platform iphoneos  \
     -additionalcontentfile \
        ~/Library/Developer/.../Main-SBPartialInfo.plist  \
     -additionalcontentfile \
        ~/Library/Developer/.../assetcatalog_generated_info.plist  \
     -o ~/Library/Developer/.../Passer Rating.app/Info.plist
```

I've been telling you all along that the Info.plist in your project window is only a precursor for the one that is sealed into your finished app. Here's where the transformation happens. The process includes information provided by the storyboard

(`Main-SBPartialInfo.plist`) and the asset catalog (`assetcatalog-generated_infoplist`).

```
GenerateDSYMFile ~/Library/Developer/.../Passer\ Rating.app.dSYM  \
        ~/Library/Developer/.../Passer\ Rating.app/Passer\ Rating
...
Touch ~/Library/Developer/.../Passer\ Rating.app
...
Stripping ~/Library/Developer/.../Passer\ Rating.app/Passer\ Rating
...
SetOwnerAndGroup fritza:staff ~/Library/Developer/.../Passer\ Rating.app
...
SetMode u+w,go-w,a+rX ~/Library/Developer/.../Passer\ Rating.app
...
```

The excitement is dying down. Xcode generates a `.dSYM` package as an external repository for the app's debugging information; `touch`es the app to ensure it is newer than any of its components, which keeps modification-date dependencies straight; removes the last debugging information from the app; and sets the filesystem permissions.

```
ProcessProductPackaging \
  ~/Library/MobileDevice/Provisioning\ Profiles/...0bca.mobileprovision \
  ~/Library/.../Passer\ Rating.app/embedded.mobileprovision
 cd "~/projects/Passer Rating"
 export PATH="Xcode.app/.../usr/bin:/usr/bin:/bin:/usr/sbin:/sbin"
 builtin-productPackagingUtility \
   ~/Library/MobileDevice/Provisioning\ Profiles/...0bca.mobileprovision \
   -o ~/Library/.../Passer\ Rating.app/embedded.mobileprovision
```

Xcode finds the distribution profile for the application, and binds it into the `.app` package.

```
CopySwiftLibs ~/Library/Developer/Xcode/.../Passer\ Rating.app
    cd "~/projects/Passer Rating"
    export ACTION=build
    export AD_HOC_CODE_SIGNING_ALLOWED=NO
    export ALTERNATE_GROUP=staff
...
    export arch=arm64
    export variant=normal
    Xcode.app/.../swift-stdlib-tool --verbose --copy

Copying libswiftCore.dylib from \
  Xcode.app/.../usr/lib/swift/iphoneos to ...Passer Rating.app/Frameworks
Copying libswiftCoreGraphics.dylib from \
  Xcode.app/.../usr/lib/swift/iphoneos to ...Passer Rating.app/Frameworks
Copying libswiftFoundation.dylib from \
  Xcode.app/.../usr/lib/swift/iphoneos to ...Passer Rating.app/Frameworks
...
```

iOS 7 and OS X 10.9 have no built-in support for Swift-generated code—they don't have the runtime libraries the compiled binaries rely on. The solution is to embed the runtimes in the application itself.

The `CopySwiftLibs` pseudo-command goes on:

```
Codesigning libswiftCore.dylib at .../Passer Rating.app/Frameworks
    /usr/bin/codesign '--force' '--sign' '376...780' '--verbose' \
        '.../Passer Rating.app/Frameworks/libswiftCore.dylib'
Codesigning libswiftCoreGraphics.dylib at .../Passer Rating.app/Frameworks
    /usr/bin/codesign '--force' '--sign' '376...780' '--verbose' \
        '.../Passer Rating.app/Frameworks/libswiftCoreGraphics.dylib'
...
```

... one by one, it applies the distribution signing identity to all the copied runtime libraries.

```
ProcessProductPackaging Passer\ Rating/Passer\ Rating.entitlements \
        .../Passer\ Rating.app.xcent
    cd "~/projects/Passer Rating"
    export PATH="Xcode.app/.../usr/bin:/usr/bin:/bin:/usr/sbin:/sbin"
    builtin-productPackagingUtility \
        ~/Target-Folder/Passer\ Rating.entitlements \
        -entitlements -format xml -o .../Passer\ Rating.app.xcent

CodeSign ~/Library/Developer/.../Passer\ Rating.app
    cd "~/projects/Passer Rating"
    export CODESIGN_ALLOCATE=Xcode.app/.../codesign_allocate
    export PATH="Xcode.app/.../usr/bin:/usr/bin:/bin:/usr/sbin:/sbin"
    /usr/bin/codesign --force --sign 37...80 \
        --entitlements ~/Library/Developer/.../Passer\ Rating.app.xcent \
        ~/Library/Developer/.../Passer\ Rating.app

Validate ~/Library/Developer/.../Passer\ Rating.app
    cd "~/projects/Passer Rating"
    export PATH="Xcode.app/.../usr/bin:/usr/bin:/bin:/usr/sbin:/sbin"
    export PRODUCT_TYPE=com.apple.product-type.application
    Xcode.app/.../usr/bin/Validation \
    ~/Library/Developer/.../Passer\ Rating.app

Touch ~/Library/Developer/.../Passer\ Rating.app.dSYM
    cd "~/projects/Passer Rating"
    export PATH="Xcode.app/.../usr/bin:/usr/bin:/bin:/usr/sbin:/sbin"
    /usr/bin/touch -c ~/Library/Developer/.../Passer\ Rating.app.dSYM
```

And now the process wraps up. The app claims privileges from the system, if only the privilege of allowing itself to run under the supervision of a debugger. The `Process-ProductPackaging` pseudo-command generates the final `.entitlements` file and processes it into the application package.

The signing identity gets applied to the .app package as a whole, then the product is examined for consistency. (This is not the same as the validation you can request before submitting an application to the App Store.) Last, the .dSYM debugging-symbol package is touched, bringing its modification date current, so it too will be immune to rebuilds until some file up the chain is changed.

> **Note**
>
> The .dSYM package is crucial, even if this is a distribution article, and not for debugging. Both the compressed binary (.ipa) and the .dSYM go into the archive (.xcarchive from which you extract the final product. The .dSYM is matched exactly to that build: It carries a unique ID that is duplicated in the product; Spotlight indexes the ID so the system can match any binary or crash report to its debugging information. Crash reports will have none of your application's symbols—they've been stripped. If Xcode or other tools can find the corresponding symbol directory, it can "symbolicate" the reports into intelligible stack traces. *Always* preserve the archive packages of anything you distribute.

Summary

This was an important chapter if you want to know how Xcode really works. It explains how the build system built into Xcode itself takes the place of traditional makefiles and the effort needed to keep them current. It showed how a build is divided into phases that "contain" files to be worked on. Settings for compilers and other tools are an essential part of configuring a build, and you saw how Xcode organizes them by project, target, and configuration.

You saw how you can use the build system from a script, so your builds can be managed without having to trigger them manually from the IDE.

Finally, you examined the Report navigator, how to get a transcript of the commands that underlie the build process, and how to analyze a transcript.

## 26

Instruments

Instruments is a framework for software-measurement tools called. . . instruments. (Capital-I Instruments is the application, small-i instruments are components of the Instruments application.) The analogy is to a multi-track recording deck. Instruments records activity into tracks (one per instrument), building the data on a timeline like audio on a tape.

You've seen Instruments before, in Chapter 16, "Measurement and Analysis," where it helped you track down some memory and performance bugs in the Passer Rating iPhone app. It deserves a closer look. You'll learn how to navigate the Instruments trace window, and how to choose instruments to fit your needs.

What Instruments Is

The focus on a timeline makes Instruments unique. Historically, profiling and debugging tools did one thing at a time. You had Shark (available with Xcode 2 and 3), which sampled a running application to collect aggregate statistics of where it spent its time. Shark had several modes for taking different statistics; if you wanted another mode, you ran Shark again. Shark's profile data was aggregated over the whole session; if you wanted to profile a particular piece of your application, there was a hot key for you to turn profiling on and off.

Separately, there was a profiling application called MallocDebug, which collected cumulative, statistical call trees for calls to malloc and free. The results were cumulative across a profiling session, so you'd know how the biggest, or most, allocations happened, but not when.

If you needed the distribution and history of *object* allocations, by class, there was an Object Alloc application.

And if you wanted to know how the application was spending its time while it was making those allocations, you quit MallocDebug or Object Alloc and ran the target app again under Shark, because the other apps did only one thing.

Instruments is different. It is comprehensive. There are instruments for most ways you'd want to analyze your code, and Instruments runs them *all at the same time*. The results are laid out by time, in parallel. Did pressing a **Compute** button result in Core Data fetches? Or had the fetches already been done earlier? Did other disk activity eat up bandwidth? In the application? Elsewhere in the system? Is the application leaking file descriptors, and if so, when, and why? If you're handing data off to another process, how does the recipient's memory usage change in response to the handoff, and how does it relate to the use of file descriptors in both the recipient and master applications?

Instruments can answer these questions. You can relate file descriptors to disk activity, and disk activity to Core Data events, with stack traces for every single one of these, because Instruments captures the data on a timeline, all in parallel, event by event. And, you can target different instruments on different applications (or even the system as a whole) at the same time.

For events—like individual allocations or system calls—Instruments keeps a complete record each and every time. For time profiling, Instruments does statistical sampling, but it keeps each sample. That means that even if you want an aggregate, *you get to pick the aggregate.*

Say the list of passers in Passer Rating stutters when you scroll it. With Shark, you'd have to start Passer Rating, get to where you'd be scrolling as quickly as you could, do the scrolling, and then kill it at once so your statistical sample wouldn't be polluted by whatever followed the part you were interested in. And you'd be too late, because the CPU time soaked up by initialization would swamp the little spikes incurred by reloading the passer table cells.

> **Note**
>
> Shark mitigated the problem by allowing you to set a delay before it started sampling, and a duration for the sample.

In Instruments, by contrast, you don't have to worry about one part of the program polluting your statistics. You can select just the part of the timeline that has to do with scrolling, and you can see what your app was doing just then.

> **Note**
>
> Most of the power of Instruments lies in the analysis tools it provides after a recording is made, but don't ignore the advantage it provides in showing program state dynamically: If you can't see when a memory total or file I/O begins and settles down (for instance), you won't know when to stop the recording for analysis in the first place.

Running Instruments

In the "Measurement and Analysis" chapter (16), you started Instruments from Xcode by issuing **Product → Profile** (⌘ I), or selecting the **Profile** variant of the large **Action** button at the left end of the Xcode toolbar. You could set the trace template you wanted in the **Profile** panel of the Scheme editor; there's even a shortcut: Hold down the Option key while making any other gesture that starts profiling, and you'll be offered the **Profile** panel of the Scheme editor before you go on. With profiling integrated into the Xcode workflow, this will be the most common way you'll use Instruments.

For specialized uses, you'll want to go beyond the few templates the **Profile** action gives you. Instruments can run and attach to applications independently, and you can set up any instruments you like for the trace.

As delivered, Instruments does not appear as an application anywhere in the Finder. As with other developer tools, it is kept inside the `Xcode.app` bundle. The Profile build action launches Instruments and points it at your target application. If you want to use Instruments with a different target (another app, or a running process), select **Xcode →Open Developer Tool →Instruments**. Instruments will launch like any other application. Its icon will appear in the Dock, and I advise you to keep it there by right-clicking its icon and selecting **Options →Keep in Dock**.

When you start Instruments, it creates a document (called a *trace document*) and displays a sheet offering you a choice of templates populated with instruments for common tasks (see Figure 26.1). A list of templates Apple provides can be found in "The Templates" later in this chapter.

At the top of the New Trace assistant is a hierarchical menu, **Choose a profiling template for:**. The first segment lets you select a device—your computer; an attached iOS device; an iOS Simulator type; or, if you saved targeting information in a custom template, the option simply to go along with the saved target. You'll be able to change the target once the trace document is open.

Figure 26.1   When you create a new trace document in Instruments, it shows you an empty document and a sheet for choosing among templates prepopulated with instruments for common tasks.

The Trace Document Window

The initial form of a trace document window is simple: A toolbar at the top, and a stack of instruments in the view that dominates the window. Once you've recorded data into the document, the window becomes much richer. Let's go through Figure 26.2 and identify the components.

Toolbar

The toolbar falls into three parts for five major functions. The controls at left ① control recording and the execution of the target applications. There is a **Record/Drive & Record/Stop** button to start and stop data collection, and a **Pause** button for suspending and resuming data collection.

> **Note**
>
> When you start recording, you will often be asked for an administrator's password. The kind of deep monitoring many instruments do is a security breach, and the system makes you show you are authorized to do it.

The **Target** chooser designates the device and the process all instruments in the document will target, unless you specify a different target for individual instruments. The choices are

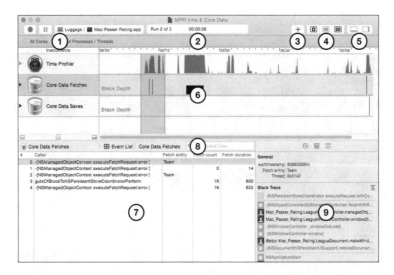

Figure 26.2   A typical Instruments window, once data has been recorded. The Extended Detail area (at right) has also been exposed. I discuss the numbered parts in the text.

- The first segment of the menu allows you to choose a device, either your computer or a mobile device attached to it. The second segment will fill with the eligible targets on that device.

- **All Processes**—Data will be collected from all of the processes, user and system, on the target device. For instance, the Core Data instruments (Mac only) can measure the Core Data activity of all processes. Not every instrument can span processes; if your document contains no instruments that can sample system-wide, this option will be disabled.

- **Choose Target...** —A sheet will drop, presenting a browser for selecting a target binary. This includes applications, dynamic libraries, extensions, and processes that may be started by `launchd` daemons.

- **Edit `target name`...** —Drops the `Choose Target`... sheet, focused on the executable you've already set for the trace document. From here, you can set the arguments and environment variables to pass to the chosen target when it is launched.

- **Recent Executables**—A section for the applications and other processes you've most recently examined.

- **App Extensions**—A section for extension plugins that have registered themselves with the system.

- **Running Applications**—This section is what it sounds like. Data will be collected from an application that is already running; select it from the submenu. Some instruments require that their targets be launched from Instruments and cannot attach to running processes. If you use only non-attaching instruments, this section will be disabled.

- **System Processes**—The same, for system daemons currently running in the background. What you see at first is a selection of the currently most-active processes. If you select the **More...** item, the menu will extend to all running system processes.

The **Target** popup is not selectable while Instruments is recording.

While recording is in progress, the clock ② displays the total time period recorded in the document. Otherwise, it shows the position of the triangular "playback head" slider in the time scale at the top of the Track area (Figure 26.3). Trace documents can store more

Figure 26.3   The left half of a trace document's toolbar displays a clock and controls for selecting and running the main target to be traced. The clock view shows the duration while recording is in process, and the time marked by the triangular "playback head" when it is not. It also shows the run being displayed if there is more than one.

than one run of a trace; click the disclosure button at the left end of a track to see all previous runs for comparison. The clock shows the currently selected run.

You can move between runs without expanding a track through the **Previous Run** (⌘ **Quote**) and **Next Run** (⌘ **Apostrophe**) commands in the **View** menu.

The right section of the toolbar provides convenient controls for display.

Library ③, with a **+** icon, shows and hides a palette of available instruments, which you can drag into the Track area.

The **Strategy** control ④ selects among perspectives on the Trace area.

- It's easiest to start with the middle segment, **Instruments**, because the Time display is the most intuitive: Each instrument has its own track, showing the instant-by-instant statistics it has collected for the whole process.

- **CPU**, the first segment, splits the instrument tracks to show the collected data identified with the processor core responsible for the event.

- **Threads** also splits instrument data, but by the thread subprocess responsible for the event; threads are not necessarily confined to a single core over its lifetime, and often threads are created for single purposes, allowing you to analyze the events roughly by purpose.

> **Note**
>
> The **CPU** and **Threads** perspectives aren't available for every instrument.

The Detail selector ⑤ is like the control in the Xcode toolbar that discloses the specialized areas in a project window. The first segment shows and hides the Detail area ⑦, which presents the data behind a trace raw, or analyzed by various criteria. The second segment exposes the Extended Detail area, which is used for configuring an instrument, filtering its data, and displaying a stack trace for events and statistical aggregates.

Track Area

The Track area ⑥ is the focus of the document window and the only component you see when a document is first opened. This is the area you drag new instruments into. Apple describes the Track area as being divided between the *Instruments Pane* on the left, and the *Track pane* on the right. For clarity, I'm going to avoid yet another sense of the word "instruments," and treat track rows as single units, with a name block on the left and a trace on the right.

Most instruments will display subsets of the data they collect if you select a time span within the recording. To do so, drag the playback head across the span you're interested in. The span will be highlighted, and the Detail area ⑦ will be restricted to data collected in the span. Click anywhere in the Track area to clear the selection.

Sometimes, you're interested in the shape of your app's performance throughout its run; sometimes you need to see the sequence of events during a single interaction with the app; and you may even be interested in processor events recorded over the course of a millisecond. Different tasks need different scales.

The scale of the Track area can be controlled by what looks like a slider below the configuration blocks. In fact, it behaves like a joystick: The track compresses while you hold it to the left, and expands while you hold it to the right.

You can also change scale by dragging in the Track area while holding a modifier key down: Shift-dragging will zoom in, spreading the interval you select to the breadth of the window. Control-dragging zooms out. The location or direction of the drag doesn't matter; the time interval you sweep out will be the size of the currently displayed interval within the new, expanded interval. The shorter your drag, the further the track will zoom out.

Selecting **View** → **Snap Track to Fit** (^ ⌘ Z) will scale the Track area so the entire recording is given the full breadth of the window.

You can also scale a track vertically, by selecting it and using **Decrease Deck Size** (⌘ −) or **Increase Deck Size** (⌘ +) in the **View** menu.

The name block shows the instrument's name and icon. To the left is a disclosure triangle so you can see the instrument's tracks for previous runs in the document. To change the vertical order of instrument tracks, drag them by the name block. You can't drag an instrument out of the document; if you want to delete a track, click the name block to select the track, and press Delete.

The trace to the right of the name block displays a timeline of the data the instrument collected. Most instruments have many options that determine what data they collect, and how. Before you run your first trace (if you're given the chance—Instruments launches and traces immediately if it's started from Xcode), examine each instrument's configuration in the Settings inspector (first tab in the Extended Detail area) to see that you'll get what you need. You can change a configuration at any time between runs.

Detail Area

The Detail area ⑦ appears when you've run a trace. Click the first segment of the toolbar's Detail selector to display it.

When you select an instrument in the Track view, the Detail area shows the collected data in tabular form. What's in the table varies among instruments, and most instruments have more than one kind of table. The first segment of the Detail jump bar ⑧ controls which table is displayed. As you drill down into the data for a detail row, elements are added to the jump bar; click higher-level elements to return to the corresponding views. The Display Settings inspector (second tab in the Extended Detail area) provides filters to further refine the currently displayed table.

Extended Detail Area

The Extended Detail area ⑨ consists of three tabs that roughly correspond to your progress in analyzing your application.

- **Record Settings** configures an instrument in preparation for a recording run.
- **Display Settings** offers filters that refine the data displayed in the Detail area.
- **Extended Detail** shows some kind of expansion on a datum in the Detail table.

Record Settings

The Record Settings tab configures the instrument you have selected in the Trace area. Each instrument has its own configuration options, but some are common to most of them.

In the **Track Display** section, there are two popups, for **Style** and **Type**.

The usual **Style** menu selects among graphing styles for the numeric data the instrument records. These may include

- **Line Graph.** The track is displayed as a colored line connecting each datum in the series of collected data. You can choose the color in the list of the available series.

- **Filled Line Graph** is the same as **Line**, but the area under the line is colored.

- **Point Graph.** Each datum is displayed as a discrete symbol in the track. You can choose the symbols in the list of available series in the inspector.

- **Block Graph** is a bar graph, showing each datum as a colored rectangle. In instruments that record events, the block will be as wide as the time to the next event.

- **Peak Graph** shows the data collected by an instrument that records events (like the Core Data instruments) as a vertical line at each event. Every time something happens, the graph shows a blip.

- **Stack Libraries** draws a bar for each event the instrument measures. The height of the bar depends on the depth of the call stack at the event; the bars are divided into colored segments, with a different color for each library that owns the caller at that level.

- Some instruments have graph styles of their own. The Time Profiler instrument has three custom styles:

  - **CPU Usage** is the classic format: An area graph shows the moment-to-moment time demands the application makes on all processor cores.

  - **Deepest Stack Libraries** shows a bar chart in which the height of the bars represents the depth of the call stack at each moment. The bars are color-coded to identify the libraries responsible for each call in the stack. The color code is the same as the one used in the icons in the Extended Detail area.

  - **User and System Libraries** is the same bar chart, but there are only two colors showing how much of the stack passed through system libraries.

- The Allocations instrument also has three custom styles:

  - **Current Bytes** is an area graph showing how much memory is in use.

  - **Allocation Density** shows how many allocations were made in each increment in time. When your app makes a flurry of allocations, it shows up as a peak in the graph.

  - **Active Allocation Distribution** filters the allocation-density graph to show where the allocations were made that were still alive at the end of the trace.

> **Note**
>
> Most instruments record events, not quantities that vary over time. In fact, the data displayed may not even be a continuous variable, but may be a mere tag, like the ID of a thread or a file descriptor. The Peak Graph style is the most suitable style for event recordings. Such displays are still useful, as they give you a landmark for examining the matching data in the other tracks. Stack Libraries would also be good, but it takes a very sharp eye to discern patterns in the call stacks of infrequent events.

The **Type** menu offers two choices for instruments that can record more than one data series. **Overlay** displays all series on a single graph. The displayed data will probably overlap, but in point and line displays this probably doesn't matter, and filled displays are translucent, so the two series don't obscure each other. **Stacked** displays each series in separate strips, one above the other.

You can change the **Track Display** settings even after the instrument has collected its data.

For instruments that can collect more than one series, a **Select statistics to list** section shows a checkbox for each available series, with a popup to select the shape of points for a Point Graph, plus a color well.

Display Settings

The Display Settings tab filters the table's contents after you've collected data. The options vary by instrument and table type, but most instruments collect call trees, and will have a "Call Tree" section among the options. The call-tree display options are

- **Separate by Category**—In the Allocations instrument, the normal call tree displays all allocations of any kind. This is useful if you need to know how much memory was allocated in any one function, regardless of what the allocations were for. If you select **Separate by Category**, the call tree list is sorted by the type of the allocation. You can expand the row for the symbol name NSImage and see code paths that led to the creation of OS X image objects.

- **Separate by Thread**—Call trees are normally merged with no regard for which thread the calls occurred in. Separating the trees by thread will help you weed out calls in threads you aren't interested in.

- **Invert Call Tree**—The default (top-down) presentation of call trees starts at the runtime start or main function, branching out through the successive calls down to the leaf functions that are the events the instrument records. Checking this box inverts the trees, so they are bottom-up: You start at the function (usually objc_msgSend in Objective-C applications) where the event occurred, and branch out to all the successive callers.

- **Hide Missing Symbols**—Checking this box hides functions that don't have debugging symbols associated with them. Most of the libraries in the system frameworks include symbols for their functions, and those can at least suggest what's going on. (And, of course, your code has symbols, because you've made sure your

"Debug Information Format" build setting is set to "DWARF with dSYM File"—it won't inflate the size of your code.)

- **Hide System Libraries**—This skips over functions in system libraries. Reading the names of the library calls may help you get an idea of what is going on, but if you are looking for code you can do something about, you don't want to see them. Using this option along with **Invert Call Tree** will often tell a very explicit story about what your code is doing. objc_msgSend is so ubiquitous in Cocoa code that finding it in a stack trace doesn't tell you much; paring the trees down to where all those calls came from tells you everything.

- **Flatten Recursion**—This lumps every call a function makes to itself into a single item. Recursive calls can run up the length of a call stack without being very informative.

- **Top Functions**—This is a very useful filter, but hard to describe. You remember in Chapter 16, "Measurement and Analysis" that we wanted to know specifically what Passer Rating function was taking up the most time as the Game database was being built.

The initial display of the call tree told us that main took up 100 percent of the app's time; we could then disclose the functions main called and see how much time they took; and so on down the stack, eventually passing, at one level or another, through our code.

Then we inverted the call tree; that told us what the most expensive functions were, no matter how they got to be called. We could work through the disclosures until, again, we could see our functions on this or that call chain.

Finally, we checked Hide System Libraries, which cut off the tree at our own functions. At that point, we could see our most expensive functions, listed by the total time spent running them—the time spent in the system calls they made was added up and attributed to our code. That aggregated time was the most valuable information we got from this technique.

Top Functions does the same thing, without having to prune any functions out of the tree. The Call Tree list in the Detail area shows every function in the app, with the total time spent in them. The first line would be main, which was running or calling the rest of the app code 100 percent of the time. (The Self column will still show the amount of time spent executing the function's own code.)

Suppose main called functionA and functionB; the next line in the table might be functionA with 80 percent—nevermind that it was already counted in main. The next line might be functionC, called by functionA, taking 50 percent; and next functionB at 20 percent.

With a comprehensive list like this, you have a guide to one of the most fruitful strategies in optimizing an application—not the speed of a run of instructions, but the algorithm that runs them. Top-function analysis gives you the total call pattern, including a loop in Cocoa that calls into your code.

> **Note**
>
> Stack traces in the Extended Detail inspector also reflect your settings of these filters.

You can also add call-tree constraints, such as minimum and maximum call counts. The idea is to prune (or focus on) calls that are not frequently made. Another constraint that may be available (for instance, in the Time Profiler instrument) can filter call trees by the amount of time (minimum, maximum, or both) they took up in the course of the run.

There's one feature that will do you a lot of good, but it's easy to miss: At the far left end of the Detail jump bar is what looks like a label that identifies the selected instrument. That's what it usually happens to show, but it's a popup menu. You can use it as another way to select an instrument track for the Detail view, but at the top is another item, **Trace Highlights**. Many instruments—especially Activity Monitor—can render their data as bar or pie charts, broken down by process, thread, or event type, or share of resources. When you select the highlights view, the Detail area will fill with the available charts.

Extended Detail

The third tab in the Extended Detail area is itself named Extended Detail. It typically includes a stack trace when you select an item in the Detail area that carries stack information. When the selected item is part of a call tree, the Extended Detail area shows the "heaviest" stack, the one that accounts for most of whatever the instrument keeps track of. There's a **Hide system calls in the stack trace** button at top-right to truncate the list to your own code and its immediate callers and callees.

Selecting a frame in the call stack highlights the corresponding call in the call-tree outline. Double-clicking on a frame shows the corresponding source code in the Detail area, with banners showing where the instrument "hit" in the function, and what proportion of those function hits fell on which lines.

> **Note**
>
> When you double-click a stack frame to see the source code in the Detail area, the Extended Detail area fills with annotations on the function call that generated that frame. The Detail area's jump bar adds a segment for the listing (**Call Trees →Call Tree →-[SimpleCSVFile run:error:]**. You can return to the call tree in the Detail area and the stack trace in the Extended Detail area by clicking the previous segment (**Call Tree**).

Library

Instruments are made part of an Instruments trace document either by being instantiated from a template or by being dragged in from the Library window.

The Library palette (**Window →Library**, ⌘ **L**, or the **+** toggle button in the toolbar) lists all of the known instruments. Initially this is a repertoire of Apple-supplied tracks, but it is possible to add your own. The palette lists all known instruments. Selecting one fills the pane below the list with a description. See Figure 26.4. Some descriptions include a **(?)** button, which only takes you to the root page of the Instruments manual in Xcode's Documentation browser.

Figure 26.4   A scrolling list of available instruments dominates the Library palette. The selected instrument is described in the panel below. Selecting a category from the popup menu narrows the list down by task, and the search field at the bottom allows you to find an instrument from its name or description.

The Library gathers instruments into groups; these are initially hidden, but they can be seen if you select **Show Group Banners** from the **Action** (gear) popup at the lower-left corner of the palette. The **Action** menu will also allow you to create groups of your own—drag an instrument into your group to add it; or smart groups, which filter the library according to criteria you choose. The popup at the top of the palette narrows the list down by group, and the search field at the bottom allows you to filter the list by searching for text in the names and descriptions.

Note

Note the split-view dimple under the group popup; drag it down, and the popup is replaced by a table of sections.

Tracing

Now we can turn to the trace document as a document—how to get data into it, how to save that data.

Recording

There is more than one way to start recording in Instruments.

The most obvious is to create a trace document and press the **Record** (red-dot) button in the toolbar. Recording starts, the target application comes to the front, you perform your test, switch back to Instruments, and press the same button, now displaying the black-square "stop" symbol.

The first time you record into a document that contains a Mac User Interface instrument (Mac targets only), the instrument captures your interaction with the target app into a list of events like key presses, mouse moves, and clicks. The Record Settings inspector's **Action** popup allows you to have the next run **Record** UI events as before, or **Drive** them, replaying the recorded actions, on the next run.

> **Note**
>
> The iOS side of Instruments gives you the same facility through the Automation instrument. Drop the instrument into the Track area, and attach a JavaScript script that will drive your application. When the Track runs, Automation will perform the UI actions you prescribed, and the other instruments will accumulate traces that you can compare directly between runs. Search the Documentation browser for "UI Automation JavaScript Reference" for details.

A second way to record is through a global hot key combination. To set the combination, Open the **Keyboard** panel in System Preferences, select the **Shortcuts** tab, and seek out the **Development** group under **Services**. The group includes a number of profiling actions, such as collecting a time profile of the application under the mouse cursor. One of the options is **Toggle Instruments Recording**. Set the combination by clicking the **add shortcut** button in that row of the table.

> **Note**
>
> I never remember these global hot keys. Do yourself a favor and check the box next to the service, so it will show up in the **Services** submenu of the application menu. The Instruments-related command will appear with its hot key combination. If there's no combination, you'll know that the app you're running has probably taken the combination for itself.

Instruments gives you a shortcut to the System Preferences window in the **General** tab in its own Preferences window: an **Open Keyboard Shortcut Preferences** button.

With the **Toggle Instruments Recording** hot key set, set up a trace document for the app you want to record—but don't run it. Run the app, then press the key combination you chose. Instruments will start recording. Press it again, and recording stops.

If you assign a key combination for other Instruments services, such as **Allocations & Leaks**, then Instruments will create a new trace document targeting the front application and record its memory activity. The same with **File Activity**, **System Trace**, and the other services that share the names of Instruments templates.

Take special note of the three **Time Profile** commands, which target the active application, the background application that has a window under the mouse pointer, or the whole system. The option of pointing the mouse at one of the target's windows allows you to start simultaneous traces on more than one application without having to disturb their place in the window ordering.

Displaying an ongoing trace, especially for more than one application, puts a significant performance burden on the system; I'll get into the details shortly. This can be a particular problem if you use hot keys to record more than one application. If you check **Always use deferred mode** in the **General** tab of the Preferences window, you can ensure that your hot-key traces will be as lightweight as possible.

The third way to record is through the Mini Instruments window. Selecting **View →Mini Instruments** hides all of Instruments' windows and substitutes a floating heads-up window (see Figure 26.5) listing all of the open trace documents.

The window lists all of the trace documents that were open when you switched to Mini mode; scroll through by pressing the up or down arrowheads above and below the list. At the left of each item is a button for starting (round icon) or stopping (square icon) recording, and a clock to show how long recording has been going on. Stopping and restarting a recording adds a new run to the document.

Closing the Mini Instruments window activates Instruments and restores the trace windows.

As with the hot keys, Mini Instruments has the advantage that it's convenient to start recording in the middle of an application's run (handy if you are recording a User Interface track that you want to loop). It eliminates the overhead of updating the trace displays.

I mentioned the burden a tracing session can put on the performance of your computer. While a trace runs, Instruments analyzes the data it collects, building up profiles and tables. Often it has to refer back to earlier data (like matching memory events to blocks and updating living-versus-transient counts) to keep the analysis current.

Computers are fast, but the process takes resources away from the target application (thus making it difficult to measure your app against real-world conditions) and can force Instruments to skip data points. You can prevent this by deferring analysis until the trace stops. **File →Record Options. . .** (⌥⌘R) sets parameters for tracing, like delaying data collection until a fixed time after launching the application, or limiting collection to a

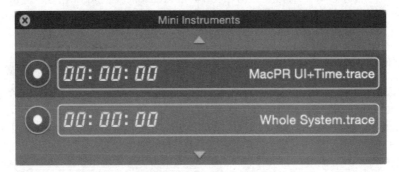

Figure 26.5   The Mini Instruments floating window. It lists each open trace document next to a clock and a recording button. Scroll through the list using the arrowheads at top and bottom.

fixed period. The option you're interested in is the **Deferred Mode** checkbox. While it's checked, Instruments will black out the trace window until the run ends. Once the run does end, the blackout will continue as Instruments conducts the postmortem analysis, and then you'll see your trace. See Figure 26.6.

Saving and Reopening

Like any other Macintosh document, a trace document can be saved. The document will contain its instruments and all the data they've collected. There can be a lot of data—potentially, full stack traces for events only microseconds apart—so expect a trace document to be large. Gigabytes are not uncommon. Trace documents generally respond well to ZIP archiving.

Another option is to save your document as a template. It's likely that you will come to need a uniform layout of instruments that isn't included in the default templates provided by Apple. You can easily create templates of your own, which will appear in the template sheet presented when you create a new trace document. Configure a document as you want it, and select **File → Save as Template....**

The ensuing save-file sheet is the standard one, focused on the directory in which Instruments looks for your templates, `~/Library/Application Support/ Instruments/Templates`. The name you give your file will be the label shown in the template-choice sheet. At the lower-left of the sheet is a well into which you can drag an icon to be displayed in lists that include your custom templates. For instance, if your

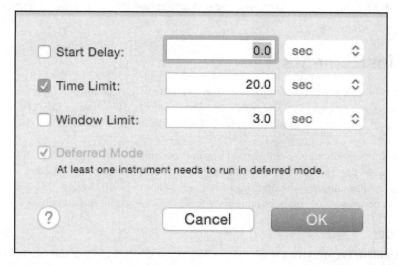

Figure 26.6   File → Record Options... (⌥⌘R) produces a sheet in which you can restrict the scope of an Instruments tracing session and improve the efficiency of the trace by deferring analysis until after the trace is done. In this case, an instrument in the trace document *requires* deferred analysis.

template is for testing your application, you'd want to drop your application's icon file here. Holding the mouse button over the well will display a popup menu so you can choose Apple-provided icons. The panel provides a text area for the description to be shown in the template-choice sheet.

- The document's suite of instruments, and their configurations, will be saved in the template.
- The template will include the target you set.
- If you include a prerecorded User Interface track, the contents will be saved. This way you can produce uniform test documents simply by creating a new trace document and selecting the template.

As you'd expect, you can reopen a trace document by double-clicking it in the Finder, or by using the **File** →**Open. . .** command. All of the data is as it was when the document was saved. Pressing **Record** adds a new run to the document.

Tracing without Instruments

There are three ways to run traces without having to launch Instruments. With the `instruments` command-line tool, you can select the target application and either a template or an existing trace document to capture the trace data. The `DTPerformance-Session` framework allows you to initiate traces from your source code without having to bother with the Instruments app's template and document infrastructure. And `iprofiler` provides the same lightweight profiling service from the command line. See `man instruments`, `man iprofiler`, and the `DTPerformanceSession` documentation for details.

The Instruments

There are 44 instruments that come with the Instruments application, plus any custom instruments you might create yourself. The Library palette, **Window** →**Library** (⌘ L), lists them all. The list in this section follows the Library's organization, adding details as I've gleaned them.

Some instruments aren't documented beyond the sentence or two they get in the Library, plus what is implied by the data they display. The listing rarely identifies which platform the instrument can target. In some cases, I can make up the gap; in others, my guess is as good as yours, often because they crash before you can see the results.

Behavior

- **Sudden Termination** (Mac only)—Audits the OS X feature of directly killing apps that volunteer that they'd be safe to kill. This instrument flags all of your filesystem activity that happens while you've signaled the system that a sudden kill would be okay. If you're actively reading and writing files, it may not be a good idea to subject yourself to termination without notice.

Core Data

- **Core Data Saves**—At each save operation in Core Data, records the thread ID, stack trace, and how long the save took.

- **Core Data Fetches**—Captures the thread ID and stack trace of every fetch operation under Core Data, along with the number of objects fetched and how long it took to complete the fetch.

- **Core Data Faults**—Core Data objects can be expensive both in terms of memory and in terms of the time it takes to load them into memory. Often, an NSManagedObject or a to-many relationship is given to you as a *fault*, a kind of IOU that will be paid off in actual data when you reference data in the object.

  This instrument captures every firing (payoff) of an object or relationship fault. It can display the thread ID and stack depth of the fault, as well as how long it took to satisfy object and relationship faults.

- **Core Data Cache Misses**—A faulted Core Data object may already be in memory; it may be held in its NSPersistentStoreCoordinator's cache. If, however, you fire a fault on an object that *isn't* in the cache (a "cache miss"), you've come into an expensive operation, as the object has to be freshly read from the database. You want to minimize the effect of cache faults by preloading the objects when it doesn't impair user experience.

  This instrument shows where cache misses happen. It records the thread ID and stack trace of each miss, and how much time was taken up satisfying the miss, for objects and relationships.

Dispatch

- **Dispatch** (Mac only)—Records Grand Central Dispatch events, the status of queues, and the duration of dispatched tasks.

Filesystem

- **Directory I/O** (Mac only)—Records every event of system calls affecting directories, such as creation, moving, mounting, unmounting, renaming, and linking. The data include thread ID, stack trace, call, path to the file directory affected, and the destination path.

- **File Activity** (Mac only)—Records every call to open, close, fstat, open$UNIX2003, and close$UNIX2003. The instrument captures thread ID, call stack, the call, the file descriptor, and path.

- **File Attributes** (Mac only)—For every event of changing the owner, group, or access mode of a file (chown, chgrp, chmod), this instrument records thread ID, a stack trace, the called function, the file descriptor number, the group and user IDs, the mode flags, and the path to the file affected.

- **File Locks** (Mac only)—Records the thread ID, stack trace, function, option flags, and path for every call to the flock system function.

- **I/O Activity** (iOS only)—Combines the functionality of all the Mac-only instruments in this category into one comprehensive instrument for iOS. By default, it only collects how long each call lasted, but click the **Configure** button to see what else is available.

Graphics

- **Core Animation** (iOS)—Collects statistics for the current state of OpenGL, including wait times for callers, counts of surfaces and textures, and how full video RAM is, as it relates to your app's use of the high-level Core Animation framework.

- **GPU Driver** (Mac or iOS)—collects the same statistics as the Core Animation instrument, at the lower level of OpenGL/OpenGL ES. There are two instruments of the same name. Drag one of them into your trace document; if you guess wrong, a yellow warning triangle will appear in the lower-right corner of the track, and you should try the other.

- **OpenGL ES Analyzer** (iOS)—Analyzes your app's usage of OpenGL ES, flagging stalls and other errors, yielding a ranked table of problems and suggestions on how to avoid them.

Input/Output

- **Reads/Writes**—`reads` and `writes` to file descriptors. Each event includes the thread ID, the name of the function being called, a stack trace, the descriptor and path of the file, and the number of bytes read or written.

Master Tracks

- **User Interface** (Mac only), on first run, records mouse and keyboard events as you use your OS X application. You'll be asked to authorize Instruments to control your application, through the System Preferences application → **Security & Privacy** → **Privacy** → **Accessibility**. After that, running the trace plays your UI events back so you can have a uniform baseline for your program as you make adjustments.

- **Cocoa Layout** (Mac only) records any changes to `NSLayoutConstraint` objects, either in the target application or anywhere in the system. It's not very easy to pick what you need out of the collected data; the best approach is to track down the view you're interested in, and enter its address in the search field.

  My copy of Instruments puts Cocoa Layout in the "Custom Instruments" category, not Master Track, but it makes more sense for me to put it next to User Interface.

Memory

- **Allocations** (iOS and Mac)—Collects a comprehensive history of every block of memory allocated during the run of the trace. Every event is tagged with the block address and the current stack trace. Configuration options let you track Cocoa reference-counting events and create "zombie" objects. You learned how to use it in Chapter 16, "Measurement and Analysis."

- **Leaks** (iOS and Mac)—Tracks the allocation and deallocation of objects in an application in order to detect the objects' being allocated and then lost—in other words, memory leaks. Leaks does not rely simply on balancing allocations and deallocations; it periodically sweeps your program's heap to detect blocks that are not referenced by active memory. If the Allocations instrument is set to monitor zombies, Leaks won't record because zombie objects, which are never deallocated, are all leaked. For an extensive example, see Chapter 16, "Measurement and Analysis."

- **Shared Memory** (Mac only)—Records an event when shared memory is opened or unlinked. The event includes calling thread ID and executable, stack trace, function (shm_open / shm_unlink), and parameters (name of the shared memory object, flags, and mode_t). Selecting an event in the Detail table puts a stack trace into the Extended Detail pane.

- **VM Tracker** (iOS and Mac)—Takes a "snapshot" of the virtual-memory zones associated with your application, recording the size of each zone, and whether it is shared or private. The trace shows total usage, but the real story is in the "dirty" trace: The VM system can share things like system libraries across applications from a single chunk of physical RAM, and memory that the app hasn't written to is "clean"—the system can simulate that memory as zeroes without taking up any actual RAM. As soon as your app writes to memory, those addresses become dirty, and they must consume precious physical memory.

  Don't bother with VM Tracker on the iOS Simulator; at the virtual-memory level, it's a Mac application with no relation to how memory would be used on an iOS device.

  By default, you have to click a **Snapshot Now** button in the Options view to collect heap data. You can check **Automatic Snapshotting** if you want to collect data periodically.

System

Two kinds of instruments fall into the System category: instruments that actively record the state of the target machine, and those that read logs an iOS device had recorded as it had been used untethered to a Mac. I'll treat them as if they were separate.

- **Activity Monitor** (iOS and Mac)—An analogue to the Unix top command, with the option to focus on only one process. This instrument is too varied to explain fully here, but its features should be easy to understand if you explore its configuration inspector. It collects 31 summary statistics on a running process, including thread counts, physical memory usage, virtual memory activity, network usage, disk operations, and percentages of CPU load. Remember that you can have more than one Activity Monitor instrument running, targeting different applications or the system as a whole.

- **Connections** (iOS only)—Measures all IP networking activity for an iOS device or any of its processes, in real time.

- **Counters** and **Event Profiler** (Mac only)—Track CPU and low-level system events using hardware diagnostic counters built into each core of the CPU. The data are eye-wateringly primitive, but if you've come to optimizing your code instruction by instruction, such as locating possibly inefficient branches, these instruments are the way to go.

  Window →**Manage Flags. . .** (⇧⌘ T) controls which flags are to trigger a count in Counters. Expect a noticeable performance hit when Counters is running. For Event Profiler, **Window** →**Manage PM Events. . .** (⇧⌘ P) sets the flags to audit.

- **Process** (Mac)—Records thread ID, stack trace, process ID, exit status, and executable path for each start (`execve`) and end (`exit`) event in a process.

- **Sampler** (iOS and Mac)—Periodically samples the target application at fixed intervals (1 ms by default, but you can set it in the inspector), and records a stack trace each time. This instrument has been superseded by Time Profiler, except in cases, like measuring graphics performance, when it is essential to minimize the effect of CPU sampling on other measurements.

- **Spin Monitor** (Mac only)—Focuses on one OS X application, or all, and logs stack traces when they become unresponsive. An application is "unresponsive" when it has spent more than a few seconds without attempting to collect a human-interface event. This is when the multicolored spinning "beachball" cursor occurs. This is a serious fault in an application, but you can't often reproduce spins. Spin Monitor sleeps most of the time, taking up very few resources until a spin activates it.

- **Time Profiler** (iOS and Mac)—Periodically samples the target application at fixed intervals (1 ms by default, but you can set it in the inspector), and records a stack trace each time. You can then get a statistical picture of what parts of your application are taking up the most time. This is an essential tool, doing what most people mean when they speak of profiling an application. Chapter 16, "Measurement and Analysis," demonstrated the use of Time Profiler.

  When Time Profiler is in a trace document, a bar is added above the Track area that lets you refine the profile: The segment control at the left provides an overview trace (middle), or it can divide the trace among CPU cores (left) or by thread (right). A series of popup menus let you restrict the trace by processor core, process, and thread; and they let you color-code by user and kernel load. A popup at the right end of the bar shows the colors used in the chart.

Note

A number of instruments from Xcode 5 have been removed—almost all the ones with "Monitor" in their names. These weren't really unique instruments, just Activity Monitor with a couple of statistics enabled. If you miss them, use Activity Monitor and check off the statistics that interest you. If you use the **Stacked** graph type and **Increase Deck Size** to make the track taller, you'll have the same effect.

System—iOS Energy Instruments

The Instruments Library puts iOS energy instruments in the "System" category, but they are different. They don't rely on Instruments to run the trace, because running them only when the device is tethered to a Mac would be counterproductive. When you designate a device for development, Xcode (or Instruments) installs a daemon on the device that can log activity that influences power drain.

You can analyze the logs when the device is plugged into Instruments again. Open Instruments and select **File →Import Energy Diagnostics from Device**.

By default, logging is off and must be turned on with the Settings app. The daemon itself can be turned off with the **Developer** panel in Settings or by an untethered reboot. If the battery runs out entirely, the daemon won't restart.

These are the instruments that analyze the usage logs:

- **Bluetooth**, **GPS**, and **WiFi**—Log when the respective radios are on.

- **CPU Activity**—This instrument is a compact version of Activity Monitor showing the total load on the CPU, with breakouts for the foreground app, audio, and graphics.

- **Display Brightness**—This instrument records the on/off state and brightness setting of the device's backlight. Ambient-light adjustments don't get logged.

- **Energy Usage**—Overall power drain on a scale of 20. When the device is plugged or unplugged to a power source, the event is flagged.

- **Network Activity**—Logs overall network usage in terms of bit and packet rates.

- **Sleep/Wake**—Logs whether the device is asleep, along with sleep-transition states.

Threads/Locks

Thread States (Mac only)—Represents each thread in the target application by a block, colored to indicate the state of the thread—running, waiting, suspended, etc.—at each moment. The Record Settings inspector has the color code (see Figure 26.7).

Trace

Scheduling, **System Calls**, and **VM Operations** (iOS, Mac)—These keep a complete record of the transitions between threads; between your user code and the underlying kernel; and of the layout of your working memory as managed by the virtual-memory system. You can read the duration of the time your code had to wait for kernel-level processing to complete. The track has two "strategies" for display, selectable through a segmented control at the left end of the bar that these instruments will insert above the time track.

These instruments force the use of deferred mode, and they insert a bar above the time scale to select display "strategies": bar graphs of "event density," or timelines that show state and flag transitions—click a flag and get a description of the transition type, timing, and a stack trace.

The bar includes a popup to narrow the display to specific processes and threads.

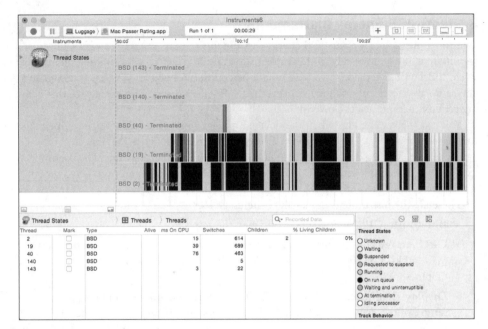

Figure 26.7   The Thread States instrument shows the state of every thread in a process as a stack of color-coded bars.

UI Automation

Automation (iOS only)—Executes a JavaScript script that exercises the UI of an iOS application on a device or the iOS Simulator. Add other instruments to the trace document to produce a package that can reproduce a test and record the performance of your app as you develop it. You configure the instrument in the Options view of the Detail area. The most important part is the Scripts section, where the **Add** drop-down menu allows you to **Import...** a .js file to the track or **Create...** one in an editor within the Detail area.

UI Automation comes with an extensive class tree; consult the "Instruments User Guide" and the "UIAutomation Reference Collection" for details.

User Interface

Carbon Events (Mac only)—Monitors events returned from WaitNextEvent. Carbon Events records an event at every return from WaitNextEvent and its cousins. It captures the thread ID, the stack trace, the event code, and a string (like "Key Down") that characterizes the event.

Cocoa Events (Mac only)—Records the event objects dispatched through every call to -[NSApplication sendEvent:]. It captures the thread ID, the stack trace, the event code, and a string (like "Left Mouse Down") that characterizes the event.

Custom Instruments

Many of the instruments included in Instruments consist of code specially written for the task, but most involve no native code at all. They are made from editable templates: You can examine these instruments yourself—this may be the only way to get authoritative details on what an instrument does—and you can create instruments of your own.

Let's see what a scripted instrument looks like. Create a trace document from the File Activity template, select the Reads/Writes instrument and then **Instrument →Edit 'Reads/Writes' Instrument** (or simply double-click on the instrument's label). An editing sheet (see Figure 26.8) will appear with fields for the instrument's name, category, and description, and a long scrolling list of *probes*, handlers for events the instrument is meant to capture.

Figure 26.8 shows the event list scrolled to the condition called **PWrite**, in the domain **System Call**, for the symbol pwrite. It is to trigger when pwrite is entered. Next comes the text of a script to be executed when the probe is triggered. Instruments uses the *DTrace* kernel facility, which has its own scripting language; for instance, this event might

Figure 26.8   The Edit Instrument sheet for the Reads/Writes instrument. The sheet is dominated by an editable list of events the instrument is to capture. The portion that specifies how to record entries to the system pwrite function is shown here.

put the time at which the event occurred into a thread variable of the probe, so that a `pwrite`-exit probe could calculate the duration of the call and record it. In this case, the scripting text is blank.

Then comes a series of items specifying what information is to be kept, for the trace graph or for the Detail view. In the case of Reads/Writes, this is

- The name of the function.
- The name of the executable.
- The first argument (the file descriptor), which is an integer to be labeled "FD."
- A string, to be labeled "Path," calculated from an expression in the DTrace language: a file path, derived from the file descriptor within the executable.
- The third argument (the size of the write), which is an integer to be labeled "Bytes."

At the bottom of the edit sheet is a drop-down menu that controls whether the instrument records a stack trace for its events, and whether the stack should be taken from user, kernel, or no space.

Integer-valued records are included in the configuration inspector's list of **Statistics to Graph** and are eligible to display in the instrument's trace. This accounts for the odd presence of "tid" (the thread ID) in the list of available plots you'll see if you click the **Configure** button in the instrument-configuration popover.

The customization sheet is a front end for the scripting language for the kernel-provided DTrace tool; only kernel-level code is capable of detecting call events in every process. The section "Creating Custom Instruments," in the *Instruments User Guide*, offers enough of an introduction to the language to get you started on your own instruments.

To make your own instrument, start with **Instrument →Build New Instrument. . .** (⌘ B). An instrument editing sheet will drop from the front trace document, and you can proceed from there.

If visiting `https://wikis.oracle.com/display/DTrace/Documentation` has made you a DTrace expert, you may find it more convenient, or more flexible, to write your scripts directly, without going through the customization sheet. Select **File →DTrace Script Export. . .** to save a script covering every instrument in the current document, and **File →DTrace Data Import. . .** to load a custom script. You can export DTrace scripts only from documents that contain DTrace instruments exclusively.

The Templates

Between iOS, OS X, and the iOS Simulator, there are 22 trace-document templates built into Instruments, and as you've seen, you can add your own. The Templates assistant presents these in four sections: one for each platform, plus yours.

This section lists all of the available templates, with the instruments they contain, sorted by platform. iOS Simulator shares some instruments with both iOS and OS X; I'll call them out in the platform lists.

All Platforms

Six templates are platform independent: They appear in all three parts of the source list.

- **Blank**: a document with no instruments in it
- **Activity Monitor**: Activity Monitor
- **Allocations**: Allocations, VM Tracker
- **Leaks**: Allocations, Leaks
- **System Trace**: Scheduling, System Calls, VM Operations
- **Time Profiler**: Time Profiler

iOS Only

These seven templates are for iOS targets only, though one of them, Automation, is also available in the iOS Simulator.

- **Automation**: Automation (also on iOS Simulator)
- **Core Animation**: Core Animation, Time Profiler
- **Energy Diagnostics**: These are the analyzers for logs a device accumulates while it's untethered from Instruments—Bluetooth, CPU Activity, Display Brightness, Energy Usage, GPS, Network Activity, Sleep/Wake, WiFi
- **GPU Driver**: GPU Driver, Time Profiler
- **Network**: Connections
- **OpenGL ES Analysis**: GPU Driver, OpenGL ES Driver
- **System Usage**: I/O Activity

Mac Only

Nine templates are for OS X applications, which in a few cases includes the simulator.

- **Cocoa Layout**: Cocoa Layout
- **Core Data**: Core Data Cache Misses, Core Data Fetches, Core Data Saves (also on iOS Simulator)
- **Counters**: Counters
- **Dispatch**: Dispatch
- **File Activity**: File Activity, File Attributes, Directory I/O, Reads/Writes (also on iOS Simulator)
- **Multicore**: Dispatch, Thread States
- **Sudden Termination**: Activity Monitor, Sudden Termination

- **UI Recorder**: User Interface
- **Zombies**: Allocations, preconfigured to track zombie objects (also on iOS Simulator)

Summary

Instruments is a big topic, and I've put you through most of it. You started with a tour of the trace document window and moved on to populating it from the Library window. You learned general principles of how to configure an instrument track.

You saw the various ways to start and stop recordings, including human-interface recordings that can be played back to generate repeatable tests for your applications.

You walked through a partial inventory of the instruments and document templates Apple supplies and how to create your own.

As your needs and expertise progress, you'll want to consult the *Instruments User Guide*, to be found in Xcode's Documentation browser.

## 27

Debugging

Debugging is intrinsic to the development process. The first parts of this book tell the story of a development process, and basic debugging techniques followed naturally. In this chapter, I want to call out a few subjects to provide you with a better grasp of how you can get the most out of the Xcode debugger and the `lldb` debugging system that underlies it.

We'll take a look at the Run action in a build scheme and how it sets the conditions for your debugging session. Then, I'll help you build the skills to make breakpoints more than mere stopping places. And we'll have a look at the command line for the `lldb` debugger, as it's used both in the Terminal and in the debugger console. Finally, a few short tips and techniques.

Scheme Options

Schemes have come up repeatedly in *Xcode 6 Start to Finish*, but I want to go through the scheme editor for the Run action, from which you'll do most of your debugging. It includes many options to access the OS's debugging features. The Run scheme editor has four tabs, and here they are, one by one.

Info

The options in the **Info** tab can be seen in Figure 27.1, top.

- You can choose whether to **Debug** the **Executable** at all.
- You have a choice of the privilege level at which the target will run.
  - You can run and debug with your user privileges (**Me**).
  - You can run with **root** privileges (so long as you can provide admin credentials).
- Ordinarily, you want to run and debug your application **Automatically**, as soon as the build completes. But sometimes you have an app that needs specific inputs and conditions from some other process that launches it. The **Wait for executable to be launched** radio button makes `lldb` wait until your app starts, and attach once it's running.

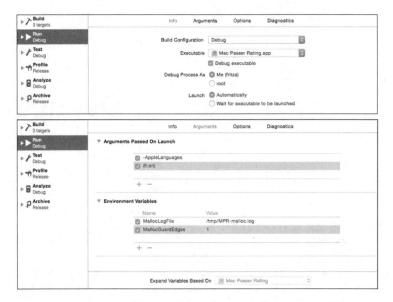

Figure 27.1   Info (top) and **Arguments** (bottom) tabs for the scheme's Run action.

Arguments

The **Arguments** panel (Figure 27.1, bottom) has two tables: one for command-line arguments, and one for environment variables. Use the **+** and **−** buttons to add and remove them. A checkbox will appear next to each item so you can choose which settings should be passed to your application on a particular run.

Argument entries can contain spaces, which will be treated as delimiters when the application is launched; that is, they will result in separate items in the traditional `argv` array. If you mean to pass an argument that contains a space, escape it with a backslash as you would on a command line.

The **Expand Variables Based On** popup menu lets you use the value of a build variable in your arguments and environment values; just include the variable's name like this: `${SETTING_NAME}`. Each target has its own set of build variables, and this menu lets you choose which set is used.

Options

The **Options** tab for the Run action is different depending on whether the target is for Mac or iOS. These controls affect runtime conditions that don't directly match up to system-defined environment variables—like location, working directories, graphics state, and whether you have to deal with potentially frustrating features like launch-time state restoration.

Mac

If you check **Allow Location Simulation**, you'll be given a choice of locations for the debug environment to report to Location Services. You can select from a menu of locations, or add a GPX file for a custom location.

In OS X, Cocoa applications are subject to automatic state restoration, wherein the OS will attempt to reopen previously open documents and configure them as they were. By checking **Persistent State: Launch application without state restoration**, you can save yourself the headaches that may come when you simply want your app to start from zero.

The Versions browser works by loading the previous versions of a document into separate document objects and having them draw themselves. Debugging a plethora of transient, near-identical documents would be... a challenge, but if you need to do it, check **Document Versions: Allow debugging when using document Versions Browser**.

The POSIX working directory is a sore point in Mac development, because when Xcode debugs an application, the working directory is set to the one that contains the app; whereas applications launched from Finder get /, the root of the filesystem (though this is not guaranteed). Checking **Working Directory: Use custom working directory:** sets the working directory for debugging runs. There's a field for entering the path and a button to open a get-directory sheet.

We saw **Localization Debugging: Show non-localized strings** in Chapter 21, "Localization." Any text that isn't drawn from the .lproj localization directory is rendered as all-caps or uninterpreted format strings. We also explored the use of the **Application Language** and **Application Region** popups.

XPC services are small executables that isolate parts of an OS X application that might threaten security or make the app less stable. You're probably aware that modern web browsers do much the same thing to prevent plugins from gaining access to the browser proper.

If you check **Debug XPC services used by this application**, Xcode will attach the debugger to XPCs as they launch, as separate process objects in the lldb session.

View Debugging is a new feature in Xcode 6. If you enable it, you can see an explosion of your application's view hierarchy in the debugger. More on that soon.

iOS

The iOS options deal with configuring the simulator and setting up debugging on devices. Here are the options that are unique to iOS.

- When you plug a development-enabled device into your Mac, you can use the Devices organizer to navigate to an application and extract its data into a data package. This is vital if you need to reproduce a bug that's dependent on the state of your application. Once you've added the data package to your project, the **Application Data** popup can select it for loading into the simulator at application startup.

- Apple expects that routing (turn-by-turn directions) applications can provide data only for parts of the globe; you'll upload a coverage (GeoJSON) file to iTunes Connect so the App Store knows what parts of the world your app should be sold in. **Routing App Coverage File** configures the simulator to restrict your app to those regions.

- The Xcode debugger provides comprehensive tools for debugging OpenGL ES and Metal on iOS devices. **GPU Frame Capture** enables or disables the frame-capture button on the debugger's control bar, allowing you to examine your builds step by step.

- iOS can launch apps in the background if they need to poll net resources for data they can download behind the scenes. Checking **Launch due to a background fetch event** simulates this kind of launch, instead of forcing the app onto the screen.

- **XPC Services** are worth mentioning, because Xcode 6 adds support for iOS extensions with this option.

Diagnostics

The **Diagnostics** tab controls a number of diagnostic and logging options for both OS X and iOS that historically were controlled by environment variables. The most famous is detecting overreleased objects by setting NSZombieEnabled to YES. **Diagnostics** presents the most frequently used options as checkboxes. Search the Documentation browser for Technical Note TN2124, "Mac OS X Debugging Magic," for a description of them and their use. The "Debugging Magic" notes (the iOS version, TN2239, isn't available as I write this, but tech notes with changeable content often drop out of sight from time to time) are worth reading all the way through.

> **Note**
>
> The "zombie" technique is a useful way to track down attempts to use an object that had been deallocated by Cocoa's memory-management system. Ordinarily, accessing a disposed-of object would crash, usually in objc_msgSend as your app tries to send the dead object a message. Sometimes the access would go to a completely different object that had been allocated into the same address as the dead object. Either way, it's difficult to determine what the overreleased object had been. When you enable zombies, objects' memory is never freed; they are simply replaced by "zombie" objects that remember what the class of the old object was, and halt execution whenever you try to send them a message. The result is that your app crashes at the *first* attempted access—there's no chance of a succession of accesses that turned out to be harmless—and you have at least a class name to narrow your search for the cause. Zombies are available through this panel, through environment variables, and as an option for the Allocations instrument.

Doing More with Breakpoints

Many developers, even if they regularly use breakpoints, believe logging is the only way to pull control flow and state out of their programs when it's not practical to stop dead at

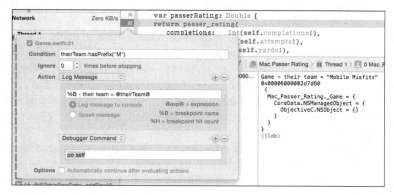

Figure 27.2   A breakpoint action can provide a more refined log than an `NSLog()` in the source code.

every pass through a segment of code. Not so. If you take nothing else away from this chapter, remember this: Almost never do you have to compile `println()`, `NSLog()`, or other printing functions into your application for debugging.

Use breakpoint options instead of `NSLog()`s. The options popover (Figure 27.2) is a little intimidating, but everything in it has a purpose, and once you understand what you can do, it all falls into place.

Let's start with some code from `Game.swift` based on `println()`:

```swift
var passerRating: Double {
    let rating = passer_rating(
        completions:    Int(self.completions!),
        attempts:       Int(self.attempts!),
        yards:          Int(self.yards!),
        touchdowns:     Int(self.touchdowns!),
        interceptions:  Int(self.interceptions!))

    if theirTeam.hasPrefix("M") {
        println("\(__FUNCTION__) - their team = \(theirTeam)")
        println("\(self.description)")
    }

    return rating
}
```

Imagine that the problem we're tracking somehow involves passer ratings coming in `Games` in which the opponent's team name begins with "M." It could happen.

1. Delete the `if` statement, including its body. The whole point is that you don't need it.
2. Click the margin at `return...` to make a breakpoint appear.

3. Right-click the breakpoint arrow and select **Edit Breakpoint. . .** , or simply option-command-click it, to expose the breakpoint options popover.

4. You're only interested in "M" teams, so in the **Condition** field, reproduce the condition in the `if` statement: enter **`theirTeam.hasPrefix("M")`**. Breakpoint conditions can execute expressions in any language being debugged. For Objective-C expressions, you must cast method return types—`lldb` can't infer the return type of every possible method implementation. Swift is tight enough about typing that you don't need to specify.

5. In the **Action** popup, select **Log Message**, and type **`%B - rating = @rating @`**. Anything you bracket with @ signs is interpreted as an expression, which is substituted into the message. You have the option of speaking the message instead of printing it.

> **Note**
>
> You also have the option of playing a sound or executing a debugger command, a shell script, or an AppleScript.

6. However, the @ . . . @ notation isn't as useful as you'd think. If you want to print an object value, this syntax doesn't help because the interpreter sees only a pointer, and prints the hexadecimal address. Your alternative is to use the `expression` debugger command, such as `expr -O -- self`, where the `-O` option tells `lldb` to print the object's description; for the comfort of `gdb` veterans, `lldb` provides the old `po` as an alias.

So click the **(+)** button and add a **Debugger Command**. Type **`po self`** in the text field.

7. In the Options section, check **Automatically continue after evaluating**. The `NSLog()`s didn't stop execution, so neither will this breakpoint.

8. Click away from the popover to close it.

> **Note**
>
> The replacement of `NSLog()` calls is complete when you check **Automatically continue after evaluating actions** in the options popover for a breakpoint. When the breakpoint hits, it will perform all its actions, but it won't halt the program.

Now run your app, and find that your debugger console fills with the breakpoint location, rating, opponent's name, and the contents of the `Game` object.

To be sure, in this simple case, it's trivial to construct logging code that does what you need—that's what we started with. But if you first notice the error only after the app had built up state for a long time, and you decide to instrument the problem, it is not practical to kill the app, insert the logging code, rebuild it, and work it to the point where it triggers the bug. Breakpoints don't need a rebuild, their presence doesn't change the state of the program itself (unless you want it to), and they can be modified on the fly.

> **Note**
>
> In earlier versions of Xcode, when you set exception or symbolic breakpoints in the Breakpoint navigator, you got a popover with breakpoint options immediately. This was useful for exceptions because the exception breakpoint can limit itself to Objective-C or C++ exceptions. Some of the Cocoa internals are implemented in C++ that makes liberal use of exceptions, which opens you up to a lot of false positives. Right-click on the new breakpoint and select **Edit Breakpoint...** from the contextual menu.

View Hierarchy

I mentioned the **Enable user interface debugging** checkbox in the Options panel of the Run action in the Scheme editor. When UI debugging is on, a ⊓⊔ button appears in the Debug area's control bar. When you click it, the target app pauses, and the editor area of the project window fills with an exploded view of the active window. The usual scrolling gestures pan over the model, dragging rotates it, and the –, =, and + buttons zoom in and out. See Figure 27.3, top.

The Debug navigator picks up a popup menu at its top-right corner. When you click the ⊓⊔ button, the menu sets to **View UI Hierarchy**, the other choices being **View Processes by Thread** and **View Processes by Queue**, which show the more traditional stack traces. In the UI hierarchy view, the Debug navigator shows a complete outline of the window's views, similar to the document outline in Interface Builder, but much more thorough.

With the UI panel visible, two new inspector tabs appear in the Utility area.

- The Object inspector (third tab) provides comprehensive information about any view you select.
- The Size inspector (fourth tab) shows the location and size of the view's frame, and a list of the Auto Layout constraints.

The controls at the bottom of the view adjust the presentation.

- The slider at the left sets the spacing between the view layers.
- There is a toggle for showing and hiding views that exist, but are not visible because they are beyond the bounds of their containers. Figure 27.3, bottom, shows that Cocoa has prerendered the rows of the game table below the visible bottom of the table.
- The box with the I-beam across it, when highlighted, shows the constraints on any view you select in the panel. All views are replaced with wireframe outlines, and its constraints are drawn in blue around it. Selecting a constraint ought to give you full details in the Object inspector, but as of Xcode 6.1, it's not all there yet.
- The third button restores the scale of the view layout, centers it, and turns it face-on.
- The fourth control is a popup menu to display just the contents, or the wireframe boundaries, or both.

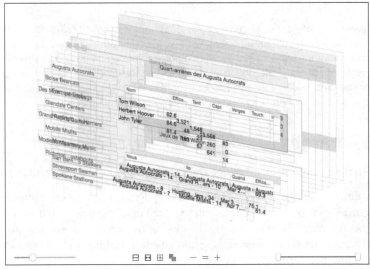

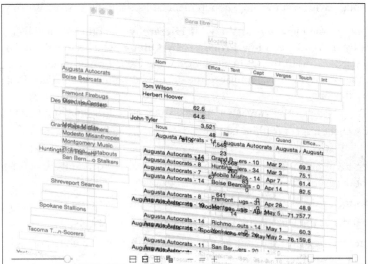

Figure 27.3 (top) Clicking the 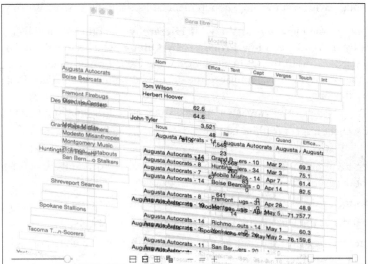 button in the debugger control bar presents an exploded view of the front window of the target application. (bottom) The controls at the bottom of the view adjust the contents: The lower-left slider has spread the views apart; the first of the toggle buttons reveals the views that had been clipped from view by their containers; and the range slider at lower-right hid the layers farther to the rear.

- Next, three buttons to zoom the view in or out, or to restore the scale to normal.
- The double slider on the right controls how much of the hierarchy will be visible. Moving the left slider to the right filters the back views from the display; moving it to the right side removes the forward views.

The `lldb` Command Line

The conditions and commands that you can put into a breakpoint-options popover are just a taste of what you can do with the `lldb` command line. The `lldb` command language is large but much more compact and consistent than `gdb`'s. Nobody can say for sure that it's more powerful, but one of the reasons Apple replaced `gdb` is that the complex of `gdb` settings and command options is so intricate that few users can get the maximum value out of it.

The general pattern of `lldb` commands is

```
noun verb options... arguments...
```

The *noun* portion classifies the available commands. The subsequent verbs and options refine your input to specific actions. The following is a list of built-in, permanent debugger command categories. A few of them are useful only on the command line, but most are wrapped in Xcode's debugging UI. Almost all can be used from the Xcode debugger's own console.

- **quit**—If you're using `lldb` on the command line, the first thing you'll want to know is how to get out.
- **apropos** and **help**—These are the commands you'll be using the most, at least for a while. The `lldb` web site has a good tutorial, but it can't cover every subcommand and option you'll want to use. The command-line help system is your best resource. Enter **help breakpoint**, and you'll get a list of all the verbs for the `breakpoint` noun; `help breakpoint set` will show you the available options for setting a breakpoint.

  > **Note**
  >
  > The tutorial at `http://lldb.llvm.org/tutorial.html` is a great starting place.

- **platform**—`lldb`'s central concept is a hierarchy of containers to organize and control a debugging session. `platform` is the outermost. This noun lets you examine and select the various devices and architectures that `lldb` can target—a single instance of the debugger can target more than one at a time—and discover the processes `lldb` can access.
- **target**—With `target`, you designate an executable as the focus of a session. You can designate more than one target, so you don't need to run a second instance of `lldb` to debug both a server and a client. Xcode provides this service when you run a target while another is running: It drops a sheet asking whether you want to quit

the existing target, but if you choose to leave it running, the debugger will work on both simultaneously.

- **process**—This is the third layer of `lldb` containers. You can launch a target (thus creating a process) or attach to an existing process. The process level is where you'd interrupt execution, send POSIX signals, or kill the process.

- **thread**—Most of what you think of when you think about debugging is in this container. The thread level is where you get stack traces and control execution by stepping through the program.

- **frame**—This is the innermost layer. It allows you to focus on the chain of frames—levels of the stack trace—at the point where execution is currently stopped. You can get a dump of variables at each level. The `frame variables` command alone gives you just the local variables (Objective-C and `@objc` objects will be expanded if you add the `-O` option). But it's much more flexible than that; type **`help frame variable`** for the extensive list of options.

- **breakpoint**—This category creates, deletes, lists, and attaches conditions and scripts to breakpoints. Because you can attach `expression` commands to a breakpoint, you can get away with executing anything you like in an application when the breakpoint triggers. **watchpoint** manages special breakpoints that trigger whenever a variable or memory region is changed—on the Mac or an iOS device.

- **expression**—The `expression` command is incredibly powerful. It will evaluate and print the result of any expression in the language of the file you're stopped in; `lldb` embeds the `llvm` compiler library, so it uses exactly the compiler that was used to build your application. The `expression` interpreter will even compile your expression into machine code before evaluating it.

  It can be any kind of expression: You can do assignments and increments. You can declare local or global variables. You can execute conditionals and loops. Remember the `-O` option if you want to print the description of an Objective-C object.

- **command**—You'll start out with the `alias` verb to create shortcuts for commonly used commands; `lldb` comes with a set of aliases that map many `gdb` commands. `command` verbs also let you load Python modules for more sophisticated commands using the `lldb` module, which gives Python complete access to `lldb`'s internal state; `lldb` will even give Python plugins access to the target program's memory space, so you can format the internal data of an object without having to run any of the object's methods.

There are many more command categories than I can list here, useful as they are: commands for manipulating memory and registers, listing source code and disassembly, and building a custom configuration. Look for *LLDB Quick Start Guide* in the Documentation browser. In the console, the `help` command is your friend.

For daily use, however, most people find debugging a program through printing its state from a command line to be like sucking the app through a straw. Xcode's debugging UI wraps most of these commands in a much more usable presentation that puts the whole state of the program on-screen at a glance. You can even use features like summary for-matters and Python-defined functions by putting them in user-, target-, or directory-specific .lldbinit configuration files.

Tips

Here are a few quick tips to help you in debugging your apps.

- By default, breakpoints are private to you—it's not likely that others on your team are interested in how you're working on your part of an app. But you can make a breakpoint public. Right-click on it in the Breakpoint navigator (sixth tab), and select **Share Breakpoint**. The breakpoint will move to a section marked "(Shared)," and it will be visible to users with different user names.

- Breakpoints are also private to the projects in which they were set. By default, a breakpoint applies only to the project that was active when it was set. If you share a source file among projects in a workspace, the breakpoint will trigger only during the run of its project's target. If you want it to trigger regardless of the project, right-click on it in the Breakpoint navigator, and select **Move Breakpoint To →User**.

- The variables view takes up the left side of the Debug area (so long as you select the left-side button from the two at the bottom-right corner of the Debug area. One big improvement is the "Return Value" pseudo-variable. Often you will have a (not very) complex statement like

  ```
  labelString = masterObject.descriptionDictionary.objectForKey("name")
  ```

  where -descriptionDictionary is a method you had defined. Step into descriptionDictionary. Step out; the program counter is now just before the call to objectForKey:. What dictionary will objectForKey: be sent to? Previously, there was no way to know without digging around through the stack pointer. Now, the "Return Value" line of the variables view will show you.

  > **Note**
  >
  > As I write this, "Return Value" didn't always show up or was easy to miss—at the machine-code level, a returned value has a very short lifetime; the bits get assigned or passed elsewhere, and the fact that they came from a function call is quickly forgotten.

- Perhaps you want a console window, just a command-line interface to see your printed output and type application input and debugger commands. Xcode 6's default appearance is discouraging, but it's more adaptable than it looks.

  Double-click any file in a navigator, or tear a tab away from the top of a project window. Either way, you'll have a separate window. Use the toolbar in that window to show the Debug area and hide the Navigator area. Drag the bar at the top of the Debug area to the top of the window, so the editor views disappear. Select **View**

→**Hide Toolbar** to make the toolbar go away. Use the visibility control at the bottom-right corner of the window to make the variables and console view visible, according to your taste.

You now have a console window. It's not perfect: The title of the window will show the name of whatever was in the window's editor when you started. And, as always, it's fragile. If one of your behaviors changes the format of the front window, you've lost your layout. If you close what you're going to think of as your "project" window, the "console" window will be the last surviving window, and when you reopen the project, you'll have only your console, and you'll have to get busy with the **View** menu to dig yourself out.

- You may find you have to authenticate yourself—possibly repeatedly—to enable the debugger and Instruments to breach security to the extent of permitting you to examine and change the state of another application (the one you're trying to debug). To silence the security dialogs, enter **sudo DevToolsSecurity -enable** on the command line.

- The po (print-object) command in the lldb console will print the results of the object's description method (or debugDescription, which is usually the same thing). The default implementation, from NSObject, just prints out the object's class and address, which is of little help. If, instead, you enter **p** ***objectVariableName**, lldb will treat the object as a C struct and display all of its instance variables.

> **Note**
> The print-object/po command is just an alias for lldb's expression -O -- objectVariable.

Another strategy worth trying for objects responding to the Swift Printable protocol is to enter expr println("object.description").

- I mentioned the watchpoint command family in the lldb command line, which allows you to set a kind of breakpoint that triggers when a variable changes value, not necessarily at any one line of your source. Watchpoints allow you to catch bugs where a value changes, and you can't determine how.

  Xcode provides a graphical interface for watchpoints, but it's not obvious. To set a watchpoint, first set an unconditional breakpoint at the first moment the variable comes into scope—you can't work on the variable until lldb can identify it, and the variable has to be in the current scope for lldb to do that. Look for the variable you're interested in in the variables pane. You may have to use the disclosure triangle on an object to expose an instance variable, if that's what you're interested in. Right-click on the variable's row and select **Watch "variableName"**. The next time something changes the value of the variable, Xcode will break in.

Watchpoints having no fixed location in the source code, there's no marker in any editor view that represents one. You can find watchpoints in a special category in the Breakpoint navigator, where you can edit, deactivate, or delete it.

Watchpoints work on iOS devices as well as on Macs.

- When you're debugging, the top bar of the Debug area, containing all the stepping and other flow-control buttons, is visible at the bottom of the project window, even if you've hidden the Debug area. At the left end of the bar is a control that expands and retracts the Debug area. If anything has been printed in the console since you last looked at the full Debug area, this control will highlight in blue.

- The **Debug** menu provides menu and key equivalents to all the flow-control buttons in the debugger. **Add/Remove Breakpoint at Current Line** (⌘ \) and **Create Symbolic Breakpoint...** (⌥ ⌘ \) will be useful if you prefer to avoid mousing as you type.

- The **Step Over** and **Step Into** commands (both in the **Debug** menu and in the debugger bar) have two additional variants:

  - **Instruction** advances the program counter to the next machine instruction in the current function (Over) or the next instruction in the course of execution, even if that means descending through a function call (Into). The variants appear in the menu; clicking the buttons with the Control key pressed does the same thing.

  - **Thread** is a little more subtle. Cocoa applications are threaded; there's no way around it. When you do a step-over or a step-into, not only does the thread you see in the debugger advance, so does any other thread that was executing at the same time. You have no control over what thread that would be, still less what code it is executing or what effect it might have on the state you are debugging. **Step Over Thread** and **Step Into Thread** freeze all other threads while you advance the thread you're debugging. Hold down Shift and Control while clicking the buttons, or select the commands in the **Debug** menu, to get the effect.

- If you're comfortable with using lldb from the command line, you can set symbolic breakpoints that match a regular-expression pattern. Say you want to stop at entry to any method whose selector begins with passer. You can do that by using the -r option of the breakpoint set command:

```
(lldb) breakpoint set -r passer.*
Breakpoint created: 8: regex = 'passer.*', locations = 8,
                    resolved = 8
```

lldb says you just created breakpoint 8; breakpoint list lets you examine it:

```
(lldb) breakpoint list 8
8: regex = 'passer.*', locations = 8, resolved = 8
    8.1: where = Mac Passer Rating`
                      -[LeagueDocument passerTable] + 16 ...
    8.2: where = Mac Passer Rating`
                      -[LeagueDocument passerArrayController] + 21 ...
```

```
8.3: where = Mac Passer Rating`
                -[PRGame passerRating] + 19 at PRGame.m:117 ...
    ...
```

It turns out the command set the breakpoint at eight locations (I'm showing only three of them). lldb separates *locations* from the breakpoints that have effect at them. You can clear the breakpoint from all eight locations by deleting it: **breakpoint delete 8**.

Multi-location breakpoints don't show up in Xcode's Breakpoint navigator, nor in editor margins.

- Sometimes breakpoints get set in your code with no indication in the Xcode UI. It's not supposed to happen, but it will happen to you. You can repair this by typing **breakpoint list** at the lldb command line, finding the number of the phantom breakpoint, and listing the numbers of the breakpoints you want to clear at the end of a typed **breakpoint delete** command.

- Here's something that isn't in the menus, and I really wish it were: If you use **Step Into** enough times in a debugging session, inevitably you will find you've stepped into a function for which there is no debugging information, or no source code. If you're good enough to reliably navigate through such code on your own, you don't need this book.

  lldb has a way out: Entering **thread step-in -a true** (-a is short for --avoid-no-debug) at the lldb command line gets you past frames for which there is no debugging information, so the debugger doesn't come back to you until it hits your code again.

- If you don't remember to break on exceptions, you will inevitably find that you'll hit one, and you won't get control of the debugger until the exception stack has wound down to the run loop, or even your main function.

  You can forestall this for OS X applications by setting the user default (preference) NSApplicationShowExceptions to YES in the Terminal command line:

```
$ # Set it for an app whose ID is com.yourdomain.application.id
$ defaults write com.yourdomain.application.id\
> NSApplicationShowExceptions YES
$ # Set it for every app you run:
$ defaults write -g NSApplicationShowExceptions YES
```

Summary

Most of *Xcode 6 Start to Finish* is an examination of how to integrate Xcode's debugger into your daily workflow. That made this chapter into an opportunity to examine some details that can guide you on the way from effectiveness to mastery.

First, we'd been leaving the debugging environment to the defaults Xcode's project templates provide. The defaults are useful, but there are details—environment variables, location sensing, background processing, and cooperation with subtasks—that have to be addressed as your application becomes more sophisticated. That's the job of the Run action in the Scheme editor.

Next, we explored the power of Xcode's breakpoints. They aren't just for halting the application for you to poke around. You can set up your breakpoints so they automate the way you gather information about how your app works. With conditions and counts and prints, they can all but eliminate the need to change your code just to get a log of how the app executes, or to flick the **Continue** button time after time while you wait for a critical piece of data to arrive.

The power of breakpoints comes from the power of the `lldb` debugger. Xcode's debugger is a wrapper on `lldb`, and it's a good one. But some day, you'll need even more control and insight. `lldb`'s command language is direct and elegant, and I showed you the outlines and the philosophy that makes sense of its design.

The UI Debugging view is pretty—and useful. I showed you how to get a live perspective on the visual presentation of your apps. Bugs in visualization are almost by definition difficult to visualize; this will take you a long way to bringing more bugs under control.

Finally, I passed along some small—but I hope, helpful—tricks that have helped me in my long hours of debugging.

Snippets

X*code 6 Start to Finish* relies mostly on narrative to take you on a tour of using Xcode for Cocoa development. I tried to cover as much as I could in the first three parts, and I mopped up the remaining big topics in the fourth. That leaves some small topics—tricks and traps—that didn't fit anywhere else.

Tricks

General

- If you're used to Unix or Linux development in C-family languages, you're accustomed to global macros like NDEBUG and DEBUG, and expect them to be set for you.

  If the argument to the standard C assert() macro is zero, it halts the program. If NDEBUG is set, assert() does nothing, so you can publish code that may still exhibit the bug you put in the assertion for, but at least it won't crash.

  The NS_BLOCK_ASSERTIONS macro does the same with Cocoa's NSAssert family of assertion macros; as do optimization levels for Swift assertions.

  Many developers like to define a DEBUG macro to guard logging and assertion code. It's not a standard macro, but it's very common.

  Xcode's project templates define DEBUG=1 for the Debug configuration; NDEBUG and NS_BLOCK_ASSERTIONS are never set. An easy way to cut down on the size of your released code is to open the **Build Settings** tab in the Target editor and double-click the value for the Release version of the "Preprocessor Macros" setting. You'll get a table to enter the definitions; click the **+** button to add lines. Set NDEBUG and NS_BLOCK_ASSERTIONS, and don't set DEBUG at all. Remember to include $(inherited) to preserve definitions made at other levels.

  > **Note**
  >
  > Don't prefix the symbols you put in "Preprocessor Macros" with -D, even though that's what would go into the clang command line; the setting does that.

> **Note**
>
> A shorthand for setting NS_BLOCK_ASSERTIONS is to set "Enable Foundation Assertions" (ENABLE_NS_ASSERTIONS) in the **Build Settings** tab, setting **Yes** for debugging builds, and **No** for release.

- The **Editor** menu is extremely variable—it adjusts to the type of file in the active editor. If you're sure there's a feature for doing what you want, but you can't find it by typing in the field at the top of the **Help** menu, be sure to bring up a related file, and click on it to adjust the **Editor** menu.

- In a complex project, an object in a XIB may take part, as provider or recipient, in dozens of outlets, actions, and bindings, each with its own context-limited editor. You don't have to click through all of the editors; select the object, select the Connection (sixth) inspector, and all of the connections will be there in one place.

- If you command-click on a system-provided symbol in a Swift file (including Swift itself, in import Swift), you will see a fully commented interface file for the class that defines the symbol, in Swift. There is no such file (at least not yet). It is an on-the-fly translation of the Objective-C @interface file.

  This is ingenious, but there is one omission: API that Apple has marked as deprecated in the ObjC header doesn't carry over into the translation. You can see the point—Apple doesn't want to encourage the use of deprecated API, nor to maintain that API so it will be Swift-compatible.

  But what happens when you use a method that was okay when you wrote it, but was then deprecated? This shouldn't happen with API Apple has released as final—at least not for another year or two—but it does happen for preview software, and during Apple's process of settling on the methods that should carry over to Swift. The nice thing about the .h files that have to accommodate legacy code is that the deprecations are still there, usually with comments telling you what to use instead. In the Swift interface, all you're told is that the method you're trying to use doesn't exist and never has.

  If Swift gaslights you like this, open an Objective-C source file, **File → Open Quickly…** (⇧⌘O), and begin typing the symbol you're looking for. (You can't do this when a .swift file is showing—Xcode will force you into the Swift interfaces.) When you see the header you need, double-click it, and you'll see the old API and (you hope) what you should use instead.

- You can't subclass a Swift class in Objective-C. Ever. Not even if you declare everything @objc and public. clang will tell you "Cannot subclass a class with objc_subclassing_restricted attribute." Every Swift class has that attribute. If you define a class in Swift, you can extend it with an ObjC category, but its subclasses are Swift forever.

- You may find some user-defined items at the bottom of the **Build Settings** table. In general, this is how Xcode preserves settings it doesn't recognize. What it recognizes depends on the context: If, for instance, you have a project that doesn't have any compilable files, Xcode won't load its list of compiler options, and those options will be shown as user-defined.

Older projects are another source of unrecognized settings. Some options are no longer supported in Xcode 6. When you open a project, Xcode may even offer to "modernize" your project by removing them. What you do about this is up to you. Usually, it's a good idea, but if you're sharing the project file with others who are building for older Xcodes or OSes, in which those settings might still be relevant, you will want to preserve those settings for their benefit.

- One setting that I haven't mentioned is $(inherited). Targets inherit build settings from the project, which in turn inherits settings from Xcode's defaults. Sometimes you want to add to, not replace, a setting from the next-lower level. Use $(inherited) to insert the inherited value in your setting.

- You've seen Xcode's offer to incorporate directories as "folder references" when you add files to a project. The Project navigator shows two different kinds of folder icon: What you've seen throughout this book are "group" folders. Basically, these are simply organizational tools, a way to gather files you've decided are related. Each file in a group is itself a member of the project.

  But sometimes adding a folder to a project means adding the folder itself. Suppose that you were building an educational program about presidents of the United States and wanted the Resources directory of the application to include a subdirectory containing a picture of each president. Your intention is that the application copy that directory in, with whatever it may contain—as new administrations or replacement portraits come in—not the particular files.

  In such a case, when you add the portrait folder, you check **Create folder references for any added folders** in the add-files sheet. The folder you dragged in will appear in the list in the same blue color as folders in the Finder, not in the yellow of Xcode's file-grouping folders. The folder reference can then be dragged into the Copy Bundle Resources build phase; the folder and its contents, whatever they might be at build time, will be copied into the product's Resources directory.

- In Chapter 4, "Active Debugging," I mentioned how OS X usually supersedes the default debugger-control keys (the **F** keys) for hardware control. You aren't stuck with Xcode's choices. The **Key Bindings** panel of the Preferences window lists all of the editor functions and application commands, and allows you to set or change the key equivalents for any of them. The default set can't be changed, but click the + button to create a customizable copy.

  The **Conflicts** button in the key table's header is particularly useful. It will show you all of the Xcode assignments that are superseded by the system or by other key assignments in Xcode.

> **Note**
>
> The number of text operations available in Xcode is staggering; the list in the **Key Bindings** table is worth a look. You'll find useful editing actions, like move-by-subword (underscores and internal caps) (**^ Left-** or **Right-Arrow**), you'd never have known about.

- I've made much of the fact that the Project navigator is not a directory or filesystem tool; that it reflects the way you want to structure the project, and not the placement of files in the filesystem's directories. This isn't *quite* true.

  If an Xcode project's file references were arbitrary, they'd have to be absolute paths. That would mean that all of the files would be identified by a path that ran through your home directory. Suppose you were sharing the project with another developer. The project and its files would be in *her* directory, and the reference to your home directory would be wrong.

  The solution would seem to be to keep the path relative to the project file—and indeed that is one of the options. It is not, however, the option Xcode uses by default. The default is **Relative to Group**, as shown in the **Location** popup in the File inspector. There are other choices, such as relative-to-build-products, relative-to-Xcode's internal `Developer` and SDK directories, and, yes, the absolute path. If you have defined source trees, you can make the path relative to one of those, too.

  But what does "relative to group" mean? If you click on a group folder, you'll see in the File inspector that groups, too, have paths (which can, in turn, be absolute or relative). Groups still aren't directories: More than one group can refer to the same file directory, and not all members of a group have to be in the same place.

  Putting a filesystem location on a group has the advantage that you can have two directories in your filesystem containing files that have the same names. Maybe the one contains live classes, and the other "mocks" for testing. Switching between the two would then be a simple matter of changing the path of the corresponding group.

  If the group's directory does not enclose a file in the group, that file's path will be stored as project relative.

- Renaming is another file-management service the Project navigator provides. It uses the same gestures as in the Finder: To rename a file or group, click once to select it, then again a couple of seconds later. The item becomes editable. Or, select the item and press Return.

  If the project is under version control, Xcode will do the necessary work to ensure that the change is noted in the repository.

- Suppose you've written something like this in an Objective-C header file:

```
extern NSString * const    PRPFirstNameKey;
extern NSString * const    PRPLastNameKey;
extern NSString * const    PRPCurrentTeamKey;
```

and you want to add the corresponding declarations to an implementation file. The first thing you would naturally do is to paste the declarations from the header. Stop there. Hold down the Option key, and notice that the mouse cursor has changed to crosshairs. Drag from the first letter of the first `extern` to the space after the last one.

You have a column selection. Press Delete. The `externs` are gone.

This is an editor feature, and isn't specific to Objective-C.

It would be nice if you could type into the column and have your text appear on each line; or copy a column, click elsewhere in the text, paste, and have the column content inserted into the insertion point and the lines below. TextMate does this. Xcode does not.

- By default, the Find navigator does a straightforward search across all the text files in the project. As you saw in Chapter 7, "Version Control," global search has some simple options, readily understood. There are some deeper features:

  - You don't have to search just for text. The cascading popup menus at the top of the Find navigator offer not just text and regular expressions, but **References** (only the uses of the symbol you entered) and **Definitions** (definition of a method, function, or global variable). Doing a search for **Find → Definitions → Matching stat (Ignoring Case)** turns up eight matches for the `StatView` class, its `statLayer let` variable; the `StatsLabel` enum constant in `GameListController.swift`; and the five `@IBOutlets` for the `StatViews` in `TodayViewController`. No uses or other substrings, just definitions.

  - Below the left end of the global search field is a label that says something innocuous like **In Project** or **In Workspace**. This is a button that slides in an outline of the groups in the project (and of the projects in a workspace). If you've been disciplined about keeping all of the files for a subsystem tucked away each in their groups, you have a great way to narrow your searches by subsystem.

  - There is another category in the scope outline, "Search Scopes," which starts out empty except for a placeholder named **New Scope. . . .** Clicking it triggers a popover for you to name and define a custom search scope. In Figure 28.1, a "Property Lists" scope is defined as files that are included in the workspace and have the `plist` extension. If I search for text containing `wt9t` in that scope, I'll be shown only the bundle and document IDs in my `Info.plist` precursors.

Code-Folding Ribbon

When I had you abate some Xcode features in Chapter 2, "Kicking the Tires," you went to the **Text Editing** panel of the Preferences window and turned off **Show: Code folding ribbon**. The feature is useful, but "noisy"—with the ribbon visible, mousing into the left margin of the editor puts transient highlights in the content.

Many text editors implement folding: You click on a control, usually in the margin, or use a menu command or key equivalent, and the editor collapses the selected block of text.

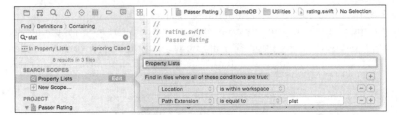

Figure 28.1   Clicking the scope button below the global-search field opens a list of potential search scopes and an affordance for defining scopes of your own—in this case, property-list files within the workspace.

A possibly long stretch of code is elided to a single line, and you're able to see the higher-level structure of a function.

The code-folding ribbon does the same thing: Turning it on adds a stripe between the gutter and the text area of the editor. The deeper the text next to the ribbon is nested, the darker the ribbon gets. When you mouse into the ribbon, Xcode highlights the text to show the extent of the code block containing that line. Clicking the ribbon collapses that block. See Figure 28.2.

The collapsed text is replaced by a yellow bubble with an ellipsis in it. Double-clicking the bubble or clicking the disclosure triangle in the ribbon expands the text. You can find menu commands for code folding, and their key equivalents, in the submenu at **Editor → Code Folding**.

The Assistant Editor

You've done a lot with the Assistant editor, but let me cover the basics all in one place: The Assistant editor is shown when you click the middle segment of the **Editor** control in the Workspace window's toolbar; when you press ⌥⌘Return, or when you navigate to a file while holding down the Option key.

- The wow feature of the Assistant editor is that it can track what file is displayed in the primary editor and show a counterpart, like the .h file for a .c file. If there is more than one counterpart—for instance, when there is a second header file for a private interface—the Counterpart assistant will rotate among the three when you click the arrow buttons in the assistant's jump bar or press ∧⌘**Up-** or **Down-Arrow**.

  The options for autofilling the Assistant editor go beyond counterparts: You can direct the assistant to related files in the class hierarchy, related Interface Builder files, files that include or are included by the primary editor, and processed content, like assembly and disassembly. As I mentioned in Chapter 5, "Compilation," the assistant can display the callers or callees of a selected function; and it can show the test methods that exercise the selected function.

```
114    var arrangedGames: [Game]? {
115        if let passer = detailItem {
116            if arrangedGames == nil {
117                // The game array isn't known, and there's a Passer to supply one.
118                // Get the array and remember it.
119                let gameSet = passer.games as NSSet
120                let dateSort = NSSortDescriptor(key: "whenPlayed",
121                                                ascending: true)
122                arrangedGames =
123                    gameSet.sortedArrayUsingDescriptors([dateSort])
124                    as? [Game]
125            }
126        }
127        return arrangedGames
128    }
```

```
114    var arrangedGames: [Game]? {
115        if let passer = detailItem {
116            if arrangedGames == nil {
117                // The game array isn't known, and there's a Passer to supply one.
118                // Get the array and remember it.
119                let gameSet = passer.games as NSSet
120                let dateSort = NSSortDescriptor(key: "whenPlayed",
121                                                ascending: true)
122                arrangedGames =
123                    gameSet.sortedArrayUsingDescriptors([dateSort])
124                    as? [Game]
125            }
126        }
127        return arrangedGames
128    }
```

```
114    var arrangedGames: [Game]? {
115        if let passer = detailItem {
116            if arrangedGames == nil {…}
126        }
127        return arrangedGames
128    }
```

Figure 28.2   When enabled in the **Text Editing** panel of the Preferences window, the code-folding ribbon appears as a strip at the left margin of the editor views. It shows progressively darker bands for each level of nesting in the code. Hovering the mouse pointer over the ribbon (top) highlights the lines at that level of nesting (or deeper). (middle) Moving to a deeper level dims the areas outside the highlighted scope. (bottom) Clicking the ribbon collapses the highlighted scope; its contents are replaced with an ellipsis bubble, and a disclosure triangle appears in the ribbon next to it.

- The Option-key gesture to put a destination file into the assistant pane can be modified. The **Navigation** panel of the Preferences window lets you customize how Xcode responds to navigational gestures:
  - Simple click navigation can go to the primary editor (the big one on the left) or whatever editor you're using at the moment.
  - Adding the Option key can send the selected file to the Assistant editor, an additional assistant pane, a new tab, or a new window.
  - Double-clicking can direct the file to a new window or a new tab.

- Further, if you navigate with the Option and Shift keys, Xcode will offer you a heads-up display offering you a graphical picker for placing the file in an existing or a new view. See Figure 28.3.

- You can have more than one Assistant view; there's a **+** button at the top-right corner of the view to add another. The **x** button next to it, of course, closes the pane.

- You aren't stuck with the side-by-side arrangement of the primary and Assistant editors. The **View → Assistant Editor** submenu offers you a choice of dividing the primary and Assistant areas vertically or horizontally, or cascading all editors in coequal rows or columns. Putting the assistant below the main editor makes dragging outlet and action connections between Interface Builder and source files much easier.

Instruments and Debugging

- It bears repeating: Apple keeps two technical notes, "Mac OS X Debugging Magic (TN2124)," and "iOS Debugging Magic (TN2239)," continually updated with the latest techniques for making debugging easier. Search for `Debugging Magic` in the Documentation browser. It's worth 20 IQ points.

- The Leaks and Allocations instruments take care of most memory problems, but not all of them. Sometimes, unused objects persist in memory, but because they have residual references, they aren't visible as leaks. Allocations has a button in its options area titled **Mark Heap**. Get your application started up and stable, and click **Mark Heap**. Then do something that will consume memory, but *should* return it to its

Figure 28.3   The Navigation Chooser appears when you select a file with the Option and Shift keys depressed. It is a graphical browser that lets you choose where the file is to be displayed. The menu equivalent is **Navigate →Open in...** (⌥⌘ <). A new window appears to the left in Cover Flow; placeholders for existing tabs, and a new one, run across the top of the presentation.

original state—like opening a document, editing it, and closing it. Do it repeatedly. Mark the heap again.

The heapshot-analysis table will show you all of the objects that were created, but not deallocated, at the end of the process. Not all will be leftovers—objects can legitimately accumulate in caches—but you should satisfy yourself that they are what they should be.

Apple engineer Bill Bumgarner has an excellent tutorial on this. Search the web for his name and "heapshot."

Building

- Not an Xcode tip, but something every programmer should take to heart: Compiler warnings are there for a reason. `clang` and `swiftc` are very, very good at catching common programming errors and violations of the coding conventions on which Cocoa relies. Many of the questions raised on support forums (see Appendix B, "Resources") arise from novices ignoring warnings. Fix every warning. Then run the analyzer (**Product → Analyze, ⇧⌘B**) and fix those, too.

- Xcode assumes that products built with the **Run** action (or **Product → Build** (**⌘B**), which is a synonym for **Build for Running**) are debugging articles and not fit for release to other users; and that Archive builds, which are fit for release, are comparatively rare. Xcode therefore does not take much trouble to make build product files easy to find.

  For archive builds, open the Archives organizer (**Window → Organizer**, second tab), select the archive, and click **Export. . .** ; you will have several options that will save an executable. The simplest are **Export as a Mac Application** or **Save for iOS App Store Deployment**.

  For run builds, do the build, find the product in the Products group in the Project navigator, and choose **Show in Finder** in the contextual menu.

- In Chapter 25, "The Xcode Build System," I said there is no way to change the set of files in a target, so if you have debug and release versions of a file, you can't switch between them in the Debug and Release configurations of your target. As applied to libraries, this isn't strictly true. The trick is to take the library *out* of the Link Binary With Libraries file, which will keep the build system from adding it to the linker command; and instead pass the name of the desired library in the "Other Linker Flags" (OTHER_LDFLAGS) build setting.

  In the **Build Settings** tab of the Target editor, search for **other** to find the setting. Open the disclosure triangle next to it, double-click the value for the Debug configuration, and click the **+** button to add an item to the list. Add the library (suppose it's named libmyname_debug.a) by typing -lmyname_debug into the new row. Do the same, for the release version of the library, in the Release item.

At build time, those flags will be added to the command lines for linking, with either the name of the debug version or the release version, depending on the configuration.

- The linker has strong opinions on what libraries it should link into an executable. In particular, for OS X builds, it will *always* link dynamic libraries (`.dylib`) in preference to static libraries (`.a`). You can override this by making sure the full path to the `.a` appears in the link command line. Just add the full path to the library, including the suffix and the `lib` prefix, to the "Other Linker Flags" (`OTHER_LDFLAGS`) build setting. You can reduce the dependency on the file paths on your machine by using the `BUILT_PRODUCTS_DIR` build variable instead of the directory path.

- The optimization-setting flag for `clang`—C-family languages, including Objective-C—goes in a progression from `-O0` (none at all) to `-O3` (everything). The temptation, when driving for the sleekest, whizziest application, is to turn the knob up full and let the optimizer fly. And yet the standard Release setting for optimization in Xcode is `-Os`—optimize for *size*. What's going on?

  The problem is that `-O3` optimization can dramatically increase the size of the generated code: `llvm` will autonomously convert function calls to in-line code, so that the content of those functions will be repeated throughout the application. It will turn counted `for` loops into *n* iterations of the loop body, one after the other, because it's quicker to run straight through four copies of the same code than to keep a counter, test it against four, and conditionally branch.

  All of these optimizations are ingenious, but they can be short-sighted. Modern processors are much faster than the main memory buses that serve them; waiting for loads of data or program instructions can stall a processor for a substantial portion of time. Therefore, very fast cache memory is put between the processor and RAM, to make the instruction stream available at a pace that keeps up with the CPU. But cache sizes are limited. An application that has been doubled in size by unrolling and inlining everywhere will overrun the cache and hit RAM to fetch instructions at least twice as often. In the usual case, "faster" code runs more slowly than smaller code. Keep the Release configuration at `-Os`.

  > **Note**
  >
  > Swift's optimization options are different, running from `-Onone` to `-Ofast` to `-Ounchecked`. The Swift compiler has no legacy of uncached CPUs to accommodate; `-Ofast` is roughly equivalent to `-Os` in `clang`, plus runtime safety checks.

- For Objective-C, `clang` is diligent about policing memory-management practices and API deprecations. Use a deprecated method, pass a `@selector` with retain/release semantics `clang` can't guess, or use a string variable for a format string, and you will be warned.

Fine, but sometimes you know what you're doing, and you don't want to be harried by warnings you have soberly decided are nothing to worry about. `clang` selects the warnings it gives through command-line flags like `-Wdeprecated` for deprecated methods.

- You could suppress the deprecation warning for the whole target by searching for it in the build settings and turning it off. You probably don't want to do this: You're doing this upon sober reflection on the warnings you got, right? You'll want to know when other deprecations arise that you do care about.

- You can turn the warning off for just one file. Find it in the table in the Compile Sources build phase, and double-click on its row. You'll get a popover in which you can enter compiler flags for just that file—in this case `-Wno-deprecated`. This is finer-grained, but usually unwise.

- You can isolate the lines that concern you: Bracket it with #pragmas that save `clang`'s warning state, tell it to ignore deprecations, and then restore the warning after the problem line:

```
#pragma mark -UISearchDisplayContollerDelegate
#pragma clang diagnostic push
#pragma clang diagnostic ignored "-Wdeprecated"

// UISearchDisplayController is deprecated in iOS 8.
// Low priority; won't fix for now.
- (BOOL) searchDisplayController:
        (UISearchDisplayController *) controller
    shouldReloadTableForSearchString: (NSString *) searchString
{
    // ...
}
#pragma diagnostic pop
```

Traps

Development is hard. Therefore Xcode is hard, both because it has to do a lot, and because any application that has to do a lot is subject to bugs and annoyances. Here are a few things to watch out for.

- In most OS X apps that edit documents, the title bar includes a "proxy icon" that stands for the document file. You can drag and drop it with the same effect as if you had dragged the document icon from the Finder. If you control- or command-click in the title, a menu of the directory chain to the document drops down. Selecting an item opens it in the Finder.

  Xcode moves its entire toolbar into the title-bar space, so there's no room for the filename or proxy icon. When a file is displayed in one of the editor views, its item in the jump bar behaves just as the proxy and title do in regular windows.

- When you remove an `@IBOutlet` from your source, `clang` and Swift react immediately, flagging errors and warnings on all references in your project—*except* for outlet connections in your XIBs and storyboards. You won't hear of it until the NIB loader starts throwing exceptions that say the target object "is not key-value coding compliant" for the missing outlet name. As soon as you change an outlet (or an `@IBAction`), audit the related objects in Interface Builder. Most of these will be in File's Owner or the view controller; select it and look in the Connection (sixth) inspector for orphaned connections.

  If you're just changing the name of an Objective-C outlet, use **Edit →Refactor →Rename. . . .** The refactoring mechanism will change the IB documents accurately and safely.

- In the name of simplicity, Xcode presents a bare search field for in-document search. There are options to be had. The magnifying-glass icon at the left end of the search field anchors a drop-down menu, and the first item is **Show Find Options. . . .** Selecting it gets you a popover presenting options for case sensitivity; prefix, suffix, partial, or whole-word matching for text; or regular expressions.

  Clicking anywhere else—such as to execute the search—makes the popover disappear. There is now no visible indication of what the next search will do. Your selections will persist, and you are expected either to remember them or to click on the tiny magnifying glass and select an item in a miniaturized menu. If your in-file searches yield surprising results, check the settings.

  If the results are surprising, but you don't know they are (if you knew what was in the file, you wouldn't need to search it), and you ship a bug because of it, that's too bad. But you got to use an uncluttered search field.

- Traditional regular-expression engines use `&` in replacement fields to stand for the full string that matched the search expression. Xcode uses `$0` instead.

- One big gap in Xcode's version-control support is *tags*. When your work comes to a significant milestone, like a version release, you'll want to mark the revision with a name that will allow you to return the project to that point. All version-control systems allow for this. Xcode won't set, display, or revert to tags. You'll have to go to the command line and use the `git tag` or `svn cp` subcommands.

- If you look in the AppleScript Editor application for the Xcode dictionary, you'll see what purports to be an extensive scripting interface that you could use, for instance, to create and configure Xcode projects programmatically. It might disquiet you to see many references to Xcode 3. Experiment, if you'd like—some of the commands perform as promised. Most do not.

- However: You *can* script Xcode for things like text transformations—say, to generate documentation comments from a function declaration. OS X, and NeXTStep before it, features *services*, filters and utilities you can find in the **Services** submenu of an application menu, or in contextual menus. Services are sensitive to the current selection—OS X knows to offer a text-based service only when text is selected—and can replace the selection with the output of the service tool.

The Automator feature of OS X produces applets from chains of scripts and services; you can use Automator to create a service. The editor is in `/Applications` `/Utilities`. Create a document, and select the **Service** type. Browse the **Library** sidebar to see the actions the system and your applications offer you.

An example: Swift, like C++, achieves its symbol-overloading and namespacing features by identifying objects internally with names derived from a full description of their scope and attributes. The compiled binaries are full of identifiers like `_TFC17Mac_Passer_Rating20LeagueViewControllerm19teamArrayControllerGSQCSo17NSArrayController_`.

- Set the context to **Service receives selected (text) in (any application)**.
- Drag the "Run Shell Script" tile from the Library list.
- Set **Pass input: (to stdin)**, so the selected text will go as an input stream into the script.
- Enter `xcrun swift-demangle -compact` as the script.
- Drag the "Copy to Clipboard" tile under the script tile, so that the connectors mate.
- Save the Service under some convenient name like `Demangle Swift Symbol` (there will be no file location associated with it—it goes into a directory reserved for Automator services).
- Quit and reopen any application (such as Xcode) you want to use the service.
- Select the symbol, and **Xcode** → **Services** → **Demangle Swift Symbol** (or the same, from the **Services** submenu of the contextual menu).
- Paste. The result should be `Mac_Passer_Rating.LeagueViewController.teamArrayController.materializeForSet : ObjectiveC.NSArrayController!`.
- You can give your action a system-wide hot key in the **Keyboard** panel of System Preferences.

- Most of the targets you'll build with Xcode will be bundles that include an `Info.plist` that the build system will process and install in the final product. By misadventure, this file might find its way into the target's Copy Bundle Resources build phase. That conflicts with the build system. Xcode will warn you if it sees this happening in a build.

- In general, source files should not end up in the Copy Bundle Resources phase. This can happen if you check the box that assigns a C-family `.h` file to a target. This isn't necessary to build the product; the compiler will find and interpret the header on its own. Xcode interprets your adding the target membership as meaning you want to treat the file as a bundle resource.

- You can't have a XIB or storyboard open in more than one editor. Interface Builder products are literal archives of Cocoa objects. Concurrent access to an object network is a tremendous headache, and I don't blame Apple for allocating its resources elsewhere.

- When you drag an NSTextView into a view in Interface Builder, you're really dragging the NSTextView *inside* an NSScrollView and the clipping view that comes between them. (You saw the same thing in Chapter 20, "Bindings: Wiring an OS X Application" with NSTableView.) If you attempt to connect an outlet to the text view, you may end up connecting to the scroll view (or to nothing, if your outlet is typed to accept only a text view).

  The problem is that the scroll view can be larger than the text view; the text view is only as tall as the text it contains. Add some "Lorem ipsum" text to the view, drag the connector to that, and you'll connect to the text view.

- Being a dynamic language, the Objective-C compiler allows any object to receive any message. Implementations may be completely unrelated; all the compiler has to do is load the receiver, the selector, and the parameters onto the stack and call for the message to be dispatched.

  > **Note**
  >
  > Swift's AnyObject type affords the same flexibility, but it won't let you send the object a message until you cast it to a class or prototype that implements the method—which pins down the return type, and eliminates this problem.

  This works well, but the ideal breaks down with the return value: It might be an integer, a float, a pointer, or a struct, and depending on the processor architecture, those results may be stored in completely different locations. The compiler has to generate the instructions to take the result from the correct place.

  Things are still fine if all implementations of methods with a given signature return the same result type; so long as the compiler has seen some declaration of the method, it can proceed. Even if the compiler has seen declarations of different return types, it can still do the right thing if the receiving object's class is known.

  Where it breaks down is when the receiver is declared to be id or Class, and so provides no indication of what methods it implements or how they return. In the past, the compiler would silently guess what return type you expect, an abundant source of obscure bugs. clang now demands that you use a cast on the receiver of the method call to remove the ambiguity.

- HFS+, the recommended filesystem for OS X, is case preserving—files will get names in the same case as you provide—but case insensitive: Xcode.txt, XCODE.TXT, and xcode.txt all refer to the same file. Most other Unix variants are case sensitive, so if you import code, be on the lookout for the assumption that the following two lines refer to different files:

```
#include "polishShoes.h"
#include "PolishShoes.h"
```

By the same token, make sure that your code uses filenames with consistent letter casing. Even if you don't expect to port your work, HFS+ isn't the only filesystem a Macintosh application sees, and on iOS, HFS+ *is* case sensitive. **But:** The iOS Simulator runs on the OS X filesystem. On the "iOS" that runs in the simulator, HFS+ *is not* case sensitive.

Part V

Appendixes

A

Some Build Variables

This appendix offers a brief (though you may not believe it) list of the major build variables that control the Xcode build system. Build variables determine compiler flags, search paths, installation behavior, and essential information like product names. A comprehensive explanation of Xcode's build variables can be found in the Documentation browser by searching for `Build Setting Reference`.

You can see all the build variables that are available to Run Script build phases by creating a phase that consists of only one line like `echo`, then checking **Show environment variables in build log**. Do a build, find the build at the top of the Log navigator (eighth tab), and select the **All** and **All Messages** filters. Click the script phase, and then on the lines-of-text button that appears at the right end of the row.

You'll find there are nearly 350 variables. This appendix lists the more useful ones. For the purposes of example, the conditions of the build are those shown in Table A.1.

Table A.1   Build Environment for the Settings Examples

Project	PasserRating
Target	Passer Rating Target
Product	Passer Rating.app
Scheme	Passer Rating
Configuration	Debug
SDK	iOS 8.2
Xcode	6.2
Build OS	10.10.2
User	fritza

> **Note**
>
> I've chosen distinct names so you can identify the origins of the automatically set variables. The templates start projects with the main target, scheme, and product name having the same values. You wouldn't ordinarily change that, but it is possible. I did leave the target and build scheme names the same, because the build system never sees scheme names. Schemes merely organize build configurations for targets; the configurations and their settings are what matter to the build system, not how they were selected.

Some of these settings have no corresponding interface in the **Build Settings** tabs of the Target or Project editor. You can set these—if they are not read-only—by selecting **Editor → Add Build Setting → Add User-Defined Setting**. Xcode will add a new line to the list, and you can enter the setting's name in the Setting column and the value under the level at which you want to set it. Boolean values should be entered as YES or NO.

The authoritative name for a build variable is its "setting name"—the name of the actual build variable, as visible in environment variables and substitutable into other settings and Info.plist expansions. You can find the corresponding entries in a **Build Settings** tab by typing the setting name, plain-language name, or any part of the long-form description into the tab's search field.

> **Note**
>
> Settings can be made conditional according to what processor architecture the product is being built for or what SDK is being used. See Chapter 25, "The Xcode Build System," for details.

The **Build Settings** tab can display setting names instead of the plain-language "setting titles." The **Show Setting Names/Show Setting Titles** item in the **Editor** menu toggles between the "real" names and the descriptive titles.

Similarly, you can control how setting values are displayed. A setting may be defined in terms of another setting, as when you specify an installation directory by $(HOME) /Applications. By default, Xcode displays embedded build variables by expanding them, because the build system will see only the fully expanded strings. The **Show Definitions/Show Values** (for the unexpanded value expressions) item in the **Editor** menu changes the display so that variable references are shown either literally (**Definitions**) or as interpreted (**Values**).

Useful Build Variables

With no further ado, here is a list of selected build variables. I've grouped them by general function, and then by a rough general-to-specific order within those groups.

Some of these variables appear to be obsolete: Apple no longer documents them, and the target templates no longer use them by default. The build system still sets them as environment variables, presumably to preserve compatibility with old run-script build phases, but the best bet is not to use them for new development.

Others are obviously used, but Xcode does not expose predefined descriptions or defaults for them. Often, these settings must have values that are strictly derived from other settings, and overriding them would break the build.

Environment

These are read-only variables that you can use in scripts or to build up other build settings.

- PROJECT—The name of the Xcode project, without extension. Unless you override it, PROJECT_NAME follows this setting.
  (PasserRating)
- ACTION—The name of the xcodebuild action that was entered in the command line or generated by Xcode to match the **Product** action that triggered the build.
  (build)
- PROJECT_NAME—The name of the project that contains the target that is being built. Most intermediate and project paths go through a directory with this name.
- PLATFORM_NAME—The name of the target platform, macosx, iphonesimulator, or iphoneos. This setting appears to be obsolete; Apple no longer documents it.
  (macosx)
- PRODUCT_NAME—The name of the target package and binary, unadorned by prefixes, suffixes, or extensions.
  (Passer Rating)
- FULL_PRODUCT_NAME—The file or directory name of the target package.
  (Passer Rating.app)
- PRODUCT_TYPE—A reverse-DNS-style identifier for the kind of product the target produces. This defines the endpoint in the build process, from which the build system infers all the steps necessary to generate the product.
  (com.apple.product-type.application)
- HOME—The path to your home directory, just as it would be in bash.
- USER—The user name of the person doing the build. There is a corresponding UID variable for the numeric user ID.
- GROUP—The group name of the person doing the build. There is a corresponding GID variable for the numeric group ID.
- PATH—The standard Unix PATH environment variable, specifying the order in which directories should be searched when Unix commands are invoked.
  (various paths to Xcode's toolchain and shadow bin and libexec directories; followed by the standard directories in the general filesystem)
- MAC_OS_X_VERSION_ACTUAL—A six-digit number designating the version of OS X on which the build is being done. The first two digits will be 10, the next 10, and the last, the minor version. The format changed with Yosemite; before, the setting was 10, followed by one each for the major and minor versions.
  (101002)

- MAC_OS_X_VERSION_MAJOR—A six-digit number that is the same as MAC_OS_X_VERSION_ACTUAL, but with the minor set to zero.
(101000)

- MAC_OS_X_VERSION_MINOR—A four-digit number that designates the current OS version, omitting the leading 10. In Yosemite, the first two digits will always be 10; the second two are the minor version.
(1002)

- MAC_OS_X_PRODUCT_BUILD_VERSION—The build number for the current OS.
(14C*nnn*)

- XCODE_VERSION_ACTUAL
(0620),
XCODE_VERSION_MAJOR
(0600),
and XCODE_VERSION_MINOR
(0620)–This is the same version information as in the MAC_OS_X_VERSION settings, but for Xcode itself.

Code Signing

These settings control provisioning issues, including the selection of the provisioning profile and the signing identity.

- AD_HOC_CODE_SIGNING_ALLOWED—Controls whether an ad hoc distribution profile will be accepted for this build.
(NO)

- CODE_SIGN_IDENTITY—The signing identity to be used for the build. This may be in a reduced form such as iPhone Developer or iPhone Distribution. If so, the build system will consult the provisioning profile for the full common name of the required certificate.
You should not explicitly set the identity if you can avoid it: Otherwise, team members will force their own certificates, and then check the project into source control. The other team members get project files that require a certificate they don't have. This sets off an arms race in which developers compete to jam their own certificates into the common project file.
Use the generic identities. Xcode will figure it out. If it can't, you have a provisioning problem that will probably get worse when you start building for distribution. It's hard to fix, but you have to do it.
(iPhone Developer)

- CODE_SIGNING_ALLOWED—Signify whether the code-signing step will be performed at all. The "allowed" switch must be YES before "required" is even considered.
(NO)

- `CODE_SIGN_ENTITLEMENTS`—The path to the `.entitlements` plist claiming permission to use certain privileged services, relative to the project folder. (`Passer Rating Target/Passer Rating.entitlements`)

- `CODE_SIGN_RESOURCE_RULES_PATH`—The path to a property list that directs `codesign` to ignore some files in the product package, so as not to freeze files that have to be modified after signing.

- `OTHER_CODE_SIGN_FLAGS`—Identifies any additional command-line flags you need to pass to `codesign`. You usually don't want to change Xcode's choice of settings for iOS builds, or for Mac builds destined for Developer ID or the Mac App Store.

- `PROVISIONING_PROFILE`—This was the UUID of a valid provisioning profile that matches the bundle ID set in `Info.plist`. New targets will not set this; Xcode will find the correct profile on the basis of the application ID and the signing identity you choose. There's no point in setting the profile independently, as anything other than the one that matches is in error.

Locations

Source Locations

- `PROJECT_DIR`—The directory that contains the project file. (`/Users/fritza/Desktop/PasserRating`)

- `PROJECT_FILE_PATH`—The full path to the project file. (`/Users/fritza/Desktop/PasserRating/PasserRating.xcodeproj`)

- `SDKROOT`—The root of the tree in which to search for system headers and libraries; this is simple for OS X SDKs, but it gets more involved once you get into the platform and OS options in the iOS SDK. This should be the same as `SDK_DIR`, and the last component should be the same as the base name in `SDK_NAME`. (`/Applications/Xcode.app/.../iPhoneSimulator8.2.sdk`)

- `SRCROOT`—The folder containing the source code for the project, usually the project document's directory. `SOURCE_ROOT` is a synonym. (`/Users/fritza/Desktop/PasserRating`)

Destination Locations

These are the directories to which object files, derived files, and products are directed in the course of a build. Many of these are somewhere in the "derived-data" directory for your project. You can set that directory using the **File → Project (or Workspace) Settings...** command, in the **Build** tab, but typically you'll use the default directory, within the `Library` folder of your home directory. The path to the default directory goes deep and involves a unique identifier string, so it's not practical for me to spell out in this list; you can depend on its beginning with the name of your target. If you see a path beginning with `/Users/fritza/Library`, you can assume that it's the derived-data directory.

The whole idea of the derived-data directory is to put all the files—they are many and large—that Xcode generates in managing and building your projects, all in one place.

These files are "derived" in that they contain only information that can be reconstructed from your source files and settings. *You do not want to put derived files in your project directory tree* if you intend to share it or put it under revision control. If you must put the derived-data directory in your project directory, make sure to give it a name you can match in the ignored-files patterns in your Subversion or Git configuration.

If you want to inspect the derived-data directory, open the Organizer (**Window** →**Organizer**), and select the **Projects** panel. Find your project in the list on the left, and see the panel at the top of the detail view. The full path to the directory will be shown (middle-truncated if the window is too narrow). Next to it will be a small arrow button that will show the directory in the Finder.

- OBJROOT—The folder containing, perhaps indirectly, the intermediate products, such as object files, of the build. Unless you override the location for intermediate files, this folder will be buried deep in your user Library directory. (/Users/fritza/Library/Developer/Xcode/DerivedData/ /Passer Rating-... /Intermediates)

- SYMROOT—The container for folders that receive symbol-rich, meaning not-yet-stripped, versions of the product. This, too, is buried in your own Library directory. (/Users/fritza/Library/Developer/-... /ArchiveIntermediates/ /Passer Rating/-BuildProductsPath)

- DSTROOT—The directory into which the product will be "installed." For iOS targets, this is simply a holding directory. For OS X, it is usually in the /tmp tree, and the project will make and populate subdirectories in DSTROOT as though it were the root of your filesystem. It is relevant only in install builds. Nowadays, it's useful only if you're building and testing system or kernel software. (/tmp/Passer Rating.dst)

- BUILT_PRODUCTS_DIR—The full path to the directory that receives either every product of the project or, if the products are scattered, symbolic links to every product. A script can therefore depend on reaching all of the products through this path. By default, $(SYMROOT)/$(CONFIGURATION), and therefore deep within your Library directory. CONFIGURATION_BUILD_DIR is a synonym. (/Users/fritza/Library/Developer/-Xcode/DerivedData/ Passer_Rating-... /Build/Products/Debug-iphonesimulator)

- TARGET_BUILD_DIR—The directory into which the product of the *current* target is built. (/Users/fritza/Library/Developer/-Xcode/DerivedData/ Passer_Rating-... /Build/Products/Debug-iphonesimulator)

- DERIVED_FILE_DIR—The directory that receives intermediate source files generated in the course of a build, such as the sources generated by the bison parser generator. This variable is paralleled by DERIVED_FILES_DIR and DERIVED_SOURCES_DIR. If you have a more general need for a place to put a

temporary file, consult the Xcode documentation for PROJECT_TEMP_DIR or
TARGET_TEMP_DIR.
(/Users/fritza/Library/Developer/... /Build/Intermediates/
Passer Rating.build/Debug-iphonesimulator/Passer
Rating.build/DerivedSources)

- OBJECT_FILE_DIR—The directory containing subdirectories, one per architecture,
  containing compiled object files. It's in the derived-data folder, which by default is
  deep within your Library directory.
  (/Users/fritza/Library/Developer/... /Build/Intermediates/
  Passer Rating Target.build/Debug-iphonesimulator/Passer
  Rating.build)

- SKIP_INSTALL—If NO, the build system will take all actions necessary to distribute
  the build products in their final directory locations. In practice, there is no actual
  installation; the "installation" tree is confined to an Xcode archive package.
  Exporting the archive will merge the tree into whatever root you choose.

  If you want to create a stand-alone framework, you must set SKIPINSTALL to NO;
  otherwise the framework will exist only as a partially built temporary in the
  derived-products directory, for the use of other products while they are in
  development.
  (NO)

Bundle Locations

- If the product is a bundle, like an application or a framework, WRAPPER_NAME is the
  base name of the bundle directory.
  (Passer Rating)

- WRAPPER_EXTENSION and WRAPPER_SUFFIX—The extension and extension-with-
  dot for the bundle directory, if the target is a bundle.
  (app and .app)

- If SHALLOW_BUNDLE is YES, the other settings in this section are moot, because the
  product bundle is like an iOS application—all of the files, except for localizations,
  are to be found immediately inside the bundle directory, without the OS X bundle
  structure.
  (YES)

- CONTENTS_FOLDER_PATH—The path, within the target build directory, that
  contains the structural directories of a bundle product.
  (Passer Rating.app)

- EXECUTABLE_FOLDER_PATH—The path, in a bundle target in the target build
  directory, into which the product's executable file is to be built. Not to be confused
  with EXECUTABLES_FOLDER_PATH, which points to a directory for "additional
  binary files," named Executables.
  (Passer Rating.app)

- EXECUTABLE_PATH—The path, within TARGET_BUILD_DIR, to the executable binary.
  (Passer Rating.app/Passer Rating)

- FRAMEWORKS_FOLDER_PATH—The path, in a bundle target in the target build directory, that contains frameworks used by the product. This is set for iOS builds even though you can't have a framework in an iOS application. For MyMacApp.app, it would be MyMacApp.app/Contents/Frameworks. There are variables for other possible bundle directories; see the Xcode documentation for more.
  (Passer Rating.app/Frameworks)

- UNLOCALIZED_RESOURCES_FOLDER_PATH—The directory, within a bundle product in the target build directory, that receives file resources that have no localization—not even the base localization. For MyMacApp.app, it would be MyMacApp.app/Contents/Resources.
  (Passer Rating.app)

Compiler Settings

These settings control how the build system produces executable code. Many of these have the prefix CLANG_ or GCC_, even though gcc is no longer included in Apple's developer tools, substituting clang. They carry over the prefix for backward compatibility.

> **Note**
>
> While the build variables expose a great number of clang settings, bear in mind that your scripts will have read-only access to them; any changes you make won't be visible outside your script. The GCC_ and CLANG_ variables are primarily useful as substitutes into other build settings, including those you might create yourself. You might, for instance, assign a setting string to a preprocessor variable in GCC_PREPROCESSOR_DEFINITIONS so you could experiment with compiler settings and permit your code to print the build settings directly.

- ARCHS—The CPU architectures for which Xcode is to generate product code. These must come from among the VALID_ARCHS list; by default, this is the value of ARCHS_STANDARD. (See Chapter 25, "The Xcode Build System," for how the build system handles multiple-architecture products.) Note that iOS apps bound for the simulator will use your Mac's hardware, so this setting will point to an Intel processor.
  (x86_64)

- ARCHS_STANDARD—The default set of architectures Xcode will build for.
  (i386 x86_64)

- ARCHS_STANDARD_32_BIT
  (i386), ARCHS_STANDARD_64_BIT
  (x86_64), and ARCHS_STANDARD_32_64_BIT
  (i386 x86_64)—The standard architectures you'd use instead of ARCHS_STANDARD if you're particular about whether the target should be 64-bit, 32-bit, or both.

- NATIVE_ARCH—The architecture on which the current build is taking place. This is the same as CURRENT_ARCH and (if the target is OS X) NATIVE_ARCH_ACTUAL. Note that you can't really use CURRENT_ARCH in a script—Run Script build phases are run only once per build, so the value you see for CURRENT_ARCH is only one of the architectures that will actually be built. If your script must hit every architecture being targeted, have it iterate through ARCHS.
  (i386)

- NATIVE_ARCH_32_BIT and NATIVE_ARCH_64_BIT—These are like NATIVE_ARCH, but refer to the 32-bit and 64-bit variants of the *development* architecture. On an iOS build, these settings are moot—they are the respective Intel architectures.
  (i386 and x86_64)

- CLANG_CXX_LANGUAGE_STANDARD—The dialect of C++ clang should accept.
  (gnu++0x)

- CLANG_ENABLE_MODULES—Whether C-family languages should accept @module directives, and in turn should be compiled into modules. Swift code always uses modules.
  (YES)

- DEFINES_MODULE—Whether the code generated by the build will constitute a module.
  (NO)

- MODULE_NAME—The name of the module the generated code defines.
  (empty—not defining a module)

- PRODUCT_MODULE_NAME—The name of the module the generated code will be sorted into. This is important now that APIs and Swift code are all segregated into by-module namespaces.
  (Passer_Rating)

- CLANG_ENABLE_OBJC_ARC—Whether clang should generate Automatic Reference Counting code, and enforce ARC conventions, for Objective-C code. Swift code always uses ARC.
  (YES)

- GCC_OPTIMIZATION_LEVEL—The strategy clang is to use in rearranging the code it generates for efficiency, by one measure or another. The possible values include -O0 a literal translation, best for debugging; -O3, the most while still maintaining standards compliance; -Ofast, "aggressive," going for speed at the possible sacrifice of standards compliance; and -Os, "fastest, smallest," which will probably be fastest of all, because the other methods generate much more code, which will likely overrun the processor's code cache and introduce halts to wait for code to load from memory.
  (0)

- SWIFT_OPTIMIZATION_LEVEL—The optimization strategy for Swift. The levels are -Onone, no optimization, best for debugging; -O, optimized as much as possible

while maintaining runtime consistency checks; -Ounchecked, with all the consistency checks removed. Gamble on releasing an -Ounchecked product only after you've exhausted every possible means to trigger a check in -Onone code, and again with -Ounchecked.
(-Onone)

- GCC_VERSION and GCC_VERSION_IDENTIFIER—The compiler version to use, which is fixed at Apple clang 1.0; there have been no backward-compatibility issues so far. The difference between the two is that the identifier uses underscores instead of dots.
(com.apple.compilers.llvm.clang.1_0)

- GCC_PREPROCESSOR_DEFINITIONS—A space-separated list of symbols to be defined in all compilations. Items of the form *symbol=value* assign values to the symbols. Symbols defined in this way will be incorporated in precompiled headers. Related is GCC_PREPROCESSOR_DEFINITIONS_NOT_USED_IN_PRECOMPS, which specifies symbols defined in every compilation but not incorporated in precompiled headers. This allows you to share precompiled headers between build configurations, with variants in global definitions taken as options in the respective configurations.

  Swift will accept preprocessor symbols for testing by preprocessing directives like #if. The directives accept only simple values; they will not do any expansions the way C-family languages expand macros. If you want to define these, add -D *symbol* to OTHER_SWIFT_FLAGS.
(DEBUG=1)

- GCC_ENABLE_OBJC_GC—Controls whether the project compiles Objective-C source with support for garbage collection. This setting is no longer available in the Build Settings editor, as Apple forbids garbage collection in all new development.

- It's good practice to treat a build as failed even if the only issues were warnings, not errors: Even if an executable binary could be generated, it won't be. GCC_TREAT_WARNINGS_AS_ERRORS isn't set by default, but maybe it should be; in most cases, warnings point out logical mistakes that you'll have to debug anyway.
(NO)

- GCC_WARN_INHIBIT_ALL_WARNINGS—The inverse of GCC_TREAT_WARNINGS_AS_ERRORS. clang won't emit any warning messages. If doing this seems to you like a good idea, please warn your customers.

- OTHER_CFLAGS, OTHER_CPLUSPLUSFLAGS, and OTHER_SWIFT_FLAGS—Catchall variables for compiler options that do not have their own build variables for C or Swift compilation. OTHER_SWIFT_FLAGS is the only way you can set preprocessor symbols for Swift code.

  Apple tries to incorporate every reasonable flag in the **Build Settings** tab, so you should rarely need to use this setting. It's a good idea to type a flag into the settings tab's search field to see whether a direct setting is available. For linker flags, the equivalent is OTHER_LDFLAGS (empty).

- GCC_WARN_...—clang accepts a *lot* of warning flags, and most of them have equivalents in the build variables. Click around in the **Build Settings** tab with the Quick Help inspector (Utility area, on the right, second tab) to see what the warnings do and what the build-variable equivalent is.

  Many developers use -Wall as a shortcut for a comprehensive set of warnings, and the clang engineers provide an even stricter -Weverything, which they insist is mostly for debugging the compiler. The **Build Settings** tab doesn't expose those options, so put them in OTHER_CFLAGS if you need them.

- EMBEDDED_CONTENT_CONTAINS_SWIFT—If your target uses Swift in its main code, the build system knows to include the Swift runtime libraries for compatibility with OS X 10.9 and iOS 7. The system will not detect Swift code in your plugins and helper apps for itself; if your app includes such, set this to YES to add the runtime to them as well.

Other Tools

As you saw in Chapter 25, "The Xcode Build System," compilers aren't the only build tools. Here are some settings for the others.

Asset Catalog Compiler

The images in an .xcassets catalog archive must be processed into more compact forms, and Info.plist must be patched to identify the application's icons and launch images.

- ASSETCATALOG_COMPILER_APPICON_NAME—The name of the image set containing the application's icon.
  (AppIcon)

- ASSETCATALOG_COMPILER_LAUNCHIMAGE_NAME—The name of the image set for the launch image.
  (LaunchImage)

- COMPRESS_PNG_FILES—Whether to compress PNG image files before adding them to the product package.
  (YES)

Info.plist

The Info.plist file in the project is just a source file for the Info.plist that will appear in the final package. The build process includes a step for resolving build-setting references, inserting mandatory keys, and, optionally, applying a C-style preprocessor.

- INFOPLIST_FILE—The name of the file that will be the *source* for the bundle's Info.plist file, if the product of this target is a bundle. This should not be Info.plist, as a project with more than one target will need to specify more than one Info.plist file.
  (Info.plist)

- If YES, INFOPLIST_PREPROCESS preprocesses the INFOPLIST_FILE, using a C-style preprocessor. You can specify a prefix file with INFOPLIST_PREFIX_- HEADER and set symbols with INFOPLIST_PREPROCESSOR_DEFINITIONS. (NO)

- INFOPLIST_EXPAND_BUILD_SETTINGS—Controls whether build settings should be expanded in the generated Info.plist. This allows you, for instance, to fill the CFBundleExecutable key with ${EXECUTABLE_NAME }, and be assured that if you ever change the name of the product, Info.plist will always be in sync. (YES)

- INFOPLIST_OUTPUT_FORMAT—Your choice of the possible file formats for the Info.plist property-list file. This is binary if you want the binary format; anything else gets you an XML plist. (binary)

- INFOSTRINGS_PATH—The path, starting with the application package, to the InfoPlist.strings file for the development locale. The development locale is identified by DEVELOPMENT_LANGUAGE. (Passer Rating.app/English.lproj/InfoPlist.strings)

- CREATE_INFOPLIST_SECTION_IN_BINARY—Some single-file products, such as stand-alone libraries and command-line tools, must contain information for Launch Services and Finder. There can't be a separate Info.plist file, so this option adds a Mach-O binary section for the Info.plist data. (NO)

- STRINGS_FILE_OUTPUT_ENCODING—.strings files map symbolic strings (usually English-language names) to strings that would be used for display in a particular language. (See Chapter 21, "Localization.") This is the encoding for the processed string, historically UTF-16, but there is now a binary format that Cocoa can use more efficiently. (binary)

Java

Apple abandoned Java as an OS X development language around 2002. (Java seemed like a good idea at the time; it always does.) There are a dozen Java-related settings still around, mostly with the prefix JAVA_. Xcode does not expose them. They don't do anything. Ignore them.

Others

Some variables point to standard Unix tools. Development tools are usually found inside the Xcode.app package; others are simply the standard Unix commands to be found in the /bin, /usr/bin, /sbin, or /usr/sbin trees. Most Make-like systems factor tool names out this way, so switching to a custom tool is simply a matter of changing the single definitions.

The pointer variables (the tools they point to should be obvious to anyone who needs them) include CHOWN, CHMOD, CP, ICONV, LEX, SED, and YACC.

There are four commands of the form REMOVE_*something*_FROM_RESOURCES. These YES/NO switches determine whether version-control directories, and headers, should be ignored when copying files into the product bundle.

Search Paths

- HEADER_SEARCH_PATHS—A space-delimited list of paths to directories the compiler is to search for headers, in addition to standard locations, such as /usr/include. If you add your own paths, carry the default paths through by putting $(inherited) at the beginning or end of your list. If the headers in question are in frameworks, set FRAMEWORK_SEARCH_PATHS instead. SDKROOT is prepended to the paths of system headers and frameworks.
(/Users/fritza/Library/... Build/Products/Debug-iphone-simulator/include/Applications/Xcode.app/... /usr/include)

- LIBRARY_SEARCH_PATHS—A space-delimited list of paths to directories the linker is to search for libraries. If set, SDKROOT is prepended to the paths of system libraries. Developers sometimes are given libraries in production and debug forms, as binaries, with no source; they'd like to use one version of the library in Debug builds and the other in Release builds. A solution is to put the two library versions in separate directories and specify different LIBRARY_SEARCH_PATHSes for the two build configurations.
(/Users/fritza/Library/... Build/Products/Debug-iphone-simulator)

- IPHONEOS_DEPLOYMENT_TARGET—The minimum version of iOS on which the product can run; symbols in the SDK from later versions of the OS are weak-linked. There is also a MACOSX_DEPLOYMENT_TARGET.
(8.2)

The DEVELOPER_ Variables

The settings that begin in DEVELOPER_ were a big part of the build environment in previous versions of Xcode, and the build system still sets them for the benefit of run-script build phases. They are read-only, so they appear nowhere in the default values in the **Build Settings** tab. Apple no longer documents them. I'm including them in case you have no alternative.

Many of the DEVELOPER_ paths had parallel SYSTEM_, SYSTEM_DEVELOPER_, PLATFORM_, and PLATFOTM_DEVELOPER_ settings, as the tool and frameworks sets may vary depending on whether you're developing for OS X or iOS.

The only survivor is SYSTEM_LIBRARY_DIR, the root of the installation path for OS X frameworks.

If you're looking for the paths to Xcode's development tools, you're better off using xcrun --find to pick out the ones that fit the current Xcode and any particular SDK you want. See man xcrun for more details.

- DEVELOPER_DIR—The directory you chose for the Xcode installation. The DEVELOPER_ variables are important, because they track the currently selected Xcode if you have more than one installed. See man xcode-select. (/Applications/Xcode.app/Contents/Developer)

- DEVELOPER_APPLICATIONS_DIR—The folder inside DEVELOPER_DIR containing Xcode and the other developer applications. You may be better served by using open -a *application-name* if all you want to do is to launch a user application. (/Applications/Xcode.app/Contents/Developer/Applications)

- DEVELOPER_BIN_DIR—The folder inside DEVELOPER_DIR containing the BSD tools, like clang, that Xcode uses. If you write scripts that execute development tools like clang or yacc directly, use this path *instead* of /usr/bin. The tools in this directory are the versions that correspond to the version of Xcode you're using. (/Applications/Xcode.app/Contents/Developer/usr/bin)

- DEVELOPER_FRAMEWORKS_DIR—The folder inside DEVELOPER_DIR that contains development frameworks, such as for unit tests. There's also a QUOTED variant that you can use with the confidence that a shell interpreter won't mangle it. (/Applications/Xcode.app/Contents/Developer/Library/Frameworks)

- DEVELOPER_LIBRARY_DIR—The folder inside DEVELOPER_DIR containing files (templates, plugins, etc.) that support the developer tools. (/Applications/Xcode.app/Contents/Developer/Library)

- DEVELOPER_SDK_DIR—The folder inside DEVELOPER_DIR that contains the software development kit for the platform the target will run on. (Simulator targets run on OS X.) (/Applications/Xcode.app/Contents/Developer/Platforms /MacOSX.platform/Developer/SDKs)

- DEVELOPER_TOOLS_DIR—Contains BSD tools, like SetFile, that are specific to OS X development and would not be expected to be in /usr/bin. (/Applications/Xcode.app/Contents/Developer/Tools)

- DEVELOPER_USR_DIR—The folder inside DEVELOPER_DIR that you should use as a prefix for the standard include, sbin, share, and other directories you'd ordinarily look for in the root /usr directory. (/Applications/Xcode.app/Contents/Developer/usr)

Source Trees

A source tree provides a particular kind of build variable, a path to a directory or to the root directory of a tree with a known structure. The path can be a location to receive build results or provide access to a system of libraries and headers. When used to build source paths, a source tree provides a reliable shorthand for packages that do not belong in the directory tree of any one project.

For example, I use the eSellerate libraries in my OS X projects. I define a source tree for the eSellerate libraries by opening the Preferences window, selecting the **Source Trees** tab of the **Locations** panel, and clicking the **+** button to add an entry. I choose ESELLERATE_DIR for the setting name and **eSellerate Directory** for the display name, and I type the full path name for the root of the eSellerate SDK into the path column.

Now, when I add a file reference to my project, I can use the File inspector in the Utility area to set **Location** to **Relative to eSellerate Directory**. Regardless of who copies or clones my project, so long as they have defined an ESELLERATE_DIR source tree, the project will find that file in their copy of that directory. I don't have to care about the details of the path, and I especially don't have to set up double-dot relative directory references.

Source trees are global—they span projects—but are per-user.

B

Resources

I've tried to make this book thorough, but it isn't comprehensive. Xcode is too big to cover exhaustively, and Apple constantly updates it. Further, your needs as a Cocoa programmer go beyond simply using the tools. This appendix is a brief reference to resources you can use to go further and keep current.

Books

Before the iOS gold rush, there were few books about Cocoa and Xcode, and they were mostly pretty good. Now, there are a lot more, and there is more... diversity. These are a selected few.

- Buck, Erik, *Cocoa Design Patterns* (2009). Cocoa conforms to a few fundamental patterns, and once you have those down, you've gone a long way toward understanding most of iOS and OS X programming. Erik Buck's book is six years old, but the fundamentals haven't changed.

- Conway, Joe, and Hillegass, Aaron, *iOS Programming: The Big Nerd Ranch Guide*, fourth edition (2014). What Aaron Hillegass's *Cocoa Programming for OS X* (see below) did for Mac programmers, this book does for iOS. A stand-alone book from the ground up, it takes you from a dead start (or at least from C programming) to some advanced topics.

- Hillegass, Aaron, and Preble, Adam, *Cocoa Programming for OS X*, fourth edition (2011), and Claude, Juan Pablo, and Hillegass, *More Cocoa Programming for OS X: The Big Nerd Ranch Guide* (2013). This book was a classic from the first edition. The series is where Mac programmers have started for more than a decade. A fine introduction, and a tour by example from beginning to advanced topics. Highly recommended.

- Kochan, Stephen, *Programming in Objective-C*, sixth edition (2013). The leading book about Objective-C, teaching it as your first programming language—it does not assume you have any grounding in C or object-oriented programming. Kochan teaches the Foundation framework, but treads only lightly on the Cocoa application frameworks.

- Lee, Graham, *Test-Driven iOS Development* (2011). Test early, test every day: Lee's book shows you how.

- Napier, Rod, and Kumar, Mugunth, *iOS 6 Programming Pushing the Limits: Advanced Application Development for Apple iPhone, iPad and iPod Touch* (2012). Napier goes deep into subjects that will get beginning-plus developers well into advanced techniques.

- Neuberg, Matt, *Programming iOS 8: Dive Deep into Views, View Controllers, and Frameworks* (2014). Matt Neuberg offers an exhaustive (800 pages) introduction to all aspects of iOS programming. Many regard this as the capstone of iOS instruction: Other books will lead you through the steps to producing applications that exhibit some advanced features of iOS. Neuberg takes a thousand pages because he explains the underlying principles step by step. You will not merely have *done*; you will have *understood*.

- Neuberg, Matt, *iOS 8 Programming Fundamentals with Swift: Xcode and Cocoa Basics* (2015). This is a lighter (400+ pages) book, more a tutorial than a text.

- Sadun, Erica, *The Core iOS Developer's Cookbook,* fifth edition (2014). Or any book with Erica as the author, particularly with the word "Cookbook" in the title. She is one of the clearest and most readable technical writers in the business. Many people swear by her iOS books.

- Sharp, Maurice; Sadun, Erica; and Strougo, Rod, *Learning iOS Development: A Hands-on Guide to the Fundamentals of iOS Programming* (2013). This book starts you at the beginning of the development process and hits all of the major issues in bringing an iOS app to App Store quality.

Books about Swift

Swift poses a problem for this list. It's a new language, still changing, and the only people who can really claim to be masters aren't writing any books, because Apple doesn't let its employees do that. Nobody has made a name, and most of those who have made names in Cocoa-related technical writing are publishing just as *Xcode 6 Start to Finish* goes to bed, or even months thereafter.

Here are what I see in the preorder lists that look good to me, on the basis of blurbs and the reputations of the authors and publishers. I can't offer details.

- Kochan, Stephen, *Programming in Swift (Developer's Library)*, sixth edition (2015).

- Manning, Jonathon and Buttfield-Addison, Paris, *Swift Development with Cocoa: Developing for the Mac and iOS App Stores* (2015).

- Mark, David and Nutting, Jack, *Beginning iPhone Development with Swift: Exploring the iOS SDK* (2014).

- Nahavandipoor, Vandad, *iOS 8 Swift Programming Cookbook: Solutions & Examples for iOS Apps* (2014).

On the Net

Do you have a question? *Use Google.* Or whatever search engine you prefer. Somebody has probably asked your question before and gotten a satisfactory answer. Even if you intend to ask on a public forum or list, search first. Apple's documentation is on the web, and the search engines' indices are still better than the one in the Documentation browser. If you're having trouble pinning down a query, remember to include some unique symbol from the related API, or at least something like `iOS`.

Then, if you can't find a good answer, consider whether the Cocoa API documentation makes the answer to your question obvious. Reread Apple's documentation one more time. Then ask. If you can say you've made a diligent attempt to find the answer yourself, the people who can help you will be satisfied that you've done your homework, and you are worth helping.

Forums

Early editions of *Xcode Unleashed* praised mailing lists (and mailing-list archives), and even USENET groups. Time has moved on. People have become comfortable getting and keeping their knowledge in the cloud. Lists that carried more than 100 messages a day a few years ago now tick along with 20 or fewer. If you want to ask a question, a web forum may be the better bet.

- I'll put the second-best first. The Apple Developer Forums *ought* to be the main resource for finding solutions to OS X and iOS problems. They were established to solve the problem that, before iPhone OS 2 went public, there was no way to discuss unpublished API. As a paid developer-programs member, you can ask questions about nondisclosed topics freely. (The Developer Tools section is available to the general public with a free registration as an Apple developer.) Some Apple engineers, having started with the private forums, never branched out to public venues like mailing lists and Stack Overflow.

  The drawbacks, however, are crippling. The forums are closed to external search engines, and the internal search facilities are ludicrous. The indexer is not customized to the subject of the forums, so if you look for a symbol declared in one of the Apple frameworks, the search engine may suggest that you really meant some technical term from veterinary medicine. You can narrow your search by time, but you can't go back 12 months (unless you conduct your search on New Year's Eve) because the search engine offers only the *calendar* year.

  The big, universal search engines prioritize results by the number of responses they attract—solutions usually float to the top. Not so on the Apple forums: When you enter your search terms, some encouraging result might flicker past in the Web 2.0

windowlet that pops up, but when it settles down, most of what you get are single messages from other hapless seekers.

But if you're looking for solutions for NDA software, the Apple Developer Forums are the only game in town. `http://devforums.apple.com/`.

- Better, much much better: *Stack Overflow*, `http://stackoverflow.com/`. It's open to search engines, the postings have usable metadata, and most of the threads you'll find will have at least one high-quality answer (though it is sometimes a trick to decide which answer that is). Very little chat, a whole lot of solutions. If your mission is problem solving, and not just reference, save yourself some trouble and prefix your search queries with **site:stackoverflow.com**.

Mailing Lists

Apple hosts dozens of lists on all aspects of developing for its products. The full roster can be found at `http://www.lists.apple.com/mailman/listinfo`. Remember that like all technical mailing lists, these are restricted to questions and solutions for specific problems. Apple engineers read these lists in their spare time, and they are not required to answer postings; they cannot accept bug reports or feature requests. Take those to `http://bugreport.apple.com/`.

These three lists will probably be the most help to you:

- **xcode-users**—Covers Xcode and the other Apple developer tools. It does not deal with programming questions; if you want to ask about what to do with Xcode, rather than how to use it, you'll be better off asking in cocoa-dev. `http://www.lists.apple.com/mailman/listinfo/xcode-users/`

- **cocoa-dev**—This is for questions about the Cocoa frameworks, for both OS X and iOS. `http://www.lists.apple.com/mailman/listinfo/cocoa-dev/`

- **objc-language**—Handles questions about the Objective-C programming language. Questions about Cocoa programming (except for the primitive data types in Foundation) are *not* on-topic here. `http://www.lists.apple.com/mailman/listinfo/objc-language/`

There is no consensus favorite for a Swift mailing list; there may never be one. The **swift-language** Google group, `https://groups.google.com/forum/#!forum/swift-language`, attracts just over a post a day. Swift questions also crop up in xcode-users and objc-language.

Developer Technical Support

One resource is in a class by itself. As part of your $99 developer-program membership, you get two incidents with Apple Developer Technical Support (DTS). (You can get more in 5- or 10-packs at about $50 per incident.) If you have a critical question that needs the right answer right away, forums and mailing lists aren't the way to go. The people who really know the right answer aren't required to be there, aren't required to answer, and are not allowed the time to research your problem for you.

If you file a DTS incident, you will be assigned an engineer who will respond within three days. He will have access to OS source code and to the engineers who wrote it. He (usually) will be able to come up with a solution to your problem that works and will work even if Apple revises the OS under you.

DTS isn't a gatekeeper for insider techniques. Almost everything that has an answer has (or will have) a public answer. What you'll be getting is an engineer with good communications skills, and enough of a knowledge base to respond to your particular problem.

Sites and Blogs

- For reference problems, the first place on the web to go is `http://developer.apple.com/`, the site for Apple Developer Programs. It has everything you'll find in Xcode's documentation packages, plus more articles, downloadable examples, business resources, screencasts, and a portal to the iOS, OS X, and Safari developer pages. A good strategy for getting official (public) information from Apple is to do a Google search restricted to `site:developer.apple.com`.

- If you find a bug in Apple software, or need a feature, go to `http://bugreport.apple.com` (you'll need to register with Apple as a developer, but the free program will do). Be sure to file a complete report (Apple has guidelines for you), and if you're looking for a new feature, be sure to make a concrete case for how it will improve your product or workflow. `https://developer.apple.com/bug-reporting/` will bring you up to speed on the details.

- Apple has an official blog for Swift: `https://developer.apple.com/swift/blog/`. Posts come a little more than once a month, but they go into detail, and of course, they are authoritative.

- `https://www.cocoacontrols.com`—is a clearinghouse for UI components for iOS and OS X. As I write this, its catalog listed 1,763 components.

- NSHipster, `http://nshipster.com/`, is a weekly blog of "overlooked bits in Objective-C, Swift, and Cocoa." Each article surveys one aspect of Cocoa programming—#pragma directives, `UICollectionView`—and reduces it into a concise, accessible introduction. With just a *little* bit of irony.

- You can get a commented listing of the interfaces in the Swift standard library by typing **import Swift** in a playground or Swift source file, and command-clicking on `Swift`. It's nearly 10,000 lines in a single page. There's a cleaned-up and organized version at `http://swiftdoc.org`.

- Mike Ash's Friday Q&A blog covers iOS and OS X topics in depth and breadth. The blog itself (updated, as you might expect, nearly every week) is at `http://www.mikeash.com/pyblog/`. You can buy it in ebook form from the links at `http://www.mikeash.com/book.html`. Send him money; he deserves it.

- There are many sample-code projects on GitHub, `https://github.com`. Plug "ios sample code github" (or "os x" or "cocoa" instead of "iOS") into your search engine, and browse at leisure.

Face to Face

Sitting down with a more experienced developer, and asking how you can accomplish what you want to do, can do more to get you on your way, and faster, than any book (except this one). There are user groups all over the world where you can get help and share your experiences; and there are classes you can take to get up to speed.

Meetings

- CocoaHeads, `http://cocoaheads.org/`, is an international federation of user groups for Cocoa programmers. They meet every month in more than 100 cities worldwide. The web site depends on each group's keeping its information up-to-date; my local group hasn't updated in nearly two years. You can still use the list for contacts.

- NSCoder Night is more a movement than a user group; it has no central (and very little local) organization. Cocoa programmers gather as often as weekly in pubs and coffee houses to share experiences and code. The get-togethers occur in nearly 60 cities around the world. Unfortunately, the web site hasn't been updated since 2011, and the link to a promised wiki is dead. Google **NSCoder night *your city***, ask around at user groups and colleges, and if all else fails, start one!

Classes

There are any number of companies and educational institutions that will teach you Cocoa programming. I'll mention two good ones, one at the high end, and one at the low, but check with your local college; you may be pleasantly surprised.

- Stanford University, CS 193, *Developing Apps for iOS*, available through iTunes U at `https://itunes.apple.com/us/course/developing-ios-7-apps-for/ \penalty-\@M%toendlongline~comp.id733644550`. This is a 20-part lecture series from a course taught by the Computer Science department at Stanford University.

- Big Nerd Ranch, `http://bignerdranch.com/`, Aaron Hillegass's training company, provides week-long boot camps on OS X, iOS, Cocoa, Rails, Android, and OpenGL at locations in North America and Europe. Your fee (starting at $3,500) includes lodging, meals, and transportation to and from the airport.

Other Software

The Xcode tools aren't everything. There are things they can't do, and there are things they don't do well. This section examines some tools that can make your life easier.

There's more to consider: You'll be using any number of productivity tools to organize your efforts and provide resources for your apps. (I recommend a good, lean bitmapped-graphics editor, for instance.) I can only survey a few programming tools.

Prices are US dollar equivalents as of late 2014, rounded to the nearest dollar (I have to round for Euro-denominated prices, so x.99 dollar amounts get rounded, too.)

Text Editors

The Xcode editor is a machine for producing Cocoa source code. It is crafted to a specific ideal of how a text editor should work. Maybe you don't share that ideal; maybe you need more direct access to text formats for which Xcode interposes a higher-level editor; maybe you need your own tools to customize your work environment.

Even if you're happy with Xcode for most tasks, as a committed Cocoa programmer you'll probably use one or more of these editors as well.

- *BBEdit*, from Bare Bones Software, is particularly good with large files and HTML. It will open anything. Its support for AppleScript, Unix scripting, and "clipping" macros make it readily extensible. This book was written in LATEX with BBEdit. It is available from Bare Bones directly.
  `http://www.barebones.com/products/bbedit`—$50.

  > **Note**
  >
  > I should disclose that Bare Bones sometimes sends me documentation work; I'm in the credits for BBEdit 11. I'd been a happy user of BBEdit for more than a decade before, and had recommended it in earlier editions of this book, before Bare Bones approached me.

- Bare Bones provides a capable "light" version of BBEdit, *TextWrangler*. What you'll miss are BBEdit's extensive tools for web development, text completion, version-control support, built-in shell worksheet, and ponies.
  `http://www.barebones.com/products/textwrangler/` - Free.

- *TextMate 2 beta*, from MacroMates, is a text editor with a huge capacity for customization. Syntax coloring and powerful keyboard shortcuts are available for dozens of languages and applications. TextMate has an active user community, and many developers whose products consume formatted text provide free TextMate extension bundles.

  TextMate 2 was declared "90 percent complete" in 2009. A "pre-alpha" went public at the end of 2011, and it has attracted fans. The source was published under the GNU General Public License in August 2012. You can purchase a license for the current, supported build at `http://macromates.com`—$50 (EUR 39).

- *Sublime Text 2* is a GUI editor for Mac, Windows, and Linux. You can customize it with JSON-based scripts and Python plugins. It recognizes dozens of language syntaxes, and it indexes both source and library code. Multiple selection allows you to edit common occurrences of a string simultaneously. I hear that skeptics of the future of TextMate are gravitating to Sublime Text and finding that TextMate bundles carry over. `http://www.sublimetext.com`—$59.

- `emacs` and `vi` are supplied with every standard installation of OS X. If you have any background in the Unix command line, you probably know how to use one of these and have nothing but contempt for the other.

  There are graphical variants of both. Check XEmacs, `www.xemacs.org`, for an X Window graphical `emacs`. MacVim is the most popular Mac-native graphical editor in the `vi` family, available at `http://code.google.com/p/macvim/` as source and installable binaries. Vico, `http://www.vicoapp.com`, is an editor with `vi` key bindings that can use TextMate language bundles. All are free of charge.

Helpers

There are many, many supplemental tools for Cocoa developers—check the "Developer Tools" category in the Mac App Store for scores of choices. Here are a few of the most useful:

- *Dash* styles itself a "documentation browser and code snippet manager." You can start with Cocoa document sets, but you can add scores of references for Ruby on Rails, Java, jQuery, Arduino… on and on. The application is built around a search interface that leads you to matches in all the active documentation sets; you're encouraged to build task-specific groups of the docsets you need for one project. Select a page (for instance, a Cocoa class reference), and all of the categories and entries on that page are displayed in a convenient index at the left edge of the window.

  The snippet manager holds code in any of dozens of languages. Select the abbreviation for one, and trigger the Dash service. The selected snippet will appear in a heads-up window so you can edit placeholders. These are more intelligent than Xcode's because editing one placeholder will edit other appearances of the same placeholder to match. Press Return to paste the completed code. Dash does a lot, and it's getting better at making everything it does accessible to an untrained user—but it still routinely posts popovers (you can suppress them) explaining fundamental uses. `http://kapeli.com/dash/`, and the Mac App Store. Free to download, $10 for full features.

- *Hopper Disassembler*, you remember, was the tool I used to produce pseudocode from a compiled C function in Chapter 5, "Compilation." If you need an analytical disassembler for your work, you're either an optimization wizard or in deep trouble with what you suspect is a compiler bug. Either way, you need it.

  You present the app with your compiled code, and it presents its best-guess partition of the byte stream into data, dynamic-linkage jump tables, and code, which it tries to break down into functions and sub-blocks within them. Then it's up to you to correct the partitions and to rename objects (including the stack offsets that define local variables) as you cycle through the task of making sense of the machine code.

As you saw, Hopper will give you pseudocode, which is great for presentation and essential to solving the puzzle.

It has hooks into the debugger. The promotional material says it works with `gdb`, but we can hope it can get by with `lldb`.

The developer (a very patient man as he dealt with me) designed the UI for his own needs. The application is meant to be run from the keyboard, using letter (not Command-key) commands. It takes some getting used to, but it's the best game in town.

A limited demo is available for free from the developer's web site, `http://www.hopperapp.com`. Purchase directly from the developer for $89.

- *Kaleidoscope* is a first-class file-comparison and merging editor. The first time you use it, you'll think of it as a glorified diff—a display of the differences between two files, little different from the comparison editor in Xcode. But the Xcode comparison editor goes only one way, to accept or refuse changes between versions of a file; it's a merging tool. Kaleidoscope lets you transfer divergent lines of text from one file to the other. So it's a general merge tool. It can be integrated into Versions, SourceTree, and the `git` and `svn` command-line tools.

  And it does whole directories. And if you have more than two versions of a file, you can queue them up so you can select any two to compare.

  And it compares images, giving you a flip comparison, a split view, or a bitmap of the changed pixels.

  And that's why it's worth 70 bucks. `http://www.kaleidoscopeapp.com`—$70 from the Mac App Store or direct.

- `mogenerator`—In Chapter 8, "Starting an iOS Application," I showed you that even though Xcode's Data Model editor can generate `NSManagedObject` subclasses from your data model, it's much better to rely on `mogenerator`. There's no reason to repeat the reasons. Use it.

  > **Note**
  >
  > The `mogenerator` package includes the `xmod` plugin, which in Xcode 3 could monitor your data-model files and regenerate the machine-side classes automatically. Unfortunately, plugins disappeared from Xcode at version 4.

- *PaintCode* is just cool. At first glance, it's a vector-based drawing application, moderately well featured. It's interesting that you can define colors by name, base other colors on variants of the plain ones, and produce gradients from the defined colors. If you have a shape filled with the named gradient, and change the base color, the derived color and gradient change to match.

  The thing is, *this is a code editor.* As you build your drawing, PaintCode generates the Swift, Objective-C, or C# code that will reproduce it. It includes expression editors for things like bounds or offsets, and variables that can be coded as locals or function parameters. I rarely use PaintCode's code unchanged, but it saves me half a day's

fooling around to get my arcs to go the right way.
`http://www.paintcodeapp.com`—$100 from the Mac App Store.

Package Managers

Xcode comes with most of the tools you'd need to build most free and open-source software (FOSS). However, even though you have all the tools you need to build everything from scratch, you don't have time to research the dependencies among libraries and the build options necessary to make them work together. That's why most operating systems and most scripting languages come with *package managers*, which take care of all the details and simply get you what you need to get on with your work.

OS X doesn't have a package manager, but four volunteer communities' projects provide the manager software and ports of many FOSS packages. All of them work from the command line; at their simplest, it's just a matter of invoking the manager's command (`fink`, `brew`, `port`, `pod`) with the package name. There are also graphical wrappers.

Third-party package managers have a problem in that they will not be the only mechanism for installing software on a system. If you run a makefile of your own, or open an installer package that installs its own components, or even use another package manager, the installed products will interfere with each other. Each manager has its own strategy for at least protecting its products from outsiders.

- *Fink* is the oldest of the four, having been founded in 2000. It is a Mac/Darwin derivative of Debian's package-management tools like `apt-get`. Build products go into the `/sw` directory. Fink has not had a binary installation since OS X 10.5 (Leopard); you will have to bootstrap by building the source distribution. The installation instructions list PowerPC as an available platform, which is good news if you are still nursing a PPC Mac along (as I did with my PowerMac G4, 2000-2013). `http://fink.thetis.ig42.org`

- *CocoaPods* is specifically for Objective-C projects. The client software is distributed as the `cocoapods` Ruby gem. The web site consists of some background information and a search field so large, you may not realize it is one. (It's the red "SEARCH★" at the top.) Enter author, name, keyword, or other relevant information, and the incremental search shows you the matching pods. `http://cocoapods.org`

- *Homebrew*, "The missing package manager for OS X," is the newest. Based on Ruby and Git, it's clean, and many new projects make it their preferred method of delivery. Build products go into the `homebrew` directory of your home directory and are then linked from `/usr/local`. `http://brew.sh`.

- *MacPorts* (formerly DarwinPorts) is old enough that it once identified itself with Darwin, not the Mac, when Darwin was still a serious contender as an open-source Unix. The project strives to keep its packages compatible with the current version of OS X, plus the two before. Its library has grown to nearly 18,000 packages. The MacPorts tree is rooted at `/opt/mports`. `http://www.macports.org`.

Version Control

As Chapter 7, "Version Control," showed, source control is a big subject, with many subtleties, and the bare command-line interfaces for the systems are a bit tangled. I've already recommended *Pro Git* and *Version Control with Subversion* as the best guides to the command-line tools.

Xcode's source-control system insulates you from the worst of it, but most developers find they still get into tangles, or need functions—tagging being the leading example—that Xcode simply doesn't provide.

The people best equipped to deliver an easy way to use source-control systems are programmers. They are their own market, and this has produced a great number of finely crafted, feature-filled graphical source-control managers. Too many for me to evaluate and list here.

A few stand out.

- *Git* itself comes with some cross-platform (Tk) tools for managing repositories. Before I switched to SourceTree, `gitk`, which you launch from the command line, was my favorite way to visualize the branching structure of a repository. It gives you diffs between a revision and its immediate predecessor. If you've installed Xcode, you've installed all the Git tools - Free.

- *SourceTree*, from Atlassian, is a well-regarded, comprehensive application for managing Git and Mercurial repositories. When you first launch it, you give it your credentials for any of the major remote-repo providers, allow it to scan your directories for repositories, and approve the set of repos you'll allow it to manage.

  The UI is... busy, with 19 controls in the toolbar. But comprehensive management of a Git repo is a busy task, and the presentation becomes quite accessible after a few minutes. Ignoring the `doc` directory from Chapter 24, "Documentation in Xcode," was a matter of a few clicks; the feature was easy to find.

  It's compatible with OS X 10.6 and up. Atlassian promotes its own cloud software-management services, including Bitbucket, a repository service that is free to projects with up to five participants. `http://www.sourcetreeapp.com` - Free.

- *GitHub* is the dominant provider of public Git-repository hosting. It provides a simple interface for managing your GitHub-hosted repositories, showing version diffs and branches. It concentrates on keeping you up-to-date in synchronizing your projects with their remotes—on GitHub. GitHub means their app to be a simple, powerful interface for its product. Nothing wrong with that; it's very good at what it does. `http://mac.github.com` - the application is free.

- *Versions* is the leading Subversion client for OS X, having won an Apple Design award for its UI design. It provides the usual services—version comparisons, commits, branch management—and communicates with the Subversion repository using its built-in implementation of Subversion 1.7—there's no need to install anything else, and no worries about possible mismatches between the app and whatever version of svn is installed on the system.

http://www.versionsapp.com—$59, $39 for students, and a free 30-day demo.

AppCode

JetBrains AppCode is an evolution of the free IntelliJ IDE specifically for iOS and OS X development. Its refactoring facilities dwarf those of Xcode, and its code analysis will do everything from correcting the spelling of program symbols in your comments to detecting dead methods, to offering to implement functions and methods you've used without defining, to automated testing, and more. It is a machine for sitting down and ripping through code. If that's your priority, you should download the demo. It includes embedded builds of clang for static analysis, lldb for debugging, and several unit-test systems, including XCTest.

Xcode still does some things better. Its version-control facilities are easier to work with day to day. It has a better debugger. It supports an integration system that eliminates much of the pain of unit testing, analysis, and beta distribution. It has Interface Builder; AppCode has "UI Designer," which works with storyboards and XIBs, but that requires faith in reverse-engineering those formats with every new release of Xcode. AppCode can't build iOS distributions. AppCode can work off of Xcode projects, but Xcode is still the best way to create Xcode projects. So, frequently, developers who use AppCode use it as a complement to Xcode—an external tool—rather than make it their primary IDE. Even Xcode fanatics (if there are such) should root for AppCode, to keep up the arms race that Apple has to run against it.

There are four tiers of licenses, including $99 for individual use, $199 for organizations, and free for education. http://www.jetbrains.com/objc/

Alternatives to Cocoa

Xcode 6 Start to Finish teaches Xcode, and incidentally Cocoa, but there are alternatives. Here are some you should explore.

Titanium and PhoneGap are frameworks for writing cross-platform mobile applications, including iOS. Both are built around JavaScript. They provide callouts to native libraries for access to features like GPS, accelerometers, and cameras. Both are open source, with support from their parent companies—Adobe for PhoneGap and Appcelerator for Titanium.

You will still need an iOS Developer Program membership to run your apps on a device.

Adobe PhoneGap

You develop PhoneGap applications mostly with whatever tools you are most comfortable using to build web sites, including Adobe Dreamweaver. UI specification comes from HTML5 and CSS. The programming language is JavaScript. To test apps, you come back to Xcode for building and running in the iOS Simulator. PhoneGap applications are wrapped in a native application that hosts the app in a UIWebView (in iOS).

PhoneGap is praised as good, for what it is: a "write once, run everywhere" development tool. It restricts itself to common-denominator features among the target devices (in part driven by the fact that HTML browsers vary among platforms, even if they mostly use WebKit). The communication between the HTML and native sides pass through a narrow pipe of JavaScript injection (to the HTML side) and a specialized URL scheme (to the "real" app).

`http://phonegap.com/`—Open source; no charge, premium support and training are available through an "enterprise" service.

Shotts, Kerri, *PhoneGap 3.x Mobile Application Development* (2014).

Appcelerator Titanium

Titanium is more ambitious. What's common among platforms is provided in the common Titanium API, but it also provides platform-specific libraries so you can adopt native-code views and UI idioms. For the IDE, you use Titanium Studio, based on Eclipse, and complete your builds for simulation and installation with Xcode (for iOS).

You code a Titanium application in JavaScript, but that's (mostly) not what the app runs. The build process translates parts of your JS code into Objective-C (for iOS) code, which is compiled into the application. There remains a JavaScript-like interpreter in your app to handle language features that only JS can do—it's where your app gets the dynamism that JS provides. These shims call down into native code that implements most of your application. Slick.

Titanium UIs are built from JavaScript specifications. Independent developers are working on interface-building tools but, as I write this, there are none in Titanium Studio. You *can* build HTML views, but HTML is not the native form for Titanium—you simply feed your HTML source into a web view, which is the "real" view so far as Titanium is concerned. For native components—navigation bars, buttons—Titanium gives you the native objects, not images that are never quite lookalikes.

`http://www.appcelerator.com/`—Open source; no charge, premium support and training available for a fee.

Brousseau, Christian, *Creating Mobile Apps with Appcelerator Titanium* (2013).

A Biased Assessment

The opinion of a developer who has sunk decades into native development: There is a place for alternative frameworks, but not as big as some hope. If you are developing in-house applications, you are usually looking to leverage time and talent into producing an application with specific functionality, without having to commit to a single vendor, and without having to satisfy a public market. Write-once-run-anywhere (WORA) is a reasonable choice for those goals.

This strategy is a disaster when applied to commercial products. The non-captive market has paid a premium for its iPhones (and Nexuses. . .), and demands apps that pay off on the latest features and capabilities. Non-native development will never keep up, and native-code competitors will have a time-to-market advantage. The temptation is to believe that a WORA app can afford to work like one platform, or the other, or neither, and paying customers won't care; they do. WORA tools are like any modern application frameworks—they can deliver prototypes that look pretty good, and run fairly well; then comes the remaining 95 percent of the development effort, making something worth charging money for. This can involve months of chasing down special cases on each platform (even WebKit behaves differently on different phones). By that point, performance becomes a serious problem: Facebook's Mark Zuckerberg called HTML-only development "the biggest mistake we made as a company."

And even for in-house development, you have to ask the question: You're relying on a BYOD (bring your own device) policy. Did your people buy iPhones and iPads (and Nexuses. . .) because they are portable, or because the apps on those devices are quick, efficient, and easy to use? If the latter, you have to deliver value on a par with those other apps, and WORA may be a waste of money.

Both frameworks tempt developers who want to avoid learning native APIs and (for iOS) a new language. It's a false economy: You end up learning a large API anyway; to the extent the API is smaller, it reflects platform features you won't have access to. A cross-platform framework is a different platform altogether, and the hope that you can just drop your web developer into a large mobile project, without a long learning curve, is likely forlorn.

Index

E

M

O

P

T

V